MENTAL
HEALTH
and the
EDUCATIVE
PROCESS:

Selected Readings

Edited by

HARVEY F. CLARIZIO
Michigan State University

RAND McNALLY COMPANY   Chicago · New York · San Francisco

RAND MCNALLY EDUCATION SERIES

B. Othanel Smith, *Advisory Editor*

MENTAL HEALTH and the EDUCATIVE PROCESS

Preface

INTRODUCTION

At the personal level, my interest in the mental health of children dates back to my experiences, first of all, as a recreation center director with socially maladjusted youth, then as a practicing psychologist in residential, child guidance and public school settings with psychoeducationally handicapped and emotionally disturbed children, and finally as a college teacher with adolescents experiencing normal personality crises.

At the national level, mental health remains a major concern. This concern has been most recently reflected in the establishment of a new Joint Committee on Mental Health of Children. This nonprofit, non-governmental, multidisciplinary agency is scheduled to report to the Congress at the time of this writing. The Commission's report, hopefully, will provide the impetus and support needed to strike out in new directions in the children's field.

One trend, which is already evident and will in all probability be intensified, is that of community psychology. And as the mental health field moves further and further into the community, it is reasonable to expect that the schools will be given an even greater responsibility for the emotional well-being of their charges. While the treatment of emotional and learning disorders will continue to receive considerable attention, preventive actions will be given greater emphasis than in the past. This collection of readings addresses itself to the school's role in mental health. Basic to the theme of this collection is the notion that the teacher is the mainstay of the school mental health program.

CRITERIA FOR SELECTION

Variety. The mental health field is characterized by various research stances and theoretical positions. In keeping with this diversity, an eclectic approach (hopefully of a selective nature) was undertaken. In this volume, the student will find empirical reports of longitudinal data and studies which involve the manipulation of experimental variables. In addition to the above types of articles, there are authoritative reviews of research on particular topics as well as papers which are more philosophical and speculative in nature. Variety is also evident in the theoretical frameworks sampled. There are, for example, selections based on a Neo-Freudian rationale, learning theory framework, Piaget's developmental psychology, self-theory and factor analytic theory.

Relevance. The selections in this volume have been made on the basis of their relevance to topics appearing with regularity in the literature. Thus, there are selections on such subjects as classroom management, prevention, cognitive development and mental health of teachers. The articles are also relevant to a wide educational audience in that they focus on the mental health of youngsters from the preschool through the college levels. Finally, the selections are relevant in the sense that they deal with issues meaningful to teachers. Discipline, adjustment difficulties and group aspects of classroom functioning have long been, for example, topics of concern to those on the front lines.

Recency. Preference was given to articles published within the last decade. The majority of articles, in fact, appeared in journals within the past three or four years. The choice of recent literature in no way denies the value of earlier research and opinion. Rather, this criterion was employed in an effort to provide a feeling for current concepts and trends in the field. Collections of earlier research are available to the student who wishes to read the literature which gave impetus to the current trends presented herein.

Readability. Since this text is intended primarily for advanced undergraduates and beginning graduate students in the field of education, preference was given to articles which minimized difficulties in communication. In accordance with this criterion, articles requiring appreciable statistical competencies as well as highly technical, esoteric papers have been avoided for the most part. Despite the above effort, the reader should, nonetheless, find himself intellectually challenged by ideas and information presented in this set of papers.

SPECIAL FEATURES OF THE BOOK

The distinctive features of this volume center around its special emphases on a number of areas. (1) First of all, there is attention devoted to a developmental view of personality crises among normal children—a topic frequently overlooked by teachers and mental health specialists alike. (2) The articles sample a broad number of more chronic and severe adjustment problems that are of interest and concern to both professional and lay groups. Special attention, for instance, is devoted to problems confronting the poor. Papers on creative thinking and mental retardation are also represented. Moreover, consideration is given to the college student whose mental health needs have been largely neglected. (3) A wide spectrum of topics on cognitive function and its relationship to mental health are explored. For example, the influence of intellectual competence on personal adequacy is considered from the vantage point of the teacher. (4) A whole chapter is addressed to classroom discipline. This topic, often a source of controversy and bewilderment for both educators and psychologists, is broached not only from various theoretical positions but from a practical standpoint as well. Specific management techniques deriving from learning theory as well as some concrete guidelines for interviewing are presented as possible means for coping with troublesome behaviors. (5) The major problems confronting the mental health field are presented succinctly and explicitly. The critical professional manpower shortage and the doubtful efficacy of psychotherapy are illustrative of current dilemmas confronting the children's field. (6) Finally, there is a focus on innovative treatment and preventive programs. New approaches characterized by flexibility and ingenuity run the gamut from brief but intensive residential treatment programs to early identification and prevention programs in the public schools.

Whatever credit this book of readings deserves must go to the authors and publishers who consented to have their material reproduced. My grateful acknowledgement is extended to each of them. Without their kind permission, this collection of papers would not have been possible. I also wish to express my sincere appreciation to Mrs. Carol Teasdale for her secretarial assistance and to Dr. Don E. Hamachek for his support throughout this project. Special appreciation is extended to Eli M. Bower and Robert D. Strom for their critical appraisals of this work.

H. F. C.

Table of Contents

PART III   MENTAL HEALTH IN TEACHING

PART IV INTERVENTION PROCEDURES

PART I

GENERAL INTRODUCTION

SCOPE OF THE PROBLEM

It is difficult to determine with any degree of accuracy the incidence of emotional disturbance in children since estimates of maladjustment will vary with the definition of disturbance used, the agencies sampled (school, child guidance clinics, juvenile court, residential hospitals) and the identification methods employed (referrals to professional specialists, rating scales, self-report inventories and sociograms). With these limitations in mind, let us briefly review some statistics on the incidence of maladjustment among children.

White and Harris (1961) after carefully reviewing six major studies on the frequency of serious maladjustment in public school children, arrived at a working estimate of 4 to 7 per cent. These figures relied primarily on teachers' judgments and were based on studies conducted between 1927 and 1958. The most recent and wide ranging study on public school children which was carried out by Bower (1960) in California indicates that approximately 10 per cent are sufficiently disturbed to warrant the label emotionally handicapped and that about 2–3 per cent of this group need immediate psychiatric attention. Using this 10 per cent figure, Eli Bower (1969), consultant at the National Institute of Mental Health, recently estimated that there are approximately 5½ million children with moderate to severe degrees of emotional disturbances in the kindergarten through college age group.

In 1965 there were approximately 697,000 juvenile delinquents seen by juvenile courts in the United States. This means that about 2 per cent of all children in the country between the ages of 10 to 13 were handled by juvenile courts that year (U.S. Children's Bureau, 1966). This figure represents a 2 per cent increase over the previous year's number of court cases. Further, this upward trend has been noticeable each year since 1949.

Granted that nobody knows exactly how many maladjusted youngsters there are, we do know that personal and social maladjustment in children constitutes a sizeable problem and one that we cannot afford to neglect.

1

THE SCHOOL'S ROLE IN MENTAL HEALTH

The rather sobering statistics presented above indicate the need for constructive intervention. In all probability, the schools are the most strategically placed institution to attack this problem. The schools have a tremendous mental health potential in that the teacher is the only trained professional person who is in contact with such large numbers of children. Moreover, the teachers have access to the youngsters for a prolonged period of time at a stage in life when personality is still presumed to be malleable. To secure a fuller appreciation of the potential impact that a school can have upon mental health, you have only to dwell upon the estimate that a pupil will spend approximately 14,000 to 16,000 hours in a classroom setting during the course of his 12 years of schooling. Can you imagine the number of ego-enhancing and/or ego-debilitating experiences that a student experiences over such an extended period of time? If the psychology of learning has taught us anything, it is the idea that overlearned activities become a part of us, for better or for worse.

Fortunately, as mental health programs have moved out of the isolated chambers of the therapist's private office and into the community, there has been a definite movement in the direction of greater teacher involvement in the mental health of children. Professional workers now realize that all problems do not stem from factors inside the individual and that we must carefully consider the child's life conditions, e.g. the school, as factors in a production of maladjustment. During the past decade, the need for a more reality-based mental health approach has become increasingly evident. And as the mental health team continues to expand in keeping with this new outlook, it might well be the teacher who assumes a primary role and the mental health specialist a secondary role in the promotion and protection of our youth's mental health. This seems especially likely since there will probably not be enough mental health specialists.

Chapter One

Chapter 1—Mental Health and the Schools—is designed to provide the reader with an orientation to the evolving mental hygiene role of our educational system. The first two selections constitute a critique of traditional treatment approaches. The last two articles examine the school's expanding role in mental health. The following themes are developed in this introductory section:

the inappropriateness of the intrapsychic model to the problems of today's youth;

the questionable outcomes of psychotherapeutically-oriented efforts with disturbed children;

mental health and the educational enterprise; and the teacher's role in an expanded mental health team.

CHAPTER 1

Mental Health and the Schools

1. Crisis in the Children's Field

Fritz Redl

While we have traditionally modeled intervention procedures after the clinic concept of treatment, the need for a more reality-based mental health approach is becoming increasingly recognized. The current realization that the child's life conditions, e.g., the school, are as important as his personal feelings must obviously involve teachers as members of an expanded mental health team to a greater extent than was true in the past. What professionally trained person is in a better position to deal with youngsters on a daily reality-oriented basis than the classroom teacher?

THE OBSOLETE MODEL AND THE LATEST FAD

If we talk about "obsolete models," we should separate them into two categories: obsolete models of service and obsolete models of theory. I have plenty of complaints about both but will confine myself here to those of service. Let me breathe in passing only my complaint that I really think

---

In *American Journal of Orthopsychiatry*, 1962, 32, 772–774. Copyright, the American Orthopsychiatric Association, Inc. Reprinted by permission of copyright owner and author.

even the best "models of personality" with which we operate today are very obsolete, indeed—and that includes the ones I myself favor. Watching the change in the complexity of our concept of the model of an atom that has taken place in my lifetime and comparing it with the still two-dimensional proportions of most of our theories of personality, I feel that we have a long stretch to make up for.

However, that is too large a topic to treat here, so let me hurry on to just a few illustrations of what bothers me about the service models that seem to me totally obsolete and that we hang on to with a tenacity worthy of a better cause.

First of all, though, let me remind you again of what I mean when I call something "obsolete." Maybe reference to the more commonly understood military situation might help to keep straight our lines of thought. It is my impression that military men in the highest strategic positions are never so much afraid of an enemy as they are panicked by the idea that the equipment they have may be found obsolete at the moment when they need it. No matter how brave and courageous they may be, they are desperately worried that something that may be in itself quite wonderful may simply prove to be not enough or obsolete at the time when it is needed. It seems to me that in the field of human behavior we have not yet reached as wise, frank, and clean a point of view. Let me add to that: When somebody says, for instance, that the institution of foot soldiers, in modern warfare, must be considered obsolete, he does not mean that his soldiers are cowards or no good or that the men in uniform don't know what to do. He doesn't even mean that they are poorly trained. He means to say that our foot soldiers need to be even better and more marvelous than ever and that all glory should go to them. He also means, though, that the total danger situation implied in the term "warfare" can no longer be met by the institution of foot soldiers, no matter how well trained. I remind you of this point because we are likely to think less clearly when we apply the term "obsolescence" to the field of mental health and child service. When I say that certain of our institutions are "obsolete," it is in this spirit that my remarks are made.

The Holy Trinity of the Child Guidance Team

For professionals, this point should need little clarification, though it may be a painful one to contemplate. I grant you that the original model of the trinity of psychiatrist, social worker, and psychologist as "the" ortho-psychiatric team—under the leadership of a medically licensed psychiatrist, no matter what the issue might be—has become classic. It was a good beginning and still has a place in our over-all service designs. In fact, most child-guidance clinics are still designed that way. This model has not become wrong. It still serves a wonderful purpose for the kids who need it. I even venture to say at least 3,000 more institutions on this model are needed right now, with no alteration at all. However, as a "model" for treatment services for the youth of our time, this holy trinity with its clear-cut "inside" status is totally obsolete. There are loads of kids whose disturbances are so different from the one for which this model was designed—and is still adequate—that new patterns are also needed for them. That we produce such new mixtures of disturbances is neither the fault of the trinity nor of the kids who show them. Some of the types of pathology we produce need services in closer proximity to the daily-life situations of the kids than the "clinic" concept allows, and other disciplines and professions are just as necessary as are the three original ones.

Other people—and their professional skills—must be involved in the "team" effort, even though they do not sit in on the clinic discussions and are not paid out of the same till. The need for team members has spread from the "psychiatric caseworker" to the caseworker to the social group worker, recreation worker, nurse, nurse's aid, and even the clinically sophisticated attendant who remains with the kids on a ward long after everybody else has gone home. The idea that the psychiatrically sophisticated nurse, the pediatrician, the public-health nurse, the teacher, and the educational therapist should never be included and the fact that even organizations committed to the interdisciplinary approach are still struggling with this idea is a hangover from obsolete concepts beyond what we can afford. We have begun to respond to the impact of these facts of life, and the struggle to incorporate "other than trinity" professions into the concept of the treatment team has made some progress during the past years. It is an arduous job to confront the original team members with the awareness that most kids spend major parts of their lives in classrooms; that the healthy learner is as important a commodity, whose mental health needs to be preserved, as is the one on your waiting lists; and that those who regulate the children's learning experiences are "psychiatrically" as important partners in our efforts as is the clinic's paid staff. I complain bitterly that we have not gone far enough at all in coming to grips with the changed reality with which we have to deal. If there is a job to be done in correcting obsolescence we have a wonderful chance to go right ahead and do it. Not tomorrow, right now. The old and "classical" trinity has become obsolete as a model for mental-health services to children. Let's not be seduced by the classical simplicity of the lines of the model into hanging on to it when it has outlived its usefulness. It takes more than "three" professions to give our kids what they need.

2. Psychotherapy with Children: A Further Evaluation

E. E. Levitt

There have been relatively few objective efforts made toward evaluating the effectiveness of psychotherapy with children. We have typically assumed that psycho-

Behavior Research and Therapy, 1963, 1, 45–51. Reprinted with the permission of the Pergamon Press and author. (Footnotes have been renumbered.)

therapy has beneficial effects and have consequently felt little, if any, need to assess the effectiveness of our intervention efforts. The review of research by Levitt on the outcome of psychotherapy with children under-scores the fact that we can no longer afford to roman-tically assume that our idealistic desires and attempts to help others are being magically fulfilled. Needless to say, this review has stirred considerable controversy in the children's field. Though certainly discouraging to the proponents of child psychotherapy, the results are heartening in that they testify to youth's tremen-dous adaptability and capacity for self-repair.

PRELIMINARY CONSIDERATIONS

In 1957, the author reviewed articles involving the evaluation of the results of psychotherapy with children for the period 1929–1955 (Levitt, 1957a). A total of 18 reports of evaluations at close and 17 at follow-up were found. Of the total of nearly 8000 child patients, two-thirds were rated as improved at close and three-quarters at follow-up. Using 'defectors' from treatment (i.e. children who had been accepted for treatment but who never began treatment) as a control baseline, approximately the same per-centages were found for respective control groups. It was concluded that the results failed to support the contention that psychotherapy with chil-dren is effective.

This conclusion was supported by the results of a long-range, follow-up study at the Institute for Juvenile Research in Chicago (Levitt, 1959), one of the largest community child guidance clinics in the United States. Treated groups were compared with defector controls from the same clinic population on 26 variables, and no differences were found.

The review has been criticized by Eisenberg and Gruenberg (1961), Heinicke (1960) and Hood-Williams (1960).[1] The major point is that de-fectors (alternatively 'terminators' or 'discontinuers') constitute an inap-propriate control group because they may be less disturbed individuals who are able to respond favourably to the diagnostic procedure alone. The hypothesis certainly appears reasonable, though none of the critiques

---

[1] By restricting his analysis of data to only two studies, Heinicke was able to arrive at the conclusion that treated children at least showed a greater degree of 'successful ad-justments,' while the control cases showed a greater percentage of 'partial improve-ments.' In addition to the obvious potential effect of selecting two investigations from many, those who are experienced psychotherapists cannot help but be struck by the greater difficulty in distinguishing among degrees of improvement, as opposed to dis-tinguishing between any improvement and no improvement whatsoever. This suggests

actually cite experimental findings which bear directly on it. There are, however, a number of investigations which do have direct bearing.

One study (Levitt, 1957b) shows that defector cases and those who have had some treatment do not differ on 61 factors, including two clinical estimates of severity of symptoms, and eight other factors relating to symptoms. Another study (Levitt, 1958a) found that experienced mental health professionals were unable to detect a difference in severity of symptoms between treated and defector child cases, based on case records. On a 5-point scale, the mean severity ratings were 3.02 for the defector children and 2.98 for the treated cases. Judgments of motivation for treatment also did not distinguish the two groups.

Ross and Lacey (1961) found that the defector cases had fewer histories of developmental difficulties, fewer 'unusual behaviours' (confusion, disorientation, panic reactions, unpredictable, meaningless and self-destructive acts), a lower incidence of specific somatic complaints, and less parental 'marital disharmony' (not including divorce and separation). The defectors also tended to have had shorter waiting periods between application and intake interview. There was no relationship to socio-economic status. Lake and Levinger (1960) did find a relationship with socio-economic status, with the defectors tending to come from lower strata, but they found no relationship between continuing into therapy and the length of the waiting period. They report positive correlations between continuing into treatment and motivation of the parent for treatment.

A follow-up study of 142 defectors (Levitt, 1958b) disclosed that a family member was clearly resistant to treatment in 24 per cent of the cases, but 52 per cent attributed defection to deficiencies of the clinic, or to environmental circumstances.

Overall, the findings seem to be in conflict. Some of the studies appear to indicate that the defectors are less disturbed, but some appear to show no differences. One study shows a relationship to the socio-economic status, while another does not. The waiting period and parental motivation were found to be associated with termination in one study, but not in another.

The problem in attempting to reconcile these conflicting findings is that the definitions of 'treated' and 'defector' vary among studies. In the Levitt (1957b, 1958a) studies, a treated case was one which had at least 5 treatment interviews; in the Ross and Lacey study (1961) a minimum of 16 interviews. The term is not defined specifically in the Lake and Levinger investigation (1960). A defector in the Levitt studies is a case which had had a complete diagnostic work-up, had been accepted for therapy, and had failed the appropriate appointment when it was offered. For Ross and Lacey, a defector is one who had less than 5 treatment interviews, and

that the distinction between 'successful' and 'partial' will usually be relatively unreliable. Eisenberg classified neurosis in children as a "disorder for which there is reasonable likelihood of response to treatment," but admits that no definite conclusion concerning the efficacy of psychotherapy can be ventured at present. Despite his criticisms, Hood-Williams accepts the defectors as a control group, "albeit with reservations, whose very nature demands that conclusions drawn from them should be highly tentative." A detailed rebuttal of his critique has already appeared (Levitt, 1960).

terminated against clinic advice. In the Lake and Levinger study, a defector is a case which broke contact with the clinic after a complete application procedure, including an interview, but no diagnostic work-up. It is entirely possible that these differences in definition lie at the root of the discrepancies in findings.

Ideally, the defector should be an individual who has been procedurally identical with the treated case except for the factor of formal treatment itself. In the Ross-Lacey investigation, the defectors could have had as many as 4 treatment interviews. In the Lake-Levinger study, the defectors had not been subjected to diagnostic evaluation, and had evidently, therefore, not actually been accepted for treatment. Only in the Levitt investigations does the handling of the defector case appear to satisfy the criterion. If we accept the results of these studies (Levitt, 1957b; Levitt, 1958a) then the conclusion is that there does not seem to be any basis for the view that the defector cases were more or less seriously disturbed than treated cases, at the time of diagnostic evaluation.

It is probably true that a defector group contains a percentage of cases which have noticeably improved in the interim between the diagnostic evaluation and the offer of therapy.[2] The critics of the 1957 review speculate that the defector group may be a poor control because it is likely to contain substantially more of such cases than will the group which eventually goes on to formal treatment.

There are several arguments against this contention. It has been pointed out (Levitt, 1960) that follow-up interviews with parents of defector cases suggest that about 18 per cent terminated contact with the clinic because of the interim symptomatic improvement. Only about 12 per cent offered this as the sole explanation for termination. This percentage could, of course, affect an inter-group comparison, but it hardly seems sufficient to account for an overall improvement rate of some 65 per cent.

The second point is simply that the treated group might also have an interim improvement rate, which would balance, or partly offset, this phenomenon in the defector group.

Interim improvement is usually a corollary of the hypothesis that the defectors are less seriously disturbed initially, since such a child is more apt to be improved by a brief contact. Another argument against the idea of interim improvement as a bias follows from the evidence which appears to suggest that the defectors are not, in fact, less seriously disturbed.

Summing up, we can say that the defectors may be a biased control group, though the available evidence appears to indicate otherwise. The need for such a control is undeniable and no one has yet suggested a superior method of establishing the baseline of spontaneous remission.

Eisenberg and Gruenberg (1961) and Eisenberg, Gilbert et al. (1961) believe that failure to distinguish among diagnostic categories tends to

---

[2]It is a common belief among clinic workers that this improvement is a function of therapeutic properties of the diagnostic procedure. If this is indeed true, then the amount of such improvement is likely to vary considerably from clinic to clinic, as the evidence (Filmer-Bennett and Hillson, 1959; Phillips, 1957) indicates that the diagnostic procedure varies. However, the etiology of the improvement is not relevant to the argument.

obfuscate an evaluation of outcome. They argue that it would be more revealing to match treated and defector control groups by diagnosis. The contention appears reasonable; spontaneous remission is usually variable among illnesses. Unfortunately, data on defector groups by diagnostic categories are not available. It is possible, however, to determine whether outcome varies by diagnosis among treated cases, which is the logical first step. The present review of evaluation studies will attempt to accomplish this.

THE PRESENT REVIEW

The present review is based on 22 publications in which evaluative data are presented.[3] More than half of these are evaluations at follow-up rather than at close, but no distinction is made in this review. Some of the follow-up intervals are very short, and the interval is not stated in some studies. Furthermore, the combined breakdowns into diagnostic categories and into follow-up and close studies would fractionate the data to the point where comparisons would be unfeasible.

Data from the investigations are divided into five groups according to diagnostic criteria. Two groups are reasonably clearcut; psychotic children (Annesley, 1961; Bender and Gurevitz, 1955; Hamilton et al., 1961; Kane and Chambers, 1961; Kaufman et al., 1962), and those with special symptoms such as enuresis, tics, and school phobia (Hersov, 1960; Lazarus and Abramovitz, 1962; Phillips, 1961; Rodriguez et al., 1959; Zausmer, 1954). A third group deals with cases of delinquency, aggressive behaviours, anti-social acting-out, etc. (Annesley, 1961; Cytryn et al., 1960; Eisenberg et al., 1958a; Morris et al., 1956; Rexford et al. 1956). The fourth group is roughly analogous to the adult neurotic (Annesley, 1961; Dorfman, 1958; Eisenberg, Gilbert et al., 1961). The fifth group, which is by far the largest, is a mixed one in which a number of different diagnostic categories are represented, and includes accounts of general or unclassified child guidance clinic samples (Chess, 1957; La Vietes et al., 1960; Miller, 1957; O'Neal and Robins, 1958a; Phillips, 1960; Seidman, 1957). The groupings are not entirely pure, but there is little overlap. By and large, cases of organicity have been excluded.

The establishment of a separate category for children with special symptoms does not imply that such a symptom may not be pathognomic of a more extensive psychological disorder. The distinction is required by the fact that the evaluation of therapy in these cases is based solely on outcome of treatment of the special symptom.

---

[3]As in the earlier review, several studies have been excluded because of overlapping, and other reasons. Eisenberg's data (1958b) are included in the later study of Rodriguez et al. (1959). A second publication by O'Neal and Robins (1958b) includes data of an original publication (1958a). The latter is used because of its more complete presentation. The general improvement-nonimprovement findings are similar. Most of the results of the study by Cytryn et al. (1960) are included in the subsequent paper by Eisenberg et al. (1961). The article by Cunningham et al. (1956) appeared in the earlier review as an unpublished paper. The study of Michael et al. (1957) is inappropriate since only 25 of 606 treated cases were located at follow-up.

The therapy procedures which are represented in the studies cover a fairly broad range, including counseling with parents, environmental manipulation, techniques based on learning theory, nondirective counselling of children, and the use of adjunctive drugs. Shock therapies, chemotherapy as the exclusive approach, and other somatic treatments have been excluded. Several recent innovations in therapeutic methods are also excluded, largely because the numbers of cases are small, or because a systematic evaluation procedure does not appear in the study. Included in this category are Charny's 'isolation treatment' (Charny, 1961), and the operant conditioning techniques of Ferster and DeMyer (1961).

RESULTS

The data from the 22 evaluation studies are summarized in Table 1. The customary trichotomous breakdown is employed: Much Improved includes any classification indicating great improvement, or 'cured'; any classification indicating lesser degree of improvement, such as 'partly,' 'moderately,' or 'slightly,' is subsumed under Partly Improved; the No Improvement class also takes in 'worse.'

The overall improvement rate for the 1741 cases in the present review is 65.2 per cent. Since evaluations at close and follow-up are not separated, the pooled defector rate of 72.5 per cent must be used as the baseline (Levitt, 1957a). This rate is significantly greater than the 65.2 per cent rate found in the present study. However, if we eliminate the psychotic and acting-out children (an attempt was made to do this in the earlier review) the adjusted figure becomes 68.3 per cent, which does not differ significantly from the defector rate of 72.5 per cent.

If we pool all evaluation studies in the 1957 review, we find that 73.3 per cent of the cases show improvement. This is significantly higher than the improvement rate for studies in the present review. Again, an elimination of the psychotic and acting-out children from the present group makes the comparability more exact. We find, nonetheless, that the adjusted improvement rate of 68.3 per cent in the present study is still significantly lower than the rate for studies in the 1957 review. However, a difference of 5 per cent could easily be due to differences in sampling, treatment procedures, evaluation methods, and other sources of variation. Its clinical significance is certainly negligible.

TABLE 1. SUMMARY OF EVALUATION DATA FROM TWENTY-TWO STUDIES

Type of disorder	Number of studies	Much Improved		Partly Improved		Unimproved		Total	Overall (%)
		(N)	(%)	(N)	(%)	(N)	(%)	(N)	Improved
Neurosis	3	34	15	107	46	89	39	230	61
Acting-out	5	108	31	84	24	157	45	349	55
Special symptoms	5	114	54	49	23	50	23	213	77
Psychosis	5	62	25	102	40	88	35	252	65
Mixed	6	138	20	337	48	222	32	697	68
Total	24*	456	26.2	679	39.0	606	34.8	1741	65.2

*The study of Annesley (1961) contributed data to three classifications.

The 3×5 matrix of frequencies of Table 1 yields a chi-square which is significant far beyond the 0.1 per cent level. It appears that much of the variation among diagnostic categories is a function of differences between the Much Improved and Partly Improved classifications. However, even if we aggregate the data for the two classifications of improvements, the 2×5 matrix still results in a chi-square which is significant beyond the 0.1 per cent level. If the two groups which seem to provide the greatest variation, the acting-out children and those with special symptoms, are eliminated, the resulting 2×3 matrix yields a nonsignificant chi-square.

DISCUSSION

The results of this second review of evaluations of outcome of therapy with children are similar to those of the earlier review, and like those earlier findings, do not differ markedly from results obtained with defector cases. And again, the inescapable conclusion is that available evaluation studies do not furnish a reasonable basis for the hypothesis that psychotherapy facilitates recovery from emotional illness in children.

Apart from this global inference, the data suggest that there is merit in Eisenberg's contention that comparisons of treated and defector cases ought to be made within diagnostic categories. It appears that the improvement rate with therapy is lowest for cases of delinquency and antisocial acting-out, and highest for identifiable behavioural symptoms, like enuresis and school phobia. However, until the required comparisons are actually made, it would be incautious to conclude that therapy is more or less successful with any diagnostic group. It is perfectly possible that the spontaneous remission rate, as indicated by appropriate defector control groups, is also lower for the delinquents and higher for the special symptoms, and that the differences which are found in Table 1 simply reflect these facts.

Strupp's statement (1962) that we have not yet arrived at the appropriate time for a definitive outcome study is probably quite true. It also appears true that in recent years, research attention has turned away from the evaluation of outcome per se and has taken up the therapist and the therapy process as phenomena for investigation. However, the study of therapeutic dyad or of the personality of the therapist as a variable, or other process phenomena, does not obviate the need for precise measurement of outcome. To find the personality or the process which makes for successful treatment, we must still have an appropriate evaluation of that treatment. As Strupp (1962) says, "Concerted effort is needed to develop meaningful and measurable criteria of therapeutic outcome." It is hard to see how this can be done without continuing to evaluate the outcome of therapy itself.

Indeed, the definitive investigation may already be in process. An evaluation study sponsored by the Jewish Board of Guardians in New York City (Bloch and Rosenfeld, 1962) is now entering its eighth year and will continue for at least two more years. The enormous care and attention to detail of this investigation makes it possible that it may evolve into Strupp's 'missing link' of psychotherapy with children.

REFERENCES

Annesley, P. T. (1961) Psychiatric illness in adolescence: Presentation and prognosis. *J. ment. Sci.* 107, 268–278.

Bender, L. and Gurevitz, S. (1955) The results of psychotherapy with young schizophrenic children. *Amer. J. Orthopsychiat.* 25, 162–170.

Bloch, D. A. and Rosenfeld, E. (1962) *Evaluation (process-outcome) studies of the psychiatric treatment of children.* Progress report and research plans for the years 1962–1964. Unpublished memorandum, Jewish Board of Guardians, New York.

Charny, I. W. (1961) *Regression and reorganization in the "isolation treatment" of children: A clinical contribution to sensory deprivation research.* Paper presented at the meeting of the Amercian Psychological Association, New York.

Chess, S. (1957) *Evaluation of the effectiveness of an interracial child guidance clinic: diagnosis and treatment.* Unpublished paper, New York.

Cunningham, J. M., Westerman, H. H. and Fischhoff, J. (1956) A follow-up study of patients seen in a psychiatric clinic for children. *Amer. J. Orthopsychiat.* 26, 602–611.

Cytryn, L., Gilbert, A. and Eisenberg, L. (1960) The effectiveness of tranquilizing drugs plus supportive psychotherapy in treating behaviour disorders of children: A double blind study of 80 outpatients. *Amer. J. Orthopsychiat.* 30, 113–128.

Dorfman, E. (1958) Personality outcomes of client-centered child therapy. *Psychol. Monogr.* 72, No. 456.

Eisenberg, L., Marlowe, B. and Hastings, M. (1958a) Diagnostic services of maladjusted foster children: An orientation toward an acute need. *Amer. J. Orthopsychiat.* 28, 750–763.

Eisenberg, L. (1958b) School phobia: A study in the communication of anxiety. *Amer. J. Psychiat.* 114, 712–718.

Eisenberg, L. and Gruenberg, E. M. (1961) The current status of secondary prevention in child psychiatry. *Amer. J. Orthopsychiat.* 31, 355-367.

Eisenberg, L., Gilbert, A., Cytryn, L. and Molling, P. A. (1961) The effectiveness of psychotherapy alone and in conjunction with perphenazine or placebo in the treatment of neurotic and hyperkinetic children. *Amer. J. Psychiat.* 117, 1088–1093.

Ferster, C. B. and DeMyer, M. K. (1961) The development of performances in autistic children in an automatically controlled environment. *J. chron. Dis.* 13, 312–345.

Filmer-Bennett, G. and Hillson, J. S. (1959) Some child therapy practices. *J. clin. Psychol.* 15, 105–106.

Hamilton, D. M., McKinley, R. A., Moorhead, H. H. and Wall, J. H. (1961) Results of mental hospital treatment of troubled youth. *Amer. J. Psychiat.* 117, 811–816.

Heinicke, C. M. (1960) Research on psychotherapy with children: A review and suggestions for further study. *Amer. J. Orthopsychiat.* 30, 483–493.

Hersov, L. A. (1960) Refusal to go to school. *J. child Psychol. Psychiat.* 1, 137–145.

Hood-Williams, J. (1960) The results of psychotherapy with children: A revaluation. *J. cons. Psychol.* 24, 84–88.

Kane, R. P. and Chambers, G. S. (1961) Improvement: Real or apparent? A seven year follow-up of children hospitalized and discharged from a residential setting. *Amer. J. Psychiat.* 117, 1023–1026.

Kaufman, I., Frank, T., Friend, J., Heims, L. W. and Weiss, R. (1962) Success and failure in the treatment of childhood schizophrenia. *Amer. J. Psychiat.* 118, 909–913.

Lake, M. and Levinger, G. (1960) Continuance beyond application interviews in a child guidance clinic. *Soc. Casewk.* 91, 303–309.

LaVietes, R. L., Hulse, W. and Blau, A. (1960) A psychiatric day treatment center and school for young children and their parents. *Amer. J. Orthopsychiat.* 30, 468–482.

Lazarus, A. A. and Abramovitz, A. (1962) The use of "emotive imagery" in the treatment of children's phobias. *J. ment. Sci.* 108, 191–195.

Levitt, E. E. (1957a) Results of psychotherapy with children: An evaluation. *J. cons. Psychol.* 21, 189–196.

Levitt, E. E. (1957b) A comparison of "remainers" and "defectors" among child clinic patients. *J. cons. Psychol.* 21, 316.

Levitt, E. E. (1958a) A comparative judgmental study of "defection" from treatment at a child guidance clinic. *J. clin. Psychol.* 14, 429–432.

Levitt, E. E. (1958b) Parents' reasons for defection from treatment at a child guidance clinic. *Ment. Hyg. N. Y.* 42, 521–524.

Levitt, E. E., Beiser, H. R. and Robertson, R. E. (1959) A follow-up evaluation of cases treated at a community child guidance clinic. *Amer. J. Orthopsychiat.* 29, 337–347.

Levitt, E. E. (1960) Reply to Hood-Williams. *J. cons. Psychol.* 24, 89–91.

Michael, C. M., Morris, H. H. and Soroker, E. (1957) Follow-up studies of shy, withdrawn children—II. Relative incidence of schizophrenia. *Amer. J. Orthopsychiat.* 27, 331–337.

Miller, D. H. (1957) The treatment of adolescents in an adult hospital: A preliminary report. *Bull. Menninger Clin.* 21, 189–198.

Morris, H. H., Escoli, P. J. and Wexler, R. (1956) Aggressive behavior disorders of childhood: A follow-up study. *Amer. J. Psychiat.* 112, 991–997.

O'Neal, P. and Robins, L. N. (1958a) The relation of childhood behavior problems to adult psychiatric status. *Amer. J. Psychiat.* 114, 961–969.

O'Neal, P. and Robins, L. N. (1958b) Childhood patterns predictive of adult schizophrenia. *Amer. J. Psychiat.* 115, 385–391.

Phillips, E. L. (1957) Some features of child guidance clinic practice in the U.S.A. *J. clin. Psychol.* 13, 42–44.

Phillips, E. L. (1960) Parent-child psychotherapy: A follow-up study comparing two techniques. *J. Psychol.* 49, 195–202.

Phillips, E. L. (1961) Logical analysis of childhood behavior problems and their treatment. *Psychol. Rep.* 9, 705–712.

Rexford, E. N., Schleifer, M. and Van Amerongen, S. T. (1956) A follow-up of a psychiatric study of 57 antisocial young children. *Ment. Hyg. N.Y.* 40, 196–214.

Rodriguez, A., Rodriguez, M. and Eisenberg, L. (1959) The outcome of school phobia: A follow-up study based on 41 cases. *Amer. J. Psychiat.* 116, 540–544.

Ross, A. O. and Lacey, H. M. (1961) Characteristics of terminators and remainers in child guidance treatment. *J. cons. Psychol.* 25, 420–424.

Seidman, F. (1957) A study of some evaluation variables in a child guidance center. Paper presented at the meeting of the American Association of Psychiatric Clinics for Children.

Strupp, H. (1962) Psychotherapy. *Annu. Rev. Psychol.* 13, 445–478.

Zausmer, D. M. (1954) The treatment of tics in childhood. *Arch. Dis. Childh.* 29, 537–542.

3. Mental Health in Education

Eli Bower

Ever since the Russian sputnik sailed into orbit, there has been mounting pressure upon the schools for increased academic excellence. The "new" math, science

Review of Educational Research, 1962, 32, 441–454. Reprinted with the permission of the American Educational Research Association and author.

curricula and team teaching were ushered in as subject matter competencies were stressed. This trend has not, however, lessened the school's role in the mental health of its students. Indeed, the school has now been given greater responsibility for the emotional robustness of its students. While some teachers might perceive a basic incompatibility between personality-enhancing experiences and educational experiences of a more cognitive nature, Bower notes that one cannot separate "the nature of the child's learning experience in school from his total growth as a personality," for mental health is part and parcel of the teaching-learning process.

In attempting to identify some of the major concepts of mental health in education, one should find the presentation by Ryan in the December 1956 issue of the REVIEW to be both informative and stimulating. In this current review of research concerning aspects of mental health in education, attention is given to (a) concepts of mental health and of education, including their interrelationships, (b) ego development in educational processes, (c) mental health factors in school achievement, (d) early identification of children with developing mental health problems, and (e) psychoeducational approaches to the education of emotionally handicapped children.

CONCEPTS OF MENTAL HEALTH AND OF EDUCATION

Concepts of Mental Health

Considerable confusion has long existed regarding what is meant by mental health. Nevertheless, the report by Jahoda (1958) to the Joint Commission on Mental Illness and Health concerning the nature of positive mental health made a courageous and productive attempt to clarify value dilemmas, to summarize past efforts, and to offer empirical indicators for recognizing positive mental health. Jahoda identified such indicators as having to do with attitudes toward self, with relations of the individual and reality, and with active efforts to master one's environment. Jahoda also noted that, while the meaning of positive mental health is elusive, the concept of mental illness is no closer to a consensus. Indeed, Szasz (1961) questioned the assignment of mental and emotional disorders to the realm of illnesses and suggested that "problems in living" be considered as a more realistic and meaningful substitute.

Investigators such as Klein (1960) and Smith (1961) have utilized Jahoda's definition to explore further the interrelations of three dimensions of mental health: self, reality testing, and environmental mastery. Does a deficit in one imply that an individual no longer enjoys positive mental health? Or must one's standing in all three dimensions be reduced for ill health to ensue? To answer these questions, Klein (1960) proposed that mental health be appraised in terms of three connotations: (a) "soundness," an enduring state of a "healthy" personality recognizable in such qualities as the presence of adaptability, the use of social skills, the demonstration of a high degree of initiative, and the possession of a general perfusion of modest optimism; (b) "well-being," an immediate or current state of health or effectiveness in dealing with stress or crisis; and (c) "emotional stability," the ability of the individual to cope with specific environmental stresses over a period of time, while maintaining a state of emotional well-being. Klein pinned down four kinds of emotional stability: (a) general stability, (b) specific stability, (c) inherited stability, and (d) acquired stability. He was particularly concerned with the ways in which acquired stability could be used in the organism's adjustment to potentially stressful situations.

Such stability would be acquired by organisms which have had experience with stress-inducing agents and in the process have developed successful nonillness-producing ways of coping with the stress. In this conceptual framework of positive mental health, it might be possible to discover situations in which small amounts of stress could render individuals increasingly able in the future to tolerate greater degrees of stress of a similar nature. For example, sibling rivalry, often regarded as a circumstance contributing to a variety of behavioral and emotional disorders, could be thought to serve as a potential immunity-producing experience that would help one to manage stress-accompanying competitive relationships. One could hypothesize that a home in which there is reasonable and affectionate access to parental guidance would appear to offer one the opportunity for learning how to cope constructively with stress-inducing situations.

Smith (1961), who has considered the conceptual problems of mental health, commented on the shift from exclusive concern with mental illnesses toward an interest in positive mental health. Such a shift, however, has not been accompanied by any real gains in research or scientific understanding. Mental health or illness is still concerned with the evaluation of the personality in terms of criteria that are value oriented. Values, which are inherent in definitions of mental illness, are taken for granted primarily because there is little disagreement about them. It is natural to assume that something is wrong with a person who behaves "strangely" or whose thinking is disordered. What is "right" about a person with positive mental health is another matter. The variety and breadth of values that underlie such definitions are rarely acceptable or explicit to all. Consequently, in his reconsideration of the problem of mental health, Smith questioned the bases with respect to which mental health has been conceptualized.

Why has there been an increased emphasis on defining concepts of *positive* mental health? The demand, concluded Smith (1959), comes increasingly from those practitioners who are concerned with the socialization and education of children. Many practitioners, educators, parents, and social and behavioral scientists who are on the firing line must seek direction for their efforts. Smith (1961) suggested four prerequisites for dealing adequately with the nonscientific value-laden aspects of positive mental health: First, the values in mental health goals should be made explicit. For example, if the "good life" is one of the goals, the term *good* needs to be defined explicitly and, if possible, operationally. Second, such positive mental health concepts as are proposed should be capable of some measurement. Third, they should fit within the framework of an acceptable personality theory. Fourth, they should be relevant to the social context in which they are conceived; for example, mental health in education should concern itself with goals relevant to educational institutions and educational processes.

At this point, reference needs to be made to Kubie's relentless pursuit of the concept of mental health in psychiatric and educational literature. Kubie (1957, 1959) argued that behavior judged to be socially desirable or undesirable can be the consequence of many factors, but that the main difference between the individual with sound mental health and the individual with impaired mental health is basically one of organismic elasticity, or homeostasis. The essence of behavior reflecting favorable mental health is flexibility; in contrast, frozen or relatively unalterable behavior is characteristic of the neurotic process, whether it be in impulses, purposes, acts, thoughts, or feelings.

Kubie (1957) also stated that behavior can be regarded as neurotic if it is the product of processes that predetermine its automatic repetiton. Such processes usually stem from unconscious forces in the personality. In another paper, Kubie (1959) declared that behavior which is motivated primarily by unconscious forces will, in fact, become recurring and repetitive, since the goals of such behavior are rarely attainable. Although behavior motivated by unconscious forces may be useful and valuable in maintaining the health and personality integration of the individual, nevertheless, such behavior does become relatively unresponsive to changing environmental conditions.

One might well question the assumption, as does Redlich (1957), that acts determined by conscious or preconscious forces are "healthier," in the sense of being freer, than acts motivated by unconscious forces. Is it not probable that unconscious defense mechanisms are health-producing in their adaptive and self-protective goals? These defenses can be said to be health-maintaining or health-producing to the extent to which the individual needs to utilize them to maintain what may be termed his self-esteem and to mediate noxious forces in his environment. Yet it would seem obvious that the increased and continuous use of such unconscious mechanisms would in the long run render the organism less able to choose alternative modes of behaving.

Bower and others (1958) proposed the concept of degrees of freedom, or the number of behavioral alternatives available to an individual, as a measure of positive mental health. In a similar vein, Kubie (1959) reported that restrictions of personality freedom are universal components of common early childhood experiences. However, the restrictions that pose a neurotic potential can be directed and modified by educational experiences, stresses, and exceptional circumstances. According to Kubie

(1959), the basic question that mental health and educational leaders and planners need to ask is "How can we equip a child with the facts, skills and understandings which he will need in life without interfering with his freedom to use such facts, skills and tools productively and creatively?"

Concepts of Education in Relation to Mental Health

Today public education has found itself facing the task of providing the intellectual, social, and affective nutrients to children and adolescents, many of which could formerly be obtained from other sources. As pointed out by Kotinsky and Coleman (1955), this perception of successful education as a prerequisite for adequate personality development of children and adolescents may be reflected in the general tendency to blame the school for all that goes amiss with the state of the nation, including increases in the rate of divorce, delinquency, automobile fatalities, and mental illness.

Education can be regarded as those experiences that mediate the culture to children. Such experiences can be provided in a variety of ways —through reading groups, teaching machines, television, lectures, seminars, individual study, group discussions, and reading. The important link that the behavioral sciences have provided to educational practice is a circular one that connects cognitive mastery as represented in the acquisition of the meanings of symbols, participation in problem solving, and attainment of reading and other intellectual skills with the emotional satisfactions and development that lead to self-identification, maturity, and freedom to relate to others.

One cannot readily separate the nature of the child's learning experiences in school from his total growth as a personality. It may be hypothesized that educational experiences contribute to the potential of favorable mental health or ill health. A variety of different kinds of research can be utilized to support this hypothesis. In a 30-year follow-up study of children who were referred to a child guidance clinic, O'Neal and Robins (1958) related childhood behavioral problems to adult psychiatric states. The investigators chose from the files of the public schools a control group of students who were similar to children referred to the clinic in age, sex, intelligence, ethnic membership, and residence. Although they had intended to use the control group for comparison purposes only, they were struck by the results, which showed that the simple criteria used to choose the control subjects—no excessive absences, no full grades repeated, no disciplinary action recorded, and an intelligence quotient of 80 or higher— had yielded a group with a high level of emotional health. The difference between the control sample and the clinical group was particularly striking in view of the fact that the former group was drawn largely from a neighborhood of low socioeconomic status. Moreover, in about one-third of the cases there was a history of broken homes.

Another kind of longitudinal study was carried out by the President's Commission on the Conservation of Human Resources. The Commission sought to understand why one out of every seven men was judged to be mentally and/or emotionally incapable of serving in the U.S. Armed Forces in time of war. In a report of the work of the research staff of the Commission, Ginzberg and others (1959) concluded that although a high level of educational attainment was not a safeguard against emotional disorders, the lower the educational level of a region, the higher the incidence of failure in the Armed Forces attributable to emotional disorders. Ginzberg noted that inadequate education and emotional problems tend, over a period of time, to reinforce one another and that learning difficulties and home difficulties seemingly combine to produce inadequate adults. This circular phenomenon was illustrated in an investigation by Bower and others (1958), in which measures of reading and arithmetic achievement of emotionally disturbed children and of their classmates were compared in grades 4, 5, and 6. The emotionally disturbed children achieved below their classmates. Moreover, the differences increased at each successive grade level.

Additional evidence for the circular phenomenon was apparent in studies of children who, unable to function in school, sought to leave or to escape from it. In an extensive investigation of 105 high school students who were on the verge of dropping out, Lichter and others (1962) found that, in general, such adolescents had budding character disorders that dated back to elementary school. The school difficulties were judged to be either the outcomes of or the antecedents to a psychodynamic conflict from which the child sought refuge.

Mental Health Within the Educational Process

What is mental health in education? One cannot consider mental health activities apart from the educational or social processes in which personality growth is embedded. Neubauer and Beller (1958) noted that the contribution of mental health to education is the facilitation of learning and the learning process—not the pursuit of particular activities or objectives of its own. Biber (1961) suggested that mental health is better derived from the intrusive quality of the intellectual educational experience than from any therapeutic regime specifically planned for the school. Biber also commented on the past emphasis placed upon the human relations aspect of school life as the main line to mental health. The error in this lay in making the teacher-child relationship and the child-child relationship the content rather than the bridge of learning. When one talks of education as a part of a program of mental health promotion or mental illness prevention, one needs to spell out the theoretical assumptions in terms of which specific educational procedures may be said to enhance mental health.

Sanford (1962a, b) argued that if educational processes are to be effective they must involve a change in the structure of development of personality through its expansion, differentiation, or integration. Sanford perceived education as a process which, among other things, frees and encourages the impulse life of children and adolescents. Sanford (1962b) urged that students need to be shown that the world of literature, drama, art, and science offers the best means by which the impulses and imagination of childhood can find gratification.

Hollister (1959) and Hollister and Goldston (1962a, b) diagrammed and described the emerging pattern of relationship between education and mental health. In the education of all children, including children with mild emotional handicaps, the relationship should be one of utilizing all social and behavioral science research in the development of curriculums and in the training of teachers, pupil-personnel workers, health workers, and administrative staffs. In addition, mental health personnel should assist school personnel in the pivotal function of establishing and building close liaison with parents. This latter function, as suggested by Conant (1961), is especially critical in slum and low socioeconomic areas. What a school should do and can do is to a large extent determined by the statuses and ambitions of the families being served. Similarly, the Joint Commission on Mental Illness and Health (1961) pointed out that society at present has no pervasive mental health resources that encompass the family within their structures, except as home-school liaison might be so conceived.

Educational and mental health agencies have become closer and more integrative than previously in their efforts to provide effective educational experiences for moderately to severely handicapped children. In the education of emotionally disturbed children, close collaboration of teachers and clinicians has been taking place. Hollister (1961) described how working with parents of this group has been assumed by trained community and residential mental health personnel. For moderately handicapped children, curricular adjustments have been made. Pupil personnel services within the school as well as assistance from outside mental health agencies have been available. Helpful descriptions of such activities may be found in the recently published textbook by White and Harris (1961). It is important to note, as have Allinsmith and Goethals (1962), that in this continuing relationship between specialists in mental health and personnel in education, both groups have exchanged skills and techniques in realizing the goals of both education and mental health. In a recent publication, the National Society for the Study of Education (1959) has described how schools, in their efforts to carry out the responsibility of educating all the children of all the people, have enlisted the mental health profession as a helpful ally in realizing educational objectives.

EGO DEVELOPMENT IN EDUCATIONAL PROCESSES

Behavior can be regarded as the result of an interaction between an organism and the environment (internal and external) mediated or interpreted by personality processes called ego processes. Such ego processes are undoubtedly learned in the course of an organism's early adaptive struggles. In time they become a polarized window through which the world and the self are conceptualized. Behavioral sciences have come to regard the construct of ego strength (that is, ego processes which enhance a positive perception of self and others, encourage a vigorous relationship to the environment, and enable the organism to manage stress in a heathful manner) as a function of the processes of growth and learning. This implied assumption of a unity between intellect and personality is to a large degree based on clinical experiences and research on an ego process called identification, from which it appears that children often introject the opinions and attitudes of key adult figures.

Of major concern to behavorial scientists and educators are those factors which encourage a defensive reaction of a person to an event and those which encourage a coping pattern. In terms of the thinking of such writers as Klein and Ross (1958) and Murphy (1961), coping is an approach to the handling of stress or a problem of living in such a manner that the result is a stronger and healthier organism—an organism in a more fluid and effective homeostasis, or balance. On the other hand, a defensive pattern constitutes an approach by the organism to the stress or problem that results in a less resilient state—that is, a more fixed and rigid homeostasis. Consequently an organism that employs defensive ego processes will, in time, lose the ability to function freely with new problems. Murphy (1961) suggested some major factors in evaluating and enhancing the positive coping resources of children. Among these are (a) the range of gratification available to the child, including his interests; (b) his positive outgoing attitude toward life, including pride in himself; (c) the range and flexibility of his defense devices; and (d) his capacities to regress, to let down, and to retreat to a safer level of functioning. Increased use of defenses will in time produce the repetitive, rigid pattern of behavior which Kubie (1959) has labeled the neurotogenic component of education. To Kubie, this component represents the failure of education since its presence prevents or limits man's ability to change.

The relationship of ego development and educational processes has only begun to be identified and described. Future research should provide operational definitions or analogues of ego strength and should identify the specific educational processes that can be expected to influence the development of ego-strengthening processes in the personality.

MENTAL HEALTH FACTORS IN SCHOOL ACHIEVEMENT

Investigators have frequently reported the existence of a positive relationship between successful school experiences and the ability to do productive work. For example, Miller (1958) considered reading disability as a syndrome that could be studied epidemiologically and that could be used as an index of antisocial behavior. In one school, Miller found that 16.1 per cent of fifth-graders were reading below third-grade level. In a two-year follow-up study, the reading status was found to remain relatively constant. Those children identified as retarded in reading exhibited, almost without exception, serious problems in social and academic adjustment. A compilation and analysis of a large body of research by Traxler and Townsend (1955) confirmed the high positive relationship between reading achievement and personal-social adjustment.

Although it would be difficult to support the hypothesis that reading difficulties are necessarily the result of emotional difficulties (since emotional disturbances could also result from a child's inability to compete effectively with other children in reading skill), the secondary effects of this disability were apparent in the chapter by Bower and Holmes in the December 1959 REVIEW. Delacato (1959) reported upon studies concerning cerebral dominance and mixed laterality as possible contributors to lack of achievement in reading. The basic premise suggested by Delacato is that hemisphere dominance, which is the last step in the phylogenetic development of the brain, is most easily affected by damage or arrested development. Another dimension of reading disability is undoubtedly that of social deprivation, as indicated in the writings of Conant (1961), Lambert and Bower (1961), and Pressman (1962).

Yet, from whatever etiology or combination of factors reading disability arises, its impact on a child's school progress is pivotal. Achievement probably precedes all other factors as a basic factor in school success. For example, Bower (1960) found that in kindergarten (before academic values are stressed) the future achiever is not perceived any differently from the nonachiever. In the first and subsequent grades, however, those children who become successful achievers also become the most socially acceptable.

Although lack of achievement in arithmetic does not seem to be so ominous a sign as reading disability, it is worthy of study. Bower (1960) noted that when the arithmetic achievement of emotionally handicapped children was compared with that of their classmates, the differences were found to be relatively greater than those in reading skill. This may be due in part to the impact of reading difficulties on certain of the arithmetic tests in which reading is a factor. It is also possible that arithmetic is more abstract and less meaningful to children with mental health problems. Undoubtedly, it is a type of learning that requires a high degree of concentration and attention.

The inability of children to concentrate and to attend because of emotional anxiety has been a subject of research for a number of investigators. Pickrel (1958) found that persons scoring high on a test of "manifest anxiety" were able to solve problems which contained only a few alternative solutions faster than a group of individuals scoring low on the same test. However, on tasks that involved a greater number of alternatives or degrees of freedom, students with lower scores on the measure of anxiety did better than the students with higher scores. McKeachie, Pollie, and Speisman (1960) tested the hypothesis that the anxiety resulting from test items that were difficult or ambiguous could be reduced if the testees were encouraged to write comments about those test items that disturbed them. Such opportunities did indeed produce higher achievement scores for those students who participated. Calvin, McGuigan, and Sullivan (1957) confirmed these findings and also reported that those subjects who made the most comments showed the greatest improvement. An additional dividend to the investigation of McKeachie, Pollie, and Speisman (1960) was the finding that when students who were asked to comment on their "feelings" about an item were compared to another group who were asked to comment in terms of further explanations of the item, the latter group made slightly higher scores. It was suggested that such talking activity may not be effective in learning unless it involves verbalizing cognitive as well as affective elements.

Stress and anxiety in the school seem to be related to dropout. In an intensive study of 45 girls and 60 boys who were about to drop out of school, Lichter and others (1962) indicated that the reason was not the result of any specific learning failure but a broad educational disability. They interpreted the dropping out to be an escape, or a turning away, rather than a positive kind of action. They found that the problems for boys tended to start in elementary school and that those for girls tended to originate in adolescence.

What has research revealed about the relationship of mental health to the achievement of the college student? Jacob (1957) concluded that college experience had only a minor effect on the quality of student judgment, social responsibility, and understanding. His findings did not support the widely held assumption that college education exerts a liberalizing influence upon adolescents. In a methodological examination of Jacob's study, Barton (1959) questioned Jacob's conclusion, which he felt had not been substantiated. Barton stated that, at best, Jacob's work was a set of challenging hypotheses. In finding substantial changes of attitude in students during their college experiences, Webster (1958) interpreted his results as supporting those personality theories that emphasize increasing complexity, differentiation, and acquisition of independence in psychological development.

Spielberger (1962) studied the relationship of measures of manifest anxiety to college achievement for two samples of comparable ability. The group of students judged to be highly anxious, when compared with the group thought to be low in anxiety, did less well in terms of their over-all college grades. Although several high-anxiety students were found to be academic failures at all levels of ability, interestingly enough an analysis of the achievement level of students with both high academic ability and high anxiety level suggested that a high anxiety level may actually facilitate achievement. These findings may be consistent with Spence's (1958) suggestion that anxiety may provide increased motivation for students.

Unfortunately, there are those individuals whose emotional problems may contribute to their dropping out of college. Harrison (1958) studied 179 students who left Yale between 1947 and 1952 supposedly because of emotional difficulties. He noted that 86 of the 179 returned and that, of these, 69 per cent were graduated. He also reported that those diagnosed as neurotic or psychotic had better than a 3 to 1 chance of succeeding upon return. Thus, the hypothesis that the appearance of a psychosis or neurosis in this age group (and socioeconomic level) usually leads to a major disruption in academic or life career is not too strongly supported. In fact, Harrison found that dropping out frequently led to an apparently effective resolution of the emotional conflict, perhaps because of the opportunity afforded for extensive therapy.

EARLY IDENTIFICATION OF CHILDREN WITH DEVELOPING MENTAL HEALTH PROBLEMS

Comprehensive summaries of procedures aimed at the early identification of children with learning and behavioral disorders of a developmental nature were given by Bower (1960), Gildea and others (1958), and Ullman (1957). Bower pointed out the social and value conflicts inherent in such programs and the strategic position of the school in the early identification of emotional problems in children.

A recent publication of the California State Department of Education (1961) reported that children's judgments of the personalities of other children were surprisingly accurate and predictive of emotional disturbances, that teachers' judgments of emotional statuses of children were similar to those of clinicians, and that teachers identified about the same proportion of children to be either overly withdrawn or overly aggressive. It was noted that about three children in each classroom had moderate to serious emotional problems and that differences between emotionally handicapped children and their classmates increased in each succeeding grade. Useful adaptation of materials used in the California investigation was described in a manual for teachers prepared by Lambert and Bower (1961).

PSYCHOEDUCATIONAL APPROACHES TO THE EDUCATION OF EMOTIONALLY HANDICAPPED CHILDREN

The problem of educating emotionally handicapped children has been one of the major factors in the increased liaison between the mental health and education professions. Three general trends in mental health programming in the classroom were identified by Hollister (1959) as follows: (a) increased confidence and experience in the impact of group settings as a basis for healing or change, (b) increased use of mental health intermediaries, such as teachers, as the major dispensers and carriers of mental health programs along with the help and support of behavioral scientists and practitioners, and (c) greater and more imaginative use of psychoeducational classroom and diagnostic techniques and of special educational and guidance programs. Hollister and Goldston (1962a) pointed out the need to identify the essential psychoeducational processes used in educating disturbed children and attempted to develop a preliminary taxonomy of the procedures and considerations involved. In another publication, Hollister and Goldston (1962b) identified 13 kinds of psychoeducational processes as relevant to the education of emotionally disturbed children in special classes: administrative processes, screening and diagnosis, planning, placement and continuous assessment, classroom relationship, classroom-motivation developmental processes, perceptual-retraining processes, behavior management, behavior re-education, academic education, rehabilitation to the regular classroom, clinician-educator liaison, and school-time liaison.

That mental health consultation as a method of helping teachers has emerged and grown is also evident in a publication of the California State Department of Mental Hygiene (1961). The use of a school mental health unit to assist school staff in their work with all children was described by Lawrence, Spanier, and Dubowy (1962). The objective of the unit in relation to the teachers was to increase their awareness of their own strength and resources in educating children. Basically, these and other programs supported Prescott's (1957) premise that the multitudinous daily decisions made by teachers are the fundamental bases of the educative process.

The education of moderately or severely emotionally disturbed children has emerged as another area of concern and of collaboration between educators and mental health personnel. The previously cited publication of the California State Department of Education (1961) reported on a state-wide research program that included 13 different kinds of classroom approaches. Morse (1958) discussed the educational poblems of disturbed children in relation to differential diagnosis as well as to the kind of teaching required. Haring and Phillips (1962) suggested one specific approach: use of the structured classroom.

It is apparent that research in the development, preparation, and coordination of pupil personnel workers including psychologists, social workers, counselors, nurses, and physicians has increased. Formation of the National Research Commission on Pupil Personnel Services, as announced by the U.S. Office of Education and the National Defense Education Act funds have encouraged new developments in this field.

Some of the challenges for additional or new research include the development of ways to (a) identify, as early as possible, children with emotional disturbances, (b) demonstrate the effectiveness of teacher education programs and of pupil personnel programs that have been designed largely for the promotion of improved mental health, (c) determine the advantages of curricular experiences that are planned to enhance the ego of the child with positive mental health as well as the one with moderate or serious mental health problems, (d) ascertain whether use of emotionally hazardous situations and crises are effective in building satisfactory coping patterns in children, and (e) evaluate the effectiveness of various school-community programs intended to improve mental health.

BIBLIOGRAPHY

Allinsmith, Wesley, and Goethals, George W. *The Role of Schools in Mental Health.* Joint Commission on Mental Illness and Health, Monograph Series No. 7. New York: Basic Books, 1962. 337 pp.

Barton, Allen H. *Studying the Effects of College Education: A Methodological Examination of Changing Values in College.* New Haven, Conn.: Edward W. Hagen Foundation, 1959. 96 pp.

Biber, Barbara. "The Integration of Mental Health Principles in the School Setting as Part of a Program of Primary Prevention." *Prevention of Mental Disorders in Children.* (Edited by Gerald Caplan.) New York: Basic Books, 1961. Chapter 15, pp. 323-52.

Bower, Eli M. *Early Identification of Emotionally Handicapped Children in School.* Springfield, Ill.: Charles C Thomas, 1960. 120 pp.

Bower, Eli M., and others. *A Process for Early Identification of Emotionally Disturbed Children.* Bulletin No. 6. Sacramento: California State Department of Education, August 1958. 111 pp.

California State Department of Education. *The Education of Emotionally Handicapped Children.* Report to the California Legislature. Sacramento: the Department, 1961. 76 pp.

California State Department of Mental Hygiene. *Programming Consultation Services to Schools by Mental Health Specialists.* Sacramento: the Department, 1961. 45 pp.

Calvin, Allen D.; McGuigan, F. J.; and Sullivan, Maurice W. "A Further Investigation of the Relationship Between Anxiety and Classroom Examination Performance." *Journal of Educational Psychology* 48: 240-44; April 1957.

Conant, James B. *Slums and Suburbs.* New York: McGraw-Hill Book Co., 1961. 147 pp.

Delacato, Carl H. *The Treatment and Prevention of Reading Problems: The Neuropsychological Approach.* Springfield, Ill.: Charles C Thomas, 1959. 122 pp.

Gildea, Margaret C.-L., and others. "Community Mental Health Research: Findings After Three Years." *American Journal of Psychiatry* 114: 970-76; May 1958.

Ginzberg, Eli, and others. *The Ineffective Soldier: Lessons for Management and the Nation, Patterns of Performance.* New York: Columbia University Press, 1959. Vol. 3, 340 pp.

Haring, Norris G., and Phillips, E. Lakin. *Educating Emotionally Disturbed Children.* New York: McGraw-Hill Book Co., 1962. 322 pp.

Harrison, Robert W. "Leaving College Because of Emotional Problems." *Psychosocial Problems of College Men*. (Edited by Bryant M. Wedge.) New Haven, Conn.: Yale University Press, 1958. Chapter 5, pp. 95–112.

Hollister, William G. "Current Trends in Mental Health Programming in the Classroom." *Journal of Social Issues* 15:50-58; January 1959.

Hollister, William G. "The Care and Feeding of Consultants." *Programming Consultation Services to Schools by Mental Health Specialists*. Sacramento: California State Department of Mental Hygiene, 1961. Chapter 7, pp. 35–43.

Hollister, William G., and Goldston, Stephen E. *Considerations for Planning Classes for the Emotionally Handicapped*. Washington, D.C.: Council for Exceptional Children, 1962. 30 pp. (a)

Hollister, William G., and Goldston, Stephen E. "Psychoeducational Processes in Classes for Emotionally Handicapped Children." *Journal of Exceptional Children* 28: 351–56; March 1962. (b)

Jacob, Philip E. *Changing Values in College: An Exploratory Study of the Impact of College Teaching*. New York: Harper & Brothers, 1957. 174 pp.

Jahoda, Marie. *Current Concepts of Positive Mental Health*. New York: Basic Books, 1958. 136 pp.

Joint Commission on Mental Illness and Health. *Action for Mental Health*. New York: Basic Books, 1961. 338 pp.

Klein, Donald C. "Some Concepts Concerning the Mental Health of the Individual." *Journal of Consulting Psychology* 24: 288–93; August 1960.

Klein, Donald C., and Ross, Ann. "Kindergarten Entry: A Study of Role Transition." *Orthopsychiatry and the School*. (Edited by Morris Krugman.) New York: American Orthopsychiatric Association, 1958. pp. 60–69.

Kotinsky, Ruth, and Coleman, Jules V. "Mental Health as an Educational Goal." *Teachers College Record* 56: 267–76; February 1955.

Kubie, Lawrence S. "Social Forces and the Neurotic Process." *Explorations in Social Psychiatry*. (Edited by Alexander Leighton and others.) New York: Basic Books, 1957. Chapter 3, pp. 77–104.

Kubie, Lawrence S. "Are We Educating for Maturity?" *NEA Journal* 48: 58–63; January 1959.

Lambert, Nadine, and Bower, Eli M. *Teachers' Manual: In-School Screening of Emotionally Handicapped Children*. Princeton, N.J.: Educational Testing Service, 1961. 72 pp.

Lawrence, Margaret Morgan; Spanier, Irene J.; and Dubowy, Mildred W. "An Analysis of the Work of the School Mental Health Unit of a Community Mental Health Board." *American Journal of Orthopsychiatry* 32: 99–108; January 1962.

Lichter, Solomon O., and others. *The Drop-Outs*. Chicago: Free Press, 1962. 302 pp.

McKeachie, J. W.; Pollie, Donald; and Speisman, Joseph. "Relieving Anxiety in Classroom Examinations." *The Adolescent: A Book of Readings*. (Edited by Jerome M. Seidman.) New York: Holt, Rinehart and Winston, 1960. pp. 408–20.

Miller, Alan D. "The Role of the School System in a Mental Health Program." *Orthopsychiatry and the School*. (Edited by Morris Krugman.) New York: American Orthopsychiatric Association, 1958. pp. 135–40.

Morse, William C. "The Education of Socially Maladjusted and Emotionally Disturbed Children." *Education of Exceptional Children and Youth*. (Edited by William M. Cruickshank and G. Orville Johnson.) Englewood Cliffs, N.J.: Prentice-Hall, 1958. Chapter 13, pp. 557–608.

Murphy, Lois Barclay. "Preventive Implications of Development in the Preschool Years." *Prevention of Mental Disorders in Children*. (Edited by Gerald Caplan.) New York: Basic Books, 1961. Chapter 10, pp. 218–48.

National Society for the Study of Education. *Personnel Services in Education*. (Edited by Nelson B. Henry.) Chicago: National Society for the Study of Education, 1959. 303 pp.

Neubauer, Peter B., and Beller, Emanuel K. "Differential Contributions of the Educator and Clinician in Diagnosis." *Orthopsychiatry and the School*. (Edited by Morris Krugman.) New York: American Orthopsychiatric Association, 1958. pp. 36–45.

O'Neal, Patricia, and Robins, Lee N. "The Relation of Childhood Behavior Problems to Adult Psychiatric Status: A 30-Year Follow-Up Study of 150 Subjects." *American Journal of Psychiatry* 114: 961–69; May 1958.

Pickrel, E. W. "The Differential Effect of Manifest Anxiety on Test Performance." *Journal of Educational Psychology* 49: 43–45; February 1958.

Prescott, Daniel A. *The Child in the Educative Process.* New York: McGraw-Hill Book Co., 1957. 502 pp.

Redlich, F. C. "The Concept of Health in Psychiatry." *Explorations in Social Psychiatry.* (Edited by Alexander H. Leighton and others.) New York: Basic Books, 1957. Chapter 5, pp. 138–64.

Reissman, Frank. *The Culturally Deprived Child.* New York: Harper & Brothers, 1962. 140 pp.

Sanford, Nevitt, editor. *The American College: A Psychological and Social Interpretation of the Higher Learning.* New York: John Wiley & Sons, 1962. 1084 pp. (a)

Sanford, Nevitt. "Implications of Personality Studies for Curriculum and Personnel Planning." *Personality Factors on the College Campus.* (Edited by Robert Sutherland and others.) Austin, Tex.: Hogg Foundation for Mental Health, 1962. Chapter 1, pp. 3–28. (b)

Smith, M. Brewster. "Research Strategies Toward a Conception of Positive Mental Health." *American Psychologist* 14: 673-81; November 1959.

Smith, M. Brewster. "Mental Health Reconsidered: A Special Case of the Problem of Values in Psychology." *American Psychologist* 16: 299-306; June 1961.

Spence, Kenneth. "A Theory of Emotionally Based Drive (D) and Its Relation to Performance in Simple Learning Situations." *American Psychologist* 13: 131–41; April 1958.

Spielberger, Charles D. "The Effects of Manifest Anxiety on Academic Achievement of College Students." *Mental Hygiene* 46: 420–26; July 1962.

Szasz, Thomas. *The Myth of Mental Illness.* New York: Paul B. Hoeber, 1961. 337 pp.

Traxler, Arthur E., and Townsend, Agatha. *Eight More Years of Research in Reading.* New York: Educational Records Bureau, 1955. 283 pp.

Ullman, Charles A. "Teachers, Peers and Tests as Predictors of Adjustment." *Journal of Educational Psychology* 48: 257–67; May 1957.

Webster, Harold. "Changes in Attitudes During College." *Journal of Educational Psychology* 49: 109–77; June 1958.

White, Mary Alice, and Harris, Myron W. *The School Psychologist.* New York: Harper & Brothers, 1961. 431 pp.

4. Some Misconceptions Regarding Mental Health Functions and Practices in the School

David P. Ausubel

There is much confusion about the teacher's role in mental health, especially as it relates to classroom discipline. David P. Ausubel, who enjoys the advantage of

Psychology in the Schools, 1965, 2, 99–105. Reprinted with the permission of the publisher and author.

being a psychiatrist and a psychologist, clarifies in his customary incisive manner the mental hygiene role of the school, examines the impact of authoritarian classroom atmospheres, exposes distortions of democratic classroom guidance and points out some steps needed to achieve a sounder concept of discipline.

Most reasonable persons would agree today that the legitimate functions of the school extend beyond the development of intellectual skills and the transmission of subject-matter knowledge. The school also has undeniable responsibilities with respect to mental health and personality development, simply because it is a place where children spend a good part of their waking hours, perform much of their purposeful activity, obtain a large share of their status, and interact significantly with adults, age-mates, and the demands of society. Hence, as long as the organizational, administrative, disciplinary, and interpersonal aspects of the school environment inevitably affect the mental health and personality development of its future citizens, it obviously behooves society to arrange these matters as appropriately and constructively as possible. Nevertheless, because the mental hygiene role of the school has been oversold and misrepresented so frequently by educational theorists, I would like to consider in this article what I believe to be some of the more serious misconceptions about mental health functions and practices in the school setting.

THE PRIMARY RESPONSIBILITY OF THE SCHOOL

To begin with, I think we need to recognize that the primary and distinctive function of the school in our society is not to promote mental health and personality development but to foster intellectual growth and the assimilation of knowledge. The school admittedly has important responsibilities with regard to the social, emotional, and moral aspects of the pupil's development, but certainly not the primary responsibility; the school's role in intellectual development, however, is incontrovertibly primary. Furthermore, much of the school's legitimate concern with interpersonal relations in the classroom does not stem merely from interest in enhancing healthful personality development as an end in itself. It also reflects appreciation of the negative effects which an unfavorable social and emotional school climate has on academic achievement, on motivation to learn, and on desirable attitudes toward intellectual inquiry. For example, if pupils feel unhappy and resentful about the discipline and social environment of the school, they will neither learn very much while they are in school nor remain much longer than they have to. And if they are goaded by fear to accept uncritically the views of their teachers and to memorize materials they do not really understand, they neither learn how to think for themselves nor build the foundations of a stable and usable body of knowledge.

THE SELECTION AND EVALUATION OF TEACHERS

Over the past three decades, in selecting and appraising school personnel, educators have tended to overvalue the personality attributes of the teacher and the mental health implications of teacher-pupil relationships, and to undervalue the teacher's intellectual functions and capabilities. But although teacher training institutions and teachers themselves overemphasize the importance of personality and interpersonal factors in the classroom, there is some evidence that pupils are primarily concerned with their teachers' pedagogic competence or ability to teach, and not with their role as kindly, sympathetic, and cheerful adults (Taylor, 1962). Despite the recent trend in such fields as government and business administration to place ability in getting along with people ahead of professional competence, it is self-evidently a dangerous state of affairs when professional personnel in any field of endeavor are judged mainly on the basis of personal qualities. It is obvious that because teachers deal with impressionable children and affect their personality development, they should not have unstable or destructive personalities. Nevertheless, the principal criterion in selecting and evaluating teachers should not be the extent to which their personality characteristics conform to the theoretical ideal promoting healthful personality development, but rather their ability to organize and present subject matter effectively, to explain ideas clearly, and to stimulate and competently direct pupil learning activity.

THE LIMITS OF NORMALITY

As was long true in the area of physical hygiene, some educators also tend to exaggerate the seriousness and permanence of the effects on mental health of minor deviations from the norm of desirable hygienic practice. There is every reason to believe, however, that a wide margin of safety is the rule both in physical and mental health. Within fairly broad limits, many different kinds of teacher personality structure and ways of relating to children are compatible with normal mental health and personality development in pupils. This principle applies when either mildly undesirable classroom practices prevail over an extended period of time, or when more serious deviations from optimal standards occur occasionally. In general, children are not nearly as fragile as we profess to believe, and do not develop permanent personality disabilities from temporary exposure to interpersonal practices that fall short of what the experts currently regard as appropriate.

THE CULT OF EXTROVERSION

In education, as in many other vocational fields, we have succumbed to the cult of the warm, outgoing, amiable, and extroverted personality, and have tended to regard any deviation from this standard as axiomatically undesirable from a mental hygiene standpoint. Formerly a pupil would be referred to the school psychologist if he was boisterous, aggressive, and refractory to discipline. Now it is the child who is reserved, contemplative, and unconcerned about the opinion of his peers who arouses the clinical concern of the child guidance specialist. Similarly, many excellent teachers who happen to be shy and introverted are viewed with alarm by their psychologically oriented superiors. Yet there is absolutely no evidence that they impair their pupils' mental health, even though they may conceivably be less popular as individuals than their extroverted colleagues; and as far as pupils are concerned, it has been definitely established that popularity may be a grossly misleading index of social adjustment. An ostensibly popular individual may be little more than a "stranger in his group" in terms of the depth of his attachments, or may be popular simply because he is docile, conforming, and willing to be directed and "used" by others (Wittenberg & Berg, 1952). Contrariwise, the pupil who is unpopular because of temperamental shyness or strong intellectual interests is not necessarily socially maladjusted or inevitably fated to become so (Morris, Soroker, & Burruss, 1954).

THE EFFECTS OF AUTHORITARIANISM

Many educators have uncritically accepted the ethnocentric psychological dictum that only democratic teacher-pupil relationships are compatible with normal mental health and personality development. Yet there are many examples of authoritarian western cultures (e.g., Germany, Italy, Switzerland) in which all of the indices of mental health and mature personality development compare very favorably with those prevailing in the United States. Hence, it is obviously not authoritarianism per se that has damaging mental health consequences, but rather the existence of authoritarian practices in home and school that are incongruous with the general pattern of interpersonal relations in the culture at large. Children *are* able satisfactorily to internalize adult personality traits and mature attitudes toward authority, even in an authoriarian home and school environment, providing that (a) personal, social, and working relationships among adults are similarly authoritarian, and (b) that adults generally make as stringent demands on themselves as they do on young people. In countries like Germany and Switzerland these latter conditions prevail, and therefore authoritarianism in home and school has few adverse effects on mental health and personality development. In New Zealand, on the other hand, authoritarianism in the home and secondary school has more serious effects because it contrasts sharply with the egalitarian and generally relaxed character of vocational and social life in the adult world.

Older children and adolescents do not satisfactorily internalize values that are indoctrinated in an authoritarian fashion if the adult culture itself is organized along democratic and egalitarian lines. Under these circumstances they feel unjustly treated and discriminated against; and not only do they tend to resent the authoritarian discipline that is imposed upon them, but also to conform to adult standards only under threat of external compulsion. This is particularly true if they perceive that many adults do not honor these standards but nevertheless presume to punish them whenever they are guilty of lapses. Hence, when adults preach the virtue of hard work, ambition, responsibility, and self-denial, but do not practice these virtues themselves in occupational life, children tend to emulate their example rather than their precepts. They become habituated to striving and working hard under external pressure but fail adequately to internalize these values. Thus when they finally enter the adult vocational world and the customary authoritarian demands for conscientious effort are lifted, the tenuous structure of their disciplined work habits tends to collapse in the absence of genuinely internalized needs for vocational achievement.

Furthermore, when a teen-ager in New Zealand obtains a job he dresses as an adult, is treated as an adult, and, from the age of eighteen, is paid on an adult wage scale. Even in the armed forces where working relationships are traditionally authoritarian, he is treated no differently than anyone else. Neither a shop foreman nor an army sergeant would ever think of using a cane on a seventeen-year-old factory hand or recruit who broke one of the rules or failed to do his work neatly. Yet in the secondary school this same teen-ager is treated very much as a child, wears short pants, and is growled at or caned for similar lapses. Hence, when he perceives the vastly more egalitarian treatment accorded his contemporaries in occupational life and in the military services, it is small wonder that he often feels resentful and sometimes manifests anti-adult and antisocial tendencies.

It also seems reasonable to suppose that as children enter adolescence, disciplinary practices should be progressively liberalized to meet increasing needs for self-determination and growing capacities for self-discipline. Quite paradoxically, however, since the primary school in New Zealand has always been much less authoritarian than the secondary school, and especially so over the past two decades, discipline tends to become stricter, more rigorous, and more explicit as children pass from the former to the latter. It is entirely understandable, therefore, that when the adolescent is unexpectedly subjected to a more restrictive discipline than he was in primary school—despite his greater physical, intellectual, emotional, and social maturity—he tends to become bewildered, dismayed, and resentful.

Attributable in part to the incongruous authoritarianism of the secondary school in New Zealand are many immature attitudes toward authority. First, in public situations, New Zealanders tend to defer excessively to the opinions of authority figures and to overconform to their dictates. Second, coexistent with this exaggerated public deference to authority, particularly among University students, is a puerile species of defiance, and an irresistible impulse to reject traditional values out-of-hand, to take outrageously extreme positions, and to shock the sensibilities of conventional folk with sacrilege, profanity, and the desecration of revered symbols. Third, because of resentment toward a discriminatory type of authoritarianism and overhabituation to external controls, many secondary school pupils fail adequately to internalize recognized social norms and individual restraints. Hence they feel quite justified in violating rules and asserting themselves when authority turns its back. Finally, the distinctive feature of adolescent misbehavior in New Zealand is simply a more exaggerated and generalized expression of anti-adult feeling and puerile defiance of adult authority. In its most extreme form, bodgieism, it is basically a cult of exhibitionistic nonconformity, out-of-bounds lout-ishness, and of studiously labored rejection of adult respectability. Among its multiple causes must certainly be counted widespread adolescent re-sentment of an inappropriately authoritarian type of discipline and sub-ordination relative to other age groups in New Zealand society. It bears some relation to the beatnik movement in the United States, but occurs in a younger age group, is less intellectual in its manifestations, and is more directly aggressive rather than philosophical in its protest.

DISTORTIONS OF DEMOCRATIC DISCIPLINE

Proponents of democratic classroom discipline believe in imposing the minimal degree of external control necessary for socialization, personality maturation, conscience development, and the emotional security of the child. Discipline and obedience are not regarded as ends in themselves but only as means to these latter ends. They are not striven for deliberately, but are expected to follow naturally in the wake of friendly and realistic teacher-pupil relationships. Explicit limits are not set routinely or as ways of showing "who is boss," but only as the need arises, i.e., when they are not implicitly understood or accepted by pupils.

Democratic discipline is as rational, nonarbitrary and bilateral as pos-sible. It provides explanations, permits discussion, and invites the partici-pation of children in the setting of standards whenever they are qualified to do so. Above all it implies respect for the dignity of the individual, and avoids exaggerated emphasis on status differences and barriers to free communication. Hence it repudiates harsh, abusive, and vindictive forms of punishment, and the use of sarcasm, ridicule, and intimidation.

The aforementioned attributes of democratic classroom discipline are obviously appropriate in cultures where social relationships tend to be egalitarian. This type of discipline also becomes increasingly more feasible as children become older, more responsible, and more capable of under-standing and formulating rules of conduct based on concepts of equity and reciprocal obligation. But contrary to what the extreme permissivists would have us believe, democratic school discipline does not imply free-dom from all external constraints, standards, and direction, or freedom. from discipline as an end in itself. And under no circumstances does it presuppose the eradication of all distinctions between pupil and teacher roles, or require that teachers abdicate responsibility for making the final decisions in the classroom.

Many educational theorists have misinterpreted and distorted the ideal of democratic discipline by equating it with an extreme form of permis-siveness. These distortions are most commonly encountered in the United States, but have also found acceptance in some New Zealand primary school circles. They have been dogmatically expressed in various psycho-logically unsound and unrealistic propositions that are considered sacro-sanct in many teachers' colleges. Fortunately, however, most classroom teachers have accepted them only for examination purposes—while still in training—and have discarded them in actual practice as thoroughly un-workable.

According to one widely held doctrine, only "positive" forms of discipline are constructive and democratic. It is asserted that children must only be guided by reward and approval; that reproof and punishment are authoritarian, repressive, and reactionary expressions of adult hostility which leave permanent emotional scars on children's personalities. What these theorists conveniently choose to ignore, however, is the fact that it is impossible for children to learn what is *not* approved and tolerated, simply by generalizing in reverse from the approval they receive for behavior that *is* acceptable. Even adults are manifestly incapable of learning and respecting the limits of acceptable conduct unless the distinction between what is proscribed and approved is reinforced by punishment as well as by reward. Furthermore, there is good reason to believe that acknowledgment of wrong-doing and acceptance of punishment are part and parcel of learning moral accountability and developing a sound conscience. Few if any children are quite that fragile that they cannot take deserved reproof and punishment in stride.

A second widespread distortion of democratic discipline is reflected in the popular notion that there are no culpably misbehaving children in the classroom, but only culpably aggressive, unsympathetic, and punitive teachers. If children misbehave, according to this point of view, one can implicitly assume that they must have been provoked beyond endurance by repressive and authoritarian classroom discipline. Similarly, if they are disrespectful, then the teacher, by definition, must not have been deserving of respect. It is true, of course, that much pupil misconduct *is* instigated by harsh and abusive school discipline; but there are also innumerable reasons for out-of-bounds behavior that are completely independent of the teacher's attitudes and disciplinary practices. Pupils are also influenced by factors originating in the home, the neighborhood, the peer group, and the mass-media. Some children are emotionally disturbed, others are brain-damaged, and still others are aggressive by temperament; and there are times when even the best behaved children from the nicest homes develop an irresistible impulse—without any provocation whatsoever—to test the limits of a teacher's forbearance.

Both of the aforementioned distortions of classroom democracy are used to justify the commonly held belief among educators that pupils should not be reproved or punished for disorderly or discourteous conduct. I have, for example, observed classrooms where everybody talks at once; where pupils turn their backs on the teacher and engage in private conversation while the latter is endeavoring to instruct them; and where pupils verbally abuse teachers for exercising their rightful disciplinary prerogatives. Some educators contend that all of this is compatible with wholesome, democratic teacher-pupil relationships. Other educators deplore this type of pupil behavior but insist, nevertheless, that punishment is unwarranted under these circumstances. In the first place, they assert, reproof or punishment constitutes a "negative" and hence axiomatically undesirable approach to classroom management; and, secondly, the misbehavior would assuredly have never occurred to begin with, if the teacher's attitudes had been less autocratic or antagonistic. I have already answered the second group of educators, and to the first group I can only say that

I am still sufficiently old-fashioned to believe that rudeness and unruliness are not normally desirable classroom behavior in any culture.

When such misconduct occurs, I believe pupils have to be unambiguously informed that it will not be tolerated and that any repetition of the same behavior will be punished. This action does not preclude in any way either an earnest attempt to discover why the misbehavior occurred, or suitable preventive measures aimed at correcting the underlying causes. But, by the same token, the mere fact that a pupil has a valid psychological reason for misbehaving does not mean that he is thereby absolved from moral accountability or rendered no longer subject to punishment.

Still another related distortion of democratic discipline is reflected in the proposition that it is repressive and authoritarian to request pupils to apologize for discourteous behavior or offensive language. However, if we take seriously the idea that the dignity of the human being is important, we must be willing to protect it from affront; and apology is the most civilized and effective means mankind has yet evolved for accomplishing this goal. In a democratic society nobody is that important that he is above apologizing to those persons whom he wrongfully offends. Everybody's dignity is important—the teacher's as well as the pupil's. It is no less wrong for a pupil to abuse a teacher than for a teacher to abuse a pupil.

If apologies are to have any real significance in moral training, however, it is obvious that, even though they are explicitly requested, they must be made voluntarily, and must be reflective of genuine appreciation of wrong-doing and of sincere regret and remorse. Purely formal and mechanical statements of apology made under coercion are less than worthless. Apologies are also without real ethical import unless their basis is reciprocal, i.e., unless it is fully understood that under comparable circumstances the teacher would be willing to apologize to his pupils.

In seeking to correct these undesirable permissive distortions of classroom democracy, it would be foolhardy to return to the equally undesirable opposite extreme of authoritarianism that flourished in the United States up to a quarter-century ago, and still prevails in many western nations. Democratic school discipline is still an appropriate and realistic goal for education in a democratic society; hence there is no need to throw away the baby with the bath water. It is only necessary to discard the aforementioned permissivist doctrines masquerading under the banners of democracy and behavioral science, and to restore certain other traditional values that have been neglected in the enthusiasm of extending democracy to home and school.

More specifically, we first have to clear up the semantic confusion. We should stop equating permissiveness with democratic discipline, and realistic adult control and guidance with authoritarianism. Permissiveness, by definition, is the absence of discipline, democratic or otherwise. We should cease instructing teachers that it is repressive and reactionary to reprove or punish pupils for misconduct, or to request them to apologize for offensive and discourteous behavior.

Second, we should stop misinterpreting what little reputable evidence we have about discipline, and refrain from misrepresenting our personal biases on the subject as the indisputable established findings of scientific research. The available evidence merely suggests that in a democratic cultural setting, authoritarian discipline has certain undesirable effects—*not* that the consequences or laissez-faire permissiveness are desirable. As a matter of fact, research studies (Cunningham, 1951) show that the effects of extreme permissiveness are just as unwholesome as are those of authoritarianism. In the school situation a laissez-faire policy leads to confusion, insecurity, and competition for power among pupils. Assertive pupils tend to become aggressive and ruthless, whereas retiring pupils tend to withdraw further from classroom participation. The child who is handled too permissively at home tends to regard himself as a specially privileged person. He fails to learn the normative standards and expectations of society, to set realistic goals for himself, and to make reasonable demands on others. In his dealings with adults and other children he is domineering, aggressive, petulant, and capricious.

Third, we should stop making teachers feel guilty and personally responsible for all instances of misconduct and disrespect in the classroom. We do this whenever we take for granted, without any actual supporting evidence, that these behavior problems would never have arisen in the first place if the teachers involved were truly deserving of respect and had been administering genuinely wholesome and democratic discipline.

Finally, teachers' colleges should terminate the prevailing conspiracy of silence they maintain about the existence of disciplinary problems in the schools. Although discipline is the one aspect of teaching that the beginning teacher is most worried about, he receives little or no practical instruction in handling this problem. Many teacher training institutions, as pointed out above, rationalize their inadequacies in this regard by pretending that disciplinary problems are relatively rare occurrences involving the disturbed child, or more typically the disturbed teacher. Due respect for the facts of life, however, suggests that prospective teachers today not only need to be taught more realistic propositions about the nature and purposes of democratic discipline, but also require adequately supervised, down-to-earth experience in coping with classroom discipline.

REFERENCES

Cunningham, Ruth. *Understanding group behavior of boys and girls.* New York: Teachers College, Columbia Univer., 1951.

Morris, D. P., Soroker, E., & Burruss, G. Follow-up studies of shy, withdrawn children. I. Evaluation of later adjustments. *American Journal of Orthopsychiatry,* 1954, 24, 743–754.

Taylor, P. H. Children's evaluations of the characteristics of the good teacher. *British Journal of Educational Psychology,* 1962, 32, 258–266.

Wittenberg, R. M., & Berg, J. The stranger in the group. *American Journal of Orthopsychiatry,* 1952, 22, 89–97.

PART II

DEVELOPMENT AND MENTAL HEALTH

In this unit, development and its relationships to mental health are examined from three related, but somewhat different perspectives.

Chapter Two

The basic theme in Chapter Two—Developmental Problems in Becoming—is that most children, though emotionally healthy, experience adjustment problems at various stages. In accordance with this theme, adjustment difficulties confronting youngsters at various stages of development are presented. Among the topics presented are the following:

the widespread existence of such phenomena as fears and hyper-activity among elementary school youngsters;
the "types" of behavior problems among early adolescents;
the shortcomings of today's breed of adolescents;
the stresses confronting achieving adolescents; and
the later adjustment of disturbed children.

Chapter Three

The emotional aspects of education have, for the most part, been neglected by the schools. Altogether too frequently, the academic values of the school predominate to the extent that only minimal consideration is given to the affective components of the teaching-learning situation. In response to this neglect are the five selections contained in Chapter Three—Social and Emotional Aspects of Educational Adjustment. These are the topics discussed in this section:

the importance of feeling in the educative process;
alienation in the schools;
the role of self-concept and its effects on school adjustment;
sex differences in socialization and their relationships to classroom interactions; and

the significance of achievement motivation in the educational performance of disadvantaged youth.

Chapter Four

Not only have the social and emotional aspects of the teaching-learning
situation been deemphasized, but, up until the present time, even the interrelationships between cognitive processes as an aspect of the socialization
process and positive mental health remained largely unexplored. Fortunately, in recent years there has been a gradual turning away from pathology
and greater stress placed on the encouragement of intellectual mastery and
creativity as a significant aspect of pupil mental health. Indeed, there
seems to be an ever increasing recognition of the role played by cognitive
development or the ego processes in the facilitation of personality and
social development. According to this viewpoint, the school can enhance
emotional robustness by developing the ego processes which take in,
organize and utilize information so as to benefit the student. That is, the
schools can help develop a socially competent individual by focusing on
the conflict-free areas of personality—an objective consistent with the
teacher's role. The following topics provide an overview of Chapter Four—
Cognitive Development and Mental Health:

ways in which the teacher can promote personal development without
sacrificing scholastic achievements;
the relationship between creative thinking and mental health;
more adventuresome forms of intervention to offset the impact of
early adverse experiences on intellectual development;
how intellectual development allows for the possibility of new emotional experiences among adolescent youth; and
the potentially deleterious emotional effects associated with the
evaluation of cognitive abilities and skills.

CHAPTER 2

Developmental Problems in Becoming

5. The Epidemiology of Behavior Disorders in Children

Rema Lapouse

*Contrary to popular belief, the typical child is beset by
many problems during the course of his development.
As Lapouse notes, normal development does not run a
smooth and untroubled course. Rather, all youngsters
experience adjustment difficulties. The data in this
study suggest that such difficulties are far more common and far less pathological than most parents, teachers and psychologists believe.*

A comparative review of research into children's behavior disorders brings
into sharp focus the major problems in such studies. Variability in the
definitions and methods used by different investigators makes it difficult
to select the more valid findings among the discrepant data reported.

An aspect of the dilemma is illustrated by Goldfarb's study[1] of the
relative ability of school teachers and psychiatrists to identify psychiatric
cases among school children. He found that these two professional groups
disagreed on the identification of specific children with mental health
problems and concluded that the teachers required further training to increase their sensitivity to psychiatric cases. The assumption that the correct definition of a psychiatric case is a secure part of the psychiatrist's

American Journal of Diseases of Children, 1966, 3, 594–599. Reprinted with the permission of the publisher and author.

armamentarium is open to question when psychiatric diagnosis still lacks the means for objective validation. Far more than in other medical fields, psychiatric diagnosis is known to vary with the theoretical system espoused by the diagnostician, which in turn influences his concept of normality and his diagnostic formulations.

The attachment of exaggerated psychopathologic significance to single behavior items such as nail biting, nose picking, and casual masturbation, says Kanner,[2] arises from the use of statistics contributed by selected groups of children from child guidance clinics and juvenile courts. He points out that, for the general population of children, neither the occurrence nor the ultimate psychiatric fate of the so-called symptoms is known, and he suggests that the unfavorable prognostic implications of these behaviors may be unwarranted.

How behavior disorders are defined is an issue crucial to their study. For the most part, psychiatrists, social workers, psychologists, and other workers in the field accept the assumption that some rather ordinary behaviors, like those mentioned by Kanner, have pathological import and predict future psychiatric casualty. As we have pointed out elsewhere,[3] this is as if observers, noting the presence of a cough in tuberculosis, interpreted all coughs as definitive evidence of this disease. Based solely on such an inclusive definition, prevalence studies will inevitably overreport the amount of tuberculosis in the population.

By the same token, an inclusive definition of behavior disorders overcounts the occurrence of this morbid state among children and creates a situation with dangerous implications. Among the dangers are: failure to distinguish between sick and nonsick children, with accompanying tendencies to treat the nonsick; invidious iatrogenic effects stemming from those tendencies which affect children, families, teachers, and other child-caring professions; consequent misapplication of existing psychiatric personnel and services and distortion of estimates for their need; and, finally, stimulation of misleading hypotheses which affect the theoretical structure of child psychiatry.

To compound the confusion created by the diagnostic dilemma, the methods used by most investigators in studying children's behavior disorders suffer not only from the problem of selection already mentioned by Kanner, but additionally from the difficulty of establishing the validity and reliability of findings, and their comparability from one study to another. The common practice of placing reliance on the skill of the interviewer or observer in obtaining and interpreting information about children introduces subjective elements which defy verification.

METHOD

The study of children's behavior described in this paper was designed to overcome some of the more obvious shortcomings of previous investigations. The aims of this research were (1) to gain knowledge regarding the prevalence of a number of behavior characteristics of children in relation to sex, age, race, and socioeconomic status; (2) to determine the interrelationships of these behaviors; (3) to correlate these behaviors with adequacy of function in the individual child; and (4) ultimately, to devise an effective means of identifying the psychiatrically sick child in the community.

The methodologic features of the design were the selection of a representative sample of children, the use of a structured interview schedule for obtaining comparable information on all children, and the avoidance of a priori definitions of so-called symptomatic behavior. Such avoidance is an applicable procedure where the diagnosis or definition of a pathological entity is uncertain.

In this study we investigated the frequency, intensity, and duration of a wide variety of behaviors, and from these dimensions were derived criteria by which the definition of a behavior disorder may be formulated. By these criteria, a behavior is considered to be disordered when it deviates from the prevailing norms and when it is accompanied by impaired function as shown by maladjustment and poor performance.

The child behavior study was based on 482 children, aged 6 through 12 years, randomly selected from households which were systematically sampled in Buffalo. In 1½ hour sessions, trained interviewers administered more than 200 closed-end questions to the mother of the selected children. Of the mothers approached, 94% consented to the interview. Mothers were selected as respondents because direct examination or observation of nearly 500 children would have been neither feasible nor reliable, and because, as Luton Ackerson[4] remarked, "While the child's mother cannot be assumed to know the truth concerning the many aspects of his behavior, there is probably no other available class of informant which would know nearly as much." Also, evidence was available supporting the relative accuracy of mothers' observations.[5]

Subsequently, two substudies were undertaken to test the reliability and validity of the mothers' reports. In one instance, the interviews were exactly replicated on a 10% subsample of the mothers originally interviewed, and in the second, a new sample of children was selected, and both the mother and child were simultaneously interviewed by different interviewers using a part of the questionnaire.

The information obtained on the children was grouped to facilitate the analysis of the data. Several areas were identified, including behavior, adjustment, social relations, achievement, health, anxiety, and environment. The items comprised in these areas and the method used in classifying them have been discussed at length in previous papers.[3,6,7] Scores were established by assigning points reflecting the presence, frequency, intensity, and sometimes duration of the various items reported. For any given area, the points were accumulated to form a single area score. Each of these overall scores summarized the scores of the contributing items. The highest scores indicated that children with these scores had more of the behaviors studied, that these behaviors occurred more frequently and more intensely, and perhaps persisted longer in high-score children than in those with lower scores.

By selecting a proportion of children with the highest or most extreme scores for behavior, the first criterion defining abnormal behavior could be fulfilled, namely, deviation from the prevailing norm. The second criterion, malfunction, could be met by separating out a proportion of children with extreme scores for adjustment, social relations, and achievement. By this means it becomes possible to assess the extent to which deviant behavior and malfunction are associated, and to examine in greater detail the characteristics of the child whose aberrant behavior is coupled with impaired function.

RESULTS

Of the 482 children comprising the sample, half were boys and half were girls; half were 6 through 8 years old and the other half were 9 through 12. Division into socioeconomic halves was predetermined by the sampling method. The proportion of nonwhites in the sample was 15%, which mirrored the proportion of nonwhites in Buffalo.

In the investigation of the prevalence of various behaviors, the first finding of significance was the surprisingly frequent occurrence of some characteristics commonly considered to be symptomatic of psychiatric disorder.[8] Over 40% of the children were reported as having seven or more fears and worries; about 30% were said to have nightmares, to be restless, and to bite their nails; and between 10% and 25% to engage in various other body manipulations. Mothers reported that almost 20% of the children wet the bed within the previous year and that over 10% lost their tempers once a day or more often.

With reports of such high prevalence of suspect behavior characteristics, it became very important to examine the possibility that these items were being inaccurately reported by mothers. In one substudy, the reliability of mothers' reports was tested by comparing the agreement between their first interviews and the reinterviews which took place on an average of six weeks later. It was found that for the more explicit and specific behaviors agreement occurred at a median of 91% of the paired answers. These behaviors are bedwetting, thumbsucking, stuttering, nailbiting, temper loss, biting clothing, chewing lips, tics, picking sores, picking nose, grinding teeth, and similar behaviors. For the more implicit and non-specific behaviors such as nightmares, fears and worries, restlessness, over-activity, and amount of food eaten, the median percentage agreement was 78. This finding indicates that the responses of mothers are fairly consistent over time, but that this consistency is greater when the reported behavior is more concrete and objectively observable. In a second substudy, the paired responses of mothers and children were examined. Their median agreement was lower than for the comparison of mothers with mothers, but the same phenomenon was observed of greater accord between mother and child on explicit-specific (68%) than on implicit-non-specific behaviors (54%).[3,8]

The most striking finding in the mother-child comparison was that, contrary to expectation, mothers in general reported fewer positive items than did children. If the child's report is accepted as the criterion, the prevalence of so-called symptomatic behaviors appears to be even greater than reported above. This finding points to the need for reassessment of the serious implications which the presence of these behaviors connotes to many workers in the field. We have raised the question whether these characteristics are truly indicative of psychiatric disorder, or whether they occur as transient developmental phenomena in essentially normal children.

Further evidence bearing on this question comes from an examination of the occurrence of high-scoring (worst) behaviors as these are examined within subgroups of the sample divided by sex, age, race, socioeconomic status, and number of siblings in the family. The greatest difference was found in children aged 6 through 8 years as compared with 9 through 12-year-olds. A statistically significant excess of high scores in younger children was found for speech difficulties; for body manipulations, also called tension phenomena, including biting nails, grinding teeth, sucking thumb or fingers, chewing lips or tongue, sucking or chewing clothing, picking nose and picking sores; for wild behavior, bedwetting, nightmares, and masturbation; and for the overall area score for behavior. This finding is also consistent with the thesis that deviant behavior occurs as a transient developmental phenomenon in school-aged children.

Although marked differences in highscoring behavior are commonly believed to exist between boys and girls, and were therefore anticipated, the only differences of any consequence were the excess of high scores among boys for bedwetting, masturbation, physical inactivity, and daydreaming. There was no sex difference in the overall behavior area score.

There were only minimal differences between white upper and lower social classes, possibly due to the dilution of the extremes in each half with intermediate socioeconomic groups. When Negro and white children were compared, however, the Negro children showed an excess of high scores for body management, including posture, gait, and coordination; for speech difficulties; and for thumbsucking, compulsive behavior, and daydreaming. No significant difference by race was observed in the overall behavior area scores.

When the sample is divided into only children and those with siblings, only one important difference appears: children from multiple child families seem more likely to suck their thumb or fingers. Since Negro families in this sample include fewer singlechild families than do the white families, the excess in thumbsucking for Negro children may well be related to family size. Evidence is also very persuasive that Negro-white differences are due less to race than to socioeconomic disparity, since the Negro children in this sample, compared with the white lower class children, live under more adverse social and economic conditions. One-third of the white lower class children have annual family incomes under $4,000, while this income level describes almost three-quarters of the Negro children. Similarly, one-third of the Negro children suffer the handicaps of poor housing and low status of the father's occupation in comparison with one eighth of the white lower class children.

In analyzing the interrelationships between various behaviors and the fears and worries of children, the evidence failed to support the thesis that fearful or anxious children (defined here as those with seven or more fears and worries) have more tension phenomena, nightmares, bedwetting, stuttering, temper loss, and tics than other children.[9] Because there is always the danger that mothers reported inaccurately, we repeated this analysis using data from interviews with children alone. The results showed an even lower correlation between a large number of fears and worries and these behaviors. Fearfulness, moreover, does not seem to be related to high scores for somatic complaints. Finally, the evidence also failed to support the expectation that the worrying mother would either *have* a worrying child or *report* a worrying child. The widespread occurrence of many fears and worries among children and the negative association between these fears and the various deviant behaviors tends to suggest that such anxieties, like many behaviors, may be a concomitant of the wide range of essentially normal developmental phenomena in children.

The search for the functional correlates of high-scoring or deviant behavior has been only partially completed. Analysis of the relationship between adjustment, as one aspect of function, and behavior has produced some interesting findings.[7] Adjustment was assessed from a series of so-called continua, described in previous papers.[3,7] Each continuum contains five statements delineating a range of adaptational possibilities among which the mother was asked to select the one which most nearly fitted her child. The statements chosen were scored according to whether they were extreme, intermediate, or middle, with the last being considered normal.

For the purpose of comparing behavior and adjustment in the subgroups, the distribution of high scores signifying maladjustment was examined.[7] It was interesting to find that, in contrast to high-scoring behavior, there was no difference in the occurrence of high scores denoting maladjustment between younger and older children. Nor, in fact, were there any notable differences between pairs of subgroups divided by sex or by number of siblings. The dramatic differences occurred among the social classes in a sharp stepwise ascent as socioeconomic status went down. The proportion of children who were judged to be maladjusted by their high scores was twice as high for the white lower class subgroup as for the white upper class; for the Negro subgroup, it was four times as high.

Although there was a significant correlation between overall scores for the behavior and adjustment areas, it was at a low level, and prediction of coexisting maladjustment from the presence of deviant behavior was quite insecure. However, some individual behaviors showed a significant relationship to scores for maladjustment. Without regard to age, the tension phenomena, restlessness, temper loss, eating habits, and eating behavior are so related. Younger children are more likely to be maladjusted in the presence of speech difficulties, tics, and physical inactivity. Older children have a greater likelihood of maladjustment when they display thumbsucking and nailbiting. No significant association with maladjustment was found in the total sample or in either age group for wild behavior, overactivity, bedwetting, disturbed sleep or bedtime behavior, and daydreaming.

For the foregoing analyses, the criterion for extreme or deviant scores for each item was arbitrarily chosen as the highest 25% of the distribution of scores in the total sample. Such a large percentage was selected because of the small sample size. As the criterion was progressively narrowed, the predictive accuracy of deviant behavior for coexisting maladjustment was increased. At the 25% level for each area, the risk of deviant adjustment is twice as great for children with, as it is for those without, deviant behavior. At the 5% level, this relative risk is increased to a ninefold difference. A definition of deviation limited to 5% of the distribution of scores would probably be optimal for the detection of children with behavior disorders.

Currently, possible associations are being looked for between behavior and adjustment on the one hand, and adequacy of function on the other. How well the sampled children function is judged by scores measuring their achievement at school and their success in family and community relationships. The finding of consistent and significant interrelationships among these modalities will increase the security of the criteria for the diagnosis and detection of behavior disorders in children.

The present child behavior study is most useful in demonstrating a method of collecting and analyzing information which reduces the subjective elements that plague most psychiatric studies related to children. Insofar as other data exist, some of the findings of this research, for example, those regarding the prevalence of enuresis and its relationship to adjustment, are borne out by other investigators. Most of the findings need confirmation. Further validation studies and tests of reliability need to be done. A much larger sample of children needs to be surveyed to permit adequate analysis of subgroups. A similar study replicating the present procedures on a larger population in other areas needs to be done to test independently both the prevalence data and the findings on interrelationships of the current work. The standardized instrument and methods developed in this study lend themselves to replication by other investigators.

Moreover, the same instrument and method used here for determining the prevalence of behavior and its correlates may also be applicable to other kinds of epidemiologic investigations. For example, comparison of findings in children with and without a particular condition is a technique which has numerous possibilities in the search for etiologic clues. The use of the replicable methods described makes it possible to compare the characteristics of children of different ethnic or cultural backgrounds, of varying family origins, and of disparate health histories.

Finally, the instrument and methods can be adapted to serve as a detecting device for the early identification of children with disturbances of psychiatric import. The successful accomplishment of this objective will make it possible to find early or mild psychiatric cases, to distinguish specific subgroups of the population with the highest risk of mental disorder, and to base estimates of psychiatric need on a more realistic foundation than exists today.

SUMMARY

Methods and findings are presented from a study of the prevalence of various behaviors and their correlates in 482 children aged 6 through 12, comprising a representative sample of children in Buffalo. Behavior disorders are defined as those which deviate from prevailing norms and are associated with functional impairment.

A major finding was that behavior deviations were much more frequent in younger than in older children, but expected differences in occurrence between boys and girls were not observed. In contrast, no age differences were seen for maladjustment, but the latter showed a stepwise increase as socioeconomic status decreased.

Fearfulness, as reported both by mothers and children, failed to demonstrate an association with various kinds of behaviors considered to have psychiatric significance. The correlation between such behaviors and adjustment was positive and significant but at a sufficiently low level that prediction of coexisting maladjustment from the presence of behavior deviations was not usually possible.

The strikingly high prevalence of so-called symptomatic behaviors, their excessive presence in younger as contrasted with older children, and the weak association between these behaviors and adjustment give rise to the question whether behavior deviations are truly indicative of psychiatric disorder or whether they occur as transient developmental phenomena in essentially normal children.

This study was supported in part by U.S. Public Health Service grants M-1507 and M-3191, and the American Child Guidance Foundation.

REFERENCES

1. Goldfarb, A.: Teacher Ratings in Psychiatric Case Findings, *Amer. J. Public Health* 53:1919–1927, 1963.
2. Kanner, L.: Do Behavioral Symptoms Always Indicate Psychopathology? *J. Child Psychol. Psychiat.* 1:17–25, 1960.
3. Lapouse, R.; Monk, M. A.; and Street, E.: A Method for Use in Epidemiologic Studies of Behavior Disorders in Children, *Amer. J. Public Health* 54:207–222, 1964.
4. Ackerson, L.: *Children's Behavior Problems*, Chicago: University of Chicago Press, 1954, vol. 1.
5. Glidewell, J. C.; Mensch, I. N.; and Gildea, M. C.-L.: Behavior Symptoms in Children and Degree of Sickness, *Amer. J. Psychiat.* 114:47–53, 1957.
6. Lapouse, R., and Monk, M. A.: Behavior Deviations in a Representative Sample of Children: Variation by Sex, Age, Race, Social Class and Family Size, *Amer. J. Orthopsychiat.* 34:436–446, 1964.
7. Lapouse, R.: The Relationship of Behavior to Adjustment in a Representative Sample of Children, *Amer. J. Public Health* 55:1130–1141, 1965.
8. Lapouse, R., and Monk, M. A.: An Epidemiologic Study of Behavior Characteristics in Children, *Amer. J. Public Health* 48:1134–1144, 1958.
9. Lapouse, R., and Monk, M. A.: Fears and Worries in a Representative Sample of Children, *Amer. J. Orthopsychiat.* 29:803–818, 1959.

6. Behavior Problems in Early Adolescence

Herbert C. Quay and Lorene C. Quay

The classification of childhood disorders has long plagued mental health specialists. Though more than thirty such approaches have been developed over the years, none has proven satisfactory. In recent years, psychologists at the University of Illinois have attempted to identify the major dimensions underlying behavior deviations in childhood. Quay and Quay note that as personality becomes increasingly complex, the number of dimensions needed to classify behavior deviations likewise increases. Though some may criticize the statistical approach to classification as abolishing theoretical concepts central to advancing the understanding of personality development and psychopathology, the hard-nosed mental health specialist should welcome what appears to be a reliable and objective procedure for the determination of meaningful syndromes or dimensions of disturbed behavior.

In a search for a conceptually meaningful way of classifying children's behavior problems Peterson (1961) had the 58 most common problems of children referred to a guidance clinic rated as to their presence or absence

Child Development, 1965, 36, 215–220. Copyright 1965 by The Society for Research in Child Development, Inc. Reprinted with the permission of the copyright owner and senior author.

This research was supported in part by a Grant M-5627 from the National Institutes of Health, U.S. Department of Health, Education and Welfare. The authors wish to express their appreciation to Mr. James Higgins, principal, Old Orchard Junior High School, Skokie, Illinois, and his entire staff for their interest and co-operation in the study. Herbert Quay's present address: Children's Research Center, University of Illinois, 1007 W. Nevada, Urbana, Ill. 61801.

in a sample of 831 children in kindergarten through Grade 6 by public school teachers. A factor analysis of the interrelationships among the items indicated that the majority of the variance could be accounted for by two factors, labeled "conduct problem" and "personality problem," which were remarkably similar in their item content for the kindergarten group, the first and second grades combined, the third and fourth grades combined, and the fifth and sixth grades combined. Factor scores were satisfactorily reliable when the independent ratings of teachers were compared, and the results of the study suggested a useful way of conceptualizing children's behavior problems at these age levels.

This study represents an attempt to further the description and understanding of the behavior problems of children by extending the findings of earlier studies to public school children in early adolescence.

SUBJECTS AND PROCEDURES

Subjects were 259 children in the seventh grade and 259 children in the eighth grade of a suburban junior high school, drawing children from predominantly upper middle-class families. These children represented only that proportion of the entire student body considered by at least one rater (teacher) to have one or more of the 58 items on the Peterson checklist as a behavioral characteristic. It should be noted that behavior problems in this particular school seem at a minimum and that the findings obtained in this study are no doubt attenuated by this restriction of range.

Each child in the sample was rated by his social studies teacher; a subsample of children was also rated by another teacher for purposes of estimating the reliability of factor scores. In those cases where two ratings were obtained both ratings were used in the factor analysis so that the correlations were actually based on 317 ratings in the eighth grade and 329 ratings in the seventh grade.

When each child was rated on the 58-item scale many of the items were noted in fewer than 10 per cent of the cases and were not subjected to further statistical analysis. The majority of these deleted items referred to behavior obviously not to be expected in children of this age group: thumb sucking, enuresis, difficulty with bowel control, crying, etc. Twenty eight items were retained for statistical analysis for the eighth grade and 26 for the seventh grade.

Correlational and factorial analysis were accomplished by electronic computer. A principal-axis factor solution was obtained using the squared multiple correlation as the communality estimate; rotation was then carried out to meet Kaiser's (1958) varimax criteria. Experimenter judgment entered only in the a priori decision to rotate only those factors with at least one loading of 0.40 or greater.

RESULTS

Factor Structure
Rotated-factor loadings may be found in Table 1; in addition the loadings for the same variables as found in Peterson's (1961) fifth- and sixth-graders, a sample of adolescent delinquents (Quay, 1964a) and a sample of preadolescent delinquents (Quay, 1964c) are presented.

TABLE 1. ROTATED FACTOR LOADINGS WITH LOADINGS FROM OTHER STUDIES FOR COMPARISON[a]

	Factors															
	Seventh Grade			Eighth Grade				Peterson's Fifth and Sixth Grades		Quay's Adolescent Delinquents			Quay's Preadolescent Delinquents		
Variable	I	II	h²	I	II	III	h²	I	II	I	II	III	I	II	III
Restless	12	63	40	15	70	−04	51	20	70	14	46	37	03	44	04
Attention-seeking	22	48	28	19	61	−08	42	02	76	−07	70	20	01	49	−09
Inability to have fun	19	−27	11	03	−15	31	12	48	−09	60	23	22	39	−12	10
Self-conscious	55	−22	35	−11	00	54	30	63	16	48	−05	39	59	−08	00
Disruptive	14	64	43	21	70	−12	56	11	76	−05	77	11	00	67	15
Feelings of inferiority	66	01	43	17	−07	57	36	62	17	47	05	29	65	06	05
Boisterousness	07	60	36	15	60	−03	39	−09	68	−14	71	18	00	69	08
Preoccupation	52	13	28	62	−04	21	43	41	37	60	14	28	18	−21	48
Shyness	42	−35	29	00	−42	38	31	51	−13	54	−28	13	59	−27	08
Withdrawal	55	−11	31	12	−18	15	07	60	05	67	−06	04	41	−34	27
Short attention span	25	59	41	56	44	11	51	29	60	11	59	28	19	37	55
Lack of confidence	59	−13	36	22	−17	63	47	58	16	66	12	30	57	03	22
Inattentive	21	64	45	58	46	−08	54	28	69	24	64	18	22	50	25
Easily flustered	41	04	16	02	14	34	13	58	24	55	19	46	60	21	25
Lack of interest	47	44	42	48	−02	−02	23	28	51	49	49	−02	29	−03	47
Reticence	..	..	..	08	−23	18	09	41	14	..	..	..	14	−04	25
Laziness in school	33	57	42	59	22	−15	41	31	37	20	55	00	09	24	66
Irresponsibility	38	67	58	51	29	00	34	20	65	34	75	00	..	..	..
Daydreaming	48	32	34	57	13	20	38	47	49	70	08	26	−07	41	50
Disobedience	01	58	34	22	62	00	43	11	86	11	74	00	−03	64	06
Uncooperativeness	..	..	..	25	36	−07	19	21	71	15	74	01	−04	59	13
Aloofness	13	−27	09	20	−32	22	18	31	05	29	−01	02	20	−30	27
Passive, suggestible	12	47	23	38	13	14	18	30	52	21	47	30	28	12	27
Hyperactivity	−16	48	25	−01	54	08	29	03	49	03	37	53	−05	60	09
Distractibility	09	62	40	36	59	−11	48	26	72	30	34	62	03	46	53
Impertinence	13	47	24	11	33	07	12	08	76	21	62	29	−16	57	02
Lethargy	47	06	22	27	−17	02	10	43	31	62	22	−05	29	−16	58
Nervous, jittery	11	26	07	−14	28	35	22	26	50	42	22	43	40	39	17

[a] Decimal places omitted

For the seventh grade two factors accounted for 83 per cent of the communality. Factor I is obviously related to inferiority, shyness, withdrawal, etc., and has been labeled "personality problem" in accordance with Peterson's (1961) designation. The factor loadings were compared to loadings found for the same variables in the previous studies by means of Tucker's coefficient[1] (see Table 2). A considerable degree of concordance with conceptually similar factors in the other studies is apparent. Factor II

[1] Ledyard R. Tucker, personal communication. This coefficient is obtained by dividing the sum of the cross-products of the loadings by the square root of the products of the two sums of squares. It is essentially a correlation coefficient, uncorrected for origin.

TABLE 2. COEFFICIENTS OF FACTOR SIMILARITY FOR LOADINGS IN TABLE 1[a]

| | Seventh Grade | | | Eighth Grade | |
	I Personality	II Conduct	I Immaturity	II Conduct	III Personality
Eighth grade:					
Immaturity (I)	.67	.70			
Conduct (II)	.09	*.83*			
Personality (III)	*.70*	−.15			
Peterson's fifth **and sixth grades:**					
Personality (I)	*.91*	.23	.61	.13	*.80*
Conduct (II)	.50	*.91*	.75	*.88*	.12
Quay's adolescent **delinquents:**					
Neurotic (I)	*.91*	.20	.60	.02	*.75*
Psychopathic (II)	.42	*.93*	.72	*.84*	.00
Immature (III)	.55	.58	*.44*	.55	.58
Quay's preadolescent **delinquents:**					
Neurotic (I)	*.84*	.08	.27	−.09	.72
Psychopathic (II)	.10	*.88*	.45	*.93*	−.06
Immature (III)	.70	.56	*.89*	.29	.26

[a]Validity values are italicized

is clearly one of aggressive, acting-out behavior and has been labeled, again in accordance with Peterson, "conduct problem." Table 2 indicates an even greater degree of comparability with the earlier studies for this factor.

For Grade 8 three factors were rotated; these three factors accounted for 84 per cent of the total communality. Factor I has its highest loadings on the variables of preoccupation, short attention span, lack of interest, inattentiveness, laziness, irresponsibility, and daydreaming. This cluster of behaviors suggested an "immaturity" or perhaps regressive syndrome which was not found in the seventh grade but had been identified, at least tentatively, in studies of juvenile delinquents. Table 2 indicates that it is, in fact, substantially related to a factor which was labeled "inadequacy-immaturity" in the study of the younger delinquents. However, the picture is clouded by its relationship with both the conduct and personality factors in the other two studies. The interpretation of this factor, and perhaps even its existence as independent from the two larger factors, must await further clarification. Factor II is obviously the conduct-problem factor and has been so labeled. Factor III seems a definite counterpart of the personality-problem factor found both in the seventh grade and in the earlier studies.

Reliability of Factor Scores

In a subsample of both grades it was possible to obtain ratings on an individual child by both his social studies teacher and another of his instructors. Table 3 presents the reliability coefficients for the factor scores. As

TABLE 3. INTERRATER RELIABILITY COEFFICIENTS FOR FACTOR SCORES

	Grade	
Factors	Seventh	Eighth
Personality	.31	.22
Conduct	.58	.71
Immaturity	—	.31

might be expected the conduct-problem dimension was rated with a good deal more reliability than were the other dimensions. The limited reliability of the personality-problem dimension in both grades is disappointing, but it must be remembered that these teachers were not especially well-trained raters and, due to the departmental system in the school, generally had only 1 hour of contact per day with those children whom they rated.

Relationships Among Factor Scores

The relative independence among the factorial dimensions is attested to by the correlations among the factor scores. In the seventh grade the personality-problem and the conduct-problem factor scores correlated .10. For the eighth-grade the immaturity factor correlated .09 with personality problem and .59 with conduct problem. Finally, conduct problem correlated $-.18$ with personality. With the exception of the immaturity versus conduct-problem correlation in the eighth grade, these dimensions are both factorially orthogonal and empirically independent.

DISCUSSION

Not only do the results of this study substantiate and extend those of Peterson's (1961) earlier work, but the factors isolated also bear considerable similarity to studies of rated problem behavior in other populations. Similar-appearing factors have also been found in factorial studies of personality questionnaires in samples of juvenile delinquents and normals (Peterson, Quay, & Cameron, 1959; Peterson, Quay, & Tiffany, 1961) and in the analyses of case histories of delinquent boys (Quay, 1964b; Quay, 1964c).

Thus it appears that at least the general outlines of the personality and conduct factors are ubiquitous when children of age range 5–19 are studied. The salient variables may vary due to developmental changes, but the basic conceptual nature of the factors remains constant. It also may be that at about age 12–14 the personality dimension is subdivided so that a cluster of problem behaviors which seem related to immaturity, or regression, appears as a separate syndrome. The finding of additional factors at the upper age levels, both here and in the studies of the other populations, is not too surprising, since it is generally assumed that children become more complex in personality development and behavior as they grow older.

REFERENCES

Kaiser, H. F. The varimax criterion for analytic rotation in factor analysis. *Psychometrika*, 1958, 23, 187–200.

Peterson, D. R. Behavior problems of middle childhood, *J. consult. Psychol.*, 1961, 25, 205–209.

Peterson, D. R., Quay, H. C., and Cameron, G. R. Personality and background factors in juvenile delinquency as inferred from questionnaire responses. *J. consult. Psychol.*, 1959, 23, 395–399.

Peterson, D. R., Quay, H. C., and Tiffany, T. C. Personality factors related to juvenile delinquency. *Child Develpm.*, 1961, 32, 355–372.

Quay, H. C. Personality dimensions in delinquent males as inferred from the factor analysis of behavior ratings. *J. Res. crime & delinqu.*, 1964, 1, 33–37. (a)

Quay, H. C. Dimensions of personality in juvenile delinquency as inferred from the factor analysis of case history data. *Child Develpm.*, 1964, 35, 479–484. (b)

Quay, H. C. Personality patterns in preadolescent delinquents. Unpublished manuscript, 1964. (c)

7. American Adolescents of Today—A New Species

Elizabeth Hurlock

This article moves further along the developmental trail by focusing on the current breed of American adolescents. Dr. Hurlock paints a rather bleak picture of the "new species." Many mental health professionals would not agree with the portrait presented and would argue that the characteristics depicted—irresponsibility, anti-intellectualism, disregard for rules, and so forth—have probably been equally true of every generation of adolescents. The position expressed nonetheless reflects the views and sentiments of a given segment of the adult society. What is your reaction to her depiction of the "new species"?

American adolescents of today are different from adolescents of past generations and from adolescents in many other cultures throughout the world. This is not due to mutation in their hereditary endowment but to cultural factors which did not exist in past generations.

Adolescence, 1966, 1, 7–21. Reprinted with the permission of the publisher and author.

Because adolescents of today are so different in so many different ways from their parents' and even more so from their grandparents' generation, the gap between the generations grows progressively wider. Adolescents complain that their parents "don't understand them" while parents and teachers of their parents' generation frankly admit that this is true.

Newness does not necessarily mean improvement. Today's adolescents may have more knowledge, more sophistication, and many cultural advantages which, in past generations, were limited to a few, but that does not make them "better" as potential adult citizens in a democracy.

In fact, the behavior of some of today's adolescents and the social problems they create make many members of the older generation question whether the "old-fashioned" adolescent was not superior to the new species. From a source as high as the Vatican, Pope Paul warned the young people of Italy recently to "avoid the fashionable weakness for skepticism and decadence of certain young people."[23]

WHAT IS RESPONSIBLE FOR THE "NEW SPECIES"?

The finger of blame has, to date, been pointed in every conceivable direction. Some maintain that growing up in the suburbs, with the freedom of the "wide open spaces," does not instill in children the desire to conform to social expectations as was true when people lived mainly in cities and had to learn at an early age to behave in a civilized way. Others claim that the break-down in family solidarity, with divorce, remarriage, social mobility, and the break-up of the elongated family system are at the basis of the trouble. Still others claim that the trend toward teenage marriages and teenage parenthood is indeed a case of the "blind leading the blind." The immaturity of the parents makes them incapable of bringing up their children to be law-abiding, socially conforming young people.

The most commonly accepted explanation is the radical change that has taken place in our child-rearing attitudes in the last generation—especially among parents of today's adolescents who went to college and who learned the evils to come from frustration and the advantages from self-expression. As a result, ever since their children were born, they shied away from "thwarting" them. If, as a small child, the adolescent of today wanted to explore, he was permitted to do so regardless of whether or not he broke some of his parents' choicest possessions or turned the parents' hair prematurely gray for fear that he would hurt or kill himself. He was permitted to say what popped into his mind, regardless of whether what he said hurt peoples' feelings or deflated their egos. Permissiveness, once established, is hard to change, especially if parents believe it is "good for the child" even though hard for them to take.

Many schools in recent years have adopted the policy of permissiveness—the "progressive education movement"—where pupils literally run the schools and where teachers and school authorities cater to their wishes and whims. Even worse, law-enforcing officers in recent years have been imbued with the philosophy of permissiveness, accepting pranks serious enough to justify arrest for juvenile delinquency on the grounds that "kids will be kids." A reputable lawyer had the gall, recently, to go to the parents of a girl who had been raped by a boy from a socially prominent and well-to-do family to ask them not to press charges against the boy on the grounds that "boys will be boys." And this occurred in a state where rape by boys eighteen years of age or older carries the death penalty while those younger—as this boy was—faced imprisonment of fifteen years for the crime.[24]

Why, one may justifiably ask, has this philosophy of child-rearing gained such widespread acceptance when any mature adult, with even the fundamental knowledge of how to bring up children, should know that no child is capable of knowing what society will tolerate and what it will not unless his parents and teachers guide him? There is no one answer. Some attribute it to parental revolt against their own strict upbringing. As children, they vowed that when they became parents they would not thwart their children as their parents had thwarted them. Others attribute it to the experiences of many fathers of today's adolescents in World War II. As a revolt against the regimentation of their lives in the armed services, they went to the extreme of wearing and doing what they pleased when they returned to the college campuses to complete their education. And, later, when they became parents, they carried over this attitude of permissiveness into their parental roles.

The more widely accepted reason for permissiveness is to point the finger of blame at Freud and the psychoanalytic school. Although it is true that the Freudian doctrine blames the thwarting of strong innate drives—such as the sex drive—for many cases of adult maladjustment, there is nothing in it that could be possibly interpreted to mean that it advocates permissive upbringing of children.[10] However, misinterpretations of Freudian doctrines by laymen have been used to justify their own permissiveness.

It is a well-known fact that young people tend, on the whole, to be more lax and more permissive than older people. This stems, in part, from feelings of insecurity about what they should do and, in part, from a desire to have fun while they are still young enough to enjoy themselves. While there are no statistics available at the present time to show whether problem adolescents are more likely to have parents below the age norm for law-abiding adolescents, there is a widespread opinion among those who deal with juvenile delinquents that their parents are younger, less serious about their parental responsibilities, and less sure of how to cope with any trouble that might arise than are parents of non-troublesome adolescents.[12,14]

The affluence of the American society of today which has permeated every social class means that adolescents' earnings from after-school or vacation jobs are not needed to supplement the family income and that, in many cases, it is not even necessary for them to work. The family provides them with generous enough allowances to "live up to the Joneses." Affluence means independence and free time to get into mischief. Put in another way, today's adolescent can literally thumb his nose at his parents and do as he pleases. If his parents become too demanding, the adolescent has a powerful weapon to silence them—he will threaten to leave home and get a job. Knowing that his parents want him to "better himself" and knowing that the stepping stone to rising in the social ladder is education, today's adolescent is fully aware that his parents will back down and let him do as he pleases.

Another explanation for the new species of adolescents in America today is the tendency to model their behavior, their clothes, their speech, and most important of all, their values, along the lines of the new American heroes and heroines—people from the world of sports and of entertainment. In the past, the heroes were the people who made contributions to the greatness of our country—soldiers, statesmen, writers, scientists, or just good citizens. Today's adolescent puts on a pedestal people who make money overnight, who live a glamorous life rivaling the luxuries of ancient Rome, and whose methods of rise to the top may not always be in keeping with the American tradition. While many people who are in the limelight of popular attention are law-abiding citizens, worthy of being imitated, far more are not. If the adolescent is dazzled by their quick and apparently easy success, it is not surprising that he puts them on a pedestal to serve as models for his life instead of some sturdy plodder who lacks glamour.[1,7]

The final explanation often given for our new species of American adolescent is the education emphasis placed on democracy. From the moment the American child steps on the doorstep of first grade until he graduates from high school, college, or graduate school, he is exposed to teaching which lauds the advantages of a democracy and stresses the evils of an autocracy. He is not only permitted to think independently and to express these thoughts freely, but is encouraged to do so. To parents of adolescents who were brought up to "respect their elders," this comes as a shock and often causes a real trauma.

From the above outline it should be apparent that no one aspect of American culture is responsible but rather the total American culture. And, because of the economic and military power of the United States in the eyes of the world, it is not surprising that young people in the less prosperous and less successful nations would want to model themselves on the American adolescent as he is depicted in the mass media. Because adolescents in these cultures are dissatisfied with existing conditions and feel that there is little hope for improvement, it is only logical that they would want to model themselves on the American adolescent, believing that by doing so they too will improve their lot in life.

CHARACTERISTICS OF THE NEW SPECIES OF AMERICAN ADOLESCENT

1. *Peer Conformity*. While adolescents in all cultures tend to want to be alike, because being different is interpreted by them to mean being "inferior," today's adolescents seem to be driven by a compulsion to follow the herd, whether for good or for bad. They are afraid that any indication of originality, in thought, in action, or in appearance, will make them into "squares." The herd they follow is their own peer group—the group within the adolescent culture with which they have achieved acceptance and identity. When there is a conflict between peer-group values and

adult values, they will accept the former and reject the latter. If, for example, it is the thing to do among their friends to cheat, they will cheat; if it is not the thing to be a virgin, they will quickly give up their virginity.

Naturally, not all American adolescents are driven by an equally strong compulsion to follow the herd but few escape it. The ones most affected are those whose status within the group is somewhat precarious or those who want to improve the status they already have. The only adolescents who seem to be able to retain their individuality are those whose status is so secure that nothing can shake it—the adolescent the sociologist calls the "star," those whose status is so hopeless that nothing they can say or do will lead to their acceptance by the peer group, and those who are not interested enough in peer activities to care whether they are acceptable to the group or not. Few fall in any one of these three categories.

There are two major reasons for the adolescent's willingness to relinquish his individuality in favor of peer conformity. The first is that our status-seeking, "live-up-to-the-Joneses" culture provided the adolescent with a model of conformity since he has left his crib. Everywhere he goes, he is confronted with conformists, whether in the home, in the neighborhood, in the school, in the community, or in the mass media. It is not surprising, under such conditions, that he grows up with the idea that a nonconformist is a "square" and that he will never be able to make a success of life.

The second reason for obsessive conformity is the high value placed on popularity. If it is essential to follow the crowd to gain acceptance by the crowd, he will pay the price. If, on the other hand, being an individual means loneliness and, even worse, a derogatory attitude from members of the peer group, he will do all within his power to avoid having this happen to him.

2. *Preoccupation with Status Symbols.* In our social-class-conscious culture of today, it would be surprising if the American adolescent of today were not anxious to be identified in the minds of the peer group members with the leading crowds. He knows that the way to make this identification possible is to have status symbols that create the impression that he is one of the crowd. That is why clothes that equal or surpass in quality and quantity those of his classmates, a car of his own, money for dates and good times, trips to Florida or Bermuda at Easter and to Europe in the summer, are so important to him. The less secure he is in his status, the more preoccupied he becomes with status symbols which, he hopes, will make his status more secure.

That status symbols are important to an adolescent becomes apparent when one examines the juvenile delinquency statistics and discovers that the major crime is theft—clothes and costume jewelry among girls and cars among boys. Another line of evidence of the importance status symbols play in the adolescent's life comes from studies of school and college dropouts. While it is true that some dropouts are academic failures, most are social failures. Boys and girls who cannot have the status symbols their classmates have are not socially acceptable to them. As a result, school and college lose their appeal and the boys and girls drop out, get jobs, and hope to improve their social status by earning money to buy the status symbols they believe are essential to this.

3. *Irresponsibility*. Today's adolescents tend to follow the philosophy of "let John do it." "John" may be their parents, their teachers, or even "Uncle Sam." "John" is rarely the adolescent himself. They may be meticulous about their appearance, but their school assignments are thrown together, home chores are either neglected completely or done so badly that someone has to do them over, they are constantly late for appointments with only the flimsiest excuses, they do not bother to answer party invitations but appear anyway, they raid the refrigerator without a thought as to whether the food was meant for the next meal, they ask a girl to "go steady" and then drop her if they find someone else who strikes their fancy, they appear late for part-time jobs and often drop them without notice, and, worst of all, they rush into marriage because they are "fed up with the family" but with no thought as to how they are going to support the marriage.

The finger of blame can be pointed only in one direction—to parents and teachers who have tolerated such behavior since the adolescents were young children. The philosophy of life that fosters such behavior is that of the "happy, carefree childhood." Parents and teachers who believe that lack of responsibility will lead to happiness, bend over backwards to assume the responsibilities the adolescent should have been assuming. By the time he reaches adolescence, he expcts things to be handed to him on a silver platter, and if he does not get what he expects, he complains that his parents and teachers are "mean." The more parents and teachers try to instill in the young people a sense of responsibility, the more they are accused of "yakity-yaking."

4. *Anti-Work Attitude*. Closely related to the lack of responsibility that characterizes far too many of our American adolescents of today is their unfavorable attitude toward work. Having been waited on hand and foot, and having had everything made easy for them in the hopes that this will make them happy, they develop the habit of putting forth as little effort as possible. Even worse, they look upon work as an evil that should be avoided at any cost. If they can get reasonably good grades by cheating, why study? If they can hold down a job by turning out some work, why "kill oneself for a slavedriver"? If they can get the prestige of being on a committee, why not let the person who is chairman of the committee do the work? If they can get the gist of a classic by reading a "true comic" or by seeing a movie based on the book, why bother to wade through the book itself? Even more important is the grumbling he hears from mother about how tired she is after a day of housework or from father about his exhausting day in the office. How could an adolescent look upon work other than unfavorably with such models before him and how could he be expected to do anything but develop the attitude that he wasn't going to "kill himself" with work?

5. *Anti-Intellectualism*. In spite of the fact that more and more adolescents are finishing high school, going on to college and even to graduate school than ever before, this is definitely not evidence of intellectual curiosity or interests. Instead, it is a way to "better themselves"—to climb the

ladder by getting a better job which, in turn, will enable them to live better and be associated with the "right people." Even more so than in the past, a person with intellectual interests is an "egghead," a "square" in a population where the important holes are for "rounds."

To achieve the goal of getting ahead, good grades are essential but cheating makes this possible. At the same time, it gives more time to have fun—to participate in extracurricular activities. Thus, they can literally kill two birds with one stone—they can have good grades and they can have their fun. Not all students, of course, suffer from the prevailing anti-intellectualism. But they are in such a small minority that they must literally hide their brains to avoid the stigma of being labelled a "brain." If they must make a choice between intellectual and non-intellectual interests, it is generally not in favor of the former. That is why our underachievers among the bright students—students who in the past would have been our real intellectuals because they wanted knowledge for knowledge's sake, not for grades—are growing at such an alarming rate.

6. *New Values.* When adolescents complain that members of the older generation "don't understand" them, they are speaking the truth. Some of the cherished American values that have come down from our founding fathers have literally been dumped in favor of new values which members of the older generation cannot understand or accept. A few examples, from the superficial to the more serious, will serve to illustrate what a revolution there has been in the past generation. Having manners has always been a value in the American culture, as it is in every civilized culture. Today's adolescents do not agree. To them, these are only superficialities that are too trivial to bother with. Dressing up and being well groomed had always been an accepted part of the party pattern until today's adolescents put their stamp of disapproval on such "non-essentials." Having a "nest egg" for the proverbial rainy day is a value preached to people throughout the world but the American adolescent of today rejects it on the grounds that one should "eat, drink and be merry today" and let the future take care of itself or let Uncle Sam take care of you. Virginity at the time of marriage is a value that every civilized culture has accepted but today's adolescents reject it as "mid-Victorian."

Where, one may justifiably ask, do these new values come from? Not from one source alone but from several, the most important of which are the new types of individuals adolescents choose as their heroes and ideals, mass media that glamourize extravagance and paint thrift as dawdy or imply that virginity belongs to another era, and from the adolescent's lack of sense of social responsibility which is part of his general irresponsibility. Some of these new values unquestionably arise within the peer group itself. If the group as a whole gives its stamp of approval to behavior that is expedient, though not in accordance with the standards of the larger social group, it is accepted as "right" by the adolescent. When, for example, it is important to get high grades but this might make having fun difficult, the adolescent will cheat and justify his doing so by claiming that "everyone does it" and, therefore, it is all right. Similarly, if it is important to be popular and if popularity with members of the other sex can be guaranteed by saying "Yes" rather than "No," a girl will engage in premarital sex behavior and then justify her doing so on the grounds that it is quite all right, so long as you love the boy—at least at the time.

7. *Disrespect for Older Generations.* With values of their own which are often so different from those of their parents and grandparents, it is not surprising that today's adolescents feel that all members of the older generations are out of step with the times. This, in turn, is interpreted by them to mean that the young generation, if it wants to get along in today's world, must reject the influence of the older generations. In doing so, they develop a derogatory attitude not only toward their relatives but toward all people over thirty.

This unfavorable attitude toward older people is reinforced by what they see or hear around them. Father complains about the "old dodos who run our country," mother shows obvious annoyance at the thought of the inconvenience she will experience when elderly relatives come to visit or become permanent members of the household, older workers are replaced by young ones in jobs, and the mass media are constantly emphasizing the "plight of the elderly." Lack of respect and esteem for age and experience are so much a part of the American culture of today that it would be unrealistic to expect today's adolescents to have attitudes that are other than unfavorable.

There are two important consequences of these unfavorable attitudes. The first is that it deprives adolescents of the guidance of anyone old enough and experienced enough to offer it. Since adolescents reject the values and attitudes of older people on general principles, it is not surprising that they would consider any advice from older people so out of step with modern times that it would not fit into their problems or help them to solve them.

Equally as serious is the second consequence: the constant friction that it engenders in the home. While expecting parents to pay their bills and assume many responsibilities for their daily living, they literally say "Hands off" when it comes to doing what their parents advise and expect from them. Furthermore, their derogatory attitude can do nothing but infuriate parents. While family friction has always existed in homes where there are adolescents striving to gain their independence, the derogatory attitude toward the very people adolescents expect to do so much for them is a bitter pill for parents to swallow. In time, it weakens family solidarity and leads to a break-up of the family loyalty which has always characterized the American family.

8. *Criticism and Reform.* Adolescents have always had a critical attitude toward their elders, whether parents or teachers, and have always vowed that, when they grew up, they would do things differently. However, it would have been unthinkable for them to verbalize their criticisms to their elders and even more unthinkable for them to tell their elders how they should do things. For many American adolescents of today, one of the favorite indoor sports is debunking those in authority, and this they do directly, not indirectly. An adolescent daughter will tell her mother, to her face, that she is "too fat," that her dress is "too long," that she is "inefficient" in her running of the home, and that she is "allowing her mind to go to seed" by not keeping up-to-date on the latest music, popu-

lar books, and movies. Father is not spared a similar critical analysis by his adolescent son. While the parent of the same sex is usually the target of critical attacks, parents of the opposite sex come in for their share.

Nor are teachers and school authorities spared in the adolescent's zeal to reform. He does not hesitate to tell his teacher, to her face, that the assignments are too long, that the grade he received was "unfair," that she treats the class like a "lot of kids," and that she has "old-fashioned ideas," if they differ from his. Many times he will even go to the extreme of telling the teacher how she should run the class, what assignments she should give, and how she should deal with troublesome students.

When school authorities impose rules the students think are unfair, they send a delegation to the principal to tell him what the students will tolerate and what they won't. If he is unwilling to reform to meet their demands, they may picket the school, go on a sit-down strike and refuse to study, or absent themselves from school until their "wrongs" have been righted. Older adolescents, on college campuses, protest the dismissal or lack of promotion of a teacher they like and literally demand that the college reverse its stand. If they are forbidden by the college authorities to talk about any subject they wish on the campus, they will picket the administration building and, when told to disperse, will start a riot.[30]

All of this, it should be very evident, is a case of the effects of overly permissive child-training come home to roost. If the adolescent has been permitted, from his earliest childhood, to say what he thinks, regardless of how it might affect others, and if he has been given little or no training in learning the manners that govern the lives of all civilized peoples, it would be surprising if he turned into a tactful, respectful person. No adult would want adolescents not to make their contribution to progress. If they can see flaws in the ways their parents and teachers are doing things, and can offer practical, constructive suggestions for improvement, few adults would object to having this new and fresh perspective. However, it is not the criticism and suggestion for reform *per se* that angers adults: it is the excessively rude and derogatory manner that is used to present them. It becomes a case where the adolescent sits in judgment on his parents and teachers, rather than a co-operative working together for the improvement of the home or school.

9. *Disregard for Rules and Laws*. Every generation of adolescents has, to some extent, felt that the rules and laws that govern society were too strict, but today's adolescents seem, in far too large numbers, to feel that they are to be disregarded or broken. Parents of today complain that their adolescent sons and daughters are impossible to control—that they do just as they please, go where they please, and return home when they please. In today's schools, most teachers spend more time on maintaining order in the classrooms than on actual teaching of subject matter. In many communities, the police are busier with the antics of teenage gangs than with adult criminality. The rise in juvenile delinquency, especially among the "affluent" members of society, is one of the shocking facts of American life of today.

To members of the older generation who believe that the only way to bring up children is by authoritarian control and that to "spare the rod means to spoil the child," the ready explanation is the laxity of our child-training methods. This is too pat an explanation to be tenable, though in part it is unquestionably true. Not, of course, because corporal punishment is the only way to make a child into a law-abiding citizen but rather because parents who spare the rod also spare the child of any necessity of toeing the mark. It is the general laxity of their training that has resulted in the child's belief that he can be a law unto himself that has resulted in the child's disregard for rules. By the time he reaches adolescence, the belief is so firmly fixed in his mind that he disregards the laws of the land just as he earlier learned to disregard family rules.

Added to this explanation is that of lack of responsibility. The adolescent who finds it easier to "let John do it" than to assume responsibility for his own affairs except when it suits his convenience to do so, has little motivation to think of the good of the social group.

10. *Unrealistic Levels of Aspiration.* Adolescence is always a period of dreaming, of making plans for the future that will lead to a better life. Today's American adolescents share that dreaming with adolescents of the past and of other cultures but they go much further. Their dreams are not only far more unrealistic but they are convinced that they will reach the rainbow at the end of their dreams with minimum effort. When their unrealistic aspirations are not realized, it is always someone else's fault, never theirs. If they aspire unrealistically high in their academic goals, for example, they seek a ready scapegoat to blame. It may be their parents who made them do home chores or take parttime jobs, thus giving them too little time to study; it may be their teachers who had a "grudge against them"; or it may be the "curve-raisers" in the class who make it "tough" for the other students.

What is responsible for this new trend toward unrealistic thinking and planning? And it is new because in past generations an adolescent who engaged in it would be told that he was getting "too big for his britches" and quickly brought down to reality. Parents, unquestionably, are the biggest offenders. Far too many believe that the reason they did not get further ahead in life than they did was that they never had the opportunities. To see to it that their children are not handicapped in the same way, they give them every possible opportunity, even at great personal sacrifice. And because today's adolescents are growing up in a period of affluence where every social class is sharing the rewards, and in a culture that has eliminated any barriers to opportunity for any groups, parents believe that their children have as good a chance to get ahead as anyone else. This belief they foster in their children so that, by the time their children reach adolescence, it is not surprising that they believe the sky is the limit.

Teachers are not completely blameless in fostering unrealistic thinking on the part of adolescents. Many a teacher who finds a student doing well in one subject tells him he can do equally well in other subjects if he will only study harder. This, of course, is not necessarily true. Abilities of unequal levels of excellence are far more common than of equal levels. Nor is it necessarily true that if a student will study harder he can do better. Some students are doing the best they can with what ability they have. Studying harder may result in higher grades, based more on effort than on achievement but, when these students must compete with other students of greater ability and when they are judged on the basis of achievement only—as in the case of the College Entrance Examinations— they will be forced to recognize that their achievements are inferior.

IS THE "NEW SPECIES" SUPERIOR?

From the brief survey of some of the outstanding characteristics of American adolescents of today, there can be no question about the fact that they are a "new species." However, newness is not synonymous with superiority. Unquestionably, in some respects the American adolescent of today is superior to the adolescent of past generations. Certainly he has had more advantages, socially, culturally, and educationally, than the majority of adolescents in the past. As a result, he has more knowledge and sophistication about the world in which he lives than adolescents of past generations. But this does not mean that he is superior as a person, or that when he reaches adulthood he will be prepared to help our nation become a stronger and better place in which to live than it is today. Some adolescents of course will, but they are not typical of the "new species."

On the other hand, there is ample evidence that far too many American adolescents of today whose hereditary endowments and cultural advantages would normally lead to high achievements are turning into second-rate students, second-rate workers, and second-rate citizens. The increase in underachievement among our most able high school and college students and in dropouts testifies to this as does the attitude of their employers toward the slipshod quality of work they do and their preoccupation with coffee-breaks and clock-watching. The shocking rise in juvenile delinquency among the affluent, not among the "slum kids" alone, is further evidence that today's adolescent is not superior to adolescents of past generations.

Another important criterion is that of happiness. Today's adolescents are not happy. Instead, they are bored, jaded, and disillusioned to the point where they turn to drink and narcotics to "drown their sorrows" and give them a stimulant that will make them feel more adequate and self-important. Even without going to the extreme of using stimulants to bolster their egos, there are far too many who suffer from feelings of inadequacy and failure to the point where they question their own worth, who wonder if life is worth living, and who talk glibly about committing suicide.

To be happy, a person must not only have a feeling of confidence that he can achieve success within his capacities but he must retain a sense of individuality and identity. Today's adolescents do not have this. Even before they leave the high school and college campuses, they have become the adult men and women in the "gray flannel suits." Even worse, they are so imbued with the fear that they will be regarded as "squares" if they discard the gray flannel suits for garb more to their liking that they are headed for a life where conformity to the herd will rule their every thought and action. This is not a good prognostication for happiness ahead.

REFERENCES

1. Berger, B. M. Teen-agers Are an American Invention. *The New York Times*, July 13, 1965.
2. Bernard, H. W. *Human Development in Western Culture*. Boston: Allyn & Bacon, 1962.
3. Cole, L., and I. N. Hall. *Psychology of Adolescence*, 6th ed. New York: Holt, Rinehart, and Winston, 1964.
4. Coleman, J. S. *The Adolescent Society*. New York: The Free Press of Glencoe, 1961.
5. Conant, J. B. *The American High School Today*. New York: McGraw-Hill, 1959.
6. Crow, L. D., and A. Crow. *Adolescent Development and Adjustment*, 2d ed. New York: McGraw-Hill, 1965.
7. Esquire Magazine. Special Edition: Teen Time. *Esquire*, July, 1965.
8. Frank, L. K., and M. H. Frank. *Your Adolescent, at Home and in School*. New York: Viking, 1956.
9. Friedenberg, E. Z. *The Vanishing Adolescent*. Boston: Beacon Press, 1959.
10. Freud, S. *The Standard Edition of the Complete Psychological Works of Sigmund Freud*. London: Hogarth, 1953–1962.
11. Gallup, G., and E. Hill. Youth: the Cool Generation. *Saturday Evening Post*, December, 1961.
12. Glueck, S., and E. T. Glueck. *Family Environment and Delinquency*. Boston: Houghton, Mifflin, 1962.
13. Gottlieb, D., and C. Ramsey. *The American Adolescent*. Homewood, Ill.: Dorsey Press, 1963.
14. Hechinger, F. M. Affluent Delinquency. *The New York Times*, September 5, 1963.
15. Hechinger, G., and F. M. Hechinger. *Teen-Age Tyranny*. New York: Morrow, 1963.
16. Hechinger, G., and F. M. Hechinger. College Morals Mirror Our Society. *The New York Times*, April 14, 1963.
17. Horrocks, J. E. *Psychology of Adolescence*, 2d ed. Boston: Houghton, Mifflin, 1962.
18. Jersild, A. T. *The Psychology of Adolescence*, 2d ed. New York: Macmillan, 1963.
19. Journal of Marriage and the Family. American Adolescents in the Mid-sixties. *Journal of Marriage and the Family*, 1965, 27, No. 2.
20. Kelley, E. C. *In Defense of Youth*. Englewood Cliffs, N.J.: Prentice-Hall, 1962.
21. Mohr, G. J., and M. A. Despres. *The Stormy Decade: Adolescence*. New York: Random House, 1958.
22. Muus, R. E. *Theories of Adolescence*. New York: Random House, 1962.
23. New York Times Report: Pope warns youth on wild outbursts over entertainment. *The New York Times*, July 5, 1965.
24. New York Times Report: Raped girl's family says father sought exoneration of son. *The New York Times*, July 10, 1965.
25. Packard, V. *The Status Seekers*. New York: Pocket Books, 1961.
26. Remmers, H. H., and D. H. Radler. *The American Teenager*. New York: Bobbs Merrill, 1957.
27. Strang, R. *The Adolescent Views Himself*. New York: McGraw-Hill, 1957.
28. U.S. News and World Report: Changes in Today's College Students, *U.S. News & World Report*, February 17, 1964.
29. U.S. News and World Report: Why Young People "Go Bad." *U.S. News & World Report*, April 26, 1965.
30. U.S. News and World Report: A Cure for Campus Riots. *U.S. News & World Report*, May 17, 1965.

8. Problems of the Successful

Robert D. Strom

(1) Have we, in our emphasis on the maladjusted student, overlooked problems confronting the successful student? (2) What are some of the more common problems confronting the achieving student? (3) How much impact do teachers and counselors have on the achieving student's personal and intellectual development? These are some of the questions examined by Dr. Robert D. Strom in the stirring article which follows.

Within any field of endeavor one finds that even the most accomplished individuals admit to having experienced obstacles in learning. Like their less successful counterparts, they can recall a number of school-related problems which gave them cause for anxiety. But these recollections, however vivid, seldom receive due consideration in discussions which supposedly are concerned with needed change in educational structure and process. Indeed there are few schoolmen who solicit the negative reports of graduates; an even fewer number view such information as essential for deliberations relating to modification of curricula, evaluative techniques or classroom procedures. To understand something of the reason behind this strange oversight, one must bear in mind recent vocational changes which have thrust undereducated persons into positions of national attention. Given the economic necessity for increased holding power, the growing visibility of unskilled dropouts, and the consequent adverse image of schools where many pupils do not complete secondary grades, it is understandable that more teachers than ever before are devoted to helping low-achievers remain students.

The High School Journal, 1968, 51, 310–317. Reprinted with the permission of the publisher and author.

Certainly assisting youngsters whose scholastic outlooks appear bleak is a noble undertaking and our collective effort in this venture needs to improve. Yet, to simultaneously disregard problems of the successful or to assign them a level of priority so low as to be without influence in altering classroom operation is indeed unfortunate. If our pattern of educational change is to have a beneficial input for greater numbers of pupils, we cannot omit or undervalue the school assessment of those who graduate. To infer that, because successful pupils make it through, they must find school satisfying is an error; neither can it be assumed that because the group members meet academic requirements and earn diplomas, they therefore have not been subject to undue pressures. Moreover, lacking the problems of successful students as a source of comparison, it has been possible for many faculties to persist in viewing the testimony of failing youngsters as simply rationalizations, magnified excuses for a lack of drive and concentration. Consider this question: Are certain difficulties shared by students of every prospect? To favor the well-being of all adolescents first requires that we ascertain what difficulties they mutually share, identify issues unique to the failing group, and to the remainder who succeed. As we continue to gain knowledge about the obstacles faced by dropouts, we ought at the same time begin an examination of the negative school experience of pupils who are regularly progressing, being promoted, succeeding—this represents a move toward enabling mental health for the entire pupil population.

At The Ohio State University we have conducted several inquiries regarding 'problems of the successful.' One of these studies involving a selected sample of 300 college sophomores began with an attempt to identify the kinds of obstacles to achievement which they had encountered during their elementary and secondary school years.[1] As an aggregate the students identified 50 obstacles which directly or indirectly relate to mental health, achievement and satisfactory completion of academic requirements. After indicating on a checklist the frequency of occurrence with which they, as individuals, were confronted by each of the obstacles, every student was interviewed relative to his written response. Before describing certain of our findings, it is necessary to remind the reader that limitations of the sampling do not permit an exercise of generalization. That is, the author makes no claim that the results presented here would necessarily be corroborated in every collegiate setting. However, given this predicate of caution, it is believed that thoughtful secondary teachers, administrators and supervisors will wish to use the outcomes as a take-off for discussion and investigation, a resource in the determination and resolution of local-individual issues.

THE ISSUE OF DIRECTION

Many of the students in The Ohio State University's 'success sample' cited matters of direction as their major obstacle to achievement. Understandably direction is important for whenever objectives are obscured, response tends to be random, energy is without focus and doubt impedes progress. On the checklist, the term 'direction' subsumed a number of items relating to goals, counseling and motivational support. When subpopulation distinctions were introduced for purposes of comparing members of the sample, it was found that the frequency of occurrence of confusion about goals directly relates to parental education. That is, the more schooled one's parents are, the less likely it is he will be confused about goals. Adolescents from homes in which parents do not complete high school show an incidence of goal confusion nearly twice as great as pupils from homes in which both parents are college graduates.

While this information would tend to merit better-educated homes, subsequent data obtained from student interviews discouraged any such inference. It seems that one reason the offspring of well-educated parents are less often confused about goals is that goals are often imposed upon them, chosen early by mother, father and other close relatives. Again and again pupils recounted the adult intrusion of goal selection. In some cases only a professional vocation would be considered. ("You can be any kind of doctor you wish!") Apparently being less confused about goals does not favor mental health. In certain cases it may simply mean that one's option is forfeit; that others choose for him what he is to become. On the other hand, less-educated parents of students—mothers and fathers who probably know less about the diversity of vocations—insisted only that 'be what you wish to be; hopefully you'll have a more easy time of it than we (the parents) have had.' The latter parental group was less specific in providing direction but at the same time more tolerant in allowing the student latitude in making choices about his own future.

Lack of counseling assistance was mentioned by students of every subpopulation. Although there is evidence that better-educated parents make available more guidance, they also seem to limit the kinds of occupational information their youngsters receive and restrict outside sources of counsel to those individuals who will reinforce or confirm earlier choices recommended by either parent. It is well to recognize that adolescent confusion about goals and lack of counseling assistance are not exclusive to the 'success sample.' Indeed, that these are problems which should be of concern to all is evidenced by the results of Project Talent at the University of Pittsburgh.[2] This project, involving 440,000 students in secondary schools across the nation, represents the first national census of aptitudes and abilities. The Pittsburgh researchers found that students in the ninth grade were greatly confused about goals, had very unrealistic educational and career plans but improved them somewhat during the high school years. About half of them made relatively radical changes during the first year after graduation from high school.

The failure of boys to develop realistic career plans is well illustrated by the following Project Talent findings:

> Of all young men who plan to become physicians when they are nearly through high school, half abandon the idea by the time they finish the freshman year of college.
>
> Forty-one per cent of twelfth grade boys planning a career in law obtain general academic aptitude scores below the 50th percentile.

Thirty-three per cent of the twelfth grade boys planning careers as mathematicians obtain scores below the average of all boys in this grade in general academic aptitude.

This distortion of unrealistic objectives becomes even more poignant when considering the outcomes of local studies. In the city of Cincinnati, 1,658 students in 35 public schools were asked to state their occupational choices. Results of the inquiry were summarized by Hoppock like this:[3]

> What would Cincinnati be like if these students became the sole inhabitants of the city in the jobs of their choice, ten years from now? . . . Health services would be very high, with every 18 people supporting one doctor. . . . It may be, however, that they would all be needed in a city that had no garbage disposal workers, no laundry workers, no water supply personnel, since no one chooses to do that kind of work. . . . The two bus drivers will find that their customers get tired of waiting, and use the services of the 67 airline pilots. It may be difficult getting to Crosley Field to see the 40 baseball players.

Evidence that the guidance program was not functioning very effectively in American high schools during the early 1960's was obtained from the fact that between 50 and 60 percent of the Project Talent national twelfth grade student sample indicated that they had not discussed college or career plans with a school counselor during the past year. It also seems clear that a large number of pupils do not have sufficient information regarding the world of work at the present time; the problem is even more serious for many students who are not in college preparatory courses.

ADEQUATE MOTIVATIONAL SUPPORT

A well-known impediment to achievement is lack of motivational support. Teachers generally lament the short supply of parental encouragement in certain types of homes but seldom entertain the possibility that motivational support might be at a discount in their classrooms. Our data show that approximately five times as many of the 'success sample' report lack of teacher encouragement as a 'sometimes' or 'often' obstacle than the number who so indicate lack of parental support as a problem of similar frequency. Comparisons among subpopulations show that the likelihood of teachers failing to provide encouragement for pupils declines as educational background of the home increases. This inverse relationship would seem to lend credence to the assertion that teacher response is influenced by the schooling status of parents, that we may allow parental success to influence our judgment of student prospect.[4,5] An indeterminate number of the teacher population perhaps reason that as children of 'better' homes will more likely succeed than others, it is they who should receive encouragement. Undoubtedly, this conviction translates into instructional favor for a limited element of the class membership.

The research findings presented here do not confirm the popular notion that parents ordinarily are remiss in offering encouragement for their youngsters, that the home often fails to provide school-favored motivation. On the contrary, although educational circumstances of the family may effect the extent to which encouragement for learning is present, the home seems to fare better in fulfilling its responsibility than does the school. Apparently much remains undone in teacher training with reference to understanding that all pupils share a need for encouragement, praise and support from those who instruct them. It is germane to cite also several of the motivational outcomes for which students feel some responsibility: one-fourth of the sample considered disinterest in school as an obstacle; one-third disliked the curriculum; and half labeled their response to school work as 'lazy.'

THE VITAL RELATIONSHIP

Prospective educators are told that optimal personality development is contingent upon satisfactory relationships, that during the growing up process each of us needs the kinds of affiliation which promote a healthy self concept, and a promising outlook toward life. Teachers are in a unique position to implement this counsel since their role permits extended periods of time with students and offers the chance for great influence. It follows that we who fail to register a positive impact, a favorable influence under such opportune conditions, have been in a sense obstacles to achievement. Many of us have a considerably less profound effect on students than we would imagine. In a study of 100 undergraduates at Harvard University, Allport[6] learned that more than 75 per cent of the students' teachers are remembered only vaguely, and credited with no appreciable influence, whether intellectual or personal. Only about 8 per cent of the teachers are reported as having a very strong influence and about 15 per cent are credited with a less strong but well remembered influence. Another way of stating this finding is to say that the average teacher (assuming that all teachers are equally effective) "gets through" to less than a quarter of the class and exerts a really strong influence on not more than one student in ten.

An obstacle of greater dimension than the failure of teachers to exercise any influence is the exercise of negative influence. Too many of us fail to use wisely our opportunities for impression. As the type of influence we convey depends on the nature of rapport, we should strive to establish confidence and respect as the basis of relationship with students. Judging from data obtained through interviews of the 'success sample,' it is common for teachers to violate principles of good rapport. Nearly 30 per cent of the students indicate they disliked certain instructors—ordinarily because of teacher recourse to punitive behavior when confronted by difficult classroom situations. Some pupils who received teacher favor in class resented their being used as examples and the consequent effect of this on peer relationship—from exclusion to the simple taunting or label of "teacher's pet." Others recall their reluctance to challenge certain teachers or question a presumably authoritarian statement because they feared the penalty of a low mark. An astonishing number believe that some teachers graded them more on the basis of conduct than on achievement, for good behavior as much as for progress.

CONCLUSION

A greater percentage of students now complete high school than the proportion who do not. This statement is gratifying when compared with holding power rates during earlier years in our century. However, it does not mean that most students elude academic difficulty or are without obstacles to achievement. A substantial body of evidence reveals that difficulty in school is not exclusive to any segment of the pupil population. To be sure, there is wide variance in the severity of obstacles and the frequency with which they are encountered by different students. But if an investigation of pupil dissatisfaction in relation to school experience is to have the widest benefit, then as nearly as possible the combined judgment of both unsuccessful and successful youngsters should be included. In times past the negative report of successful students has been absent or given only perfunctory attention in affecting school change since they made it through. As a result, without problems of successful pupils as a source of comparison, schoolmen have tended to minimize the importance of complaints by failing students. Little support was given the proposition that certain difficulties might be shared by students of every prospect.

From our study it appears students of every level share the problem of confusion about goals. Among the successful especially, there is a good deal of familial influence in goal selection but a relative lack of guidance as to how objectives might be achieved. Apparently this circumstance has not been rectified in schools to the extent that it should, or there would be a less persistent lament among students regarding lack of counseling assistance. In addition, both low and high scoring students negatively perceive unrealistic teacher expectation for performance and the overemphasis on grades. Most everyone seems to view external evaluation as a threat which creates a need for defensiveness. Pressures for accomplishment also give rise to a high index of cheating and can pose difficulties for relating with the peer group. Finally, student experience indicates that conditions of learning at home and in school need improvement if the students are to profit more from solitary pursuits.

Time has shown that an unjust society or institution cannot endure as those outside its benefit will revolt. In the educational setting the revolt translates into disinterest, delinquent behavior, truancy or dropout. In turn, such issues can escalate so as to evolve into matters of unemployment, family disruption and crime. This ought not to be. Neither should there be unconcern about the negative judgment of successful pupils relative to school process, for these grievances, too, require consideration if student experience is to improve. Every teacher and faculty interested in pupil mental health needs to remain sensitive toward the obstacles to achievement faced by today's students. Since many of these obstacles are unique in history to adolescence, grownups cannot count upon retrospect as a singular guide for advice. It may be there are some things we are too old to know, too old to have experienced. But we are not too old to learn, and learn we must if the young would have the chance our generation has promised them.

REFERENCES

1. Strom, Robert D., *Educational Psychology*. Englewood Cliffs: Prentice-Hall, Inc., 1968. 450 pp. (In press)
2. Flanagan, John C., *A National Inventory of Aptitudes and Abilities*. Pittsburgh: University of Pittsburgh, Project Talent Bulletin No. 4, 1965.
3. Hoppock, Robert, "The Use and Misuse of Occupational Information," an address to Ohio Guidance Personnel delivered in Columbus, Ohio, June 17, 1965.
4. Passow, A. Harry, "Diminishing Teacher Prejudice," in *The Inner-City Classroom: Teacher Behaviors*, edited by Robert D. Strom. Columbus: Charles E. Merrill Books, 1966, pp. 93–109.
5. Strom, Robert D., "Teacher Aspiration and Attitude," in *The Inner-City Classroom: Teacher Behaviors*, edited by Robert D. Strom. Columbus: Charles E. Merrill Books, 1966, pp. 21–39.
6. Allport, Gordon W., "Crises in Normal Development," in *Mental Health and Achievement*, edited by E. Paul Torrance and Robert D. Strom. New York: John Wiley & Sons, 1965, pp. 354–362.

9. Stability of Deviant Behavior Through Time

Harvey Clarizio

While it is generally agreed that most youngsters out-grow problems of a minor nature, controversy continues to exist as to whether more serious problem behaviors are transitory or permanent in nature. Following a review of the major long-term follow-up studies on a variety of deviant youth, the author argues that change seems to characterize the course of most behavior deviations as much as stability. These findings should not, however, be construed as suggesting "an easy way out" or as implying that help should be withheld from youth whose difficulties are believed to be nonpersistent. What factors in your opinion make for stability? for change?

Most children experience problems in the course of development. The question arises, however, as to whether childhood problems are transient or permanent in nature. In other words, does a child grow out of his prob-

Mental Hygiene, April 1968, 52, 288–293. Reprinted with the permission of the publisher and author.

lems with increasing age or does he become a mentally ill adult? The answer to this question is of interest to theoreticians as well as practitioners. To the theorist, knowledge pertaining to the stability of deviant behavior furthers understanding of both normal personality development as well as childhood psychopathology. To the clinician, such knowledge would not only better enable him to predict the course and outcome of various behavior problems but also enable him to focus treatment on the cases most in need of professional intervention.

Clinicians and developmental psychologists have traditionally differed in their answers to this question of stability. The former are more inclined to view childhood problems as being of a chronic nature whereas the latter view them as being of a nonpersistent nature. The conflicting views may, in large measure, be a function of the populations studied. Studies based on fairly typical samples of children, for example, indicate that developmental problems are not particularly stable over time. Macfarlane[11], for example, notes that the magnitude of interage correlations of problems suggest a nonpersistence over a long age span. Lapouse and Monk[9] found age to be the variable most closely associated with the amount of behavior deviations with young children surpassing older children. These authors conclude that behavior deviations in children are an age bound phenomenon. In brief, studies based on nonpsychiatric populations indicate that behavior problems do not tend to be chronic in nature.

The above evidence is based on a developmental approach using samples of normal children whose problems may be less numerous and less severe than those cases typically referred to psychiatric clinics. How about the child whose problems are sufficiently visible to warrant referral to professional agencies? Does he grow up to be a mentally ill adult or does he too tend to grow out of his problems? Investigations bearing on this issue have been of two kinds—retrospective studies and follow up studies.

In retrospective studies mentally ill adults are selected as subjects and their childhood histories are reconstructed through the use of case studies, interviews with parents, teachers, etc. and inventories. Illustrative of this approach is the study by Kasanin and Veo[7] in which school histories were obtained through teacher interviews on 54 hospitalized adult psychotics. The subjects had a mean age of 20 years and were classified into one of five categories on the basis of their earlier school histories. Of the 54 psychotics, half were placed in the three categories which represented adequate adjustment (fairly well-adjusted, well-adjusted, and school leaders). Fifteen of the subjects were the nobodies, that is, those whom the teachers could not remember. Only fifteen of the 54 patients fell into the "peculiar and difficult" category. This latter finding is rather striking since from the standpoint of rater bias, one would have expected that the teacher's knowledge of the former student's hospitalized status to have influenced her recall of the deviant aspects of his earlier behavior. Thus, even though the method should have facilitated the findings of a closer relationship between child and adult disorder, only moderate support was found to support such a hypothesis.

Bower et al.[3], despite efforts to control teacher rater bias, found relatively similar results in his retrospective studies. While teachers seemingly recognized the onset of schizophrenia among their former students, those who later became schizophrenic were not typically viewed as being emotionally sick or as having major problems by the teachers. The subjects did differ from control subject with respect to teacher ratings; yet, on the basis of high school ratings, predictions would not have been accurate as to later adult pathology.

A major methodological difficulty with retrospective studies is that we do not know how many other children showed similar symptoms during the school years and yet grew up to be normal. This limitation is well exemplified in a study by Renaud and Estes[16] who studied 100 mentally healthy adults and found that a significant proportion of them had pathogenic childhoods. Traumatic and pathological events were so common that had the subjects been plagued with psychosomatic or neurotic disorders, background factors could easily have been identified with the erroneous conclusions drawn that disturbed children become disturbed adults. Schofield and Balian[19] in studying 150 normal adults also found that nearly one-fourth of their subjects had traumatic histories.

Another serious limitation in studies of this sort involves reliance on the memories of adults who knew the subject as a child. The memories of informants are, unfortunately, most likely influenced by knowledge of the psychiatric adult status. Informants may thus selectively forget certain incidents or tend to remember the unusual. It would appear that in light of present findings and methodological limitations, retrospective studies offer at best only moderate evidence to support the notion that the maladjusted child grows up to be the maladjusted adult.

The other major approach involves follow up studies wherein children seen by child guidance clinics are reevaluated after a period of time has elapsed. The results of this approach vary appreciably with the criterion of mental health or illness used at the time of follow up. When clinical judgment of the psychiatric interviewer is used as the criterion, the results suggest that subjects who show maladjustment as children will show maladjustment at adult status. In one of the best known follow up studies, Robbins[17] studied 525 children who had been referred to the same St. Louis Municipal Clinic between 1924 and 1929. Thirty years later the adult psychiatric and social status of these subjects was compared with that of 100 control subjects. In checking the adult psychiatric status of these subjects available for follow up, only 20% of these former patients fell into the "no disease" category whereas 52% of the control group were so classified. As adults, 34% of former child guidance patients were characterized by seriously disabling symptoms as compared to 8% of the matched group of control subjects. Differences were markedly higher in the incidence of sociopathic personalities and somewhat higher for psychotic disorders and alcoholism. There was, however, little difference between the two groups in the rate of neurotic disturbances. Such behaviors as shyness, nervousness, fears, tantrums, seclusiveness, hypersensitiveness, tics, irritability and speech defects were not related to adult psychiatric outcomes. This finding suggests that neurotic symptoms in childhood are not predictive of adult neurosis. In fact, control group subjects had a slightly higher rate of neurosis as adults than did the former patients. Interestingly enough, it was not withdrawn behavior that characterized the preschizophrenic group but aggressive acting-out behavior of an anti-social nature.

In general, the findings of this study imply that former childhood patients, especially those who engage in seriously antisocial behavior, contribute more than their share to adult mental disorders. The emphasis on clinic treatment of delinquency in the 1920's, differences between the groups with respect to socioeconomic status, the question as to how representative the sample is of other clinic populations, and possible contamination of psychiatric judgments through the awareness of the subjects' past history illustrate some of the difficulties associated with this long-term follow up study.

Another major follow up study which used a more demanding criterion of mental illness, namely, admission to a mental hospital, arrived at a somewhat different conclusion (Morris, Soroker and Burrus)[14]. The subjects were 54 childhood patients who had been classified as internal reactors at the Dallas Guidance Clinic some 16 to 27 years earlier. Upon follow up the majority of these subjects were seen as having achieved a satisfactory adjustment. Just one-third of the group was seen as marginally adjusted and only one subject had been hospitalized. Later analysis of data obtained from this same clinic suggests, as was true in the St. Louis follow up study, that withdrawn and introverted youngsters have a low probability of developing schizophrenia. Schizophrenics were found more among the children with both antisocial and non-antisocial complaints (the "ambiverts") than among the "introverts" and "extroverts." Former child patients at the Judge Baker Clinic who later became hospitalized as schizophrenics also had histories characterized by theft, truancy, running away, and antisocial sexual activity.[15]

What can we conclude in the light of available evidence? It should be noted that conclusions must be tentative because there has been no study specifically designed to measure the stability of deviant behavior over time and because of the methodological shortcomings of past studies. Bearing the above limitations in mind, the following tentative conclusions are advanced: (1) It appears that certain "types" of disturbed children do contribute more than their share to the population of adult psychiatric disability. The extent of overlap between childhood and adult disturbance remains, however, uncertain. This is an area badly in need of additional extensive longitudinal research, for it is neither judicious nor pragmatic, especially in view of the shortage of mental health specialists, to treat all disturbed children if, for example, only 25% will become significantly maladjusted as adults. (2) While it is commonly assumed that adult behaviors and personality are established in early life experiences and while there is a body of empirical research demonstrating the stability of personality over them, there is nonetheless a genuine danger in overgeneralization. The possibility of this type of error is well illustrated in Robbins'[17] finding that more than one-third of diagnosed sociopaths showed a marked decrease in antisocial behavior in later life. Though these improved sociopaths by no means became ideal citizens, the fact that more than one-third of this seriously antisocial population did improve noticeably challenges the notion of incorrigibility commonly associated with this diagnosis. (3) In large measure, the stability of the behavior deviation depends on the nature of the problem in question as well as the child's environment. Normal problem behavior which occurs as a developmental phenomena seems to have a very high probability of being resolved with increasing age. Clinical problems, though having a lower probability of improvement than those of a developmental nature, also seem to have a reasonably high probability of spontaneous remission. Since it is obviously misleading to speak of clinical problems as a homogeneous entity, we have in Table 1 categorized specific clinical problems on the basis of follow up studies as tending to be either chronic or transitory in nature.

We must not lose sight of the environment in which the individual must function as a major factor in one's total adjustment. A dependent adult may, for instance, achieve an adequate adjustment if he has a supportive employer who will take time to give him the attention and direction he needs. Similarly, an individual with strong oppositional tendencies may not experience adjustment difficulties if he has a job in which he is able to work under conditions of minimal supervision and has an easy going, submissive wife. Thus, even if personality characteristics remained perfectly constant, we could expect some change in the individual's behavior as a consequence of environmental contingencies. (4) Somewhat contrary to prevailing clinical belief, it is aggressive, antisocial, acting-out behavior of a severe nature that is most predictive of later significant adult disturbance and most deserving of our treatment efforts. In addition to evidence cited earlier, Roff[18] found that reliable group predictions of military adjustment could be made on the basis of earlier social adjustment in school. Children who were mean and disliked by their classmates commonly had bad conduct records in military service. (5) Although two of three unsocialized aggressive youngsters continue in their antisocial ways, it must not be assumed that the majority of young norm violators become adult criminals. For as Kvaraceus[8] points out, it is widely agreed that much juvenile delinquency does not inevitably terminate in adult criminal activity. There appears to be a curvilinear relationship between delinquent activity and age. After reaching a peak at age sixteen, the "delinquency curve" begins to level off.[13] (6) Shyness or withdrawn behavior tends to disappear with advancing age. Moreover, there is little evidence to suggest that shyness is predictive of later scrizophrenia despite the fact that clinicians often view introverted behavior as having dire consequences for mental health. There is a vast difference between the child who can relate and does not, or who wants to relate and lacks the necessary social skills, and the child who cannot relate because of a severe basic incapacity. The best evidence to date suggests that the preschizophrenic child is characterized by both antisocial behavior and serious non-antisocial symptoms.[17] (7) Neurotic symptoms (fears, hypersensitiveness, tics, etc.) often presumed to be the precursors of adult neurotic disturbances have also been found lacking in prognostic power. The findings of current empirical research challenge the long-held assumptions that adult neurotic behaviors result from disturbances in parent-child relations or from parental loss in childhood.[17] (8) The probabilities of remission characterizing childhood schizophrenia and infantile autism are indeed low. Yet, although these severe disabilities definitely tend to persist through time, about one in four of those so diagnosed apparently achieves a reasonably adequate adjustment.[6] (9) Generally speaking, it is very difficult to postulate any direct causal relationships between early childhood maladjustment and later specific psychiatric disability. We do know that a goodly number of disturbed children will grow up to attain a reasonably adequate adult adjustment. The truth of the matter is, however, that we still do not fully understand the role of later experiences on personality adjustment. Also, we must not overlook the possibility that some adult disturbances arise independently of childhood problems.

In our present state of knowledge, we can conclude that there is at best only mild or moderate evidence to support the notion that disturbed children turn into disturbed adults. Since the less noxious childhood disorders e.g., shyness, are more common than the more severe disorders, e. g., childhood schizophrenia, it would seem that, all in all, change appears to characterize the course of behavior deviations in children as much or more than chronicity or stability. The concept of emotional disturbance in children as a progressively deteriorating condition is thus called into question.

TABLE 1. STABILITY OF CLINICALLY DEVIANT BEHAVIOR THROUGH TIME

Investigator	Relatively transitory	Relatively permanent
Robbins[17]	Tics Seclusiveness Nervousness Fears Tantrums Hypersensitiveness Speech defects	
Michael, Morris and Soroker[12]	Shyness	
Coolidge, Brodie and Feeney[4]	School phobia (47 of 49 returned to school)	
Balow[1]		Severe reading problems (needed continued supportive instruction)
Levitt, Beiser and Robertson[10]	Neurotic disorders (three-fourths improved)	
Berkowitz[2]	Predelinquent behavior (three-fourths had no record of delinquency)	
Robbins[17]	Sociopathic behavior (one-third showed moderate improvement)	Sociopathic behavior (two-thirds unimproved)
Eisenberg,[5, 6]	Autistic behavior (if useful speech was present by age 5)	Autistic behavior (if mute by age 5)
Eisenberg,[5, 6]	Childhood schizophrenia (one-fourth achieved a moderately good social adjustment)	Childhood schizophrenia (three-fourths either attained a marginal adjustment or required continuous institutional care)

REFERENCES

1. Balow, B., & Blomquist, M. 1965. Young adults 10–15 years after severe reading disability. *Elem. Sch. J.*, 66:44–45.
2. Berkowitz, B. 1955. The juvenile aid bureau of the New York City police. *Nerv. Child.* 11:42–48.
3. Bower, E., Shellhammer, T., Daily, J., & Bower, M. 1960. High School students who later become schizophrenic. Sacramento, California: State Department of Education.
4. Coolidge, J., Brodie, R., & Feeney, B. 1964. A ten year follow up study of sixty-six school-phobic children. *Amer. J. Orthopsychiat.* 34:675–684.
5. Eisenberg, L. 1956. The autistic child in adolescence. *Amer. J. Psychiat.* 112:607–612.
6. Eisenberg, L. 1957. The course of childhood schizophrenia. *A.M.A. Arch. Neurol. and Psychiat.* 78:69–83.
7. Kasanin, J., & Veo, L. 1932. A study of the school adjustments of children who later in life become psychotic. *Amer. J. Orthopsychiat.* 2:212–230.
8. Kvaraceus, W. 1966. Early identification and prevention. In W. Wattenberg (Ed.) Social Deviancy Among Young. Chicago: University of Chicago Press, 189–220.
9. Lapouse, R., & Monk, M. 1964. Behavior deviations in a representative sample of children. *Amer. J. Orthopsychiat.* 34:436–446.
10. Levitt, E., Beiser, H., & Robertson, R. 1959. A follow up evaluation of cases treated at a community child guidance clinic. *Amer. J. Orthopsychiat.*, 29:337–347.
11. Macfarlane, J., Allen, L. and Honzik, M., 1954. A developmental study of the behavior problems of normal children between twenty-one months and fourteen years. Berkeley, California: University of California Press.
12. Michael, C., D. Morris, and E. Soroker. 1957. Follow up studies of shy withdrawn children. II. Relative incidence of schizophrenia. *Amer. J. Orthopsychiat.* 27:331–337.
13. Miller, W. Quoted by W. Kvaraceus. 1966. In W. Wattenberg (Ed.) Social Deviancy Among Youth. Chicago: University of Chicago Press. 189–220.
14. Morris, O., Soroker, E. and Burrus, G. 1954. Follow up studies of shy withdrawn children: Evaluation of late adjustment. *Amer. J. Orthopsychiat.* 24:743–754.
15. Nameche, G., Waring, M., and Ricks, D., 1964. Early indicators of outcome in schizophrenia. *J. Nerv.: Ment. Dis.* 139:232–240.
16. Renaud, H. and F. Estes. 1961. Life histories with one hundred normal American males: Pathogenicity of childhood. *Amer. J. Orthopsychiat.* 31:786–802.
17. Robbins, L. 1966. Deviant Children Grown Up. Baltimore: Williams and Wilkins Company.
18. Roff, M. 1961. Childhood social interactions and young adult bad conduct. *J. Abnorm. Soc. Psychol.* 63:333–337.
19. Schofield, W. and L. Balian. 1959. A comparative study of the personal histories of schizophrenic and nonpsychiatric patients. *J. Abnorm. Soc. Psychol.* 59:216–225.

CHAPTER 3

Social and Emotional Aspects of Educational Adjustment

10. The Place of Affective Learning

Earl C. Kelley

How a student feels is more important than what he knows. This is the message conveyed by Earl C. Kelley as he emphasizes the significance of emotion in the educative process. Altogether too often, we overlook the fact that one of the fundamental tasks of the teacher is to develop in students favorable attitudes toward the self and the subject matter. Can you think of ways in which the teacher can serve as a conditioner of emotional responses? That is, how does a teacher help a student to feel good about himself and the course he is studying?

I was pleased to be invited to write this editorial because the topic for this month is of the utmost importance. It could well come about that this is one of the most important issues in the history of this publication.

The reason for this statement is that it has now become abundantly clear, from research and from reason, that *how a person feels is more important than what he knows.* This seems true because how one feels controls behavior, while what one knows does not. What one knows is used in behavior, to be sure, but the way it is used depends upon positive

Educational Leadership, 1965, 22, 455–457. Reprinted with permission of the Association for Supervision and Curriculum Development and the author. Copyright © 1965 by the Association for Supervision and Curriculum Development.

or negative feelings. It is possible to be a saint or a demon with similar knowledge. History furnishes ample illustrations of knowledge being put to evil uses. The Nazis who slaughtered six million innocent people knew too much but felt too little.

We in education are slowly waking up to the fact that feelings are really important. This can be seen in educational literature. There is much discussion of the self-concept, the self-image, and of the fact that if one thinks too little of himself he becomes immobile and unable to learn. In fact, the person who has come to hate himself and others does not take in much subject matter.

All of this causes us to take another look at subject matter and its uses. None of the above is to imply that what one knows is not important. One's proper subject matter is the universe around him, and without some comprehension of that universe and his relation to it, he could not know how to deal with it, no matter how he felt.

Subject matter and feeling are so closely intertwined that they can no longer be considered a duality. Everyone who learns something has some feeling about it, and so, as in so many other areas, they are inseparable. No matter what we do, affective learning goes on anyway. When this affective learning is positive, the learner becomes constructive in his behavior.

We need to reconsider our ideas and attitudes toward subject matter itself. It has long been considered an end in itself. If the learner came through in possession of a large store of subject matter, we have said he is "good." If the subject matter was something the learner could not or would not store, and be able to prove that he had stored it, he has been considered "bad," or at least a failure.

We ought to be able to reconsider the role of subject matter in the education of our young without being accused of not valuing subject matter. It is not a question of reducing the importance of what is learned, but of seeing the relationship between accumulated information and the unique learner. I have on occasion been charged with not wanting learners to learn anything, but only to feel good. This is not true. One of my basic criticisms of the traditional school is that those in attendance do not learn nearly enough. We have reared a generation of people who have been schooled but not educated.

The main reason for this outcome is that with our rigorous subject matter approach we have closed personalities when we should have been opening them. We have used fear and anxiety as motivating devices, and this has repelled the learner when we should have been attracting him. When the learner has not, because of these destructive feelings, learned what we adults purpose him to learn, we have had to resort to coercion of one form or another. Coercion sets in motion a whole cycle of negative affects, often resulting in open hostility and rejection on the part of both learner and teacher. Many such learners are then headed toward the human scrap-heap—the rejects known as dropouts, the educationally disinherited, who in most cases will be unable to cope with the society of the future. It is from this human scrap-heap that most of our delinquent and mentally ill are drawn.

The basic error in most of our curriculum work is that we start with the materials, which are the tools of education, not the product. We choose our tools first, and then look around to see what we are going to do with them. These materials are usually chosen without regard to the individual differences among the learners, often without regard to the culture of the community where the school is located. Curriculum building is the only operation I know about where the tool is chosen before what is to be built is known or decided upon.

We have for so long chosen the curriculum with little regard for the feelings of the learner that we are of course unskilled in planning curriculum with affect in mind. When new understandings show us that how a person feels is more important than what he knows, our old assumptions and procedures will no longer suffice. We are faced with a requirement to learn new methods of using materials. If we had spent as much time in considering the feelings of the learner as we have in choosing and presenting information, we would by now know how to go about it.

We cannot say that, although planning curriculum with affective learning in mind is a clear necessity, we do not know how to do it, and so we will continue to ignore it. Since such planning is a requirement, we will have to learn how to do it, just as any other workman must do when his past methods have become obsolete.

GETTING STARTED

I cannot of course tell others how to do this. Each school system and each individual teacher must solve this problem in his own way, taking into account his own resources, the nature of his unique learners and the community in which he works. I can, however, make a few general suggestions, which may provide a way of getting started.

Many schools have committees which work on curriculum. Every school needs some organization of this sort. A school cannot in these changing times continue to operate well without somebody examining what is being done, and what ought to be done in the light of new evidence and new conditions. Even in a factory someone has to spend some of his time in planning.

I would like to see such a committee not address itself to the material first, since this had been done many times. I would like the committee members to ask themselves a new set of questions.

How can we secure commitment to the learning task on the part of our learners? *Educational Leadership* had a whole issue on commitment recently, and some articles on the topic even splashed over into another issue. I know of no way to get anybody committed to any task anywhere without consultation and some choice. This raises another question.

What are the ways of bringing about consultation and some choice with the learner? In other words, how go about teacher-pupil planning, so that what is to be done makes some sense to the learner? There is a rich supply of literature in this field.

How can we take advantage of the learner's uniqueness, rather than considering it a handicap?

How can we give the academically gifted a chance to use his ability without depriving him of many of his peers? In our own form of segregation, the gifted are actually deprived.

How can we make available to the learner his proper subject matter, which is not alone held in a book but consists of the whole world around him?

What shall we do about marks? Do they on the whole bring about more negative than positive feeling?

What are our devices for rejection, and how may they be reduced?

These are only a few of the questions which might be raised. Any committee sensitive to the feelings of learners will find more. Eventually, after all of these questions are effectively dealt with, the committee will finally come to this one: What materials shall we use, and how shall we use them?

I have a strong belief that every learner should feel better, more able to cope with unknown vicissitudes, more courageous at the end of a class than he did at the opening. If he feels worse, less able and less courageous, then the class has damaged him, rather than helped him. If this is oft repeated then he is on his way to the human scrap-heap.

I further strongly believe that if a teacher behaves in such a way as to open selves, open personalities, and then has something around for people to learn, they will learn. And this learning will be greater in quantity and in usefulness than would be the case if learners are driven to close themselves. We cannot open selves and render them receptive if we start our classes with threats.

The future must appear promising, not threatening, if learners are to come toward the teacher rather than retreat from him. The learner must have confidence in the teacher, feel that there is no double-cross in prospect, before he can open up. This confidence is not conveyed alone by what we say but mostly by our behavior.

11. Alienation in the Classroom[1]

Philip W. Jackson

This is the day and age of alienation. The culturally disadvantaged, the protestors on college campuses, the hoods on street corners, the creative thinkers, the drug

Psychology in the Schools, 1965, 2, 299–308. Reprinted with the permission of the publisher and author.

[1]Revised version of a paper read at the Institute for Administrators of Pupil Personnel Services, Harvard University, Summer, 1964.

*users, the hippies—all feel a sense of divorce from the
mainstream of American life. In the following article,
Philip W. Jackson not only examines the symptoms
and extensiveness of classroom alienation, but speaks to
the school's role in reaching the apathetic student. Suggestions for change include: (1) an expanded definition
of achievement; (2) a clarification of academic standards together with the means for achieving them; and
(3) a greater emphasis on teacher genuineness.*

Every child experiences the pain of failure and the joy of success long
before he reaches school age, but his achievements, or lack of them, do
not really become official until he enters the classroom. From then on,
however, a public record of his progress gradually accumulates, and as a
student he must learn to adapt to the continued and pervasive spirit of
evaluation that will dominate his school years. For most, the adaptation
is not too difficult. Ideally, they will experience far more success than
failure, and will feel appropriately elated or depressed depending on the
judgment their work receives. But, naturally, the ideal is not always
realized. Many students do less well than they should and, more important, many—including some of the most able—do not seem to care, one
way or the other, how they are doing. Although the two forms of difficulty—the academic and the motivational—are interrelated and both are
serious, the apathetic student (irrespective of his achievement status) is
a more disturbing example of classroom failure than is the youngster who
is not doing well but who cares deeply about his lack of progress. The
student who is willing but unable to do his work indicates, most frequently, the breakdown of a particular instructional sequence; but the
student who no longer cares how well he does or who otherwise gives
signs of being dissatisfied with school life, may signal the breakdown of
social identification—a much more serious state of affairs. The remarks
that follow focus chiefly on this second type of classroom failure: the
student who cannot or will not respond appropriately to the values, the
rewards, and the expectations that combine to form the culture of the
school.

  Our understanding of social and psychological problems has been
enhanced in recent years by the development of the concept of alienation. As the term was originally used by social theorists, such as Marx
and Weber, alienation referred to the psychological discomfort suffered
by the worker in an industrialized society. Cut off from both the means
and the ends of production, the industrial worker lost the feeling of
pride and commitment that had characterized the earlier craftsman.
Labor, which was once a unified and intrinsically satisfying activity, had
become fragmented and meaningless. The link between the product and
the producer was broken, and with nothing to sell but himself, the
worker began to feel curiously adrift in a world that seemed to be fashioned increasingly by and for the desires of others.

That which began as a theoretical description of the worker's plight has since been verified empirically, and as it is used today, the concept of alienation has been broadened to include not only the factory worker, but, to some extent, all who live in today's industrialized urban societies. The estrangement of modern man from himself and from others is viewed by many as the major psychological problem of our time. In the present paper ideas derived from empirical and theoretical studies of alienation will be applied to the examination of classroom problems.

SIGNS OF ALIENATION IN THE SCHOOL

As a group, educators are highly achievement-oriented. And understandably so. Not only have their own academic careers been relatively successful—indicating that typically they have embraced the school's values from the beginning—but, in addition, their professional energies are focused almost exclusively on the promotion of achievement in others. It is hardly surprising, therefore, that many teachers view scholastic success as an all-encompassing good, and have a difficult time understanding people who do not share this basic value. Normally the teacher expects the student to be delighted by high grades and deflated by low ones (as he himself was when he was a student). Even when the rewards and punishments of grades are not operating, the student is thought to be gaining personal satisfaction from the growth of his own ability (as the teacher supposedly did), and, therefore, he is expected to undertake school tasks eagerly. When these expectations are not met, the teacher may become puzzled or annoyed by what he perceives as a complete disregard for an obvious virtue. Yet as the statistics on dropouts and delinquents, and the extensive literature devoted to the topic of classroom boredom indicate, there are many students who do not share the teacher's enthusiasms.

One of the first and most important signs of disturbance in a social unit—and, hence, one of the most reliable indicators of alienation—appears when individuals or sub-groups within the unit hold fundamentally different views of either the value of the rewards dispensed to group members or the conditions under which the rewards are distributed.

It is commonly recognized that there are two major reward systems operating in the classroom: the "intrinsic," which arises naturally from the growth of ability, and the "extrinsic," which comprises the evaluations given by teachers, fellow students, and outsiders. When either of these systems begins to misfire, the danger signals of more serious difficulties have been sounded. As has been suggested, the misfiring may occur in two ways: through the devaluation of the reward system or through its misapplication (either real or fancied).[2]

The student who gets no pleasure from his own progress has devaluated the *intrinsic* reward system. Similarly, the student who doesn't

---

[2]Rewards may also be overvalued and, thus, sought more fervently than some people think they should be. The "money-hungry" adult and the "grade-hungry" student are two examples of such overstriving. These forms of pathological motivation will not be discussed in the present paper.

care what the teacher or others think has devaluated the *extrinsic* reward system. If the student is unable to see his own progress (or sees some when there is none) the *intrinsic* reward system is being misapplied. Similarly, if the student deserves praise or punishment from others (or thinks he does) and it is not given, the *extrinsic* reward system is being misapplied.

These two forms of malfunctioning—the devaluation and the misapplication of the school's rewards—are clearly interrelated. Indeed, in many instances there seems to be a causal relationship between the two. Devaluation (in the form of student indifference) is often a reaction to the suspicion of unfairness or illogic in the handling of rewards. The student who thinks he is being treated unfairly and who feels unable to do anything about it learns to remain detached and uninvolved. The possibility of there being this kind of causal link is important because it implies that beneath the student's bland indifference harsher feelings may lurk. These feelings may stem from a basic distrust of the classroom environment in general and of school authorities in particular.

A first step, then, in the diagnosis of alienation is to examine the degree of concordance between the objective and the subjective aspects of evaluation, between what society thinks of a person and what he thinks of himself. A lack of agreement in these matters would be interpreted as a serious danger signal. Even when there is a perfect agreement, however, and the reward system appears to be operating flawlessly, the search for symptoms of alienation cannot be abandoned. A second important diagnostic query focuses on the person's perception of the powers that give direction to his life. The important question here is how the individual believes his successes and failures come about. Who is responsible?

Basically, there are two sources of action—the self and the non-self—to which the burden of responsibility can be affixed. In extreme terms, we can believe either we are what we are because of our own actions or because of what others, or fate, or "Lady Luck," did to us. In the first instance, we feel in control of our life, as if we are masters of our own destiny. In the second instance, helpless and victimized, as if our destiny is in the hands of forces over which we have little or no control. The beliefs of most people are commonly somewhere between these two extremes, although one point of view may be more dominant than the other.

The student who does not accept personal responsibility for his achievement status is the educational equivalent of society's alienated man. Both his gains and his losses are a function of what others have done to him. Therefore, he cannot honestly feel pride in his achievements or shame for his failures.

Of the many manifestations of alienation, the one dealing with the assignment of responsibility has received the greatest amount of attention from researchers. An example of how this psychological condition is translated into empirical terms and used in studies of children is contained in an investigation by Crandall, Katkovsky, and Preston (1962). These researchers studied a group of forty primary-grade children for whom they constructed a special test, called the Children's Intellectual Achievement Responsibility Questionnaire (abbreviated by the letters IAR). This questionnaire was designed to assess the degree to which the children believed their successes and failures to be the results of their own efforts or to be caused by what others did. The questionnaire contains descriptions of several common experiences of grade school children—some involving success and praise, others involving failure and criticism—and asks the child to tell whether these experiences, when they happen to him, are usually the result of what he does or of what others do. An example of a success item is: "Suppose you did better than usual in a subject at school. Would it probably happen (a) because you tried harder or (b) because someone helped you?" The following is a failure item: "When you make a mistake on a school assignment, is it usually (a) because the assignment the teacher gave was a particularly hard one or (b) because you were careless?" A high self-responsibility score is obtained by choosing the alternatives that imply the acceptance of personal blame or credit for failure or success.

Scores on the IAR were essentially unrelated to achievement behavior for girls, but not for boys. Indeed, the correlations between IAR scores and achievement were positive consistently for boys and were higher than similar statistics obtained with other predictor variables, including measures of need for achievement and general manifest anxiety.

An investigation of a similar phenomenon was conducted by Battle and Rotter (1963) who administered a newly designed projective test of internal-external control to a group of sixth- and eighth-grade students. The test consists of 29 cartoon items about which subjects are questioned concerning the assignment of responsibility for the conditions depicted (e.g., Why is she always hurting herself? Why is her mother always hollering at her?). The most important finding to come out of this study was that differences in attitudes toward internal and external control were related to social class and ethnic group. Lower-class Negroes were significantly more external than were middle-class Negroes or whites. Middle-class children, in general, were significantly more internal than were lower-class children.

A recent study by Bialer (1961) provides a third illustration of how the assignment of personal responsibility is used as a variable in research on children. Bialer developed a scale consisting of 23 questions of the following sort: "Do you really believe a kid can be whatever he wants to be?" "When nice things happen to you, is it only good luck?" "Do you often feel you get punished when you don't deserve it?" He administered this questionnaire, together with other tests, to a combined group of 89 mentally retarded and normal children selected from special classes and from regular elementary classrooms of a public school system. The tendency to perceive events as being under internal control (the opposite of being alienated) increased with age and was positively related, in particular, to the mental age of children. Bialer suggests that in the early stages of development there is no conception of the relationship between the outcome of events and one's own behavior. Consequently, he argues, young children, as a group, tend to view all of their experiences as being controlled by the whims or fancies of fate, other people, and external forces. Young children tend, then, to perceive events hedonistically, as merely pleasant or unpleasant, without considering whether or not their own actions might have contributed to the outcome.

The brief descriptions of these three studies give a general impression of how the concept of alienation is being used in studies of children. They also highlight the major findings with respect to the assignment of personal responsibility. They indicate that the tendency to perceive success and failure as being bestowed by outside forces (a) is more characteristic of those who fail in school than of those who succeed; (b) is likely to occur more frequently among lower-class than among middle-class children; (c) is associated with other types of psychological disability, such as anxiety; and (d) is particularly evident in very young and mentally immature persons.

A logical reaction to a life over which one has little control would be to withdraw or to become resigned to the inevitable. It would seem, then, that an attitude of indifference might flow as naturally from the denial of personal responsibility as from the perception of injustice in the distribution of life's rewards. This indifference—which students sometimes describe as "playing it cool"—is the most important single indicator of alienation in the classroom. Underlying it are likely to be found feelings of being mistreated or manipulated by school officials.

THE PERVASIVENESS OF ALIENATION

Only the surface manifestations of alienation have been treated thus far. To probe more deeply requires a consideration of how the syndrome of alienation may permeate many areas of behavior. Also, to this point, alienation has been described more as an individual psychological ailment, than as a shared mode of adaptation to some of the harsher features of social reality. In the comments that follow, the adaptive aspects of this behavioral strategy will be emphasized.

Social theory and research of the last few decades emphatically warns us not to assume that the alienated person is sick, and society well. Indeed, many social analysts believe that the opposite is true. This being so, when the sign of alienation appears in a student it is imperative to determine to what extent the symptoms arise from a unique personal history, and to what extent they stem from the reality of present school and home conditions. Sometimes, for example, the reward system of the school does operate illogically, and sometimes teachers do exert so much control that their students no longer have a feeling of personal power. When these conditions hold it is not surprising to find indifference or apathy in the classroom. Also, many children live in homes and neighborhoods in which there is little or no support for academic values. Small wonder that such students have difficulty working up more than lukewarm enthusiasm over the tasks and the rewards of school life. The badly functioning school and the unsupportive home environment are part of the everyday experience of many children. For these youngsters the syndrome of alienation is more understandable and the steps that might be taken to eliminate it are more obvious than is true for students who do not suffer from such immediate environmental disadvantages.

As he confronts an indifferent student, then, the teacher or counselor must ask whether the signs of motivational withdrawal are situationally confined or whether they pervasively color the student's view of the world. There is a difference between the student who is apathetic during his hours in the classroom, but engrossed in other contexts, and the one who is as indifferent to life outside the classroom as he is to life inside.

Two major difficulties, however, are connected with attempts to determine whether or not alienated behavior is situationally confined. The first arises from the fact that even when the behavior seems to occur only within clearly specified limits—such as a classroom—the question of how much the present situation contributes to the student's attitude is still to be answered. Although our typical reaction might be to place blame for the condition on the immediate setting, the student's present attitudes may be almost exclusively the result of his previous experience. Consider the high school student whose poor attention in mathematics classes stems from bad experiences with arithmetic instruction during his grade school years.

A second difficulty involved in fixing the limits of alienation derives from the fact that the disorder tends to spill over from one area of behavior to another. A major assumption underlying much of the theoretical writing is that when alienation arises in connection with the performance of a person's major social roles—such as worker, or mother, or soldier—it tends to spread to the performance of other roles as well. The alienation of the factory worker, arising out of conditions of the assembly line and mass production, shows up in his home life and his leisure hours as well as in his behavior on the job. In other words, alienation, even when situationally aroused, is not like a set of dirty coveralls that can be left behind when the whistle blows. Rather, it is an enduring perceptual set, which, if unchecked, may be expected to affect larger and larger portions of a person's life. Therefore, when students are identified whose total world view seems to be described appropriately as "alienated" it is unreasonable to assume that the source of this alienation is as diffuse as the symptom itself, although it might be quite difficult to identify the specific area of experience that served as the origin of the general ailment.

One way, then, of thinking about the degree of seriousness of a person's feeling of alienation is to consider the spread of the feeling in time and space; to ask, in effect, in how many different settings does he feel like this, or how many of his waking hours are tainted by these feelings? Another way is to consider the social or psychological depth, so to speak, at which the feeling seems to operate. In this regard, a helpful set of distinctions is suggested by Scott (1964), who argues that the condition of alienation may stem from four major "social sources." In order of increasing seriousness, these are: facilities, roles, norms, and values.

At the most rudimentary level, alienation consists of being unable to control facilities. Among the working class, with whom it was first identified, this feeling of powerlessnes was created by the fact that the laborer no longer was able to control the speed of production (because of assembly line production) and was heightened as other major decisions concerning the means and ends of production were taken from him. At the second level, that of role, the alienated person no longer feels the need to adhere to the set of expectations society holds for him. Some of the many roles each person is expected to perform carry more status than others and, hence, are felt to be more important. The failure to accept responsibility for these "primary status-carrying roles" is naturally more serious psychologically and sociologically, than is a comparable failure with respect to more peripheral expectations.

Alienation from norms—Scott's third level—is reflected in the refusal to conform to the rules and regulations by which goals are obtained. The condition of being separated from the norms of society has received the label "anomie" from social theorists, notably Durkheim and Merton. The victim of this condition shares the values of most other men, but he cannot or will not use the normal channels for obtaining them. For such a person the usual relationship between means and ends has undergone a radical change. This change oftens brings with it a distrust of others, for when the means-ends relationship is altered a person can no longer believe that the motives of others are what they seem to be.

The fourth and most serious source of alienation occurs when the individual rejects, or simply fails to develop, a commitment to one or more fundamental values of his society. The person who is alienated in this sense not only rejects the means of his fellows; he rejects the ends as well. In the most extreme case he does not transfer his allegiance to a set of substitute goals but, instead, turns away from all values. When this "devaluation of valuation" begins, the victim of alienation has entered upon the final separation that threatens to cut him off from all others, and, ultimately, from himself.

There are certain important and perhaps obvious resemblances between recurring forms of student behavior and the four types of alienation suggested by Scott. It is dangerous, however, to assume that these signs of difficulty have the same meaning when observed in students as when observed in adults. It may be, for example, that the separation between the world of children and the world of adults creates strains that produce, in turn, signs of a temporary alienation that will disappear by the time the child becomes an adult. It is equally possible, of course, that the greater social dependency of the child may make it more difficult for him than for the adult to turn away from the expectations and values of other people. Consequently, the behavioral indicators of alienation may signify a much more serious condition when observed in young people than when observed in adults. A variant of the latter argument is offered by Bettelheim (1961), who points out that "with the whole pressure of school, parents, educational system, and society at large favoring success in learning, it often takes a great deal more determination on the part of the non-learner to fail than for the good learner to do well in school." The comparison between adult and juvenile forms of alienation requires much more study than it has been given to date and must, therefore, be made with caution. Nonetheless, the resemblances are there and deserve comment.

The student who is separated from the facilities of scholarship (the first level of alienation in Scott's conceptual scheme) is the one who does not know how to handle the basic tools of learning. With respect to a particular subject (and possibly to all of his work) he may feel "lost" or "at sea." This student might also be overwhelmed by the amount of work he is expected to do and may despair of ever being able to catch up with his classmates.

The classroom equivalent of the adult's separation from role would be the young person's struggles with the responsibility of being a student. It is generally overlooked that the student role involves much more than the satisfactory performance of specific academic skills. A student is expected to maintain severe restrictions on his physical movement and his speech (even in the most "progressive" classroom!); he is expected to show the proper deference to the teacher and other authorities, while demonstrating, at the same time, his growth in autonomy and independence; he is expected to become intensely absorbed in the subject of the teaching session, but he is also expected to shift his interest and his focus of concern at the sound of a bell. He is expected to compete for the approval of the teacher and other educational rewards, but he is also admonished not to be a "show-off," for the reputation he earns in the classroom has to be lived with on the playground and in the dormitory. Given these varied and, at times, conflicting demands, it is hardly surprising that some people find the role of student difficult to perform.

The goals of the school, broadly considered, have to do with learning how to become a productive member of a particular segment of society. But the school is not alone in contributing to this end. Family, friends, and other formal agencies also play a part, and, depending on the particular group in which a person is seeking acceptance, the school's contribution may be great or small compared with that from other sources. It is possible, in other words, for a person to be highly achievement-oriented (in the general sense), to have an intense desire to learn certain things, and to care very much about his status in the eyes of others, without, at the same time, viewing the school as instrumental in helping him to attain these goals. Such a person may be forced, of course, to be in school and, while there, his condition might best be described as alienation from a set of norms. For him the entire education institution, not just the role of student, is senseless. He may seek the same general goals as his classmates, but he does not perceive the classroom as a place where they may be obtained.

Separation from values, the most serious form of alienation in Scott's view, may show up in the classroom in two ways. First, some students may fail to shift from the value system of children—with its hedonistic orientation—to the value system of adults—with its emphasis on the virtues of responsibility, the control of impulse, and the like. Second, some students may fail to shift from the value system of their family and friends to the value system espoused by the school. The school, in other words, extols the virtues that characterize the mature middle-class adult (or are supposed to). Students who are uninterested or unable to become either mature or middle class might exhibit signs of this fourth form of alienation. Such students need not be openly defiant, although rebellion often springs from this condition; they may, instead, behave as if the "proper" values guided their action, but their lack of commitment rarely escapes the eye of the watchful teacher.

The four levels of alienation suggested by Scott—from facilities to values—do, then, seem to be crudely identifiable within the classroom. Also, although much more needs to be known about the relationship between juvenile and adult forms of alienation, the increasing seriousness as the source of the separation moves from facilities to values seems to be as applicable to students as to adults. The task remaining is to consider, even though it can only be at the level of conjecture, some of the steps the school might take to check or reverse the progress of this disorder.

THE TREATMENT OF ALIENATION

First, we must admit that no one really knows what to do about the alienated student. At best we can point to some of the common sources of classroom difficulty that seem to be related logically to the development of alienation and trust that improvement in these areas will have beneficial results. Second, we must recognize that extreme forms of alienation may be too difficult for teachers to handle and may require outside help. The student who is extremely disgruntled with school life may also be disgruntled with life in general, and may need individual therapy if he is to begin to change his perceptions of himself and others.

One of the most badly needed changes in school practice is that of broadening our conventional definition of achievement. At present the assessment of achievement typically involves a normative judgment. That is, the student's work is compared with the achievement of his peers, locally and nationally, rather than with some absolute criterion or with his own previous level of performance. The normative approach is unavoidable in those school subjects where a precise statement of objectives is impossible—and there are many such subjects. But this type of evaluation often puts the student at the mercy of his classmates. If, on the one hand, he is "lucky" enough to have fellow students who do not want to work or who are not too bright, he can emerge successful from the experience. If, on the other hand, he happens to be among brilliant, hard-working students, he emerges looking a bit like a dolt. Either way, the student's evaluation is independent, to some extent, of his own efforts. Like the factory worker, he has little to do with setting the standards by which his work is judged.

If, however, some measure of growth were used or some absolute criteria set, the standards of achievement might not be as capricious as they now must seem to some students. The establishment of specific criteria of achievement is an extremely difficult job. Not enough is known about the structure of most school subjects to set anything but arbitrary standards. The use of gain scores as measures of achievement also presents problems. The interpretation of the size of gains, for instance, almost invariably reintroduces the concept of norm. Despite these difficulties, it is likely that any improvement in the variety and the logical compellingness of our achievement measures would help to reduce one of the common sources of discontent in the classroom.

Closely related to the goal of improving the assessment of achievement is the goal of clarifying academic expectations and the methods of attaining them. Students not only need to know how far they have come; they also need to know where they are headed, and precisely how to get there. Yet scholastic goals and the best methods of reaching them are anything but clear in many classrooms. The clarification of ends and means does not require necessarily that students have a hand in setting their own goals, although it is probable that in some instances student planning would increase the appeal of educational objectives. In many instructional areas, however, it is doubtful that the students are capable of establishing their own goals or of determining how best to achieve them. Clear goals, regardless of how they are set, would help to reduce some of the uncertainty that likely contributes to the development of student indifference.

Academic standards are not the only expectations that operate in the classroom. In addition, there are the requirements that have to do with performing the role of student, and, as indicated earlier, these requirements are often ambiguous and conflicting. Most of the overt disturbances in the classroom appear to result from failure to meet student role expectations rather than from failure to meet academic standards. Therefore, efforts to clarify the student role or to decrease the internal conflict among the various role expectations would almost certainly make life in the classroom easier and more attractive.

Evidence in support of the benefits of greater clarity in the definition of the student role is presented by Kounin and Gump (1958), who conducted an observational study of kindergartens. They found that when teachers made their expectations clear, defined rules precisely, and suggested positive actions the misbehaving child might take, the incidence of unruly behavior diminished. Even when it occurred under these conditions, the misbehavior did not seem to have a negative effect on the rest of the children.

The student is not alone, of course, in his discomfort. The role of the teacher contains its own peculiar stresses, which serve indirectly as an additional source of classroom difficulty. Because teaching is a moral enterprise, the teacher often is encouraged to maintain a public image that is more virtuous, more omniscient, and more altruistic than is humanly possible. When students perceive the discrepancy between what the teacher professes to be and what he truly is, they are likely to charge the teacher with being "a phony." It is not difficult to understand why the student who perceives the teacher as being a bit of a fraud might feel disillusioned and might have some difficulty remaining involved in his role. In modern fiction many of the characters of J. D. Salinger—Holden Caulfield and Franny Glass, in particular—reflect the disillusionment and disgust (harbingers of alienation) that accompany the perception of the "phony" teacher.

Contradictions between preaching and practicing are not new, and teachers are surely not the only offenders. Furthermore, in many instances the charge of phonyness is a bit too severe. As long as people strive to better themselves, a gap of some kind will exist between the real and the ideal. Failure to live constantly in accord with the ideal hardly provides grounds for applying the label "phony." Nonetheless, when students behave as if they believe such a label is appropriate, teachers must be alert enough to recognize this major sign of difficulty and to take steps to remedy it.

The classic educational solution for dealing with chronically failing students is to shower them with "success experiences." The engineering of success is certainly an important remedial strategy, but it is not the all-purpose palliative some educators believe it to be. First, if it is to be effective, the success must be in an area that is significant to the student. Success in building a doorstop or in winning a footrace is not very likely to ease the pain of failing to learn how to read, no matter how much we might believe in the benefits of compensation. The student cannot, in other words, make up for important failures by experiencing trivial successes. Second, success, if it is to have its expected therapeutic impact, must not only be perceived by the student as important, it must also be seen as resulting directly from something the student does. Success may be pre-planned, but it must not be rigged. Educational hand-outs are of doubtful value to the alienated student.

In summary, the prevention and remediation of alienation involves first and foremost the clarification of the school environment. Students need to have a clearer picture of how they are doing, they need to understand the school's expectations and they need to be shown exactly how those expectations can be fulfilled. They need help in resolving the ambiguities of the student role and they need to be surrounded by teachers and administrators who are unequivocal in the perception of their own adult roles.

Finally, a repeated word of caution. Despite the similarities that have been discussed here, the alienated student and the alienated adult are really two distinct phenomena. It would be a mistake, therefore, to exaggerate the prognostic significance of signs of alienation in young people; to imagine, for example, that every indifferent student will become an indifferent adult. Fortunately, many of our least promising students turn out to be models of self-fulfillment when they mature. Not all, however, overcome the stresses of their student days, and others show no signs of difficulty until many years after they have left the classroom. Consequently, although we should not become prophets of despair each time we encounter a student who is less enthusiastic about schooling than we are, neither should we ignore early signs of danger that might erupt into a serious form of classroom failure.

REFERENCES

Battle, Esther S., and Rotter, J. B. Children's feelings of personal control as related to social class and ethnic group. *Journal of Personality*, 1963, 31, 482–490.

Bettelheim, B. The decision to fail. *School Review*, 1961, 69, 377–412.

Bialer, I. Conceptualization of success and failure in mentally retarded and normal children. *Journal of Personality*, 1961, 29, 303–320.

Crandall, V. J., Katkovsky, W., and Preston, Anne. Motivational and ability determinants of young children's intellectual achievement behaviors. *Child Development*, 1962, 33, 643–661.

Kounin, J., and Gump, P. The ripple effect in discipline. *Elementary School Journal,*
1958, 59, 158–162.
Scott, M. B. The social sources of alienation. In I. F. Horowitz (Ed.) *The new sociology: essays in honor of C. Wright Mills.* Oxford Univer. Press, 1964. Pp. 239–
252.

12. Self-Concept as Related to Motivation and Learning

Don E. Hamachek

*What one believes about himself is related to his per-
formance in school. This is the theme developed by
Dr. Hamachek in his analysis and review of self-concept as a determinant of school adjustment.*

As William James put it, "The Self is the sum total of all that a person
can call his." More than that, it is a person's awareness of his individual
existence in terms of all of the beliefs, attitudes, and opinions which he
holds about himself.

Increasing evidence indicates that student failures in basic school
subjects—as well as the misguided motivation and lack of academic involvement characteristic of the underachiever, the dropout, the culturally
disadvantaged, and the failure—may be due in part to unhealthy perceptions of the self and the world. Many students, for example, have difficulty
in school, not because of low intelligence or poor eyesight, but because
they have learned to consider themselves unable to do academic work.
This seems to be equally true in special school activites, such as athletics,
dramatics, club participation, or public speaking.

A pioneer in this area was Prescott Lecky (1), who was one of the
first to point out that low academic achievement may be related to a
student's conception of himself as unable to learn academic material. He
observed, for example, that some children made the same number of er-

In *Motivation in teaching and learning,* What Research Says to the Teacher, No. 34.
Washington, D. C.: Association of Classroom Teachers, a department of the National
Education Association, 1968. Pp. 5–9. Reprinted with the permission of the publisher
and author.

rors in spelling per page regardless of the difficulty of the material. Although one would normally expect more errors on harder material, these children spelled as though they were responding to a built-in upper limit beyond which they could not go. It occurred to Lecky that they were responding more in terms of how they thought they could spell than in terms of their *actual* spelling abilities. He arranged to have a group of these children spend some time with a counselor who helped them explore their feelings about their spelling abilities. As a consequence of these discussions and despite the fact that these children had no additional work in spelling whatever, there was a notable improvement in their spelling!

There is evidence to suggest that the way a student feels about himself and his ability to do schoolwork is positively related to what he thinks others expect of him. For example, students with low academic self-concepts are likely to perceive parents and teachers as having low expectations for them. That is, they perceive others as having little faith in their (the students') ability to do well in school in the first place (2).

Experiments in behavioral research have shown that the experimenter's *expectations* for his subjects' performance can be a significant determinant of how the subjects actually respond. For example, within each of the six grades in a particular school were three classrooms, one each of children performing at above average, average, and below average levels of scholastic achievement. In each of these classes, an average of 20 per cent of the children were identified to the teachers as having scores on the *Test for Intellectual Blooming* which suggested that they would show unusual academic gains during the academic year. Actually, the children had been picked at random from the total population of children taking the same test. Eight months after the experimental conditions were instituted, all children were retested with the same IQ test. What were the results? For the school as a whole, those children from whom the teachers had been led to expect greater intellectual gain showed significantly greater gain in IQ score than did other children in the school! In fact, the lower the grade level, the greater the IQ gain (3). Apparently teachers treated the "brighter" children more positively and more favorably, and the children responded in kind by showing greater gains in IQ.

The results of these and other studies should serve to remind us that a student's learning and motivation in school may be more closely related to his perception of our expectations for him than we think.

SELF-CONCEPT AND LEARNING: RESEARCH CONCLUSIONS

A considerable fund of research evidence relating self-concept to school learning has been accumulating in recent years. To give you a feeling for the relationships which have been uncovered, following are summary statements drawn from the major conclusions of seven different self-concept studies. Among other things, it has been found that—

1. In terms of their perception of self, individuals have a definite commitment to perform as they do. Other things being equal, those who do not achieve *choose* not to do so, while those who do achieve *choose* to do so (4).

2. There was a significant positive relationship between immature self-concepts and reading disabilities in a third- and a sixth-grade class (5).
3. There was a significant positive relationship between high self-concept and school achievement in a group of 102 fifth- and sixth-grade children (6).
4. There was a significant positive relationship between self-concept of ability and school achievement over a six-year period from grade 6 through grade 12 (7).
5. Measures of self-concept and ratings of ego-strength made at the beginning of kindergarten were found to be more predictive of reading achievement two and one-half years later than were measures of intelligence (8).
6. Male achievers feel more positive about themselves than do male underachievers (9).
7. Underachieving academically capable high school boys were found to have more negative perceptions of self and of others and were less emotionally stable than achievers (10).

When it comes to motivation and learning, self-concept research points to a simple conclusion: Underachievers sadly underestimate themselves. Which leads us to the next logical question.

WHAT CAN TEACHERS DO?

Just as a child *learns* to walk and *learns* to talk, he *learns* about himself. Each of us learns who he is and what he is from the ways in which he was treated while growing up, not to mention how he is treated on a daily basis by those around him. This is what the psychiatrist Harry Stack Sullivan called "learning about the self from the mirror of other people." Like each of us, our students learn to view themselves as liked, acceptable, and capable from *having been* liked and accepted, and from *having been* successful. The crucial key to increasing the proportion of students with adequate self-concepts, with adequate feelings of self-esteem, is to help students toward success experiences that teach them they are worthwhile people.

How can we provide more students with positive self-concepts—with the "I can" feeling? First we must understand that a positive sense of self is teachable. If one's ideas about himself are a function of experience, then, whether we like it or not, young people learn about themselves in the classroom. And what is learned can be taught. The question is not whether we approve or disapprove of enhancing motivation and learning through teaching for a positive sense of self but whether the effects of our teaching are positive or negative. For the 7.5 million youngsters expected to drop out of school in the 1960's, the effect will clearly have been the latter.

If we, as teachers, are to facilitate motivation and learning through self-concept enhancement, we must—

1. Understand that we teach what we *are,* not just what we *say.* We teach our own self-concepts far more often than we teach our subject matter.

2. Understand that anything we do or say could significantly change a student's attitude about himself for better or for worse. Further, we must understand the implications of our role as persons who are important or "significant" to students if we are to utilize that role properly.
3. Understand that students, like us, behave in terms of what seems to be true, which means that many times learning goes on, not according to what the facts are, but according to how they are perceived,
4. Be willing not just to teach subject matter, but to deal with what the subject matter *means* to different students. In the truest sense of the word, we must be as willing to deal with the *interpretation* of a subject as we are to deal with the *information* about it.
5. Understand that we are not likely to get results simply by telling someone he is worthy. Rather, we imply it through trust and the establishment of an atmosphere of mutual respect. One good way to start is to take time to listen to what the students have to say and to use their ideas when possible.
6. Understand that teacher behavior which is distant, cold, and rejecting is far less likely to enhance self-concept, motivation, and learning than behavior which is warm, accepting, and discriminating.

REFERENCES

1. Lecky, P. *Self-Consistency—A Theory of Personality*. New York: Island Press, 1945. 154 pp.
2. Brookover, W.; Thomas, S.: and Paterson, A. "Self-Concept of Ability and School Achievement." *Sociology of Education* 37, 271–78; Spring 1964.
3. Rosenthal, R., and Jacobson, L. "Teachers' Expectancies: Determinants of Pupils' IQ Gains." *Psychological Reports* 19, 115–18; 1966.
4. Roth, R. M. "Role of Self-Concept in Achievement." *Journal of Experimental Education* 27, 265–81; June 1959.
5. Bodwin, R. F. *The Relationship Between Immature Self-Concept and Certain Educational Disabilities*. Doctor's thesis. East Lansing: Michigan State University, 1957. Abstract: *Dissertation Abstracts* 19, 1645–46; January 1959.
6. Coopersmith, S. A. "A Method for Determining Types of Self-Esteem." *Journal of Educational Psychology* 59, 87–94; 1959.
7. Brookover, W.; Erickson, E. L.; and Joiner, L. M. *Self-Concept of School Ability and School Achievement, III*. Educational Research Series, No. 36, U. S. Department of Health, Education and Welfare, Office of Education, Cooperative Research Project No. 2831. East Lansing: Michigan State University, February 1967.
8. Wattenberg, W. W., and Clifford, C. "Relationship of Self-Concept to Beginning Achievement in Reading." U. S. Dept. of Health, Education, and Welfare, Office of Education, Cooperative Research Project No. 377. Detroit: Wayne State Univ., 1962. 62 pp.
9. Shaw, M. C.; Edson, K.; and Bell, H. "The Self-Concept of Bright Underachieving High School Students as Revealed by an Adjective Check List." *Personnel and Guidance Journal* 39, 193–96; November 1960.
10. Combs, C. F. "Perception and Self: Scholastic Underachievement in the Academically Capable." *Personnel and Guidance Journal* 43, 47–51; September 1964.

13. Teacher Interactions with Boys and with Girls

Pauline S. Sears and David H. Feldman

Boys typically encounter more difficulty in school than girls. School maladjustment, in fact, is largely a male phenomenon. Why is this so? A partial answer might well hinge around the manner in which teachers react differentially toward boys and girls. Pauline Sears and David Feldman tell how a significant aspect of socialization—sex role development—influences school adjustment.

One of the important developmental tasks facing children of elementary school age is the adoption and maintenance of a sex role which will help them eventually to reach a sense of real identity. Many factors affect the way a child works at—and works out—this developmental task, but we are particularly concerned here with the teacher's part in this task. In our elementary schools, which have long been coeducational, teachers work with boys and girls. Do the teachers react differently to boys than they do to girls? If they do, what effect does this have on the intellectual and social development of the individual boy and girl?

We began exploring these questions by preparing a short questionnaire in which we asked for teachers' opinions about their own behavior in relation to boys and to girls. We wanted to know whether teachers think they do, or should, behave differently toward boys than they do toward girls. In about half of our sample, both the men and the women teachers said that they do make some differentiation in their behavior. However, a majority of the teachers in the sample did not think that the aims of their teaching are different for boys than they are for girls, nor did they think

The National Elementary Principal, 1966, 46, 30–35. Reprinted with the permission of the publisher and senior author. Copyright 1966, Department of Elementary School Principals, National Education Association. All rights reserved.

The research and development reported herein was performed pursuant to a contract with the U. S. Office of Education under the provisions of the Cooperative Research Program.

that specific techniques of approval and disapproval are more effective with one sex than with the other.

A logical next question is: Do teachers actually behave in the classroom as they think they behave? The next section of this article presents information from studies that involved classroom observation of various samples of elementary school teachers.

TEACHER BEHAVIOR AND PUPILS' SEX

What we actually know about teacher behavior in regard to the sex of children is not really very much. The monumental *Handbook of Research on Teaching*[1] lists 73 references reporting measurement of teacher classroom behavior by systematic observation. But not one of these studies, it appears, indicates to whom—boy or girl—the teacher behavior was directed.

There are several studies testing the hypothesis that boys receive a larger number of disapproval contacts from their teachers than girls do. The earliest of these, by Meyer and Thompson,[2] was carried out by time sample observation spread over an entire school year. Three sixth-grade classes, all taught by women, were used. In each classroom the boys received significantly more disapproval or blame than the girls did. And, interestingly enough, boys also received more praise or approval than the girls did, although this difference was significant in only one classroom.

Why the greater disapproval and blame for the boys? The boys may have been more outwardly aggressive in the classroom than the girls were, and we suggest that the teachers may have been responding by counter-aggression. And why the greater praise and approval for boys, as shown in one classroom particularly? Perhaps the teachers were trying to reduce the aggressive and reinforce the positive behavior of the boys by praising any positive behavior they exhibited. Or perhaps the praise reflected guilt on the teachers' part over their own overtly critical reactions to the boys' behavior.

A larger study by Spaulding,[3] using 21 fourth- and sixth-grade classes (13 men teachers and 8 women teachers), produced similar results on disapproval. But these teachers interacted more with boys than with girls on every one of the four major categories of teaching behavior: approval, instruction, listening to the child, and disapproval. Thus it appears that boys receive more of the teacher's active attention than girls do. Is this because they demand more attention from the teacher than do the more passive, dependent girls? Informal observations in elementary classrooms have suggested that boys in upper elementary grades participate more than girls do in classroom discussion, making more statements and asking more questions. Perhaps in some sense their independent talk pushes the teacher to respond to them.

Further light on the disapproval question is shed by Spaulding's breakdown as to how, and for what, the disapproval was conveyed. Seven categories were devised for the aspect of behavior disapproved: violation of rules, personal qualities of child, thoughtlessness, task mechanics, lack of knowledge or skill, lack of attention, poor housekeeping. Lack of attention was the most frequent cause for disapproval: around 40 per cent for both boys and girls. But another 40 per cent of the total disapproval received by the girls was for lack of knowledge or skill ("No, Mary, not 24!"), whereas when the boys were disapproved, only 26 per cent of the time was it for this reason. As expected, boys considerably exceeded girls in the frequency of disapproval received for violation of rules: boys, 17 per cent; girls, 9 per cent. These differences were significant.

Another difference appeared in the tone of voice used for disapproval. Teachers criticizing a boy were more likely to use a harsh or angry tone; criticism of girls was more likely to be conveyed in a normal voice. Jackson's recent work (personal communication[4]) divides teacher interaction with children into three categories: instructional, managerial, and control or prohibitory. Sixth-grade boys, according to these results, get into at least eight times more trouble than girls do on the last two categories. Probably they have a more difficult time than girls have in adjusting to the institutional aspects of the classroom. Alternatively, it is possible that much of the "trouble" teaches at least some of the boys that they can create some interesting effects in the classroom by being independent of the teacher.

If these results are typical for elementary classrooms generally, what should we expect the social learnings of boys and girls to be as they go through many hours of interaction with teachers during their elementary school years? One consequence might be a cumulative increase in independent, autonomous behavior by boys as they are disapproved, praised, listened to, and taught more actively by the teacher. Another might be a lowering of self-esteem generally for girls as they receive less attention and are criticized more for their lack of knowledge and skill. In fact, the Sears study[5] found bright fifth- and sixth-grade girls to be significantly lower than boys of the same intelligence in their own self-concepts of mental ability. Of course, a number of rival explanations are possible for this finding.

A fourth study of teacher interaction with boys and girls was done by Lippitt and Gold.[6] Generally, teachers made more supportive remarks to girls and more critical remarks to boys. However, when the children were divided as to whether they were judged high or low on social power (the ability to get other children to follow), striking sex differences emerged in the low social power groups. Teachers were much more supportive (and less critical) of low power girls than of low power boys.

INDIRECT MEASURES OF TEACHER BEHAVIOR

Direct observation of teacher behavior is obviously the clearest indication of what is actually going on in the way of teacher-pupil interaction. However, we can make some inferences about behavior from indirect measures: teachers' reports of students' behavior, their ideas on the kind of child who gives them the most satisfaction, grading practices, and perceptions by the students themselves of teacher behavior.

Torrance[7] asked a large number of teachers to describe incidents in which they believed they had rewarded creative behavior in the classroom. Rewards were thought to consist of such behavior as being respectful of the unusual questions and ideas of children, providing for periods of non-evaluated practice, and helping children to see the consequences of their ideas. Of 224 incidents reported, 172 mentioned the sex of the child—74 per cent involving boys and 26 per cent, girls. Torrance concludes that this ratio is only fair since other evidence suggests that girls receive more rewards than boys do for conforming school behavior. One wonders if girls receive the implicit message that creative thinking is for boys and conformity is for girls.

Torrance also reports two separate but identical studies in which boys and girls were observed as they experimented with science toys and suggested how they might be used. The first study showed that boys have many more good ideas than girls have. This finding startled Torrance who discussed with the teachers and parents the possibility of misplaced emphasis on sex roles during the early years, with consequent interference in the development of potentialities.

The following year the project was repeated with a new group of students. This time the girls came up rather strikingly, demonstrating and explaining as many ideas as the boys, according to the observer recording. But when the students were asked who contributed the better ideas, they said—and they said it both years—that the contributions of boys were better than those of girls. It is possible that this occurred because the subject matter was science, which may be thought to be a "masculine" field. It would be interesting to see how contributions would be evaluated if the task were composing poems.

GRADES AND ACHIEVEMENT

Although the evidence is by no means conclusive, there seems to be a trend toward differences in grading and evaluation in favor of girls, even though there is a contrasting trend indicating that boys achieve at least as well as girls. Most of the research in the area of grading practices has been focused on the secondary school, so we are not free to assert that the same trends would be found at the elementary level. However, many of the same classroom conditions exist at both levels, and what small data there are point in the same directions as those of the secondary school studies.

There are six possible combinations of teachers and students which could be studied for sex differences in grading and achievement: single sex classes with male or female teachers and mixed classes with male or female teachers. Of these six possibilities, only mixed classes are commonly found in the United States. However, a comparative study of twelve countries[8] shows differences in interest and achievement in mathematics between boys and girls taught in single-sex, as opposed to coeducational, schools. This study finds that boys do better than girls in mathematics in both kinds of schools, but especially in countries with a large proportion of single-sex schools (Belgium and France).

At least two things must be kept in mind with regard to the above study: it is a study of *achievement* on a standardized test, not grades; and it is a study of mathematics achievement among junior high school and high school children. We would first have to compare achievement with grades and then run the entire study for elementary school children in order to speak with authority about sex differences at this level. This study does, however, include all six possible combinations of teachers and pupils; other studies are less complete.

Two such less complete studies, cited by Waetjen and Grambs,[9] corroborate Husén's findings and, to an extent, expand them. Carter[10] tested achievement versus grades in beginning algebra, holding IQ constant. Although the differences in achievement slightly favored boys, their grades were significantly lower. As in Husén's study, the sex of the teacher was not as important as the sex of the child. All of the classes in this sample were mixed classes with male or female teachers. It would be interesting to see if the discrepancy between grades and the achievement would hold true for Husén's cross-cultural data as well.

Hanson's study[11] included students at both primary and secondary levels, but it was done twenty years ago. He found that a much larger percentage of the boys in his sample (N–3000) received A or B grades on an achievement test than received A or B grades from their teachers (48 per cent versus 29 per cent).

Coleman's data for adolescents[12] agree with the above findings. Coleman also shows that girls' grades vary less than boys', presumably because social pressures affect the sexes differently.

Thus, from the limited evidence we have, it seems that girls are given even higher grades than boys despite the fact that boys achieve at least as well as girls and, in some cases, better.

CHILDREN WHO SATISFY TEACHERS

It seems likely that the children the teacher likes best are those whose talents and behavior facilitate the teacher's own satisfactions in his teaching. With this in mind, Sears[13] asked a group of elementary teachers to rate the children in their classes in terms of how much the teacher enjoyed having each one in the group. Since a number of personality and ability measures on the children were available, it was possible to obtain a composite picture of the kind of child these teachers like to teach. For data analysis, the children were divided into ability groups by sex, so results appear for the bright and less bright (average ability) boys and the same for girls.

Bright boys are liked by the teacher if they are friendly and self-sufficient. Quite different correlates appear in the boys of average ability whom the teacher likes. Here the teacher welcomes affiliative, dependent motivation; good feelings of confidence; and solid work habits. If the boy has only average ability, these characteristics may permit the maximum influence by the teacher. Independence is not so much desired for these boys. For girls, teachers' values appear to be met if girls show good student behavior and are friendly. Work habits should be good in the girl of average ability, but are not so important for the bright girl. Emphasis is on friendly, agreeable qualities for both groups of girls.

PERCEPTIONS OF STUDENTS

Making systematic observations of teacher-child interaction requires hours of time in the classroom by outside observers. Several studies have avoided this by using the children, who are present in the classroom anyhow, as the "observers."

For example, in Meyer and Thompson's study,[14] children were asked to nominate four fellow class members for a number of situations in which children receive approval or disapproval from their teacher for some behavior. The responses given by boys and girls were analyzed separately. Highly significant differences appeared. Both boys and girls believed that boys received more disapproval than girls. There were no sex differences in their beliefs about the teacher's distribution of praise.

McNeil[15] obtained first-grade childen's ratings on teacher behavior toward boys and girls in reading groups. The children's perceptions were that boys had fewer opportunities to respond than girls and received more negative comments on their performances.

Davidson and Lang[16] had boys and girls respond to an adjective checklist containing favorable (for example, "generous") and unfavorable (for example, "a sloppy worker") traits. The children did this by completing the following statements: "My teacher thinks I am . . . ." and "I think I am . . . ." More girls than boys believed the teacher thought of them favorably. However, for all the children there was a strong positive relation between how favorably they believed the teacher saw them and how favorably they viewed themselves. This may indicate a response set toward optimism or pessimism as the children filled out both forms, or it may show that at the elementary level, children's self-concepts are considerably influenced by their ideas of how that "significant other," the teacher, feels about them. According to Coleman,[17] the teacher does not have a very significant influence, apart from his instructional role, at the high school level. But it seems likely that for younger children, perhaps particularly for young girls, the influence is more profound.

MALE AND FEMALE TEACHERS

There have been periodic complaints that the elementary school is a feminized organization in which young boys lack masculine models for good academic achievement. Thus Kagan,[18] in an ingenious experiment, found that second-grade children view common objects in the classroom (blackboard, book, page of arithmetic, school desk) as more clearly associated with femininity than with masculinity.

But Clapp[19] found no differences in fall-spring achievement gains of fifth-grade boys studying with men or with women teachers. This was a large study: over 600 boys with 28 women and 17 men teachers. Husén, working with the international sample of thirteen-year-olds previously mentioned, found mathematics performance superior among students taught by men, but this difference disappeared when related variables were taken into account.

Ryans' study[20] of teacher characteristics involved a national sample of over 1,400 elementary teachers, of whom 86 per cent were women. Differences between the sexes in personal-social characteristics were as follows: men were less responsible and businesslike in classroom behavior, more favorable toward democratic classroom practices, more inclined toward permissive, child-centered educational viewpoints, and more emotionally stable than women.

One suspects that the last word on this subject has not been said. It is likely that selection of men teachers at the elementary level proceeds according to somewhat different rules than selection of women, resulting in samples which are not really comparable on dimensions other than that of sex. Still to be carried out is the crucial experiment of having equal numbers of enthusiastic and talented men and women to teach primary children.

ACHIEVING MAXIMUM INTELLECTUAL FUNCTIONING

Other articles in this issue have presented evidence on sex differences in children, some of which may be innate. The authors of this article suggest that social learning of sex roles is also important. It is likely that parents, mainly unconsciously, start the process of teaching "sex roles," and that teachers, also without being fully aware of what they are doing, continue the process. Artistic production is not expected of boys; excellent problem solving is not expected of girls. But society might benefit by having all children develop both these skills to the fullest. A chapter by Maccoby[21] provides thorough documentation of temperamental differences (not known to be innate or a product of social learning) between boys and girls—differences which are associated with intellectual, rather than social or emotional performance. Here we clearly get into the teacher's chief function—the development of children's ability to think reasonably, independently, and creatively.

Maccoby proposes that optimal intellectual performance comes about in children when boys are less bold and impulsive than the "real" boy and when girls are less timid and inhibited than the "real" girl. This hypothesis suggests a reduction and modification of maximum differential treatment of the sexes. If we are interested in maximizing *intellectual* functioning, we may have to revise our ideas about what constitutes a "proper" sex role and what experiences best contribute to its function.

A complication is that we are not sure of the effects on children of specific teacher behaviors. Spaulding, as we mentioned previously, found that teachers criticizing boys were more likely to use a harsh or angry tone, while their criticisms of girls were more often conveyed in a normal tone. We do not know the effects of these behaviors. Quite possibly the harsh tones, intended to cause boys to conform, actually foster a defiant, independent attitude which reinforces the very behavior the teacher wished to subdue. Associated with this may be the boldness and impulsiveness which Maccoby has found to be detrimental to good thinking in boys.

Our goal, then, will be to specify the kinds of teacher behaviors that will focus boys' and girls' interest on intellectual tasks. The behaviors may or may not be quite different for each sex. McNeil[22] has found, for example, that first-grade boys made more progress in learning reading under programed instruction while girls did better in the usual reading groups under teacher direction.

In similar vein, Kagan[23] has the following to say: "There are strong semantic associations between the dimensions of 'masculinity' and 'femininity' and specific areas of knowledge for most adult members of western culture. This is an unfortunate marriage for one would hope that knowledge would retain some neutrality amidst the warring factions of the mind. It may be possible, however, to alter this associational link between domain of knowledge and the sex roles through modification in the procedures and atmosphere in the elementary schools."

TEACHERS AS MEDIATORS OF THE CULTURE

In some degree, certainly, teachers must support the values current in the culture in which they teach. Probably in most instances the teachers themselves wish to do this because their own values are similar to those of parents and the culture in general. Such agreement leads to harmony. Now in what circumstances does the elementary teacher have a unique role in that he may or should consciously deviate, for a planned useful purpose, from the mores he sees around him?

A current example is the excitement about the so-called "culturally deprived" child. His teacher is regarded as needing to provide compensatory stimulation for the kinds of stimulation the child receives in his own home environment. This is for the ultimate good of the child and of society. The teacher here is taking an active, interventionist, reconstructive role rather than reflecting the mores of the child's surrounding culture. In a more general sense, what changes would we suggest in the desired outcome of the educational process?

We begin here by suggesting that society needs men who carry some of the "feminine" characteristics of sensitivity to other people and responsiveness to emotion, as well as tougher "masculine" characteristics. Society also needs women who are somewhat tougher in their thinking processes than they now are, more confident of their own ability to solve problems, less conforming to social pressures. As teachers can contribute by their own attitudes and behaviors to the development of these abilities and attitudes, so will society profit.

Or, should we say, "Vive la différence"?

REFERENCES

1. Gage, N. L. *Handbook of Research on Teaching.* Chicago: Rand McNally and Co., 1963. 1,172 pp.
2. Meyer, William J., and Thompson, George G. "Teacher Interactions with Boys as Contrasted with Girls." In Raymond G. Kuhlens and George G. Thompson (Editors), *Psychological Studies of Human Development.* New York: Appleton-Century-Crofts, 1963.
3. Spaulding, Robert L. *Achievement, Creativity, and Self-Concept Correlates of Teacher-Pupil Transactions in Elementary Schools.* Cooperative Research Project No. 1352, U. S. Department of Health, Education, and Welfare, Office of Education, Washington, D. C., 1963.
4. Jackson, Philip W. Personal communication, 1966.
5. Sears, Pauline Snedden. *The Effect of Classroom Conditions on the Strength of Achievement Motive and Work Output of Elementary School Children.* Cooperative Research Project No. OE-873, U. S. Department of Health, Education, and Welfare, Office of Education, Washington, D. C., 1963. 311 pp.

6. Lippitt, R., and Gold, M. "Classroom Social Structures as a Mental Health Problem." *Journal of Social Issues* 15: 40–50; 1st quarter 1959.
7. Torrance, E. P. *Guiding Creative Talent.* Englewood Cliffs, N.J.: Prentice-Hall, 1962. 353 pp.
8. Husén, Thorsten, and others. *A Comparative Study of Outcomes of Mathematics Instruction in Twelve Countries.* New York: Wiley, 1966.
9. Waetjen, Walter B., and Grambs, Jean D. "Sex Differences: A Case of Educational Evasion?" *Teachers College Record* 65: 261–71; December 1963.
10. Carter, E. S. "How Invalid are Marks Assigned by Teachers?" *Journal of Educational Psychology* 43: 218–28; April 1952.
11. Hanson, Earl H. "Do Boys Get a Square Deal in School?" *Education* 79: 597–98; May 1959.
12. Coleman, James. *The Adolescent Society.* New York: The Free Press, 1961. pp. 252–53.
13. Sears, Pauline Snedden. (See footnote 5.)
14. Meyer, William J., and Thompson, George G. (See footnote 2.)
15. McNeil, John D. "Programed Instruction Versus Usual Classrooms Procedures in Teaching Boys to Read." *American Educational Research Journal* 1: 113–20; March 1964.
16. Davidson, H. H., and Lang, G. "Children's Perceptions of Their Teachers' Feelings Toward Them Related to Self-Perception, School Achievement, and Behavior." *Journal of Experimental Education* 29: 107–18; December 1960.
17. Coleman, James. (See footnote 12.)
18. Kagan, Jerome. "The Child's Sex Role Classification of School Objects." *Child Development* 35: 1051–56; December 1964.
19. Clapp, Rufus C. "The Relationship of Teacher Sex to Fifth Grade Boys' Achievement Gains and Attitudes Toward School." (Unpublished doctoral dissertation, Stanford University, 1966.)
20. Ryans, David G. *Characteristics of Teachers.* Washington, D. C.: American Council on Education, 1960. 416 pp.
21. Maccoby, Eleanor. *The Development of Sex Differences.* Stanford, Cal.: Stanford University Press, 1966. about 230 pp.
22. McNeil, John D. (See footnote 15.)
23. Kagan, Jerome. "Personality and the Learning Process." *Daedalus* 94: 588; Summer 1965.

14. Negro Academic Motivation and Scholastic Achievement

Robert Lee Green and William W. Farquhar

The topic of achievement motivation has in recent years been the focus of active inquiry. This is an important personality construct to educators in that the

Journal of Educational Psychology, 1965, 56, 241–243. Copyright 1965 by the American Psychological Association. Reprinted with the permission of the copyright owner and senior author.

setting of standards of excellence bears directly on student performance. In the following article, Drs. Green and Farquhar relate this concept to the academic accomplishments of Negro and Caucasian high school students. The most significant finding was that among Negro males, measures of achievement motivation proved to be more accurate predictors of grade point average than measures of scholastic aptitude. The implications for school administrators and counselors are noted.

Recent studies have indicated that the typical Negro student fails to achieve as well (Boykin, 1955; Bullock, 1950), drops out of school more frequently (Conant, 1961), and demonstrates a lower need for achievement than his Caucasian counterpart (Lott & Lott, 1963). Many educators assert that the school achievement (grade-point average) of both groups is related to achievement motivation and academic aptitude.

Norton (1959) found that the total Differential Aptitude Test (DAT) correlated significantly with science-achievement scores of white ninth-grade males and females. Jacobs (1959) found that the DAT Verbal Reasoning correlated significantly with grade-point averages (GPA) for senior high school males and females.

Additional studies (Bennett, Seashore, & Wesman, 1959) have demonstrated that cognitive and personality factors correlate with achievement for Caucasian students. However, few have attempted to explore the relationship between the latter factors and achievement for Negro student populations.

The purpose of the present study was to investigate the relationship of personality and cognitive factors with academic achievement (GPA) for eleventh-grade Negro and white students of both sexes.

METHOD

Subjects

The Negro sample consisted of 104 males and 129 females selected from two Detroit-area high schools with a total eleventh-grade school enrollment of 700 students. The schools were selected a priori in order to represent a full range of socioeconomic environments.

The Caucasian sample, tested by the second author, consisted of 254 males and 261 females randomly selected from a population of 4,200 eleventh-grade students from nine high schools in eight Michigan cities.[1]

[1]For a full description of the sample-selection procedure and the development of the Michigan State M scales, see Office of Education Cooperative Research Project No. 846.

Measures

Three measures were gathered on both samples:

1. Michigan State M Scales—a theoretically based objective measure of academic motivation. The M scales consist of four subtests which were designed to assess the following motivational components: (*a*) the need for academic achievement (Generalized Situational Choice Inventory), (*b*) academic self-concept (Word Rating List), (*c*) occupational aspirations (Preferred Job Characteristics Scale), and (*d*) academic personality factors (Human Traits Inventory). The total scale contains 139 male and 136 female items.

2. Aptitude Measure—the verbal score of the School and College Ability Test (SCAT) and the Verbal Reasoning score of the DAT were obtained from the school records of the Negro and Caucasian students, respectively.[2]

3. School Achievement (GPA)—each student's GPA was computed using ninth- and tenth-grade subjects. Only academic subjects were included, that is, those requiring homework.

RESULTS

The correlations between achievement (GPA) and aptitude for both races and sexes are shown in Table 1. As indicated in this table, there is no correlation between verbal aptitude and achievement (GPA) for Negro males despite the significant correlation between verbal aptitude and GPA for Negro females. All motivation subtests—except the male Human Traits Inventory (HTI)—correlate significantly with achievement for both Negro males and females. The self-concept—Word Rating List (WRL)—is the best single prediction of achievement for the Negro sample.

Both verbal aptitude and the motivation scales correlate significantly with achievement for the white male and white female samples. The best single predictor of achievement is, for the white male sample, verbal aptitude (.62) and, for white females, the self-concept (WRL) scale (.34). The M-scale total correlates significantly with achievement for all groups.

DISCUSSION

The most important finding of the study was the lack of correlation between aptitude and achievement (−.01) for Negro males. This finding is noteworthy in light of the correlation between aptitude and GPA (.64) for white males. The relationship between aptitude and achievement for Negro males must be qualified as pertaining to a northern urban educational system. It may be hypothesized that in a rural southern segregated educa-

---

[2]Both the SCAT and DAT Verbal tests correlate comparably with the American Council on Education (ACE) Linguistic test. SCAT Verbal and ACE Linguistic = .89, DAT Verbal and ACE Linguistic = .84 females, .74 males.

TABLE 1. CORRELATIONS BETWEEN APTITUDE AND M-SCALE SUBTESTS WITH GRADE-POINT AVERAGE AS A FUNCTION OF RACE AND SEX

Sample		Aptitude and M-scale Subtests Correlated with Grade-Point Average						
Race and Sex	Verbal Aptitude	GSCI	HTI	PJCS	WRL	M total	N
Negro								
Male	−.01	.26*	.14	.30*	.36*	.37*	104
Female	.25*	.46*	.40*	.34*	.64*	.55*	129
White								
Male	.62*	.50*	.42*	.32*	.51*	.50*	254
Female	.21*	.21*	.29*	.18*	.34*	.43*	261

Note. Abbreviations used: GSCI, Generalized Situational Choice Inventory; PJCS, Preferred Job Characteristics Scale. The variability of verbal aptitude and the HTI subtest for the Negro Male sample did not exceed the variability of the other subtests.

*$p < .05$.

tional system, verbal aptitude might again be a significant predictor for Negro males because, in most segregated educational systems, those scoring high on aptitude tests would be given priority on the typically meager educational facilities. Thus, in a segregated system verbal-aptitude results may become a self-fulfilling prophecy. However, in our northern sample, educational opportunity was available in sufficient abundance to reach a reasonably wide range of youngsters, irrespective of aptitude.

Among the subtests of the M scales, the self-concept scale (WRL) is the best predictor of achievement for Negro males (.36) and females (.64) and white females (.34). This finding is supported by the recent research of Payne and Farquhar (1962) and indicates the strong relationship between the students' self-perception and school achievement.

For the Negro males, the M scales appear to be more valid predictors of achievement than verbal aptitude. This finding has implications for school administrators and counselors since scores on aptitude tests are often used in making student educational-vocational decisions. Because verbal aptitude was shown to be a poor predictor of achievement for the Negro male students of this sample, critical examination should be given before making decisions concerning Negro students solely on verbal measures.

The finding that verbal aptitude was a significant predictor of achievement for Negro females in contrast to Negro males should be more fully explored.

Obviously, cross validation of these correlations is needed. Furthermore, the value of the M scales in estimating achievement for this sample of Negro students emphasizes the relationship between nonintellectual factors and school performance. It may well be that many Negro students (especially males) are being graded on other than academic performance (e.g., social desirability). Future studies employing other forms of standard achievement tests are needed to isolate the pertinent factors which determine school achievement of this minority group.

SUMMARY

Separate samples of 233 Negro and 515 Caucasian high school students of both sexes, randomly selected to represent a wide range of socioeconomic environments, were tested as to verbal aptitude, academic achievement, and academic motivation. Except for Negro males, both samples obtained significant correlations between verbal aptitude and achievement. The Negro males showed no such relationship between aptitude and achievement, but academic-motivation tests (the M scales) correlated significantly with achievement for all groups of interest.

REFERENCES

Bennett, G. K., Seashore, H. G., and Wesman, A. G. *Differential Aptitude Test manual.* (3rd ed.) New York: Psychological Corporation, 1959.

Boykin, L. L. The reading performance of Negro college students. *Journal of Negro Education,* 1955, 24, 435–441.

Bullock, H. A. A comparison of the academic achievements of white and Negro high school graduates. *Journal of Educational Research,* 1950, 44, 179–192.

Conant, J. B. *Slums and suburbs.* New York: McGraw-Hill, 1961.

Jacobs, J. M. Aptitude and achievement measures in predicting high school academic success. *Personnel and Guidance Journal,* 1959, 37, 334–341.

Lott, Bernice E., and Lott, A. J. *Negro and white youth; a psychological study in a border-state community.* New York: Holt, Rinehart & Winston, 1963.

Norton, D. P. The relationship of study habits and other measures to achievement in ninth grade general science. *Journal of Experimental Education,* 1959, 27, 211–217.

Payne, D. A., and Farquhar, W. W. The dimensions of an objective measure of academic self-concept. *Journal of Educational Psychology,* 1962, 53, 187–192.

CHAPTER 4

Cognitive Development and Mental Health

15. Intellectual Mastery and Mental Health

Millie Almy

What is the primary goal of the teacher—to develop
intellectual competence or emotional well-being among
his students? Can these two viewpoints be reconciled?
If so, in what specific ways can the teacher develop an
emotionally robust person without slighting academic
competence? These and other issues are treated in the
following selection by Millie Almy.

A pencilled slogan, "Kill mental health," has appeared on so many bill-
boards of late that it no longer excites comment. Is the demise of "mental
health" perhaps to date from the moment it became a cliché? So far as the
schools are concerned, the answer seems all too clear.

Since the 1930's, most American schools have had an avowed concern
for children's social relations, their personal problems, and their personal
adjustment. In many instances extensive psychological services have been
developed for the early detection of emotional disturbance and mental illness. But the main responsibility for the promotion of mental health has
lain with the teachers. Imbued with the notion that they must teach the
"whole child" (as though there were some other kind), they have struggled to understand the complexities of a child growing up in his family

Teachers College Record, 1962, 63, 468–478. Reprinted with the permission of the
publisher and author.

and the intricacies of his life with his peers. Beyond this, many have attempted in various ways to help children to cope more or less directly with these problems.

LIMITS ON TEACHERS

But the teacher's influence, however good it may be, is spread over some 25 individuals (or in the case of many high school teachers, 125). How effective can he be? This question becomes particularly acute, in view of the fact that the mental health function of the teacher has so often been seen as something apart from his teaching functions. One of the first mental hygiene specialists to call attention to this was Ruth Kotinsky.

In an article with Jules Colemen (9), she put the issue very directly: What is the school's business? Have the schools the personnel, the facilities, the time to take on mental health responsibilities beyond those inherent in carrying through the functions traditionally accepted as their business? Are there not potentialities for influencing mental health in teaching the skills and understandings necessary to cope with the environment, the skills of communication, the ways of identifying and solving problems rationally, and the rudiments needed for a vocation?

The decade in which Ruth Kotinsky raised these questions was, by and large, a decade of retreat for the schools. Beset by criticism from within and without, many schools abandoned so-called frills and fads and placed renewed emphasis on the fundamentals, on skills and content and subject matter.

So far as mental health is concerned, the decade may perhaps be labeled one of beginning clarification. The appearance in 1958 of *Current Concepts in Mental Health* by Marie Jahoda (7) indicated initial progress toward the eventual establishment of some empirical indicators for mental health. One of the six components of the multiple criterion proposed by Jahoda seems especially relevant for the school. This is the component of environmental mastery.

Environmental mastery encompasses adequacy in love, work, play, and in interpersonal relationships, in adaptation and adjustment, and in problem solving. The child undoubtedly formulates his basic attitudes toward love, work, play, and other people in considerable part before he enters school, but the school confronts the child with new possibilities. It introduces him to persons whose ways of responding are different from those he has known at home. It provides him with knowledge of many sorts of work and play. It develops skills that enable him to investigate and to cope more effectively with the world of people and things. Although the knowledge and the skills the school offers can be acquired elsewhere, no other agency can be held so directly responsible for this aspect of mental health.

To say this does not deny that developments in other components of the personality may affect environmental mastery. Mastery obviously also involves attitudes toward self, the development of autonomy, and the perception of reality. Conversely, progress toward mastery has repercussions on each of the other facets of the mental health criterion.

CHILDREN'S REACTIONS

We can only conjecture about how effectively the schools further environmental mastery at the present time. Everyone knows youngsters who have not only found satisfaction from their schooling, but have emerged from it with real convictions about their own abilities and their future. They anticipate mastery. One 15-year-old, shortly following the announcement of Sputnik, wrote this about his reactions:

> What a time to live! In five years we'll be on the moon!
> Every time I hear someone moaning about how he should have lived in the days of the Old West when men were men and about how the world today is a hopeless mess, I nearly throw up.
> And I want to be a part of it. So the Russians did it first. More power to them. They're going to need it to keep ahead of us now. 18,000 miles an hour. Ten years ago Bell had just finished going eight hundred and astonishing the world. Now, we're on our way. Vanguard will succeed, and Sputnik will have a couple US type companions.
> And then in a few years, I come along. I and my generation are going to be the ones to see this thing off. We may not get to Mars, but the first men to leave the earth's atmosphere are going to be my contemporaries. Maybe me, if I can be so lucky. What a chance! How can a pioneer of three thousand miles of earth be compared to a pioneer of forty thousand miles of space? I'm on my way. Just watch my smoke!

But, in contrast to the youngsters who regard the future with equanimity and see themselves taking active part in it, there are others who are resigned to passivity. They spend their days in waiting—waiting to be old enough for first grade, waiting to graduate from elementary school, waiting to graduate from high school, and then waiting for college, or waiting for marriage, or waiting for a job that involves waiting for quitting time. Then they wait for the coming of their children, who, unless war comes, will carry on the endless waiting, the endless rounds of meaningless activity. Or, as one commentator on the American scene has put it, "America will not perish from a bomb. It will perish from boredom."

The picture is exaggerated of course. But its prototype does exist. And to the extent that youngsters emerge from our schools without commitments, with little sense of personal challenge, beset by apathy, the schools appear to have failed in furthering environmental mastery. Furthermore, children who lack any real feelings of involvement, who evade using their intellectual powers, are probably to be found both in schools that are clearly traditional and in schools that still bear some of the trappings of progressivism.

The crucial test of any school's contribution to mental health lies not so much in the skills and knowledge it purports to teach as in its effectiveness in helping youngsters to incorporate these into their day-to-day living. It is a matter of using such skills and knowledge to strengthen and enhance each child's personal resources. But the question of whether the average school makes an appreciable difference in these respects is an open one. It is a question unlikely to be answered satisfactorily until certain basic issues have been resolved.

One such issue has to do with the matter of individuality in learning and thinking. To what extent can the school, predicated on the notion that children are to be taught in groups, provide adequately for each individual? Related to this is the problem of differences in the ways of learning and of thinking at different ages. When there is so much to be learned, how much leeway can the school have to adapt its instruction to these differences?

Still another issue relates to the fact that the glib use of words does not always reflect genuine understanding. Traditionally, the school has emphasized the verbal transmission of knowledge to the exclusion of other ways of knowing. How long can this continue if students are to develop the critical, creative thinking demanded for mastery in a complex modern world?

TEACHING VS. LEARNING

An issue of somewhat different but nonetheless critical order has to do with the relationship between teaching and learning. Schools are prone to describe their curriculum in terms of what is taught. The more important question, of course, is "What has been learned?" But the nature of the learning very likely turns as much on *how* something is taught as it does on *what* is taught.

Around each of these issues are many questions that schools must face before they can hope to fulfill their mental health roles adequately.

First, the matter of *individuality in learning*. Although schools have long paid lip service to "individual differences," most school practice assumes common, average, or typical ways of learning. Yet, it is a specific emotional concern, a specific tendency to see a problem differently from the way others see it, a specific sensitivity to what one sees or hears or feels, that either inhibits or enhances learning. Clinical studies have shown that children's propensities for learning are related to their ways of coping with the emotional conflicts inherent in growing up. The accomplishment of a particular learning task may lead toward a constructive resolution of conflict for one child. The same task may be unproductive or even defeating for another child. Without training in recognizing the influence of these deeper motivations, can a teacher adequately diagnose the child's needs as a learner? To what extent can the curriculum provide leeway for the child to make the appropriate use of his unique ways of learning at the same time that he adapts to the ways of others? To further environmental mastery, where shall the balance between the nurturance of individuality and conformity to group trends be struck?

At a time when the furore of "keeping up with the Russians" puts a premium on the acceleration of learning, many persons press the schools to begin the "fundamentals" earlier, to start mathematics, science, and foreign languages sooner, and to push the "gifted" ahead. Although many children have already demonstrated their abilities to learn more than has typically been expected, many questions about pacing learning to development arise. For example, evidence from the administration of thousands of IQ tests, from other studies of conceptual development, from Piaget's research on children's thinking, as well as from psychoanalytic studies of young children, indicates that the young child's learning and his thinking is of an imaginative, manipulative, exploratory kind. Not until the middle school years does he begin to organize and systematize his knowledge in a truly logical fashion. Even then, he is still very much bound to the concrete in his thinking, and not until near adolescence do abilities to deal meaningfully with abstractions emerge.

PRICE OF HURRY

What are the effects of the early introduction of generalizations and abstractions for which the child may have few experimental referents? Is it possible to further a kind of verbal environmental mastery at an early age, but at a price? The price, perhaps, of a lack of empathy toward one's fellows or what Jerome Bruner (4) has termed a lack of "passion" for ideas? Conversely, what happens to the child who is held in school to a concrete level when his mind is already taken up with the abstract? Is the concrete *always* enriching?

Many schools, from the kindergarten through the college, have reacted to current criticisms by putting more stress on "knowledge," which may be anything from the alphabet and the multiplication tables to the dates of the Punic Wars or the basic principles of atomic theory. Such knowledge often is acquired largely by memorization and repetitive drill and all too often is tested in similar fashion. No one doubts the importance of many of the facts youngsters are supposed to learn, but in relation to a mental health criterion of environmental mastery, the crucial question is their relevance to an individual coping with and understanding a changing world. A youngster needs to know facts; he also needs to know how and when to apply them. He needs, further, to know how to appraise and evaluate a given situation. Above all, he needs to know that there are many ways of knowing. The scientist does not always arrive at new ideas through processes of logical deduction. New insights often arise from undirected fantasy or from periods of conscious preoccupation with some other activity. A particular event can be "known" through direct sensory participation; it can be weighed, measured, analyzed into its components, put into a larger context, but often it may also be played with, painted, or danced.

Does the school contribute to environmental mastery when it leaves the student with the impression that there are so few ways of knowing? Or are *all* the ways of knowing not the business of the school?

With appalling frequency, many young teachers say today, "What I learned in my education courses does not help me in the classroom." Those of us who teach teachers often retort that they are merely looking for "recipes." But are they? Are they not saying that we taught them about children, about learning, and about thinking without teaching them *how* to direct learning or *how* to change thinking?

In dealing with the nature of teaching as related to the nature of the learning and the thinking that ensues, we have come to what is likely the basic issue for mental health in the schools. Not until we know more specifically how teaching affects thinking can we know how extensively teachers can influence the development of environmental mastery.

When John Dewey formulated his ideas about learning and thinking, he surely intended to help youngsters toward a meaningful, intellectual mastery of the environment. But neither Dewey nor his followers spelled out in sufficient detail how a teacher may appraise the many kinds of thinking he encounters among his pupils, nor how he may help them to shift from ineffective to effective kinds. Too often the teacher, receiving his notions of Dewey's philosophy fourth or fifth hand, has been left with no better criterion for the value of a particular activity than "they learn by doing." Once a teacher loses sight of the intellectual goals to be realized in the pursuit of any activity, it often deteriorates into a free-for-all in which the immediate emotional concerns and needs of the youngsters dominate the situation. Many teachers are ill-equipped to deal directly with these and retreat from them to a more stereotyped and sterile but "safe" kind of teaching.

When the teacher's *primary* function is clearly seen to be that of teaching skills and understandings and ways of solving problems, it is clear that knowledge of children's ways of thinking and learning is an essential part of his professional repertoire. But, in addition, he needs skill in influencing that thinking and learning. Without such skills, it is doubtful that any teacher can effectively fulfill the mental health functions which are inherent in his role.

A few educators and psychologists are now beginning to examine the nature of the relationship between what the teacher does and what the children think. Such examination promises much for eventual understanding of the specific ways teachers can further environmental mastery. Current research programs at Bank Street College (3), for example, include an analysis of the teacher's involvement in the processes of the child's learning and thinking. Along with this goes study of the various ways the teacher offers emotional support to the child and helps him to build inner controls.

Many other centers are carrying on research related to thinking, and interest in the nature of teaching increases steadily. Examination of some of the research dealing with the nature of teaching on the one hand, and the nature of thinking on the other, suggests that both of these areas constitute important new resources for mental health in education.

ANALYSES OF TEACHING

Most of the research related to teaching is directed toward the questions of what it means to be teacher and what it is that a teacher *does* in relation to his pupils that results in their learning and their thinking.

There is nothing new in the notion that effective teachers present material, ask questions, clarify understanding, and so on, in different ways from less effective teachers. What is new is the attempt to arrive at a framework for analyzing the teacher's behavior so that it becomes possible to pinpoint the places where his questions or his comments either enhance or forestall good thinking.

Interest in such analysis has arisen spontaneously in several different centers. Bellack and Huebner (2), discussing the need for a theory of teaching, point out that in the 25 years prior to 1956, little if any research was directed specifically toward teaching. Apparently, in what would seem to be equally important activities in the school—the *giving* and the *taking* of instruction—much more systematic attention has been given to taking than to giving. B. O. Smith (*14*), an educational philosopher at the University of Illinois, is engaged in an attempt to describe and classify the actions, both verbal and expressive, that compose the teacher's repertoire. A colleague of Smith's, M. J. Aschner (*1*), describes the teacher as a strategist and tactician in the campaign for learning, noting that the teacher's repertoire includes not only what he does to instruct pupils, such as defining, explaining, showing, and admonishing, but also observing what his pupils do and say in response to these actions. "He does so in order to predict—to diagnose and adapt his teaching to the pupils' present state of comprehension and progress in learning, to appraise the quality of their reasoning and to assess their emotional reactions to the situation of the moment." This notion of prediction, Dr. Aschner cautions, is not the same as that implied in much current research in the psychological laboratory. Teachers do not see themselves as manipulators of student behavior by push-button techniques: "It is the teacher's task and purpose not to condition the responses or the learnings of his pupils, but to develop in them their own capacities to think and to act responsibly."

Marie Hughes (*5*) and her colleagues at the University of Utah have also attempted to analyze teachers' behavior in the classroom. They have studied teaching functions relating to the obviously intellectual content of the classroom experience, such as stimulating interest, clarifying content, and evaluating results, and also functions relating to the affective aspects of the learning situation. Many of the immediate outcomes of their study offer real cause for discouragement about the effectiveness of teachers in furthering active environmental mastery. Teachers judged "good" by their administrators exercised the controlling functions most frequently and most pervasively. They told the children both what they should do and how they should do it, what they should answer and how they should answer. The teacher gave the children very little opportunity to explore ideas, or to make comparisons and inferences. The thinking processes they demanded were almost exclusively limited to identification and memory.

Dreary as these findings are, they also seem to hold some promise. These teachers were not "bad" teachers; they were not mean; they were simply ineffective. The reason for this probably lies in the fact that no one had ever helped them to see the variety of specific ways they could respond to children and, having so responded, the specific ways they could build on the ideas of the children. Given an opportunity to study an analysis of their own behavior and to discuss it with a nonthreatening consultant or counselor, could they not learn to modify their approach and to direct it toward opening new and richer avenues of enquiry?

SAUCE FOR THE GOOSE

Lawrence Kubie (*10*), in a devastating critique of education, has suggested that overemphasis on repetitive drill (and much that these teachers were doing *would* fall under the heading of repetitive drill) is symptomatic of anxiety, anger, and repression. But we may ask whether some (though by no means all) of the anxiety and the anger which teachers bring to the teaching situation may not arise in part out of the frustration involved in knowing that they are expected to do *something* about the learning of these children, while they remain basically uncertain as to *what* to do.

If we expect the acquisition of knowledge, skills, and understandings to enhance the ego development of youngsters, it is no less reasonable to anticipate that knowledge, skills, and understanding—provided always that their relevance to the teaching situation is clear—should also strengthen the teacher.

Some oblique evidence on this point comes from a current study by Jersild (*8*), relating to the effects of personal psychotherapy and psychoanalysis on teachers. Some of these teachers reported that as their therapy progressed, they were able to see more clearly and specifically how their own behavior in the classroom influenced the learning and the thinking of their pupils. At the same time, some of them noted an increasing ability to understand and hence to clarify the youngsters' confusions. Although, in these instances, the teachers' insights into their own functioning as teachers came only after therapy, their comments often suggested that they would not only have welcomed but could have benefited at an early point in their careers from a more penetrating analysis of what was involved in teaching.

Studies of teacher behavior by Levin (*11*) and others provide good evidence that teachers who have a high interest in children are most likely to remain in teaching. Such individuals, it would seem, would not be frightened but, rather, rewarded by an opportunity to examine their own techniques. They might welcome study of their own ways of relating to children with a view to seeing how these affect children's learning and thinking.

The notion that teachers and teachers-in-training would benefit from analysis of their teaching implies that such analysis would not be directed toward a single "right" way. Rather, consideration of the *variety* of ways one might respond in a given situation should lead to flexibility and help in the quick "on the spot" decisions which are part of the challenge and the fun of teaching.

Ultimately, of course, any analysis of the task of teaching leads back to the question of its effectiveness in relation to the achievement of the pupil. Some of the teacher's actions may further the pupil's learning and thinking. Others may serve only to block and confuse him. It is no accident that much of the current interest in the analysis of teaching comes from centers where there has also been continuing research related to thinking as revealed in the classroom.

RESEARCH ON THINKING

The theoretical views on thinking held by two psychologists, Jean Piaget and Jerome Bruner, appear to have particular significance for the eventual resolution of some of the issues raised earlier.

Piaget's position, although well formulated, has been difficult for American investigators to interpret. But many skeptics are now impressed by his later work and by independent research validating a number of his ideas. These relate particularly to the question of developmental differences in thinking. Piaget uses the principles of formal logic as a basis for his analysis of thinking. He has arrived at a schematization of the emerging developmental stages of the abilities to deal either with increasingly complex problems or with simple problems in more efficient ways. Within the period covered by the years of schooling, there are three such stages. A preoperational or representational stage extends into the early childhood period. During this phase, much of the child's thinking is characterized by an inability to separate his own goals from the means for achieving them. In the later stage of concrete operations, extending from approximately 7 to 11 years, the child becomes increasingly able to organize the means for achievement of the goal independently of the goal itself. His operations are internalized and reversible, but he is still bound very closely to the immediately present object world. In the stage of formal operations, beginning around the age of 12, a stage which is preparatory to adult thinking, the ability to use hypothetical reasoning and controlled experimentation develops. The child is no longer bound to the concrete, but can deal directly with abstractions.

By and large, Piaget has seemed to his American colleagues to neglect the important role of motivation in thinking. Indeed, he has specified that the "structures" of intellect and affect must be regarded separately. Nevertheless, as various psychoanalytic writers have shown, and as he and his colleague, Inhelder (6), have brilliantly demonstrated in an analysis of adolescent thinking, the shift from one level of thinking to another is in many ways very closely bound up with the individual's life situation and with the changing nature of his needs, wishes, and desires.

Piaget is a genetic psychologist and biologist. He has never fully developed the implications of his position for the schooling of children. The main implication is, however, almost immediately apparent. If there are, as his theory indicates, built-in limitations in thinking at a particular level, then to confront the pupil with problems whose solutions are based on logical operations beyond his comprehension at that level must be to confront him with a meaningless task. If the solution his teacher expects is beyond him, it appears that for the moment at least, he and his teacher are really speaking in different languages. The student can, perhaps, if the teacher demands it, learn a solution by rote memory; but the words he mouths are little more than gibberish so far as real insight is concerned.

Jerome Bruner, unlike Piaget, does not deal with developmental differences in thinking, and his emphasis on motivation is somewhat different. Nevertheless, his viewpoint is in many ways compatible with Piaget's. His mode of attack on the nature of thinking seems likely to provide new insights into both the problem of individuality and that of the variety of ways of knowing.

Bruner views thinking as a complex process involving categorization, organization, transformation, and evaluation. Motivation is implied in and gives direction to each of these. This scheme for analyzing intellectual performance is currently being tested with children. Although children younger than ten years have not been involved in this study, the results are assumed to have general application, certainly to older children and probably to younger ones.

These youngsters under Bruner's observation have encountered a wide range of intellectual tasks, many of them clearly parallel to those usually involved in school learning. Examination of their performances in detail has indicated some of the dimensions on which this theory can be measured. One such dimension is *power,* which has to do with the youngster's perseverance and the range and order of approaches he uses in attempting to solve a problem. Another dimension involves individual *style* in thinking, a matter of the way the concepts the child brings to the problem are organized. A third referred to as *conceptual distance,* reflects the child's ability to avoid becoming bound in the immediate and obvious and to keep his eventual goal in view. A dimension of *involvement* measures the degree of separation of the task from personal needs and demands. In this connection, it may be noted that some children appear to be almost exclusively task-oriented, whereas others are always much more directed toward pleasing the experimenter. Finally, there is a *rigidity-flexibility* dimension, related to the ability to recognize errors and change one's plans accordingly.

Bruner (4), has recently reported a study comparing learning effectiveness in normal children and in children with learning blocks—those with adequate or superior intelligence who were unable to learn in school.

LEARNING BLOCKS

The findings bear directly on the question of the school's responsibility for mental health. The children with learning blocks revealed cognitive organizations differing radically from those of the normal youngsters. Their thinking was dominated by what Bruner calls "pre-emptive metaphors," principles of organization biased toward over-inclusion and over-generalization. For example, a child whose early experiences have reinforced the idea that "things can hurt me" views his environment as a source of potentially disruptive events. A youngster of this sort is so busy reading possible destruction into the learning problems set for him and defending himself against it that he never copes with the reality problems.

Bruner believes that the thinking of persons who are "defenders" rather than "copers" has never moved beyond the action-and-affect-laden conceptualization characteristic of the young child. Such conceptualization, of course, also survives in the creativity of the artist and sometimes serves the disciplined thinking of the inventor and initiator. But it is not pre-emptive and distorting as it is in the child who thinks only defensively.

Bruner theorizes that the prevention of learning difficulties is dependent on three factors in the early history of the child. These include opportunities for play, opportunities for identification, and freedom from excessive drive and anxiety. Undoubtedly the family contributes most importantly to these, but the influence of the school is not negligible. A closer examination of these factors indicates some of the ways the school may function to further children's abilities to think adequately and to cope with their environment realistically rather than merely defensively.

Play, according to Bruner and others, reduces the pressures of impulse and incentive and makes intrinsic learning possible. Piaget also indicates that play is important, especially during the period when the child is developing basic notions about the nature of the world. Thus, a first step toward the conviction that intellectual activity has an inherent worth comes in doing things for fun, and an early childhood education program based on play takes on added significance.

So far as identification is concerned, the child first emulates the models he finds in his own family. But teachers, provided they are individuals for whom children can have warm and positive feelings, may also serve as models and, if they are competent, importantly influence children's ways of thinking.

The third factor mentioned by Bruner also relates to the behavior of the teacher. Excessive drive and anxiety inhibit effective thinking. Too much pressure on learning, too many external rewards and punishments, lead to blocking and functional stupidity on the part of the would-be learner.

Illustrative of the inevitable enmeshing of teaching and thinking is a recent six-year study by Sarason (12) and others. This inquiry revealed many children with good intellectual potential who were unable to function adequately in school. It appeared that very often the techniques used by their teachers mobilized rather than allayed these children's anxieties. Unfortunately, relatively few of the teachers were able to identify the anxiety-prone children in their classrooms. Nor were they able to avoid anxiety-arousing techniques in dealing with them.

Undoubtedly, many teachers are benignly unaware of the inhibiting effects certain comments and expressions have on many children. Others deliberately push and prod in the mistaken notion that they are thus providing needed motivation. They assume that learning is necessarily painful and overlook the fact that success in learning often provides a powerful incentive to further learning.

LEARNING BY MACHINE

Evidence on this point comes from current research on teaching machines. This research also throws considerable light on many of the relationships between teaching and thinking. Teaching machines, as developed under the direction of B. F. Skinner (13), operate on the principle that a very complex concept can be broken down into a series of related ideas—learning these ideas step by step according to a "program," leads to eventual comprehension of the large idea. Unlike a textbook, which may skip an essential step for the student, each step in the program for the machine must be made explicit. The person who sets up a program must not only know the subject matter to be taught, but also the thinking processes through which it can be mastered. The record of the student's errors indicates the places where the programmer failed to anticipate confusion. The machines may thus contribute to improved knowledge of both teaching and thinking.

Many educators have taken a dim view of the development of the machines for a variety of reasons. The machines do involve the manipulation of student behavior by push-button techniques. Some of their appeal to the learner may depend on their novelty, and that appeal may diminish. They promote some kinds of thinking and learning, but are inappropriate for others. The effectiveness of any machine is entirely dependent on the nature of the program given it. This, in turn, depends on the person who develops the program, how well he understands the subject the machine is to teach, and the thinking processes involved in mastering it.

But the machines appear to have some very positive attributes. The student makes an active response. He does not parrot an answer, but must compose or select the appropriate idea. The machine is set up so that he makes progress through making the correct responses in a sequence intended to lead him to increasing competence and understanding. The machine eliminates the kinds of verbal and expressive behavior on the part of the teacher that may either enhance or confuse learning in the usual classroom situation. The child is "in contact" only with the person who made the program on which the machine operates. For some children, a machine may be considerably less threatening than a teacher! In general, however, the purposes of mental health and environmental mastery would seem best served only when the machine is used as an adjunct to the teacher. It could provide opportunities for individuals to proceed at their own rates, obviate much of the needless repetition which is now so prevalent, and free the teacher to function in a more truly creative and individualized way with youngsters.

In the long run, of course, the question of whether or not the school can promote mental health lies directly with the teacher. The teacher, more than most other persons, can, I believe, further the youngster's efforts toward active, healthy mastery. He can help him with the specific skills and knowledge traditionally held to be the business of the school. He can also help him toward the critical, evaluative, creative kinds of thinking needed to cope with an environment that is ever changing.

But if the teacher is to accomplish these things, he too must have help. His mental health function needs to be clarified and reduced to comprehensible size. He needs more than a firm grasp of the skills and knowledge he is expected to teach his pupils. He needs to understand thinking processes. He needs to know very specifically what it means to teach and how what he does as a teacher influences the thinking and the learning of those he teaches.

REFERENCES

1. Aschner, M. J. The language of teaching. *Teachers College Record*, 1960, 61, 242–252.
2. Bellack, A., & Huebner, D. Teaching. *Rev. educ. Res.*, 1960, 30, 246–250.
3. Biber, Barbara. Integration of mental health principles in the school setting. In G. Caplan (Ed.) *Prevention of mental disorders in children*. New York: Basic Books, 1961.
4. Bruner, J. On coping and defending. Address to the American Psychological Association, September, 1959.
5. Hughes, Marie, *et al. Assessment of the quality of teaching in elementary schools*. Salt Lake City: Univer. Utah, 1959.
6. Inhelder, Barbel, & Piaget, J. *The growth of logical thinking from childhood to adolescence*. New York: Basic Books, 1958.
7. Jahoda, M. *Current concepts of positive mental health*. New York: Basic Books, 1958.
8. Jersild, A., & Allina, Eve. *The influence of psychotherapy on a teacher's life and work* (in process).
9. Kotinsky, Ruth, & Coleman, J. V. Mental health as an educational goal. *Teachers College Record*, 1955, 56, 267–276.
10. Kubie, L. *Education and the process of maturation*. New York: Bank Street Publications, 1958.
11. Levin, H., *et al*. Studies of teacher behavior. *J. exp. Educ.*, 1957, 26, 81–92.
12. Sarason, S. B. *Anxiety in elementary school children*. New York: Wiley, 1960.
13. Skinner, B. F. Teaching machines. *Science*, 1958, 128, 969–977.
14. Smith, B. O. A concept of teaching. *Teachers College Record*, 1960, 61, 229–241.

16. Mental Health, Creative Thinking, and Values

Kaoru Yamamoto

In the following article, Dr. Yamamoto grapples with these issues: Is the mentally healthy person characterized by more than a freedom from mental illness? Is creative environmental mastery associated with emotional robustness? Is creative thinking desirable or nec-

Elementary School Journal, April, 1966, 361–367. Copyright 1966, by The University of Chicago Press. Reprinted with the permission of the copyright owner and author.

essary for effective functioning? Is creativity really
something we cherish sufficiently to nurture? Are we
ready to accept the consequences it might produce?

The history of man's understanding of man has many instances of an approach from the negative side, or entry through the back door, so to speak. Our definition of a healthy person seems to be based on our knowledge about the sick, and our idea of a well-functioning person stems from our understanding of a malfunctioning human being. Pathology has been the mainstay of our medical science, or psychoanalysis, and of our behavioral sciences. Health has been defined as the absence of, or freedom from, defects, pain, or disease. Mental health has usually been defined as the absence of, or freedom from, neurosis or psychosis. We know far more about the deviant minority in the population than about the healthy. In general, our assessment of personality has been more effective in the detection of malfunctions than in the prediction of effective functions.

Nevertheless, the importance of a positive approach to this problem has not entirely escaped keen observers. In 1933 Adolf Meyer said, "It has . . . seemed strange to me that we should, after the fashion of pathology and a defensive and narrow attitude of health interests, focus our attention so exclusively upon 'what is wrong.' . . . Why the lack of interest in the positive facts of life as found?" (1: 577). Meyer's major interest was clearly shown in the following statement: "It is spontaneity that I want to study and inquire into and cultivate and respect as the all-important characteristic quality of a person" (1: 581).

Alfred Adler was another person who tried to explore the positive aspects of health. Hall and Lindzey have this to say about him: "By endowing man with altruism, humanitarianism, cooperation, creativity, uniqueness, and awareness, he restored to man a sense of dignity and worth that psychoanalysis had pretty largely destroyed" (2: 125).

WHO ARE THE HEALTHY?

A concept of the fully functioning person has been expounded by Maslow (3). He suggested that the fully functioning person might be as deviant from the normal person as the abnormal person is, only in the opposite direction. We cannot define the healthy person merely by pointing out the lack of pathologies or the absence of disturbances. A fully functioning person should be identified by characteristics or qualities he possesses and not by those he lacks.

Guilford presented a similar viewpoint when he objected to the idea of applying knowledge based on sick people to the normal group. Instead, he proposed "the extension of descriptive variables of the normal population into pathological groups, thus accounting to a large extent for their syndromes" (4: 491).

Shoben also expressed doubts about the traditional approach to mental health. He asked, "Is it most fruitful to regard normality or integrative behavior as merely reflecting a minimal degree of pathology, or may there be a certain merit in considering the asset side of personality, the positive aspects of human development?" (5: 183). Shoben then presented a five-facet model of integrative adjustment in terms of self-control, personal responsibility, social responsibility, democratic social interest, and adequate ideals and standards.

Similar models of the healthy person have been advocated by Allport, Rogers, and Combs. All of them emphasized such characteristics as openness to experience, trust in one's organism, warm and deep relation to others, imaginativeness and creativity, and a unifying philosophy of life (6–8).

From the empirical side, MacKinnon provided interesting information based on a series of studies of a large number of "highly effective" individuals. These individuals were defined in terms of their ability to perform their duties and tasks successfully under high psychological and physical tension, for example, during the war years. To the investigators' surprise, they repeatedly found that individuals of the most extraordinary effectiveness had had life histories marked by severe frustrations, deprivations, and traumatic experiences. MacKinnon then postulated that two variables determine effective functioning—emotional stability, or personal soundness, and originality, or creativity of thought and action. Personal soundness seemed better described by an individual's response to problems than by an absence of problems (9).

The combat effectiveness of a group of fighter-intercepter pilots during the Korean conflict, studied by Torrance and his associates, gives further insight. Ace pilots with five or more "kills" (enemy planes destroyed) were contrasted with pilots who were not aces. The two groups were matched for rank, age, and previous combat experiences. It was learned that the aces were characterized by singleness of purpose, intensity of efforts, willingness to take calculated risks, lesser rigidity, and higher imaginativeness (10).

CREATIVE THINKING

In this brief review of conceptual schemes of the healthy person, I would like to point out that one recurrent element appears to be a quality called *creativity, originality,* or *imaginativeness.* Could this, then, be the missing factor in the sick-average-healthy continuum that is to replace the traditional abnormal-normal bipolar scheme? Could creative thinking be the quality that characterizes the healthy and differentiates them both from the sick group and from the middle group, who are not sick but not particularly healthy? These questions have stimulated many recent explorations into creative thinking and behavior. Let us examine some formulations and evidence.

The first efforts to explain man's creative endeavors came from, among others, psychoanalysts and clinical psychologists. Kris, for example, coined the famous phrase, "regression in the service of the ego," and pointed out the paradoxical requirement of a creative mind to be both unrestricted and well-disciplined (11). Thought should be open, novel, and free-wheeling, but, at the same time, it should be relevant, harmonious, and constructive (12).

Kubie put it this way: "The uniqueness of creativity, i.e., its capacity to find and put together something new, depends on the extent to which preconscious functions can operate freely between these two ubiquitous concurrent and oppressive prison wardens" (13: 47). By *wardens* he meant conscious and unconscious processes of the mind.

A DETACHED DEVOTION

One difficulty in studying creative thinking empirically would seem to be the fact that "creative thinkers can tell us so little about it" (14: 31)— about the birth and death of ideas, that is. Analyses by careful observers, however, tend to confirm the paradoxical balance suspected by clinical workers. Thus, both Henle (14) and Bruner (15) agreed on a characteristic feature of creative thinkers, namely, their "detached devotion." Creative work demands a passionate, sustained interest on the part of the thinker and also a certain detachment from his ideas. He must be deeply committed to and immersed in his work, but, at the same time, he should be able to keep his distance from it so that he may be free to examine it, develop it, or even reject it.

ARCHITECTS

MacKinnon's accounts of male creative architects revealed that there was evidence of psychopathology in the Minnesota Multiphasic Personality Inventory protocols of these men. But there was also clear evidence of adequate control mechanisms in their creative and productive life as architects. The creative ones showed an openness to their own feelings and emotions, keen self-awareness and positive self-regard, wide interests, and a clear preference for the complex and the asymmetrical. They tended to show high theoretical and aesthetic values and revealed tolerance of the tension created by strong opposing values, for example, rational, cognitive, theoretical as opposed to sensual, emotional, aesthetic (16).

The creative architects were found to be less conforming than their less creative colleagues. One indication of this quality was found in the high feminine interests of the creative architects. Another indication was found in the architects' sense of responsibility. The creative architects felt that their primary responsibility was to their own professional standards and not, as in the case of the less creative architects, to the client, to colleagues, and to society. The creative architects prized independence in their thought and action (16).

CHEMISTS

Although research scientists work in a world that is somewhat different from that of architects, patterns of needs revealed by creative members of these two groups seem to have much in common. Stein reported that a group of creative chemists were characterized by striving and internal freedom that appeared to be well organized and purposeful. In pursuing the unknown and in seeking novel accomplishments, a creative chemist is further aided by his strong need to play. In other words, he can engage in activities that have no immediate purpose. He can break down an existing whole into its component parts and study them to see how the parts can be integrated into new and useful ideas. In this activity, he is also aided by his high aesthetic sensitivity (17).

Roe pointed out the tendency of eminent social and behavioral scientists to avoid complex, emotional interpersonal relationships. Their behavior was goal-oriented, and they could be called well adjusted only in the broader sense of being socially useful and happy in their work and not necessarily in the sense of being free from psychological stress (18).

GOOD OR BAD?

With all this and other information, can we now say that creative thinking is desirable or necessary if a person is to be healthy and effective? Can we agree with the popular opinion (19:8) that creativity is "a kind of psychic wonder drug, powerful and presumably painless" and that "everyone wants a prescription" for it?

I wish our answer were simply and clearly affirmative, but, alas, the situation is not that simple. Before we can answer these questions, we are forced to re-examine many of our cherished dreams and beliefs, and reformulate many concepts and practices.

First, we must realize that our traditional interpretation of human motivation needs to be revised. A person interacts with his environment for more than one reason. To be sure, he wants to reduce tension, conflict, and other unpleasant experiences to regain equilibrium. Further, however, he actively seeks to disturb the present balance of his own accord and for the sake of challenge. He goes out of his way to "encounter, explore, and master that which is intriguing and challenging" (20: 254). In this connection, the concept of "competence motivation" suggested by White seems to deserve careful attention and expansion (21).

Second, the psychology of thinking must be built on this conception of "life as actively pushing forward, of man as not only coping with but also as seizing control of his environment" (22: 200). In such a formulation, the emphasis will be on the process of thinking rather than on the elements of thought or the end products of thinking. Some daring and original methods of inquiry in addition to (or in place of) the traditional analytic approach may be required to answer the challenge.

Third, we shall be faced with the question of how to nurture creative behavior. This is at one and the same time an academic problem of behavior control and a practical problem of education. For the moment at least, we do not know much about the precedents and the consequents of such behavior (23, 24). Even if longitudinal studies suggest some causal relations between a set of child-rearing and schooling procedures and later behavior of a creative nature, we shall be confronted with at least one difficulty in using this knowledge. MacKinnon has described the problem. As he wrote, we "would still have no assurance that the conditions in the home, in school, and society, the qualities of interpersonal relations between instructor and student, and the aspects of the teaching-learning process which would appear to have contributed to creative development a generation ago would facilitate rather than inhibit creativity if these same factors were created in today's quite different world and far different educational climate" (16).

WHAT DO WE PRIZE?

Last but not least is the crucial question of values in psychology and education. Any judgment on mental health inescapably involves a value decision, and any study reveals more about the investigator's own values and preferences than it does about positive mental health as such, since so much depends on the kind of people the investigator selects as representing a healthy personality (25).

Elsewhere, I argued that no one can and should insist on cultivating man's dormant potential without fully realizing what this entails. "No one can judge whether creativity is 'good' or 'bad.' This is a value judgment involving the evaluator as deeply as the evaluated. Are we ready and willing to re-examine our societal values and to revise them if necessary? Or are we merely offering lip service because 'everybody is talking about creativity'?" (26: 21).

A simple example illustrates the disparity between our lip service to creativity and prevalent attitudes. Researchers find that highly creative children are often described as difficult or as silly and wild by their parents, teachers, and friends. Highly creative children are independent and tend not to identify with values held by teachers. Highly creative children are not described as popular among their peers (27–29). To state the problem bluntly, we do not know what to do with these crazy kids.

If we really commit ourselves to creative thinking, "we should be prepared for many new and often shocking things, new concepts of social order, new definitions of aims of personality development, new patterns of child rearing, new systems of efficiency or productivity rating, new ways of supervision and management, new curricula, new evaluation instruments, and many, many others" (26: 21). Are we ready for all these changes?

REFERENCES

1. A. Lief. *The Commonsense Psychiatry of Dr. Adolf Meyer*. New York: McGraw-Hill Book Company, 1948.
2. C. S. Hall and G. Lindzey. *Theories of Personality*. New York: John Wiley and Sons, 1957.
3. A. H. Maslow. *Motivation and Personality*. New York: Harper and Brothers, 1954.
4. J. P. Guilford. *Personality*. New York: McGraw-Hill Book Company, 1959.
5. E. J. Shoben, Jr. "Toward a Concept of the Normal Personality," *American Psychologist*, XII (April, 1957), 183–89.
6. G. W. Allport. *Personality and Personal Encounter*. Boston: Beacon Press, 1960.
7. C. R. Rogers. "Toward Becoming a Fully Functioning Person," in *Perceiving, Behaving, Becoming*. Edited by A. W. Combs. Washington, D.C.: Association for Supervision and Curriculum Development, 1962.

8. A. W. Combs. "A Perceptual View of the Adequate Personality," in *Perceiving, Behaving, Becoming*. Edited by A. W. Combs. Washington, D.C.: Association for Supervision and Curriculum Development, 1962.

9. D. W. MacKinnon. "The Highly Effective Individual," *Teachers College Record*, LI (April, 1960), 367–78.

10. E. P. Torrance, C. H. Rush, Jr., H. B. Kuhn, and J. M. Doughty. *Factors in Fighter-Intercepter Pilot Combat Effectiveness*. Lackland Air Force Base, Texas: Air Force Personnel and Training Research Center, 1957.

11. E. Kris. *Psychoanalytic Explorations in Art*. New York: International Universities Press, 1952.

12. D. Rapaport. *Organization and Pathology of Thought*. New York: Columbia University Press, 1951.

13. L. Kubie. *Neurotic Distortion of the Creative Process*. Lawrence: University of Kansas Press, 1958.

14. Mary Henle. "The Birth and Death of Ideas," in *Contemporary Approaches to Creative Thinking*. Edited by H. E. Gruber, G. Terrell, and M. Wertheimer. New York: Atherton Press, 1963.

15. J. S. Bruner. "The Conditions of Creativity," in *Contemporary Approaches to Creative Thinking*. Edited by H. E. Gruber, G. Terrell, and M. Wertheimer. New York: Atherton Press, 1963.

16. D. W. MacKinnon. "The Nature and Nurture of Creative Talent." *American Psychologist*, XVII (July, 1962), 484–95.

17. M. I. Stein. "Explorations in Typology," in *The Study of Lives*. Edited by Robert W. White. New York: Atherton Press, 1963.

18. Anne Roe. "A Psychological Study of Eminent Psychologists and Anthropologists, and a Comparison with Biological and Physical Scientists," *Psychological Monographs*, LXVII (1953), No. 2.

19. J. W. Gardner. "Renewal in Societies and Men," *Annual Report of Carnegie Corporation*. New York: Carnegie Corporation, 1962.

20. J. W. Getzels. "Creative Thinking, Problem-solving, and Instruction" in *Theories of Learning and Instruction*. Edited by Ernest R. Hilgard. Chicago: National Society for the Study of Education, 1964.

21. R. W. White. "Motivation Reconsidered: The Concept of Competence," *Psychological Review*, LXVI (September, 1959), 297–333.

22. R. B. MacLeod. "Retrospect and Prospect" in *Contemporary Approaches to Creative Thinking*. Edited by H. E. Gruber, G. Terrell, and M. Wertheimer. New York: Atherton Press, 1963.

23. K. Yamamoto. "Creative Thinking: Some Thoughts on Research," *Exceptional Children*, XXX (May, 1964), 403–10.

24. K. Yamamoto. "Training for Creative Thinking: A Case of an Iceberg?" A paper read at the American Educational Research Association, Chicago, February, 1965.

25. M. Smith. "Research Strategies Toward a Conception of Positive Mental Health," *American Psychologist*, XIV (November, 1959), 673–81.

26. K. Yamamoto. "Relationships between Creative Thinking Abilities of Teachers and Achievement and Adjustment of Pupils," *Journal of Experimental Education*, XXXII (Fall, 1963), 3–25.

27. J. W. Getzels and P. W. Jackson. *Creativity and Intelligence*. New York: John Wiley and Sons, 1962.

28. E. P. Torrance. *Guiding Creative Talent*. Englewood Cliffs, New Jersey: Prentice-Hall, 1962.

29. K. Yamamoto. "Creativity and Sociometric Choice among Adolescents," *Journal of Social Psychology*, LXIV (December, 1964), 249–61.

17. What is the Optimal Learning Environment for the Young Child?

Bettye M. Caldwell

This paper challenges the assumption that the child's natural family provides the only effective learning environment for young children. Because of the importance of the preschool years for intellectual development and because of the inability of some parents to provide adequate intellectual priming, it is imperative according to Bettye M. Caldwell that we consider novel and bold patterns of care to supplement deficient homes.

A truism in the field of child development is that the milieu in which development occurs influences that development. As a means of validating the principle, considerable scientific effort has gone into the Linnaean task of describing and classfying milieus and examining developmental consequences associated with different types. Thus we know something about what it is like to come of age in New Guinea,[29] in a small Midwestern town,[4] in villages and cities in Mexico[25] in families of different social-class level in Chicago[12] or Boston,[27,31] in a New York slum,[46] in Russian collectives,[9] in Israeli Kibbutzim,[23,34,41] in the eastern part of the United States,[33] and in a Republican community in Central New York.[10] Most of these milieu descriptions have placed great stress on the fact that they were just that and nothing more, i.e., they have expressed the customary scientific viewpoint that to describe is not to judge or criticize. However, in some

American Journal of Orthopsychiatry, 1967, 37, 8–21. Copyright, the American Orthopsychiatric Association, Inc. Reproduced by permission of copyright owner and author.

* Presented at the 1965 annual meeting of the American Orthopsychiatric Association, New York, New York.

The author's work is supported by Grant Nos. MH-07649 and MH-08542, NIMH, U.S. Public Health Service, and by Grant No. D-156(R), Children's Bureau, Social Security Administration, Department of Health, Education, and Welfare.

of the more recent milieu descriptions which have contrasted middle- and lower-class family environment as highlighted conditions in extreme lower-class settings, [31,46] often more than a slight suggestion has crept in that things could be better for the young child from the deprived segment of the culture. Even so, there remains a justifiable wariness about recommending or arranging any environment for the very young child other than the type regarded as its natural habitat, viz., within its own family.

Of course, optimizing environments are arranged all the time under one guise or another. For example, for disturbed children whose family environments seem effectively to reinforce rather than extinguish psychopathology, drastic alterations of milieu often are attempted. This may take the form of psychotherapy for one or both parents as well as the disturbed child, or it may involve total removal of the child from the offending environment with temporary or prolonged placement of the child in a milieu presumably more conducive to normal development. Then there is the massive milieu arrangement formalized and legalized as "education" which profoundly affects the lives of all children once they reach the age of five or six. This type of arrangement is not only tolerated but fervently endorsed by our culture as a whole. In fact, any subculture (such as the Amish) which resists the universalization of this pattern of milieu arrangement is regarded as unacceptably deviant and as justifying legal action to enforce conformity.

For very young children, however, there has been a great deal of timidity about conscious and planned arrangement of the developmental milieu, as though the implicit assumption has been made that any environment which sustains life is adequate during this period. This is analogous to suggesting that the intrauterine environment during the period of maximal cellular proliferation is less important than it is later, a suggestion that patently disregards evidence from epidemiology and experimental embryology. The rate of proliferation of new behavioral skills during the first three years of life and the increasing accumulation of data pointing to the relative permanence of deficit acquired when the environment is inadequate during this period make it mandatory that careful attention be given to the preparation of the developmental environment during the first three years of life.

CONCLUSIONS FROM INADEQUATE ENVIRONMENTS

It is, of course, an exaggeration to imply that no one has given attention to the type of environment which can nourish early and sustained growth and development. For a good three decades now infants who are developing in different milieus been observed and examined, and data relating to their development have made it possible to identify certain strengths and deficiencies of the different types of environments. Of all types described, the one most consistently indicted by the data is the institution. A number of years ago Goldfarb[19] published an excellent series of studies contrasting patterns of intellectual functioning shown by a group of adopted adolescents who had been reared in institutions up to age three and then transferred to foster homes or else placed shortly after birth in foster homes. The development of the group that had spent time in the institution was deficient in many ways compared to the group that had gone directly into foster homes. Provence and Lipton[33] recently published a revealing description of the early social and intellectual development of infants in institutions, contrasting their development with that of home-reared children. On almost every measured variable the institutional infants were found wanting—less socially alert and outgoing, less curious, less responsive, less interested in objects, and generally less advanced. The findings of this study are almost prototypic of the literature in the field, as pointed out in excellent reviews by Yarrow[47] and Ainsworth.[1]

Although there are many attributes in combination that comprise the institutional environment, the two most obvious elements are (1) absence of a mother and (2) the presence of a group. These basic characteristics have thus been identified as the major carriers of the institutional influence and have been generalized into an explicit principle guiding our recommendations for optimal environments—learning or otherwise—for young children whenever any type of milieu arrangement is necessary. This principle may be stated simply as: the optimal environment for the young child is one in which the child is cared for in his own home in the context of a warm, continuous emotional relationship with his own mother under conditions of varied sensory input. Implicit in this principle is the conviction that the child's mother is the person best qualified to provide a stable and warm interpersonal relationship as well as the necessary pattern of sensory stimulation. Implicit also is the assumption that socio-emotional development has priority during the first three years and that if this occurs normally, cognitive development, which is of minor importance during this period anyway, will take care of itself. At a still deeper level lurks the assumption that attempts to foster cognitive development will interfere with socio-emotional development. Advocacy of the principle also implies endorsement of the idea that most homes are adequate during this early period and that no formal training (other than possibly some occasional supervisory support) for mothering is necessary. Such an operating principle places quite an onus on mothers and assumes that they will possess or quickly acquire all the talents necessary to create an optimal learning environment. And this author, at least, is convinced that a majority of mothers have such talents or proclivities and that they are willing to try to do all they can to create for their children the proper developmental milieu.

But there are always large numbers of children for whom family resources are not available and for whom some type of substitute milieu arrangement must be made. On the whole, such attempts have followed the entirely logical and perhaps evolutionary approach to milieu development—they have sought to create substitute families. The same is usually true when parents themselves seek to work out an alternate child-care arrangement because of less drastic conditions, such as maternal employment. The most typical maneuver is to try to obtain a motherly person who will "substitute" for her (not supplement her) during her hours away from her young child.

Our nation has become self-consciously concerned with social evolution, and in the past decade a serious attempt has been made to assimilate valid data from the behavioral and social sciences into planning for social action. In this context it would be meaningful to examine and question some of the hidden assumptions upon which our operating principle about the optimal environment for the young child rests.

EXAMINING THE HIDDEN ASSUMPTIONS

1. *Do intermitten, short-term separations of the child from the mother impair the mother-child relationship or the development of the child?* Once having become sensitized to the consequences of institutionalization, and suspicious that the chief missing ingredient was the continued presence of the mother, the scientific and professional community went on the *qui vive* to the possibly deleterious consequences of any type of separation of an infant from its mother. Accordingly, a number of studies[10,18,21,35,39] investigated the consequences of short-term intermittent separation and were unable to demonstrate in the children the classical syndrome of the "institutional child." In reviewing the literature, Yarrow[47] stressed the point that available data do not support the tendency to assume that maternal deprivation, such as exists in the institutional environment, and maternal separation are the same thing. Apparently short cyclic interruptions culminated by reunions do not have the same effect as prolonged interruptions, even though quantitatively at the end of a designated period the amount of time spent in a mother-absent situation might be equal for the two experiences. Also in this context it is well to be reminded that in the institutional situation there is likely to be no stable mother-child relationship to interrupt. These are often never-mothered rather than ever-mothered children, a fact which must be kept in mind in generalizing from data on institutional groups. Thus until we have data to indicate that such intermittent separation-reunion cycles have similiar effects on young children as prolonged separations, we are probably unjustified in assuming that an "uninterrupted" relationship is an essential ingredient of the optimal environment.

2. *Is group upbringing invariably damaging?* In studies done in West European and American settings, social and cognitive deficits associated with continuous group care during infancy have been frequently demonstrated. Enough exceptions have been reported, however, to warrant an intensification of the search for the "true" ingredient in the group situation associated with the observed deficits. For example, Freud and Dann[17] described the adjustment of a group of six children reared in a concentration camp orphanage for approximately three years, where they were cared for by overworked and impersonal inmates of the camp, and then transported to a residence for children in England. The children, who had never known their own mothers but who had been together as a group for approximately three years, were intensely attached to one another. Although their adjustment to their new environment was slow and differed from the pattern one would expect from home-reared children, it was significant that they eventually did make a reasonably good adjustment. That the children were able to learn a new language while making this emotional transition was offered as evidence that many of the basic cognitive and personality attributes remained unimpaired in spite of the

pattern of group upbringing. The accumulation of data showing that Kibbutz-reared children[34] do not have cognitive deficits also reinforces the premise that it is not necessarily group care *per se* that produces the frequently reported deficit and that it is possible to retain the advantages of group care while systematically eliminating its negative features. Grounds for reasonable optimism also have been found in retrospective studies by Maas[26] and Beres and Obers,[6] although in both cases the authors found evidence of pathology in some members of the follow-up sample. Similarly Dennis and Najarian[14] concluded from their data that the magnitude of the deficit varied as a function of the type of instrument used to measure deficit, and Dennis[13] showed that in institutions featuring better adult-child ratios and a conscious effort to meet the psychological needs of the infants the development of the children was much less retarded than was the case in a group of children residing in institutions with limited and unsophisticated staff. It is not appropriate to go into details of limitations of methodology in any of these studies; however, from the standpoint of an examination of the validity of a principle, it is important to take note of any exceptions to the generality of that principle.

In this context it is worth considering a point made by Gula.[20] He recently has suggested that some of the apparent consistency in studies comparing institutionalized infants with those cared for in their own homes and in foster homes might disappear if it were possible to equate the comparison groups on the variable of environmental adequacy. That is, one could classify all three types of environments as good, marginal, or inadequate on a number of dimensions. Most of the studies have compared children from palpably "inadequate" institutions with children from "good" foster and own homes. He suggests that merely because most institutions studied have been inadequate in terms of such variables as adult-child ratio, staff turnover, and personal characteristics of some of the caretakers, etc., one is not justified in concluding *ipso facto* that group care is invariably inferior or damaging.

3. *Is healthy socio-emotional development the most important task of the first three years? Do attempts to foster cognitive growth interfere with social and emotional development?* These paired assumptions, which one finds stated in one variety or another in many pamphlets and books dealing with early child development, represent acceptance of a closed system model of human development. They seem to conceptualize development as compartmentalized and with a finite limit. If the child progresses too much in one area he automatically restricts the amount of development that can occur in another area. Thus one often encounters such expressions as "cognitive development at the *expense* of socio-emotional development." It is perhaps of interest to reflect that, until our children reach somewhere around high school age, we seldom seem to worry that the reverse might occur. But, of course, life is an open system, and on the whole it is accurate to suggest that development feeds upon development. Cognitive and socio-emotional advances tend on the whole to be positively, not negatively correlated.

The definition of intelligence as *adaptivity* has not been adequately stressed by modern authors. It is, of course, the essence of Piaget's definition[32] as it was earlier of Binet.[7] Unfortunately, however, for the last generation or so in America we have been more concerned with how to measure intelligent behavior than how to interpret and understand it. Acceptance of the premise that intelligent behavior is adaptive behavior should help to break the set of many persons in the field of early child development that to encourage cognitive advance is to discourage healthy socio-emotional development. Ample data are available to suggest that quite the reverse is true either for intellectually advanced persons[42,43] or an unselected sample. In a large sample of young adults from an urban area in Minnesota, Anderson[3] and associates found that the best single predictor of post-high school adjustment contained in a large assessment battery was a humble little group intelligence test. Prediction based on intelligence plus teacher's ratings did somewhat better, but nothing exceeded the intelligence test for single measure efficiency.

It is relevant here to mention White's[45] concept of competence or effectance as a major stabilizing force in personality development. The emotional reinforcement accompanying the old "I can do it myself" declaration should not be undervalued. In Murphy's report[30] of the coping behavior of preschool children one sees evidence of the adjustive supports gained through cognitive advances. In his excellent review of cognitive stimulation in infancy and early childhood, Fowler[16] raises the question of whether there is any justification for the modern anxiety (and, to be sure, it is a modern phenomenon) over whether cognitive stimulation may damage personality development. He suggests that in the past severe and harmful methods may have been the culprits whenever there was damage and that the generalizations have confused methods of stimulation with the process of stimulation *per se.*

4. *Do cognitive experiences of the first few months and years leave no significant residual?* Any assumption that the learnings of infancy are evanescent appears to be a fairly modern idea. In his *Emile,* first published in 1762, Rousseau[38] stressed the point that education should begin while the child is still in the cradle. Perhaps any generalization to the contrary received its major modern impetus from a rather unlikely place—from longitudinal studies of development covering the span from infancy to adulthood. From findings of poor prediction of subsequent intellectual status[5] one can legitimately infer that the infant tests measure behavior that is somewhat irrelevant to later intellectual performance. Even though these behaviors predictive of later cognitive behavior elude most investigators, one cannot infer that the early months and years are unimportant for cognitive development.

Some support for this assumption has come from experimental studies in which an attempt has been made to produce a durable effect in human subjects by one or another type of intervention offered during infancy. One cogent example is the work of Rheingold,[36] in which she provided additional social and personal stimulation to a small group of approximately six-month-old, institutionalized infants for a total of eight weeks. At the end of the experimental period, differences in social responsiveness between her stimulated group and a control group composed of other babies in the institution could be observed. There were also slight but nonsignificant advances in postural and motor behavior on a test of infant development. However, when the babies were followed up approximately a year later, by which time all but one were in either adoptive or boarding homes or in their own natural homes, the increased social responsiveness formerly shown by the stimulated babies was no longer observed. Nor were there differences in level of intellectual functioning. Rheingold and Bayley[37] concluded that the extra mothering provided during the experimental period was enough to produce an effect at the time but not enough to sustain this effect after such a time as the two groups were no longer differentially stimulated. However, in spite of their conservative conclusion, it is worth noting that the experimentally stimulated babies were found to vocalize more during the follow-up assessments than the control babies. Thus there may have been enough of an effect to sustain a developmental advance in at least this one extremely important area.

Some very impressive recent unpublished data obtained by Skeels, offer a profound challenge to the assumption of the unimportance of the first three years for cognitive growth. This investigator has followed up after approximately 25 years most of the subjects described in a paper by Skeels and Dye.[40] Thirteen infants had been transferred from an orphanage because of evidence of mental retardation and placed in an institution for the retarded under the care of adolescent retardates who gave them a great deal of loving care and as much cognitive stimulation as they could. The 13 subjects showed a marked acceleration in development after this transfer. In contrast a group of reasonably well matched infants left on the wards of the orphanage continued to develop poorly. In a recent follow-up of these cases, Skeels discovered that the gains made by the transferred infants were sustained into their adult years, whereas all but one of the control subjects developed the classic syndrome of mental retardation.

The fact that development and experience are cumulative makes it difficult ever to isolate any one antecedent period and assert that its influence was or was not influential in a subsequent developmental period. Thus even though it might be difficult to demonstrate an effect of some experience in an adjacent time period, delayed effects may well be of even greater developmental consequence. In a recent review of data from a number of longitudinal studies, Bloom[8] has concluded that during the first three to four years (the noncognitive years, if you will) approximately 50 per cent of the development of intelligence that is ever to occur in the life cycle takes place. During this period a particular environment may be either abundant or deprived in terms of the ingredients essential for providing opportunities for the development of intelligence and problem solving. Bloom[8] states:

> The effects of the environments, especially of the extreme environments, appear to be greatest in the early (and more rapid) periods of intelligence development and least in the later (and less rapid) periods of development. Although there is relatively little evidence of the effects of changing the environment on the changes in intelligence, the evidence so far available suggests that marked changes in the environment in the early years can produce greater changes in intelligence than will equally marked changes in the environment at later periods of development. (pp. 88–89)

5. *Can one expect that, without formal planning, all the necessary learning experiences will occur?* There is an old legend that if you put six chimpanzees in front of six typewriters and leave them there long enough they eventually will produce all the works in the British Museum. One could paraphrase this for early childhood by suggesting that six children with good eyes and ears and hands and brains would, if left alone in nature, arrive at a number system, discover the laws of conservation of matter and energy, comprehend gravity and the motions of the planets, and perhaps arrive at the theory of relativity. All the "facts" necessary to discern these relationships are readily available. Perhaps a more realistic example would be to suggest that, if we surround a group of young children with a carefully selected set of play materials, they would eventually discover for themselves the laws of color mixture, of form and contour, of perspective, of formal rhythm and tonal relationships, and biological growth. And, to be sure, all this *could* occur. But whether this will necessarily occur with any frequency is quite another matter. We also assume that at a still earlier period a child will learn body control, eye-hand coordination, the rudiments of language, and styles of problem solving in an entirely incidental and unplanned way. In an article in a recent issue of a popular woman's magazine, an author[22] fervently urges parents to stop trying to teach their young children in order that the children may learn. And, to be sure, there is always something to be said for this caution; it is all too easy to have planned learning experiences become didactic and regimented rather than subtle and opportunistic.

As more people gain experience in operating nursery school programs for children with an early history deficient in many categories of experience, the conviction appears to be gaining momentum that such children often are not able to avail themselves of the educational opportunities and must be guided into meaningful learning encounters. In a recent paper dealing with the preschool behavior of a group of 21 children from multiproblem families, Malone[28] describes the inability of the children to carry out self-directed exploratory maneuvers with the toys and equipment as follows:

> When the children first came to nursery school they lacked interest in learning the names and properties of objects. Colors, numbers, sizes, shapes, locations, all seemed interchangeable. Nothing in the room seemed to have meaning for a child apart from the fact that another child had approached or handled it or that the teacher's attention was turned toward it. Even brief play depended on the teacher's involvement and support. (p. 5)

When one reflects on the number of carefully arranged reinforcement contingencies necessary to help a young child learn to decode the simple message, "No," it is difficult to support the position that in early learning, as in anything else, nature should just take its course.

6. *Is formal training for child-care during the first three years unnecessary?* This assumption is obviously quite ridiculous, and yet it is one logical derivative of the hypothesis that the only adequate place for a young child is with his mother or a permanent mother substitute. There

is, perhaps unfortunately, no literacy test for motherhood. This again is one of our interesting scientific paradoxes. That is, proclaiming in one breath that mothering is essential for the healthy development of a child, we have in the very next breath implied that just any mothering will do. It is interesting in this connection that from the elementary school level forward we have rigid certification statutes in most states that regulate the training requirements for persons who would qualify as teachers of our children. (The same degree of control over the qualifications and training of a nursery school teacher has not prevailed in the past, but we are moving into an era when it will.) So again, our pattern of social action appears to support the implicit belief in the lack of importance of the first three years of life.

In 1928, John B. Watson[44] wrote a controversial little trade book called *The Psychological Care of Infant and Child.* He included one chapter heretically entitled, "The Dangers of Too Much Mother Love." In this chapter he suggested that child training was too important to be left in the hands of mothers, apparently not because he felt them intellectually inadequate but because of their sentimentality. In his typical "nondirective" style Watson[44] wrote:

> Six months' training in the actual handling of children from two to six under the eye of competent instructors should make a fairly satisfactory child's nurse. To keep them we should let the position of nurse or governess in the home be a respected one. Where the mother herself must be the nurse—which is the case in the vast majority of American homes—she must look upon herself while performing the functions of a nurse as a professional woman and not as a sentimentalist masquerading under the name of "Mother." (p. 149)

At present in this country a number of training programs are currently being formulated which would attempt to give this kind of professional training called for by Watson and many others. It is perhaps not possible to advance on all fronts at the same time, and the pressing health needs of the young child demanded and received top priority in earlier decades. Perhaps it will now be possible to extend our efforts at social intervention to encompass a broader range of health, education, and welfare activities.

7. *Are most homes and most parents adequate for at least the first three years?* Enough has been presented in discussing other implicit assumptions to make it unnecessary to amplify this point at length. The clinical literature, and much of the research literature of the last decade dealing with social-class differences, has made abundantly clear that all parents are not qualified to provide even the basic essentials of physical and psychological care to their children. Such reports as those describing the incidence of battered children[15,24] capture our attention, but reports concerned with subtler and yet perhaps more longstanding patterns of parental deficit also fill the literature. In her description of the child-rearing environments provided by low lower-class families, Pavenstedt[31] has described them as impulse determined with very little evidence of clear planfulness for activities that would benefit either parent or child. Simi-

larly, Wortis and associates[46] have described the extent to which the problems of the low-income mother so overwhelm her with reactions of depression and inadequacy that behavior toward the child is largely determined by the needs of the moment rather than by any clear plan about how to bring up children and how to train them to engage in the kind of behavior that the parents regard as acceptable or desirable. No social class and no cultural or ethnic group has exclusive rights to the domain of inadequate parentage; all conscientious parents must strive constantly for improvement on this score. However, relatively little attention has been paid to the possibly deleterious consequences of inadequacies during the first three years of life. Parents have been blamed for so many problems of their children in later age periods that a moderate reaction formation appears to have set in. But again, judging by the type of social action taken by the responsible professional community, parental inadequacy during the first three years is seldom considered as a major menace. Perhaps, when the various alternatives are weighed, it appears by comparison to be the least of multiple evils; but parental behavior of the first three years should not be regarded as any more sacrosanct or beyond the domain of social concern than that of the later years.

PLANNING ALTERNATIVES

At this point the exposition of this paper must come to an abrupt halt, for insufficient data about possible alternative models are available to warrant recommendation of any major pattern of change. At present there are no completed research projects that have developed and evaluated alternative approximations of optimal learning environments for young children in our culture. One apparent limitation on ideas for alternative models appears to be the tendency to think in terms of binary choices. That is, we speak of individual care *versus* group care, foster home *versus* institution, foster home *versus* own home, and so on. But environments for the very young child do not need to be any more mutually exclusive than they are for the older children. After all, what is our public education system but a coordination of the efforts of home plus an institution? Most of us probably would agree that the optimal learning environment for the older child is neither of these alone but rather a combination of both. Some of this same pattern of combined effort also may represent the optimal arrangement for the very young child.

A number of programs suggesting alternatives possibly worth considering are currently in the early field trial stage. One such program is the one described by Caldwell and Richmond.[11] This program offers educationally oriented day care for culturally deprived children between six months and three years of age. The children spend the better part of five days a week in a group care setting (with an adult-child ratio never lower than 1:4) but return home each evening and maintain primary emotional relationships with their own families. Well child care, social and psychological services, and parent education activities are available for participating families. The educational program is carefully planned to try to help the child develop the personal-social and cognitive attributes conducive to learning and to provide experiences which can partially compensate for inadequacies which may have existed in the home environment. The strategy involved in offering the enrichment experience to children in this very young age group is to maximize their potential and hopefully prevent the deceleration in rate of development which seems to occur in many deprived children around the age of two or three years. It is thus an exercise in circumvention rather than remediation. Effectiveness of the endeavor is being determined by a comparison of the participating children with a control group of children from similar backgrounds who are not enrolled in the enrichment program. Unfortunately at this juncture it is too early for such projects to do more than suggest alternatives. The degree of confidence which comes only from research evidence plus replicated experience will have to wait a little longer.

Effective social action, however, can seldom await definitive data. And in the area of child care the most clamorous demand for innovative action appears to be coming from a rather unlikely source—not from any of the professional groups, not particularly from social planners who try to incorporate research data into plans for social action, but from *mothers*. From mothers themselves is coming the demand that professionals in the field look at some of the alternatives. We need not be reminded here that in America at the present time there are more than three million working mothers with children under six years of age.[2] And these mothers are looking for professional leadership to design and provide child-care facilities that help prepare their children for today's achievement-oriented culture. The challenge which has been offered is inevitable. After almost two decades of bombarding women with the importance of their mothering role, we might have predicted the weakening of their defenses and their waving the flag of truce as though to say, "I am not good enough to do all that you are saying I must do."

It is a characteristic of social evolution that an increased recognition of the importance of any role leads to the professionalization of that role, and there can be no doubt but that we are currently witnessing the early stages of professionalization of the mother-substitute role—or, as I would prefer to say, the mother-supplement. It is interesting to note that no one has as yet provided a satisfactory label for this role. The term "baby-sitter" is odious, reminding us of just about all some of the "less well trained" professionals do—sit with babies. If English were a masculine-feminine language, there is little doubt that the word would be used in the feminine gender, for we always speak of this person as a "she" (while emphasizing that young children need more contact with males). We cannot borrow any of the terms from already professionalized roles, such as "nurse" or "teacher," although such persons must be to a great extent both nurse and teacher. Awkward designations such as "child-care worker," or hybridized terms such as "nurse-teacher" do not quite seem to fill the bill; and there appears to be some reluctance to accept an untranslated foreign word like the Hebrew "metapelet" or the Russian "Nyanya." When such a word does appear, let us hope that it rhymes well and has a strong trochaic rhythm, for it will have to sustain a whole new era of poetry and song. (This author is convinced that the proper verb is *nurture*. It carries the desired connotations, but even to one who is not averse to neologisms such nominative forms as "nurturist," "nurturer," and "nurturizer" sound alien and inadequate.)*

Another basis for planning alternatives is becoming available from a less direct but potentially more persuasive source—from increasing knowledge about the process of development. The accumulation of data suggesting that the first few years of life are crucial for the priming of cognitive development call for vigorous and imaginative action programs for those early years. To say that it is premature to try to plan optimal environments because we do not fully understand how learning occurs is unacceptable. Perhaps only by the development of carefully arranged environments will we attain a complete understanding of the learning process. Already a great deal is known which enables us to specify some of the essential ingredients of a growth-fostering milieu. Such an environment must contain warm and responsive people who by their own interests invest objects with value. It must be supportive and as free of disease and pathogenic agents as possibly can be arranged. It also must trace a clear path from where the child is to where he is to go developmentally; objects and events must be similar enough to what the child has experienced to be assimilated by the child and yet novel enough to stimulate and attract. Such an environment must be exquisitely responsive, as a more consistent pattern of response is required to foster the acquisition of new forms of behavior than is required to maintain such behavior once it appears in the child's repertoire. The timing of experiences also must be carefully programmed. The time table for the scheduling of early postnatal events may well be every bit as demanding as that which obtains during the embryological period. For children whose early experiences are known to be deficient and depriving, attempts to program such environments seem mandatory if subsequent learning difficulties are to be circumvented.

SUMMARY

Interpretations of research data and accumulated clinical experience have led over the years to a consensual approximation of an answer to the question: what is the optimal learning environment for the young child? As judged from our scientific and lay literature and from practices in health and welfare agencies, one might infer that the optimal learning environment for the young child is that which exists when (a) a young child is cared for in his own home (b) in the context of a warm and nurturant emotional relationship (c) with his mother (or a reasonable facsimile thereof) under conditions of (d) varied sensory and cognitive input. Undoubtedly until a better hypothesis comes along, this is the best one available. This paper has attempted to generate constructive thinking about whether we are justified in overly vigorous support of (a) when (b), (c)

---

* In a letter to the author written shortly after the meeting at which this paper was presented, Miss Rena Corman of New York City suggested that the proper term should be "nurcher," a compound of the words, "nurse" and "teacher." To be sure, a "nurcher" sounds nurturant.

or (d), or any combination thereof, might not obtain. Support for the main hypothesis comes primarily from other hypotheses (implicit assumptions) rather than from research or experimental data. When these assumptions are carefully examined they are found to be difficult if not impossible to verify with existing data.

The conservatism inherent in our present avoidance of carefully designed social action programs for the very young child needs to be re-examined. Such a re-examination conducted in the light of research evidence available about the effects of different patterns of care forces consideration of whether formalized intervention programs should not receive more attention than they have in the past and whether attention should be given to a professional training sequence for child-care workers. The careful preparation of the learning environment calls for a degree of training and commitment and personal control not always to be found in natural caretakers and a degree of richness of experience by no means always available in natural environments.

REFERENCES

1. Ainsworth, Mary. 1962. Reversible and irreversible effects of maternal deprivation on intellectual development. Child Welfare League of America, 42–62.
2. American Women. 1963. Report of the President's Commission on the Status of Women. (Order from Supt. of Documents, Washington, D.C.)
3. Anderson, J. E., et al. 1959. A survey of children's adjustment over time. Minneapolis, Minn. University of Minnesota.
4. Barker, R. G., and H. F. Wright. 1955. Midwest and Its Children: The Psychological Ecology of an American Town. Row, Peterson, New York.
5. Bayley, Nancy. 1949. Consistency and variability in the growth of intelligence from birth to eighteen years. J. Genet. Psychol. 75, 165–196.
6. Beres, D., and S. Obers. 1950. The effects of extreme deprivation in infancy on psychic structure in adolescence. Psychoanal. Stud. of the Child. 5, 121–140.
7. Binet, A., and T. Simon. 1916. The Development of Intelligence in Children. Elizabeth S. Kite, trans. Williams and Wilkins, Baltimore.
8. Bloom, B. S. 1964. Stability and Change in Human Characteristics. John Wiley and Sons, New York.
9. Bronfenbrenner, Urie. 1962. Soviet studies of personality development and socialization. In Some Views on Soviet Psychology. Amer. Psychol. Assoc., Inc. pp. 63–85.
10. Caldwell, Bettye M., et al. 1963. Mother-infant interaction in monomatric and polymatric families. Amer. J. Orthopsychiat. 33, 653–64.
11. Caldwell, Bettye M., and J. B. Richmond. 1964. Programmed day care for the very young child–a preliminary report. J. Marriage and the Family. 26, 481–488.
12. Davis, A., and R. J. Havighurst. 1946. Social class and color differences in child-rearing. Amer. Sociol. Rev. 11, 698–710.
13. Dennis, W. 1960. Causes of retardation among institutional children. J. Genet. Psychol. 96, 47–59.
14. Dennis, W., and P. Najarian. 1957. Infant development under environmental handicap. Psychol. Monogr. 71, (7 Whole No. 536).
15. Elmer, Elizabeth. 1963. Identification of abused children. Children. 10, 180–184.
16. Fowler, W. 1962. Cognitive learning in infancy and early childhood. Psychol. Bull. 59, 116–152.
17. Freud, Anna, and Sophie Dann. 1951. An experiment in group upbringing. Psychoanal. Study of the Child. 6, 127–168.
18. Gardner, D. B., G. R. Hawkes, and L. G. Burchinal. 1961. Noncontinuous mothering in infancy and development in later childhood. Child Develpm. 32, 225–234.
19. Goldfarb, W. 1949. Rorschach test differences between family-reared, institution-reared and schizophrenic children. Amer. J. Orthopsychiat. 19, 624–633.

20. Gula, H. January, 1965. Paper given at Conference on Group Care for Children. Children's Bureau.
21. Hoffman, Lois Wladis. 1961. Effects of maternal employment on the child. Child Developm. 32: 187–197.
22. Holt, J. 1965. How to help babies learn—without teaching them. Redbook. 126(1), 54–55, 134–137.
23. Irvine, Elizabeth E. 1952. Observations on the aims and methods of child-rearing in communal settlements in Israel. Human Relations. 5, 247–275.
24. Kempe, C. H., et al. 1962. The battered-child syndrome. J. Amer. Med. Asso. 181, 17–24.
25. Lewis, O. 1959. Five families. New York: Basic Books.
26. Maas, H. 1963. Long-term effects of early childhood separation and group care. Vita Humana. 6, 34–56.
27. Maccoby, Eleanor, and Patricia K. Gibbs. 1954. Methods of child-rearing in two social classes. In Readings in Child Developm. W. E. Martin and Celia B. Stendler, eds. Harcourt, Brace & Co., New York, pp. 380–396.
28. Malone, C. A. 1966. Safety first: comments on the influence of external danger in the lives of children of disorganized families. Amer. J. Orthopsychiat. 36, 3–12.
29. Mead, Margaret. 1953. Growing up in New Guinea. The New American Library, New York.
30. Murphy, Lois B., et al. 1962. The Widening World of Childhood. Basic Books, Inc., New York.
31. Pavenstedt, E. 1965. A comparison of the child-rearing environment of upper-lower and very low-lower class families. Amer. J. Orthopsychiat. 35, 89–98.
32. Piaget, J. 1952. The Origins of Intelligence in Children. Margaret Cook, trans. International Universities Press, New York.
33. Provence, Sally, and Rose C. Lipton. 1962. Infants in institutions. International Universities Press, New York.
34. Rabin, A. I. 1957. Personality maturity of Kibbutz and non-Kibbutz children as reflected in Rorschach findings. J. Proj. Tech. pp. 148–153.
35. Radke Yarrow, Marian. 1961. Maternal employment and child rearing. Children. 8, 223–228.
36. Rheingold, Harriet. 1956. The modification of social responsiveness in institutional babies. Monogr. Soc. Res. Child Develpm. 21, (63).
37. Rheingold, Harriet L., and Nancy Bayley. 1959. The later effects of an experimental modification of mothering. Child Developm. 30, 363–372.
38. Rousseau, J. J. 1950. Emile (1762). Barron's Educational Series, Great Neck, N.Y.
39. Siegel, Alberta E., and Miriam B. Hass. 1963. The working mother: a review of research. Child Developm. 34, 513–42.
40. Skeels, H. and H. Dye. 1939. A study of the effects of differential stimulation on mentally retarded children. Proc. Amer. Assoc. on Ment. Def. 44, 114–136.
41. Spiro, M. 1958. Children of the Kibbutz. Cambridge, Mass.: Harvard U. Press.
42. Terman, L. M., et al. 1925. Genetic studies or genius: Vol. 1. Mental and physical traits of a thousand gifted children. Stanford University, Calif.: Stanford University Press.
43. Terman, L. M., and Melita H. Oden. 1947. The gifted child grows up: twenty-five years' follow-up of a superior group. Stanford University, Calif.: Stanford University Press.
44. Watson, J. B. 1928. Psychological care of infant and child. Allen and Unwin, London.
45. White, R. W. 1959. Motivation reconsidered: the concept of competence. Psychol. Rev. 66, 297–333.
46. Wortis, H., et al. 1963. Child-rearing practices in a low socio-economic group. Pediatrics. 32, 298–307.
47. Yarrow, L. J. 1961. Maternal deprivation: toward an empirical and conceptual re-evaluation. Psychol. Bull. 58, 459–490.

18. Cognitive Structure and Adolescent Experience

David Elkind

Borrowing heavily from a Piagetian model of intellectual development, David Elkind delineates the basic differences in thought processes between high school and elementary school students. The author notes that any comprehensive explanation of the adolescent's social-emotional characteristics must entail not only a study of psychodynamic and physiological forces but also the intellectual expansion which occurs at this stage of development.

Every affective experience whether it be a simple sensation, a general **feeling or a** complex emotion presupposes some form of cognitive structuring. With respect to a simple sensation, for example, the recognition of its location presupposes a general body schema. Similarly, in the case of a general feeling, say of malaise, the recognition of the feeling as distinct demands a comparison with previous states which at the very least involves judgmental and memory structures. The same holds true for emotions, the ability to recognize and label one's emotions has as a prerequisite the capacity to discriminate amongst the many possible emotions and this in turn must involve cognitive structures.

From the developmental point of view, i.e., from the point of view which sees mental structures as manifesting a progressive evolution, we should therefore expect to find changes in experience coincident with changes in cognitive structure. Put rather more directly, if the child lacks some of the cognitive structures he will have as an adult, he must of necessity lack some of the affective experiences he will encounter when he is mature. On a purely descriptive level this appears to be patently true. Prejudice, for example, does not usually appear until adolescence and the formation of cliques based on social class lines. It is also rare for a child to bear a long-lasting grudge towards another young person. Depressive

Adolescence, 1967, 2, 427–434. Reprinted with the permission of the publisher and author.

states are, as a last example, also a phenomena of adolescence except in rare cases.

In the present paper, I wish to trace some of the experiences, which make their first appearance in adolescence, to the new cognitive structures which come to fruition at about the time of puberty. I do not wish to imply that these new structures *cause* the experiences in question but only to suggest that they are a necessary if not a sufficient condition for their occurrence. Indeed, the majority of adolescent experiences can only be fully understood within the context both of the new mental capacities which mark the advent of this age period and in the context of the new affective transformations which have been described by writers such as Anna Freud (1946), Erikson (1959), and Blos (1962). If I here ignore the psychodynamics of adolescence it is for the purpose of emphasizing the role of cognitive structure and not to imply that motivational factors are unimportant.

COGNITIVE STRUCTURE OF ADOLESCENCE

Our knowledge about the cognitive structure of adolescents is due, in large measure, to the work of Jean Piaget and his colleague Bärbel Inhelder (Inhelder and Piaget, 1958). In their work on adolescent thinking, these investigators have pointed out some of the ways in which the thought of the adolescent differs from that of the child. The adolescent is, in the first place, capable of combinatorial logic and can deal with problems in which many factors operate at the same time. For example, consider the problem of arranging four differently colored poker chips into all possible combinations. There are 16 possible combinations in all. If the colors are red; blue, yellow and green the combinations would be: R; B; Y; G; RB; RY; RG; BY; BG; YG; RBY; RBG; BYG; RYG; RBYG; and none. Now most adolescents can easily form all of these combinations whereas children cannot and it is in this sense that the combinatorial reasoning of the adolescent goes beyond the more elementary syllogistic reasoning of the child.

A second feature which sets the thought of the adolescent off from that of the child is his ability to utilize a second symbol system, i.e., a set of symbols for symbols. It is not without reason, for example, that algebra is never taught to elementary school children. The capacity to symbolize symbols makes the adolescent's thought much more flexible than that of the child. Words carry much more meaning because they now can take on double meanings, they can mean both things and other symbols. It is for this reason that the understanding of metaphor, double entendre and cartoons seldom occurs prior to adolescence (Shaffer, 1930). It also explains why adolescents are able to produce many more concepts to verbal stimuli than are children (Elkind, Barocas and Johnson). For our purposes, the most significant result of this aspect of adolescent thought is that it enables the adolescent to take his own thought as an object, which is to say that he can now introspect and reflect upon his own mental and personality traits.

Still a third characteristic of adolescent thinking is the capacity to construct ideals, or contrary to fact situations. When a child is told, for example, to suppose that coal is white, his reaction tends to be "But coal is black." The adolescent, on the contrary, can accept this contrary to fact premise and proceed with the argument as if the premise were correct. Once again, the capacity to deal with the possible as well as the actual liberates the adolescent's thought so that he can now deal with many problem situations in which the child is stymied. Most importantly, for our purposes, the capacity to deal with the possible means that the future is now as much of a reality as the present and is a reality which can and must be dealt with.

In addition to expanding the adolescent's adaptive potentials, these aspects of adolescent thinking also pave the way for new experiences and reactions unknown to childhood. It is these experiences, for which the new cognitive structures of adolescence are necessary prerequisites, that we now need to consider.

STRUCTURE AND EXPERIENCE

The capacity to deal with combinatorial logic and to consider all possible factors in a given problem solving situation, paves the way for some characteristic adolescent reactions. One consequence of the capacity for combinatorial logic is that, particularly in social situations, the adolescent now sees a host of alternatives and decision making becomes a problem. He now sees, to illustrate, many alternatives to parental directives and is loath to accept the parental alternatives without question. He wants to know not only where a parent stands but also why, and is ready to debate the virtues of the parental alternative over that chosen by himself and his peers. Indeed, the adolescent's quarrels with parental decisions are part and parcel of his own indecisiveness. While he is having trouble making decisions for himself, at the same time he does not want others making decisions for him. Paradoxically, but understandably, the adolescent's indecisiveness also frequently throws him into a new dependence, particularly with regard to the peer group, but also with respect to his parents. The adolescent demands that his parents take a stand if only so he can rebel against it.

Without denying the validity or importance of the dynamic factors which lie beneath the adolescent's difficulties with his parents, the cognitive aspects of the struggle must be recognized. Were the adolescent not capable of grasping alternatives to parental directives and if he was not in turmoil over making his own decisions, at least some of the storm and stress of this period would never appear or at least would appear in quite a different form. In primitive cultures, for example, where the more advanced mental structures may not be attained, there may be little storm and stress. In short, the presence of structures which enable the adolescent to construct multiple alternatives, sets the stage for characteristic conflicts between young people and their parents as well as for the increased dependence upon the peer group for final decision making.

Another structural feature of adolescent thought with repercussions for adolescent experience is the capacity to think about thinking, to introspect. For the first time, the adolescent can take himself as an object, evaluate himself from the perspective of other people with respect to personality, intelligence and appearance. The adolescent's self-consciousness about himself is simply a manifestation of this new capacity for introspection. Now that the adolescent can, so to speak, look at himself from the outside he becomes concerned about the reactions of others to himself. Many adolescents undertake a regime of physical or intellectual exercise because in examining themselves they find a discrepancy between what they are and what they wish to be, between the real and the ideal self. For the child, this discrepancy is seldom conscious but in adolescence, the capacity to introspect and examine the self from the standpoint of others brings it home in full force. It is for this reason, perhaps, that a child with a physical handicap (such as a deformed arm) who has been a happy "gutty" kid experiences his first real depression in adolescence.

This introspection has another consequence that might well be mentioned. The adolescent becomes secretive about his thoughts. He recognizes now that his thought is private and, more importantly, that he can say things which are diametrically opposed to his thoughts. When a child fabricates, he tends to believe the fabrication so that once it is constructed he defends it as the truth. This is not the case with the adolescent, who knows very well that what he is saying and what he is thinking are quite different and who doesn't believe his fabrications although he can make them sound entirely convincing. The adolescent thus begins creating the social disguises, so common in adults and so rare in children, behind which the young person conceals thoughts and wishes that are quite at variance with his verbal professions. At one extreme these disguises are tact and politeness while at the other extreme they are deceit and exploitation. The potential for both are present as soon as the young person can say one thing and think another and be aware that he is doing so.

The capacity to construct ideals and to reason about contrary to fact propositions also plays a considerable role in adolescent experience and behavior. For one thing, the young person can conceive of ideal families, religions and societies and when he compares these with his own family, religion and society he often finds the latter wanting. Much of adolescent rebellion against adult society derives, in part at least, from this new capacity to construct ideal situations. These ideals, however, are almost entirely intellectual and the young person has little conception of how they might be made into realities and even less interest in working towards their fulfillment. The very same adolescent who professes his concern for the poor spends his money on clothes and records, not on charity. The very fact ideals can be conceived, he believes, means that they can be effortlessly realized without any sacrifice on his part.

It is for this reason that young people feel that adults have compromised and sold out, that while adults profess justice, integrity, obedience to the law, they hypocritically fail to put these ideals into practice. In effect, the adolescent not only constructs ideal families, religions and societies, he also constructs ideal persons. The short-lived adolescent crush is a case in point. It is short-lived just because no human person can match the ideal created in adolescent thought. The adolescent, moreover, tends to lack compassion for human failings both with respect to himself and to others. But while he is down on adults for ethical hypocrisy, he flails himself for personal shortcomings such as the control of masturbation, the making of social blunders and academic or athletic failures. Perhaps it is because the adolescent is relatively uninvolved with serious issues of justice, integrity and obedience to the law, that he feels so superior to adults in these regards.

These exaggerations of adolescence come gradually to an end as the young person is forced to adapt to the realities of adult life. As he begins to engage in productive work, he reassesses the adult world as well as his own limitations and becomes more accepting of both.

SUMMARY AND CONCLUSION

In this paper I have suggested that the appearance of new mental structures in adolescence helps to account for many of the experiential and behavioral characteristics of this age period. The capacity for combinatorial thought, i.e., for taking all factors into account in problem solving situations, sets the stage for indecision, rebellion, dogmatism, and dependence. Likewise, the capacity to introspect leads to self-consciousness, self-examination and to the construction of social façades which mask true feelings and thoughts. Finally, the capacity to construct ideal families, religions and societies leads the adolescent to derogate his own family, religion and society and to regard adults as having sold out and compromised their principles. The adolescent, on the other hand, berates himself for personal lapses and lacks compassion for others as well as for himself. These phenomena of adolescence diminish as the young person begins to engage in productive work and to accept the limitations of others as well as his own. In short, what I have tried to demonstrate here is that a full understanding of adolescent phenomena must take into account not only the psychodynamic changes and conflicts of adolescence but also the new cognitive structures which make their first appearance during this age period.

REFERENCES

Blos, P. On adolescence. New York: The Free Press, 1962.

Elkind, D., Barocas, R., and Johnson, P. Concept production in children and adolescents. (Submitted).

Erikson, E. H. Identity and the life cycle. Psychol. Issues, I, No. 1, New York: International Universities Press, 1959.

Freud, Anna. The ego and the mechanisms of defense. New York: International Universities Press, 1946.

Inhelder, Bärbel, & Piaget, J. The growth of logical thinking from childhood through adolescence. New York: Basic Books, 1958.

Shaffer, L. F. Childrens' interpretation of cartoons. Contributions to Education, No. 429. New York: Teacher's College, Columbia University, 1930.

19. The Marking System and Poor Achievement

Eugene D. Alexander

Discussion surrounding the evaluative aspects of our educational system has had a long and polemical history. In the following article, Dr. Alexander expresses the viewpoint that the uses of tests and grades is not only antithetical to the objectives of education but is also harmful psychologically. What do you think?

Today with the tremendous mass of students being exposed to our education system we are deeply and sincerely concerned about the standards of our education. We are afraid that the level of learning is approaching mediocrity. In a desperate effort to bolster our standards, we become more strict in our marking system and we emphasize the test situation as a means of discouraging those students unable to compete. We see marks as an incentive to study and learning. We feel that the student will work harder and learn better in order to obtain higher grades. We see marks as a method of reward for the better student and as a means of "realistic" evaluation for all students. Unfortunately the relationship of marks with ability and interest in learning is not so simple. In fact there are a great number of influences affecting achievement that have no relationship at all to ability and interest in learning. There is some evidence that, for many people, marks become a barrier to learning and are seen more as punishment for poor achievement than as a reward for successful accomplishment.

FACTORS RELATED TO POOR ACHIEVEMENT

Of the large number of factors related to poor achievement, some are part of the immediate school experience, but many are outside the control of the school situation. McMillan found that children showed more success and less failure when (a) they were female rather male, (b) their

The Teachers College Journal, 1964, 36, 110–113. Reprinted with the permission of the publisher and author.

parents had more education, (c) their parents came from a higher educational level, (d) they were high in socioeconomic status, (e) parents had higher incomes, (f) they had not moved in 10 years, (g) they belonged to a relatively small family. Kurtz (1951) found that under-achievers more often came from homes with unhappy emotional climate, had fewer friends and these friends had a less favorable attitude toward school than over-achievers, felt inferior and unhappy, preferred non-academic to academic tasks, had minimum ambition and did not have high prospects for themselves, a feeling shared by their teachers. Walsh (1956) compared 20 low achieving boys from grades 2 to 5 with 20 adequate achieving boys with equal ability. She examined their attitudes toward themselves by analyzing the roles projected in a boy doll with which they played. The low achievers consistently differed from the adequate achievers in portraying the boy doll as restricted in action; unable to express his feelings appropriately and accurately: being criticized, rejected or isolate; and acting defensively through compliance, evasion or negativism. Alexander (1963) discovered that for 10th grade students there was a significant relationship of expressed self-concept and self-acceptance with marks when the effect of intelligence was partialled out. From his data he concluded that a student's self-perception could be an important factor in school achievement and often operated independently from intelligence. Stevens (1956) found that academically unsuccessful students showed poor self-insight into their intellectual abilities and showed poor self-acceptance. Tallent (1956) in examining 9th graders observed a direct relationship between behavior control and intellectual achievement. The controlled group was superior on concentration, and tasks demanding a high order of conceptualization. The impulsive group was superior on sensory-motor speed and coordination and tasks with very little intervening mental manipulation.

Baer (1956) reported that children entering school at a later age consistently achieved better than children of the same IQ entering earlier. Spivak (1956) found that children in self-contained 7th and 8th grades achieved significantly better than youngsters from a departmental organization. This difference was maintained throughout the ninth grade when all students entered a departmental situation. Malpass (1953) observed a significant relationship between perception of school and end of semester grades. Youngsters with a better perception of school received better grades. Bond (1952) found that reading was an important factor that presented itself as an obstacle to low ability pupils. Repeated failure led to a "don't care attitude" and the students learned to retreat when confronted with a problem situation. They were fearful about achieving and this impeded studying.

Thus, developmental factors, socioeconomic factors, emotional climate in the home and peer relationships all relate to school achievement, but are relatively outside the school situation. Teacher-pupil relations, perception of school and basic ability are close to the school situation. Poor self-concept, self-rejection, anxiety, poor self-control and feelings of powerlessness are reflections of the individual's inner life. As can be seen, there are many characteristics and influences that have absolutely nothing to do with the school environment, yet which very profoundly relate to the student's performance. There are many influences inside the school situation that relate to achievement yet are not academic in nature. All of these the student brings with him as he faces the evaluative experience and this experience leaves him with no alternative other than success or failure. Let us examine what actually takes place in the poor achievement or failure situation.

FAILURE LEADS TO MORE FAILURE

Smith (1952) experimentally induced the belief of failure by verbal instructions and found that throughout a series of 15 trials there was an impairment of learning whether actual failure took place or not. Osler (1954) gave 15 classrooms of students an arithmetic test. She then divided the students into groups matched for ability, age, and scores on the arithmetic test. She randomly assigned these groups to treatment conditions. She informed one group that they were among the lowest 10% on the test. She informed another group that they were among the most successful students on the test, and she gave another group no set at all. She then administered an arithmetic test comparable to the first test. She found that the students in the success and control groups did significantly better than students in the failure group. In both these studies it was not actual failure that led to poor achievement, but the feeling of failure that the individual had. The individual perceived himself as a failure so he functioned as a failure.

FAILURE LEADS TO DEFENSIVE ACTION

Van Holt (1955) discovered that *under neutral conditions achievement is related to imaginal and creative processes, but that under failure conditions, achievement is related to emotional processes and their control.* Thorne (1954) compared a low self-acceptance group with a high self-acceptance group after an induced failure situation. The low group raised their self-evaluation in the task while the high group lowered their ratings. *Those with low self-acceptance became so preoccupied with loss of self-esteem that they could not make a realistic evaluation of their performance.* Diller (1954) found that after a failure experience, self-attitudes are not positively correlated with attitudes toward others. A disrupted pattern of attitudes appears. An individual may either raise his self-esteem while lowering his esteem of close friends, or he may lower his own self-esteem while rating his close friends higher. Martine (1953) examined the self-concepts of college students after placing them in a relaxed situation and later placing them in a situation where they were pressured to achieve. He found two groups that did poorer under pressure. One of these groups was successful in the relaxed situation though doing poorly under pressure. They had the need to achieve but this need was blocked by conflict and anxiety over either succeeding or failing. "They probably have experienced considerable failure. Possibly, competition leads to anxiety over the possibility of failure which in turn causes further disorganizing emotion and consequent failure." Another group did poorly under both relaxed and pressured situations. *"These individuals have the motive to succeed, but fear of failure is so strong that anxiety results in an avoidance of response, which disallows even the imagination of positive striving for achievement."*

Thus, under pressure of failure, people tend to get so involved in anxiety over their feelings about themselves that their efficiency of achievement suffers.

THE PICTURE OF THE POOR ACHIEVER

Putting this information together, a clear picture slowly emerges. The key concept is the student's own self-perception. A student enters the academic situation with a certain self-concept which may be good or poor, depending on his previous experience and environment. Success and failure operate on this self-concept either to enhance or to depreciate it. Generally speaking, the poorer the early environment the greater the need for a good school experience and the more difficult it is to get one. Much of this depends on the pupil-teacher relationship. Of course it is more difficult for the teacher to give the poor ability student a good experience than to give one to a good student.

When the student experiences failure he begins to perceive himself as a failure and his achievement drops. This seems to be operative with high as well as low ability students. As this feeling of failure increases, the student becomes defensive. He becomes more involved in protecting his self-concept than in achieving. This may take the form of depreciation of the academic situation, increased involvement with non-academic experiences, devaluation of others and hostility toward them, or, more subtly, an involvement with the rote aspects of learning at the expense of creativity. Pressure only leads to greater defensiveness or poorer achievement. The culmination of repeated failure is "an avoidance response which disallows even the imagination of positive striving for achievement."

Thus, the self-concept and achievement interact with mutual effect. That is, poor achievement leads to a depreciation of the self-concept which leads to continued poor achievement; and, to a lesser extent, good achievement leads to an enhancement of the self-concept which leads to better achievement. One of the best defenses that the poor achiever can use to escape this cycle is to devaluate or de-emphasize the academic situation so that achievement becomes unimportant to the maintenance of the self-concept. It is then possible for him to maintain an adequate self-esteem in spite of his poor performance in the school situation. At its worst this may lead to a depreciation of thinking and learning in general.

With this picture in mind, it is now much easier to understand some of our typical poor-achievers. There is the hostile aggressive student who maintains a "good" self-concept by being "tougher than the other guy." There is the congenial student, often of high ability, who never gets his homework done or never pays attention in class. He then can protect his self-esteem by telling himself that he is failing not because he is an incapable student, but because he doesn't do his work. There is the average student who tries and tries and gets nowhere because he "knows" he is a failure. There is the student who doesn't even try because he is convinced that he is a failure from the start. More subtly, there is the student who maintains high marks because he can regurgitate but who is unable to think creatively. And on and on.

To call the poor achiever lazy, to say he has no motivation is just to describe the symptom. The student is trying to maintain a good self-concept. The individual can not live with himself unless he can see himself as worthwhile. He will avoid or defend himself from any situation that threatens his self-esteem. If feelings of repeated failure in the academic situation threaten his self-concept, he will avoid or protect himself from experiences that stimulate this feeling. The only way in which he will meet a situation head on and try to achieve is if it enhances his self-esteem and does not give him feelings of failure.

HELPING AND HINDERING THE POOR ACHIEVER

Thus, to help the poor achiever we can either strengthen his self-esteem by helping him see that he is a worthwhile individual no matter what his past experience, or we can give him successful experiences of achievement so he can see that he is not a failure. In evaluating any method we must ask ourselves if that particular experience will enhance the student's self-concept. If it doesn't, we must reject it. The same method can meet with success or failure, depending on the total situation in which it is applied. It is the human interpersonal relationship between teacher and pupil that determines whether the method is a success or failure. If conditions such as an impossible home environment or rigid marking system act as obstacles it will make it very difficult for the teacher to give the pupil feelings of self-esteem and success.

Low marks function more as a threat of failure than as a motivation for improvement. As often as not they are actually punishment for previous failure, poor past environment or emotional difficulty. As a student continues to get low marks he begins to perceive himself as a poor achiever. As he perceives himself in this light he begins to function this way, no matter what his ability. He may decide that school is too threatening to his self-concept and may discount school so it is no longer important enough to be a threat.

Tests do not help to motivate the poor achiever, either. They represent the failure situation and are to be avoided and feared by him. They only raise his anxiety and increase his poor self-concept. Tests may motivate the good achiever, but often only to memorize and repeat than think and originate.

Nor is external pressure the answer to poor achievement. It leads to anxiety and blockage in some students and almost complete immobility in others. For some a relaxed situation with understanding guidance and support may help, but others need even more than this.

For the severe poor achiever direct counseling may be the only answer. Only through exploration of his self-concept can he begin to see himself in a more worthwhile light. Only then can he begin to believe that he does not have to continue to be a failure.

The low-ability pupil is defeated before he begins. He can seldom hope to obtain an average grade. School is one failure experience after another. The havoc wreaked on his self-concept can be imagined. Special consideration and often a special program are necessary if he is to have the opportunity to feel successful.

The marking system with its normative criteria leads continually to more difficult goals for the poor achiever. He can see no progress. It represents continued failure. The only way he can begin to experience some success is under a system with more obtainable goals. Perhaps the most realistic criteria are his previous experiences. He can see that he is not really a failure.

The most surprising thing that research points out is that even students with skills and ability tend to continue to fail after they experience failure. Thus, of equal importance to teaching skills is the supportive role of the teacher. A good deal of her time must be spent believing in, and supporting her students. She must support them to exploring in their own way and not in terms of what she decides they should explore, for rejection of the student's own initiative in itself implies failure on his part. Inflexible direction can lead to the most dismal failure of all—the A student who functions brilliantly in a structured situation but is so dependent on external approval that he is unable to produce anything really creative. Conforming is his protection against feelings of failure.

An educational system that evaluates its students on their ability to memorize, recall and repeat is actually penalizing the students whose talents are expressed in the unique and original. Often such students appear as poor achievers when evaluated by the usual marking criteria. Any system that substitutes extrinsic incentive for intrinsic motivation creates conditions for conformity, manipulation and control. A student does not have the opportunity to learn to evaluate himself independently. He actually depends on the judgment of others. The evaluation situations that he faces are imposed upon him and he automatically reacts to them without searching deeply within himself. A failure experience and being a failure are often felt to be synonymous when judged extrinsically. When a person has the opportunity to establish intrinsically his own conditions of experience, failure acts to give the individual insight into the limitations of his abilities. He more willingly exposes himself to the anxieties of the unknown and in not having to protect his self-esteem, he does not interpret a failure experience as a failure of himself.

Our society is often accused of anti-intellectualism. Maybe the extrinsically imposed testing and evaluative functions of our educational system are partially to blame. Perhaps this attitude, to some extent, is an avoidance response and a defense feeling of failure engendered when individuals had been confronted previously with intellectual experiences.

REFERENCES

Alexander, Eugene D., "The Relationship Between Self-Concept, Self-Acceptance and School Marks." *Dissert. Abs.* 1963, 23, 3229.

Baer, Clyde, "A Comparison of the School Progress and Personal Adjustment of Underage and Overage Students of Comparable Intelligence During Eleven Years of School." *Newsletter*, Division of Sch. Psychologists, A.P.A., Vol. 10 No. 2 Winter 1955-6.

Bond, Jesse A., "An Analysis of Factors Adversely Affecting Scholarship of H. S. Pupils." *J. of Ed. Res.* 46, 1–15, Sept. 1952.

Diller, Leonard, "Conscious and Unconscious Self-Attitudes After Success and Failure." *J. of Per.* 23, 12, Sept. 1954.

Kurtz, John J., Swenson, Esther J., "Factors Related to Over-Achievement and Under-Achievement in School." *Sch. Rev.* 59, 472–80, Nov. 1951.

Malpass, Leslie F., "Some Relationships Between Student's Perception of School and Achievement." *J. Ed Psy.* 44, 475–82, Dec. 1953.

Martine, John George, "Relationship Between the Self-Concept and Differences in the Strength and Generality of Achievement Motivation." *Dissert. Abs.*, 1953, 13, 877.

McMillan, R. T., "School Acceleration and Retardation Among Village Children in So. Oklahoma."

Osler, Sonia F., "Intellectual Performance as a Function of 2 Types of Psychological Stress." *J. Exp. Psy.* 47, 115–121, 1954.

Smith, George Joseph, "Influence of Failure, Expressed Hostility, and Stimulus Characteristics on Verbal Learning and Recognition." *Dissert. Abs.* 1952, 12, 600.

Spivak, Monroe L., "Effectiveness of Departmental and Self-Contained Seventh and Eighth Grade Classrooms," *Sch. Rev.* 64, 391–6, Dec. 1956.

Stevens, Peter H., "An Investigation of the Relationship Between Certain Aspects of Self-Concept Behavior and Students' Academic Achievement." *Dissert. Abs.* 1956, 16, 2531–2.

Tallent, Norman, "Behavioral Control and Intellectual Achievement of Secondary School Boys." *J. of Ed. Psy.* 47, 490–503, Dec. 1956.

Thorne, Robert Bernard, "The Effects of Experimentally Induced Failure on Self-Evaluations." *Dissert. Abs.* 1954, 14, 1817.

Van Holt, Jr., Henry William, "A Study of Personality Processes Under Neutral, Failure and Success Condition." *Dissert. Abs.* 1955, 15, 1660.

Walsh, Ann M., *Self Concepts of Bright Boys with Learning Difficulties*. New York: Teachers College, Columbia University, 1956.

PART III

MENTAL HEALTH IN TEACHING

This unit addresses itself to various aspects of mental health in the teaching-learning process—the social psychological aspects of the educational setting, pupils with persistent adjustment difficulties, classroom management and, finally, teacher adjustment.

Chapter Five

Chapter Five—Group Aspects of Classroom Functioning—deals with a neglected topic. Ironically, though the teacher is basically a group worker, most of what we know about mental health pertains to the individual apart from the group. The five selections contained in this chapter reflect the gradual accumulation of knowledge about group dynamics and the increasing awareness of their importance for both the affective and cognitive aspects of the educative process. By way of overview, the following list of topics is presented for your perusal:

a new method for classroom grouping;

the influence of variations in classroom climate on student productivity and morale;

the influence of peer culture on academic achievement;

the uses of sociometry in studying classroom groups; and

the impact of racially integrated classes on social acceptance.

Chapter Six

Chapter Six—Students with Special Needs—deals with youngsters whose problems, for the most part, are more chronic and severe than the transient difficulties characteristic of normal developmental crises. The adjustment difficulties chosen for discussion are those of intense and contemporary concern to educators, mental health specialists and, in certain instances, parents. The following list of problems to be discussed in this section can be conceived as falling roughly into two categories—those whose difficulties derive largely from sociological or cultural forces (articles 25–28) and those whose difficulties originate in psychological forces (articles 29–30):

stresses operating on disadvantaged teen-agers;
controversy in the field of mental retardation;
the campus adjustment of college students;
the plight of creative thinkers;
the dynamics and treatment of school phobia; and
the effects of passive aggressiveness in the classroom.

Chapter Seven

Chapter Seven—Classroom Discipline—focuses on an aspect of the school mental health program that is of particular concern to teachers. Though classroom management problems can be minimized through sound program development, there comes a time in every teacher's life when he must cope with student misbehavior. Yet he must do it in the most hygienic manner possible. Discussion of the following aspects of classroom management will hopefully prove helpful in this regard:
the new mental hygiene outlook on classroom management;
on-the-spot interviewing with troublesome students;
group determinants of classroom disruption;
teacher style and its influence on disruptive behavior; and
a behavior modification approach to classroom control.

Chapter Eight

In Chapter Eight—Mental Health of Teachers—there is a shift from the student's mental health problems to those of his teacher. Teachers, like workers in other occupational groups, are subject to maladjustment. While all forms of teacher maladjustment are not necessarily harmful to students, teacher personality is undeniably one of the most significant determinants of the school's mental health program. Irritability, constant nagging, intensive anxiety and unfair disciplinary practices are certainly not conducive to a healthy classroom climate. The cumulative impact of teacher maladjustment is indeed a source of apprehension, especially at the elementary school level where a teacher has the same pupils for approximately 175 days per school year. The mental health of teachers as discussed in this chapter centers around the following themes:
teaching as a vocational expression of basic personality needs;
the necessity of self-understanding;
common stresses leading to teacher anguish and disillusionment; and
tips to teachers for sound mental health.

CHAPTER 5

Group Aspects of Classroom Functioning

20.   Matching Teachers and Pupils

Herbert A. Thelen

The topic of classroom grouping has been a lively one in educational circles for some years now. In the following selection, Dr. Thelen advances, in truly creative fashion, the notion of teachability grouping and presents some research findings on this approach. What is your reaction to this intriguing innovation?

If you ask Teacher A what would most improve his teaching and he replies, as well he might, "Get John and Stephanie out of my class; I can't do a thing with them," the chances are that Teacher B will say, "Those two were fine in my room last year. I've got a couple I'd be better off without this year, though."

This exchange would surprise no one. Everybody seems to realize that some pupils perform better with certain teachers than with others. Indeed, toward the end of a school year, a group of teachers will often sit down to figure out which students should be assigned to certain teachers.

At the University of Chicago Laboratory School, for example, it has been a long-standing custom for kindergarten teachers to recommend the

NEA Journal, April, 1967, 18–20. Reprinted with the permission of the publisher and author.

Dr. Thelen has written at greater length on this subject in *Classroom Grouping for Teachability*. Copyright © 1967 by John Wiley & Sons, Inc. New York.

first grade teacher to which every kindergartner should be assigned. Frequently, school counselors make similar recommendations. Many parents try hard to get their children with certain teachers.

Surprisingly enough, although everyone recognizes that the interpersonal relationship between child and teacher is at the heart of the learning situation, most systems used for grouping children overlook this factor completely.

During the year 1957–58, three teachers (Robert Boyd, Paul Moulton, and Howard Gordon), 50 sophomores in the Laboratory School of the University of Chicago, and I set out to test some educational innovations—team teaching, closed-circuit TV, feedback panels, telephones, etc.

At the end of a year, we realized that the truth of any of our statements would depend upon the human beings we were talking about. We became convinced that the nature of classroom teaching and learning is so dependent upon the particular combination of students and teacher that until this combination could be clarified, we could not say under what conditions any teaching method or concept could be expected to make sense.

We discovered that what made sense for one student did not do so for another. It was as though the students represented different types, with different approaches to learning, different ways of using social relationships, different kinds of rewards and punishments, and different degrees to which any learning experience has importance for their own needs.

The following examples illustrate our discoveries:

• In solving algebra problems, 12 students seemed to work best by themselves, seeking help from the teacher after school; 10 seemed to work best in groups of 2 or 3; 12 seemed to work best in a rather formal setting, with the teacher in direct charge and always available for help; the remaining 14 students seemed to work equally well or poorly under any of these three methods.

• Six students who had achieved outstandingly were excused from work during the last month of the school year in order to investigate on their own any subject which they and their teachers decided would be worthwhile. Three of these students turned out creative, perceptive work; their experiences were exciting and highly productive. The other three—equally bright and equally good achievers—probably did not do as well as they would have done in their regular classes.

• The three teachers involved in the experiment taught by quite different methods. One was an excellent lecturer; another made use of committee-planned projects; the third guided intellectual discussion to analyze problems and to explain steps in problem solving. A few students, possibly 12 out of the 50, worked well under all these methods. Most of the students, though, had decidedly different preferences, standards, and abilities under these different methods.

We were not surprised to find that the students reacted in different ways. We had not expected, though, that these individual differences would play such a vital role. Our findings made clear to us that the reason much discussion of teaching seems vague and opinionated is that the validity of any statement depends upon what the students—both individually and in a group—are like.

And what are students like? What do teachers think they are like? Ever since we were soberly assured by a very fine elementary teacher that pupils are either "wrigglers" or "squirmers," the three teachers and I had wanted to talk with more teachers about types.

We asked 70 Oklahoma City teachers, supervisors, and principals to write descriptions of the types of students in their classrooms. We received 300 descriptions, which we found could be classified into four categories—good, bad, indifferent, and lost. Other than these, we came up with few neat and all-inclusive categories of students.

It seemed to us that whether a teacher categorizes students as good, bad, indifferent, or lost may partially depend on the teacher's mental image of what a class looks like when it is learning. To some, the picture is of an orderly, attentive, responsive, cooperative, respectful, good-natured group; others visualize enthusiastic students, hard-working, full of interesting ideas, noisy at times, encouraging of individual opinions.

Teachers with such disparate mental pictures would not have the same conception of a successful student. Our observations brought us to the conclusion that perhaps the best way to compose a class would be to select students for each teacher like those who, in his opinion, had been most successful with him in the past—had been what we called *teachable*.

This conclusion about how to compose a class led to our idea of teachability grouping. With a grant from the Cooperative Research Branch of the U.S. Office of Education, we set about testing the idea.

The goals of our test were to determine:

Is the idea of teachability grouping valid?

To what extent is teachability a general factor, described the same way by all teachers?

To what extent is it a unique factor, defined very differently from one teacher to the next?

Can we describe this factor at all?

If we can describe it, does it make sense in the light of other knowledge?

In the spring of 1960, 13 teachers in eight schools in Illinois, Wisconsin, and Indiana agreed to participate in our experiment in teachability grouping. The grades ranged from 8 through 11; the subjects taught were English, American literature, social studies, geometry, advanced algebra, biology, world history, and American history.

Each of the 13 teachers was assigned two classes. In one, the students were carefully chosen on the basis of a 405-item assessment battery to resemble closely the students the teacher felt had benefited the most from his teaching; in the other class, which served as a control group, students were chosen by the school's regular selection process.

Some of the premises, conclusions, and findings from the study follow:

• We decided that the extent to which teachability is a general factor could be assessed by asking teachers to name the students who, in their opinion, had the most worthwhile experiences in their classes. If they all chose students with the same characteristics, we could conclude that teachability meant the same thing to all teachers. If, however, they chose different students, it would mean that the definition of teachability differed from teacher to teacher.

Our 13 teachers varied widely in the factors which they thought made a student teachable. They showed a mild tendency to select factors which indicate a high degree of personal adequacy, but other than this mild tendency, teachable students as selected by the 13 teachers had little in common.

• The classes chosen on the basis of teachability showed greater group solidarity than the control group. As classes, they were more work-oriented, less inattentive, less distractable, and more manageable. The students had a greater sense of common purpose. The teacher gave more of himself and was more of a person in a teachable class; his teaching was more flexible; he was more permissive with respect to disruptive behavior, which, however, occurred less frequently.

These differences in the teacher and the teaching again represent only a mild tendency. They seem to be mostly subconscious changes in the responses of the teacher to the high-solidarity, more manageable class.

• Compared to the corresponding regular classes, 11 of the teachable groups received higher grades from the teacher, 1 received lower grades, and 1 received the same grades. When the 26 classes were divided into top and bottom halves by means of the teachability scores of the students, 75 per cent of the students in the top halves got better grades than the average student in the bottom halves.

In respect to gain on achievement tests from the start of the experiment in the spring, as contrasted with overall grades for the total year's work, members of only five of the teachable classes made greater gains than did students in the regular classes, whereas those in 8 of the regular classes gained more than the one in the experimental classes. This seems to indicate that the teachers thought that their educational goals (on which the final grades were based) were better achieved by the teachable classes even though the pupils in them actually gained less than those in regular classes on whatever it is that achievement tests measure.

Nine of the teachers preferred the students in their experimental classes as individuals to "work with" or "chat with" to those in their regular classes, and six preferred members of the teachable class for both purposes. On the other hand, more students in the regular classes expressed a preference for working with or chatting with their teachers than did students in the corresponding teachable classes.

One explanation of this might be that the more work-oriented, cohesive experimental classes set higher standards for themselves, thus creating hidden resentments which focused on the teacher. Another explanation might be that a bit of personal exploitation was involved in the teachable classes. That is, the kinds of students a teacher considers teachable may have characteristics that meet his needs.

To the extent that a teacher's needs are met through his participation in activities that also meet the needs of the students, no exploitation is involved. If, however, a teacher has needs that cannot be so channeled, and if these needs are somehow threatening to the students, the students may feel resentment toward him even though they go ahead and help meet his needs (after all, that's partly why they were selected).

When rating preferences among themselves, students in 11 of the teachable classes had greater preferences for chatting with one another than did regular students; in 8 teachable classes they indicated greater preferences for working with one another than the regular students did.

Teachers in the experiment wanted and got very different things from their teachable classes. One teacher appeared to want a more vigorous, personality-involving interaction with his students; another wanted a class that could penetrate more deeply into principles of his subject; a third wanted a class he could move faster with; another wanted a pleasant, friendly, nonwork-oriented class that would make him feel more adequate; one wanted a class in which he could combine counseling and teaching.

Is the idea of teachability grouping valid? Our experiment convinced us of its soundness, despite the fact that some of the results did not appear to confirm its desirability. Teachability grouping makes sense in the light of the modern conception of education as an active experimental process. A child learns by experiencing. His reactions to the attitudes, enthusiasms, aversions, interests, public goals, and private purposes of his teacher affect or even largely determine the nature of his experience.

Since no two students are identical, no two will react in the same way and no two will have identical experiences. By the same token, different teachers will affect different students with varying degrees of impact. The child-teacher relationship is unique with every combination of child and teacher, and thus every teacher is a more effective teacher for some students than for others. What we call teachability results from a quality of the relationship between child and teacher.

21.   The Student's World

Philip W. Jackson

What is life in the classroom really like? What impact can such unpublicized aspects of institutional life as delay, denial and interruption have on student scholarship? What is the hidden curriculum which each pupil must

The Elementary School Journal, April, 1966, 345–357. © 1966 by The University of Chicago Press. Reprinted with the permission of the copyright owner and author.

master? What adaptive strategies are developed in re-
sponse to the demands of institutional membership? Are
the demands for institutional conformity and intellec-
tual mastery incompatible? These and other thought
provoking issues are raised by Dr. Jackson as he exam-
ines the student's world. What solutions would you
offer?

And I have seen dust from the walls of institutions,
Finer than flour, alive, more dangerous than silica,
Sift, almost invisible, through long afternoons of tedium,
Dropping a fine film on nails and delicate eyebrows,
Glazing the pale hair, the duplicate gray standard faces.

Theodore Roethke, "Dolor"

Prehensile sophomores in the tree of learning
Stare at the exiled blossoming trees, vaguely puzzled.

John Malcolm Brinnin, "Views of the favorite colleges"

When you were a child, how many times did you find yourself cornered by an adult, usually a strange aunt or uncle, who opened the conversation with that oldest of all gambits: "Well, how do you like school?" As an adult how often have you been left alone with someone else's child and, not knowing what else to say, found yourself falling back on some variant of the standard query: "How's school?" If you have not had both of these experiences, and each of them several times, you must be something of a recluse, for talk about school, when the dialogue is between an adult and a child, is almost as popular a social maneuver as talk about one's health or the weather.

Yet such talk, despite its popularity, rarely yields much information about what life in school is really like or how that life is experienced by the student to whom we are speaking. There seem to be two major reasons why this is so. First, in most instances neither the child nor the adult takes the query seriously. Both know that questions about school, like questions about personal health, are polite social gestures and usually are not intended to be answered fully or honestly. Thus, when asked about his classroom experiences, the fourth-grader who is having a miserable time with long division and who hates his teacher with a deep and abiding passion knows that he is expected to respond in much the same way as the victim of a migraine headache whose health is inquired into. Custom requires both sufferers to grin and say, "Fine, thank you."

A second limit to what we can learn about school life by talking to students arises from the fact that students may themselves not be acutely aware of what is happening to them in the classroom. Or, more precisely, they may never have tried to express the vague feelings and intuitive knowledge engendered by that experience. School life, like life in the military service, is not easy to describe to outsiders. You have to have been there.

But even being there is not enough, for when fellow students, or army veterans, discuss their common experience they often overlook or fail to mention some of the obvious and pervasive aspects of that experience. And often it is these familiar and seemingly trivial features of life that are the most revealing when it comes to capturing the flavor or unique quality of membership in a social institution. Accordingly, the remainder of this essay will focus on some aspects of school life that students rarely talk about in the presence of adults or even, in all probability, in the presence of other students.

The subjects to be discussed are not dramatic, or even intrinsically interesting, though I shall do my best to keep them from becoming deathly dull. What is more important, they concern things we all know, even though we do not think about them too much. My only justification for asking you to attend to such mundane matters is my hope that a consideration of these trivial but neglected events will deepen our insight into the character of the student's world and, hence, might lead us to ask new questions about our responsibility for establishing and maintaining that world.

Two warnings are necessary. First, I do not bring words of uplift and inspiration. In fact, some of the things I am going to say about schools and schooling will not be pleasant. They may even sound harsh. But I am convinced that educators are ready for such talk, provided it stems from good intentions, and that they prefer frankness, even though it may hurt, to the sticky sentiment and clichés that have come to characterize educational discussions from college courses to inservice workshops. Second, I am not going to present a plan of action for your consideration. Indeed, I am going to raise many more questions than I shall answer. Here again, I believe that more and more teachers are becoming tired of hearing experts, whether from the university or the central office, hand out the latest panacea for eliminating our educational woes. For a change, therefore, I will ask you to do nothing but think. If there are practical implications that follow from what I have to say, it is up to you to find them.

THE SOCIAL TRAFFIC OF THE CLASSROOM

Anyone who has ever taught knows that the classroom is a busy place, even though it may not always appear so to the casual visitor. Indeed, recent attempts to describe that busyness have yielded data that have proved surprising even to experienced teachers. For example, we have found in our studies of elementary-school classrooms that the teacher engages in as many as a thousand interpersonal interchanges each day. No comparable data are available for high-school teachers, but there is reason to believe that the interpersonal demands are equally severe at that level. A look at these and other demands is instructive as we try to understand what life in the classroom is really like.

First, consider the rapidity of the teacher's actions. What keeps her hopping from Jane to Billy to Sam, and back again, in the space of a few seconds? Clearly much of this activity is done in the interest of instruction. In most classrooms the teacher acts as a gatekeeper who manages the flow of interaction. When more than one person wishes to say something (a common condition in educational gatherings), it is the teacher who decides who will speak and when. Or we might turn our observation around and say that it is the teacher who determines who will not speak, for usually the number of students who want to say something exceeds the number who are granted the privilege.

SUPPLY SERGEANT

Another time-consuming task for the teacher, at least in the elementary school, is that of serving as a supply sergeant. Classroom space and material resources are limited, and the teacher must allocate these resources judiciously. Not every student can use the big scissors at once; only one child at a time can look through the microscope or drink from the drinking fountain or use the pencil sharpener. Again, it is important to recognize that the number of students who want to use these resources at any given moment is often greater than the number that can use them.

Closely related to the job of doling out material resources is that of granting special privileges to deserving students. The teacher frequently must decide whether a student is to be allowed to hand in his homework paper late or make up a quiz that he missed or have an extra day to finish his laboratory assignment. In elementary-school classrooms it is usually the teacher who assigns coveted duties, such as serving on the safety patrol, running the movie projector, or clapping the erasers. Students soon learn that in school, as in life in general, many are called, but few are chosen.

OFFICIAL TIMEKEEPER

A fourth responsibility of the teacher, and one that calls our attention to another important aspect of classroom life, is that of serving as an official timekeeper. The teacher sees to it that things begin and end on time, more or less. He determines the proper moment for switching from discussion to workbooks, or from spelling to arithmetic. He decides whether a student has spent too long in the washroom or whether those who take the bus may be dismissed. In many schools the teacher is assisted in this job by elaborate systems of bells and buzzers, but even when the school day is mechanically punctuated by clangs and hums, the teacher is not relieved of his responsibility for watching the clock. School is a place where things often take place not because people want them to, but because it is time for them to happen.

Our concern here is with the student and the quality of his life in the classroom. Therefore, the frenetic activity of the teacher, as she goes about calling on people, handing out supplies, granting privileges, and turning activities on and off, is of interest to us only insofar as the student experiences that behavior. We are interested, in other words, in what it is like to be on the receiving end of the teacher's action.

To begin, it is safe to say that for most students, some of the time, and for some students, most of the time, the classroom is a great place to be.

When new insights are formed and mastery is achieved, when the teacher's queries can be answered with confidence, when privileges are granted and praise bestowed, when natural interests and desires coincide with institutional expectations—at such moments (and such moments do occur more or less regularly for many students) life at school must be extremely satisfying. A sufficient number of such experiences might well create the desire for further education and could set the stage for a lifetime of scholarship and academic pursuits.

But it is probably also true that for most students, some of the time, and for some students, most of the time, the classroom comes close to resembling a cage from which there is no escape. When activities are dull and repetitious, when the student is not called on even though he has signalled the desire to be heard, when privileges are not granted and blame, rather than praise, is bestowed, when natural interests and desires are antithetical to the demands of the institution—at such moments (and such moments probably occur more or less regularly for many students) life in school must be extremely irksome.

The important point is that these unpleasant aspects of school life are experienced not only by those who are failing in their schoolwork (although students with low achievement might receive more than their share of these discomforts). Nor are they simply a function of the cantankerousness or maladroitness of particular classroom teachers (although poor professional preparation and psychological disorders of teachers may well add to the student's burden). It would seem, in other words, that much of the pain of school life is a natural outgrowth of the problems of institutional living and the management of social traffic. Given the arrangement in which one person is chiefly responsible for serving the educational needs of thirty or thirty-five others and for articulating the demands of this group with those of several other groups in the same building, three of the most salient features of school life—delay, denial, and interruption—are almost inevitable.

DELAY

Consider for a moment the frequency of delay. When we examine the details of classroom life carefully, it is surprising to see how much of the student's time is spent in waiting. In the elementary school, the students often line up for recess, for lunch, and for dismissal, and they frequently have to wait for the lines to be straight before they move. During individual seatwork they wait for the teacher to come around to their desk to inspect their work. When the whole class is working together, there is the waiting for the slower pupil to finish the work that the faster ones have completed. During discussion there is the waiting for fellow students to answer the teacher's query. When motion pictures or slides are shown, there is usually a delay as the room and the equipment are made ready. As time for the bell approaches, students are waiting for it to ring, even though they may still have their eyes on the teacher.

No one knows for sure how much of the student's time is spent in neutral, as it were, but it is certainly a memorable portion. How many of us who have lived thousands of days in schools can remember waiting anxiously for the minutes to tick away until the dismissal bell freed us? How many of us whose lungs are lined with chalk dust can recall the hours spent looking out the classroom window as we waited for the group in which we were imbedded to move sluggishly along? How many of us respond sympathetically to the following image of school life presented by George Santayana, as he describes his student days at Boston's Boys Latin School: "No blackboard was black; all were indelibly clouded with in-grained layers of old chalk; the more you rubbed it out, the more you rubbed it in. Every desk was stained with generations of ink-spots cut deeply with initials and scratched drawings. What idle thoughts had been wandering for years through all those empty heads in all those tedious school hours! In the best schools almost all schooltime is wasted" (1).

Idleness, unfortunately, is only part of the picture, and perhaps not even the most important part. Waiting is not so bad and may even be beneficial when the things we are anticipating ultimately happen. Indeed, Longfellow was probably speaking with the voice of wisdom when, in his *Psalm of Life,* he advises us to "Learn to labour and to wait." But he was just a shade too optimistic when, in another poem (the title of which iron-ically is *The Student's Tale*), he promises his reader that "All things come round to him who will but wait." At least it is doubtful that Longfellow was referring to things that go on in classrooms, for there the waiting is sometimes in vain.

DENIAL

The denial of desire is a commonplace in school, and likely it has to be. Not everyone who wants to speak can be heard, not all the students' queries can be answered to their satisfaction, not all their requests can be granted. It is true that, considered individually, most of these denials are psychologically trivial; but considered cumulatively, their significance increases. Part of learning how to live in school involves learning how to give up desire as well as waiting for its fulfillment.

Typically, things happen on time in school, and, as a result, activities are often begun before interest is aroused and terminated before interest wanes. Once again, there is probably no alternative to this unnatural state of affairs. If we were to wait until students requested a history class on their own, as an instance, we would have a long wait. Similarly, if we allowed students to remain in their physical education classes until they grew tired of the game, there likely would not be time for other things. There seems to be no alternative, therefore, but to stop and start things on time, even though it means constantly interrupting the natural flow of interest and desire for at least some students.

INTERRUPTIONS

But interruptions in the classroom are not confined to the beginning and ending of subject-matter periods. There are also more subtle ways in which activities are broken into. The irrelevant comment during class discussion, as an instance, often breaks the spell created by the relevant remarks that have preceded it. When the teacher is working individually with a student while others are present—a common arrangement in elementary-school classrooms—petty interruptions, in the form of minor misbehavior or students coming to the teacher for advice, are the rule rather than the exception. In countless small ways the bubble of reality created during the teaching session is punctured, and much of the teacher's energy is spent in patching up the holes, just as much of the student's energy is spent in attempting to ignore them. Students are constantly "turning back" to their studies after their attention has been momentarily drawn elsewhere.

Here, then, are three of the unpublicized features of school life: delay, denial, and interruption. As educators what do we make of them? Or better, what should we make of them? Let's dispense with extreme reactions first.

On the one hand, there is the temptation to ignore these aspects of classroom experience. After all, delay, denial, and interruption are features of life in several other settings. Why pay particular attention to these petty annoyances when they occur in school? Students themselves do not seem to be too upset by these occurrences, the argument continues; therefore, it is probably safe to ignore them, with perhaps a passing cluck of disapproval, and move to more pressing educational problems.

On the other hand, there is the temptation to magnify these undesirable events until they become all that can be seen of school life. This alternative, which might be called the school-is-hell approach, seems to be dominant on many of our college campuses these days. It is the credo of the new undergraduate religion: anti-establishmentarianism.

The trouble with these extreme positions, as with most, is that they can be maintained only by choosing to ignore certain salient features of our educational scene. Defenders of the optimistic leave-well-enough-alone point of view preserve their calm by remaining blind to the fact of widespread discontent in our schools. Defenders of the school-is-hell point of view must keep the edge on their fury by failing to acknowledge that there is massive satisfaction as well as massive dissatisfaction in our classrooms.

A more dispassionate point of view, although one that is unlikely to capture newspaper headlines, might lead us to examine the strategies that students develop to adapt to these mundane features of school life. What must be done, in other words, if the student is to live a large portion of his life in an environment in which delay, denial, and interruption are inevitable? Further, how do the strategies for adapting to these demands combine with, complement, or contradict the strategies for acquiring knowledge and developing intellectual mastery?

PATIENCE AND RESIGNATION

The quintessence of virtue in an institutional setting is contained in the single word: *patience*. Without that quality life can be miserable for those who must spend time in our prisons, our hospitals, our corporation offices, and our schools. But virtue can become soured if tested too severely. And the conditions that lead to the development of patience can also, if carried too far, set the stage for the development of resignation—a much less virtuous condition. Indeed, the distinction between the patient person and the resigned person is not always easy to make on the basis of surface appearances, even though there is a world of difference in the psychological strength of the two.

While the patient person maintains a firm grasp on his own plans for the future and, hence, retains a sense of integrity, the resigned person does not. Resignation involves an act of psychological surrender in which one's own desires, plans, and interests are abandoned and action is taken on the basis of the desires, plans, and interests of others. The resigned person has not only given up hope, he has given up many other linkages between his motives and his actions. Resignation involves, in other words, a loss of feeling and a sense of no longer caring about what happens.

Returning to the situation in our schools, we can see that if students are to face the demands of classroom life with equanimity—rather than with disappointment, anger, and rebellion—they must learn to be patient. This means that they must be able to disengage, at least temporarily, their feelings from their actions. The hope is that the disengagement will not become permanent, that patience will not fade imperceptively into resignation. Yet in expressing this hope we acknowledge a real danger, for the one condition lies just beyond the other, along the same path. The problem, for the teacher, is to help students become uninvolved when conditions demand it, but not too uninvolved. We want students to be calm in the face of some of the frustrations caused by collective life in an institution, but we do not want them, in the jargon of adolescence, to "cool it."

MASQUERADE

The second-grader who groans with disappointment when an enjoyable classroom activity is terminated, and the fourth-grade who zestfully waves his hand while his classmate is struggling to answer the teacher's question, both will likely be transformed by the time they reach high school or college into the jaded "professionals" of the classroom—those living inkblots whose enigmatic silence and languid slouch effectively mask both the presence and the absence of enthusiasm for educational affairs. Which ones are merely being patient, and which resigned? It is sometimes hard to tell.

Students also know that teachers like to see evidence of enthusiasm and involvement, and this knowledge causes alertness and other signs of interest to be worn as masks in much the same way as signs of indifference. Classroom courtesy demands that you keep your eye on the teachers and frown intensely at appropriate times even though your mind may be miles away. Again the teacher is faced with the problem of deciding which students are really with her as she goes about her work and which ones just appear to be with her.

The business of faking involvement and of masking withdrawal is not limited to the simple procedure of showing signs of attention when class is in session. These are not the only strategies by which students adapt to classroom demands. Nor are delay, denial, and interruption the only unpleasant aspects of school life with which the student must cope. The classroom, it must be remembered, is an evaluative setting in which the student must learn not just to comply with commands, but to comply in a way that yields a positive evaluation.

Thus arises the common practice of giving the teacher what she wants on written assignments and test questions, even though the assignments seem meaningless and the questions inane. Along with this practice goes the technique of disguising ignorance, of responding to the teacher's queries with sufficient ambiguity or with only thinly veiled flattery so that she will not discover and no longer care whether the student knows anything or not. (When I was a high-school student, this ploy was known as giving the teacher a "snow job." I do not know what name it goes under these days, but I am fairly confident that it is still being practiced.)

These forms of student behavior may be laughed off as harmless pranks, and sometimes they are nothing more than that. But all these acts of detachment and deception, each of which might be considered harmless, or even "cute," when used in moderation, grow out of attempts to deal with institutional constraints. When used excessively and in combination, they are the marks of the educational con-man, the student who has learned to size up teachers and give them what they want with all the shrewdness and feigned sincerity of a dishonest second-hand car dealer.

THE TWO CURRICULUMS

Much that has been said up to this point can be summarized by suggesting that every school and every classroom really has two curriculums that the students are expected to master. The one that educators traditionally have paid the most attention to might be called the official curriculum. Its core is the three R's, and it contains all of the school subjects for which we produce study guides and workbooks and teaching materials. It is the curriculum that all the curriculum reform groups are shouting about these days.

The other curriculum might be described as unofficial or perhaps even hidden, because to date it has received scant attention from educators. This hidden curriculum can also be represented by three R's, but not the familiar one of reading, 'riting, and 'rithmetic. It is, instead, the curriculum of rules, regulations, and routines, of things teachers and students must learn if they are to make their way with minimum pain in the social institution called *the school*.

THE REWARD SYSTEM

Two or three important observations might be made about the relationship between these two curriculums. One is that the reward system of the school is tied to both. Indeed, many of the rewards and punishments that sound as if they are being dispensed on the basis of academic success and failure are really more closely related to the mastery of the hidden curriculum. Consider, as an instance, the common teaching practice of giving a student credit for trying. What do teachers mean when they say a student tries to do his work? They mean, in essence, that he complies with the procedural expectations of the institution. He does his homework (though incorrectly), he raises his hand during class discussion (though he usually comes up with the wrong answer), he keeps his nose in his book during free study period (though he does not turn the page very often). He is, in other words, a "model" student, though not necessarily a good one.

It is hard to imagine any of today's elementary-school teachers failing a student who tries, even though his mastery of course content is slight. And elementary-school teachers are not alone in this respect. At higher levels of education as well rewards go to the solid citizen as well as to the budding scholar. Surely many of our valedictorians and presidents of our honor societies owe their success as much to institutional conformity as to intellectual prowess. No doubt that bright-eyed little girl who stands trembling before the principal on graduation day arrived there at least partly because she typed her weekly themes neatly and handed her homework in on time.

This manner of talking about educational affairs may sound cynical and may be taken as a criticism of teachers or as an attempt to subvert the virtues of neatness, punctuality, and courteous conduct in general. But nothing of that kind is intended. The point is simply that in schools, as in prisons, good behavior pays off.

Just as conformity to institutional expectations can lead to praise, so can the lack of it lead to trouble. As a matter of fact, the relationship of the hidden curriculum to student difficulties is even more striking than is its relationship to student success. Consider, as an instance, the conditions that lead to disciplinary action in the classroom. Why do teachers scold students? Because the student has given the wrong answer? Or because, try as he may, he fails to grasp the intricacies of long division? Not usually. A student is more likely to be scolded for coming into the room late or for making too much noise or for not listening to the teacher's directions or for pushing while in line. The teacher's wrath, in other words, is commonly triggered by violations of institutional regulations and routines rather than by the student's intellectual deficiencies.

Even with the more serious difficulties that clearly entail academic failure, the demands of the hidden curriculum lurk in the shadows. When Johnny's parents are summoned to school because their son is not doing too well in arithmetic, what explanation will be given for their son's poor performance? More than likely blame will be placed on motivational deficiencies in Johnny rather than on his intellectual shortcomings. The teacher may even go so far as to say that Johnny is *un*-motivated during arithmetic period. But what does this mean? It means, in essence, that Johnny does not even try. And not trying, as we have seen, often boils down to a failure to comply with institutional expectations, a failure to master the hidden curriculum.

There is a further question that must be asked about the relationship between the official and the unofficial curriculums in our schools: To what extent does the mastery of one interfere with the mastery of the other? In other words, how do the demands of intellectual achievement relate to the demands of institutional conformity? Are they complementary or contradictory?

We have already seen that many features of classroom life call for patience, at best, and resignation, at worst. As the student learns to live in school, he learns to subjugate his own desires to the will of the teacher and to subdue his own actions in the interest of the common good. He learns to be passive and to acquiesce to the network of rules, regulations, and routines in which he is imbedded. He learns to tolerate petty frustrations and to accept the plans and the policies of higher authorities, even when their rationale is unexplained and their meaning unclear. Like the inhabitants of other institutional settings he learns that he must frequently shrug and say, "That's the way the ball bounces."

But the personal qualities that play a role in intellectual mastery are of a very different order from those that characterize the Company Man. Curiosity, as an instance, that most fundamental of all scholarly traits, calls forth the kind of probing, poking, and exploring that is almost antithetical to the attitude of passivity that has just been described. The productive scholar must develop the habit of challenging authority and of questioning the value of tradition. He must insist on explanations for things that are unclear. The scholar must certainly be a disciplined man, but his discipline is developed in the service of his scholarship, rather than in the service of other people's wishes and desires. In short, intellectual mastery calls for sublimated forms of aggression rather than submission to constraints.

DOCILE SCHOLARS

These brief descriptions exaggerate the real differences between the demands of institutional conformity and the demands of scholarship, but they do serve to call our attention to points of possible conflict between the two sets of demands. Can both sets be mastered by the same person? Apparently so. Certainly not all our student council presidents and valedictorians are academic Uriah Heeps. Some have clearly managed to retain their intellectual aggressiveness while at the same time acquiescing to the laws that govern the social traffic of our schools. Apparently it is possible, under certain conditions at least, to breed docile scholars, even though the expression might appear at first glance to be a contradiction in terms. But how are these successes achieved? At what cost? And how many fail to achieve the synthesis of the so-called well-rounded student?

A SOCIAL PRICE

The cost of scholastic success must be measured not only in terms of the intellectual energy expended or the non-academic gratifications denied. For many students there is also a social cost. The students who accede willingly and sincerely to both the intellectual and the institutional demands of the school run the risk of being perceived as defectors by their peers. At the lower levels of education these students are likely to be called *goody-goodies, tattletales,* and *teacher's pets*; at the upper levels they are called *greasy grinds, eager beavers,* and *squares.* In the eyes of many of their classmates the students who receive the highest praise from the authorities of the school are the ones who have sold out to the system. For many students this kind of name-calling, which is often correctly perceived as reflecting envy, is not difficult to endure and is a small price to pay for the admiration of adults whom they respect. For other students it is more important to appear to be a "regular guy." Many would rather be seen as a "buddy" than as a "brain."

The number of failures in our schools is much larger than the number of students who do not come up to snuff on our achievement tests or final exams. The failures include an untold number who seemingly succeed but who turn off their intellectual motors when the dismissal bell rings. These children have learned how to give the teacher what she wants all right, but in the process they have forgotten how to use their mental powers to give themselves what they want when the teacher is not around. This group includes the students who make the honor rolls and the dean's lists during the school year but who do not know what to do with themselves during the summer vacation. It includes the thousands who, after their formal schooling is finished and diploma hung on their wall, will never again be stirred by the quest for knowledge. It includes the millions for whom a childhood of teacher-watching is followed by an adulthood of television-viewing, with hardly a change of posture or facial expression to mark the transition. One almost expects them to raise their hands and ask Johnny Carson if they can go to the bathroom. Adequate as students? Yes. Adequate as adults? No.

TWO WORLDS

And who is to blame for these failures? The schools? The society? The individual? All three share the responsibility, I suppose, but it is the school's role with which we are particularly concerned at present. The school, it would seem, asks the student for a commitment to two worlds— the world of the institution and the world of scholarship. Unfortunately, it often succeeds in obtaining only a feigned commitment to either one.

What about our own commitment to these two worlds? How have we partialled out our own loyalty? How much have we ourselves become Company Men, more interested in an up-to-date register than an up-to-date idea, more concerned with straight lines than with straight thinking? After all, we too, like our students, are rewarded for doing things neatly, and on time, with a minimum of fuss and bother. How often have we received compliments from our principals for the surface show of scholarship, for the attractiveness of our bulletin boards rather than for the vigor and imaginativeness of the ideas we present to our pupils? Nor are our administrators the villains of the piece, for they, in their turn, are caught in the same bind. The public wants its institutions to be run quietly, efficiently, and economically. The best-attended school-board meeting is almost always the one at which the budget is discussed. And who is this elusive public but the very people we educators had yesterday in our classrooms. So the circle is complete. No one is responsible, yet everyone is.

What, then, is life like in school? It would seem to be a life of contradictory demands and competing tendencies, a life in which discovery and disappointment go hand in hand, where the unpredictable and the routine are combined daily. These monotonous settings of desks and blackboards and books provide a stage for the cyclic enactment of a full drama, a play that is at once boring and exciting. No wonder our young friend only says, "Fine!" when we ask him how things are going in the classroom. School is a puzzling place, and the puzzles are not all intellectual ones.

REFERENCES

1. George Santayana. "The Latin School" in *Unseen Harvests*, p. 487. Edited by Claude M. Fuess and Emory S. Basford. New York: Macmillan, 1947.

22.   Toward a Sociology of Learning:
Peer Group Effects on Student Performance

S. S. Boocock

In recent years there has been widespread discussion of the youth culture as it affects academic accomplishments among high school and college students. Dr. Boocock discusses the impact of peer groups, notes that educational institutions must learn to use this force constructively, and briefly suggests some ways of doing so.

Before turning to groups and institutions outside of the school, I shall consider the educational implications of a sub-system which is in a sense both inside and outside the school—i.e., "youth culture," the "adolescent society," the "adolescent sub-culture," or "peer group," to mention a few of

Sociology of Education, 1966, 39, 26–32. Reprinted with the permission of the American Sociological Association and author.

the names given to this contemporary phenomenon.[1] The peer group is interesting structurally in that while its membership is made up almost entirely of high school and college students, it is not part of the formal organization of the school system.

Although Waller pointed as early as the 1930's to the basic conflict between the values and interests of the larger adult society which teachers represent and the things which are interesting and meaningful to children (Waller, 1932, Chapter 9), widespread debate and systematic analysis of youth culture has been relatively recent. Parsons (1962) sees it as an inevitable reaction to the "strains" in contemporary American society, in which rising levels of expectations for children are combined with permissive child-rearing practices and progressive educational methods. Coleman's adolescent society is a reflection of a highly industrialized society, in which the family has lost many of its former functions, especially those which made it a self-sufficient economic unit. Thus, "the child can no longer help the family economically; in turn the family has little to offer the child in the way of training for his place in the community" (Coleman, 1961, p. 3).

There has also been disagreement over the structure of these informal youth groups. Smith (1962) sees them in terms of a series of transitory group memberships through which the young person progresses, from one-sex gangs to cliques increasingly oriented toward the opposite sex and culminating in marriage and the establishment of new families. To Smith, adolescent sub-group activities are an integral part of the normal progression toward adulthood. Eisenstadt, on the other hand, feels that one reason why the integration of young people into the larger community is so problematic in modern societies is that not only does the youth group, "whatever its composition or organization, usually stand alone," but also that it "does not constitute a part of a fully institutionalized and organized series of age groups" (Eisenstadt, 1962, p. 38).

Virtually all the analysts agree, however, on the existence of such a culture, distinct from, if not entirely independent of, adult culture and institutions.[2] What makes it of concern to educators and relevant to the topic of this paper is that—

> —*the student's peer group seems to have tremendous influence upon his attitudes toward and behavior in school;*
> —*this powerful influence seems often to work at variance with the learning-achievement goals of the school.*

---

[1] While these terms are generally used interchangeably, this phenomenon can be considered on different levels, from the small friendship groups in particular schools to the general, and national, phenomenon, whose products and symbols (e.g., clothes, hair styles, music) are recognizable in almost any part of the United States.

Note also that some of the measures discussed in the last chapter under the topic of value climates are really measures of peer group opinion and thus relevant to this section also.

[2] There are a few dissenters. Elkin and Westley, 1955, see little conflict between parents and children and little evidence of any kind of separate youth culture. However, their conclusions are based upon a very small sample of cases in a rather atypical (upper middle class, professional and business, Canadian) suburb where parents and children seemed to participate in an unusually large number of joint activities.

Probably no study of adolescent sub-groups has created more interest and controversy than Coleman's, already discussed under the topic of value climate, and it is worth reformulating some of the major findings within the framework of this section.

Coleman's thesis is that not only do high school students as a whole hold academic achievement in low esteem relative to athletics and other activities peculiar to their own culture, but that peer groups in many schools "exert a rather strong deterrent to academic achievement," actually working against the formal goals of the school system (Coleman, p. 265). No matter what the value climate of the schools, the social elites were less favorable to the "brilliant scholar" value than the non-elites (although the grade averages of the former tended to be higher). Students identified as athletic stars received more sociometric status than scholars, although the athlete-scholar usually received the most of all. And in schools where anti-intellectualism was especially strong among the leading crowds, those who were willing to take an intellectual role were not those with the highest intelligence, but those willing to work at a relatively unrewarded activity (Coleman, p. 265).

Finding no relationship between per pupil expenditure and achievement of student according to their abilities, Coleman concluded that no amount of money poured into school facilities will be really effective unless students value scholastic excellence. His recommendation was rather to apply the structure of activities that are highly supported by young people (e.g., interscholastic athletics) to the classroom.

Coleman's book has had strong supporters and vehement critics. My own reservations can perhaps be summed up by saying that many of the findings are inconsistent with consistency theory. For example, the members of leading crowds tended to value academic performance less but get better grades than the non-elites; the same was true of girls as compared to boys; academic values were not high in schools (such as Executive Heights) in which the highest proportions of students planned to attend college. That is, both on the individual and system levels there seems to be an inconsistency between the values of groups of respondents and their subsequent behavior. Three possibilities are suggested: the validity of Coleman's measures of value climate can be questioned; the peer culture may not be the only, or the strongest, influence in certain areas, such as academic performance; a lot of youngsters are under a lot of strain as a result of inconsistency between their stated values and their actual behavior.

On the college level, the most intensive recent examinations of peer influence upon academic commitments were the studies of Vassar College students, sponsored by the Mellon Foundation and directed by Nevitt Sanford (cf. Sanford, 1956; Freedman, 1956; Sanford, 1959; Bushnell, 1962). Questionnaire data and diaries (in which respondents recorded all their activities for several one-week periods) were collected from all students over a five-year interval. In addition, a sample drawn from one class was intensively interviewed and tested; an anthropologist was a kind of participant observer of the student culture; and some studies of alumnae were conducted.

Sanford and his associates found peer group influences operating in much the same way as those described by Coleman, although the pressures were perhaps more subtle. There was a distinct student culture. Girls resisted acculturation on the faculty's terms, not by rebelling against studying and achievement in general (good grades were, in fact, generally respected) but by resisting wholehearted commitment to scholastic achievement at the cost of satisfactory social relations with friends. The goal of the student culture was a pleasant campus life, with agreeable interpersonal relations and a minimum of conflict and soul-searching in connection with course work. Certain student norms—e.g., proscriptions against close relationships with professors or excessive amounts of time spent on studying—functioned to maintain the relatively unruffled status quo that students thought desirable. It is interesting that the "scholar," one of several student "types" developed by Sanford, tended to be found among girls who had suffered "early and persistent awkwardness in social relations with peers" (Sanford, 1959).

The study by Hughes, Becker and Geer of student culture in a Kansas medical school acts as a kind of replication of the Vassar studies. Peer group effects showed up even more clearly in this setting because of the intense pressures placed on students by the formal requirements of medical training. The student culture was perceived to have two major functions: "first, to provide modes of adaptation that make the pressures of the school tolerable and not too upsetting to the individual student, and, second, to provide support for patterns of behavior which, though they are in the interest of the students as they see it, may be at variance with what is desired by the faculty and administration" (Hughes, *et al.*, 1962, p. 466). Thus students reach informal agreements on what *all* of them will learn in preparation for exams (Hughes, et al., p. 525), and informal norms direct which and how many case summaries out of the total assigned by professors will actually be completed and turned in (Hughes, *et. al.*, pp. 527–528).

A striking thing about these three studies is their similarity to studies of informal factory work groups, such as the Hawthorne Study Bank Wiring Room experiments. In each case the small informal group is not part of the "official" system and is sometimes not even recognized by it. It is characterized by close ties of a "primary" sort, and has a great deal of control over the productivity of its members in respect to the goals of the formal organization.

A rather different approach to the analysis of peer group influence on the college level was taken by Wallace (1965), who compared the postgraduate aspirations of an entire freshman class of a midwestern college at three times during the school year. Wallace found that the proportion of freshmen wanting to go on to graduate or professional school after graduation rose at each subsequent measurement, bringing the freshman profile ever closer to the aspiration pattern of the upper classes. Even with measures of previous academic achievement and future occupational ambition held constant, the aspiration climate created by the freshman's older peers seemed to account for an appreciable amount of his aspiration change.

There were also some interesting interaction effects among the three factors. For example, peer influence seemed to be most powerful among those students with the *lowest* past academic achievement. Wallace interprets this finding as suggesting that "the rise in low academic rank freshmen's graduate school aspirations may have had more to do with their social attitudes toward, and experiences in, college than with their expectations of graduate school success" (Wallace, p. 384), and that the student who is weaker academically is also the one most likely to be susceptible to and to conform to peer group pressures. A similar pattern was found in connection with socio-economic ambition, with a greater rise in postgraduate study aspirations being expressed among freshmen who chose relatively low status occupations for themselves when they entered college.

A major distinction of the Wallace study is in the conceptualization of peer group influence. The Coleman-type analysis seeks to characterize the climate of a given school by locating it in one cell of a multidimensional property space, and its location on each dimension is determined by the expressed attitudes of the entire student body (or a representative sample of it). The Wallace study uses a technique, originally set forth by Peter Rossi, by which *each student* has an "Interpersonal Environment" score, obtained by having him check all the names he or she recognizes from a list of the entire student body (freshmen and non-freshmen). For each student, the measure "estimates that part of the total student-body with which he had direct or indirect contact sufficient to remember the names of its members" (Wallace, p. 378).

Wallace's method of measuring aspiration climate suggests that the very notion of climate may be more complicated than the Coleman type of measure implies. In a system as large as many schools are (the college Wallace studied had a student body of 1,051), there may be two or more sub-groups each holding different sets of values. Thus a student who seems to be a deviant from the values of the student culture may be deviating from those of the most visible or "leading" clique but may be well integrated into his own sub-group. And even if one can distinguish a single— or at least a dominant—value climate, Wallace's conceptualization suggests that it may affect different students differently, depending upon which other members of the system they have contact with.

One of the reasons it is important to understand the dynamics of peer group influences and values is that people care so much about being liked and respected by their peers. A large portion of the work in the field of sociometry has centered around the measurement of peer group status. Two opposing hypotheses can be formulated relating sociometric status to learning. One hypothesis would predict a negative correlation, based on the reasoning that high achievement is an alternative or a compensation for unsatisfying interpersonal relations. The other hypothesis would predict a positive correlation, on the grounds that the student who feels accepted and secure in his interpersonal relationships will have a positive attitude in other areas as well and will be free of conflict and thus able to concentrate on school work.

Research evidence seems to favor the latter hypothesis slightly. In a review of studies of elementary school children Gronlund (1959) found positive correlations between achievement test scores and sociometric status ranging from .14 to .36, and these correlations tended to get stronger when comparisons were made between only the highest and lowest status groups. Ryan and Davie (1958) got similar results in a study of four Connecticut high schools, and concluded that social acceptance, at least in terms of their rather crude measure, accounted for "a small portion of grade variance" (Ryan and Davie, p. 102). Buswell (1953) found that the correlations tended to disappear when intelligence was controlled, I.Q. and achievement being themselves highly related. Buswell attributed the small original correlation to a tendency for children to over-choose others who are pretty similar or *slightly* above them in achievement and intelligence rather than greatly superior.

The lack of striking correlations lead Gronlund and Ryan and Davie to conclude, as Coleman did, that social acceptance is not a uniform factor but depends upon the character of the school and its component parts. "School achievement is probably most closely related to sociometric status where such achievement is highly valued by the group. . . . Thus, when the relation between school achievement and sociometric position is being considered, the level of achievement of the choosers as well as that of the chosen must be considered" (Gronlund, pp. 195–196).

In conclusion, while the true strength and nature of peer group influences are not yet known, it seems clear that educational programs that work against peer values are doomed to failure. The best thing to do with such a potentially powerful force is to use it, and the search for areas of agreement between youth and adult culture and for methods of teaching that retain the structure and channel the energies of student friendship groups seems a very fruitful kind of research. Student tutoring programs, team projects, and academic games are a few modes of instruction designed to use such groups to further learning goals.

REFERENCES

Bushnell, J. H. "Student Culture at Vassar." In N. Sanford (ed.) *The American College*. New York: Wiley, 1962, 489–514.

Buswell, M. M. "The Relationship between the Social Structure of the Classroom and the Academic Success of the Pupils." *Journal of Experimental Education*, 22 (1953), 37–52.

Coleman, James S. *The Adolescent Society*. New York: Free Press, 1961.

Eisenstadt, S. N. "Archetypal Patterns of Youth." *Daedalus*, 91 (Winter, 1962), 28–46.

Elkin, Frederick, and William A. Westley. "The Myth of Adolescent Culture." *American Sociological Review*, XX (Dec. 1955), 680–684.

Freedman, M. "The Passage Through College." *Journal of Social Issues*, 12 (1956), 12–28.

Gronlund, Norman E. *Sociometry in the Classroom*. New York: Harper, 1959.

Hughes, E. C., H. S. Becker, and B. Geer. "Student Culture and Academic Effort." In N. Sanford (ed.) *The American College*. New York: Wiley, 1962, 515–530.

Parsons, Talcott. "Youth in the Context of American Society." *Daedalus*, 91 (Winter, 1962), 97–123.

Ryan, F. J., and J. S. Davie. "Social Acceptance and Academic Achievement among High School Students." *Journal of Educational Research*, 52 (1958), 101–106.

Sanford, N. "Personality Development during the College Years." *Journal of Social Issues*, 12 (1956), 1–71 (entire issue).

Sanford, N. "Motivation of High Achievers." In O. D. David (ed.) *The Education of Women*. Washington, D. C.: American Council on Education, 1959, 34-38.

Smith, Ernest A. *American Youth Culture*. Glencoe, Ill.: Free Press, 1962.

Wallace, Walter L. "Peer Influences and Undergraduates' Aspirations for Graduate Study." *Sociology of Education*, 38 (1965), 377–392. This complete study has been published as: *Peer Groups and Students' Achievement*. Chicago: Aldine, 1965.

Waller, Willard. *The Sociology of Teaching*. New York: Wiley, 1932.

23. Sociometry and Improved Social Relations in the Classroom

Norman E. Gronlund

Since the rejection and acceptance perceived by the student can have a significant impact on his mental health, the teacher needs a reliable tool for assessing social acceptance, power and competence. To this end, sociometric techniques were developed to provide diagnostic, therapeutic and evaluative information about social relations in the classroom.

The sociometric technique has been widely used in school settings to study the social acceptance of individuals and the social relations of group members. Although its greatest use has been at the elementary school level, it is finding increasing use at the high school level. The simplicity of the technique and the variety of purposes served by the results have made it a welcome addition to the other evaluation procedures used in the classroom.

In using the sociometric technique, the teacher simply asks the students to choose a given number of companions for some group situation or activity. For example, students may be requested to select seating companions, laboratory companions, fellow committee members, or the like.

The High School Journal, 1965, 48, 391–395. Reprinted with the permission of the publisher and author.

Their choices are written on a slip of paper, or a specially prepared form, and turned into the teacher for analysis and for use in rearranging the group.

The basis for choice on a sociometric test should be a natural part of the ongoing classroom activity and the students should be assured that their choices will be put into effect. If five choices are allotted for a particular situation, it is usually possible to satisfy at least two choices for each student. Since the reliability of sociometric results has been shown to increase up to the five-choice limit, and not beyond that number, five choices seems to be a good number to use with each sociometric question.[1]

In analyzing sociometric results each choice should be given a value of one regardless of level of choice. There seems to be no logical basis for assigning weights to the various levels and the use of one point for each choice simplifies the analysis. The social acceptance of each student is determined by simply totaling the number of choices received. The social relations of the group members can be revealed by plotting the results in the form of a sociogram. This is a graphic representation of the choices made by each individual. It is especially useful in detecting cliques, cleavages, and similar social patterns existing in the group structure.

Sociometric results have been found to be surprisingly stable from one time to another, from one choice situation to another, and from one group to another. Wertheimer[2] studied the sociometric status scores of 200 high school students who stayed in the same home room classes over a two-year period and reported considerable stability over that period of time. Results obtained 20 months apart correlated .69 for boys and .62 for girls. A study by Gronlund and Whitney[3] has cast light on the extent to which classroom social status can be interpreted as a measure of general social acceptability. They asked students in 12 home room classes to choose the *classmates* they most preferred as seating companions, and then to choose from *throughout the entire school population* those students they most preferred as fellow classmates in their home room the following year. On the first choice situation all choices were, of course, confined to pupils within the same classroom. On the second choice situation, approximately 40 per cent of the choices went to pupils in classes other than those in which the choices were given. Despite the relatively large percentage of choices passing *between* classrooms on the second choice situation, the students' sociometric status scores correlated .72 over the two situations. In other words, the students' social acceptance in the classroom was significantly related to their social acceptance throughout the school. A further analysis of the results indicated that students who were isolated (i.e., received no choices) in the classroom tended to remain social isolates when choices were made on a school-wide basis. Studies such as these tend to support the significance of classroom sociometric results.

---

[1] Gronlund, Norman E. *Sociometry in the Classroom.* New York: Harper & Row, 1959.

[2] Wertheimer, R. R., "Consistency of Sociometric Status Position in Male and Female High School Students," *Journal of Educational Psychology*, 48:385–390, 1957.

[3] Gronlund, N. E. and Whitney, A. P., "Relation Between Pupils' Social Acceptability in the Classroom, in the School, and in the Neighborhood," *School Review*, 64:267–271, 1956.

There are a number of specific ways that sociometric results can be used by the classroom teacher. These can best be described in terms of diagnostic, therapeutic, and evaluative uses. All of the uses have implications for improved social relations and, hopefully, a resulting salutary effect on learning.

DIAGNOSTIC USES OF SOCIOMETRIC RESULTS

The major value of the sociometric test as a diagnostic tool resides in its ability to identify problems which originate from, or are influenced by, the social structure of the group. Such problems include the socially isolated student, social cleavages along racial, religious, or social lines, and small clique structures which may have an undesirable influence on group functioning. Sociometric results do not indicate why these social patterns exist nor what to do about them, but they do provide a good starting point for further study. The choices to and from individuals also provide clues to group rearrangement which might have a beneficial effect on the social relations of the group members.

In analyzing sociometric results, it is important to interpret the data in light of all other information known about the students. A socially isolated student, for example, may be busily pursuing his own individual interests and have little need for a circle of friends, or he may be so desperately unhappy in his social isolation that he is unable to concentrate on his school work. Similarly, a student may be socially isolated because he is shy and withdrawn, because he is hostile and aggressive, or simply because he differs from the other group members in some way (e.g., race, religion, or social class). To obtain full meaning from sociometric results, consideration must be given to a student's need for social interaction, his personal characteristics, and the social forces operating in the group. Social relations are the product of numerous factors interacting in complex ways and simple interpretations are seldom adequate.

In addition to their use in identifying social relations problems per se, sociometric results can also aid in a fuller understanding of other types of classroom problems. The social acceptance and social relations patterns of the retarded reader, the slow learner, the difficult discipline case, the truant, and the like, can aid in analyzing their difficulties and possibly provide clues for remediation. Difficulties in social relations both contribute to and are affected by problems of learning and adjustment in other areas of development.

THERAPEUTIC USES OF SOCIOMETRIC RESULTS

The most direct contribution of sociometric results to improved social relations can be seen in the arrangement and rearrangements of classroom groups along sociometric lines. Through sociometric grouping each student is given a position in which he feels psychologically comfortable, and consequently one that provides him with the greatest opportunity for developing satisfying social relations. There is some research evidence to support the claim that the sociometric arrangement of classroom groups has a beneficial effect on social interaction, but most of the studies were done at the elementary school level.

One study,[4] using high school students, is of interest because it involved the sociometric grouping of an entire freshman class. In the spring of the year, all freshmen were asked to indicate their preferences for classmates in their home rooms the following year. The home room classes for the sophomore year were then arranged by placing each student in the home room which satisfied the largest number of his sociometric choices. A follow-up sociometric test at the end of the sophomore year indicated a general increase in the students' social acceptance scores over those obtained a year earlier. Although this study was of the "action research" type, without a control group for comparison, the findings suggest that sociometric grouping at the high school level may be of therapeutic value.

When arranging sociometric groups, consideration also should be given to factors other than the students' choices. It may, for example, be desirable to break up a clique that is having a disturbing influence on the class or to provide for greater social interaction between subgroups formed along social, religious or social class lines. Such adjustments can be made within the framework of sociometric choosing, and, of course, any promises made to the students concerning the number of choices they will have satisfied must be kept. Where sociometric groups are formed in a mechanical fashion (i.e., on the basis of sociometric choices alone), there is the danger that clique formations and social cleavages will be further increased, resulting in a detrimental rather than a beneficial influence on students' social relations.

EVALUATIVE USES OF SOCIOMETRIC RESULTS

Another use of the sociometric test is in evaluating the influence of various school practices on students' social relations. Probably the most common use in this regard is in evaluating special programs designed to improve social relations. The effectiveness of our efforts to integrate racial groups in the classroom, for example, can be partially determined by noting changes in the number of sociometric choices passing between members of the different groups. Similarly, we can evaluate the success of programs aimed at improving social interaction between social classes, religious groups, rural-urban students, and the like.

Sociometric results can also contribute to an evaluation of programs not directly concerned with improving students' social relations. If ability grouping is used in the school, for example, sociometric data can help us determine if a social cleavage is developing between the various ability groups. In a like manner, we can determine the social effect of different teaching techniques, promotional practices, special classroom activities, and the like. Although numerous other factors must be considered in evaluating a particular practice, whether it has beneficial or detrimental effects on students' social relations is an important consideration.

---

[4] Amundson, C. L., "Increasing Interpersonal Relationships in the High School with the Aid of Sociometric Procedures," *Group Psychotherapy*, 6:183–188, 1954.

A study by Forlano[5] illustrates one of the many ways that socio-metric data can be used for evaluation purposes. He measured changes in students' social acceptance scores in core and noncore classes and found that core classes contributed to greater gains in interpeer acceptance. While no one would claim that the main objective of core classes is to improve students' social relations, the finding is of significance in an over-all evaluation of the influence of core classes on student development.

In summary, the sociometric test is easily administered, it provides a fairly stable and general measure of social relations, and the results can be used for diagnostic, therapeutic, and evaluative purposes. Despite the ap-parent usefulness of sociometric results, however, they provide no panacea for our educational problems. The modern classroom teacher will use many diagnostic techniques, a variety of grouping methods, and a wide array of evaluation procedures. The sociometric test is simply a useful ad-junct—one which directs special attention to students' social relations.

24.   The Social Choices of Students in Racially Integrated Classes for the Culturally Disadvantaged Talented

Verna Godman Janzen and James J. Gallagher

The topic of school desegregation is indeed a timely one. The following article by Verna Janzen and James Gallagher addresses itself to one aspect of this problem, namely, what impact does intergroup contact have on sociometric choices? The results indicate some cross racial social choices; however, the nature and kind of choice apparently depend, in part, upon factors internal to the group.

The influence of racial integration in the public schools has been more dis-cussed than researched. Many of the arguments on the influence of school integration are based upon unproven assumptions. The purpose of the

Exceptional Children, December, 1966, 221–226. Reprinted with the permission of the publisher and author.
[5] Forlano, George, "Peer Acceptance in Core and Noncore Classes," *The Journal of Educational Research,* 57:431–433, 1964.

present study is to investigate the sociometric choices of 100 gifted disadvantaged children in four intermediate grade classrooms in a midwestern university community.

BACKGROUND

Gronlund (1959) did a comprehensive review of studies on social choice and concluded that there were a large number of variables that influenced such choice. Among these were intelligence, achievement, propinquity, physical maturity and ability, physical attractiveness, social skills, and socially aggressive personality characteristics. In regard to the racial variable he commented:

> Where racial cleavages exist in a community these cleavages are reflected in children's sociometric choices. However, where racial integration has been in effect for some time, children's sociometric choices freely cross race lines (p. 218).

Moreno (1934) and Criswell (1939) both found distinct racial groupings in their studies which were conducted in large metropolitan areas where segregation was common. However, Raths and Schweikart (1946), in studying fifth and sixth graders, found that both Negro and white children were accepted by their classmates. Katz (1964), in a review of the status of Negro children, concluded that white school children in the north indicated a preference for their own racial group from an early age.

Reviews of the influence of intelligence (Campbell, 1964) and achievement (Spaulding, 1964) confirm the earlier reviews of Gronlund that each has a major influence on social choice. The one reservation to this generalization is the observation by Hollingworth (1942) and Gallagher (1958) that, if a child's intelligence greatly exceeds his classmates' (e.g., Binet IQ of 170 in a class where the average is 110), then he is less likely to be socially popular.

PROBLEM

The purpose of this study was to investigate the relation of choice of seating, working, and playing companions to race, sex, and intelligence in four intermediate level classrooms of culturally disadvantaged gifted children.

PROCEDURE

The 100 children involved in this study were enrolled in two elementary schools in Champaign, Illinois, which had established classes for culturally disadvantaged gifted children. They were involved in an experimental program supported by the Illinois Department of Program Planning for Gifted Children and designed to evaluate the effectiveness of intensive home-school contacts with parents when provided in conjunction with a special educational program for socially and culturally deprived children with high potential. The two criteria used to determine eligibility for children in the projects were as follows:

1. Subjects were from homes classified as culturally deprived according to the father's occupation and housing ratings obtained through the City Planning Commissioner's Office.
2. They were in the top 20 per cent of the culturally deprived population according to an individual psychological evaluation by a qualified psychological examiner in which scores on a battery of tests were considered. Each child was administered a Stanford-Binet intelligence test as part of the battery.

These criteria allowed children of lower Binet IQ scores to participate on the grounds that these tests measured intellectual functioning, not true potential. The media IQ for all four classes fell between 110 and 119. The children were randomly assigned to the experimental or control group. The experimental group received home visitations from the teachers, while the control group received only the special program with conventional home and school contacts.

For the purposes of description in the present article, the following descriptive labels are applied to the four classrooms:

Alfred	Experimental Class I	Fourth and Fifth Graders
Boswell	Experimental Class II	Fifth and Sixth Graders
Yodel	Control Class I	Fourth and Fifth Graders
Zader	Control Class II	Fifth and Sixth Graders

In each classroom, the homeroom teacher passed to each child an alphabetical listing of the familiar names (first or nicknames and last names) of the members of the class and a mimeographed instruction sheet with four half sheet pages containing spaces to write five choices. She then read the following directions aloud while the children read them silently.

During the next few weeks, we will be changing some seats, working in small groups, and playing some group games. Now that we all know each other by name, you can help me arrange groups that work and play best together. You can do this by writing the names of the children you would like to have sit near you, to have work with you, and to have play with you. You have been given an alphabetical list of the names of the children in this room. From this list, you may choose anyone in this room you wish, including those people who are absent today. Your choices will not be seen by any other pupils. Give the first name and the initial of the last name for each person you choose. Make your choices carefully so the groups will be the way you really want them. I will try to arrange the groups so that each pupil gets at least two of his choices. Sometimes it is hard to give everyone his first choices so be sure to make five choices

for each question. On the last page, I would like to know the names
of the pupils you think will want to sit near you.
Remember!
1. Your choices must be from pupils in this room, including those
   who are absent.
2. You should make all five choices for each question.
3. You should write the first name and the initial of the last name.
4. You may choose a pupil for more than one group if you wish.
5. Your choices will not be seen by any other pupil.

The choice of the three criteria was made on the basis of their generality and their reflection of actual possible situations which the children
can take seriously, as recommended by Gronlund (1959). The use of
three criteria was deemed necessary since, according to the same source,
"for evaluating interpersonal relationships and for determining the group
acceptance of individual pupils several criteria are usually necessary"
(p. 46). Five choices were requested of the child mainly for the sake of
the teacher who would try to fulfill at least one of each child's choices.
Only the first three choices were used in the data analyses, and, unfortunately, there were a few cases in which the children did not even record
three choices for every item.

RESULTS

Figure 1 shows the major choices of seating companions in the four classrooms. A double line indicates a mutual choice. The social stars and isolates are noted by an asterisk and a I, respectively, and these were
determined by the criteria established by Gronlund.

In Alfred it can be noted that there were four stars: two white girls,
one white boy, and one Negro boy. There were also four isolates: two
Negro girls, one Negro boy, and one white boy. Alfred shows a tightly
knit ingroup of white girls, none of whom chose outside their own race.
None of the most popular Negro girls chose outside their own race, while
three of the least popular Negro girls chose from among the closed, white
girl ingroup.

There were considerably more interracial choices among the boys,
with the two boys who were stars (one white and one Negro) showing a
mutual choice for each other.

In Boswell, neither stars nor isolates can be seen limited to one race or
sex. In contrast to Alfred, one can see the most popular white girl had
mutual choices with the two most popular Negro girls. The other three
white girls made few choices outside their own race or sex. The boys
again show greater interracial choices, with a number of mutual choices
evident. The one white boy and Negro girl mutual choice noted here was
most unusual.

In Yodel, there is a rather small white population amounting to only
29 per cent of the total, and this may have influenced the results somewhat
in this classroom. Over half of the white population were designated as
isolates, while only one white boy was a star. The one white girl in the
class seems out of place, since she is unlikely to be chosen by the boys and

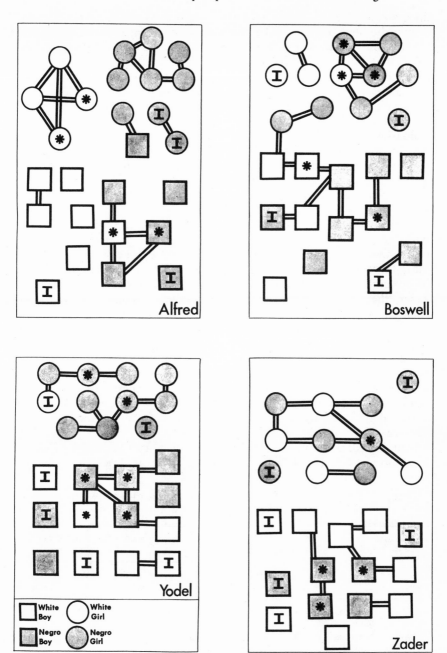

FIGURE 1.   Patterns of Sociometric Choices in Four Classrooms

does not find social status with the Negro girls. The cross sex choice among the boys seemed similar to the other two classes discussed above.

Finally in Zader, a different pattern emerges again. Here there are substantial interracial choices among white and Negro girls as well as boys. There seems to be a large number of isolate boys in the class of both races, with the majority of choices going to the three Negro boys who were the stars.

It is clear from the portrait in these four classrooms that any generalizations to be made about social structure in an integrated class would have to be made cautiously, if at all. The color of skin seemed less important than the personalities of the individuals. There did seem to be fewer interracial choices between girls than between boys. As found in practically all studies of this age level, there was very little cross sex choice in any of the classes.

Table 1 reveals the percentages of Negro and white children choosing within and outside their own racial group in each of three situations: seatmates, working companions, and playmates. As can be seen from the results, there are many differences among the four classrooms. For the Negro children in Yodel, about 90 per cent chose their own race, while in Zader, the percentage was between 50 and 60. Similarly, in the white children, their choice of whites as companions ranged from 30 to 40 per cent in Yodel and Zader to 50 to 80 per cent in Alfred and Boswell. A chi square test was calculated for each racial group to determine whether the choices exceeded chance when the racial proportions in the class were taken into account. For instance, in Yodel there was a very small group of white children, so it would not be expected that they would receive as many choices as would the 70 per cent majority of Negroes. When such a statistical test was applied, it was found that of the eight comparisons, three reached statistical significance.

In Alfred, the white children chose other white children significantly more often than would be expected by chance. In Yodel, the Negroes

TABLE 1. PERCENTAGES OF NEGRO AND WHITE CHILDREN CHOOSING
WITHIN AND OUTSIDE THEIR OWN RACIAL GROUP

Class		Per cent Choosing Negroes in Each Situation			Per cent Choosing Whites in Each Situation		
		To Sit with	To Work with	To Play with	To Sit with	To Work with	To Play with
Alfred	Negroes	71	76	71	29	22	27
	Whites**	18	27	27	82	73	73
Boswell	Negroes	67	58	73	33	42	27
	Whites	52	48	63	48	52	37
Yodel	Negroes**	88	90	90	12	10	10
	Whites	67	48	62	33	38	38
Zader	Negroes	56	54	59	44	46	41
	Whites*	69	72	75	31	28	25

*Chi square significant at .05 level.
**Chi square significant at .01 level.

chose other Negroes significantly more often than would be expected by chance; but in Zader, the white children chose Negro children at a rate significantly greater than chance. These results would tend to indicate that race does seem to be a factor in social choice in some classes under certain conditions, but not in others. In the present circumstances, it was not possible to probe further into the conditions that might have been influencing these varying results in the four classrooms. There did not seem to be substantial difference in choice whether the selection was seatmate or working or playing companion.

When the students were broken down by IQ scores and a check made on the number of social choices that were received, no significant differences were obtained for any of the classrooms for either sex in terms of the more intelligent children receiving more choices. It appears in this instance that, when the range of ability is reduced by the type of ability grouping practiced as part of the current project, intelligence ceases to be a major factor in social choice.

CONCLUSIONS AND IMPLICATIONS

In the great struggle and turmoil surrounding school integration, there have been several nagging questions regarding its impact on the students themselves. One of these has been whether placing students of different races in the same physical environment really accomplishes anything in terms of human contact and interaction. Do the children perhaps establish their own social world built on race within that physical environment, so that the possibility of increasing human understanding between races is a myth?

The results of this study would clearly show that there are substantial cross racial choices within the four classrooms, with many factors apparently influencing the nature and kind of such choices. This sample of students should provide much of the future leadership of this social class, as it represents the intellectual elite of the social class in this community. Therefore, there would seem to be reason for encouragement for those who perceive integration of schools as allowing for greater social contact and, through greater contact, more empathy and understanding.

It should be noted that these results have been obtained upon pre-adolescent students in the intermediate grades. Whether such cross racial choices can withstand the growing peer and cultural pressure that would be available during the adolescent years would be a necessary and important research question to answer.

While it should not be automatically assumed that greater contact with students of another race would increase positive feelings towards that race, it should provide a more realistic and diversified basis for judgment than the cultural stereotypes of the mass media or the fears and fantasies of frightened friends.

REFERENCES

Campbell, J. D. Peer relations in childhood. In M. L. Hoffman and L. W. Hoffman (Editors), *Review of child development research, volume 1.* New York: Russell Sage Foundation, 1964. Pp. 289–322.

Criswell, Joan. A sociometric study of race cleavage in the classroom. *Archives of Psychology*, 1939, 33, 1–83.

Gallagher, J. J. Peer acceptance of highly gifted children in elementary school. *Elementary School Journal*, 1958, 58, 465–470.

Gronlund, E. *Sociometry in the classroom.* New York: Harpers, 1959.

Hollingsworth, Leta. *Children with IQ about 180.* New York: Harcourt, Brace and World, 1942.

Katz, I. Review of evidence relating to effects of desegregation on the intellectual performance of Negroes. *American Psychologist*, 1964, 19, 381–399.

Moreno, J. L. *Who shall survive?* Washington, D.C.: Nervous and Mental Disease Publishing Company, 1934.

Raths, L., and Schweikart, E. F. Social acceptance within interracial school groups. *Educational Research Bulletin*, 1946, 26, 85–90.

Spaulding, R. L. Personality and social development: peer and school influences. *Review of Educational Research*, 1964, 34, 588–598.

CHAPTER 6

Students with Special Needs

25. As a Psychologist Sees Pressures on Disadvantaged Teen-agers

Arthur Pearl

What are the major pressures under which the cultur-
ally disadvantaged learner has to operate? What char-
acteristics must a teacher of low-income pupils possess?
These are the fundamental points examined by Dr.
Pearl as he discusses one of the most serious problems
confronting American education today.

The greatest pressure on the disadvantaged youth is caused not so much
by his environmental deficit as by what he feels is his lack of a future.
The truth of the matter is that our society provides little opportunity for
a low-income youth to find a place in the world. As a result, most of his
formal education and other kinds of social intervention are not only ineffective but often humiliating or debasing.

For example, he is compelled to go to school, but what he is presented with there has no meaning to him in terms of the way he sees the
world. He is told to stay in school so that eventually he can get a better
job, but in actuality being a high school graduate offers him little if any
more in terms of access to the opportunity structure than being a high
school dropout. He knows friends and relatives who have graduated from
high school and are either unemployed or in some undignified, degrading,

NEA Journal, February, 1965, 19 & 21. Reprinted with the permission of the publisher and author.

and debasing jobs. His real choice is often boiled down to becoming an unemployed high school graduate or an unemployed dropout.

Although society today is geared to favor the college graduate, a higher education is an impossible goal to most disadvantaged young people. Even if they could conceive of the possibility of going to college, there is little in their educational activity and nothing in their home background that prepares them for it. Many of them are in basic tracks that do not prepare for college. The slightly more fortunate are placed in a so-called general curriculum which does not prepare them for college either.

What the schools need to do is to find some way to offer these disadvantaged youth the possibility of going to college or, at the very least, some hope for a future.

Another kind of pressure on the disadvantaged youth is exerted by love—the undiscriminating sort dispensed by well-meaning teachers. Not all of these kids are lovable, and they can see through any false posture.

Not long ago I heard the dean of a school of education say that the one thing disadvantaged children need is love. If we could only give them enough love, we could solve all of our problems, he implied. He became furious with me, however, when I tried to explain to him that love given so promiscuously is known in the streets as prostitution.

By trying to give universal love, the teacher actually punishes the disadvantaged student. In effect, the teacher is asking him to feel guilty for anything he does that displeases her because he is hurting or disappointing one who loves him.

For example, take the fifth grade teacher in a Chicago slum school who, shortly after the mass demonstrations against de facto segregation, found some salacious comments scrawled on her record book. Turning to the class, she asked, "After all I've done for you, why are you being so mean to me?"

After a long silence, one of the boys finally answered, "Because you're white."

The teacher, although she had just witnessed two racial school boycotts, was dumbfounded. With tears in her eyes, she told the class that she could not teach them any more that morning; she was too upset.

Her self-righteousness was the most excruciating punishment that she could have used against the boy. He had presented himself honestly and courageously and, if anything, should have been rewarded for his contribution. Instead, he was humiliated. Not surprisingly, at the end of the class he walked up to the teacher and stamped as hard as he could on her feet.

The object lesson here is quite clear. The teacher had established a love relationship that no one had asked for. By failing to acknowledge the boy's honesty and by humiliating him, she drove him to the only kind of face-saving action he knew how to express. If she had handled the situation honestly, say by discussing this particular problem with the class, she could have built up this boy's self-respect and her own effectiveness as a teacher.

It is not love that disadvantaged children need so much as honest respect. Anything phony will force them to lash out against the teacher and whatever else the school imposes upon them.

Another pressure the schools have got to do away with if they are to deal effectively with the disadvantaged is the fierceness of individual competition. Most disadvantaged children have nothing in their backgrounds to prepare them for school, and as a consequence they are unable to compete equally with most other children.

If the school continues to punish such children with failing grades and other forms of humiliation, these youngsters will be disaffected with the whole educational process. Even if they are not actually told they are stupid, the school implies it. They are asked to read when they can't read well; they have to stand at the board and face the laughter and ridicule of their friends. If they finally decide not to go to school, they are arrested as truants.

Admittedly, some of these children are not of high or even average intelligence—in the ways that we normally measure intelligence—but they can learn to do many useful things in society.

One of the interesting results of a recent experiment in programed learning reveals that IQ does not truly indicate how *much* a person can learn but how *fast* he can learn. Experiments with programed learning in physics and chemistry indicate that a person with an IQ of 80 can learn just as much as a person with an IQ of 140, although it may take the person with the low IQ a much longer time. (Incidentally, when tested a year later, the low IQ students, who had invested much more time in learning, scored higher than the high IQ students.)

Although their rate of learning is generally slower than that of the more fortunate children, disadvantaged students need not be placed in special groups. Homogeneous grouping, I believe, is done more often for the benefit of the teacher than for his students.

Instead of depending on such gimmicks, educators ought to be moving toward what I would call team learning. We have had team learning for a long time, but we have called it cheating. In the context I am speaking of, however, all students work together to help each other learn instead of working to beat the system. The effectiveness of this type of learning has been proven in scores of experiments, particularly some conducted by the Army.

In short, we have got to be less concerned with the outcomes of education and more concerned with the process of education.

Obviously, putting the right type of teacher in the classroom is a key to relieving many of the pressures on the disadvantaged child in school. Unfortunately, we have a lot of teachers in predominantly disadvantaged schools who should not be there. A lot of them are prejudiced, not necessarily because of their children's racial or ethnic background but because the values and mores of these children are opposed to the values and mores of the middle class from which most of their teachers come.

A teacher in a disadvantaged school should be nonjudgmental. He should recognize that his students may have a different approach to life, one perhaps more suitable to the kind of world they live in than the one in which he lives.

The teacher should also be attuned to the fact that while these children have many deficits, they have assets as well. The kinds of assets a child is likely to have will largely be in tune with the kind of world with which he has learned to deal.

The disadvantaged child lives in a very physical world, one which places little value on reflective thinking. His assets, therefore, are going to be largely physical—the ability to act out his emotions and feelings freely and honestly. This is one reason why Frank Reissman and others place a great deal of emphasis on role playing as part of the learning experience of these children.

The teacher must recognize that children learn differently—that some learn by reading, some by listening, some by feeling, and some by acting out or projecting themselves.

Finally, the teacher should have a sense of humor. He should not take himself so seriously that he becomes outraged at a child's inability to respond in some preconceived way. A child should be able to come into a classroom knowing that he is going to have some fun. Even if the child looks upon learning as something incidental, it is surprising how much he learns in a relaxed atmosphere in which he is enjoying himself.

There is no reason why education has to be unenjoyable. If the teacher is nonjudgmental and free from prejudices, if he is willing to recognize the good qualities of his students, he can make of education what it is supposed to be—preparation for living in a democratic society where everyone has a chance to achieve dignity and status.

26.   Familial Mental Retardation: A Continuing Dilemma

Edward Zigler

Is it realistic to view mentally retarded youth as a homogeneous group? Or are there identifiable subgroups with differing etiologies within the total population of retardates? Is mental retardation the result of neurophysiological defects and poorer genetic stock? Or does

Science, January 1967, 155, 292–298. Reprinted with the permission of the publisher and author. Copyright 1967, by the American Association for the Advancement of Science.

mental retardation arise from motivational and emo-
tional factors which, in turn, stem from adverse envir-
onmental circumstances? In the following article,
Edward Zigler presents a scholarly and exciting analy-
sis of both theory and research as they pertain to these
controversies. What is your position on these matters?

The past decade has witnessed renewed interest in the problem of mental retardation. The interest has resulted in vigorous research activity and the construction of a number of theories which attempt an explanation of attenuated intellectual functioning. However, much of the research and many of the theoretical efforts in the area appear to be hampered by a variety of conceptual ambiguities. Much of this ambiguity is due to the very heterogeneity of phenomena included within the rubric of intellectual retardation. A portion of this ambiguity also appears to be the product of many workers' general conceptual orientation to the area of mental retardation.

The typical textbook pictures the distribution of intelligence as normal or Gaussian in nature, with approximately the lowest 3 percent of the distribution encompassing the mentally retarded (see Fig. 1a). A homogeneous class of persons is thus constructed, a class defined by intelligence-test performance which results in a score between 0 and 70. This schema has misled many laymen and students, and has subtly influenced the approach of experienced workers in the area. For if one fails to appreciate the arbitrary nature of the 70-I.Q. cutoff point, it is but a short step to the formulation that all persons falling below this point compose a homogeneous class of "subnormals," qualitatively different from persons having a higher I.Q. The view that mental retardates comprise a homogeneous group is seen in numerous research studies in which comparisons are made between retardates and normal individuals with the two groups defined solely on the basis of an I.Q. classification.

This practice gives rise to a "difference," or "defect," orientation to mental retardation. Such an approach historically included the notion of moral defect and had many origins, ranging from the belief that retardates were possessed by a variety of devils to the empirical evidence of the higher incidence among them of socially unacceptable behaviors, such as crime and illegitimacy. More recently, the notion of defect has referred to defects in either physical or cognitive structures. This defect approach has one unquestionably valid component. There is a sizable group of retardates who suffer from any of a variety of known physical defects. For example, mental retardation may be due to a dominant gene, as in epiloia; to a single recessive gene, as in gargoylism, phenylketonuria, and amaurotic idiocy; to infections, such as congenital syphilis, encephalitis, or rubella in the mother; to chromosomal defects, as in mongolism; to toxic agents, as in retardation caused by radiation in utero, lead poisoning, or Rh incompatibility; and to cerebral trauma.

The diverse etiologies noted above have one factor in common; in every instance, examination reveals an abnormal physiological process. Persons who are retarded as a result of an abnormal physiological process *are* abnormal in the orthodox sense, since they suffer from a known physiological defect. However, in addition to this group, which forms a minority of all retardates, there is the group labeled "familial"—or, more recently, "cultural-familial"—which compromises approximately 75 per cent of all retardates. This group presents the greatest mystery and has been the object of the most heated disputes in the area of mental retardation. The diagnosis of familial retardation is made when an examination reveals none of the physiological manifestations noted above, and when retardation of this same type exists among parents, siblings, or other relatives. Several writers have extended the defect notion to this type of retardate as well, although they differ as to what they propose as the specific nature of the defect. On the basis of differences in performance between retardates and normals on some experimental task, rather than on the basis of physiological evidence, they have advanced the view that all retardates suffer from some specifiable defect over and above their general intellectual retardation.

Some order can be brought to the area of mental retardation if a distinction is maintained between physiologically defective retardates, with retardation of known etiology, and familial retardates, with retardation of unknown etiology. For the most part, work with physiologically defective retardates involves investigation into the exact nature of the underlying physiological processes, with prevention or amelioration of the physical and intellectual symptoms as the goal. Jervis (1) has suggested that such "pathological" mental deficiency is primarily in the domain of the medical sciences, whereas familial retardation represents a problem to be solved by behavioral scientists, including educators and behavioral geneticists. Diagnostic and incidence studies of these two types of retardates have disclosed certain striking differences. The retardate having an extremely low I.Q. (below 40) is almost invariably of the physiologically defective type. Familial retardates, on the other hand, are almost invariably mildly retarded, usually with I.Q.'s above 50. This difference in the general intellectual level of the two groups of retardates is an important empirical phenomenon that supports the two-group approach to mental retardation, the approach supported in this article.

A TWO-GROUP APPROACH

Hirsch (2) has asserted that we will not make much headway in understanding individual differences in intelligence, and in many other traits, unless we recognize that, to a large degree, such differences reflect the inherent biological properties of man. We can all agree that no genotype spells itself out in a vacuum, and that the phenotypic expression is finally the result of environment interacting with the genotype. However, an appreciation of the importance of genetic differences allows us to bring considerable order to the area of mental retardation.

We need simply to accept the generally recognized fact that the gene pool of any population is such that there will always be variations in the behavioral or phenotypic expression of virtually every measurable trait or characteristic of man. From the polygenic model advanced by geneticists, we deduce that the distribution of intelligence is characterized by a bisymmetrical bell-shaped curve, which is characteristic of such a large number of distributions that we have come to refer to it as the normal curve. With the qualification noted below, this theoretical distribution is a fairly good approximation of the observed distribution of intelligence. In the polygenic model of intelligence (see 2–4), the genetic foundation of intelligence is not viewed as dependent upon a single gene. Rather, intelligence is viewed as the result of a number of discrete genetic units. (This is not to assert, however, that single gene effects are never encountered in mental retardation. As noted above, certain relatively rare types of mental retardation are the product of such simple genetic effects.)

Various specific polygenic models have been advanced which generate theoretical distributions of intelligence that are in keeping with observed distributions (3, 5, 6). An aspect of polygenic models of special importance for the two-group approach is the fact that they generate I.Q. distributions of approximately 50 to 150. Since an I.Q. of approximately 50 appears to be the lower limit for familial retardates, it has been concluded (4, 5, 7) that the etiology of this form of retardation reflects the same factors that determine "normal" intelligence. With this approach, the familial retardate may be viewed as normal, where "normal" is defined as meaning an integral part of the distribution of intelligence that we would expect from the normal manifestations of the genetic pool in our population. Within such a framework it is possible to refer to the familial retardate as less intelligent than other normal manifestations of the genetic pool, but he is just as integral a part of the normal distribution as are the 3 per cent of the population whom we view as superior, or the more numerous group of individuals whom we consider to be average (8).

The two-group approach to mental retardation calls attention to the fact that the second group of retardates, those who have known physiological defects, represents a distribution of intelligence with a mean which is considerably lower than that of the familial retardates. Such children, for the most part, fall outside the range of normal intelligence—that is, below I.Q. of 50—although there are certain exceptions. Considerable clarity could be brought to the area of mental retardation through doing away with the practice of conceptualizing the intelligence distribution as a single, continuous, normal curve. Perhaps a more appropriate representation of the empirical distribution of intelligence would involve two curves, as Fig. 1b illustrates. The intelligence of the bulk of the population, including the familial retardate, would be depicted as a normal distribution having a mean of 100, with lower and upper limits of approximately 50 and 150, respectively. Superimposed on this curve would be a second, somewhat normal distribution having a mean of approximately 35 and a range from 0 to 70. (That the population encompassed by the second curve in Fig. 1b extends beyond the 70-I.Q. cutoff point is due to the fact that a very small number of individuals with known defects—for example,

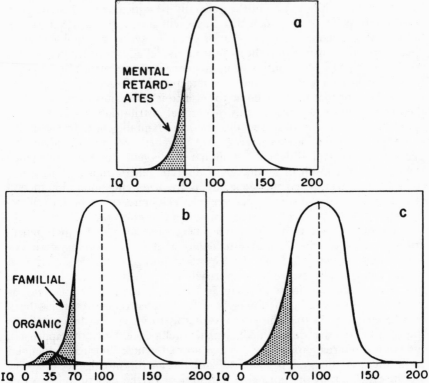

FIGURE 1.   (a) Conventional representation of the distribution of intelligence. (b) Distribution of intelligence as represented in the two-group approach. (c) Actual distribution of intelligence. [After Penrose (4)]

brain damage—may be found throughout the I.Q. continuum.) The first curve would represent the polygenic distribution of intelligence; the second would represent all those individuals whose intellectual functioning reflects factors other than the normal polygenic expression—that is, those retardates having an identifiable physiological defect. This two-group approach to the problem of mental retardation has been supported by Penrose (4), Roberts (9), and Lewis (10). The very nature of the observed distribution of I.Q.'s below the mean, especially in the range 0 to 50 (see Fig. 1c), seems to demand such an approach. This distribution, in which we find an overabundance of individuals at the very low I.Q. levels, is exactly what we would expect if we combined the two distributions discussed above, as is the general practice.

Limitations of space prevent consideration here of the controversy concerning the role of environmental factors in the etiology of familial retardation. Although such factors cannot be ignored by the serious student of mental retardation, the general dispute, discussed below, between adherents of the defect theory and of the general developmental theory can be examined somewhat independently of the environmental issue. That there will always be a distribution of a particular shape is a conclusion inherent in the polygenic argument, but the absolute amounts of intelligence represented by the various points on the distribution would still depend in large part on environmental factors.

DEVELOPMENTAL VERSUS DEFECT ORIENTATION

Once one adopts the position that the familial mental retardate is not defective or pathological but is essentially a normal individual of low intelligence, then the familial retardate no longer represents a mystery but, rather, is viewed as a particular manifestation of the general developmental process. According to this approach, the familial retardate's cognitive development differs from that of the normal individual only in respect to its rate and the upper limit achieved. Such a view generates the expectation that, when rate of development is controlled, as is grossly the case when groups of retardates and normals are matched with respect to mental age, there should be no difference in formal cognitive processes related to I.Q. Stated somewhat differently, this means that the familial retardate with a chronological age of 10, an I.Q. of 70, and thus a mental age of 7, would be viewed as being at the same developmental level intellectually as a child with a chronological age of 7 and an I.Q. of 100.

In contrast, according to the defect orientation, all retardates suffer from a specific physiological or cognitive defect over and above their slower general rate of cognitive development. This view generates the expectation that, even when the rate of cognitive development is controlled, as in the situation where mental ages are matched, differences in intellectual functioning which are related to I.Q. will be found. On their face, the repeated findings of differences in performance between groups of normals and retardates matched as to mental age have lent credence to the defect theory and have cast doubt on the validity of the developmental theory.

The developmental theorist's response to these frequently reported differences has been to point out that performance on any experimental task is not inexorably the product of the subject's cognitive structure alone but reflects a variety of emotional and motivational factors as well. To the developmentalist, then, it seems more reasonable to attribute differences in performance between normals and retardates of the same mental age to motivational differences which do not inhere in mental retardation but are, rather, the result of the particular histories of the retarded subjects.

It should be noted that most theories in the area of mental retardation are basically defect theories. These differ among themselves, however. A major difference involves the theoretician's effort to relate the postulated defect to some specific physiological structure. The theoretical language of some defect theoreticians is explicitly physiological, that of others is nonphysiological, while that of others remains vague. Particular defects that have been attributed to the retarded include the following: relative impermeability of the boundaries between regions in the cognitive structure (11, 12); primary and secondary rigidity caused by subcortical and cortical malformations, respectively (13); inadequate neural satiation related to brain modifiability or cortical conductivity (14); malfunctioning disinhibitory mechanisms (*15*); improper development of the verbal system, resulting in a dissociation between verbal and motor systems (*16, 17*); relative brevity in the persistence of the stimulus trace (*18*); and impaired attention-directing mechanisms (*19*).

Where the hypothesized defect is an explicitly physiological one, it would appear to be a simple matter to obtain direct evidence that the defect does or does not exist. Such evidence would come from biochemical and physiological analyses as well as from pathological studies of familial retardates. A number of such studies have, of course, been carried out. Although there is an occasional report of some physical anomaly, the bulk of the evidence has indicated that the familial retardate does not suffer from any gross physiological defects. Indeed, if such evidence were readily available the defect theorist would cease relying on the more ambiguous data provided by studies of molar behavior. Failure to find direct evidence of a physiological defect in familial retardates has not deterred, and should not deter theorists from postulating such defects.

In spite of the negative physiological evidence, workers such as Spitz (*14*) maintain that all retardates, including familial retardates, are physically defective, and that our failure to discover defects in familial retardates is due to the relatively primitive nature of our diagnostic techniques. This view is bolstered by Masland (*20*), who has also noted the inadequacies of such techniques. It is perfectly legitimate for the defect theorist to assert that, although not at present observable, the physical defect that causes familial retardates to behave differently from normals of the same mental age will someday be seen. These theorists operate very much as the physicists of a not-too-distant era did when they asserted that the electron existed even though it was not directly observable. Analogously, defect theorists in the area of mental retardation undertake to validate the existence of a defect by first asserting that it should manifest itself in particular phenomena—that is, in particular behaviors of the retarded—and then devising experiments in which, if the predicted behavior is observed, the existence of the hypothesized defect is confirmed. Not only is this approach legitimate but, as noted above, it has become increasingly popular as well. A relatively comprehensive review of the literature emanating from the general defect position is now available (*21*). In the following paragraphs I briefly summarize the major defect positions.

An influential defect position is that of the Russian investigator A. R. Luria (*16*), whose work has now also influenced investigators in England and the United States. In the Soviet Union no distinction is made between retardates having known organic impairment and that larger group whose retardation is of unknown etiology, nor are genetic or cultural factors considered to be determinants of mental retardation. All grades of mental retardation are attributed to central-nervous-system damage believed to have occurred initially during the intrauterine period or during early childhood. Thus the diagnosis of mental retardation necessarily involves specification of a defect in some neurophysiological system; in fact, in the Soviet Union, professionals who work with the mentally retarded are called "defectologists."

Luria's interest in defective functioning appears to be an outgrowth of his more basic concern with the development of the higher cognitive processes in man. The influence of both Vygotsky and Pavlov may be seen in his work, which has been primarily concerned with the highly intricate development of the role of speech and language in regulating the child's behavior. In his comparisons between normal and retarded children, Luria has demonstrated that the behavior of retardates resembles that of chronologically younger normal children in that verbal instructions do not result in smooth regulation of motor behavior. Luria has found that retarded subjects have considerable difficulty with tasks requiring verbal mediation. Thus, Luria has inferred that the major defect in the retarded child involves an underdevelopment or a general "inertness" of the verbal system, and a dissociation of this system from the motor or action system. This dissociation is vaguely conceptualized as resulting from a disturbance in normal cortical activitiy.

The view that the behavior of a retardate resembles that of a chronologically younger child is, of course, consistent with the general developmental position. However, several English and American investigators (see, for example, 17 and 22) have demonstrated that, even with mental age level controlled, retardates have more difficulty on tasks requiring verbal mediation than normal subjects have. On the other hand, other such investigations have failed to provide support for Luria's position (23). To date, findings related to this position can best be described as equivocal.

Another major defect position is that of Herman Spitz (14), who has extended the Köhler-Wallach (24) cortical satiation theory to the area of mental retardation. According to Spitz, all retardates suffer from inadequate neural or cortical functioning; the inadequacy is best characterized by a certain sluggishness, or les-than-normal modifiability, in the functioning of cortical cells. Thus, Spitz believes that in retardates it takes longer to induce temporary, as well as permanent, electrical, chemical, and physical changes in stimulated cortical cells, and furthermore, that once such a change is produced, it is less readily modified than in the case of normal persons.

Spitz's evidence in support of his theory has come primarily from comparisons of the performance of retardates and normals of the same chronological age on a variety of perceptual tasks—for example, figural aftereffects and Necker-cube reversals. The heuristic value of Spitz's position may be seen in his recent efforts to extend his postulates beyond the visual perception area and employ them to generate specific predictions concerning the phenomena of learning, transposition, generalization, and problem solving. The evidence in favor of Spitz's position is far from clear-cut, however. Spivack (25) has pointed out that Spitz's findings are in marked contrast to those of other investigators. The very nature of many of Spitz's measures—for example, a verbal report—raises the troublesome issue of how well they reflect the perceptual responses being investigated. It should be noted that, in respect to this point as well as to other criticisms, Spitz himself has become one of the most cogent critics of his own efforts.

Many of Spitz's findings could be encompassed by the general developmental position. The developmental theorist would argue that it is not surprising that one gets different results for normals and for retardates matched with respect to chronological age, since such groups are at different developmental levels (as defined by mental age). One would be tempted to say that Spitz's work has little relevance to the issue of whether familial retardates suffer from a defect over and above their slower and more limited rate of cognitive development. However, Spitz has been quite explicit in his views that the differences he obtains are not development phenomena but reflect a physical deficit that should manifest itself even in comparisons with normal subjects matched in mental age to the retardates.

Ellis (18) has also advanced the view that the retardate is basically different from the normal individual and that this difference is a result of central-nervous-system pathology from which all retardates suffer. Ellis views this central-nervous-system pathology as producing a short-term memory deficit which, in turn, underlies the inadequacy of much of the retardate's behavior. The theoretical model presented by Ellis includes two major constructs, stimulus trace and neural integrity.

The stimulus trace, the mechanism underlying short-term memory functions, is conceptualized as a neural event or response which varies with the intensity, duration, and meaning of the stimulus situation confronting the subject. The stimulus-trace construct is thus anchored to stimulus characteristics on the one hand and to the subject's responses to these characteristics on the other. The neural-integrity construct is conceptualized as the determinant of the nature of stimulus-trace activity, and is defined by "measures of behavioral adequacy." The typical measure of neural integrity employed by Ellis is the I.Q. Thus, a person of low I.Q. is said to suffer from a lack of neural integrity. This lack, in turn, delimits or restricts stimulus-trace activity, and such restriction results in a variety of inadequate behaviors.

In support of his theory, Ellis has noted findings from numerous experiments involving short-term retention phenomena. These include studies on serial learning, delayed-reaction tasks, fixed-interval operant behavior, electroencephalographic investigations, reaction time, and factor analyses of the WISC test (the Wechsler Intelligence Scale for Children), as well as several studies of discrimination learning in brain-damaged animals (see 18). In respect to his own experimental tests, Ellis's reliance on the I.Q. as the measure of neural integrity has produced two types of comparisons: comparison of retardates and normals of the same chronological age and comparison of retardates and normals of the same mental age. In either comparison Ellis's model would predict that the retardates would be inferior on tasks involving short-term retention, due to their lower I.Q. In general, the findings obtained with groups matched as to chronological age have supported Ellis's position, while those obtained with groups matched as to mental age have not.

It should be noted that the demonstration that retardates do less well than normals of the same chronological age on tasks requiring short-term memory is a somewhat circular undertaking. It is circular to the extent that a deficit in short-term memory would influence the I.Q. score itself through its effect on certain of the intelligence subtests—for example, the digit-span test. Again, it should be emphasized that the discovery of a difference between normals and retardates of the same chronological age is just as amenable to a general developmental interpretation as to the view that all retardates suffer from central-nervous-system pathology, since the mental age of such retardates is necessarily lower than that of normal subjects in the control group.

Perhaps the oldest of the more influential defect positions is the Lewin-Kounin (*11, 12*) formulation that familial retardates are inherently more "rigid" than normal individuals of the same mental age. This position differs from the others discussed above in that the defect is conceptualized as inhering in a hypothesized cognitive structure without reference or reduction to any specific physiological entities. By the term *rigidity*, Lewin and Kounin were referring not to behaviors, as such, but rather to characteristics of the cognitive structure. These theorists felt that the essential defect, in retardation, was the lowered capacity for dynamic rearrangement in the "psychical system." This "stiffness" in cognitive functioning was conceptualized as being due to the relative impermeability of the boundaries between cells or regions of the cognitive structure. *Rigidity*, then, referred primarily to the nature of these boundaries, and to the resulting degree of communication or fluidity between regions.

Principal support for this position was contained in a series of experiments conducted by Kounin (*11*), in which he found differences between familial retardates and normals of the same mental age on a variety of tasks involving transfer phenomena, sorting, and concept-switching. Although the Lewin-Kounin position continues to receive some support (*26*), a fairly sizable amount of work (*27, 28*) now indicates that the differences discovered by Kounin between retardates and normals of the same mental age were due to differences in motivational variables rather than to an inherent cognitive rigidity of the retardate.

Lewin and Kounin appear to be the only defect theorists who have dealt adequately with the problem of etiology, which becomes a crucial issue in the controversy over the two theories. Their formulation was limited to familial retardates, and only such retardates were employed in Kounin's experiments. The other defect theorists have tended to argue that the distinction between familial and organic retardates is misleading, and, as a result, they have used groups of retardates of both types in their experiments. This presents an almost insurmountable problem when one attempts to evaluate the degree to which any uncovered differences in behavior support the major theoretical premise which underlies most defect approaches. This premise, clearly seen in the work of Luria, Spitz, and Ellis, is that all retardates, familials and organics alike, suffer from some specifiable defect. However, until the etiological issue is attended to in the research design, there is no way of assessing how much of the revealed difference between normals and retardates of the same mental age is a product of the gross organic pathology known to exist in the organic retardates included in the retarded group and how much is a product of the defect thought by the defect theorists to exist in all retardates.

The general developmental approach is applicable only to the familial retardate, and this approach does not speak to the issue of differences discovered between normal children and organic retardates. The developmental theorist also believes that, even when a difference in behavior is found between normals and familial retardates of the same mental age, it need not be attributed to any defect which inheres in familial mental retardation. Such differences are viewed as the possible outcome of differences in a variety of motivational factors which exist between the two groups. A sampling of the literature which lends credence to this view follows.

MOTIVATIONAL AND EMOTIONAL FACTORS

The view of those of us who believe that many of the reported differences between retardates and normals of the same mental age are a result of motivational and emotional differences which reflect differences in environmental histories does not imply that we ignore the importance of the lower intelligence per se. In some instances the personality characteristics of the retarded individual will reflect environmental factors that have little or nothing to do with intellectual endowment. For example, many of the effects of institutionalization may be constant, regardless of the person's intelligence level. In other instances we must think in terms of an interaction; that is, a person with low intellectual ability will have certain experiences and develop certain behavior patterns differing from those of a person with greater intellectual endowment. An obvious example of this is the greater amount of failure which the retardate typically experiences. What must be emphasized is the fact that the behavior pattern developed by the retardate as a result of such a history of failure may not differ in kind or ontogenesis from patterns developed by an individual of normal intellect who, because of some environmental circumstance, also experiences an inordinate amount of failure. By the same token, if the retardate can somehow be guaranteed a history of greater success, we would expect his behavior to be more normal, regardless of his intellectual level. Within this framework, I now discuss several of the personality factors which have been known to influence the performance of the retarded.

It has become increasingly clear that our understanding of the performance of the institutionalized familial retardate will be enhanced if we consider the inordinate amount of social deprivation these individuals have experienced before being placed in institutions (29, 30). A series of recent studies (30–34) has indicated that one result of such early deprivation is a heightened motivation to interact with a supportive adult. These studies suggest that, given this heightened motivation, retardates exhibit considerable compliance with instructions when the effect of such compliance is to increase or maintain the social interaction with the adult. These findings would appear to be consistent with the often-made observation that the retarded seek attention and desire affection (35–36).

Recent findings suggest that the perseveration so frequently noted in the behavior of the retarded is primarily a function of these motivational factors rather than a result of inherent cognitive rigidity, as suggested by

Lewin (*12*) and Kounin (*11*). Evidence is now available indicating (i) that the degree of perseveration is directly related to the degree of deprivation the individual experienced before being institutionalized (*30*), and (ii) that institutionalized children of normal intellect are just as perseverative as institutionalized retardates, while noninstitutionalized retardates are no more perseverative than noninstitutionalized children of normal intellect (*31, 32*).

Although there is considerable evidence that social deprivation results in a heightened motivation to interact with a supportive adult, it appears to have other effects as well. The nature of these effects is suggested in observations of fearfulness, wariness, or avoidance of strangers on the part of retardates, or of suspicion and mistrust (*36, 37*). The experimental work done by Zigler and his associates on the behavior of institutionalized retarded individuals has indicated that social deprivation results in both a heightened motivation to interact with supportive adults (a positive-reaction tendency) and a wariness of doing so (a negative-reaction tendency). The construct of a negative-reaction tendency has been employed to explain certain differences between retardates and normals reported by Kounin, differences that have heretofore been attributed to the greater cognitive rigidity of retarded individuals. For instance, it has been demonstrated (*38*) that, once the institutionalized familial retardate's wariness has been allayed, he becomes much more responsive than the normal individual to social reinforcement. Thus, a motivational rather than a cognitive factor would seem to underlie certain rather mysterious behavioral phenomena frequently observed in familial retardates—for example, a tendency to persist longer on the second of two highly similar tasks than on the first.

Both positive- and negative-reaction tendencies have been recently investigated in a series of studies, with children of normal intellect (*39*), directed at further validation of the "valence position." Stated most simply, this position asserts that the effectiveness of an adult as a reinforcing agent depends upon the valence he has for the particular child whose behavior is being reinforced. (An adult's valence for a child refers to the degree to which that adult is sought or avoided by the child.) This valence is determnied by the child's history of positive and negative experiences with adults. The studies noted above have produced considerable evidence that prior positive contacts between the child and the adult increase the adult's effectiveness as a reinforcer, while negative contacts decrease it. If the experimentally manipulated negative encounters in these experiments are viewed as experimental analogs of encounters institutionalized retardates actually have experienced, then the often-reported reluctance of such children to interact with adults and their wariness of such encounters become understandable. Thus it would appear that their relatively high negative-reactive tendency motivates them toward behaviors, such as withdrawal, that reduce the quality of their performance to a level lower than that which one would expect on the basis of their intellectual capacity alone.

Another factor frequently mentioned as a determinant in the performance of the retarded is their high expectancy of failure. This failure expectancy has been viewed as an outgrowth of a lifetime characterized by confrontations with tasks with which they are intellectually ill-equippedt o deal. The work of Cromwell and his colleagues (40) has lent support to the general proposition that retardates have a higher expectancy of failure than normals have, and that this results in a style of problem-solving in which the retardate is much more highly motivated to avoid failure than to achieve success. However, the results of experimental work with retardates to investigate the success-failure dimension are still somewhat inconsistent, suggesting that even such a relatively simple proposition as this one is in need of further refinement.

Recent studies (31, 33, 41) have indicated that the many failures experienced by retardates generate a cognitive style of problem-solving characterized by outer-directedness. That is, the retarded child comes to distrust his own solutions to problems and therefore seeks guides to action in the immediate environment. This outer-directedness may explain the great suggestibility so frequently observed in the retarded child. Evidence has now been presented indicating that, relative to normals of the same mental age, the retarded child is more sensitive to verbal cues from an adult, is more imitative of the behavior of adults and of his peers, and does more visual scanning. Furthermore, certain findings (31) suggest that the noninstitutionalized retardate is more outer-directed in his problem-solving than the institutionalized retardate is. This makes considerable sense if one remembers that the noninstitutionalized retardate lives in an environment that is not adjusted to his intellectual shortcomings and, therefore, probably experiences more failure than the institutionalized retardate.

Another nonintellective factor important in understanding the behavior of the retarded is the retardate's motivation to obtain various types of reinforcement. The social-deprivation work discussed indicates that retardates have an extremely strong desire for attention, praise, and encouragement. Several investigators (40, 42) have suggested that, in normal development, the effectiveness of attention and praise as reinforcers diminishes with maturity and is replaced by the reinforcement inherent in the awareness that one is correct. This latter type of reinforcer appears to serve primarily as a cue for self-reinforcement.

Zigler and his associates (27, 43, 44) have argued that various experiences in the lives of the retarded cause them to care less about being correct simply for the sake of correctness than normals of the same mental age. In other words, these investigators have argued that the position of various reinforcers in the reinforcer hierarchies of normal and of retarded children of the same mental age differ.

Clearest support for the view that the retardate cares much less about being correct than the middle-class child of normal intellect does is contained in a study by Zigler and deLabry (43). These investigators found, as Kounin (11) did, that when the only reinforcement was the information that the child was correct, retardates were poorer on a concept-switching task than middle-class normal children of the same mental age. However, when Zigler and deLabry added another condition, reward with a toy of the child's choice for concept-switching, they found that the retardates performed as well as the middle-class normal children. Since the satisfaction of giving the correct response is the incentive typically used in experimental studies, one wonders how many of the differences in performance found between retardates and normals are actually attributable to differences in capacity rather than to differences in the values such incentives may have for the two types of subjects.

Much of this work on motivational and emotional factors in the performance of the retarded is very recent. The research on several of the factors discussed is more suggestive than definitive. It is clear, however, that these factors are extremely important in determining the retardate's level of functioning. This is not to assert that these motivational factors cause familial mental retardation but to say, rather, that they lead to the retardate's behaving in a manner less effective than that dictated by his intellectual capacity. An increase in knowledge concerning motivational and emotional factors and their ontogenesis and manipulation would hold considerable promise for alleviating much of the social ineffectiveness displayed by that rather sizable group of persons who must function at a relatively low intellectual level.

SUMMARY

The heterogeneous nature of mental retardation, as well as certain common practices of workers in the area, has resulted in a variety of conceptual ambiguities. Considerable order could be brought to the area if, instead of viewing all retardates as a homogeneous group arbitrarily defined by some I.Q. score, workers would clearly distinguish between the group of retardates known to suffer from some organic defect and the larger group of retardates referred to as familial retardates. It is the etiology of familial retardation that currently constitutes the greatest mystery.

A number of authorities have emphasized the need for employing recent polygenic models of inheritance in an effort to understand the familial retardate. While appreciating the importance of environment in affecting the distribution determined by genetic inheritance, these workers have argued that familial retardates are not essentially different from individuals of greater intellect, but represent, rather, the lower portion of the intellectual curve which reflects normal intellectual variability. As emphasized by the two-group approach, retardates with known physiological or organic defect are viewed as presenting a quite different etiological problem. The familial retardate, on the other hand, is seen as a perfectly normal expression of the population gene pool, of slower and more limited intellectual development than the individual of average intellect.

This view generates the proposition that retardates and normals at the same general cognitive level—that is, of the same mental age—are similar in respect to their cognitive functioning. However, such a proposition runs headlong into findings that retardates and normals of the same mental age often differ in performance. Such findings have bolstered what is currently the most popular theoretical approach to retarded functioning —namely, the view that all retardates suffer from some specific defect which inheres in mental retardation and thus makes the retardate immutably "different" from normals, even when the general level of intellectual development is controlled. While these defect or difference approaches, as exemplified in the work of Luria, Spitz, Ellis, and Lewin and Kounin, dominate the area of mental retardation, the indirect, and therefore equivocal, nature of the evidence of these workers has generated considerable controversy.

In contrast to this approach, the general developmental position has emphasized systematic evaluation of the role of experiential, motivational, and personality factors. As a central thesis, this position asserts that performance on experimental and real-life tasks is never the single inexorable product of the retardate's cognitive structure but, rather, reflects a wide variety of relatively nonintellective factors which greatly influence the general adequacy of performance. Thus, many of the reported behavioral differences between normals and retardates of the same mental age are seen as products of motivational and experiential differences between these groups, rather than as the result of any inherent cognitive deficiency in the retardates. Factors thought to be of particular importance in the behavior of the retardate are social deprivation and the positive- and negative-reaction tendencies to which such deprivation gives rise: the high number of failure experiences and the particular approach to problem-solving which they generate; and atypical reinforcer hierarchies.

There is little question that we are witnessing a productive, exciting, and perhaps inevitably chaotic period in the history of man's concern with the problem of mental retardation. Even the disagreements that presently exist must be considered rather healthy phenomena. These disagreements will unquestionably generate new knowledge which, in the hands of practitioners, may become the vehicle through which the performance of children, regardless of intellectual level, may be improved.

REFERENCES AND NOTES

1. G. A. Jervis, in *American Handbook of Psychiatry*, S. Arieti, Ed. (Basic Books, New York, 1959), vol. 2, pp. 1289–1313.
2. J. Hirsch, *Science* 142, 1436 (1963).
3. I. L. Gottesman, in *Handbook of Mental Deficiency*, N. R. Ellis, Ed. (McGraw-Hill, New York, 1963), pp. 253–296.
4. L. S. Penrose, *The Biology of Mental Defect* (Sidgwick and Jackson, London, 1963).
5. C. Burt and M. Howard, *Brit. J. Statist. Psychol.* 9, 95 (1956).
6. _____, *ibid.* 10, 33 (1957); C. C. Hurst, in *Proc. Roy. Soc. London Ser. B.* 112, 80 (1932); R. W. Pickford, *J. Psychol.* 28, 129 (1949).
7. G. Allen, *Amer. J. Mental Deficiency* 62, 840 (1958); C. Burt, *Amer. Psychologist* 13, 1 (1958).
8. G. E. McClearn, in *Psychology in the Making*, L. Postman, Ed. (Knopf, New York, 1962), pp. 144–252.
9. J. A. F. Roberts, *Eugenics Rev.* 44, 71 (1952).
10. E. O. Lewis, *J. Mental Sci.* 79, 298 (1933).
11. J. Kounin, *Character and Personality* 9, 251 (1941); *ibid.*, p. 273.
12. K. Lewin, *A Dynamic Theory of Personality* (McGraw-Hill, New York, 1936).
13. K. Goldstein, *Character and Personality* 11, 209 (1942–43).
14. H. H. Spitz, in *Handbook of Mental Deficiency*, N. R. Ellis, Ed. (McGraw-Hill, New York, 1963), pp. 11–40.
15. P. S. Siegel and J. G. Foshee, *J. Abnormal Soc. Psychol.* 61, 141 (1960).
16. A. R. Luria, in *Handbook of Mental Deficiency*, N. R. Ellis, Ed. (McGraw-Hill, New York, 1963), pp. 353–387.
17. N. O'Connor and B. Hermelin, *J. Abnormal Soc. Psychol.* 59, 409 (1959).

18. N. R. Ellis, in *Handbook of Mental Deficiency*, N. R. Ellis, Ed. (McGraw-Hill, New York, 1963), pp. 134–158.
19. D. Zeaman and B. J. House, *ibid.*, p. 159.
20. R. L. Masland, *Amer. J. Mental Deficiency* 64, 305 (1959).
21. E. Zigler, in *Review of Child Development Research*, M. L. Hoffman and L. W. Hoffman, Eds. (Russell Sage Foundation, New York, in press), vol. 2.
22. N. A. Milgram and H. G. Furth, *Amer. J. Mental Deficiency* 67, 733 (1963); *ibid.* 70, 849. (1966).
23. D. Balla and E. Zigler, *J. Abnormal Soc. Psychol.* 69, 664 (1964); M. Rieber, *Amer. J. Mental Deficiency* 68, 634 (1964).
24. W. Köhler and H. Wallach, *Proc. Amer. Phil. Soc.* 88, 269 (1964).
25. G. Spivack, in *Handbook of Mental Deficiency*, N. R. Ellis, Ed. (McGraw-Hill, New York, 1963), pp. 480–511.
26. M. Budoff and W. Pagel, "Learning potential and rigidity in the adolescent mentally retarded," paper presented before the Society for Research in Child Development, Minneapolis, Minn., March 1965.
27. E. Zigler, in *Readings on the Exceptional Child*, E. P. Trapp and P. Himelstein, Eds. (Appleton-Century-Crofts, New York, 1962), pp. 141–162.
28. ————, in *International Review of Research in Mental Retardation*, N. R. Ellis, Ed. (Academic Press, New York, 1966), vol. 1, pp. 77–105.
29. A. D. B. Clarke and A. M. Clarke, *Brit. J. Psychol.* 45, 197 (1954); D. Kaplun, *Proc. Amer. Assoc. Mental Deficiency* 40, 68 (1935).
30. E. Zigler, *J. Abnormal Soc. Psychol.* 62, 413 (1961).
31. C. Green and E. Zigler, *Child Develop.* 33, 499 (1962).
32. E. Zigler, *J. Personality* 31, 258 (1963).
33. ————, L. Hodgden, H. Stevenson, *ibid.* 26, 106 (1958).
34. R. Shepps and E. Zigler, *Amer. J. Mental Deficiency* 67, 262 (1962); H. Stevenson and L. Fahel, *J. Personality* 29, 136 (1961); E. Zigler and J. Williams, *J. Abnormal Soc. Psychol.* 66, 197 (1963).
35. W. M. Cruickshank, *J. Clin. Psychol.* 3, 381 (1947); E. E. Doll, in *Readings on the Exceptional Child*, E. P. Trapp and P. Himelstein, Eds. (Appleton-Century-Crofts, New York, 1962), pp. 21–68.
36. E. A. Hirsh, *Amer. J. Mental Deficiency* 63, 639 (1959); B. L. Wellman, *Childhood Educ.* 15, 108 (1938).
37. M. Woodward, *Brit. J. Med. Psychol.* 33, 123 (1960).
38. P. Shallenberger and E. Zigler, *J. Abnormal Soc. Psychol.* 63, 20 (1961); E. Zigler, thesis, Univ. of Texas, Austin, 1958.
39. H. Berkowitz, E. C. Butterfield, E. Zigler, *J. Personality Soc. Psychol.* 2, 706 (1965); H. Berkowitz and E. Zigler, *ibid.*, p. 500; N. McCoy and E. Zigler, *ibid.* 1, 604 (1965).
40. R. L. Cromwell, in *Handbook of Mental Deficiency*, N. R. Ellis, Ed. (McGraw-Hill, New York, 1963), pp. 41–91.
41. J. Turnure and E. Zigler, *J. Abnormal Soc. Psychol.* 69, 427 (1964).
42. E. Beller, *J. Genet. Psychol.* 87, 25 (1955); J. Gewirtz, *Monographs Soc. Res. Child Develop. No. 59* (1954), p. 19; G. Heathers, *J. Genet. Psychol.* 87, 37 (1955); E. Zigler, *Amer. J. Orthopsychiat.* 33, 614 (1963).
43. E. Zigler and J. deLabry, *J. Abnormal Soc. Psychol.* 65, 267 (1962).
44. E. Zigler and E. Unell, *Amer. J. Mental Deficiency* 66, 651 (1962).
45. I am deeply indebted to Susan Harter for her help in organizing this article and for her assistance in clarifying many of the ideas presented. Preparation of the paper was facilitated by research grant MH–06809 from the National Institutes of Mental Health and by the Gunnar Dybwad award of the National Association for Retarded Children.

27.   Students, Stress and the College Experience

Edward J. Shoben, Jr.

The temper of student mood on large university cam-
puses across the nation has rapidly become one of dis-
content and unrest. Against this background, the
National Conference on Student Stress was convened
in 1965 at the Airlie House in Warrenton, Virginia.
Student and faculty representatives from 33 colleges
attended as did 35 consultants in the behavioral sciences.
Three basic themes were reported—the desire for a
more functional education related to modern life, more
genuine personal relationships with faculty and a
greater voice in the determination of their education.

THE CRUCIAL ISSUE

Within the not always painless openness of the conference, a great deal of attention was predictably paid to the problem of student access to the faculty. The yearning to talk with professors on terms of equality, to have them "level with us," and to "know what they really think" was frequently expressed. When this demand for personalized attention was interpreted—significantly, by a faculty member—as dependency and an insistence on rights without responsibilities, the record was quickly and clamorously set straight. In the heated words of one student, "We don't want to have our hands held or our head patted. We want a really good education."

Here was the crucial issue: What is the nature of a good education for today's college students? The participants in Warrenton, like a hundred generations before them, wrestled valiantly if a little fearfully with the great question; and if, at the end of their days together, they fell short of unanimity, they still had cogent things to say. On at least two points,

In *Students, Stress and the College Experience.* U. S. National Student Association, May, 1966. Pp. 15–23. Reprinted with the permission of the publisher and author.

there seemed to be a considerable consensus. First, although the defining lineaments of a good education may not be conceptually clear, there is a widely shared sense that very few colleges and universities offer programs that embody them; and second, the lack of "a really good education" is the central source of student stress.

Such judgments can be ignored only by the most irresponsible of administrative leaders and faculty members, but the conference also provided more positive guides to presidents, deans, and professors who take genuine pride in the constant renewal of the college's strength and meaning. One criterion of a good education, strongly urged by a vocal and committed group of students, is relevance—relevance to the world of modern politics and social ferment, revelance to the human condition in mass society, relevance to the doubts, fears, and hopes of thoughtful youth. Three episodes describe the referent for "relevance" in this context.

Late one evening, a tall, quiet undergraduate at a big midwestern university suddenly disengaged himself from his coke to stand over one of the consultants who had been asking a group of students about their experiences in Mississippi. His voice was tight but his words were clear. "Why do you guys keep badgering us about what we do in the South or on picket lines? It's a little more exciting, but it's not very different from what we're doing when we work in mental hospitals or tutor Negro kids. That's where we really learn what kind of world we're living in and how to get along in it. We don't in your goddam classrooms." Within minutes, the student and the consultant were sketching a course in which classwork would be an exercise in disciplined and informed reflection on field work in the civil rights movement, the education of the culturally disadvantaged, or community mental health programs.

The second episode involves an analysis submitted a few days after the conference. It is worth quoting at length:

> Our position has grown paradoxically out of a new commitment to traditional liberal values. The traditional liberal accorded the individual the highest status in society; the individual is the end toward which all else was merely a means. But in serving this idea, the traditional liberal invented the seeping bureaucracies he thought necessary to reach systematically every citizen. The problem of how to maintain the identity of the individual in this process, however, has become our inheritance. The civil rights movement has most clearly pointed up this problem. The American Negro represented one of the most passive elements in our society. One of the reasons for his plight was "organized America," which kept him in his place by the sheer weight of its structures. It became the task of the civil rights worker to convince Negroes that by standing up and asserting their individual identities, they could have some impact on their communities.
>
> On the campus, a student who understands this is outraged by the individual values that have been applied to the educational process and by the bureaucratic models that the university follows in its organizational patterns. We find these things anathema to the realization of our objective, i.e., the resurrection of the individual. The structural-functional approach is itself irrelevant, or, worse, de-

structive. It's this reliance on bureaucracy, the manipulation of structures, and the analysis of functions that makes some of us say "Don't trust anyone over 30."

Our solution is to inject into the system more human qualities, the most obvious of which is emotion. Perhaps the combination of the McCarthy era and the departmental approach to knowledge has sterilized the academic process. It has certainly made it irrelevant to activist students because they have seen what a commitment to ideals can do for a group of people if it is fearlessly defended in front of the cameras of human conscience. No wonder the educational experience bugs us with its shallowness when professors aren't willing to lay their competence on the line publicly. Why load us with principles and ideals that obviously are less important than a $14,000.00-a-year job and tenure? We want ideas that are worth some passion.

The educational experience must be made relevant through a new solution. Just another new structure won't liberate the thinking of the student and open him up to the real learning experience—the one that goes on inside when we really try to examine ourselves. We need relationships with teachers who will help us face the big tough hang-ups: Am I a moral pacifist or a coward? Is abortion a humane answer to the problems of unwed motherhood, and what has the pill got to do with my answer? Who am I, where am I, where am I headed, and do I really want to go there? Is an academic career any less sterile than one in business? What are the things that make a society really worth fighting for?

No structure will ever open up the professor and the student to problems like these. Instead, we have to reshape the educational experience so the professor is more than a mechanism for dispensing information that enables the student to get the *symbols* of success.

Independently, another student had made the same point: "Everyone in the universities thinks too much about structures. They're important, but the new focus must be primarily on making the structures compatible with people, and the people more generous to each other in the structures."

The third "episode" is really a medley of interchanges defining a common theme of variety in a truly educational experience. At one point in a somewhat disjointed but heated discussion of student-faculty relationships, an animated girl took the floor, shaking her dark hair impatiently. "Look," she said. "Maybe we've grabbed onto the faculty because they're more tangible than what we really have in mind. What we're really looking for is a lot of different things, isn't it? For some of us, it's being in a community where people think and talk about human experience in perspective. For others, it's earning a ticket to a good job. For others, it's just the fun of learning new things, whether they're especially important or not. For still others of us, it's building up the skills to handle the world better—coping with each other, earning a living, knowing how to deal with kids some day, having a say in our communities. They're all all right; but they're different, and we're different, and we change. If we knew how to pick our schools, we might have better experiences; but because we change, that wouldn't work anyway. A good school has to keep up with us, to provide different experiences as we change and maybe even grow."

The girl's comments came up at dinner that evening. A stocky young man with expressive hands gestured vigorously. "She's right. I want to tap my school's resources, pick the brains of my profs, and make damn' sure I don't come out the same thing I was as a freshman. But *I* want to do the changing, not be moulded by the establishment. I just want to be sure they have something for me as I change." And one of the discussion groups reported a segment of its deliberations in this form:

> Our colleges are a bit too much like high schools, and because we're no longer high school students, we find this stressful. Students may not be very mature when they first enroll at a university, but they are looking forward to the freedom to make mistakes and the help of capable people to set them right when they are made. If we weren't going to make errors in judgment or performance sometimes, we wouldn't have to go to college. We don't want protection. We want a chance to think for ourselves about politics and morals and how we can earn good livings but keep our integrity. What we get is a choice of a profession with a lot of little packages tied to the thread that leads to medicine or business administration or engineering, and the packages are called philosophy and economics and what-have-you. They are too seldom geared to us and what we are, too seldom taught by people who want to find out about us, and too seldom informed by our efforts to make our needs known. We don't know how. That's one of the reasons we came to college—to find out, not to be filled up with facts and ideas that other people believe are important.

The crucial issue, then was that of dynamically redefining a good education for today's youth. The response of the conference, by no means unanimous but still powerful, was that any viable definition must embrace three elements: relevance to a world of rapid social change, the infusion of a passionate commitment to the individual as the *sine qua non* of value into the educational process, and a readiness to meet diverse and changing needs to explore very different developmental opportunities. What the last item means, above all, is that at least a significant segment of current student bodies are demanding a voice in the shaping of their own education—not as a right and not because they feel themselves necessarily wiser than their elders, but because they profoundly believe that exercising this responsible privilege is itself educative. A major challenge to many institutions is precisely that of devising the conditions under which students may properly test this conviction.

True enough, there were other ideas expressed at Airlie House. A number of participants reported worries about admission to graduate school as central forms of stress. Indeed, to many of the faculty members and consultants, the widely shared interest among students in ultimately joining the professoriate was a sizeable surprise. Whether these aspirations arose from a desire to set right the academic world by operating inside it or from more positive identifications with university personnel was far from clear, but the frequency of such ambitions lent an extra degree of cogency to the conferees' criticisms.

Another theme, developed as a kind of offset and corrective to the emphasis on emotion as prerequisite to humanizing the campus, was that of intellectual discipline. "Having a heart is all right," said one man, "but what about a brain to express what the heart has to say in terms that society can understand? If you alienate people by the way you say and do things, it doesn't matter whether your ideas are humane or not. You won't get anywhere." Another put it this way: "All that marching is good for society, but it doesn't really mean anything for us unless we march with a book in front of our nose." Still another reminded the conference that there is no intrinsic conflict between particular students and particular faculty members or administrators. Objecting to the phrase "straw students"—meaning academic Uncle Toms who trade their integrity for favor among the college's official personnel—he urged that "it was only reasonable" to accord teachers the authority won by their training and "to give them a chance in their own way to help us learn." Not without his supporters, this student was still stopped short by the blunt question of "Learn what?"

In conversation afterward, several of the consultants found a touch of despair in the ease by which such an articulate young man had been put down. Even for those who had made an initial commitment to it, it seemed, the intellectual life as presented to undergraduates is too vague, too fuzzy in its apparent goals, to be both compellingly attractive and easily defensible to those of more activist persuasions. The activist can formulate relatively clear aims on the basis of objectives animating social movements in the larger world; in consequence, he can give the strong impression, to himself in some instances as well as to others, that he knows and is secure in the object of his quest. Similarly, the career-oriented student typically finds his mentors able to provide goals that rationalize in at least reasonably convincing ways the steps required for their attainment. But the enterprise of intellect, disconnected from either the rewards of livelihood or the instrumental role it may play in social activism, seems to be, in the minds of some extremely able college students, a somewhat foggy and goalless affair.

For at least two of the so-called "adults" at the conference, that thought uneasily postponed sleep on that autumnal Virginia night. They hope that this report will have a more productive effect on a number of the leaders of American higher education.

TO SEE OURSELVES

That more productive effect, however, will entail more than a renovation of the curriculum and a clearer demonstration of humane commitments on the part of faculty and administrators. It must also take into account the way in which large numbers of able students perceive the campus community. The accuracy of these perceptions is, of course, a major issue; but it must be remembered that perceptions define a reality of their own, and elements of distortion in them hardly prevent their having a strongly determinative influence on attitudes and performance. A recurrent question raised at Airlie House, sometimes obliquely and sometimes directly, was that of whether we who occupy academic positions can see ourselves as students see us and respond constructively to that image.

For much of the stress that students experience in college grows out of a sense of dealing with adversaries. The corpus of institutional rules, for example—ranging from student dress through deadlines for papers to dormitory hours—are resented less because they are unreasonable than because they are disrespectful. In student eyes, these regulations are neither aimed at the personal development of youth nor formulated as embodiments of the university's distinctive values. Students understand the role of restraints, although they may chafe under them, in personal growth; and they are, for the most part, prepared to honor, even when they disagree with them, those men and organizations that take clear-cut and well rationalized stands on valuational matters. Their complaint is that many of the rules to which they are subject are imposed only to make the college run with more efficient blandness.

The editor of a student newspaper concretized the point. Expansively verbal, he became incoherent with anger in reporting that, asked to raise a proportion of his budget through advertising, he had been denied the sale of space to breweries. The reason given was that ads for beer might put in jeopardy gifts to the college from teetotaling potential donors.

One of the most dramatic events at the conference bore on the same problem. A student, arguing for the right of young men and women to visit each other in residence halls without regard to the clock, used the phrase "twenty-four-hour intervisitation rules." A young professor from a distinguished eastern university leaped to his feet, infuriated by what he took to be the hypocritical rhetoric involved, and translated the term into a taste-violating Anglo-Saxonism. After a moment of startled silence, it was the students who set him straight. While sexual intercourse is not unknown among undergraduates, it was *not* the point under discussion. The issue was one of social access and the right of privacy in conversation, unhampered by the ghosts of Victorian chaperones rattling doorknobs.

What is objectionable about the modal rules segregating men and women in dormitories is two things, both of which arouse student contempt. One is their ineffectualness: The regulations hardly prevent sexual contact among those who are interested in it; they simply change its setting. The other is their underlying assumptions—that sexual intimacy is more important to youth than the broader and deeper intimacies of friendship, that college students are incapable of exercising controls over their sexual impulses, and that undergraduate sexuality threatens the college with a fatal embarrassment. "Why the discrimination?" asked one of the conferees. "Kids from my high school class who didn't come to the university now have apartments of their own and can call on each other as they please. I'm not going to make a lot of noise about it, but I hope that college has helped me be at least as mature as they are."

The illustrations could be extensively multiplied, but the point is clear. For many thoughtful students, our halls of learning are littered with regulations enforced by bureaucrats, and the bureaucrats can only be conceived as adversaries. They are adversaries in the sense of being persons who are doing something *to* or *for* students without maintaining any ongoing relationship *with* students. Granting that curricular sequences are planned with his interests in view, the undergraduate still yearns to play a more determinative role and to enjoy more flexibility in planning his areas of concentration and distribution. Generally in agreement with the faculty on such matters, he still wants a voice in the formulation of speaker policies. Understanding the need for order in a big organization, he wonders what is so sacred about class hours, course schedules, and academic terms that they, rather than the subject matter and his own involvement, must shape the rhythms of his concern for an idea, a body of information, or a special project. Drawn to a particular school by the scholarly lustre of its faculty, he is bitterly disappointed by his lack of access to their minds and their personalities, and one feature of the conflict is his efforts, often bumbling and graceless, to achieve that access through the barricades of formal office hours, separate dining facilities, and the realities and excuses of the publish-or-perish regulation.

The experience of a faculty participant from a border-state university is relevant here. At one point in the academic year, he met with a group of Negro students, many of them juniors and seniors. Apart from the uneasiness associated with their racial identity in an institution only recently opened to Negroes, they had one major and unanimous complaint: None of them had ever had a conversation with a professor without a relatively formal and predetermined agenda. Upset by this information and inclined to interpret it in racial terms, the faculty member shortly thereafter met with the new members of Pan-Hel, attractive and advantaged girls whose college careers had been successful by virtually all the ordinary standards. They had one major and unanimous complaint: None of them had ever had a conversation with a professor without a relatively formal and predetermined agenda!

Sheer access here is far less important than the opposition, the gulf between the patterns of value that are, on both sides, far from clearly formulated and explained. An intense girl from a new midwestern university, her sorority pin worn proudly, clarified the issue. Leaning across the table in her discussion group, she addressed a faculty member:

> Look! College has been fun, and I'm glad I went. I'm going to be even more glad to get out. You lay down the requirements and set the rules. You tell us our educations are going to be a big benefit to us as people, and you teach us. Then you grade us. It's pretty clear to me that the grades don't have much to do with the big benefits we're supposed to get, but they make a big difference in what we can do in school, to our parents, and to the kinds of jobs we're likely to get. The grades are important but not for the reason you say they are. We want 'em so we can play basketball or be a May Queen candidate. That's what they're worth; they don't tell us anything about our big benefits. So to get them we try to out-psych you, and some of us even cheat.

The older members of the academic community may wonder, as its older members have always done, at the implications of this outburst—the values placed on basketball and popularity, the expressed willingness to cheat for short-term goals that seem, *sub-specie aeternitatis,* a little tawdry. But as the older and more permanent inhabitants of that community, had we better not listen carefully? It is hard to escape the inference that these learnings, regardless of what we have tried to teach, are the ones that willy-nilly we have somehow facilitated. It is even harder to avoid the sinking feeling that the liberating, growth-inducing, moral purposes of education have fallen into a rather ruinous state. Still declared, those purposes, in the light of practices perceived by students, have become words, words, words. Instead of focusing on the "big benefits" of greater self-knowledge and an enlarged and humane familiarity with a complex world, the process of evaluation becomes a duel between adversaries for the mere symbols of athletic or political eligibility.

To make the point in this fashion obviously overstates it, but our concern here is less with objective precision and more with communicating the distress and disappointment of students who, searching for the "big benefits," feel that they must settle for grades wrung, by fair means or foul, from an opponent.

Even if this view of the academy is inaccurate, it won't disappear by virtue of its being ignored, and it suggests two possible problems of considerable vitality. One is the extent to which the sense of *communitas* has been weakened as an essential setting in which humane educational objectives can be pursued. The other is the degree to which a kind of educational Gresham's law operates on our campuses where cheap motivations drive out more significant ones—where the desire for empty grades supplants the desire to learn, where memorization supersedes the quest for meaningful relationships, where out-psyching the professor displaces a common hunt for contemporary significance in our traditions and a shared and vigorous reflection on the things that matter most to living men. Again, the leaders of our colleges and universities need not always concur in the sometimes harsh judgments of some of their best students to find in them the stimulus for an imaginative review of their institutional aims, policies, and procedures.

28.   Their Stories Tell Their Feelings: Problems of Highly Creative Children

E. Paul Torrance

Evidence reported by E. Paul Torrance suggests that creative students: (1) are subjected to pressure toward conformity; (2) are pushed to develop a well-rounded

The Gifted Child Quarterly, Summer, 1961, 31–34. Reprinted with the permission of the publisher and author.

*personality; and (3) find their divergency to be equated
with emotional disturbance or immaturity. Despite the
need of a changing society for innovation, it appears
that we do not even regard positive deviancies as desirable.*

Inescapably, the individual who thinks of a new idea is in the very beginning a minority of one. Even when matters of demonstrable fact are involved, as in the Asch experiments, there are very few people who can
tolerate being a minority of one. Since creativity involves independence
of mind, nonconformity to group pressures, or breaking out of the mould,
it is inevitable that highly creative children experience some unusual problems of adjustment. Thus, the highly creative child must either repress his
creativity or learn to cope with the tensions which arise from being frequently a minority of one. Repression of creative needs may lead to actual
personality breakdown. Their expression frequently leads to loneliness, conflicts, and other problems of adjustment. Educators of gifted children need
to understand both types of problems.

SANCTIONS AGAINST DIVERGENCY

In one of our studies, we have asked approximately 5,000 children in
grades three through six to write imaginative stories concerning animals
or persons with some divergent characteristic. These have given us many
insights concerning the way children see the operation of their society's
sanctions against being different. The following story by a sixth-grade
girl illustrates many of these sanctions:

> Far into the jungle of Africa lived a flying monkey named Pepper.
> Pepper was a well-educated monkey and very cute. . . . Pepper was
> unusual too. He was not like all of the other flying monkeys. You
> see, Pepper didn't eat bananas like everybody else. He wanted to be
> different. He ate peppers!
>   No one ever went out of the jungle so Pepper, being different,
> decided to go to America! . . . When the people saw him, they began
> to laugh and then others began to scream. Then out of nowhere a
> man from a zoo came and took Pepper by surprise. . . .
>   Now Pepper was sad. He didn't like the cage they put him in.
> He made a vow that if he ever got out he would never be different
> again and ten minutes later he saw some bent bars high enough to
> fly through. All of a sudden he flew out and in two days was back
> in the jungle. He kept his promise too. He was never different
> again. He was a good little flying monkey.

I suppose *he ate his bananas!*

About two-thirds of the stories about flying monkeys tell similar tales
of conformity or of destruction. Some cultures, however, are more indul-

gent of divergency than others. Stories written by gifted children in special classes are far more hopeful in outlook than those of gifted children in regular classes. In about 70 per cent of the stories of pupils in classes for high achieving children, the flying monkey is in some way able to persist in his flying. The stories written by children in a small Oklahoma town composed of Indians, whites, and a few Negroes also reflect this tolerance of divergency. In 74 per cent of their stories, the flying monkey succeeds.

CREATIVE CHILDREN MAY NOT BE WELL-ROUNDED

The highly creative child is likely to have lagged in some phase of his development. Many investigators in a variety of fields have been disappointed to find that outstanding individuals in the field under study are not well-rounded, "all-American" boys. Verbal abilities frequently will be below some of their other abilities. Perhaps the most inventive and imaginative child we have tested is a boy who has had unusual difficulty in learning to read, yet his store of information and his ability to use it imaginatively in solving problems and developing ideas is fantastic.

This problem is particularly acute at the fourth-grade level. In a number of cases, fourth graders identified by our tests as highly creative have been reevaluated by teachers. Teachers then discover that these children are far more knowledgeable and thoughtful than they had imagined. One examiner after testing orally a certain fourth-grade boy remarked: "This boy impresses me as the kind of individual who will become a top executive who can dictate to five secretaries at the same time without becoming confused." The boy's responses gave evidence of high inventive level, flexibility, and originality. This boy, however, has a serious reading disability and ranked near the bottom of his class on the written test of creative thinking.

Because verbal skills are highly valued in our society, tremendous pressures are placed on children to be "well-rounded" in this respect. The relentlessness of these pressures is symbolized in the following story by a sixth-grade girl:

> Quack! Quack! They were after him again—the Ladies Duck Aid Society, with their hair up in pin curls and their screaming, fat ducklings swimming and holding onto their skirts. They never failed. Alas! It was getting too much for little Glob-Blob. Every day there would be quacking and screaming of ducklings while poor Glob-Blob would run as fast as he could to get away from the vicious ducks.
>
> The reason for this was because poor Glob-Blob could not quack. So every day the Ladies Duck Aid Society would chase Glob-Blob, for they said it was for the good of the ducks, and it was not only right but they were doing a good turn.
>
> It was lucky for Glob-Blob that the ducks were fat and flabby, for if they were limber, I will not mention what would happen. But one day, these lazy ducks did reduce, and when chasing Glob-Blob dealt him a good many hard blows. And the next day, poor Glob-Blob was at last doomed. The vicious quackers had come and the

chase was on. Glob-Blob was failing. It is a shame that so noble a duck should be doomed, but 'That's life,' said Glob-Blob to himself as, slowly but surely, failing, he dropped to the ground. The quackers, very pleased with themselves, sat down for a chat.

But I shall always remember Glob-Blob and his death. So I shall let him finish his journey, where there will be no more quackers and chasers, and where at last, he may have passionless peace forever.

Many children must consider their counselors, teachers, and parents as "quackers and chasers" when we work so hard to make them become "better rounded personalities." They might contribute far more to society and be far happier and more successful by capitalizing upon their unique strengths rather than spending fruitless energy trying hopelessly to compensate for some divergent characteristic or behavior. I would not, of course, deny that it is necessary for some of our highly creative youngsters to achieve basic skills necessary for success in their chosen areas of specialization.

CREATIVE CHILDREN PREFER TO LEARN ON THEIR OWN

Many creative children prefer to learn on their own and schools have been slow in providing such opportunities. Last year we conducted an exciting study in which we found that children would do a great deal of writing on their own, if properly motivated. In another it was found that gifted children in a split-shift school showed more growth in language development, science, and social studies than under a full-day schedule. Only in spelling was there significantly less growth among the split-shift children (seventh graders).

Since we have generally assumed that children do not learn on their own, we have seldom provided them with opportunities to do so. I have seen learning situations "accidentally" left "open" a sufficient number of times to have become quite excited about what would happen, if we should do so more frequently. The following story by an Oklahoma sixth grader symbolizes this situation:

Once there were some monkeys sitting in a group. They were all alike except three monkeys. They were very different because they could fly.

One day some men from a park zoo were looking for some monkeys because theirs had died. They came upon the three that flew. So they took them in a cage. The cage didn't have a top to it. They were in the sun one day and the monkey said to the other, "I wish we could get out of here."

"Then, why don't we fly out of here?" said the other.

They started to fly out. When they got about half a mile, some men came to feed them. When they couldn't find the three monkeys, they saw them flying away. One of them said, "If we would have put them in a cage with a top, we would have had a real good thing here in the zoo."

One function of the school counselor might be to help highly creative children recognize or discover the "openings" in their cages to which they might be blinded.

CREATIVE CHILDREN LIKE TO ATTEMPT DIFFICULT TASKS

Frequently highly creative children strongly desire to move far ahead of their classmates in some areas. They always make us afraid that they are not "ready." Fortunately, however, educators of gifted children are rapidly revising many of their concepts about what can be taught at various levels of education. This terrifies many. The following recent headlines reflect such a fear:

"Caution Urged in Changing Primary into High Schools"
"Can We Rush Primary Education?"
"Don't Turn Grade Schools into High Schools, Educators Warn at Parley"
"Reading for Kindergarten, Language Too Soon Attacked."

Some of the panic may have been eased by a recent report of the Educational Policies Commission of the NEA and the American Association of School Administrators (*Contemporary Issues in Elementary Education, 1960*).

A very frequent theme in our imaginative stories is related to this problem. The young animal or fowl asks, "When can I roar? When can I crow? When can I quack? When can I fly?" Almost always, the answer is, "When you are a little older." We are always afraid that the young one might not be ready to learn and that he would be forever scarred by even the most temporary failure.

A common experience in the lives of many highly outstanding individuals has been their ability to cope with failure and frustration. Certainly, almost all highly creative scientists, inventors, artists, and writers attempt tasks which are too difficult for them. Had they not attempted such tasks, it is quite unlikely that their great ideas would have been born.

CREATIVE CHILDREN ARE SEARCHING FOR A PURPOSE

It has been said of most outstanding creative achievers that they seemed to be possessed by a purpose and to be "men of destiny." Creative children need some purpose which is worthy of the enthusiastic devotion they seem capable of giving. Some of this need is symbolized in the following story by a sixth-grade boy:

> There once was a South American monkey that didn't know what he was, who he was, or why he was even alive. He decided that he didn't know even the way to figure it out, so he thought he would make up a reason.
>
> He had seen many airplanes fly overhead. He had seen many ferocious animals, many nice animals, and many machines. He had always thought that it would be nice to fly, so he pretended he was an airplane.

He had also heard that buzzing sound of the engines, so he called himself "Buzz." He also decided that he was a real fast flyer so that this was the reason he was alive.

Now we all know that monkeys can't fly, but he didn't know this. Why he didn't even know that he was monkey, so he kept trying and trying—and you know what? He flew!

Perhaps this has some implications not only concerning the need for helping children discover their potentialities but for helping them achieve their self-concepts creatively rather than by authority.

CREATIVE CHILDREN SEARCH FOR THEIR UNIQUENESS

Counselors and teachers may become irritated with creative children who seem to create problems for themselves by trying consciously to be different—searching for their uniqueness. Barron maintains that creative individuals reject the demands of their society to surrender their individuality because "they want to own themselves totally and because they perceive a shortsightedness in the claim of society that all its members should adapt themselves to a norm for a given time and place."

One way in which the creative individual searches for his uniqueness is through his vocational choice. Getzels and Jackson, for example, found that their highly creative compared with their highly intelligent subjects gave a greater number of different occupations and more "unusual" or rare occupations. Their attitudes toward adult success were also different, the high creatives being less concerned with conventional standards.

THE PSYCHOLOGICAL ESTRANGEMENT OF CREATIVE CHILDREN

In no group thus far studied have we failed to find relatively clear evidence of the operation of pressures against the most creative members of the group, though they are far more severe in some classes than in others.

When we select the most creative members of each sex in each classroom and match them for sex and Intelligence Quotient with other children in the same classroom, three characteristics stand out as differentiating the highly creative children from the less creative ones. First, there is a tendency for them to gain a reputation for having wild or silly ideas. Their teachers and their peers agree on this. Second, their work is characterized by its productivity of ideas "off the beaten track." This explains one of the difficulties of teachers and peers in evaluating their ideas and perhaps why they show up no better than they do on traditional intelligence tests. Their ideas simply do not conform to the standardized dimensions, the behavioral norms, on which responses are judged. Third, they are characterized by humor and playfulness. All of these characteristics help explain both the estrangement and the creativity.

In the next issue, I shall discuss some of the problems which arise when highly creative children repress their creative needs and abilities.

29.   School Phobia: Rapid Treatment of Fifty Cases[1]

Wallace A. Kennedy

Many teachers and counselors are baffled by youngsters suffering from school phobia. In the following study, Dr. Kennedy distinguishes between two types of school phobia, describes the difference in their symptomatology, and presents a rapid treatment program consisting of six steps for the neurotic crisis type. A follow-up study indicated that the treatment was successful.

School phobia, a dramatic and puzzling emotional crisis, has attracted considerable attention for a number of years. Phobias in general are the subjects of widely differing theories of dynamics and treatment. The controversy regarding the treatment of children's phobias dates from the earliest case studies presented by Freud (1909), continues through the laboratory demonstrations of Watson and Jones (Jones, 1924) to the more recent experimental treatment of Wolpe (1954). There have been five broad reviews since the earliest paper presented by Johnson *et al.* in 1941: Klein (1945), Waldfogel, Cooledge, and Hahn (1957), Kahn (1958), Glasser (1959), and Sperling (1961). These reviews in the main support the contention that the major weight of evidence thus far leans toward the psychoanalytic interpretation of phobias, while the work of Wolpe is more consistent with the approach presented herein.

The psychoanalytic theory stresses the role of the mother in the development of school phobia. A close symbiotic relationship, which displays itself in an overdependency, is present between the mother and child. Stemming from an unsatisfactory relationship with her own mother, the mother finds it difficult to cope with her own emotional needs. The father often is in a competing role with the mother, and seems

Journal of Abnormal Psychology, 1965, 70, 285–289. Copyright 1965 by the American Psychological Association. Reprinted with the permission of the copyright owner and author.
[1] The research reported herein was supported through the Human Development Clinic of Florida State University, Tallahassee, Florida.

to try to outdo her in little tasks around the home: in trying to strengthen his own image, he depreciates that of the mother. He too overidentifies with the child. Thus, the emotional climate of his family prevents the child from ever finding out whether or not he, of his own volition, can solve problems. Possessive, domineering parents tend to make the child's growth toward independence difficult. His guilt regarding his own impulses is transformed into depression: the anxiety can reach extreme proportions.

On the other hand, Wolpe sees the phobia as a learned reaction, which he treats through direct symptom attack with what he calls reciprocal inhibition, or desensitization.

Interest in the school phobia problem, which occurs at the rate of 17 cases per thousand school-age children per year, has been greatly intensified in the past few years. An extremely significant advance was made by Cooledge and the Judge Baker group in 1957, when they presented evidence that there were not one, but two types of school phobia, which, although sharing a common group of symptoms, differed widely in others. These are referred to as Type 1 School Phobia, or the neurotic crisis, and Type 2 School Phobia, or the way-of-life phobia. The common symptoms are: (a) Morbid fears associated with school attendance; a vague dread of disaster; (b) Frequent somatic complaints: headaches, nausea, drowsiness; (c) Symbiotic relationship with mother, fear of separation; anxiety about many things: darkness, crowds, noises; (d) Conflict between parents and the school administration.

At the Human Development Clinic of Florida State University, 10 differential symptoms between Type 1 and Type 2 School Phobia have been determined. A differential diagnosis can be made logically and empirically on the basis of any 7 of the 10.

Problem

In the Fall of 1957 the Clinic embarked upon an experimental procedure for the treatment of Type 1 School Phobia—a procedure similar to that of Rodriguez, Rodriguez, and Eisenberg (1959) with one major exception: whereas Rodriguez made no distinction between types of school phobia and treated in the same manner all cases which came to the clinic, the 50 cases reported herein were selected on the basis of the criteria mentioned (see Table on page 223). The Florida State University Human Development Clinic, as a teaching and research clinic, does not generally see deeply disturbed children, but refers them to other agencies.

In the 8-year period covered by the report, there have been 6 cases which would meet the criteria of Type 2 School Phobia. These 6 cases were treated by supportive therapy for the children and parents. None of the 6 Type 2 cases had more than three of the 10 Type 1 criteria, and the results were completely dissimilar to those reported for the 50 Type 1 cases. All of the Type 2 cases were chronic in nature. All had family histories of one or more parents seriously disturbed. Two of the cases were diagnosed as having schizophrenia; 2 were diagnosed as having character disorders with the school phobia being a minor aspect of the case. One of

TEN DIFFERENTIAL SCHOOL PHOBIA SYMPTOMS

Type 1	Type 2
1. The present illness is the first episode.	1. Second, third, or fourth episode.
2. Monday onset, following an illness the previous Thursday or Friday.	2. Monday onset following minor illness not a prevalent antecedent.
3. An acute onset.	3. Incipient onset.
4. Lower grades most prevalent.	4. Upper grades most prevalent.
5. Expressed concern about death.	5. Death theme not present.
6. Mother's physical health in question: actually ill or child thinks so.	6. Health of mother not an issue.
7. Good communication between parents.	7. Poor communication between parents.
8. Mother and father well adjusted in most areas.	8. Mother shows neurotic behavior; father, a character disorder.
9. Father competitive with mother in household management.	9. Father shows little interest in household or children.
10. Parents achieve understanding of dynamics easily.	10. Parents very difficult to work with.

the 6 was hospitalized; 1 was sent to a training school. Of the 4 remaining, 2 were able to go to college, although their records were poor and their symptoms continued. These 6 cases were in treatment for an average of 10 months. In no circumstances was a school phobia case changed from Type 1 to Type 2, or vice versa.

This experimental procedure with Type 1 School Phobia was begun with considerable caution, with only 1 case in 1957 and 2 the following Spring. The treatment involved the application of broad learning theory concepts by blocking the escape of the child and preventing secondary gains from occurring. In addition, the child was reinforced for going to school without complaint. This rapid treatment procedure has now been followed with 50 cases.

Subject Population

Subjects for the 50 cases over an 8-year period were school-age children, all suffering from the first evidence of a phobia attack, from the geographical area served by the Human Development Clinic of Florida State University. The subject distribution by year and sex is illustrated in Table 1, by symptom and sex in Table 2, by age and sex in Table 3, and by grade and sex in Table 4.

The fathers' mean age for the male subjects was 36; the mothers', 35. For the female subjects the fathers' mean age was 38; the mothers', 36. The boys' mean age was 9; that of the girls', 10. There was no definite pattern in birth order of the subjects, or in number of siblings.

TABLE 1. YEAR OF TREATMENT AND SEX OF 50 TYPE ONE
SCHOOL PHOBIA CASES

Year	Male	Female	Total
1957	1	0	1
1958	1	1	2
1959	4	2	6
1960	4	8	12
1961	6	3	9
1962	5	4	9
1963	4	5	9
1964	0	2	2
Total	25	25	50

TABLE 2. SYMPTOM CHECKLIST AND SEX OF 50 TYPE ONE
SCHOOL PHOBIA CASES

Symptom	Male	Female	Total
1. First attack	25	25	50
2. Monday onset—Thursday illness	24	25	49
3. Acute onset	25	23	48
4. Lower grades	22	18	40
5. Death theme	22	22	44
6. Mother's health an issue	23	21	44
7. Good parental marital harmony	24	23	47
8. Good parental mental health	23	24	47
9. Father helper in the house	21	21	42
10. Parents achieve insight quickly	24	25	49

TABLE 3. AGE AND SEX OF 50 TYPE ONE SCHOOL PHOBIA CASES

Age	Male	Female	Total
4	0	1	1
5	3	1	4
6	2	3	5
7	3	2	5
8	3	1	4
9	3	5	8
10	4	3	7
11	1	2	3
12	3	0	3
13	2	4	6
14	1	2	3
15	0	0	0
16	0	1	1
Total	25	25	50

TABLE 4. GRADE AND SEX OF 50 TYPE ONE SCHOOL PHOBIA CASES

Grade	Male	Female	Total
Nursery School	0	2	2
Kindergarten	4	0	4
First	4	4	8
Second	0	1	1
Third	6	4	10
Fourth	3	4	7
Fifth	2	2	4
Sixth	3	1	4
Seventh	2	2	4
Eighth	0	2	2
Ninth	1	2	3
Tenth	0	1	1
Total	25	25	50

Method and Results

During the course of the past 8 years, 50 cases of Type 1 School Phobia have been treated. Five of these cases might be considered semicontrols because they were untreated Type 1 cases of some duration, or they were Type 1 cases unsuccessfully treated elsewhere before they were seen at the clinic. One of these semicontrol cases had been out of school for 1 year, and the other 4 had been out for over 3 months.

All 50 of the cases responded to the treatment program with a complete remission of the school phobia symptoms, and follow-up study indicates no evidence of any outbreaks of substitute symptoms or recurrence of the phobia.

In the follow-up schedule the parents were phoned in about 2 weeks, and again in 6 weeks, to see if the progress had continued. They were then phoned on a yearly basis, except in 1961, when follow-up interviews were conducted reaching 19 of the 21 cases completed at that time. During the course of the 8 years, 6 families were lost because of moving with no forwarding address. Of these lost cases, none had been followed less than 2 years, 2 were followed 3 years, and 1 for 4 years.

RAPID TREATMENT PROCEDURE

The rapid treatment program for Type 1 school phobia involves six essential components: good professional public relations, avoidance of emphasis on somatic complaints, forced school attendance, structured interview with parents, brief interview with child, and follow-up.

Good Professional Public Relations

It is necessary to establish good communication with schools, physicians, and parent groups, such that the cases are likely referred on the second or third day of the phobic attack. This groundwork involves the typical mental health consultation and case-by-case follow-up with the referring source.

Avoidance of Emphasis on Somatic Complaints

If phobic qualities predominate, that is, if the child conforms to seven of the differential symptoms of Type 1 School Phobia, emphasis on somatic complaints should be avoided. For instance, the child's somatic complaints should be handled matter-of-factly, with an appointment to see the pediatrician after school hours. Abdominal pains will probably require the pediatrican to make a prompt physical examination, but this can probably be done on the way to school.

Forced School Attendance

It is essential to be able to require the child to go to school and to be willing to use any force necessary. In all of the present cases, simply convincing the parents of this necessity and having them come to a firm decision, has generally been enough. The ability to be decisive when necessary has been essential.

Have the father take the child to school. These fathers are not unkind, and they can show authority when necessary.

Have the principal or attendance officer take an active part in keeping the child in the room.

Allow the mother to stand in the hall, if she must, or to visit the school during the morning, but not to stay.

Structured Interview with the Parents

Stressing the following points, conduct with the parents a structured interview designed to give them sufficient confidence to carry out the therapeutic program even in the face of considerable resistance from the child.

Lead the interview. The confidence of the parents is greatly increased by the interviewer's verifying the history rather than taking it. Correctly anticipating 7 out of 10 variables within a family structure is well calculated to induce full cooperation.

Be optimistic. Stressing the transient nature, the dependable sequence of a difficult Monday, a somewhat better Tuesday, and a symptom-free Wednesday, tends to lighten the depression of the parents regarding their child's unwillingness to go to school.

Emphasize success. Type 1 cases always recover. Ninety percent of the Type 1 phobics stay at school most of the first day. Along with optimism comes a slight mobilization of hostility which helps the parents to follow the plan.

Present the formula. Simply but directly, with repetition for emphasis, outline a plan for the parents to follow, assuming that it is the end of the school week by the time of the referral and that the interview with the parents is conducted on Thursday or Friday.

Parent Formula.

Do not discuss in any way, school attendance over the weekend. There is nothing a phobic child does better than talk about going to school.

Don't discuss going to school. Don't discuss phobic symptoms. Simply tell the child Sunday evening, "Well, son, tomorrow you go back to school."

On Monday morning, get the child up, dressed, and ready for school. Give the child a light breakfast to reduce the nausea problem. Have the father take the child matter-of-factly off to school. Don't ask him how he feels, or why he is afraid to go to school, or why he doesn't like school. Simply take him to school, turn him over to the school authorities, and go home.

If the child therapist has not seen the child the previous week, he may see him after school on the first day.

On Monday evening, compliment the child on going to school and staying there, no matter how resistant he has been, no matter how many times he has vomited, cried, or started to leave. If he has been at school for 30 minutes on Monday, progress is being made. Tell the child Monday evening that Tuesday will be much better, and make no further mention of the symptom.

Tuesday can be expected to be a repetition of Monday, but with everything toned down considerably. On Tuesday evening, encourage and compliment the child strongly for doing so much better.

Wednesday should be virtually symptom free. Wednesday evening, with considerable fanfare, give a party for the child in honor of his having overcome his problem.

Brief Interview with the Child

The child himself should be seen only briefly by the child therapist and only after school hours. The content of the interview should be stories which stress the advantage of going on in the face of fear: how student pilots need to get back into the air quickly after an accident, and how important it is to get right back on the horse after a fall. In addition the therapist can describe real or imaginary events in his own childhood when he was frightened for awhile but everything turned out all right: all to stress to the child the transitory nature of the phobia.

Follow-Up

Follow-up by phone, being chatty and encouraging and not oversolicitous. In the long-range follow-up, chat with the parents about further school phobia symptoms, incidence of other phobias, school attendance records, academic progress, and the occurrence of other emotional problems in the child.

DISCUSSION

Two legitimate concerns have been expressed regarding preliminary reports at local meetings. The first is a concern about the claim of complete remission for all 50 cases—a claim inconsistent with the usual child guidance clinic success rate—and the consequent belief that the criterion for success is simply too narrow. Only self-report data and reports from school administrations are available regarding the symptom-free nature of these children once this phobic episode has passed. It is true that no diagnostic evaluation has been undertaken with any of these children during follow-up. It must be remembered, however, that the definition of symptom remission is restricted to those obvious symptoms which might conceivably lead the parents or school officials to re-refer the children to the clinic. In this regard, these 50 children in the Type 1 School Phobia group are symptom free.

Because of the nature of the Human Development Clinic and the nature of this project, careful selection has been exercised in accepting cases, as mentioned above. Due to the relationship between the schools and the clinic, and the clear definition of cases suitable for the project, there is reason to believe that the majority of Type 1 School Phobia cases in the five-county area the clinic serves have come to our attention, whereas the local county mental health clinic has received a high percentage of the Type 2 cases. The success of the Type 2 cases of school phobia accepted by the Human Development Clinic for teaching purposes has not been remarkable.

The second concern is that perhaps what is called Type 1 School Phobia is not really a severe phobic attack at all, but borders on malingering of a transient nature which would spontaneously remit in a few days anyway. In fact, because of the apparent sound mental health of the family as a group, its middle-class values which stress school, and the family's good premorbid history, including the academic record of the child, there is little reason to doubt that the majority of the cases would eventually return to school whatever treatment was undertaken. However, our five semicontrol cases and evidence seen from other clinics of Type 1 cases that have been out of school for prolonged periods suggest that this method of treatment may accelerate or facilitate the remission. Recommendation for the use of this technique is restricted, then, to those cases showing Type 1 symptoms which, in spite of their possible transient nature, present a rather serious problem to teachers, parents, and counselors.

REFERENCES

Cooledge, J. C., Hahn, Pauline B., & Peck, Alice L. School phobia: Neurotic crisis or way of life. *American Journal of Orthopsychiatry*, 1957, 27, 296–306.

Freud, S. *Analysis of a phobia in a five-year-old boy.* Std. Ed., New York: W. W. Norton, 1909.

Glasser, K. Problems in school attendance: School phobia and related conditions. *Pediatrics*, 1959, 55, 758. (Abstract)

Johnson, A. M., *et al.* School phobia: A study of five cases. *American Journal of Orthopsychiatry*, 1941, 11, 702. (Abstract)

Jones, M. C. A. laboratory study of fear: The case of Peter. *Journal of Genetic Psychology*, 1924, 31, 308–315.

Kahn, J. H. School refusal—some clinical and cultural aspects. *Medical Officer*, 1958, 100, 337. (Abstract)

Klein, E. The reluctance to go to school. *Psychoanalytic Study of the Child*, 1945, 1, 263. (Abstract)

Rodriguez, A., Rodriguez, Maria, & Eisenberg, L. The outcome of school phobia: A follow-up study based on 41 cases. *American Journal of Psychiatry*, 1959, 116, 540–544.

Sperling, M. Analytic first aid in school phobias. *Psychoanalytic Quarterly*, 1961, 30, 504. (Abstract)

Waldfogel, S., Cooledge, J. C., & Hahn, P. B. Development, meaning and management of school phobia. *American Journal of Orthopsychiatry*, 1957, 27, 754. (Abstract)

Wolpe, J. Reciprocal inhibition as the main basis of psychotherapeutic effects. *A.M.A. Archive of Neurology and Psychiatry*, 1954, 72, 204–226.

30.   Passive Aggressiveness and Learning

Leslie Y. Rabkin

Have you ever known a student who passively resists his teacher's authority by bringing the wrong book to class, by forgetting his assignment at home, by losing his place when reciting or by interrupting his school work to sharpen his pencil or to go to the bathroom? If so, you have probably experienced the disruptive effects associated with passive aggressive behavior as described by Leslie Y. Rabkin in the following article.

The educational process involves two basic elements. First is the imparting of wisdom, the transmission of the cultural heritage in all its diversity. Joined to this, and more wide ranging in its ultimate effect, is the development of a receptive, critical attitude, the nurturance of an enquiring mind. This two fold process implies an active participation of teacher and pupil. Passive aggressive behavior plays havoc with this participation and thus disrupts and distorts the process.

Passive aggressiveness as a transient mode of relating is engaged in by all of us. Although we are usually quite unaware of the feelings which engender our actions, such behavior represents a means of expressing our anger, annoyance, frustration, and disappointment in a socially tolerated form.

The psychiatric label of passive aggression refers to what is known as a personality or character disorder, an early and relatively permanent

---

Exceptional Children, September, 1965, 1–3. Reprinted with the permission of the publisher and author.

distortion of personality which prevents the individual from maintaining an effective, flexible, and reciprocal relationship with another person. These individuals suffer a life taken up with a struggle against a feared, hated, and envied authority, whatever its form. They see authority figures as tyrannical and unjust, and themselves as badly used by those in control. However, because of their fear of retaliation, these persons cannot directly express their angry and aggressive feelings towards authority, relying instead on passive maneuvers which veil yet release their feelings. Thus, the angry outburst gives way to stubborn, defiant pouting; the resentment against a supposed injustice develops into inefficiency and procrastination.

THE PASSIVE AGGRESSIVE CHILD

Various patterns of family interrelationships may result in the development of passive aggression behavior. The basic element appears to be that these people grow up in an environment marked by its projection of blame, most particularly on the part of the mother (Harris, 1961). This maternal need to scapegoat the world can affect the child in several ways.

He may, for example, learn by imitation and identification that the best way to deal with the world is to attack it. Feelings of guilt are quickly dispersed by finding fault with the people and objects around him and by blaming events on those with whom he interacts. The child develops what Sullivan (1953) calls the basic malevolent attitude, a feeling that one is surrounded by enemies and that any evidence of tenderness towards others will result in pain. And so, uncertain and afraid, the child "makes it practically impossible for anyone to feel tenderly toward him or to treat him kindly; he beats them to it, so to speak, by the display of his attitude" (Sullivan, 1953, p. 214).

Another result may develop if the child himself has been the mother's scapegoat. This is a well-nigh insoluble situation, fraught with frustration and muted anger. The child is in a state of chronic rage, but can find no avenue of discharge. Retaliating against mother leads to her counterviolence and the severing of all the deeply emotional ties to her. What is left is a seething anger, directed both against himself and the world.

A third path to this form of personality distortion involves the family situation in which father is the victim of mother's depreciation. Such a damaged and degraded father cannot be a suitable model to a boy in need of masculine identification. To be like father is to be open to contempt similar to that wreaked upon him. Yet to avoid father and become mother's ally involves even greater guilt and anxiety. If the child ends up in a reactively strong attachment to father, he is likely to be met with the devastating criticism "You're just like your father!" As Harris (1961) notes, ". . . if the son is thus given a bad name, he will, in his school behavior, live up to that name" (p. 73).

ACTION AND REACTION IN THE CLASSROOM

The final common pathway of behavior for all these children will be along a continuum of aggressiveness, primarily of a passive aggressive type, in any of its myriad forms. Such children enter school burdened by a residue of anger which cannot be properly channeled, frustrated to an extreme degree by the most trivial demand or problem, and suffocatingly wrapped in their internal conflicts. As a result, the potent inner energies of the child cannot be turned to constructive, reality oriented purposes. The sublimatory process, in which aggressive energy becomes the motive force behind the need to freely inquire, to dig deeply into a problem, to press on to the accomplishment of a task, never takes place. The result can only be what has been called learning impotence.

There is another reason why the passive aggressive child's chances of learning anything at school are so slight. In the classroom it is the teacher who represents hated authority to the child and who thus becomes the victim of his passive aggression. The child's wisecracks, his sullen foot dragging, his uncompleted assignments demand an excessive amount of grudging teacher attention.

It is just this type of behavior which creates a feeling in the teacher that he is being personally attacked for no reason and thus engenders retaliatory behavior. The teacher finds himself enmeshed in a power struggle, fearful that there will be a contagion of such behavior throughout the classroom disrupting all discipline. Inevitably, the teacher has an impulse to counterattack, banish the child from the classroom, and rid himself of his frustrated fury. Whatever action he takes, the teacher is likely to be left with feelings of frustration, helplessness, and guilt.

What has resulted is a vicious circle. The teacher's all too human reaction to an all too human frailty provides the *coup de grace* to any flickering chance for learning to take place. The lamp of education is extinguished.

THE PASSIVE AGGRESSIVE TEACHER

What of the passive aggressive teacher? We all know such disturbed teachers, those who harbor an endless reservoir of anger, directed both to their young charges and their superiors. Expressed in passive and not so passive ways in the classroom situation, through verbal abuse or abandonment, their hostility works to the obvious detriment of all learning. Fortunately, these disturbed individuals form only a small part of the teaching force.

There are factors involved in the teaching situation, however, which, in their own insidious fashion, create and foster anxieties which cannot help but intrude into the day by day interaction of student and teacher. How can anything but anxiety and frustration develop where there are the additive factors of the corrosive effect of constant pupil contact throughout the working day, and the esteem shattering effect of being at the receiving end of an administrative chain of command, each link of which may be ordering some behavior incompatible with that demanded by another?

The teacher, at the confluence of these forces, and himself an individual with needs, wishes, feelings and beliefs, may rebel at his lot in the only way which seems open to him. The battle against authority gets transposed into the classroom with the teacher who resents his role, taking out his frustrations on the children through direct attack or, more likely, by withdrawal and passive defiance. A similar withdrawal may take place after a period of feeling trapped within the confines of a classroom with its mind numbing hurly-burly. If the teacher is not allowed a suitable time out period, anger against the children and the forces which prescribe this constant contact may emerge in similar ways. Given this accumulated tension and unrest, the educational process will again suffer.

GUIDEPOSTS FOR PREVENTION

What can be done about passive aggressiveness, in any form so disruptive of the learning process? The child's problem stems from the distortion of what should be a tender, loving relationship into a malevolent, hateful one, with the result that he cannot effectively deal with his hostile and aggressive feelings; these then erupt in a manner designed to maintain his distance from others.

The teacher, in dealing with such a disturbed personality, can attune himself not to the outward trappings of hate, but to the inner loneliness and despair of the child. He can make an effort to pay the child some special, personal attention, attempting in this way to provide an accepting adult figure, using the power of this relationship to lead the child into a learning situation.

Should this attempt prove futile, as it often must because of the severity of the child's disturbance, the teacher must be prepared to call in professional aid. Constant cooperative interchange with the school's own guidance and psychological services can facilitate this process.

In regard to the teacher's own difficulties, it is imporant that he develop an attitude of self-appraisal and introspection. He must seek to understand and cope with his own counterfeelings when confronted in the classroom with passive aggressive or other disturbed and disturbing behavior. Should self-help prove inadequate, professional consultation can be sought.

What is most important, in the case of teacher or children, is the early detection and appreciation of the problem. Once the cycle of action and reaction begins, each moment makes the resolution of the problem infinitely more difficult.

The disruptive force of passive aggressive behavior is indeed profound. But we do have the tools with which to understand and deal with the problem. We must make use of these tools, for otherwise the classroom becomes a battleground and learning, as we have defined it, will not take place.

REFERENCES

Harris, I. D. *Emotional blocks to learning*. Glencoe: The Free Press, 1961.
Sullivan, H. S. *The interpersonal theory of psychiatry*. New York: Norton, 1953.

CHAPTER 7

Classroom Discipline

31. The Mental Hygiene Viewpoint on School Discipline

William C. Morse

*Because mental hygiene specialists have not fully under-
stood the teacher's role, they have made little available
to teachers by way of specific and concrete practical
suggestions pertaining to management of the child's
daily behavior. Dr. Morse stresses the need for more
realistic and effective approaches to classroom discipline. By expanding diagnostic and intervention techniques, redefining the concept of acceptance, and
developing more effective ways of talking with students, teachers will be in a better position to fulfill their
mental health role as it relates to school discipline.*

The mental hygiene viewpoint on school discipline stays one jump ahead
of chaos. To a large extent, practice is governed by outmoded concepts.
Methodology tends to be polarized: some advocates cling to a simple
minded hope that affection and acceptance will conquer all; others are
just as certain that the only way to manage recalcitrant youth is to get
tough and kick them out when they do not respond. Such a primitive
dichotomy, based as it is on vastly oversimplified notions of how to in-

The High School Journal, 1965, 48, 396–401. Reprinted with the permission of the
publisher and author.

fluence behavior, is no longer worthy of attention by serious students of personality dynamics.

The current effort of the mental hygienist is to work out a more appropriate and adequate basis for school discipline. As a matter of fact, mental health concepts have had less actual influence on the everyday workings of schools than we wish to admit. The reason is that proposals have lacked realism. School people are rightly concerned with concepts which will function in the educational milieu rather than esoteric ideas useful in other settings. But the mental hygiene movement in and out of schools is still dominated by concepts which, although valid in themselves, are remote from the Monday morning to Friday night routine of schools with thousands of children who must not only be "seen" in interviews but must also be controlled in the social world of the school. The new look in school mental hygiene has parallel in psychiatry where the art of helping is now moving from the interview room to social psychiatry in the community. The social psychiatry of Caplan[1] and the school assistance of the Newman group[2] are examples. These approaches consider the total milieu, the use of crisis situations and new methods of intervention to teach young people how to cope with difficulties.

One thing is certain. The new mental hygiene must provide more effective approaches than those of the past, for problems of discipline are of high priority in most schools. Perhaps it takes the form of helping a mildly deviate adolescent find a place in the school community rather than become a drop-out. More likely it is how to handle such behavior as disrespect, defiance of teacher authority, peer aggression, calculated rejection of the school's goals, or destructiveness. While the magnitude and chronicity is more evident in central urban complexes, similar behavior, though sometimes with a different format, is present in suburbia and the rural areas as well. Intensified pressures for academic accomplishment in schools produce much failure and frustration, and the many daily examples of raw aggression prevalent in society encourage impulse acting-out. At the same time there is the realignment of the socializing forces in the culture with the family influence diminishing while the school and other community agencies have yet to find the formula for replacement efforts. It has been termed a crisis in "character," which is the old fashioned term being used again.[3]

There is no miracle drug to assuage the agony of cultural change. The school's portion of the responsibility remains uncertain, but this much is clear: we can help children through the use of appropriate disciplinary procedures. The following sections are a hurried look at three parts of this extensive problem. However, these excerpts are sketches of the new mental hygiene view.

---

[1] Caplan, Gerald. "Opportunities for School Psychologists in the Primary Prevention of Mental Disorders in Children," *Mental Hygiene*, Vol. 47, No. 4, October 1963, pp. 525–539.

[2] Newman, R. G., Redl, F. and Kitchener, H. L. *Technical Assistance in a Public School System* (in press). School Research Program, 5410 Connecticut Ave., N.W., Washington 15, D.C.

[3] Peck, R. F. and Havighurst, R. J. *The Psychology of Character Development.* New York: John Wiley & Sons, Inc., 1960.

1. *Schools will broaden the techniques used in both diagnosis and intervention.* A dual system of diagnosis and intervention is proposed. Both the traditional and the new approaches are necessary, but one offers more potential for the school milieu. All involved with discipline wish to alter pupil behavior. This starts with theory regarding cause of the behavior we wish to alter. Then it is necessary to know how to produce alterations in the desired direction. In traditional terms, this is all seen as a product of one's life history, oversimplified as follows:

CASE HISTORY APPROACH

A. *The individual's life experience and its culmination is assessed* by the psychologist with projective tests, by the social worker who unravels the family dynamics, and by the psychiatrist who searches for the underlying motivations in the pupil's inner life.

B. *The individual's life experience culminates in a diagnosis* where the essence of the findings are summarized as a syndrome. This capsule description of the problem implies the major dynamics. For example, a youngster may be diagnosed as a "sociopath," "neurotic," etc. Even though there is less than complete agreement on nosology, these syndromes convey meaning to the specialists. But they frequently suggest very little to the educator of what should be done to help the child.

C. *Behavior in question is seen as an inevitable outcome* of the syndrome assigned, and a consequence of long standing personality deviations. This tends to make the educator feel there is little the school can do.

D. *Plans for intervention must then be based on altering the personality.* The traditional method to alter behavior is through one to one (or sometimes group) therapy with the child and/or parents. This suggests that schools setting out to alter behavior will need to provide traditional therapy, since this is the key to alteration.

Many barriers become apparent when this methodology is seen as the single or major channel for change. The teachers and most other school personnel are left on the sidelines. The school must depend upon outside experts to produce change. Necessary communication between the teacher and the clinical personnel is often difficult to activate and sustain. It should be made clear that, in our experience, such traditional therapy may be the only method for really changing behavior in many cases and certainly it is a significant part in getting needed control in many others.

But there is a growing awareness of a set of "causes" other than the historical. Contrasted with the case history approach is the life space approach. Here the search for causes of given behavior turns to the conditions in the contemporary scene, those here and now environmental forces which impinge upon the pupil's self at any given time. Behavior is seen as a consequence of these forces. Situational analysis suggests a new schema.

LIFE SPACE APPROACH

A. *The individual's life space is studied in terms of the major forces operating in his milieu.* In the classroom, this means a study of the nature of the task in which the pupil is involved. For example, the task may contain the seeds of acute frustration leading directly to misbehavior and a discipline problem begins to grow. The group relationships are analyzed, for this second area may be the generator of forces producing unacceptable behavior. Groups may scapegoat or put strong pressure for certain behavior on members. Thus groups "cause" behavior. Finally, the authority relationship may contain the source of misbehavior, so the adult-child interaction must be scrutinized. A youngster who is rejected or feels he is rejected by the teacher may act out to get a response. There are methods of studying a classroom milieu to better know the play of forces. In addition, more remote forces are studied to fill out the contemporary press—family, siblings, neighborhood and so on.

B. *These forces are seen as filtering through a particular "self."* Forces alone do not produce behavior. They filter through a particular self. Knowledge of self-esteem, self-aspiration and role help educators appreciate the nature of the given pupil. School personnel can do much to understand the self concept of students. From this point of view behavior and misbehavior are the consequence of contemporary forces interacting through the self.

C. *Plans for intervention can then be directed both at the nature of the self and at the field of forces.* If behavior has to be controlled, it may be possible to get alterations by modulating the tasks assigned, the group involvements or the authority relationship. In fact, it may be that these stresses, objectively viewed, are, in some instances, inducing the undesirable behavior. Through counseling with pupils, it may also be possible to change certain perceptions that need remedy.

It is clear that environmental manipulation may not in itself significantly alter the self, and case history methods as previously indicated, may be needed. But adjusting the forces to the level that the pupil can learn to cope with is in line with current theory of mental health work. The individual who is able to maintain himself within the range of acceptable behavior has already learned coping skills to manage situations. These can be taught to many other students by proper handling at crisis times. Now, schools often handle tense situations in a manner which encourages or consolidates unfortunate coping—we generate anger, we pile on rebuke, we belittle the pupil's intention and capacity to adjust all in the guise of motivation and support.

Actually, building coping strength does not imply an easy intervention course. It is certainly no easier to accomplish than are changes by traditional therapy, but it does offer the opportunity to work within the scope of school responsibility—dealing in matters of curriculum, pupil-teacher relationship, group life and so on. Flexible use of teaching personnel, new perceptions regarding evaluation and making the work relevant are all interventions to be considered along with many more. The most significant way to influence behavior and build coping capacity is to expose children to an environment reasonable for them, whatever this may be, and work through the steps until the pupil is able to accommodate to more stress. The preventive potential of this is well delineated in a recent paper by Bower[4] which includes some specific procedures. While the life space approach is not a panacea, it is a new direction proposed by school mental health.

2. *School personnel are gradually understanding the new concept of acceptance.* One of the most vexing concepts in dealing with discipline is the matter of acceptance. Is it "accepting" a pupil to exclude him from a room or school? To restrict his freedom? To put high demands on him for compliance? To give him a chance to try something we know he will fail? The answer to each statement is both yes and no because psychological acceptance is not a set pattern of adult behavior but rather depends upon the nature of each child, and what will help him learn. To do this requires "differential diagnosis," looking behind the symptom to basic patterns of behavior.[5] We accept the child psychologically only when we react in such a manner as best to teach him that which he must learn. All children do not learn to control their impulses in the same way. While there is no place for adult hostility to children, there is a place for differential handling in many other ways. This is an extensive topic and can only be touched upon here but it lies deep at the core of the new look in mental hygiene.

For example, an adolescent with a minimum of conscience will exploit permissiveness and thus learn little of how to cope with his impulses from this type of "permissive" acceptance. He needs to know that his environment will always be less rewarding if he misbehaves. He is restricted when he violates others' rights. When gratifications are denied him, however, it is never with hostility. With a youngster of this nature, words are largely wasted: clear action is necessary. He is "accepted" by being restrained. In fact, with some children in a crisis, acceptance may require physical holding though never hurting.

An anxious child, on the other hand, needs to talk and work his problem through. His "acceptance" follows another pattern even though his behavior may have to be drastically curbed. Piling on pressure for control may encourage some pupils to seek self-punishment as a relief for inner guilt. The variety of patterns of "acceptance," in effect, match the variety of personality patterns found in pupils. To accept the child requires an appreciation of the nature of the pupil's personality as indicated in the case history approach, and then selecting responses which will help him learn necessary conformity. The many faces of acceptance leave no place for a split between counselors who listen (viz accept) and principals who discipline (viz punish). The pupil needs unitary handling based upon his true nature.

3. *Schools are using new ways of talking with youngsters.* Old style moralizing gets nowhere with most young people today. The need is for a non-moralistic but still effective way to discuss behavior with pupils. As

---

[4] Bower, Eli. "The Modification, Mediation and Utilization of Stress During the School Years." *Amer. Jo. Ortho.*, Vol. XXXIV, No. 4, July, 1964, pp. 667–674.
[5] Lipman, H. S. *Treatment of the Child in Emotional Conflict.* 1963.

indicated, traditional therapeutic methods are not suited to teachers and other school personnel.

The life space diagnostic schema has also been the foundation of a new way for teachers to discuss problem situations, called Life Space Interviewing.[6] Discussion is derived from the actual behavior which has taken place, usually in the presence, or at least in the awareness, of the adult. This "situation" then becomes the focus for talking through the nature of such behavior in the future. In other words it embodies closure, a real look at what will take place next if this behavior is not controlled. Such interviewing can be used to alter certain behavior even in quite disturbed children. It is a most useful mode of confrontation for discipline situations. Again this is not easy to do and it does not always bring success even after extensive use, but it is school relevant. Teachers have found it most useful and, with supervised training, they have been able to develop real skill in such interviewing.

Our thesis is simply this. Schools need to break new paths if they are to be effective in handling discipline without resorting to excessive repressive acts. A new mental hygiene oriented methodology has already been started. The techniques offer an infusion of control techniques with mental hygiene principles.

32. Life Space Interview in the School Setting

Marcella Brenner

As noted in the preceding article, a most important skill for teachers is the ability to talk effectively with problem students. As far as teachers are concerned, what is most often needed are on the scene impromptu talks about specific troublesome incidents. To this end, Life

In R. G. Newman & M. M. Keith (Eds.), *The School-Centered Life Space Interview.* Washington, D.C.: Washington School of Psychiatry, 1967. Pp. 38–43. Reprinted with the permission of the publisher and author.

[6] Redl, Fritz. "The Strategy and Techniques of the Life Space Interview." *Amer. Jo. Ortho.*, Vol. XXIX, No. 1, January 1959, pp. 1–18.

Morse, W. C. "Training Teachers in Life Space Interviewing." *Amer. Jo. Ortho.*, Vol. XXXIII, No. 4, July 1963, pp. 727–730.

Space Interviewing was developed. Dr. Brenner offers
us some guidelines for this type of school-oriented
reality interviewing.

WHAT HAPPENS IN THE INTERVIEW?

In any exchange between teachers and children the comments and questions of the teacher—or principal—are useful if they help the child out of his difficulty. They are of no avail if they dig deeper the hole he is in. Too often we say things like:

—You apologize this minute.

—Your mind is in the gutter.

—Why did you throw the ball across the room?

—Why did you hit the little girl? She's half your size.

—Why did you write this fresh note to Mary Jane? And I want the truth!

—What makes you think you can use that kind of language to me? Is that the way you talk to your mother?

(The suggestion here is that the principal thinks it probably *is* the way Margaret talks to her mother and that lets Margaret know that he thinks that the whole family is beneath contempt.)

—A boy who doesn't have a father certainly should be more responsible.

—I'm ashamed of you. You're a big boy now.

The teacher or principal may deliver a long lecture. A lecture is not an interview. Often our remarks are moralizing, shaming or belittling. We push and probe and insist that a child tell us why he did something when he couldn't possibly tell why even if he wanted to. Then, in our effort to "close the case" with some kind of overt action, we require a public apology from the child.

It is, of course, much easier for me to list the foregoing useless if not damaging gambits than to describe interview behavior that is likely to be useful to the child. The interview which follows is presented not necessarily as a model but as case material that may be useful for our discussion.

Lee's mother had phoned to tell the principal that Lee was uneasy about coming to school. Bill was demanding money from him. Lee wanted to pay to avoid trouble with Bill.

PRINCIPAL: Hello Bill. Sit down. Do you know why I sent for you?

BILL: No.

PRINCIPAL: Strange business—requiring kids to give you money or comic books or you beat them up. Did somebody ever do this to you?

BILL: No. We made a bet. He lost. I said: "You owe me cokes."

P.: You *both* made a bet—or you said "I bet you such and such?"

B.: Well, I really set it up.

P.: And you decided what he owed you *after* he lost the bet?

B.: Yes.

P.: What about that?

B.: Guess I shouldn't.

P.: What should you?

B.: Agree first.

P.: This beating up. Now what about that?

B.: (Tears) I told him he didn't have to pay up.

P.: He doesn't think so. Do you wish you had more money for cokes or comic books?

B.: Yes.

P.: Most kids do want more money.

B.: But I have money. I go to a skating club and I pay for it from my own money.

P.: Good. How do you get your own money?

B.: I shovel snow, cut grass, do jobs.

P.: Good.

(Bill—tears dry now, Kleenex operation.)

P.: How are you going to handle this from now on? Are you feeling sore at Lee because I got hold of this?

B.: No.

P.: Well, you could be. But his mother got it out of him and she told me. Think you can be friends with him?

B.: Yes.

P.: You're a nice kid and I'm sure you're sorry. (Eyes tearful again.) Sometimes kids see TV or grownups act a certain way and try to imitate it.

(Bill smiling, clearly thinking about something he had seen or heard.)

P.: Was there some of that in this?

B.: Yes.

P.: Well, trying things out is one way to find out what won't work— That's what growing up is. Have you gotten this one out of your system?

B.: Yes.

P.: Do I need to call your mother?

B.: No.

P.: Okay—just between us, then. Come back if you need help getting things straightened out with Lee. Do you have any of his money?

B.: No—just comic books. I'll return them.

P.: You feel better now?

B.: Yes.

P.: Anything else you want to say—or ask?

B.: Is Lee's mother going to call my mother?

P.: I really don't know. I doubt it. She wasn't angry. Just wanted this stopped.

(Bill still worried and not making a move to go.)

P.: Still worried about your mother?

B.: Yes.

P.: Have you changed your mind? Want me to tell her for you?

B.: No.

P.: So?

B. I don't know. I'll see.

P.: Let me know what you decide or if you want help.

Interview behavior—all behavior for that matter—has a heavy non-verbal component. The attitude, gesture, tone of the teacher or principal are of critical importance. Silence, too, is part of the communication. Timing is significant. To say to a child "I know you're sorry about this" at the right time is extremely valuable. To say it at the wrong time may push him further into the sullen silence that got him into trouble in the first place. Certainly, meaningful communication is going on if the principal puts his hand on a boy's shoulder to give him time to recover.

As I indicated earlier, in Life Space Interviews we are working inevitably with many unknowns. Therefore it is well to try to recognize what can be known, to recognize what is happening before our eyes, to grasp the significance of the child's interview behavior. Is he trying to tell us something or to keep from telling us?

A silent partner in an interview is frustrating indeed. Is the youngster tongue-tied by embarrassment? He may be embarrassed about the reason for the interview or he may be embarrassed about having to talk to us about it. Is he keeping quiet because he knows it's a good idea not to trust adults or is he afraid he will get other kids in trouble? Are echoes of another situation interfering with his ability to hear what you are saying in this one? Is he silent because he is too upset, too angry to talk, and needs all his energies just to hold himself together? None of this necessarily means that he is resisting us or that he is unmindful of the trouble he is in. It helps to acknowledge to a child that we realize that he is too upset to talk, or that we know that some things are hard to talk about. A brief postponement may help. An older girl will appreciate the opportunity to go to the restroom, wash her face with cold water, comb her hair. A young child may need more time to finish sobbing and may be able to use a cookie or cold milk to advantage.

A child may retreat to obdurate silence to keep from crying. When a child is afraid of his own feelings, toughness is a ready armor against the kindness of a fond teacher—a kindness which if acknowledged will make him fall apart.

Another area of easy misinterpretation is the apparent stubbornness of a child who actually is trying to communicate with us but doesn't know the words to use or doesn't know how to talk about his feelings. Sometimes a child doesn't know the acceptable words for what he wants to say. Also difficult is the talker who uses language to keep us at a distance. Although we encounter this more often in Johnny's parents than in Johnny, some children learn the talking technique early and it can be extremely hard to handle, particularly with a bright child who leads you down many interesting garden paths—away from the issue at hand.

WHAT WILL BE USEFUL AND SUPPORTIVE TO CHILDREN IN THE INTERVIEW?

1. Be polite. Offer the child a chair. Produce a kleenex if it is needed. We demand good manners from children and often are guilty of exces-

sive rudeness toward them. Children want and need the adults in authority to be firm and to stick to strict rules. We can be direct and assume adult responsibilities courteously. If you are talking to a child and are interrupted by the phone, apologize to him just as you would to his mother. Don't interrupt him when he is trying to tell you something. Don't answer your own questions, "Why did you go AWOL to Bud's (the corner store which is off limits) at lunch time? To meet Chuck, no doubt. You two better look out, you'll be in trouble with the police."

2. Don't tower over a little child. Kneel or bend down to him. Have a small chair or stool in the office for really little ones and another low one for you to sit on. Be careful about lifting a kindergartner or first grader up on a desk or table. Although well-meant this may push a frightened child into a screaming panic because he feels trapped in midair and can't get down.

3. When you are sure of your ground, it can be a good approach to confront a child with your knowledge of his misdeed, and not give an inch. This can be a tremendous relief to the child who otherwise would have to clam up or spend twenty minutes denying the facts. Confrontation, however, is not likely to be successful with the child who feels that everybody is his enemy.

4. Be sparing with your use of "Why?" It is very difficult to explore reasons and all but impossible for a child to lay his motivations out on the principal's desk for dissection. It is much better to say, "We can't have this art on the lavatory walls. I'm not going to let you continue. We have to talk about this a little."

5. Get the conversation going about the actual situation. Get a description of what happened. *Listen* to what the child says.

6. If you think a child is overwhelmed with guilt or shame, begin by minimizing the weightiness of the problem at hand, "This doesn't bother me too much but we had better look at it. It can cause you trouble." This can make it easier for a child to begin to let you in. Of course, in a very important issue you eventually have to come to grips with the whole of the difficulty.

Point out that almost everybody gets into something like this at some time. "It's not so unusual. Let's talk about it." This can be useful to a child who is frightened after he has revealed an interest in sex, for example. On the other hand, the child who says "everybody does it" needs a different treatment.

7. Say what you know the child wants to say but can't put into words. "You were very disappointed, weren't you? You had been counting on this for a long time and couldn't stand to have to wait any longer." This is very different from and should not be confused with the amateur practice of psychiatry. It does not mean that you point out to a child your "understanding" of his unconscious motivations, sibling rivalry or oedipal conflict.

In the "disappointed" situation, the silver-dollar-throwing incident, the principal knew that Donny had been waiting and hoping to hear that he had been accepted in a special boarding school. His home was intolerable to him. His father had died very suddenly and his mother, with three small children, had moved to a new community and chosen for a second husband a man with no education, no grace, no profession, no trade. He was a bully and was physically cruel to the mother and children. The principal had been trying to get Donny into a boarding school but it was taking months to complete the arrangements. Each time Donny saw the principal, he hoped that she would have word for him. One day, the principal and the public health nurse walked into Donny's classroom on business that had nothing to do with Donny. He waited a moment, saw that they had not come to bring him news and hurled a silver dollar at the nurse's head.

In the interview, the principal did not, as we said above, go into the underlying forces which were making it all but impossible for this child to maintain himself at school. Rather, she helped him talk about his disappointment and helped him handle his immediate frustrations until the time when Donny was accepted in the boarding school.

8. Be aware of the kinds of thinking demanded by the particular situation. Millie Almy, in a recent article,[3] discusses "the tendency toward wishful thinking when adults assume that the thinking of the five- or ten-year-old basically resembles their own, and again when they take whatever he says to mean what they would mean if they were saying the same thing."

Bright children frequently become involved in relationships which are beyond their grasp in terms of emotional and personality maturity. ". . . . the intellectually superior child exposes himself to experience beyond his years. He perceives so much, and, sensing many of the implications, he reacts to and becomes involved in learning which makes an emotional demand beyond his stage of personality growth."

9. Help the child with plans for specific steps to improve the situation. Remember that much of the temper and anger and misbehavior of the child is born of his anxiety. Accept his right to an emotional outburst. Reassure him. If you really mean to help him, he will know it and be able to believe you. Help him look toward health and responsible behavior. A child may be so scared of severe punishment at home that he cannot consider rationally the problem at hand. If you believe it will be possible to deal with it at school, you can reassure him: "I think we can handle this here. I don't believe I need to call your father." If you think the home *should* be informed give the older child the opportunity to do it himself and report back to you. If he is afraid of possible exclusion from school he needs to hear "I mean for you to graduate and I won't let you get into serious trouble. Now, let's see what we can do about this."

10. At some point in the interview, give the child an opportunity to ask *you* questions. Or say, "Is there anything you want to tell me?" or, "Is there something you would like me to try to do for you?" Be prepared for some remarkable questions and disclosures, but after you've done this a few times you'll be convinced of how helpless and frightened the misbehavers are and you'll be moved by the depth and intensity of their desire to be "in" and to be good.

---

[3] Millie Almy, Wishful Thinking About Children's Thinking?, *Teachers College Record*, Vol. 62, pp. 396–406, Feb. 1961.

33. What Most Frequently Goes Wrong in School Groups

Fritz Redl

Fritz Redl is widely known for his work in the children's field. In the selection, he underscores the importance of group psychological factors in the production of classroom difficulties. The teacher, who is first and foremost a group leader, consequently needs skills in group analysis. Redl's discussion of common group malfunctions should prove helpful in this connection.

GROUP-PSYCHOLOGICAL FACTORS IN DISCIPLINE PROBLEMS

At this point a thorough analysis of a wide variety of discipline cases should be presented. The group-psychological factors involved in them should be carefully isolated, and multiple choices for solutions should be suggested. However, such an approach—the only one that would be of real practical use for the teacher on the job—cannot be made in the limited space of this study. Nevertheless, we shall at least try to enumerate the most frequent types of group-psychological factors contributing to discipline problems. We have to leave all interpretations and applications to the reader's own imagination but hope that we may be able to follow this presentation with more concretely helpful illustrative materials at some later date.

Remember our thesis is that many discipline problems are not the results of things wrong with the individuals involved but are the outcroppings of factors in the structures of the groups in which the individuals live. When something is wrong with the group, even the most normal individual member is likely to produce confused action leading to problem

In *Discipline for Today's Children and Youth.* Washington, D.C.: Association for Supervision and Curriculum Development, National Education Association, 1944 and 1956. Pp. 45–57. Reprinted with permission of the Association for Supervision and Curriculum Development and the author. Copyright © 1944 and 1956 by the Association for Supervision and Curriculum Development.

behavior. What we are investigating now is just *what* it is that most frequently goes wrong with school groups and, therefore, constitutes the highest disciplinary risk. We think we can classify the results of our analysis under six main headings.

DISSATISFACTIONS IN THE WORK PROCESS

The fact that bad teaching or curriculum planning automatically increases the number of discipline problems we produce has long been known in a general way. In fact, for a while we placed so much emphasis on this factor that we regarded it as the only source of discipline problems. There are still some who adhere to this theory, by the way, loudly protesting that a teacher who knows how to teach won't have any discipline problems in his classroom. This is a wild exaggeration of an otherwise very worthwhile point. Exaggeration in the opposite direction can also be heard from time to time: that discipline is based only on "personality factors" and "mental disorders in the pupils" and that it has practically no relationship to the curriculum as such.

Rejecting both extremes and trying to salvage the morsel of truth contained in both, we should like to suggest that any disturbance in the satisfactions children get out of the work they do with their teachers is likely to reflect itself in the production of problem behavior. Here are some examples.

Subject Matter Much Too Easy. Too much of the work ability of the students remains unchallenged and has to search for other outlets.

Subject Matter Much Too Difficult. Frustration accompanies great stretches of the work. Research has proved beyond doubt that exposure to the frustration of not being able to do things well produces tremendous aggression or restlessness in normal children. The results are unavoidable diversions, taking pokes at one another, dropping and throwing things, irritability, and "I-don't-care" attitudes, which lower behavioral inhibitions all over the place.

Language of Teachers Too Remote. Language can be remote from the children's development level or from the native tongue ordinarily used on their social plane. If that is the case, the child feels out of place, not really wanted, or even looked down upon and begins to show signs of social-outcast reactions and protest.

Load of Assignments Too Heavy. In this case, the school hour is loaded with the emotional strain of guilt feelings, criticisms, and a general impression of not being up to what is expected, or an attempt is made to catch up on lost play time by having a good time during class.

Load of Assignments Too Light. Then the feeling of progress in learning is lacking, which again reflects itself in a growing unwillingness to do any work because the time spent on it does not seem profitable in the end.

Assignments Badly Planned, Poorly Explained, Unfairly Judged. The result is that typical "resentment behavior" pops out in little irritations all over the place.

Type of Work and Presentation Too Advanced. They do not click with the developmental needs of the children. For instance, lectures on

nature in general should be given at an age when a strong curiosity about animals' bodies can easily be utilized for motivation.

Type of Work and Presentation Too Infantile. They are too infantile compared to the developmental level at which the children happen to be emotionally. For instance, talks about sex and the flowers are too childlike when youngsters are full of pride about their newly acquired preadolescence daring in sex exploration on a very different level indeed.

Activities Too Much on a Merely Verbal Level. Such activities leave the normal motor needs of growing children unchallenged for long stretches of time. We frequently find restlessness, noise, shuffling of feet, falling of chairs, and pushing when too much discussion or lecturing substitutes for real participation and manipulative activities.

Work Badly Scheduled. Scheduling can be bad in terms of sequences of different types or can be ill-timed in terms of exhaustion and fatigue. For instance, the English poetry class is at the end of a long day after a baseball game, at which moment it seems to be especially hard to excite manipulation-greedy sixth-graders about Shelley or Keats.

The examples could be multiplied by the hundreds. Suffice it to say in summary that any serious mistake in the planning or presentation of the curriculum in terms of the real growth needs of the children we teach produces an increase in discipline problems, even with the most normal and well-mannered groups of children. Boredom and fatigue are known to be the worst enemies of school morale. Only the moron doesn't care whether we bore him or not—he doesn't notice or care what happens around him anyway. The normal youngster instinctively searches for substitute satisfactions if taught the wrong way. This natural defense of the normal individual presents itself as a "discipline problem" at times.

EMOTIONAL UNREST IN INTERPERSONAL RELATIONS

The schools were originally designed as places in which to learn. Unfortunately, we do not invite only the various I.Q.'s of the children to come in. The youngsters bring, to our great discomfort, other parts of their personalities besides their intelligences. They bring perceptions, moral attitudes, and whatever else has to be taught. They bring their bodies—every part of them, no matter how disturbing or unnecessary for what we want to teach. And they bring the whole inventory of the emotions they use at home and on the playground, in addition to those that are relevant to the acquisition of wisdom and knowledge. No wonder they also "live" in our classrooms, whether we like it or not. This means that they form attachments and hatreds, cliques and subgroups; they hope, love, hate, and fear. They experiment with one another as potential friends, sweethearts, rivals, cooperators, bosses, even slaves.

They try to experience the whole scale of person-to-person relationships with which they have become acquainted in their private lives. In short, life goes on in spite of any curriculum plans we may have.

Conflicts arising from personal relations are reflected in the shape of "discipline problems." Such discipline problems are often not even directed at us at all, but they are there just the same.

Individual Friendships and Tensions. Strong, sudden friendships among youngsters sometimes produce stubbornness against the intrusion of the teacher through criticism or blame. Vehement antipathies, hatreds, and animosities among youngsters may encourage individual feelings to supersede reasonable adjustments to teacher demands or work interests. Sometimes even work and achievement become only a phase in this tension among individual children, instead of a serene process of intellectual growth achieved in emotional isolation.

Cliques and Subgroup Formations. These phenomena are often the backbone of group life, the greatest pillars of learner morale. Sometimes, though, they may confuse the school picture no end. You may get subgroups against one another, so that anything you say becomes unacceptable to group 1 simply because it is so enthusiastically received by group 2. Or you may find that various subgroups begin to impress one another by the degrees to which they submit to or rebel against your leadership.

Many fights and many instances of undesirable behavior are sidelines of such subgroup tensions, rather than direct attacks upon the order you represent. The basis on which such subgroup formation takes place may be developmental age, sex, degree of sophistication, social discrimination, racial or national difference, degree of academic interest, proximity to the teacher as a person, acceptance of the school code, and many others.

Disorganization in Group Roles. Every teacher knows what "group roles" are, even though he may not be familiar with the term. A few examples may suffice to show the phenomenon we refer to: Most any classroom has such typical functions filled by pupils as leader, second in command, organizer (with or against the teacher), janitorial assistant, teacher's pet, model boy, black sheep, scapegoat, bully, isolate, rejectee, group executioner, attorney-at-law, defender of the innocent, group clown (with or against the adult), hero in battle, fifth columnist (in terms of group interests), seducer and ringleader, trouble starter, rabble-rouser, appeaser, humorous rescuer of tense situations.

Whenever any one of these roles is badly filled or not needed in a group in which a lot of individuals strive to establish such roles for themselves or whenever many youngsters fight for the same group role in competition, you are likely to have a rise in your discipline problems, no matter how nice these youngsters or how smart you yourself may otherwise be.

Pupil-Teacher Frictions. The fact that strong frictions or emotional disturbances in the feelings of youngsters toward us are the source of many discipline problems has long been recognized in theory. Often, however, we are not quite aware of the degree to which pupil-teacher emotion enters the production line of discipline problems. For often these emotional elements are of low visibility, and sometimes even the youngsters themselves are unaware of their existence or deny them loudly to others and themselves. The most serious producer of discipline problems is the tendency in so many youngsters to project upon the teacher what are really basic attitudes developed in relation to the family at home. Strong feelings in youngsters of "not being liked or understood" or of "being discriminated against," for example, frequently may develop without any real mistake being committed in school.

Any tension, conscious or unconscious, among the youngsters is likely to color your classroom discipline. Especially in cases of general irritability and touchiness or widespread "uppitiness" and resistance on the part of whole classrooms, the suspicion that some of it goes back to disturbed interpersonal relationships is frequently justified.

DISTURBANCES IN GROUP CLIMATE

Without a chance really to define "group climate" adequately at this stage of the game, we still think we can put across what this peculiar term means by describing several instances. For teachers experience group climate all through their work, even though group-psychological discussions have been kept out of their teacher-training curricula. On the whole, we mean by this term the basic feeling tone that underlies the life of a group, the sum total of everybody's emotions toward one another, toward work and organization, toward the group as a unit, and toward things outside.

The Punitive Climate. The punitive climate is one of the most frequent distortions of climate in classrooms. A punitive climate is *not* identical with "a case of punishment." On the contrary, wise punishment usually does not at all imply the basic attitude of "punitiveness" of the teacher toward the child, whereas in a thoroughly punitive climate the pressure on children is often so high all the time that the teacher need make only sparse use of actual punishment as such.

However, the punitive climate is perhaps the most destructive of group morale and discipline of any classroom climate. It invariably produces these characterological side effects: The teacher shows little respect for the persons of the children in her room, being so sure he can manage their behavior by threat and fear anyway that he doesn't bother about them as human beings; the pupils usually expect absolute acceptance or rejection on the basis of the teacher's behavior code, and they usually fall into two groups—some rebel, hate, and fight back (the open "problem cases" in a punitive group), and others identify themselves with the teacher out of fear and, therefore, have to become moral hypocrites in their attitudes toward the other children. They are suspiciously submissive as long as the teacher is present, squeal on neighbors when they get a chance, and, in general, develop "holier than thou" attitudes toward their pals. The emotions of fear of reprisal and shame are in the air most of the time; the teacher, as well as the onlookers, receives sadistic enjoyment of the chronic type.

It is this kind of climate that breeds sadists, bullies, and hypocrites. In this type of group it is a sign of character and courage to become a behavior problem. The morally healthy individual is the most frequent victim of the punitive climate.

The Emotional-Blackmail Climate. This climate is another distortion of healthy group living. It is a variation of the punitive climate but sails under a different disguise. In the emotional-blackmail climate the teacher "loves" all children and says so at the rate of three times a minute. He rubs it in about how nice and unaggressive he is—how he will never punish anybody for doing wrong—while he drips with enjoyment of the self-induced guilt feelings of his crew. In the emotional-blackmail climate, you don't get punished if you do wrong, but you know you have to feel like a heel for three weeks afterward. The teacher in this climate produces a tremendous emotional dependence on him, exploiting it as the only source of influence.

The results of this type of climate are surprising absence of physical or other obvious violence between teacher and children, often confused with understanding and progressiveness in technique; an extreme fear in the children of the disapproval of their teacher, resulting in extended orgies of self-accusation by the children and hurt feelings by the adult leader after each disciplinary breach; strong rivalries among some of the children who are the "good" ones against those of the children who are not so emotionally close to the teacher as they.

The discipline problems of this group are especially strong when its members move from younger childhood into early adolescence, when so much adult dependence is unnatural for them. The main casualties of this climate are those who want to grow up and become independent and would rather take the rap for mischievous acts than turn into self-deprecatory introverts at the teacher's command.

The Hostile-Competition Climate. The hostile-competition climate is a distortion of an otherwise healthy phenomenon in our society. Normally, a good deal of competitiveness is unavoidable, even liked, by children growing into a society in which there can be little doubt of the presence of competitiveness. However, there are two things that can go wrong with a normal competitive climate: One is that there may be more competitiveness than children need or can stand without developing negative character traits or defeatism; the other is that competitiveness may deteriorate into hatefulness.

The hostile-competition climate can be characterized as one in which everybody is whipped into aggressively competing with everybody else all the time. Reward is given to the child who proudly tramples under his feet whoever dares to compete with him. Shame falls upon the head of the child who would rather get a lower grade than feel "holier than thou" toward his best pal. This climate turns a classroom into a dog race. It is highly doubtful that mutual love and friendship are instigated in the participants while the race is going on.

The results are extreme uncooperativeness among group members (all organization has to be enforced by outside rules and pressures); the development of outcasts from those who happen to be last in the line of aggressive competition; and the development of snobs from those who happen to hold the front line easily and get more than ten times the amount of praise that their efforts deserve. The result is dependence of such groups on autocratic management, no real wish for democratic cooperation and self-management, enjoyment of punishment for discipline breaches as outlets for all the hostility and moral snobbishness fostered under cover.

The Group-Pride Climate. The group-pride climate has a very healthy counterpart. What we mean here is the distorted case in which the group leader tries to develop a strong emotional relationship of every group member with the total group and then overfosters feelings of vanity and conceit related to the group as such. Good "teams" sometimes allow their team spirit to disintegrate into the climate we refer to.

The group-pride climate usually involves a high degree of group consciousness among a classroom as a whole, with a variety of positive attributes connected with such development. At the same time it produces a whole host of potential group executioners who simply wait for moments when they can swoop down upon the unlucky devils who have stained group honor or rewards. On the other hand, it develops a certain set of chronic rejectees and releases wild mob-lynching psychology against them under cover of righteous group indignation. Violent fights and the chronic problem behavior of the constantly persecuted and despised rejectee are the main types of discipline problem engendered by a climate of this kind.

We could—and should—continue this analysis of typical classroom climates for quite a while. Suffice it to say here that the total climate that governs the social relationships among teacher, children, and total group has a tremendous influence upon the type of discipline problem that will be automatically avoided or automatically produced. We also admit, though, that this factor along the production line of discipline problems is still the most difficult to analyze without further group-psychological instrumentation.

MISTAKES IN ORGANIZATION AND GROUP LEADERSHIP

Many teachers do perfect jobs of teaching, as far as the presentation of subject matter and the organization of learning experiences go, and they also have fine teacher personalities and very fair approaches to "the child." Where they get into trouble is in the mechanics of group leadership. For the successful handling of groups of certain types is as complex a task as the organization of subject matter and is a chapter entirely of its own.

As teachers receive practically no organized training in group leadership, children are exposed to a hit-and-miss technique that causes many problems that could easily be eliminated. Again we shall have to select only a small fraction of the illustrations that offer themselves.

Too Much Autocratic Pressure. Too much autocratic pressure can be a problem, especially at age ranges in which gradual emancipation from adult leadership is a natural and important trend. Program and organization may be so adult-centered that there is little feeling of real and meaningful participation by the members of the group.

Too Little Security. Too little security given the group by the adult leader leaves the children constantly exposed to the strains of responsibility and moral guilt. Tossing all responsibilities over to the group with little reference to its members' developmental needs and emotional maturity is often mistaken for "self-government" and "education for democracy," which it certainly is not.

Too High or Too Low Standards for Group Behavior. Too high standards expose children to moral defeatism, with the result that irresponsible mischievousness becomes a way out. Too low standards give them no chance to satisfy normal amounts of "group pride." As a result they get disgusted and disgruntled and develop feelings that their group life is childish and not worthwhile; they produce reactions similar to those of boredom and fatigue.

Too Much Organization. When there is too much organization, life is regimented by a thousand silly little rules that you bump into wherever you turn, resulting in trouble-avoidance, taking the place of really serious group-mindedness.

Too Little Organization. With too little organization, all issues have to be decided on a moment-to-moment basis, and the children never quite know what to expect.

Out-of-Focus Group Organization. Organization can often be out of step with age, developmental maturity, special type, background and specific needs of the group. This is often especially true when schools change their clienteles, as, for example, when new boundaries are set up for the areas served by the schools and foreign relief clienteles replace hyperambitious, overprotected groups from "refined" neighborhoods, while teachers and school organization maintain the same basic disciplinary pattern. Constant revision of the organizational pattern to fit total school structure and needs is essential.

Lack of Tact. Lack of tact is especially frequent among highly ambitious and subject-matter-minded teachers who have little imagination about how children feel. It is especially frequent also in the transition from one developmental phase to another, when teachers often try to treat youngsters as though they were much younger than they feel.

Indulgence in Personal Sensitivities and Allergies. There is also danger of superimposing one's own personal behavior code on the children, regardless of whether or not it fits. It can take the form, for example, of tremendous sensitivity to language with preadolescents of a low-protection area or extreme touchiness in terms of personal vanity with children who have little school-mindedness or security with adults at home.

Overreaction to Dignity Violations. Many serious discipline problems have little to do with discipline at all. They are the hysterical overreactions of oversensitive adults to irritating child behavior, especially when differences of social background and manners are involved.

Plan for Revenge Instead of Educational Change. To "show them" or to "give them what they have coming" is often made the prime motivation for the way discipline problems are handled, whereas the chances for real changes of attitudes among the children involved should be the only thing that counts.

Inconsistency in Promise and Threat. If extreme in nature, inconsistency undermines group security and gives children feelings of unpredictability against which they rebel; or they become defeatist in their attitudes toward group issues.

Stupidity in Carrying Out Promises or Threats. The idea that consistency in itself is a virtue and that it is better to be consistent and do the wrong thing than ever to change one's decision is a serious mistake, too. Children watch the thoughtfulness with which you plan your action. Thoughtfully documented change of decision is more conducive to respect than is silly, stupid, or inconsiderate sticking to the wrong gun.

Wrong Use of Techniques. Wrong use of punishment and rewards, reasoning, interference, and "learn by mistake" techniques is included here. Obviously wrong applications of any set of educational techniques undermine group morale and develop a "try and don't get caught" psychology. What constitutes "wrong use" is, unfortunately, a chapter too involved to be opened up here.

Wrong Arguments about Educational Techniques. More children disobey because of the silly arguments on the basis of which obedience is sold to them than because of opposition to obedience itself. The same is true all through the line of educational techniques. Especially in talking to groups, teachers are likely to support the right things they do by the wrong arguments and thus to produce resistance where there wasn't any to begin with. This is especially true during early adolescence, when the group code changes so that the same argument that would have appealed to them a few years ago is just that much provocation now.

Mistakes in Emotional Distance and Proximity. Mistakes in emotional distance and proximity are so well known as a factor in undermining group morale that we can skip them after brief mention. We add only that such emotional preferences and rejections may be noticed by children even though we are not aware of them ourselves and that class- and race-based emotional reactions are special dynamite along that line.

It would be easy to continue this list for quite a while. Let us summarize briefly by repeating that, even with excellent teaching ability guaranteed, even with a fine attitude toward "the child" from the beginning, any one mistake in the organizational or personal management of the children and the group is likely to produce problem behavior. An inspection of the group-leadership techniques we use is essential from time to time, as children, as well as the world around them, change more rapidly than does our list of generally recommended, previously practiced educational tricks.

EMOTIONAL STRAIN AND SUDDEN CHANGE

Emotional strain, affecting a whole group, may in itself be sufficient to produce upsets and problem cases. We know this is true whenever the emotional strain on groups is easily recognizable as such.

Anxiety. The stage of anxiety in which many school groups find themselves for weeks during "examination period," and afterward waiting for the results, is a frequent type of group strain. In the same way, sudden affects that sweep classrooms at times are productive of problem behavior beyond expectation. Excitement about contemporary events (community riots), extreme fury, enthusiasm, unusual hilarity, and depression and fear are among the prime dangers to stable morale. Needless to say, the constantly whipped-up excitement and aggression in times of war work as chronic irritants to the discipline of many school groups and add unnoticeably but considerably to the problems of the teacher as group leader.

Boredom. One of the most deteriorating effects of emotions upon group morale, however, does not flow from wild acts and excitement but rather from the lack of it over too long a time. Boredom will always remain the greatest enemy of school discipline. If we remember that children are bored, not only when they don't happen to be interested in the subject or when the teacher doesn't make it interesting, but also when certain working conditions are out of focus with their basic needs, then we can realize what a great contributor to discipline problems boredom really is.

In classes too large, a number of the children will of necessity be bored, while the others enjoy what goes on, for rarely can any one teaching procedure be exactly on the right level for everybody involved. Another form of boredom in classrooms comes from overemphasis on verbalization, while the manipulative needs of children are left unattended. The same thing in reverse—prolonged manipulative activity leaving the imagination no chance to come in—may also bring on boredom.

Research has shown that boredom is closely related to frustration and that the effect of too much frustration is invariably irritability, withdrawal, rebellious opposition, or aggressive rejection of the whole show.

Reaction to Change. Reaction to change is perhaps the most frequent and, as yet, unrecognized factor in discipline difficulties. Of course we expect such bad effects from changes for the worse. It is important to keep in mind, though, that such a limitation of the problem is not realistic. Any change, even for the better, tends to upset group organization temporarily and to lead to a phase of increased problem production.

Many teachers will remember how even their "nice" classrooms are sometimes hard to manage when the usually light room is darkened, when the lecture setting changes to a discussion, a subcommittee arrangement, or a picture-slide demonstration. They know how much noise and confusion often accompany changes from one room to another, from class to luncheon and the other way around and how otherwise very studious children may all of a sudden act very foolishly in the museum they wanted for so long to visit.

A change in group leadership also weighs heavily as a factor in reaction to change. Much of the trouble substitute teachers have with classes has little to do with the real quality of those classes or with the teachers' real ability for group leadership. For, when you meet a class in which someone else is substituting for the permanent leader, it automatically has already deteriorated into something more akin to a mob than a group, and the task of leadership is very different from the task under normal conditions.

Changes in program affect groups the same way and especially changes in leadership technique. The most frequent example of this kind of change is the attempt to spring self-government on a school. What you find during the first few months has nothing to do with the children's reactions to self-government. It is only their reactions to the fact of change itself. Only after a few months do their real reactions to self-government, their ability to take it, and their immaturity toward it become visible at all.

The answer, of course, is not that change should be avoided at all costs. It is that the knowledge of this law of group psychology should guide us in our evaluation of what happens and that we sometimes can meet confusion caused by too-sudden change through planning for it by means of "transition techniques."

THE COMPOSITION OF THE GROUP

The problem of "grouping" has never been satisfactorily discussed—to say nothing of being solved. The most frequent controversial disputes are concerned with "intelligence" versus "maturity" grouping. Unfortunately, neither of the two is a way out. The real picture is much too complex for that.

Without entering this very important and devious problem here, we can generalize safely to the extent that, whenever something is very wrong in the composition of a group, discipline problems are the natural and unavoidable result.

If this is true, then the discovery of what constitutes healthy divergencies, as distinct from serious mistakes, in group composition must become of prime importance.

The following principles can be suggested without too much risk:

First, it isn't a question of whether or not groups are heterogeneous but of whether or not the criteria according to which they are heterogeneous are relevant to group life or not.

Example 1. The 10A is well matched in interest in and ability for Latin. At the same time it is rather divergent in terms of developmental age. Some of the students are wildly adolescent; others have left their adolescence behind them in many ways; still others are just in the transition from delayed childhood.

As they have all been picked because of their interest in and ability for Latin and as the Latin teacher does a superb job of teaching and group leadership, they are a happy group for the Latin hour for which they are together once a week.

They would be a mess and in chaos if they were expected to live as the group they are for even a day in camp.

Example 2. The children in Cabin 8 are of widely varying I.Q.s. Yet they are well matched in terms of camp interest, degree of sophistication, and developmental maturity. So they make a superb cabin group, in spite of the fact that it would be near to impossible to teach them any one academic thing the way they are.

Second, as every group is always badly matched in some criteria, even though it has been well matched in others, the real problem is to avoid extremes in those criteria that are "marginal" to the main purpose of group life.

Example. The 10A Latin class already discussed has one mistake in it. There are only three children who are very immature in their outlooks on life and sex. The more sophisticated ones are so far in the majority that these three are pretty much out of place. In such a case we will observe that after a few weeks of concentration upon Latin, the three Benjamins will become problems to the teacher. They will be either especially fearful of expressing themselves, or they will become especially clownish and wild in their attempts to impress their otherwise more sophisticated companions. Too-great heterogeneity in a secondary criterion of grouping will still encourage discipline problems.

Just how far apart the extremes between group members in one criterion can be without disturbing the group balance is a question still unsolved. Right now the situation has to be studied anew from case to case. Research efforts to develop generally applicable standards are under way.

Third, although practically any criterion may be relevant for grouping in one case and highly unimportant in another, we find that the following are often the most important criteria to be considered in analyzing the causes of discipline problems.

Age and development. Age and development, especially in terms of physical and social maturity, are a major criterion.

Socioeconomic backgrounds, racial elements, and so forth. Especially the various differences arising from the substratification in our society are central here: for instance, the difference in codes between youngsters who are highly "manner-minded" and those who are proudly unconventional. This factor should be considered more often than it usually is.

Home acceptance or emancipation. Differences in home dependence often count heavily during the late grade-school and junior high-school years, when children make the transition from strong home identifications to greed for emancipation at varying rates.

Shyness-toughness. Some shy children together with a few more expressive ones make a good mixture. If the distance becomes too great the opposite end is achieved: The shy youngster gets more scared than he was before and becomes a problem through his withdrawal. The wild one gets more "show-offish" through the cheap admiration he gets from his more retiring colleagues.

Intelligence and knowledge. This topic is so well known that commentary is not needed.

Interest and work acceptance. Especially vital in terms of learning morale.

Physical coordination. Extreme differences tend to encourage sharp subgrouping within a group.

Leader acceptance. From open defiance to strong need for childish dependence, two tastes hard to satisfy in the same group.

Organizational maturity. When two-thirds of your group can easily be expected to be self-governing, whereas one-third is on such a different level of organizational dependence that it cannot function without the pressure of outside lures and controls, behavior problems arise.

Enjoyment of group life. The factor of enjoyment separates the happily "group-eager" youngster from his more isolationist pal.

All in all, what we want to point out is that the mere mixture of your group out of too heterogeneous elements in highly group-relevant items may in itself constitute a constant producer of discipline problem behavior without anything else being wrong. Discovery and repair of such factors in time save you much undeserved criticism and much self-accusation, so that a psychological analysis of your group composition is a job well worth undertaking from time to time.

KNOW YOUR GROUPS

Needless to say, any one of the six group-psychological factors in discipline problems may co-exist with any other. The task for the practitioner boils down to three major parts.

First, don't allow yourself to be fooled by the surface appearance of a discipline problem. What youngsters do contains no indication of what the real source of your discipline problem is.

Second, you can find the trouble, though, by analyzing your discipline problems in terms of the following questions.

What did the behavior observed really mean?

To what extent was it produced by the peculiar case history of the individual involved? To what extent did it also (or even mainly) contain elements of a group-psychological nature?

Which of the most frequent group-psychological factors producing problem behavior in school classes are involved and to what degree?

Third, on this basis you will want to add these further questions, growing out of a previous chapter of our little study, to your calculations.

As I want to do something about it, do I plan mainly for effect on the individual or effect on the group, and how can I be sure to respect the law of "marginal antisepsis"?

In which direction do I have to aim most, toward change of surface behavior or modification of basic attitudes, and how can I be sure to respect the law of marginal antisepsis with regard to this problem?

How can I possibly evaluate whether or not what I want to do will "work" without being fooled by false analogies or by the cheap sellers of "bags full of tricks" and without neglecting the less visible subsurface effects of what I do over the more visible and tangible results?

None of this is meant to substitute for the personal analysis of each case, of each situation, by the teacher who is in it. It is meant to encourage that teacher to think through his problem instead of applying otherwise recommended techniques without critical examination.

The author is convinced that the good disciplinarian, though always retaining some of the qualities of a good artist, is still closer to the modern physician than to the performer of magical tricks at a county fair.

34. Managing Emotionally Disturbed Children in Regular Classrooms: A Replication and Extension[1]

Jacob S. Kounin and Sylvia Obradovic

The following article, by Kounin and his associate, represents one of the few research studies conducted on the topic of classroom management. (1) Teachers who are successful in controlling the behavior of normal youngsters are also relatively successful with emotionally disturbed children. (2) Teachers' "with-it-ness" techniques and programming for variety in learning activities are related to desirable child behavior. These are some of the major findings stemming from this research attempt to delineate certain dimensions of teaching style that influence the behavior of disturbed and nondisturbed pupils in regular elementary school classes.

In a previous study based on observation of elementary school classrooms containing one or more emotionally disturbed children, Kounin, Friesen, and Norton (1966) concluded that teachers who were successful in managing the behavior of non-disturbed children in a classroom were also successful in managing the behavior of emotionally disturbed children in the classroom. This conclusion was based upon the following findings:

1. A significant positive correlation between the *work involvement*[2] scores of disturbed and non-disturbed children in the classroom.

2. A significant positive correlation between the *deviancy*[2] scores of the disturbed and non-disturbed children.

Journal of Special Education, 1968, 2, 129–135. Reprinted with the permission of the publisher and senior author.

[1] The research reported here was supported by Public Health Service research grants from the National Institute of Mental Health.
[2] Defined below.

3. A significant correlation between the *deviancy-contagion* scores of the disturbed children and the *deviancy* and *work involvement* scores of the non-disturbed children.

4. A delineation of specific teacher techniques that correlated significantly in the same direction and approximate magnitude with the behavior of both the disturbed and the non-disturbed children.

These findings were arrived at through analysis of videotapes recorded for a half-day each in 30 elementary school classrooms. Because there were some differences between the first two grades and the upper grades and between seatwork and recitation subsettings (e.g., arithmetic lesson, reading lesson), the breakdowns for grade level and subsetting resulted in some quite small N's.

The present study attempted both to replicate and extend the earlier study. To obtain a better sample of both seatwork and recitation subsettings for all teachers, the number of classrooms for the first two grades was increased. In addition, the recording time for each time for each class was extended.

METHOD

The activities in 50 first and second grade classrooms were videotaped for a full day each. (The recording technique was described in the previous study.) Because the recording for one classroom could not be used, the final usable N was 49 classrooms, 24 located in a predominantly middle class suburb of Detroit, Michigan, and 26 located in metropolitan Detroit.

To exclude "extreme" classrooms from the study, only schools whose average achievement scores fell between the 20th and 80th percentiles of the school system's norms were used. The schools selected were large enough to have at least two classrooms for each grade, and one "poor" and one "good" classroom were selected per school—this judgment being based upon whether the children in the classroom showed high or low degrees of work involvement. The designation of children as "emotionally disturbed" was based upon a consensus among the teacher, principal, and, in most cases, a school social worker. Where the child was on a waiting list for the school social worker but had not had a professional diagnostic work-up, the principal investigator accepted a consensus between the principal and teacher, along with some obvious pathological circumstances (such as a child in the first grade being in his fourth foster home).

The sample of children for scoring was selected by the project director from diagrams of the seating arrangements for each academic subsetting in each classroom. Each diagram was divided into four quadrants and a boy and girl from each quadrant selected for scoring. The emotionally disturbed children were scored separately.

Each child finally selected for scoring was coded for *work involvement* and *deviancy* every 12 seconds for the duration of a specific academic subsetting, the 12-second interval being used to accommodate the timing device on the videotape machine. For *work involvement*, the children were rated as to the number of times they were considered to be: (a) definitely doing their assigned work; (b) probably doing the work; or (c) definitely not working. The ratio of ratings for "definitely not working" was used as the score for *work involvement*. For *deviancy*, the children were coded as: (a) not misbehaving; (b) engaging in mild misbehavior; (c) engaging in serious misbehavior. The *deviancy* score was the percentage of 12-second units in which no misbehavior occurred. (All scores, for children and teacher, were stated in a hypothesized positive order.) Intercoder reliabilities for different sets of coders ranged from 82% to 100% agreement, with a mean of 95%.

A teacher's managerial success in the classroom was defined by her ability to induce work involvement and prevent deviancy in the children with whom she worked. A detailed description of the categories in which teachers were scored will be given below. To avoid coloring teacher scores with children's behavior scores, different individuals were used to score teachers than to score children. (There was one exception. The coder for *accountability* and *group alerting* for teachers in recitation subsettings also coded children's behavior, but a period of about one year separated the two codings.) Intercoder reliabilities for teacher styles ranged from 79% to 99% agreement, with a mean of 92% agreement.

FINDINGS

There were no significant differences, by t test, between the scores of disturbed and non-disturbed children for either *work involvement* or *deviancy,* or in seatwork or recitation subsettings. The correlation between the scores of disturbed and non-disturbed children were .764 for work involvement and .818 for deviancy in recitation subsettings and .567 for work involvement and .649 for deviancy in seatwork settings. These correlations support the conclusion that a teacher's degree of success in managing the classroom as a whole is related to her degree of success in managing the behavior of the emotionally disturbed children in the class. A more precise formulation of this conclusion requires (a) a delineation of what it is that teachers do that makes a difference in how children behave in their classrooms and (b) a determination of whether these techniques have the same effect upon disturbed and non-disturbed children.

Table 1 summarizes the correlations between various teacher techniques and the behavior of the emotionally disturbed and non-disturbed children in the classroom. The correlations for the non-disturbed children are shown in parentheses. With few exceptions, the correlations obtained for disturbed children and non-disturbed children are in the same direction and approximate magnitude.

Three conclusions may be drawn from these correlations:

1. Specific teacher techniques, which can be delineated, do determine how children behave in a classroom.

2. These techniques are *group* management techniques.

3. They have about the same effect upon emotionally disturbed children as upon non-disturbed children.

A description of the various teacher techniques rated in the study follows.

TABLE 1. PRODUCT-MOMENT CORRELATIONS BETWEEN TEACHER STYLES AND THE BEHAVIOR OF CHILDREN IN ACADEMIC SETTINGS*

Teacher Style Dimension	Recitation (N=49)		Seatwork (N=48)	
	Children's Work Involvement	Children's Deviancy	Children's Work Involvement	Children's Deviancy
Slowdowns	.528 (.656)	.621 (.641)	.494 (.198)	.409 (.490)
With-it-ness	.510 (.615)	.415 (.531)	.537 (.307)	.472 (.509)
Smoothness	.501 (.601)	.399 (.489)	.518 (.382)	.136 (.421)
Overlappingness	.485 (.460)	.213 (.362)	.414 (.259)	.271 (.379)
Group Alerting	.434 (.603)	.311 (.442)	.385 (.234)	.334 (.290)
Valence-Challenge	.335 (.372)	.406 (.325)	.304 (.308)	.346 (.371)
Accountability	.269 (.494)	.206 (.385)	.086 (.002)	.124 (−.035)
Seatwork Variety and Challenge	.042 (.061)	.043 (.033)	.284 (.516)	.154 (.276)
Highest Multiple Correction	(.812)	(.720)	(.685)	(.741)

*A correlation of .279 is significant at the .05 level; a correlation of .361 is significant at the .01 level. Correlations for nondisturbed children are given in the parentheses.

MANAGEMENT CATEGORIES AND TECHNIQUES

For the purposes of the study and categorization of teacher behavior, a set of descriptive codewords was used.

The codewords *slowdowns* and *smoothness* relate to a teacher's initiation and maintenance of the class's movement. *Slowdowns* refers to the manner in which a teacher maintains movement during a particular classroom activity and during the transition from one activity to another; it designates teacher-initiated friction that impedes the group's rate of movement. *Slowdowns* are created by the forms of teacher behavior classified and coded as follows:

Overdone. This was used when the teacher engaged in actions or a stream of talk that clearly exceeded what was necessary to get the children to understand or participate in an activity (behavior that would elicit the reaction, "All right, that's enough already!"). It was applied to the following categories of teacher behavior.

Behavior overdone. "Nagging," "preaching," or "moralizing" about the behavior of the class or of a particular child.

Prop and action overdone. Talking too much or dwelling too long on subactions (how to sit, where to put hands) or "props" (pencils, crayons, books) to the point of obscuring the task or its purpose.

Task overdone. Elaborating the task or task directions beyond the point where most children clearly understood and were ready to proceed.

Sheer overtalk. Excessive talking that could not be clearly classified in the above categories.

Target Fragmentation. This was used when the teacher directed individual children or small groups of children to do separately what the entire group could do at once—producing a drag in classroom movement and unnecessary delays for the other children. Thus, instead of directing a group of children to go to the "reading circle," the teacher might tell Johnny to go to the circle, then Mary, then Robert, until all were finally seated there.

Prop Fragmentation. Equivalent to *target fragmentation* except that the teacher causes the *slowdown* by directing the children to handle "props" separately when they could be managed in an unbroken unit of behavior.

The term *smoothness* was applied in connection with a teacher's manner of initiating and sustaining movement in the group. *Anti-smoothness* behaviors were coded as follows.

Dangles. Initiating an activity and then leaving it dangling to attend to something else (e.g., walking away from the group after giving a transition order, watering a plant after raising a question in arithmetic).

Truncations. The same as *dangles* except that in a *dangle* the teacher eventually resumes the activity, whereas in a *truncation* she drops it entirely.

Thrusts. A teacher's sudden bursting in on the children's activities with an order, statement, question, in such a manner as to indicate that the timing was dictated only by her own needs or desires, with no evidence, such as pausing or looking around, of sensitivity to the group's readiness to receive the new message. An everyday example of a *thrust* would be someone's butting in on a conversation without waiting to be noticed or attempting to ease in by listening to see what was being discussed.

Stimulus-boundedness. Equivalent to a *thrust* (in the sense of "jerkiness") except that here the teacher's behavior is a response to an event of some kind.

The *stimulus-bounded* teacher behaves as though she has no will of her own, reacting to an event as a helpless iron filing to a magnet. For example, she might be explaining an assignment or passing out papers, notice a piece of paper on the floor or a child sitting improperly (the event must be one that is not intensive, intrusive, or disruptive of the class), and become "immersed" in the event to the point of paying no attention to the major activity. This kind of behavior may be regarded as the opposite of goal-directed.

Group alerting and Accountability were used in describing the degree to which the teacher focuses her behavior on the group as a whole, rather than on a single child, when the group is the performing unit. Thus, even though only one child in a reading group might be reading aloud, the group is regarded as the performing unit, since all the children are doing essentially the same work either by listening, reading along or preparing to recite. The model for teacher behavior in this situation is an individual tutoring session in which the child is either listening to the tutor or performing for him and is held accountable for his alertness, knowledge, and performance. To what extent does the teacher make the classroom a replicate of this tutorial situation?

Group alerting refers to the degree to which the teacher focuses on all the children in a group during transition periods and recitations. Some forms of teacher behavior watched for in coding for *group alerting* are: (a) creating suspense in the classroom by pausing after a question and looking around before selecting a child to recite; (b) selecting reciters at random rather than in a predictable order; (c) alerting the children that they might be called upon to evaluate a reciter's performance; (d) circulating or deliberately looking around at the group during a child's recitation; (e) presenting a challenging issue to the group during the recitation; (f) acting in other ways indicating that the group is being kept alert and stimulated.

Accountability refers to the degree to which the teacher communicates to the children that she knows what they are doing in relation to the task during a child's recitation—her demonstrated alertness about how the children are performing the designated task. A simple measure of this alertness is the number of children called upon to recite during a given interval.

Another aspect of teacher style that was assessed was the teacher's ability to avoid satiation in the children in her group. The average duration of specific activities (a simple notion of "attention span") was found not to correlate with children's behavior. Nor did we feel that we could validly determine the children's feelings about their progress—probably the most important variable in slowing down the rate of satiation. We did attempt to arrive at a measure of variety and challenge in the day's program. In the previous study, the degree of variety in the class's activities, which included non-academic settings, did not correlate with the children's behavior. The latter's correlations with seatwork variety for *learning-related* activities were among the highest obtained. In the present study, variety and challenge were the highest predictors of the *work involvement* scores of non-disturbed children during seatwork, though not during recitation.

At transition points, *valence and challenge-arousal* were scored—the degree to which the teacher (without *overtalk*) attempts to instill in the children a zest for the upcoming task. *Valence* indicates that the teacher communicates to the children that the activity has intrinsic pleasure— "You'll like this one." *Challenge* refers to the teacher's communicating that the upcoming task will be intellectually challenging—"This next one is tricky"—and of course delivers on her promise with a task that does require some thought or creativity.

Seatwork variety-challenge was based upon the number of changes in assigned seatwork during a given period of time. Changes were scored in the following categories: (a) academic content (reading, arithmetic); (b) type of intellectual challenge (repetitive, rote copying tasks were scored negative and tasks requiring thought or creativity positive); (c) "props" (routine to unusual); (d) child responsibility (initiates own pace, pace set by other); (e) overt behavior mode (sedentary to active); (f) group configuration; and (g) geographic location.

Another aspect of teacher style that correlates with children's behavior is *with-it-ness*—the degree to which the teacher demonstrates that she is tuned in on what is going on in her classroom—has the legendary "eyes behind her head." This score was based upon the percentage of "desist events"—occasions when the teacher did something to stop a child's misbehavior, selected the correct deviant, and did so on time. The following were regarded as mistakes: (a) admonishing the wrong child; (b) stopping a minor act of misbehavior when there was a more serious one taking place (scolding a child for whispering when two other children were chasing each other around the room); (c) acting too late (after contagion had set in, or the misbehavior had grown worse).

Overlappingness is a measure of the degree to which a teacher attends to two issues when confronted with two issues to handle. (This correlates highly with *with-it-ness*.) Two types of events were scored: "desist incidents" and "child intrusion incidents" (as when a child from a seatwork group approaches the teacher while she is working with a reading group). Does the teacher give her attention to both demands for her attention or does she go all out to one and drop the other? For example, while working with a reading group and interrupted by a child in seatwork, a teacher high in *overlappingness* will do something with the reading group (scan, instruct reader to continue) while handling an intruding child, or desisting a deviant child.

DISCUSSION

As noted above, the correlations among these various forms of teacher behavior and children's behavior indicate that it is possible to delineate concrete aspects of teacher behavior that lead to managerial success in a classroom and apply to both disturbed and non-disturbed children. These are techniques that create a classroom ecology which applies to the *group* and not merely to individual children. Advocating this approach is not a simple matter of admonishing teachers to "create rapport" or "make it interesting." Nor does it entail a preoccupation with personality attributes such as "friendliness," "patience," "love of children," "understanding." Nor is it simply a matter of extrapolating from other adult-child relationships, whether with parents, psychotherapists, or even with tutors. Rather, the business of running a classroom is based upon a complicated technology directed towards developing a non-satiating learning program; programming for progress, challenge, and variety in learning activities; initiating and maintaining group and individual movement in classroom tasks; observing and eliciting feedback for many different events; coping with more than one event simultaneously; directing actions at appropriate targets; and doubtless others yet to be determined.

We would like to close with an opinion about priorities in the training and selection of classroom teachers, whether for emotionally disturbed children or others. We feel our research shows that techniques of group management and programming should be given more emphasis than they are presently receiving in curricula for prospective teachers. Classroom management techniques (and one might note that none of them necessitates punitiveness or restrictiveness) are neutral, enabling, and facilitating many different educational objectives. The lack of these skills puts a barrier in the way of promoting an effective classroom ecology and achieving educational objectives. Mastery of them frees the teacher to achieve a variety of objectives, including that of helping individual children.

REFERENCE

Kounin, J. S./Friesen, W. V./Norton, A. E. Managing emotionally disturbed children in regular classrooms. *Journal of Educational Psychology*, 1966, 57, 1, 1–13.

35. Learning Theory Approaches to Classroom Management: Rationale and Intervention Techniques

Harvey F. Clarizio and Stephen L. Yelon

In this article, the theoretical rationale for a learning theory approach to classroom discipline is discussed. Behavior therapy techniques—extinction, positive reinforcement, modeling, punishment, discrimination learning, and desensitization—are reviewed in relation to the management of deviant behavior in the school setting. Advantages and limitations of each technique are presented. What is your reaction to the notion that class-

The Journal of Special Education, 1967, 1, 267–274. Reprinted with the permission of the publisher and senior author.

*room teachers should be more concerned with the
undesirable behavior per se than with its more remote
causes?*

Today, more than ever before, there is acute concern about the mental
health of children. Traditionally, we have modeled intervention efforts
after the clinical concept of treatment. Dissatisfaction with the limitations
of psychotherapeutic intervention (Levitt, 1957) together with the professional manpower shortage in the mental health field has led, however, to
suggestions, e.g., Redl (1962), that we need new modes of treatment,
closer to real-life situations, if we are to tackle children's problems more
effectively.

When psychodynamic models were the preferred method of treatment, teachers were accorded at best a second-string status on the clinical
team helping emotionally handicapped children. The increasing popularity
of behavior therapy and other approaches based on learning theory now
offers teachers opportunities for an integral role in the quest for better
mental health for children. Indeed, it might well be the mental health
specialist who will now assume the supportive role (Gallagher & Chalfant, 1966) in the "treatment" of children.

In the application of learning theory principles to the modification
of deviant behavior, the emphasis is on the changing of behavior with little
attention devoted to the etiology of the behavior. Why should teachers
focus primarily on the behavior rather than on its causes? There are several reasons:

1. First, teachers by virtue of their orientation are not trained to
probe the causes of behavior that even mental hygiene specialists often
consider obscure and uncertain. Hence, is it really helpful to ask the
teacher to understand the causes underlying children's disturbed behavior?

2. Teachers in any case are rarely in a position wherein they can directly manipulate the causes so as to modify their influence on the child's
classroom adjustment. For example, if the problem lies in the parent-child
relations or in a brain lesion, there are few if any constructive intervention techniques that the teacher can employ. Yet the child's troublesome
behavior persists and must be handled as effectively as possible when it
occurs in the classroom.

3. Even in such occasional cases where the causes can be identified
and manipulated directly, the maladaptive behaviors may persist. Thus,
despite the discovery and correction of the contributing role of poor
vision and faulty child-rearing practices in a reading disability case, a
pupil may continue to experience difficulty with his reading until attention is *specifically* devoted to his reading behavior, and unless he can
experience success in this specific area, his mental health will continue to
be impaired.

4. Behaviors or symptoms or habits may in their own right be inca-
pacitating and disturbing, and current persisting symptoms may them-

selves be producing emotional disturbance (Franks, 1965) above and beyond the core disturbance from which the child is suffering. And, as research indicates (White & Harris, 1961), it is difficult to disentangle educational and emotional maladjustments in the school-age child (Gallagher & Chalfant, 1966).

5. There is little substantial evidence to indicate that if the teacher assists the child in modifying his behavior or symptoms, other undesirable behaviors will inevitably take their place in the manner of symptom substitution (Grossberg, 1964).

6. Finally, and most importantly as already implied, the teacher most commonly has no resort other than to deal with the pupil's behavior as it appears in the here and now. As Lewis (1965) attests:

> If we cannot aspire to reconstruction of personality that will have long range beneficial effects, we can modify disturbing behavior in specific ways in present social contexts. This more modest aspiration may not only be more realistic but it may be all that is required of the child-helping professions in a society that is relatively open and provides a variety of opportunity systems in which a child can reconcile his personal needs with society's expectations of him.

Having argued that the teacher should be primarily concerned with behavior per se rather than with its causes, let us turn to techniques emanating from learning theory which have relevance to the modification of deviant behavior in the classroom (see Glossary of Terms below). Although the techniques to be presented are discussed separately for the sake of clarity, it should be recognized that more than one of them may be operating at any given time in real-life attempts to modify behavior. Moreover, common to all of these techniques is the use of "systematic environmental contingencies to alter the object's responsiveness to stimuli" (Krasner & Ullmann, 1965).

GLOSSARY OF TERMS

Behavior Therapy. A therapeutic process in which the primary goal is to change overt behavior rather than to re-structure an individual's personality makeup. The process uses principles of learning for its methodological source.

Extinction. The decrease and eventual disappearance of a response learned under conditions of reinforcement when the reinforcement is withheld.

Reinforcement. Whatever serves to maintain the occurrence or increase the strength of a response, e.g., food, water or the avoidance of punishment.

Partial Reinforcement. A condition in which subjects receive reinforcement only at various time intervals or after a certain number of responses.

Positive Reinforcement. Much the same as reinforcement, i.e., *presenting* a pleasant stimulus when a response occurs, as opposed to negative reinforcement where an unpleasant stimulus is *removed* when a response occurs.

Modeling. A condition where the behavior to be acquired is demonstrated for the learner.

Punishment. A condition where a learner is made to feel uncomfortable by being presented an unpleasant stimulus, e.g., the infliction of pain by hitting, and/or a condition where a pleasant stimulus is withdrawn so that the learner is made to feel discomfort, e.g., having treats withdrawn.

THE TECHNIQUES

Extinction. There is a growing body of research demonstrating that simple withdrawal of reinforcers can reduce or eliminate such troublesome behavior as excessive talking, tantrum behavior and academic errors (Warren, 1965; Williams, 1959; Zimmerman & Zimmerman, 1962). Extinction is not always, however, the most economic and effective means of producing behavioral change (Bandura & Walters, 1963). Certain cautions should be recognized:

1. Spontaneous remission—the return of undesirable behavior—may occur following the extinction trials, thus necessitating additional extinction sessions.

2. When behavior is maintained on a partial reinforcement schedule, removal of the reinforcers may actually produce an increase in the frequency and intensity of the deviant responses. Moreover, it is sometimes extremely difficult not to reinforce maladaptive behaviors in a school setting, since circumstances may be beyond the teacher's control. The aggressive youngster who kicks the teacher or a classmate cannot help but be reinforced by the look of pain on the victim's face. The needed cooperation of classmates in the application of extinction procedures may also be difficult to secure, so that by necessity the deviant behavior is established on a partial reinforcement schedule.

3. General observation suggests that certain behaviors do not diminish and disappear simply because reinforcers are withdrawn, and sometimes teachers cannot or will not wait long enough to permit the completion of the extinction process. These limitations are particularly acute in situations in which emotional contagion is a distinct possibility. Behaviors seriously injurious to the self would also seemingly not lend themselves well to this technique. In brief, this method of behavior change has proven to be of value with acting-out as well as inhibited youngsters. Yet, its limitations suggest that other methods of behavioral modification are at times more economical and effective (see Ausubel, 1961, Bandura, 1965).

Positive Reinforcement. Operant conditioning techniques constitute one of the main tools of behavior modification. In this technique, emphasis is placed on the response made by the individual, and only minimal attention is given to the stimuli eliciting the response. Essentially, the teacher presents a reward whenever the child emits the desired response. While teachers have been cognizant of the value of positively reinforcing "good" behavior, there is ample evidence to suggest that even "good" teachers not uncommonly reinforce undesirable behavior. One of the merits of the positive reinforcement technique stems from its applicability to antisocial youngsters as well as to withdrawn children (Bandura & Walters, 1963).

There has been a dearth of psychotherapeutic approaches designed for the conduct problem child, despite such pupils typically being the most disruptive of classroom procedures. The application of positive reinforcement principles to seriously aggressive children involves the manipulation of three variables: the schedules of reinforcement, the interval factor and the type of reward. With respect to the concept of re-inforcement schedules, a distinction must be enforced between the acquisition and the maintenance of behavior. For the former, continuous or full-schedule reinforcement or reward after each appearance of the desied behavior is most effective, whereas for the latter, partial or inter-mittent reinforcement is most economical and effective. The interval variable merely refers to the passage of time between the production of a response and the presentation of the reward or reinforcer. The delay factor should usually be quite short initially, because acting-out children typically have difficulty in postponing gratification. Step by step, the interval can be lengthened as the child acquires more adequate behavioral controls.

The rewards for such pupils, at the start, may have to be tangible or physical in nature but should always be paired with verbal social rein-forcers, e.g., "You handled yourself well in that situation today" (Quay, 1963). Gradually, the reinforcers can be shifted away from the concrete into language and other symbolic forms of reward until the child can respond satisfactorily to them. In deciding upon the most suitable rein-forcers, consideration should be given to such factors as the child's developmental level and socio-cultural background.

The main unresolved question with the technique of positive rein-forcement centers around the question of how to make the child initiate the response in the first place so that he can be rewarded (Franks, 1965). The technique of social modeling may well provide at least a partial answer to this problem (Baer, 1963; Ferster, 1961; Hewitt, 1964; Slack, 1960; Wolf, Risley & Mees, 1964).

Modeling. Modeling is based on the premise that a child will imitate the behavior of others. Modeling is important in that children commonly acquire social skills through imitation of and identification with exam-ples of socially approved behaviors presented by suitable models. School teachers thus have a unique opportunity to influence the behavior of en-tire groups of children. However, this technique has been typically over-looked in the management or modification of deviant behavior in schools. Modeling procedures may represent a more effective means than positive reinforcement of establishing new response patterns in children (Bandura, 1965). Moreover, a behavior pattern, once acquired through imitation, is often maintained without deliberate external reinforcement, because human beings learn to reinforce themselves for behaving in certain ways. Teacher training institutions have long recognized the importance of modeling procedures in the training of future teachers and, accordingly, attempt to provide adequate models in the form of critic teachers. How-ever, attention should now be devoted to the teacher's use of modeling procedures in influencing the behavior of the pupils.

There are three effects of exposure to models: the *modeling effect,* the *inhibitory* or *disinhibitory effect,* and the *eliciting effect* (Bandura, 1965). Through the *modeling effect* children come to acquire responses that were not previously a part of their behavior. As noted earlier, model-ing procedures may be considerably more economical in establishing new responses than the method of operant conditioning based on positive reinforcement, especially when a combination of verbalizing models and demonstration procedures are used. The strengthening or weakening of inhibitory responses already existing in the observer (the *inhibitory* or *disinhibitory effect*) can also be accomplished through modeling procedures. Children, for example, who see a model punished or rewarded for aggressive behavior tend to decrease or increase their aggressive behavior accordingly. The *eliciting* or *response facilitation effect* refers to the teacher's eliciting responses that precisely or approximately match those exhibited by the model. Thus, observation of the teacher's response provides discriminative clues that trigger similar responses already in the pupil's behavior repertoire. This eliciting effect is distinguished from the modeling and the disinhibiting effects in that the imitated behavior is neither new nor previously punished.

The probability that a child will imitate a model is a function of several variables. Modeling is partly dependent upon the reinforcing consequences of the model's behavior. Thus, if a model is rewarded for his socially approved behavior, the likelihood that the observer will behave in a socially approved manner is increased. Other factors include the process of attending to the model's behavior, e.g., previous training in observation, and various environmental stimuli, e.g., the complexity of the stimuli (Baldwin, 1967; Bandura, 1962b; Bandura & Hutson, 1961; Bandura & Kupers, 1964; Bandura, Ross & Ross, 1963).

Punishment. Aversive conditioning or punishment is an intervention technique which has been used primarily to discourage undesirable behavior. This technique consists in the presentation of either physically or psychologically painful stimuli or the withdrawal of pleasant stimuli when undesirable behavior occurs. The use of punishment as a technique for behavioral modification has been contraindicated for the following reasons:

1. Punishment does not eliminate the response; it merely slows down the rate at which the troublesome behaviors are emitted.

2. This technique serves notice to stop certain negative behaviors; it does not indicate what behaviors are appropriate in the situation.

3. Aggressive behaviors on the teacher's part may provide an undesirable model for the pupil.

4. The emotional side effects of punishment, such as fear, tenseness and withdrawal are maladaptive.

5. Punishment serves as a source of frustration which is apt to elicit additional maladaptive behaviors.

Some psychologists, who are currently reconsidering the concept of punishment, contend that it can have a beneficial effect if applied to specific responses rather than to general behavior (Marshall, 1965).

Teachers, whatever their motivations, use verbal reprimands and other forms of correction in their approach to classroom management, and the judicious use of punishment as an intervention technique is most likely necessary in that it is impossible to guide behavior effectively with positive reinforcement and extinction alone. As Ausubel (1961) asserts, "It is impossible for children to learn what is *not* approved and tolerated simply by generalizing in reverse from the approval they receive for the behavior that *is* acceptable." Thus, punishment of specific responses can have an informative and beneficial effect. A particular positive value that may accrue from the use of punishment is that undesirable behaviors are held in abeyance, thus permitting the teaching of desirable modes of behavior through such intervention techniques as social imitation or positive reinforcement. Although punishment techniques have been used primarily with acting-out pupils, they have also been found to be of value in certain cases of withdrawn behavior (Bandura, 1962a; Church, 1963; Lovaas, 1965; Meyer & Offenbach, 1962; Redl, 1965; Sears, Maccoby & Levin, 1957; Solomon, 1964).

Discrimination Learning. Children sometimes engage in maladaptive behavior because they have transferred behaviors acceptable in one setting to a second setting where these behaviors are considered inappropriate and maladaptive. Thus, for example, the child who is overly dependent upon his mother may behave in a very dependent way toward his teacher. Such cases of inappropriate generalization can sometimes be remediated through the use of discrimination learning. Essentially this process consists of labeling given behaviors as appropriate within a specific environmental context. The teacher in the above case, for example, may inform the child in a nonpunitive way that she is not his mother but his teacher and that as such she will require him to become more self-reliant. This labeling by the teacher makes the child more aware of both inappropriate and appropriate behaviors. Interestingly, children do not always have to be able to express such discriminations verbally in order to achieve "insight" into their behavior. It is rather required, to insure effective results, that appropriate responses be rewarded and undesirable responses discouraged. Discrimination learning thus may be of service in conjunction with most other techniques in managing conduct and personality problems in the classroom (Ayllon & Michael, 1959; Barrett & Lindsley, 1962; Brackbill & O'Hara, 1958; Penny & Lupton, 1961; Stevenson, Weir & Zigler, 1959).

Desensitization. Desensitization as an intervention technique has been used principally with the fearful and phobic child. The basic objective is to have the child achieve a relaxed response in the presence of what were previously anxiety-producing stimuli. To accomplish this relaxed response, the subject is encouraged to perform approximations of previously punished acts within non-punishing or actually rewarding situations. Or through gradual exposure to the feared object or situation, a subject may become able to perform a formerly feared act or approach the feared object in a relaxed manner (Bentler, 1962; Garvey & Hegrenes, 1966; Jersild & Holmes, 1935; Lazarus, 1960; Wolpe, 1958).

CONCLUDING REMARKS

As evidenced by our discussion of the limitations of each technique, we do not envision management techniques emanating from learning theory as a panacea, but these intervention techniques do have certain potential advantages:

1. The fruitfulness of these techniques in modifying human behavior has been demonstrated in laboratory settings as well as in natural settings.

2. They are consistent with the teacher's role whereby she must reflect cultural expectations and set standards for her pupils' academic and social behavior.

3. Behavioral approaches offer specific and practical techniques for use in day-to-day classroom problems. While teachers already use some or all of these techniques, they frequently do so intuitively or inconsistently thereby reducing their efficacy.

4. These techniques enable the teacher to strive toward more realistic and obtainable goals relative to their pupils' mental health.

5. One of the most important attributes of these techniques is the fact that they can be taught to teachers. While there are few if any teacher training institutions currently offering didactic and practice training in such techniques, one can envision the time when teachers will acquire such skills through laboratory courses taken in conjunction with their formal course work or through in-service meetings and workshops.

REFERENCES

Ausubel, D. A new look at classroom discipline. *Phi Delta Kappan*, 1961, 43, 25–30.

Ayllon, T. & Michael, J. The psychiatric nurse as a behavioral engineer. *Journal of Experimental Analysis of Behavior*, 1959, 2, 323–334.

Baer, D. Effect of withdrawal of positive reinforcement on an extinguishing response in young children. *Child Development*, 1961, 32, 67–74.

Baer, D. Social reinforcement and behavior change. *American Journal of Orthopsychiatry*, 1963, 591–633.

Baldwin, A. Theories of child development. *Critique of social learning theory*, Chapter 16. New York: Wiley, 1967.

Bandura, A. Punishment revisited. *Journal of Consulting Psychology*, 1962, 26, 289–301(a).

Bandura, A. Social learning through imitation. In M. Jones (Ed.), *Nebraska Symposium on Motivation*, Lincoln, Nebraska: University of Nebraska Press, 1962. Pp. 211–269(b).

Bandura, A. Behavioral modification through modeling procedures. In L. Krasner & L. Ullman (Eds.), *Research in behavior modification*. New York: Holt, Rinehart & Winston, 1965.

Bandura, A. & Hutson, A. Identification as a process of incidental learning. *Journal of Abnormal and Social Psychology*, 1961, 63, 311–318.

Bandura, A. & Kupers, C. The transmission of patterns of self-reinforcement through modeling. *Journal of Abnormal and Social Psychology*, 1964, 69, 1–19.

Bandura, A., Ross, D. & Ross, S. Imitation of film mediated aggressive models. *Journal of Abnormal and Social Psychology*, 1963, 66, 3–11.

Bandura, A., & Walters, R. *Social learning and personality development*. New York: Holt, Rinehart & Winston, 1963.

Barrett, B. & Lindsley, O. Deficits in acquisition of operant discrimination and differentiation shown by institutionalized retarded children. *American Journal of Mental Deficiency*, 1962, 67, 424–436.

Bentler, P. An infant's phobia treated with reciprocal inhibition therapy. *Journal of Child Psychology and Psychiatry*, 1962, 3, 185–189.

Brackbill, Y. & O'Hara, J. The relative effectiveness of reward and punishment for discrimination learning in children. *Journal of Comparative and Physiological Psychology*, 1958, 51, 747–751.

Church, R. The varied effects of punishment on behavior. *Psychological Review*, 1963, 70, 369–402.

Ferster, C. Positive reinforcement and behavioral deficits of autistic children. *Child Development*, 1961, 32, 437–456.

Franks, C. Behavior therapy, psychology and the psychiatrist: contribution, evaluation and overview. *American Journal of Orthopsychiatry*, 1965, 35, 145–151.

Gallagher, J. & Chalfant, J. The training of educational specialists for emotionally disturbed and socially maladjusted children. In *N.S.S.E. yearbook 1966: social deviancy among youth*. Chicago: University of Chicago Press, 1966. pp. 398–423.

Garvey, W. & Hegrenes, J. Desensitization techniques in the treatment of school phobia. *American Journal of Orthopsychiatry*, 1966, 36, 147–152.

Grossberg, J. Behavior therapy: a review. *Psychological Bulletin*, 1964, 62, 73–88.

Hewett, F. Teaching reading to an autistic boy through operant conditioning. *The Reading Teacher*, 1964, 17, 613–618.

Jersild, A. & Holmes, F. Methods of overcoming children's fears. *Journal of Psychology*, 1935, 1, 75–104.

Krasner, L. & Ullman, L. *Case studies in behavior modification*. New York: Holt, Rinehart & Winston, 1965.

Lazarus, A. The elimination of children's phobias by deconditioning. In H. Eysench (Ed.), *Behavior therapy and the neuroses*. New York: Pergamon Press, 1960. Pp. 114–122.

Levitt, E. E. Results of psychotherapy with children: an evaluation. *Journal of Counseling Psychology*, 1957, 25, 189–196.

Lewis, W. Continuity and intervention in emotional disturbance: a review. *Exceptional Child*, 1965, 31, 465–475.

Lovaas, I. Building social behavior in autistic children by use of electroshock. *Journal of Experimental Research in Personality*, 1965, 1, 99–109.

Marshall, H. The effect of punishment on children: a review of the literature and a suggested hypothesis. *Journal of Genetic Psychology*, 1965, 106, 108–133.

Meyer, W. & Offenbach, S. Effectiveness of reward and punishment as a function of task complexity. *Journal of Comparative and Physiological Psychology*, 1962, 55, 532–534.

Penny, R. O. & Lupton, A. Children's discrimination learning as a function of reward and punishment. *Journal of Comparative and Physiological Psychology*, 1961, 54, 449–456.

Quay, H. Some basic considerations in the education of emotionally disturbed children. *Exceptional Child*, 1963, 30, 27–31.

Redl, F. Crisis in the children's field. *American Journal of Orthopsychiatry*, 1962, 32, 759–780.

Redl, F. The concept of punishment. In N. Long, W. Morse & R. Newan (Eds.), *Conflict in the classroom*. Belmont, Calif.: Wadsworth, 1965.

Sears, R., Maccoby, E. & Levin, H. *Patterns of child rearing*. Evanston, Ill.: Row Peterson, 1957.

Slack, C. Experimenter-subject psychotherapy: a new method for introducing intensive office treatment for unreachable cases. *Mental Hygiene*, 1960, 44, 238–256.

Solomon, R. Punishment. *American Psychologist*, 1964, 19, 239–253.

Stevenson, H., Weir, M. & Zigler, E. Discrimination learning in children as a function of motive-incentive conditions. *Psychological Report*, 1959, 5, 95–98.

Warren, A. All's quiet in the backroom. Paper read at the Council for Exceptional Children, Wichita, Kans. Oct., 1956.

White, M. & Harris, M. *The School psychologist*. New York: Harper, 1961.

Williams, C. D. The elimination of tantrum behavior by extinction procedures. *Journal of Abnormal and Social Psychology*, 1959, 59, 269.

Wolf, M., Risley, T. & Mees, H. Application of operant conditioning procedures to behavior problems of an autistic child. *Behavior Research and Therapy*, 1964, 1, 305–312.

Wolpe, J. *Psychotherapy by reciprocal inhibition*. Stanford, Calif.: Stanford University, 1958.

Zimmerman, E. & Zimmerman, J. The alternation of behavior in a special classroom situation. *Journal of Experimental Analysis of Behavior*, 1962, 5, 59–60.

CHAPTER 8

Mental Health of Teachers

36. The Mental Health of the Teacher

Robert F. Peck and James V. Mitchell, Jr.

Teaching, like other vocations, can offer an avenue for the fulfillment of healthy needs and mature interests or it can serve as an outlet for neurotic tendencies such as an insatiable, dominating need for affection and self-esteem. As Drs. Peck and Mitchell note, situational factors can also affect the teacher's emotional stability.

We could easily devote much time and effort to a consideration of the mental health needs of students and then conveniently overlook the very legitimate needs of their teachers. Perhaps we are all consciously or unconsciously influenced by the stereotypic conception of the classroom teacher as a more than human creature who has no right to any emotion except that of being "dedicated." Such a creature, of course, has no needs. Those of us who are teachers may naturally resent this conception. We not only try to avoid slipping into such a role; we also do what we can to correct the benighted souls who insist on holding fast to this conception.

Teachers *do* have needs, and the manner in which they satisfy these needs has a most important bearing on the kind of influence they have on their students. Much of the teacher's need-fulfillment (or lack thereof)

In *Mental Health,* What Research Says to the Teacher #24. Washington, D. C.: Association of Classroom Teachers, a department of the National Education Association, 1962. Pp. 18–25. Reprinted with the permission of the publisher and senior author.

must necessarily center on his activities with his students, and within this matrix, there is the possibility of both *legitimate* and *exploitative* need-fulfillment for teachers.

LEGITIMATE NEED-FULFILLMENT FOR TEACHERS

Although there are a few teachers who feel that teaching is essentially a thankless job, there are many others who find substantial satisfaction in doing work that they feel is a significant social contribution. Not only do they obtain the usual satisfaction from a task well done, but they have the added comfort of knowing that their satisfactions are not entirely selfish. They know they have significantly influenced the lives of their students in ways that will not only contribute to their individual effectiveness and contentment but may make them into better citizens as well. To fulfill one's self-esteem needs in this way is a legitimate and commendable form of need-fulfillment. In much the same way, the effective teacher achieves his own self-actualization by exerting every effort to provide for the self-actualization of his students. His self-actualization consists not of the simple, selfish kind of self-aggrandizement that characterizes many other occupations; rather, it is a realization of his own potentialities through the very act of getting the best from his students.

We are not unrealistic in saying that there inhere in the teaching situation itself certain positive influences that can make an important contribution to the teacher's mental health. A classroom teacher can usually plan his work in such a way as to provide a certain orderliness and predictability to his life, in contrast to the uncertainties that plague his friends in other professions. He can typically assume a degree of independence in conducting his classes, and he is relatively free to exercise his creative powers in developing new instructional techniques whose effectiveness will be immediately evident in student reactions. Although his relationships with other teachers may not be completely devoid of competitive aspects, he is not likely to experience or be the object of the more virulent kinds of competition that characterize other occupations. He and his colleagues are more likely to sense the importance of cooperative effort in their common professional endeavors. A teacher on tenure can enjoy a job security that would be the envy of many of his brethren in business or some of the professions. Finally, the typical teacher is likely to have more freedom than most in developing those skills which he feels are most likely to contribute to his own growth and contentment as a person and as a teacher.

These positive influences have a close relationship to the characteristics of good mental health that were outlined at the very beginning of this booklet. In effect, the teaching situation is one which provides many opportunities for the development of personal autonomy, the realization of self, self-acceptance, and a respect for others. Thus, the mental health impact of the teaching situation has a good many positive influences—or it *can* have, if one permits it.

The classroom teacher whose satisfactions in life are totally dependent on his work, however, will usually fall short of achieving a sense of balance and contentment in life. No matter how rich the satisfactions from one's work, one can rapidly reach a point of satiety with any occupation if it is the *sole* focus of one's life. It is most important, therefore, that the teacher develop out-of-school interests that are a vital and satisfying part of his life. The form that these activities should take is very much dependent on the personality involved, but in most cases, these activities should probably be quite dissimilar to typical work tasks. For most people, those involving satisfying relationships with friends of their own age group are usually a major source of reward and refreshment.

EXPLOITATIVE NEED-FULFILLMENT

The occupation of teaching is unique with respect to need-fulfillment. It can afford opportunities for an altruistic, beneficent, and constructive kind of need-fulfillment. It can, unfortunately, provide a setting for relatively vicious, destructive, or neurotic kinds of satisfactions. Even the milder forms of these neurotic satisfactions cannot be taken lightly, for their effects always extend beyond the confines of the teacher's personal life to the development and general well-being of his students.

One variety of such exploitative need-fulfillment takes the form of what we might call the "mother hen" complex. The classroom teacher who operates with the mother hen complex is the one who organizes her students like a little brood of chicks, exploiting every opportunity to suffocate them with her "mothering" and expecting a rich return in terms of their devotion. Certainly, kindliness, acceptance, and even affection are important teacher assets, especially for the primary teacher, but the mother hen type often encourages her students to develop a worshipful and totally dependent attitude toward her that provides neurotic satisfaction for the teacher's need for love and affection. This situation is hardly in the best interests of her students, who need to develop new relationships with authority and gradually achieve greater independence in their learning and living. Unfortunately, since the mother hen type seldom recognizes the real purpose of her actions, she goes blithely on assuming that her motives are above reproach.

Another kind of neurotic need-satisfaction, sometimes overlapping with the mother hen complex, may be referred to as the "habit of command" complex. Classroom teachers, continually confronted with immature minds and constantly exercising the privilege of managing groups of students, may become overimpressed with their own wisdom and power. Psychologically, it is an easy matter for a teacher to slip into the practice of using his position of pre-eminence for satisfaction of his need for self-esteem. Only too often, this conflicts with the needs of his students. Such a teacher may, for instance, become so domineering in the classroom that student initiative and responsibility are effectively quelled. The point may be reached where the insistent self-esteem needs of the teacher are routinely indulged, but those of students are largely neglected or ignored because of the priority of teacher need-satisfaction. The fact that such a teacher is seldom consciously aware of what is occurring only makes the condition more controlled in its destructive influence.

The two kinds of exploitative need-fulfillment mechanisms described are among the types of behavior which may make the teacher less effective, or downright destructive, in his efforts to accomplish the essential purpose of his teaching. The only effective antidote to such conditions is the kind of self-understanding that develops from a combination of objective self-observation, a thorough knowledge of the dynamics of adjustment, and perhaps a strong helping hand from school administrators or colleagues who can give understanding and human support while working to correct the exploitative pattern.

ON-THE-JOB HAZARDS TO MENTAL HEALTH

There are certain on-the-job hazards to the mental health of the teacher that can vitiate all of his attempts to achieve constructive need-satisfactions. These hazards are not simple problems that can be solved overnight. Many conditions are remediable in the sense that intelligent planning by classroom teachers and school authorities can certainly go a long way to alleviate many of the frustrations caused by them. For instance, classroom teachers who serve in a school with a principal who seldom demonstrates an understanding of, and appreciation for, their work are likely to be thwarted in achieving any sense of accomplishment. A creative and dynamic teacher may even appear to be a threat to some principals, who react by erecting formidable barriers to the realization of such creativity. A lack of adequate teaching resources can be discouraging to the most dedicated of teachers and can often result in reduced motivation to exert the extra effort necessary to achieve anything other than mediocre results. Poor relations between teachers can create extra frictions that dampen enthusiasm for teaching and lower school morale.

Conversely, the able school administrator knows that a little insight into the dynamics of human relations can be very beneficial. For example, required attendance at what they perceive to be "useless" meetings erodes the morale of many teachers. Administrators might well take a few extra minutes to reflect on whether a planned meeting is simply a matter of form, and a consequent waste of time, or whether it can honestly be expected to accomplish something. The investment of large amounts of time in clerical chores is likewise discouraging to many classroom teachers, who feel that a little money spent on clerical assistants would increase the effectiveness of teachers with their students. Last—but far from least—is one of the most potent of all morale busters: discipline problems. A classroom teacher who can count on help from an understanding supervisor, a consulting school psychologist, an immediate superior, or a fellow teacher can face the difficult discipline problems with more optimism and creativity than one who must face the threat alone.

The mental health of teachers thus depends on many practical problems in instruction and management, as well as on the nature of the psychological mechanisms teachers characteristically employ to satisfy their needs. In terms of the amount of effort required to effect a change for the better, the practical problems are more amenable to immediate remediation, while the latter is a matter of deep-seated personality dynamics that are more resistant to change.

EFFECT OF TEACHER'S MENTAL HEALTH
ON PUPIL LEARNING

The manner in which a classroom teacher characteristically fulfills his needs has implications not only for his own mental health but for the mental health of his students as well—a relationship which is particularly evident in the case of exploitative need-fulfillment. There are still other ways in which the teacher's mental health can have a bearing on student learning and adjustment.

GOOD MENTAL HEALTH IS CONTAGIOUS

One of the most important generalizations that can be made about the mentally healthy, well-adjusted teacher is that such a person is free to be child-oriented and problem-oriented. We say that he is "free" to be this way because he is not laboring under the burden of his own personal problems, which could sap his emotional strength and leave him little time or energy for anything else. He enjoys solving classroom problems because he has not been whipped by his own personal problems. He has patience because it has not been severely tried by his own personal exasperations. Such a teacher creates a desire for learning and an eagerness for life in the minds of his students because he himself feels this way about learning and life. And he communicates these feelings to his students not just by word but by his every action; he literally advertises in his own person that life is eminently worth living and eminently worth learning about. Because he is confident of his own learning and teaching abilities, he inspires confidence in his students that they can cope with relatively complex intellectual tasks and feel the thrill that comes with accomplishment. For students who are struggling to achieve their own patterns of self-actualization, he exemplifies the worthwhile values that can result when self-actualization is actually attained.

POOR MENTAL HEALTH HAS AN INFLUENCE

Exploitative need-fulfillment has already been discussed as a possible deleterious effect of poor mental health in the teacher. We have suggested previously that an overload of frustrating personal problems can serve as a drain on energy and as an inhibitor of teaching effectiveness. In addition to these negative influences already mentioned, there are other unfortunate consequences of poor mental health in the classroom teacher. It happens only too often, for instance, that the maladjusted teacher characteristically interprets each classroom problem as a personal threat, reacting with feelings of anxiety and insecurity when he should be performing at his clear-headed best. Not only are his thought processes generally disrupted under such conditions of threat, but when the threat involves a breach of discipline, he is only too likely to react in a personal, retaliatory manner rather than to consider the causes of such behavior in a fairly objective and analytical manner. Also, a teacher who suffers from anxiety and lack of self-confidence usually cannot avoid somehow communicating his feeling to the students. Students may react by becoming anxious themselves or by interpreting the behavior as evidence of weakness. In the latter case, they may then behave aggressively so as to create the soul-satisfying spectacle of an authority figure squirming in discomfort. Both of these student reactions are often quite unconscious in operation, and both, of course, are unwholesome reactions that are quite avoidable in the classrooms of the reasonably well-adjusted, normally healthy teacher. It is risky to generalize that poor mental health *always* affects teaching behavior adversely, but it is not an exaggeration to say that some such repercussions as those described are quite likely to appear in teaching as the concomitants of poor mental health.

37. The Voice of the Self

Arthur T. Jersild

As noted in the preceding article, self-understanding is the best antidote for overcoming behavior antithetical to the standards of good teaching and mental health. In the following selection, Dr. Jersild develops the point that teachers must first face themselves to become effective. His basic hypothesis as well as the means outlined for the achievement of self-knowledge warrant close and careful consideration from both neophytes and well-seasoned veterans.

In a recent study of a group of representative teachers, all but one reported a variety of personal problems. This lone exception said that he was not a bit anxious: He was never troubled by his anger; and his love life, social

NEA Journal, 1965, 54, 23–25. Reprinted with the permission of the publisher and author.

life, and work life were all okay. He had no personal problems. He did, however, have ulcers.

Every teacher, but particularly the typical neophyte, has personal problems. Some of them he openly admits having, but others he probably does not reveal even to himself.

The study I have mentioned brought information from about 200 teachers who had sought help in achieving self-understanding. Many of them spoke of attitudes which had interfered with their effectiveness as beginning teachers and which had persisted even after they had finished their apprenticeship.

Anger is one of the most common, pervasive, and difficult emotions in the teacher's life. From early childhood the restraints on showing anger or even feeling it are so powerful that many individuals lose touch with their anger. They fail to realize that unaccountable spells of the blues, feelings of fatigue, and headaches may be anger in disguise.

A large proportion of the teachers in the study mentioned finding it difficult if not impossible to know their own minds and assert their rights. As a rule, teachers do not tend to be aggressively self-assertive. Even veteran faculty members sometimes accept extra assignments meekly and allow themselves to be harassed without openly protesting. They may, however, store up the anger they feel, perhaps without even noticing it.

One source of anger is vulnerability growing out of the universal need to be approved and liked. This need is especially strong in a person who is feeling his way a bit uncertainly and who needs reassurance concerning his worth. Teachers in the study said that their need to be liked sometimes placed them at the mercy of their pupils.

Another condition that prevails frequently among teachers is anxiety. Everyone is anxious; the circumstances that produce anxiety are as numerous and varied as the predicaments and desires that arise in the course of human experience. The anxieties of teachers are as diverse as the anxieties of people in general. Some special conditions exist in the teaching profession, however, that may in distinct ways express or give rise to anxiety.

Anxiety springs from a condition of inner conflict. It is especially likely to prevail if a discrepancy exists between a teacher's avowed motives and the motives that actually impel him. When such a discrepancy occurs, the teacher is, in a sense, acting in a devious fashion—playing false with others, with himself, or both.

A teacher is likely to feel anxious if he uses the teaching situation to satisfy needs in his own life while trying to convince himself that everything he does is for the welfare of his pupils. One teacher reported that, as a beginner, she encouraged her pupils to be dependent upon her, to view her as a precious person. She got a great deal of satisfaction because many of them cried when they said goodbye to her on the last day of school.

Then this young woman examined her motivation. She decided that she had been fostering dependence to gratify her need for power or to be assured of her adequacy—that her reasons had been devious. She changed her tactics and encouraged independence. Instead of having the last day resemble a wake, she made a gay event of it. She ended her account by saying that she felt much happier now that she was more honest with her pupils and herself.

A teacher feels that he is being false to himself if he claims that he is a soft disciplinarian because he believes that children learn best in a free and permissive atmosphere when his softness actually springs from fear of giving offense by being firm.

By the same token, he feels false to himself if he claims that he is strict because pupils learn more from a tough teacher, when his true motivation is a need to dominate others.

A sensitive teacher becomes anxious if he is a partner in, or a silent spectator of, practices which he regards as wrong. The more idealistic his aim, the more inevitable is a hiatus between that aim and what he is able to do. If he must convince himself that everything he does is right because he is unable to accept himself as one who compromises between what he would like to do and what he can do, he is in a false position and anxiety results.

The beginning teacher often sees himself as on trial before his pupils, his colleagues, and his supervisors, and, what is likely to be the toughest trial of all, before himself.

As a beginner, he is a learner, and as such, he is bound to make mistakes but he castigates himself for these mistakes more than a realistic appraisal of the situation would warrant.

Self-criticism becomes a scourge when a beginner is constantly dissatisfied with his work even though it is satisfactory to others. He makes himself a failure in his own eyes by imposing standards he cannot fulfill, by seeking perfection he can never reach.

If teachers are to cope with their own problems and live up to their potentialities, they must grow in self-understanding. Both teacher-preparation institutions and in-service activities could and should do far more than they usually do to help teachers to take stock of themselves, to get a thoughtful conception of their worth, and to overcome barriers within themselves. What knowledge is more fundamental than knowledge of self?

From an academic standpoint, awareness of self is necessary if a person wishes to appreciate and to help his pupils appreciate the richness of many of the scholarly disciplines. We do not really grasp the truths embodied in history and literature unless we can appreciate them through an awareness of how they relate to ourselves. Napoleon remains a wooden soldier unless we can perceive him in the light of Napoleonic tendencies within ourselves. Hamlet comes alive only when we realize a kinship between his doubts and conflicts and our own.

From a humanitarian point of view, knowledge of self is even more important. Most persons move through childhood into adult years with a burden of emotional problems. Self-knowledge not only helps an individual to understand himself; it helps him understand others, too. The best way to learn about what lies hidden in the secret self of someone else is to inquire, "What lies hidden within me?"

The voice of the self, usually silent and yet sometimes audible to the inner ear, speaks a universal language. The closer any human comes to knowledge of himself the more he is in touch with a core of humanity which he shares with all others.

Knowledge of the self does not flow through the channels of instruction we usually employ in the training of children or the preparation of teachers. In most fields of scholarship, an interested, able learner can appropriate all that men's minds have wrought through generations of labor. For example, the learner can use a map without having been a pioneer explorer. But in the sphere of self, each person is an explorer almost from birth.

The most intimate and decisive aspects of learning pertaining to the self are in the domain of attitudes and emotions. If an individual is to grow in self-understanding, it is essential for him to examine these—to face them thoughtfully rather than blindly.

How can teachers-in-training or teachers-on-the-job do this? Currently, intensive psychotherapy or psychoanalysis represents the most systematic efforts in this area. Group therapy, under the guidance of a professionally trained person, is another means. These methods are available only to a few, however, and many do not want or need prolonged and costly therapy.

A resource short of such intensive methods can be cultivated in every teacher education institution and in every sizable school faculty. I refer to work groups in which the participants mutually seek to help one another explore the realm of feeling. Almost all members of such groups report that they receive great benefit from the activity.

Many practical considerations and psychological limitations are, of course, connected with work of this sort. Membership in such groups must be voluntary. A certain amount of leadership is required, at least in the beginning. Members must be committed to the idea of examining their attitudes rather than of showing how smart they are. They must have or acquire enough courage and trust to share states of mind that ordinarily are not aired in the presence of others.

Persons who use this approach, particularly for the first time, will have to undertake a good deal of groping and exploring, feeling their way at the beginning. Arrangements should be made with a minimum of fanfare, without fancy promises, and without any pretension that this is the same as a professionally supervised therapy group.

Participants should be allowed to move at their own pace. It needs to be understood that everything is confidential and that the participants are all seeking self-understanding.

One of the fascinating features of this kind of group work is that it almost invariably involves facets of the mind that usually are ignored in the academic setting, including fantasies, dreams, vagrant feelings and thoughts, and the ability latent in all of us to let the mind roam in a process of free association. Trickles of anger, fear, tenderness, and other feelings that often are barely noticed can be made articulate and can be examined.

Another reward of effective group work is the spirit of trust, sympathy, and comradeship that gradually builds up. Sometimes the very persons who have most annoyed each other establish strong bonds of affection.

A reservoir of friendliness and good will is present in any group of decent people. Often, however, feelings of kindness and compassion are hidden until a person has had an opportunity to voice his anger without being punished or rejected or has had an opportunity to reveal his fears without being called a coward.

In a genuine search for self-understanding, the accounting methods differ from those we ordinarily apply in everyday life; the uncovering and sharing of weakness often leads to previously unfound strength. The greatest kind of courage is not the courage to banish fear but to acknowledge it.

When a person delves into himself, he is likely to discover that the things which alienate him from others are outweighed by the worth of his own humanity and by his kinship with others.

The greatest reward of knowledge of self is growth in compassion— compassion which leads a person not just to say dutifully, "I am my brother's keeper," but to feel, "I am my brother's brother." If, through self-study, beginning teachers can reap this reward more fully, they and all mankind will be blessed.

38. The Straws that Break the Teacher's Back

Nicholas J. Long and Ruth G. Newman

Not all threats to a teacher's mental health derive from factors within the individual. In the following article, teachers lucidly describe their frustrations, anxieties and disillusionments growing out of associations with school administrators, the community and students. How, in your opinion, can we minimize the stresses which threaten the teacher's effectiveness and mental health?

What first appears in applying informed personal services is the variety of things teachers find particularly frustrating in their classrooms. Ask a teacher to report honestly what most drives him to distraction: sometimes

In "The teacher's handling of children in conflict." *Bulletin of the School of Education,* Indiana University, 1961, 37 (4), 12–19. Reprinted with the permission of the publisher and senior author.

it is the big things like overcrowdedness, or having no time to do a job; sometimes it is the personal idiosyncrasies that make life unbearable. There is no use in placing a hierarchy of importance on the gripes. As anyone knows, a spilled glass of orange juice at breakfast can, at a given moment, be just as upsetting as not receiving a pay raise. It is possible for both kinds of events to be devastating for the time being, or to be met and handled in proportion when awareness and support are available.

Below are some examples of teachers' frustrations as they expressed them. They represent the kinds of frustrations which carefully planned in-service or consultative programs try to meet, in an Androcles and the Lion kind of way, by seeing them as thorns which can, temporarily or perma-nently, cripple the teacher and keep him from performing, and can conse-quently hold back the child. A truly good consultative service to teachers could be of help, regardless of which of the following complaints one chooses:

Overcrowding is experienced with a sense of helplessness by some teachers:

> In our school district during the past school term there was an over-flow of children in our school causing most of the classes to have from 39 to 45 children. There was a constant assignment of new chil-dren from other schools in the city as well as from surrounding areas. This impact was felt tremendously in the school program and its operation to accomplish certain goals. As for me, this kind of "bargin'-in" (that was my inner feeling) of from one to two chil-dren each week was quite frustrating, as my concern in meeting individual differences was thwarted and my anticipated goals seemed out of reach. I found myself unconsciously resenting the fact that the child was sent to my room, and I became quite peeved if he did not have command of the skills expected of a second grader, for this meant that my job was to take time to help him if I could or at least to provide opportunities to expose him to the skills. I was not even willing to take him where he was and to work from that point, as that would take time, and time was what I didn't have, especially since time had already been sacrificed to register, enroll, and wel-come him to the class.

> I dread going to school these days—210 children a day, about 40 kids in a class. They tell me a new school is being planned to take up all the kids from the new housing settlement, but until then just try to teach English to 180 kids: the slow ones, the fast ones, the noisy ones. I thought you were supposed to know the kids you teach. I hardly know most of their names, let alone what they need from me. I love English. I have theories about teaching it. All that's been scrapped. Now I'm lucky to simply follow the prescribed dull study plan. I feel I'm not doing a thing for these kids. I'd give my soul for five classes of 20 children each!

> I teach kindergarten. Once was, when I had a nice small 16 in a class group. Now I have two sessions: 50 in the morning, 42 in the afternoon, a volunteer parent helper for each class—when they show up. By the end of the day I feel as if I have the D.T.'s, with hundreds of moppets instead of pink elephants passing by. They call this teaching? Not in any child development course I ever had.

Special rules of personal and social behavior, as well as extra and menial chores and low salaries imposed on teachers, are often bitterly resented:

> Then there is the "universal" frustration, not so much of salary (although everyone agrees that we are grossly underpaid) as of the benevolences I must cater to. I honestly hold in high esteem the virtues of the YMCA, YWCA, Boy Scouts, Girl Scouts, Red Cross, United Fund, and professional organizations, but somehow they seem to lose their flavor when I am aware that I *must* join in order to be considered a "good, cooperative" teacher. How nice it would be to join these wonderful organizations simply because I want to join them by choice only!
>
> In the community in which I reside, teachers are somewhat expected to be "saints." This notion, to me, is ridiculous, for teachers, like everyone else, are human. It struck me as funny when I was interviewed for this particular position that the principal mentioned rather pointedly that this area had many people who drank in it, but that pressure was put on to get rid of any teacher who did so. He suggested that if I drank, not to drink in this area.
>
> It would be nice to go into school in the morning and just teach and not have to be collecting money, taking attendance, playing nurse, and trying to discipline those who do not respond to the classroom role. It is difficult to be satisfied with doing just half a job all the time. It is difficult to realize that we cannot be 100 per cent effective but have to settle for much less. It is difficult for me to adjust to this situation as I am more of a perfectionist and like to get the best results all the time.
>
> I hate to quit because I like to teach, but like it or not, I have to resign. My wife is expecting our second child and can no longer work. Since our first child is ill the doctor's bills and living expenses are just too much. I am overtired, tired trying to meet expenses by working at the post office in the Christmas rush and in a factory during summer times. I've been offered a job in an insurance company and, like it or not, I've got to take it. You've got to be rich to afford to teach if you've got a family.

The policy of administration is sometimes felt by teachers to be so outrageous (whether right or wrong) that their total teaching attitudes are affected:

> To teach under an administration which focuses its attention upon creating benevolent public relations, even at the expense of school standards, seems to be my outstanding frustration. How is it possible for a high school principal to condone a student's laziness, slowness, and apparent lack of interest in subject matter, in a conference among the child's parents, the child, the teacher involved, and himself, and to state explicitly that possibly the reason for the child's failure was due to the lack of motivation and severity of grading done by the teacher. Mary, the student concerned, was a high school senior. She had failed sophomore and junior English and she was retaking both of these courses during her senior year as she needed both to graduate. Miss T. had Mary for sophomore English. She passed Mary because, as Miss T. said to me, "You can't fight city

hall." I did not pass Mary, but when she graduated, she had no record on her permanent record of a failure in junior English. She had instead a "C."

The procedure of giving a contract for eight or nine months seems to have a decidedly negative effect upon the teacher. The implication read into the action is that the employer doesn't trust his judgment and has little faith in the training and prior experience of the applicant—that there is so much possibility that the teacher will be unsatisfactory that he cannot afford to hire her for a longer period than a year at a time. The result is an undermining of the teacher's performance, self-confidence, and feeling of security.

Most permanently established teachers would not have been asked to take such a teaching load, but many principals feel that they can ask a beginning teacher to accept almost any situation. This is a particularly hard thing to do, because a beginning teacher needs all of the help and encouragement that she can get, and even in the most pleasant situation will have many problems to cope with anyway. I feel that for a teacher, especially a teacher in her first year of teaching, to be so totally out of her teaching field is an injustice not only to the teacher but to the students.

The emotionally disturbed child in the classroom often generates despair and helplessness in the teacher:

There is a child in the classroom who suffers from an emotional problem. He is withdrawn, sensitive, and nervous—a condition which I know results from his home environment—a broken home, rejection, poverty, etc. I try to work with this child, give him projects that will display his self-worth, encourage him to join in the play activities of other children, give him extra "slaps on the back" for work well done, etc. All of this I do in the limited time the child is in school and under my jurisdiction. After school he goes home, back into the same surroundings that have caused him to be emotionally disturbed in the first place. My work, seemingly, becomes undone; the child enters the classroom the next day in the same condition as he entered the day before. I know the mind, soul, or body cannot be cured in one day, but as this chain of events goes on and on each day, I cannot help but sense a feeling of failure and helplessness.

Suzy was sent to me as an incorrigible seven-year-old who followed no rules, fought with all children, and caused constant room disturbance. She had an I.Q. of 78 on the Kuhlmann-Anderson and 79 on the Stanford-Binet. She was hostile, and yet on the first day of school she threw herself on me, nearly suffocating me with an embrace. Inquiring into her background, I found she lived in a house with seven or eight adults and as many children, seemingly all related, yet no definite relationship could be determined. I could not find out where the father was or even if he were living. Three women claimed to be her mother, but none would talk to me about her. Each said that her grandmother was responsible for her and she went to work at three in the afternoon and worked all night. I was never able to contact the grandmother. The frustration came about because I could find no one who seemed to care enough about Suzy to talk about her or try to help her. During the year I worked on the theory that if I loved her enough, she in turn would feel more secure and want to conform. I felt both I. Q. scores were invalid, because Suzy could think and reason. She was quite capable of finding information and presenting it when she desired.

I can't stop worrying about one little girl in my first grade. She behaves so peculiarly. She doesn't talk most of the time, though she can talk. She answers the other children and me with animal sounds. She hides under chairs like a dog and barks at people. She even bit one little boy. She draws pictures of dogs and insists on eating her lunch on all fours. I've talked to her mother who is frantic about her behavior, but they have no money to see a psychiatrist. She's been on a clinic waiting list for six months, and I've had the child up for Special Service to test her for three months. In the meantime, the class all laugh at her, and she just gets worse, and I don't know what to do.

Parents are often experienced by teachers as an impossible cross to bear, whether this is because of the teacher's own unresolved feelings about his parents or whether the parents actually *are* obstructionists:

As a teacher, I try to give all the love, energy, consideration, and understanding to each pupil that I possibly can. To have a parent question my attention to another child over his makes me quite frustrated, baffled, and thwarted. If only parents would understand that some pupils require more attention than others and that it is not that the teacher is partial in any respect.

The most frustrating thing I've encountered has been parental attitude. Some, and I must say generally speaking it's the mothers, feel as though their children are bordering on genius. When the mothers classify their dear offsprings as such, the teacher shouldn't expect them to do such trivial things as study a lesson or do a class assignment, but should give the child superior grades in subject matters and satisfactory for attitude.

I have a parent who calls me every night to complain about her child's behavior. At first I tried to be nice and tell her what to do, but nothing is enough. Can't she see I have a right to my evenings, and can't she handle her own child? But I can't seem to cut her off, and I feel helpless to do anything. I've told the principal, and he doesn't seem interested in helping me. "Oh, she'll stop," says he. But when?

Interpersonal relations with staff, where there are differences of opinion or approach or personality conflicts, can be of determining importance to a teacher:

Although students may have difficulty in other subjects, social studies presents quite a problem to several of my students. I believe it is because it involves a great deal of reading and comprehension. Extra time is needed to give those students help who are having difficulty mastering social studies. But what is most frustrating to me is the fact that many of our teachers frown on me for giving special help to the students because the teachers feel that the administration will require them to help with special problems also. Then too, some teachers have accused me of trying to impress the administrators because I give some special help.

The school was more of the traditional type, and, although I did try many new ideas and techniques, I found that I began following a somewhat "middle-of-the-road" position. Rather than actually teaching according to the way I had planned, I began to lean more and more to the type of teaching which was customary in the school system. There was not any real pressure from my critic teacher or from the superintendent, who was a personal friend, but I somehow felt that my efforts pleased them more when I followed the line of "traditional" teaching. At the same time, I felt that I was not doing a good job when I did not follow the practices which I had studied in my methods classes. Discipline seemed to be the main objection to the newer methods. Whenever the boys and girls were working on their committees and the room was "noisy," I noticed that I worried about distracting the other rooms nearby. I even began to question the worth of my opinion. I sometimes felt that the older teachers humored me in conversations when I voiced my approval of modern methods and theory. This was not always the case, but I occasionally detected an attitude of "You'll learn. You may think this way now, but wait until you've taught several years." Perhaps this is why I began my graduate work right away rather than beginning teaching as I had previously planned.

I could do my job all right if that sixth-grade teacher would stay out of my way. We have a school where the principal is with us two days a week and with another school three days. When she's not here, that bossy, nosey Mrs. D. just takes over, calls down my kids in the hall when they're not doing anything, criticizes my bulletin board, disciplines my children in front of me, and undermines my authority. The principal is so dependent on Mrs. D. that there's no use talking to her. Anything Mrs. D. does is fine!

Sometimes deeply experienced personal conflicts can overwhelm a teacher:

I do not like having things on my desk looked at or handled. My desk is verboten. There are always children who want to rifle the papers or just look. They do not want anything, it just seems to be something they do. It doesn't matter to me that I never have anything on my desk that I do not want anyone to see or handle, I just don't want anyone to bother anything that is there. Inside, I have the feeling of "It's mine—hands off!" I know that this is silly, but I feel it strongly. The same feeling carries over to my personal things at home. I want them left alone.

When I may be about to come to a climax in a sentence experiment, or in the explanation of a transitive passive verb, or have all the attention of every eye and am about to express the punch line, there comes a knock at the door. I may as well answer it, because all hope of competing with that unknown factor of "Who's at the door?" is to no avail. Upon answering, I am handed a clarinet by a mother who says, "Would you please give this to Jeanne? She forgot she had band today." About this time I feel like a plugged-up volcano unable to blow the proverbial top.

If I were to name frustrations, they would come not from teaching but from the fact that I feel my family is shorted. I find myself, at the end of the day, weary physically and mentally, often unable to cope with home demands. I will give a short answer to those at home, whereas at school I would weigh my words and answer with a smile. Meeting the needs of two sons, ages 15 and 6, and a husband who is far from well could be a full-time job in itself. I feel frustrated in that I have little enthusiasm and patience to give at home after a full day of being enthusiastic and patient with a room full of children.

The other area of frustration is a difficult one to explain and also to admit. When I entered teaching, I had no intention of making it a career. I had hoped eventually to marry and raise my own family. After four years of teaching, I realized I would not meet many eligible men in the classroom. I realized I had to make a choice as to the type of career I wanted for myself. I knew that teaching was the one in which I would feel the happiest and gain the most satisfaction. I am going into guidance and counseling. I like working with people and think I have a reasonable amount of understanding of them. However, at times I feel very unloved and unwanted. I know this is going to hinder my working relationship in some cases. I can remember during my first few years of teaching that I threw myself wholeheartedly into helping students with extracurricular activities. I know I was looking for their appreciation and affection as an outcome of my work. But in most cases the students forgot about my help and enjoyed the activities themselves, letting me sit on the side and watch. How does a single person manage to fill this need for love and affection without becoming the embittered old maid that is often used as a stereotype for teachers? I feel this is an important problem with me. I know the solution cannot come in a short time, nor can anyone else solve it but myself. I would like some suggestions as to possible solutions.

I know one should not dislike a child, but there is one in my class who so offends me that it spoils my whole day. She is sloppy and fat. Her hair is stringy and unkempt. She sits sulky and slumped in her chair, never shows any pleasure in anything, answers in a fresh way, if at all. I know she must have a hard time at home, and I bend over backward trying to be nice. But at the end of the day, I am exhausted from the effort. I even dream about her nights.

As different as these personally recounted examples of frustrations are, there is not one of them that could not be to some degree alleviated by on-the-spot, psychologically sophisticated supervision, consultation, or whatever is called the process of airing one's difficulties, looking at them honestly with an informed and sympathetic person, and being helped not to deny them or let them grow to giant size but to perceive them in a fresh context. Whether by new pathways of communication, or by a reshuffling of the way one sees things, or by simply getting the jumble of enraging feelings into a framework of words, or by a sense of human support, *something* can grow out of this process for the teacher and the pupils. But this can only be effected when the school and the teachers are openly hospitable to this kind of help, and when the help itself becomes, with increased experience, the kind a teacher asks for. To be of use, it cannot be poured down the throat like medicine; to be nourishing, it must be sipped slowly like the good wine that it can be.

39.   Suggestions to Teachers for Keeping in Good Mental Health

Glenn M. Blair, R. Stewart Jones, and Ray H. Simpson

What can the teacher do to safeguard his mental health?
Drs. Blair, Jones, and Simpson offer several practical
and worthwhile methods for coping with the stresses
and strains associated with classroom life.

Since there are many causes of maladjustment among teachers, there are also many ways in which their personal and emotional difficulties may be alleviated. Progress toward better mental health is a goal which must be sought not only by teachers and educational organizations, but also by the community as a whole.

Perhaps no point has been more greatly stressed in this volume than the principle that needs, wants, and drives must come to fruition if people are to be well-adjusted. Consequently, the starting point for helping teachers maintain good mental health must be the determination of their drives and goals. Two needs immediately stand out as important in the job of teaching. The first is that teachers want to be liked and respected by their pupils. The second is that teachers need to feel a sense of professional accomplishment. As previously shown, several things stand in the way of the satisfaction of such needs. Pupils are not aware of the needs of teachers. To some extent, they share the community's stereotype about teachers as being a group apart—a little different from other people. Under such circumstances, it might be wise for teachers to make known to pupils what some of their own needs are. Perhaps the simple statement by the teacher that he wants all pupils to like him, and wants help from the class when he does things which the pupils do not like, would be an effective first step.

A further barrier which blocks the attainment of professional goals is that teachers may have erroneous notions about the way in which such goals may be achieved. It is apparent that teachers ought to know the

In *Educational Psychology* (3rd ed.). New York: The Macmillan Company, 1968. Pp. 619–621. Reprinted with the permission of the publisher and authors. © Copyright, The Macmillan Company, 1968.

characteristics of teachers which children like. It is also clear that a failure to realize professional goals calls for a re-examination of the teaching situation and one's objectives, as was pointed out in the preceding chapter.

Much of the progress toward the better mental health of teachers is in the hands of the larger community whose dictums about salary, teachers' conduct, school buildings, and the size of classes determine not only the kinds of teachers that are recruited, but also the morale of those presently engaged in this profession. Great strides have been made toward bettering the teacher's social status and working conditions in the past twenty years. But even under good teaching conditions there are many problems which teachers must learn to solve for themselves. These are feelings of pressure and inferiority, gnawing anxieties, fears and depressions, and inevitable frustrations and conflicts.

There is no panacea for the solution of these problems, yet much is known about the general conditions which foster good mental health. Principles from the field of mental hygiene would seem to support the following suggestions to teachers:

1. Recognize that differences of opinion are healthy and learn how to use the criticisms of others constructively.
2. Expect a certain amount of aggression and rebellion in young people. Such expression is a normal developmental pattern in our culture.
3. If you do not feel well get a medical examination. Some of your aches and pains may be real.
4. Become so absorbed in teaching and avocational activities that there is little time for worrying about petty problems and engaging in unhealthy preoccupation with yourself.
5. Put yourself periodically into a position where you must learn something new. It may be typing, ping pong, a foreign language, or anything else which keeps you active.
6. Become a member of some organization—church, community, civic, or professional. Belonging to a group tends to make one feel secure and to satisfy a need for belonging and status.
7. Develop some close personal friends. Complete self-sufficiency is undesirable.
8. Learn how to converse with, and work with, different kinds of people.
9. Work actively to help the teaching profession deserve and attain a higher status than it now enjoys.
10. Express hostile feelings once in awhile. Repressing them may lead to anxiety.
11. Make a plan for your life, but do not be overly ambitious. Overambition can be just as harmful as underambition. Cut the world down to your size. Do not aspire for things beyond the level where you have a reasonable chance for success.
12. Develop a satisfying philosophy of life. Believe in something.
13. Be yourself. Although there is always room for improvement in personality, you are probably not too bad a person as you are. No one is perfect. Excessive attempts to ape other people kill individuality and lead to unhappiness.

PART IV

INTERVENTION PROCEDURES

There have been three revolutions in the mental health field (Hobbs, 1964; Smith, 1968). The first mental health revolution brought about a humane concern for the emotionally disturbed. With the advent of institutional psychiatry in the 19th century, the insane were granted asylum, which though inhumane according to present day standards, nonetheless constituted compassionate care in comparison with the earlier incarceration in jails and almshouses. No longer were the mentally ill seen as possessed by demons. Now they were seen as sick people for whom there was some degree of hope. But alas, patients were rarely given professional treatment. For the most part, they were simply provided with custodial care in some large institution out in the countryside. Eventually, the debilitating effects of institutional care become evident.

The second mental health revolution centered around Sigmund Freud's dynamic approach to mental illness. In accordance with his views, emphasis was placed on the intrapsychic life of the patient. The locus for this type of help was the therapist's private office and the method was that of psychotherapy or treatment by talk. This type of treatment offered little to those attempting to help patients in the huge state hospitals since there were not enough professionally trained therapists to provide individualized psychotherapy.

The third revolution—a community based mental health approach— hopes to return the emotionally disturbed individual to the community and as a first class citizen. To this end, comprehensive community mental health centers are being established. Impetus to the notion of a therapeutic community can be attributed largely to the advent of the tranquilizing drugs and the report of the Joint Commission on Mental Illness entitled "Action for Mental Health" (1961). As Smith (1968) stated, "We need to invest more in working on the social context in which troubled people are involved and to count less upon the effectiveness of the isolated therapeutic hour." In this sense, deviant behavior is not seen as a private illness, but a "social, ethical and moral problem, a responsibility of a total community" (Hobbs, 1964). Selections in the final two chapters center around the implementation of the third revolution in the school setting (Chapter 9) and in the community at large (Chapter 10). Special emphasis is devoted to the professional manpower shortage, the neglect of mental health needs among low-income groups, the need for more effective treatment efforts, and the role of preventive strategies.

Chapter Nine

To be effective the school must provide a battery of mental health services. First and perhaps most basic is a sound program of mental health for all children. Healthy teacher-pupil relationships coupled with a curriculum broad and flexible enough to encompass individual differences in ability, interests, and cultural background can go far in providing a sound base for a school mental health program. Redl and Wattenberg (1959) list four specific ways in which learning can assist development: 1. Learning builds and supports the child's feeling of self worth. 2. Learning can help to satisfy the needs for belonging. 3. Learning builds confidence, which in turn increases the drive for further learning. 4. Achievement in learning helps a child to set realistic goals for himself. The finding of a close relationship between educational adjustment and personal adjustment is not unexpected since accomplishment in school-related activities constitutes one of the major developmental tasks of youth in our society.

When preventive programs prove inadequate (and often times they will for reasons beyond the school's control) then the schools must consider such forms of psychoeducational treatment as mental health consultation, student counseling, parent counseling or remedial instruction. At times, placement in a special class, day school, homebound instructional program, or residential school program might be warranted. While both the preventive and treatment aspects of a mental health program need to be developed, it appears that in the past we have neglected the preventive aspects of a school mental health program in favor of the treatment aspect. It is heartening in this connection, however, to note that the concept of prevention is in recent years being accorded a more central status. In keeping with this trend, which has arisen in part as a consequence of the manpower problem and the doubtful efficacy of conventional treatment procedures, a preventive point of view is emphasized. An overview of the chapter's content is as follows:

> obstacles that must be overcome if preventive approaches are to be effective;
> an empirical study of prevention in the school setting;
> the use of nonprofessionals in the classroom;
> the results of preschool programs for the disadvantaged;
> the immunization value of stress;
> a new function for mental health specialists which will hopefully multiply their effectiveness;
> curriculum approaches designed to promote improved mental health;
> and a learning theory framework for teaching disturbed youth.

Chapter Ten

The articles in this chapter center around the following two themes:

> the need for caution in implementing community programs, and

the bold new directions taken by various workers in the field of community mental health.

While it is too early at this writing to determine whether the third revolution will realize the wonderful promise it holds, let us hope that we will continue to have the courage to implement and to evaluate adventuresome programs in mental health.

CHAPTER 9

Intervention Procedures in the Schools

40. Primary Prevention of Mental and Emotional Disorders: A Frame of Reference

Eli M. Bower

In response to the manpower shortage and doubts concerning the feasibility of psychotherapy, many authorities are focusing their thoughts on preventive action. While the notion of prevention has acquired a high status, very little has been done to actively implement this concept. In the following article, one of the nation's leading proponents of preventive efforts—Eli M. Bower—outlines some of the principal roadblocks responsible for this state of affairs.

Let me first define primary prevention of mental and emotional disorders as operationally as possible: it is any specific biological, social, or psychological intervention which promotes or enhances mental and emotional robustness, or reduces the incidence and prevalence of learning and behavior disorders in the population at large. By way of analogy, three or four polio vaccine shots are a primary prevention of polio; after an individual has received them his resistance to polio is, hopefully, strengthened significantly. If he has not received them, but seems to show early signs of the disease, other interventions on his behalf would be termed secondary prevention. If he has succumbed to the disease, the successive application of such measures

In *The Protection and promotion of mental health in schools*, 1964, monograph #5, 1-9. Reprinted with the permission of the publisher and author.

as iron lung treatment, exercise therapy of various kinds, and later rehabilitation therapy would be called tertiary prevention. In other words, the three stages of prevention are: *primary*, what is done for population at large; secondary, what is done for identifiable vulnerable groups; tertiary, what is done by way of treatment and rehabilitation.

Primary prevention as a goal in the field of health often combines a faith in magic with an equally strong belief in man's capability to handle a virus, a protozoan, or the discrete elements of social pathology. Witch doctoring is still rather profitable in the United States; Americans spend upwards of a billion dollars annually on magical remedies. One still hears of the magic bullets and miracle drugs and to some degree these are indeed magical and miraculous. Yet polio is now preventable, and so is tetanus, smallpox, plague, typhoid, diphtheria, goiter, and several different kinds of influenza. In the field of mental and emotional disorders we can point to a few specific diseases—among them pellagra and more recently phenylketonuria—which are preventable in a primary sense. By and large, however, one needs a very high-powered microscope or telescope combined with radar and sonar equipment to find any widespread major efforts in program, demonstration, or research in the prevention of emotional disorders.

Primary prevention of these disorders is a problem with which few wish to wrestle. Many try to avoid the wrestling match by asserting that the best prevention is early treatment, but the degree of "earliness" is left in ambiguity. In other words, we need to face not only that there are few enthusiastic supporters in the mental health professions, in the community at large, or in legislative bodies for preventive programs, but also that there is a great deal of rational and serious resistance to such programs. If we hope to install programs that will have at the very least an even chance of trial, I believe it is important for those of us in this field to understand some of the reasons for the resistance.

One of the major deterrents to the development of prevention programs is the idea held by many experts that nothing much can be accomplished unless we have a thorough social overhaul. Mental and emotional disorders are seen as the exclusive result of injustice, discrimination, economic insecurity, poverty, slums, and illness. Any effort, therefore, which is not aimed directly at major social change is viewed by this school as inadequate and inconsequential—like trying to fell a giant sequoia with a toy axe. Another view sees the prevention effort as involving wheels within wheels within wheels, highly complex and sticky. The alleged magnitude of these complexities is a deterrent to psychologists and social scientists who can, with little effort, find more digestible and much neater problems to define and solve. Some who see the value of pursuing the problem's elusive solution look in vain for something akin to Archimedes' lever which could move the whole problem at once. Others are less ambitious, but simply cannot determine how or where to begin.

A second factor in the resistance to prevention programs which needs to be anticipated and managed involves the fortress of personal privacy—the much-publicized right and privilege of each person and each family in a free society to mind their own business and have others mind theirs. Primary prevention in any health matter has always meant intervention in the lives of persons in the population at large. But if the intervention takes place prior to such time as the persons needing special help are singled out, it may not then be an invasion of personal privacy but perceived as a necessary and, indeed, a mandatory step for the common good. Even at this level, public acceptance takes time. For instance, regulation of auto traffic, of school attendance, and of polio and smallpox vaccination have become generally acceptable; yet water fluoridation for dental hygiene still raises the issue of invasion of personal privacy in certain communities, which may or may not decide to accept this preventive program.

Under the pressures of an expanding population and an earth grown smaller through instant communication and quick transport, an individual's conduct is becoming more and more the business of his neighbors. The California Vehicle Code contains 1,800 laws that did not exist 40 years ago. Today's building and planning codes determine how a man may use his property—even to the kind of structure he may erect on it—and in crowded urban areas such codes are socially necessary. Restrictive traffic laws may be said to infringe upon one's right to drive as he pleases, but we all know that our freedom and our lives depend on such restrictions. One uninoculated smallpox carrier endangers all of us. Similarly, but seldom acknowledged, one child with inadequately controlled id impulses or inadequate superego development endangers his next door neighbors and his entire community. The nub of all these problems is to find a way of intervening which is right and proper, and which can be understood, and therefore sanctioned, by the majority of citizens.

In the behavioral field there are at present some institutions which have an opportunity to explore ways of increasing their potential for primary prevention. The well-baby clinic and the public school are given informal and official sanction to "interfere" and "meddle"—the former, in terms of the child's health and family environment, the latter, in terms of the child's educational progress or lack of progress. Nevertheless, these institutions, too, must be alert to the conflicts inherent in such sanctions. The school must find its leverage in its assigned task of educating children and therefore carefully define the role of such auxiliary services as psychological testing and mental health consultation in assisting the teachers to carry out their instructional tasks. To most parents the health and educational progress of their children represent important and highly significant processes; more often than not there is a strong motivation to work with the school or the well-baby clinic to enhance their children's healthiness and educational success.

Certain values of our society, however, constitute another barrier to the development of prevention programs: success is often associated with virtue, and failure with sin. Deep in our culture is the notion that in a free society each person has equal opportunity with his fellows to show his mettle as a conscientious, hardworking, and—consequently—successful citizen. If he chooses not to be conscientious (according to the majority's definition of this term) and hardworking, the prevailing mores hold that he has only himself to blame for the result. This is the stereotype. Realistically, there is increasing clinical and research evidence to support the hypothesis that children who find healthful satisfactions in relationships with family, neighborhood, and school, will as adults find these same satisfactions; and that the children who find frustration and defeat in these primary institutions also tend to be defeated as adults.

Prevention, as a specific activity, still has the major problem of interesting and involving a great many more members of the mental illness professions. Most of these men and women are involved in relationships with individual patients and of necessity, are largely concerned with the curing of illnesses. As T. F. Fox points out:

> Curative medicine has generally had precedence over preventive medicine: people come to the doctor to be healed, and most practicing physicians still think of prevention as subsidiary to their main task—which is, to treat the sick. Though they subscribe, intellectually, to prevention, they really feel more at home when the disease has "got going."[2]

In this connection, one may need to recognize and deal with a minimization or depreciation of processes of psychological change other than intensive psychotherapy. The mental health worker, whether psychiatric technician, nurse, psychologist, social worker, or psychiatrist, is often deeply impressed by the mountainous obstacles in effecting positive, healthful changes in mental patients and, consequently, finds it difficult to comprehend how less intensive types of experiences might have prevented the illness. Ian Stevenson, in his study of direct instigation of behavioral changes in psychotherapy, points out that some patients often improve markedly when they have mastered a stressful situation or relationship and that, if such patients are helped to manage a day-to-day problem, change does take place.[3]

It is possible that our overemphasis on individual therapy as a major community resource retards to some degree our interest in, or the priority given to, prevention. The fact is, however, that primary prevention is the concern of all of the mental health professions—not merely the responsibility of any one group. Much preventive gold can be mined from clinicians and therapists by encouraging them to translate their clinical experiences and knowledge into programs with preventive possibilities, and we should make use of these avenues. Such translations, however, must be within a framework of what is operationally feasible, in what Kardiner called the "Key Integrative Systems" of a society—its primary institutions which shape the basic personality structure of its members.[4]

And finally, there is the knotty problem of defining the goals of prevention. If our prime intention is the promotion of emotional robustness and of ability to *cope with life* rather than *to defend against it*, that goal

---

[2] Fox, T. F., "Priorities," *Proceedings of the 36th Annual Dinner Meeting, Milbank Memorial Fund* (1960), p. 16.

[3] Stevenson, Ian, "Direct Instigation of Behavioral Changes in Psychotherapy," *AMA Archives of General Psychiatry*, vol. 1 (1959), p. 99–107.

[4] Kardiner, Abraham, "The Individual and His Society," New York, Columbia University Press (1945).

needs to be given a base of health objectives that are specific, positive, and (hopefully) measurable. As Rene Dubois points out:

> Solving problems of disease is not the same thing as creating health. * * * This (latter) task demands a kind of wisdom and vision which transcends specialized knowledge of remedies and treatments and which apprehends in all their complexities and subtleties the relation between living things and their total environment.[5]

Evaluative baselines are difficult to define or use, because of the lack of specificity of what constitutes mental illness, plus the changing character of this illness. Nevertheless, such evaluations of the health of a community are the *sine qua non* of preventive programs. The effect or worth of any program will require evidence of its impact on the health of large groups of persons; without a conceptual and evaluative framework, such programs can neither be formulated nor tested.

A FRAMEWORK FOR PRIMARY PREVENTION

Thus, no one single problem covering primary prevention is of greater urgency than the development of a platform or position from which one can begin to organize and act. One cannot exert leverage on any field of forces except from some fixed position. Even if this framework is only theoretical it can serve us to develop hypotheses, test them, and then further develop or, if need be, abandon the original framework. The definition of primary prevention with which this paper began is one kind of platform from which action can take off. Let me repeat it here.

"Primary prevention of mental and emotional disorders is any specific biological, social or psychological intervention which promotes or enhances the mental and emotional robustness or reduces the incidence and prevalence of learning and behavior disorders in the population at large." In this framework, then, we would aim preventive programs at persons not yet separated from the general population and, hopefully, at interventions which are specific enough to be operationally defined and measured.

Taking off from this position, it seems to me that we must make the following basic value assumption: that those social, psychological, and biological factors which tend to enhance the full development of the human characteristics of man have illness-preventive potential and are therefore desirable and that factors which tend to limit or block such development have illness-producing potential and are therefore undesirable. By human characteristics, the full development of which are sought, I would propose the ability to love and the ability to work productively (Freud's "Lieben und Arbeiten"). Philosophically, one might propose those aspects of man's experience which give him the maximum ability to adapt to his own potential as well as to the realities of his environment. One can, therefore, hypothesize that forces which increase or enhance the degrees of freedom of man's individual and social behavior are mentally healthful, and that those which reduce such freedom are unhealthful.

---

[5] Dubois, Rene, "Mirage of Health" (Harper, 1959), p. 22.

What, specifically, is meant by degrees of behavioral freedom? Behavioral freedom may be regarded as the ability of the organism to develop, maintain, and enhance resiliency and flexibility in coping with problems. Operationally, the degree of such freedom may be defined as the number of behavioral alternatives available to an individual personality under normal *or* stress conditions.

In thinking of preventive action as increasing man's behavioral degrees of freedom, reference needs to be made to L. S. Kubie and his relentless pursuit of this notion in discriminating between neurotic and non-neurotic behavior. His contention is that socially positive behavior can be the consequence of either healthy or neurotic processes, but that the basic difference between the normal and the neurotic is the organism's capacity, or lack of capacity, to maintain its elasticity. This elasticity manifests itself in the individual's freedom and flexibility to learn through experience, to change, and to adapt to changing circumstances.

> Thus, the essence of normality is flexibility, in contrast to the freezing of behavior into patterns of unalterability * * * that characterizes every manifestation of the neurotic process whether in impulses, purposes, acts, thoughts, or feelings. No single psychological act can be looked upon as neurotic unless it is the product or processes that predetermine a tendency to its automatic repetition.[6]

Characteristically, behavior that is motivated primarily by unconscious personality forces becomes a recurring pattern of action, because the goals of such behavior, being basically symbolical and highly masked to the individual, are seldom attainable. The further they are pursued, the stronger and more rigid become the behavior patterns, and the slimmer are the chances of moving on to new patterns. Thus, such behavior is repetitive and relatively unresponsive to experience. On the other hand, behavior motivated by forces at a level of relative awareness is usually directed at goals which are reasonably attainable and, subsequently, reduce the need to continue the same behavior pattern. The degrees of freedom—or the number of behavioral alternatives available to an individual—are therefore enhanced to the extent to which behavior is the result of preconscious or conscious forces in the personality.

One might, however, question the assumption, as does F. C. Redlich, that the individual is moved in a more healthful direction when acts are determined by conscious or preconscious forces rather than by unconscious forces.[7] For example, are not unconscious defense mechanisms health-producing and health-oriented in their adaptive and ego-protective goals? To the extent to which the organism needs ego defenses to maintain himself and mediate noxious forces in his environment, such defenses are productive of health. Yet, with increasing use of such unconscious de-

[6] Kubie, L. S., "The Fundamental Nature of the Distinction Between Normality and Neuroses," *Psychoanalytical Quarterly*, vol. 23 (1954), pp. 167–204.

[7] Redlich, F. C., "The Concept of Health in Psychiatry," in Alexander Leighton, *et al.*, eds., *Explorations in Social Psychology* (Basic Books, 1947).

fenses the organism, in the long run, will become less and less able to choose alternative modes of behaving and will more and more weave into the personality an inflexible and repetitive behavior pattern. Nevertheless, it is undoubtedly true that some repetitive, inflexible types of behavior can produce benefits in certain relationships, particularly in specific vocations or jobs.

The operations of neurotic processes in individuals can and do result in *culturally defined* successful behavior; an individual with relatively few degrees of behavioral freedom may find himself in a life space where the demands are limited and coping is possible. Similarly, a person can be a blatant failure without benefit of personality defect or neurosis. All of this emphasizes the difficulties in defining behavioral illness or health without reference to the contest and expectations of the social milieu in which the personality must function.

The concept of degrees of behavioral freedom as representing the difference between health and illness is also a key to the main difference between coping mechanisms and defense mechanisms. *In coping with problems* the organism maintains and develops resiliency and resources; *in defending against problems* the organism develops blocks and distortions which reduce resiliency and resources and deprive it of the freedom to act in new ways. Coping can be conceived of as integrative to personality, defending as disintegrative.

Jerome Bruner points out that there is always a mixture of coping and defending in dealing with problems, and that it is highly important that we distinguish sharply between the two processes. He says that such a distinction can best be made in terms of learning effectiveness:

> Let me suggest that effective cognitive learning in school—in contrast to the gratification-demanding, action-related, and affect-infused earlier learning—depends upon a denaturing process, if I may use such a fanciful expression. This involves at least three things. It requires, first, the development of a system of cognitive organization that detaches concepts from the modes of action that they evoke. A hole exists without the act of digging. Secondly, it requires the development of a capacity to detach concepts from these affective contexts. A father exists without reference to the thinker's feelings of ambivalence. It demands, moreover, a capacity to delay gratification so that, figuratively, each act of acquiring knowledge is not self-sufficiently brought to an end either by success or failure, and whatever happens can be taken as informative and not as simply frustrating or gratifying.[8]

THE ROLE OF PRIMARY INSTITUTIONS IN PREVENTION

The zonal classifications of people and services developed by Dr. Dan Blain is another way of looking at the same conceptual framework. In this context, primary institutions are seen as increasing the degrees of freedom of the population they serve so that there is a significant reduction in the

---

[8] Bruner, Jerome S., "On Coping and Defending" (mimeographed), p. 8.

need for secondary or tertiary institutions. In this framework the goals of programs of primary prevention would be as follows:

1. To increase the biological robustness of human beings by strengthening those services that deal with prenatal care, postnatal care, and the developmental problems of early childhood and adolescence.

2. To increase the area of effectiveness of primary agencies so that they may encompass a greater variety and greater number of persons in the general population. For example, the extension and accessibility of primary zone school services for retarded or emotionally disturbed children may make it possible that a child will not need secondary or tertiary services. Again, if health services for mothers or mothers-to-be were located close to neighborhood shopping centers or laundromats, the service could be offered on posters which read "Get a little help with your health or pregnancy problems during your wash cycle." A great many such special social techniques are necessary to persuade some women to use available social and medical services.

3. To decrease excessive or unhealthy stress or, conversely, to work with institutions to build greater stress immunity and manageability into their programs. Can we, for example, build some kind of psychological immunity into children and adolescents by providing controlled exposure in small measure to certain noxious emotional forces and then assisting children to mediate or manage them healthfully?

It is evident that these primary institutions and services can be seen as the front line defenses of a community. Among the forces which may move people out of the sphere of primary institutions that are not geared to contend with such forces are (1) the vulnerability of the organism to stress, (2) the number and character of the emotionally hazardous situations and crises which the individual is required to mediate and manage, and (3) how mediation and management is accomplished. The key to this movement lies in the character of mediation process (coping or defending).

An emotionally hazardous situation is any sudden alteration in the field of social forces affecting an individual so that the individual's perception and expectation of self and others undergo change. In this definition the hazardous situation or crisis is a *normal life occurrence,* which is temporarily upsetting, not always in an unpleasant sense yet necessitating rapid reorganization and mobilization of an individual's personality resources to deal with it. Examples are such situations as birth of a sibling, death of a loved one, school entrance, school failure, marriage, job promotion, divorce, or inheritance of a large sum of money from a dead uncle's estate. The greatest hazard is that the individual may find himself unable to manage the increased stress in a healthful way. Yet, since these situations are part of the normal process of living, they are, in a large part, the cutting edges which sharpen and crystallize personality development and integration.

Whether for good or for bad, emotionally hazardous crisis situations have these aspects in common: (1) they cause a rise in inner tension and uneasiness, (2) they cause some disorganization in normal functioning, (3) and they necessitate some internal change in self. An individual in such a situation can be said to be lightly balanced, so as to be able to move quickly in any direction. During this period of relative instability, minimal forces have their greatest effect, much like the effect of a one-gram weight at one end of an extremely delicately balanced seesaw. Such a small force would have little effect if the other forces governing the organism were relatively stable.

The implications of the emotionally vulnerable situation or crisis as a fulcrum for preventive action by the primary institution is clear. To the extent to which the institution or service can identify such situations and is prepared—or strengthened—to make the most of this opportunity, to that extent can it place grams of force on the side of health and personality growth. In some cases, institutions are capable of being aware of certain crises and can thus do a great deal to help individuals deal effectively with them. In other cases, however, the service may fail to recognize relevant crises or, in still other cases, recognize the crisis but fail to take advantage of the health-producing potential of the situation.

For example, a school may be well aware of the effect of the birth of a child on his siblings, but as an institution seldom may be in a position to obtain and use this information. Yet this important and natural event is often sufficiently upsetting to the life of the sibling to warrant anticipation by the school. To capitalize on this "emotionally hazardous situation," teachers may need to plan opportunities for the sibling to be recognized, to be helpful, to be successful—in short, to help the child by managing and mediating his crisis within the structure and role of the institution. The child may need no more than an extra pat on the back by the teacher; in other cases, a planned teacher-parent conference may be of help. What is critical here is (1) recognition by the institution of the emotionally vulnerable position of the child and (2) readiness to act positively upon it.

There is evidence that one-parent families are more vulnerable than intact families to stress and emotional hazards. This provides another opportunity for preventive action by another primary institution—the child-care center. Properly staffed and oriented, this facility can be a force in developing and maintaining some type of social intervention for the mothers and children utilizing its services. In theory, the child-care center would be reinforced as a primary institution if its staff included specially trained personnel who could work with a parent or the regular staff on the normal problems of people who are bringing up children but must work as the breadwinner at the same time.

WHITHER PREVENTION?

Prevention is at present a high-status word in the mental health field and generally applicable to almost all professional endeavors. It may be applied to newer and more effective treatment methods for schizophrenia, to custodial hospitalization of suicidal patients, or to the use of quieting drugs for overactive patients. It may also be used vaguely to mean improved housing, better human relations, better schools, more staff, and so on.

This lack of pinpointing of what we mean by prevention is especially critical in a field which already has a large element of vagueness and ex-

pansiveness. If, as Freud noted, thinking is action in rehearsal, it behooves individuals interested in preventive action to get ideas into rehearsal which are primarily preventive, which are specific enough to be duplicated in more than one locality, and which are operational enough to be evaluated within one's lifetime. We must also keep in mind that the preventive battlegrounds are the primary institutions or services of a society. It must be determined what interventions or modifications these institutions can make to reduce the emotional vulnerability or enhance the strength of the human organisms which they serve.

Prevention, it would seem to me, has to do with building a greater degree of immunity-producing experience in our primary institutions, through specific interventions at points where the psychological discomfort of an individual can be predicted and where a little help can go a long way. The nature of these interactions and experiences should enhance the degrees of psychological freedom of an individual to discover and select new behavioral alternatives in dealing with the slings and arrows of life.

The rigid and unchanging elements in human nature tend to entrench themselves in institutions which in turn become rigid and unchanging. Similarly, professional groups tend to entrench their ideas and interests with the result that the professional person understands everything about his job except its primary purpose. Often we are slaves to our training, both personally and professionally, and do the things we know how to do instead of trying to do the things we ought to do. School psychology is a relatively new profession, to which fate has given an unequaled opportunity. For good or bad, its practitioners are bound to a primary institution —the school—and must find the profession's identity and uniqueness in this institution's efforts to serve the health and educational needs of children. As Mark Twain said, "Soap and education are not as sudden as a massacre but they are more deadly in the long run."

A telling model of the need for prevention is embodied in an old Cornish custom which was at the same time a simple and valid test of what might be called social insanity. In the 1600's a person suspected of being insane was put in a small room in front of a sink in which was placed a bucket. The faucet was then turned on. The subject was given a ladle and asked to empty the water from the bucket. If he tried desperately to bail the water out of the bucket without curtailing or attempting to reduce the flow at its source, he was considered insane. Any society or community which atempts in this 20th century to provide bigger and better buckets of cure for behavior disorders without at the same time trying to reduce or stop the flow of their sources is equally suspect of insanity. I urge all of us to examine the tap, and to look for the tools and the methods by which we can begin to turn it down or turn it off.

41.   Prevention of Emotional Disorders in the School Setting: A Further Investigation

Emory L. Cowen, Melvin Zax, Louis D. Izzo, and Mary Ann Trost

Is it possible to develop and evaluate a preventive mental health program in a school setting? To answer this question, Emory L. Cowen and his associates exposed primary grade pupils for three years to a comprehensive program designed for early detection and treatment of emotional disorders. Evidence demonstrating the salutary effects of this program on a variety of criterion measures is presented in the following selection.

In a recent report (Cowen, Izzo, Miles, Telschow, Trost, & Zax, 1963), a preventive mental health program, established in the primary grades of a public elementary school in Rochester, New York, was both described and evaluated. This program was conducted over a 3-year period in a single experimental (E) elementary school, with two geographically contiguous and demographically comparable control (C) schools, maintaining traditional mental-health-related services, as controls. When the E group was nearing completion of its third-grade experience, a comprehensive series of evaluations was undertaken comparing E and C school children on a variety of school-record, achievement, behavioral, self-rating and rating-by-others indexes.

In another phase of this study, a dichotomous clinical judgment (Red-Tag versus Non-Red-Tag) was rendered for each child, soon after he

Journal of Consulting Psychology, 1966, 30, 381–387. Copyright 1966 by the American Psychological Association. Reprinted with the permission of the copyright owner and senior author.

[1] The authors acknowledge, with appreciation, support of the project by the New York State Department of Mental Hygiene. The present write-up was done in connection with the investigators' further work in this area, supported by the Community Services and Research Branch of the NIMH (MH 01500-01).

[2] Our appreciation is extended to Robert Klein, Department of Psychology, Stanford University, who contributed significantly to the data processing and analysis.

entered the first grade, on the basis of currently available information. A Red-Tag was applied to the folders of all children who, in terms of psychological testing data obtained during social work interviews with mothers and actual observed behavior, seemed to have already manifested moderate to severe maladjustment or in whom there was considered to be a high probability that such pathology was incipient. In the particular locale studied, this figure ran to 37% of the total group in the original sample. The Red-Tag classification, which was entirely internal to the project staff, was recognized to be an arbitrary and fallible clinical judgment.

Some suggestions of the possible effectiveness of the preventive program were noted, in the earlier study, in terms of significantly "healthier" anxiety scale scores for E school children in comparison to their C school peers, and several significantly more favorable attitudes by E as opposed to C teachers and parents. However, such differences were not generalized to all, or even the preponderant majority, of criterion measures. Others, among the latter, either showed only a trend in the predicted direction or, in some instances, no differences whatsoever. When, however, Red-Tag children in the E school were compared to their Non-Red-Tag counterparts, significant differences favoring the latter were found on several achievement measures, an achievement-aptitude discrepancy score and on two behavioral rating indexes completed by teachers and professional specialists, respectively.

The model reflected in the foregoing program is one which emphasizes early detection of emotional disorders and an attempt at their prevention. This is in some contrast to the more traditional clinical model, calibrated to deal with evident and relatively more entrenched symptomatology primarily through the vehicle of individual clinical diagnosis and treatment. Increasingly, socially oriented analysis (Albee, 1959, 1963; Joint Commission on Mental Illness and Health, 1961; Nichols, 1963) points up the facts that the demand for mental health services far outstrips the present supply, that new sources of professional manpower are sorely needed in the mental health area, and that more parsimonious and far-reaching approaches to our societal mental health problems merit careful exploration.

This earlier research program was, in no sense, a "clean" one; indeed, we have ourselves described, at some length, many of its principal pitfalls (Cowen, et al., 1963). While it was our feeling that the total array of our earlier findings contained some encouraging aspects, the results in no sense resolved with finality the principal issues being examined. It was, for one thing, not clearly demonstrated in any generalized way that the E school preventive program had positive consequences. Moreover, there was the uncertainty of not knowing which of the "positive" findings were stable, replicable ones. The general paucity of data in this area, in addition to the foregoing considerations, pointed up the need for further empirical data.

The present investigation, largely a cross-validation of our earlier study, seeks in the main to answer the same two questions that guided the original research: (a) what is the effectiveness of the preventive program itself? and (b) what are the sequelae of early detected pathology? The fundamental methodology and techniques of evaluation used in this study are highly comparable to those used in the preceding one, with the exception of several relatively minor changes in program and techniques of evaluation which were introduced to replace procedures or assessment methods found to be ineffectual in the earlier work.

The research was carried out in the same settings (both E and C schools) as was the original study. The nature of this setting has been described more fully elsewhere (Cowen et al., 1963). Briefly, both E and C schools were located in largely "upper-lower" socioeconomic status (SES) districts and housed children making up a representative cross section of the city of Rochester, ethnically, except for some substantial underweighting of Negro and Jewish youngsters.

The target group, in the present case, consisted of those youngsters who reached third grade the year immediately following the original group. These youngsters, like their predecessors, had been exposed to the early detection-preventive program for a full 3-year period.

METHOD AND PROCEDURES

Subjects

The total initial sample of third graders consisted of 103 from the E school and 136 from the two C schools. The E and C schools were the same as those used in our earlier investigation (Cowen et al., 1963). Initial selection of the C schools had been determined by a variety of demographic and census tract data taken from the Rochester City School District, demonstrating their high degree of comparability to the E school on the basic indexes of concern. Post hoc comparison of the earlier E and C samples (Cowen et al., 1963) revealed no significant or near significant differences on the three Otis IQ measures.

For the present sample, we again began by attempting to verify our assumptions about the demographic comparability of the E and C schools through comparison of the three Otis IQ scores of the two groups. The resulting three t ratios, each significant at $p = .01$ with higher scores for the C school, made it clear that assumptions about group comparability of IQ measure were untenable. Apparently, due to some combination of actual change in neighborhood and or sampling fluctuation, the initial E ($N = 84$) and C ($N = 123$) samples were, in fact, quite disparate on this essential set of control indexes. Since IQ is a variable which is likely to covary systematically with many of the dependent measures used in the present study, we felt it essential that its effects be partialled out. Accordingly, more restricted subsamples of E and C group youngsters were selected, and in order to obtain an approximate IQ matching of our E and C groups, it was necessary to reduce our sample size to 65 for each group. For these new subsamples the Otis total IQ of the E group averaged 100.89 and that for the C group 102.98. Verbal and Nonverbal IQ scores for the two groups were also closely matched.

It should be emphasized that the restriction of sample size to achieve relative IQ comparability was relevant *only* to the E versus C school comparisons. In the case of the Red-Tag versus Non Red-Tag comparisons within the E school, the entire E school sample of 103 was usable, since there were no significant or near significant IQ differences between subgroups. The Ns of the Red-Tag and Non-Red-Tag samples were 31 and 72, respectively, the current Red-Tag figure thus running about 30% of the total group (slightly less than the 37% figure reported for the preceding year group (Cowen et al., 1963).

Procedure and Evaluation Measures

The basic experimental (prevention) program, as applied in the E school, represented a continuation of the program described in detail in our earlier publication (Cowen et al., 1963). As such, it featured early diagnostic evaluation of first-grade youngsters, social work interviews with mothers, a consultative service established by the school psychologist and social worker in the primary grades, after-school activity programs, a consulting psychiatrist and parent and teacher discussion groups.

Since the majority of the E school sample was in attendance at this school for the full 3-year period, up to the point of evaluation, these youngsters were exposed to the program for its entire duration. Those youngsters who transferred into the E school during the first, second, or third year had an exposure which was reduced accordingly.

Evaluation of the program both in E and C schools took place in the last month of the third school year. The criterion measures used for the evaluation of the children roughly approximated those used in the preceding year, although there were several modifications and additions. The criterion battery covered a wide range of indexes including school-record measures, teacher evaluation scales, peer evaluation instruments and self-report and self-evaluation techniques. More specifically, the following indexes were used:

School-record measures. Nurses Referrals (third grade); Cumulative Nurses Referrals; Days Absent; Grade Point Ratio based on final third-grade report card; Science Research Associates (SRA) Comprehension, Vocabulary Reasoning, Concepts and Computation (the latter three of these SRA measures having been added for the present year's analysis) and an Achievement-Aptitude Discrepancy (D) score.

Adjustment measures. The anxiety (A) and lie scales of the Children's Manifest Anxiety Scale (CMAS) (Casteneda, McCandless, & Palermo, 1956) were used. In addition we employed a 17-item teachers' behavior rating scale. For this measure the teacher indicated those characteristics (e.g., dependency, moodiness, disruptiveness, etc.) that were descriptive of a given child's behavior, and for each item so checked, provided an intensity rating along a 3-point scale. This measure yielded two scores: Teachers Rating (sum)—a simple arithmetic summation of the items checked with their intensity ratings—and Teachers Rating (overall)—a single global adjustment estimate, along a 5-point scale made for each of the children.

Finally, a single overall adjustment rating by the Mental Health Clinical Services (MHCS) project staff, also based on a 5-point scale, was provided for each of the children in the experimental school. The foregoing scales have been described in greater detail in our earlier publication (Cowen *et al.,* 1963).

The other adjustment measures used in this study were the Bower Thinking About Yourself (TAY), an instrument for assessment of self-concept in young children, and the Bower Class Play, a sociometric peer-evaluation technique (Bower, 960, 1961; Bower & Lambert, 1961; Zax, Cowen, Izzo, & Trost, 1964). In essence, the TAY consists of a series of descriptions of specific attributes of young children. The respondent is asked to indicate the extent to which each of these actually describes him (self-concept) and the extent to which he would like them to describe him (ideal-self). The discrepancy between these two estimates is taken as the index of self-dissatisfaction. The Bower Class Play is a two-part test. The child is presented with a series of hypothetical roles half positive and half negative, for an imaginary play to be put on by his class. For Part I, essentially a free-response sociometric choice situation, the child simply lists for each item, good or bad, as many children in his class as he feels would fit each role. From the cumulative pattern of nominations by the entire class group, two scores—total negative choices (1B) and percentage of negative choices (1C)—are derived. Though there is some correlation between the two, the percentage estimate is nevertheless useful since it partials out the varying factor of total number of choices. Part II consists of a series of 30 four-role sets, each containing two positive and two negative roles. The child indicated for each set the one for which he or his teacher or his peers would think him best suited. Once again, two principal scores are derived—total negative roles (IIB) and percentage roles (IIC), in this case the two scores being highly intercorrelated and, in fact identical, unless the child omits one or more items.

RESULTS

Results are presented within the framework of the two principal questions raised pertaining (*a*) to the effects of the preventive program itself and (*b*) to the sequelae of early-identified pathology or incipient pathology. For either of these two basic sets of comparisons, the tabled subject Ns may differ for differing variables, always falling short of the earlier-stated maximal Ns, as a function of such factors as absence from school on a testing day, incomplete or lost records, etc.

Comparisons of E and C Groups

Table 1 presents means and variances for E and C school subjects, for each of the school-record and adjustment measures. For each measure, a t ratio testing the significance of the difference between E and C group means is included. It may be noted that of the total of 19 criterion school record and adjustment measures, seven differentiate significantly between E and C groups, each of these favoring the former.

Comparisons of Red-Tag and Non-Red-Tag Children

Table 2 presents means and variances of Red-Tag and Non-Red-Tag groups, for each of the school-record and adjustment measures. Once again a t ratio testing the significance of the differences between means of

TABLE 1. COMPARISON OF SCHOOL RECORD AND ADJUSTMENT
MEASURES FOR *E* VERSUS *C* GROUPS

Measure	E school			C schools			t	p
	Mean	Variance	N	Mean	Variance	N		
School-record measures								
Nurses referrals, third grade[a]	0.88	1.95	65	1.51	4.44	65	2.02	.05
Cumulative nurses referrals	2.52	9.35	65	3.41	6.16	22	1.23	n.s.
Days absent	10.72	125.92	65	12.76	139.60	65	1.01	n.s.
Grade point ratio	24.95	17.86	65	20.98	35.83	65	4.37	.001
SRA comprehension	56.69	540.44	65	45.20	709.24	59	2.54	.02
SRA vocabulary	57.88	760.08	65	51.02	807.57	59	1.37	n.s.
SRA reasoning	62.72	785.64	65	60.71	910.55	59	0.39	n.s.
SRA concepts	42.86	394.84	65	41.51	1024.81	59	0.29	n.s.
SRA computation	43.91	709.64	65	39.48	565.68	58	0.97	n.s.
Ach-Apt D Score	3.47	0.80	65	2.59	0.63	65	5.95	.001
Adjustment measures								
Teachers' rating (Total)	3.62	176.72	65	3.30	177.62	64	0.43	n.s.
Teachers' rating (Overall)	1.94	1.03	65	2.69	0.82	64	4.41	.001
CMAS anxiety	19.61	55.74	63	22.47	70.56	65	2.03	.05
CMAS lie	3.76	4.56	63	4.63	5.20	65	2.23	.05
TAY D score	33.60	113.57	57	32.31	145.84	64	0.62	n.s.
Class Play IB	10.48	127.84	65	9.69	141.31	65	0.39	n.s.
Class Play IC	46.25	904.13	65	55.46	1026.75	65	1.69	n.s.
Class Play IIB	7.34	47.83	65	9.03	33.40	61	1.48	n.s.
Class Play IIC	24.25	554.19	65	29.61	374.15	61	1.39	n.s.

[a] Lower scores represent ideal for first three school-record and *all* adjustment measures.

the Red Tag and Non-Red-Tag group means is included for each measure. In this instance, of the 20 criterion school-record and adjustment measures used in the analyses, significant differences at $p \leqq .05$, favoring the Non-Red-Tag group, emerge for 14 of the comparisons.

A second series of structurally identical comparisons comparing the same Red-Tag sample with a reduced Non-Red-Tag sample (N = 40), excluding all students who transferred into the *E* school after the start of the program, was also carried out. The rationale for this series of analyses was that the reduced group would be a purer one, since there might be "buried" in the total Non-Red-Tag group some true Red-Tag children who had not yet been identified due to insufficient time and/or contact. All 14 significant differences noted in the original comparison remained in the second analysis. In addition, two new significant differences again favoring the Non-Red-Tag group emerged—on SRA Vocabulary and CMAS Anxiety. Since these results parallel the original ones so closely and, in fact, are even slightly "sharper," they are not tabled here.

DISCUSSION

The general effects of the experimental prevention program may be judged from the series of comparisons of the *E* and *C* schools on the

TABLE 2. COMPARISON OF SCHOOL-RECORD AND ADJUSTMENT
MEASURES FOR RED-TAG VERSUS NON-RED-TAG GROUPS

Measure	Red-Tag			Non-Red-Tag				
	Mean	Variance	N	Mean	Variance	N	t	p
School-record measures								
Nurses referrals, third grade[a]	1.93	5.50	29	0.65	1.23	71	4.13	.001
Cumulative nurses referrals	6.69	5.67	29	1.76	4.01	71	5.67	.001
Days absent	11.94	186.26	31	9.76	60.52	72	1.10	n.s.
Grade point ratio	21.35	27.64	31	24.65	22.57	72	3.37	.01
SRA comprehension	42.77	607.50	30	56.34	662.34	70	2.67	.01
SRA vocabulary	48.83	855.18	30	56.56	744.63	70	1.39	n.s.
SRA reasoning	49.13	863.77	30	60.73	863.36	70	1.99	.05
SRA concepts	43.10	471.75	30	40.97	591.94	70	0.45	n.s.
SRA computation	30.38	631.32	30	42.73	790.35	70	2.18	.05
Ach-Apt D score	2.70	1.01	29	3.25	0.85	55	2.57	.02
Adjustment measures								
MHCS Rating	4.48	0.26	31	1.19	0.27	72	32.90	.001
Teachers' rating (Total)	7.03	38.03	30	2.66	7.63	71	5.40	.001
Teachers' rating (Overall)	2.57	1.50	30	1.75	0.71	71	4.32	.001
CMAS anxiety	21.83	71.79	29	19.41	59.93	71	1.52	n.s.
CMAS lie	4.31	4.65	29	4.10	5.35	71	0.47	n.s.
TAY D score	34.00	101.33	28	33.38	112.51	61	0.24	n.s.
Class Play IB	13.35	159.57	31	8.31	78.95	72	2.48	.02
Class Play IC	57.71	1030.48	31	44.04	823.70	72	2.30	.02
Class Play IIB	9.83	68.35	30	6.35	27.38	72	2.78	.01
Class Play IIC	32.33	816.30	30	21.14	303.73	72	2.63	.01

[a] Lower scores represent ideal for first three school-record and *all* adjustment measures.

criterion school-record and adjustment measures. Although significant differences between groups are not found on all of these measures, certainly the preponderant weight of the findings point in the direction of a more favorable status for E group members, that is, those who have been exposed to the experimental program for a 3-year period. This inference is based both on the profile of directional differences between groups as well as the specific pattern of significantly differentiating criterion indexes, seven of which favor the E group at $p \leqq .05$. Thus, youngsters who have participated in the program are referred or refer themselves less frequently to the school nurse, obtain higher report card grades and higher SRA Comprehension scores, and manifest a higher level of achievement in comparison to their basic aptitude level. Moreover, they are rated as better adjusted by their teachers and obtain lower scores on both the anxiety and lie scales of the CMAS. Of particular interest is the fact that the differentiating criterion measures cover a fairly wide spectrum as to both structure and content. They include a straightforward behavioral-descriptive index, achievement criteria reflecting both everyday classroom behavior and standardized tests, and adjustment indicators of the external evaluative and self report type.

In comparison to the structurally related findings from the preceding year's data (Cowen *et al.,* 1963), the present results are considerably sharper and more clear-cut. They in no sense contradict the prior findings; rather they accentuate and clarify the earlier data. It is somewhat less certain as to whether the differential clarity of findings for the consecutive-year group is a result of sample fluctuation, strengthening of program, more effective evaluation, chance, or some complex combination of these factors.

Our second prime concern in this, as well as the preceding, investigation has been with the course of development, over a 3-year period, of youngsters who were "diagnosed" very early in their school careers as having manifest or incipient emotional problems ranging in severity from moderate to severe. For the most part, this group included youngsters with acting-out problems of shyness, timidity and withdrawal, and problems of inadequate academic achievement.

A reasonably comprehensive picture of the status of the Red-Tag child, after 3 school years, is obtained from the series of direct comparisons between the Red-Tag versus Non-Red-Tag groups on the 20 criterion measures used herein. The differences between the two groups are overwhelming, with the Red-Tags showing up, directionally as less favorable on 19 of 20 measures, significantly so at $p \leqq .05$ on 14 of them. It seems quite clear that by the end of the third school year, the child with early-diagnosed emotional disorders has suffered serious impairment in the academic, achievement, adjustment, and behavioral spheres. This seems to be the case whether the evaluation is derived from formal tests, teacher rating, peer rating, or self-rating. The extent of deficit seems to be substantial and the Red-Tag child appears to be well rutted on a globally downhill course which, by that time, is already well accelerated. These findings are entirely consistent with those emanating from our prior investigation (Cowen *et al.,* 1963). They are, however, just as was the case in the basic *E* versus *C* group comparisons, even more clear-cut here than they were in the earlier study. Despite the avowed fallibility of the Red-Tag classification, it is one with considerable predictive utility. We need to understand better the elements and components of what, up to this point, has been a gross clinical estimate. Attempts at further delineation, in this direction, are currently in progress. There are, to be sure, some fundamental limitations to the present study, many of which are intrinsic to the basic nature of the research itself. Some derive from the fact that the study is restricted fundamentally to a single experimental school and two control schools. Hence, the danger exists that factors theoretically unrelated to the content of the experimental program could be affecting the outcome.

A second major concern has to do with the network of evaluative criteria employed in the study. These represent a combination of reality, rationality, and chance and somewhere along the line, must obviously reflect the value judgment of the investigators. Since our conclusions are tied to our criteria, it could be argued that these are inadequate, insufficiently broad, too ephemeral, etc. Finally, these criterion measures are, at best, "way-station indicants." We need to know whether the demonstrated effects (*a*) endure over time and (*b*) relate to other indicators of mental health disturbance which are more of the bellweather, face-valid variety (e.g., hospitalization). This latter type of information is gained, necessarily, only via long-range follow up; such work is now being undertaken by the present investigators.

With all due allowance for the recognized limitations of the research, we believe that the results obtained establish a type of "hunting-license" or justification to probe more intensively the potential of an early detective and preventive orientation to mental health problems. Current manpower data, analyses of the limited effectiveness of traditional diagnostic-therapeutic helping structure and logic have all pointed in this direction. To these factors, we now seek to add some empirical evidence. In our view, the present findings point up the rich potential of a community-based preventive approach, anchored in, but not restricted to, the school setting. For example, the very high incidence of early pathology and its already very serious consequences within the first 3 school years suggest that there is here a fertile domain for the intense exploration of early secondary preventive measures and interventions. Certainly there is need for imaginative and innovative new program development and evaluation within the philosophical framework that has guided the present effort.

REFERENCES

Albee, G. W. *Mental health manpower trends.* New York: Basic Books, 1959.

Albee, G. W. American psychology in the sixties. *American Psychologist,* 1963, 18, 90–95.

Bower, E. M. *Early identification of emotionally handicapped children in school.* Springfield, Ill.: Charles C. Thomas, 1960.

Bower, E. M. Primary prevention in a school setting. In G. Caplan (Ed.), *Prevention of mental disorders in children.* New York: Basic Books, 1961. Pp. 353–377.

Bower, E. M., & Lambert, N. M. *A process for inschool screening of children with emotional handicaps.* Sacramento, Calif.: California State Department of Education, 1961.

Casteneda, A., McCandless, B. R., & Palermo, D. S. The children's form of the manifest anxiety scale. *Child Development,* 1956, 27, 317–326.

Cowen, E. L., Izzo, L. D., Miles, H., Telschow, E. F., Trost, M. A., & Zax, M. A preventive mental health program in the school setting: Description and evaluation. *Journal of Psychology,* 1963, 56, 307–356.

Joint Commission on Mental Illness and Health. *Action for mental health.* New York: Basic Books, 1961.

Nichols, R. S. The influence of economic and administrative factors upon the type and quality of care given to persons with psychological disorders. *Working Papers in Community Mental Health,* 1963, 1, 1–17.

Zax, M., Cowen, E. L., Izzo, L. D., & Trost, M. A. Identifying emotional disturbance in the school setting. *American Journal of Orthopsychiatry,* 1964, 34, 447–454.

42. A Teacher-Aide Program for Preventing Emotional Disturbances in Young School Children

Melvin Zax, Emory L. Cowen, Louis D. Izzo,
Angelo J. Madonia, Joseph Merenda and Mary Ann Trost

With the dawning realization that the relatively small numbers of highly trained professionals will be unable to reduce mental health problems to any very large degree, the focus of attention has shifted to the short-term training of large numbers of paraprofessionals or care-givers. Melvin Zax and his colleagues relate in the following article how they used the untapped services of warm, sensitive and intelligent women in the community as teacher-aides to head off emotional disorders in children. What services would you have had teacher-aides perform? What would you have done to prepare the regular classroom teacher for this kind of program?

A growing feeling among mental health workers, reflected clearly in the report of the Joint Commission on Mental Illness and Health,[1] is that approaches which go beyond traditional methods hold the only real answers to the mental health problems facing society today. Furthermore, studies of the manpower pool in the so-called "helping professions" indicate that mental health workers are currently in short supply and that this situation will become worse with the population growth.[2, 3] Many who have been sensitive to this state of affairs have been casting about for alternatives to the exclusive use of highly trained professionals for work in mental health.

Mental Hygiene, 1966, 50, 406–415. Reprinted with the permission of the publisher and senior author.

The program described was supported by a grant (MH-01500) from the National Institute of Mental Health, Community Services and Research Branch, Bethesda, Md. This support is gratefully acknowledged.

Prominent among those who have turned in such a direction are Rioch and co-workers,[4] who have demonstrated that intelligent housewives can be trained to do psychotherapy effectively. Their original program, though fascinating in implication, was limited to particularly bright, well-educated women, whose training was relatively intensive—i.e., nearly full time for a two-year period.

Other efforts in this direction have been undertaken on a more focused and time-limited basis, with somewhat less-select subprofessional target groups. For example, Sanders[5] and his colleagues have trained subprofessionals in a relatively short time to be extremely useful in a state hospital milieu therapy program. Several additional programs are currently being developed that utilize the subprofessional with varying amounts of training in the performance of a variety of mental-health-related functions.[6-9]

This paper is a type of case study of a specific program designed to train housewives to function as mental health aides in the classroom setting, in an effort to forestall the development of serious emotional disorders in young children. The program was a limited one, conducted over a period of four and a half months. The aim of the present report is to describe its workings and to point up some of its early successes and failures.

Actually, there have been a few well-organized programs directed toward school-children,[10-12] but for the most part these have involved the use of mental health professionals in new roles. One specific program, with features similar to the one to be described, has been reported by Donahue and Nichtern.[13] This program was directed toward the very severely emotionally disturbed child (i.e., schizophrenic and brain injured) in the school system, using the services of housewives recruited from the school district. These housewives worked on a volunteer basis as teachers of small groups of children who were unable to benefit from routine classroom exercises. The authors reported considerable success by such volunteers in effectively teaching these problem children and, moreover, in making it possible for many of them to return to regular classes. In the program to be described, a similar manpower (more accurately, womanpower) source was drawn upon to work in the primary grades of a public school.

It was felt that many children begin their years of schooling on the wrong foot, either because they cannot conform well to the limits of the school situation (feeling intimidated by such stimuli as authority figures who are not the familiar parents, or a set of strange peers who exert group pressures that have never been experienced before) or for other reasons. Some of these children manage at least a modicum of adjustment eventually, whereas others never do achieve a comfortable adaptation that allows for the realization of their abilities. These problems are often painfully obvious to the teacher in the elementary grades, whose hands are tied by the need to conform to a curriculum and a feeling of responsibility for an entire group of children.

Because such adaptation problems exist, progressive school systems have attempted to provide highly trained professionals to deal with youngsters who are not benefiting from their schooling and who may be acting as a disruptive force in the classroom. Nearly always, however, referral to the school psychologist or social worker is primarily for the child with a well-entrenched pattern of maladaptive behavior that has long been nourished by a familial constellation and the general demands of the school situation.

Hopefully, such difficulties might be avoided if attention could be given to incipient problems before a maladaptive process becomes well fixed. Since teachers have much to do, which precludes their playing a primarily mental-health-oriented role in the classroom, it was thought that mature, warm, sensitive people, provided with relevant and focused training, might serve this very useful function, working as subprofessionals. It was with this in mind that a small group of "pioneers" were recruited to serve as teacher aides in the classrooms of primary-grade teachers.

SELECTION OF TEACHER AIDES

In conceiving this program, the authors were not able to specify precisely what such aides would spend their time doing. They could only state vaguely that the teacher aides would be using whatever interpersonal skills they possessed as warm human beings to help children in the classroom who needed their help in order to remain in the mainstream of class routine. It was expected that there would be times when such adaptation would not be possible for a child and that it might be necessary for him and the aide to engage in activities that seemed, on the surface, to be orthogonal to the immediate demands of the situation. An example of this might be actually leaving the classroom with the child when he was not able to profit from the immediate experience and was disruptive for the group at large. However, even on such relatively infrequent occasions, the ultimate goal would continue to be that of fostering healthy adjustment to the school situation.

As will be noted below, this vague "job description" left open many questions for both the aides and the teachers, some of which were satisfactorily resolved and others for which solutions are still being sought. It was sufficient for the authors that, at the outset and throughout the first year of the program. all who were involved in it—aides, teachers, school mental health workers, and school administrators—applauded its purposes and accepted the notion that some such program was, in principle, desirable.

The initial problems faced in starting a program were those of recruiting personnel. It was felt that part-time personnel might well be drawn from among the vast number of good mothers in the community who, having reared their children to a point of some independence, found themselves casting about for worthwhile activities with which to occupy themselves. Such women are to be found working as volunteers in a variety of settings, in which traditionally oriented professionals have tended to use them for time-consuming and routine functions, wherever needed, rather than to incorporate them as basic elements into a comprehensive, mental-health-oriented program.

A small number of such women (six, in all) were sought for this pilot program. To avoid a massive screening procedure, which would result both in a great deal of work and in the discouragement of many good applicants, the authors chose to circulate a "Help Wanted" notice among a small group of mental health professionals in Rochester, N. Y., primarily among those employed by the city school district and the University of Rochester. Later, two or three clergymen with prominent interest in mental health were also contacted. It was felt that such resource people might be able to bring the prospective teacher-aide program to the attention of suitable candidates from among their friends or acquaintances and thereby provide a type of pre-screening.

The notice stated that a small group of women was to be trained in connection with a newly instituted program for the early detection and prevention of emotional disorders in primary-grade school-children. Duties were sketchily described as serving as the "extra pair of hands" that any good teacher might like to have in order to provide the hyperactive, withdrawn, periodically upset, or underachieving child with the extra attention he might need to become more stable and better adjusted. It was indicated that each volunteer would be required to work half a school day, each day of the week, and that for this the modest sum of $25 per week could be provided. The attributes of the women being sought were described as follows:

> The type of women we would like to recruit should possess a personal warmth and liking for children, in connection with which the experience of having successfully reared children of their own would seem to be an important prerequisite. In addition, flexibility, a genuine commitment to the type of work we describe, a life situation which would permit her to devote the necessary time to the project and an interest in the school situation would also seem important. Hopefully, the person herself would be relatively free of major personal problems. These attributes would be valued above formal education.

This method of soliciting volunteers turned up a number of excellent candidates, 11 of whom were interviewed. In addition, when the "Help Wanted" announcement was later inadvertently printed in a church newsletter, many interested women responded, which suggested that such a program might be feasible, from the manpower viewpoint, on a much broader basis than was presently being attempted.

Those who were interviewed were first seen by a team consisting of one of the two program psychologists and an advanced graduate student in clinical psychology. Though largely unstructured, these approximately one-hour interviews were guided by the need to elicit the information and impressions that would allow the interviewers to rate each applicant on a series of 21 seven-point scales, one cluster of which described personal and social attributes and the other, intellective and orientation factors. In addition, there were three scales on which global impressions of anxiety level, personal liking for the applicant, and a prediction of the applicant's likely success in the teacher-aide role were made. Each interviewer was also required to list what he regarded as assets and limitations of the candidate.

Applicants were asked to fill out a personal history form describing themselves, their spouse, and their children in terms of such variables as age, education, and employment history. Several items were also included in this form regarding the applicant's interests, hobbies, skills, group affiiliations, health, and personal goals in life. Finally, applicants were required to answer questions about their motivation for applying, what they hoped to get out of the program, and what assets and liabilities they felt they brought to it.

The rating scales and history form were thought to be useful in providing some structure for the interviews and for acquainting project staff with the backgrounds of the aides. Furthermore, it was intended that, once a large enough sample of aides had been trained and placed in schools, it might be possible to use the information contained in these instruments to develop criteria relating to successful functioning in the teacher-aide role. This has not yet been attempted because only six aides were trained in the first program year.

Following their session with the initial interviewing team, those applicants thought to be most suitable for the program were interviewed once more in the school where assignments were to be made, by the psychologist (i.e., *the project psychologist*) in charge of the basic early detection and prevention program into which the teacher-aide project was to be incorporated. [14, 15] When there was concurrence in the choice of an applicant by the interview team and the project psychologist, the applicant was accepted for the program.

The six women selected ranged from 26 to 58 years in age. None held a college degree, but three had some college training. One had not even completed high school. All were mothers who seemed to have been successful in rearing their own children, and none seemed to possess any strong need to supplant the teacher in her role as an imparter of knowledge. On the contrary, their interest in the program seemed to stem from a genuine desire to serve the emotional needs of children.

THE TRAINING PROGRAM

A five-week training program was designed to provide some background in relevant psychological theory, an appreciation of a few very basic concepts such as psychic determinism and the importance of early experience in personality development, and an opportunity to ease gradually into the classroom situation. Fundamentally, the authors were banking heavily on the personal qualities of the aides as their most potent resources. The training program was primarily intended to provide the emotional and intellectual support to assuage any feeling that they were being tossed into an arena in which they had no weapons on which to rely.

Specifically, the first week of the training program included the presentation of a two-and-a-half-hour session on the mental hygiene movement and another spelling out the history of the project in which they were to be working. A series of six two-and-a-half-hour sessions spread over the first four weeks of the program were devoted to material on personality development, behavioral disorders, and child-parent relationships. The only other such didactic sessions involved one meeting each on an orientation to the schools and on the elements of teaching methods, both of which were conducted by the project mental-health team and the principal, with the goal of providing a better understanding of classroom routine and the teacher's role. In all such sessions, materials were presented in a relatively informal, discussion-oriented, issue-centered context directed primarily toward activating a particular way of thinking.

A second major component of the training program was clinical materials and case discussion. This was introduced during the second week of training with the use of a film entitled "Unconscious Motivation." During the third training week another film, "The Quiet One," was used in one session, and a morning was spent by the aides simply observing children in several different classrooms. Both films and observation sessions were followed by discussions of what was observed and how this might be understood psychologically. During the final two weeks of training, there were three more classroom-observation sessions and a session during which actual problems manifested by schoolchildren were presented by the project psychologist and social worker and discussed by the aides and a child psychiatrist, who served initially as clinical consultant to the project and later as a resource person for the aides. In the very last week, the aides were actually assigned to classrooms and were encouraged to participate in the program that was going on. Each session was followed by a meeting with the project mental health team at which the aides' experiences were discussed.

THE PROGRAM IN OPERATION

Just prior to and during the period that the aides were being selected and trained, the six primary-grade teachers in the experimental school met twice with the two program psychologists, the project mental health team, the principal, and the consulting psychiatrist. The proposed program and its background were described to them, and they were invited to volunteer to accept aides in their classrooms. All six expressed willingness to be part of the program, and this determined the number of aides to be recruited. As the time for the actual implementation of the program approached, a meeting was held with the teachers to discuss the kinds of role conflicts that might arise between aide and teacher, who would both be "cooking in the same kitchen." The teachers were encouraged to maintain their role as the person in charge of the classroom and to define clearly the limits within which the aide might operate. It was pointed out that such limits might well vary from one teacher to another and that a certain amount of arbitrariness in such matters was thought, by program personnel, to be quite natural. This was more readily accepted intellectually than emotionally, as will be seen below when impressions about actual program operation are presented.

After the aides had been trained and placed in classrooms, they functioned independently, but were aware that they could turn at any time to the project psychologist and social worker for advice or supervision on any aspect of their functioning. In addition, regular weekly meetings were held for all the aides with the project mental-health team, and many of these included the consulting psychiatrist. The sessions involved discussions of specific interactions between the aides and the children and, inevitably, between the aides and the teachers to whom they were assigned. Similar meetings were held during the course of the program with the teachers, but on a less regular basis. A few meetings at the time the program was terminating for the year brought forth considerable comment from the teachers as a group and highlighted some of the important tactical errors in the design and functioning of the program.

Quite predictably, the first sessions with aides and teachers were devoted largely to the problems of working out role relationships. The teachers' concerns in this area were reflected in such complaints as: "Children are taking advantage of the aide's being in the room," "Some aides seem to feel they should function as teachers," and "Nobody knows what the aides are to do in the room." In addition, some teachers expressed concern that they might hurt the feelings of their aide by being critical of her activities with children during the class period. This latter problem was compounded by the fact that the aide was in virtually every case older than the teacher with whom she was working. In addition, four of the six teachers in this particular program were teaching for the first time and were facing all of the adjustment problems related to their newness on the job. The turnover rate among elementary school teachers being what it is, this problem is probably not so unique to the present program as it might seem at first blush. Finally, teachers complained that they simply felt under pressure with another adult in the room so that they couldn't relax and be themselves. One remedy suggested by a teacher, which should have been recognized as indicative of a trend perceived clearly only later, was that the aides work only during afternoons, after formal instruction was concluded during the morning. This reflected the view that the preventive and educational programs were somehow inimical.

For their part, the aides complained that the teachers seemed to want them to relate to children only around schoolwork, and they felt that this hampered them in dealing with the children on a "feeling" level. The aides also reported that "some teachers" were arranging for "free time," such as during an art period, in which aides were permitted to become involved with all the children—an example of the trend toward separating the functions of teacher and aide. In addition, the aides began to grapple with the inevitable problem of controlling their relationships with children who made excessive demands on their attention and to probe the general limits of their roles with the children.

In a second meeting with the project team and the consulting psychiatrist, the teachers seemed still to be struggling with the question of just how the aide should function. They rejected the idea that aides might best serve as tutors around school subject matter and expressed preference for their providing the child with "enriching" experiences by bringing in magazines and other materials not ordinarily provided by the school. Note again the trend toward moving the aide further from the typical goals of the educational enterprise. In this meeting, as in the limited number of teacher meetings that followed, until the short series of final evaluation meetings were held, the teachers seemed relatively reticent and inactive. It should be noted, however, that in informal individual meetings with the project team the teachers hinted at some underlying dissatisfactions with aspects of the teacher-aide program.

In their second meeting, as in most of those which followed, the aides were quite active in focusing on relationships with specific children. In this they seemed particularly concerned with the question of how they might be more effective in helping children whose needs they could recognize. They appeared to minimize the value of what they were already doing and to set unrealistically high standards for themselves. Many of these feelings resembled those of the fledgling therapist whose enthusiasm and confidence are dampened by the shock of the reality that the task of intervening in the emotional lives of others is laden with obstacles that cannot be overcome by good will alone. The remaining aide meetings followed a similar course.

In a check of their activities after the program had been in operation approximately two months, it was found that, although the aides were charged with the responsibility of looking after the needs of all the children, they were, in fact, spending the largest portion of their time with relatively few. In most cases, these were children who had been identified earlier by teachers and the project team as particularly maladjusted youngsters. In addition to helping children at their desks with schoolwork, aides were spending a large portion of their time at the back of the room with individuals or very small groups, simply chatting with them, reading to them, playing games, or working on classroom material. Similar activities ensued when the aides occasionally took a child out of the room to a vacant room, or for walks. On occasions when the teacher was called out of the room, the aide took charge of the class, generally reading to the group.

EVALUATION AND DIRECTIONS FOR FUTURE WORK

No formal evaluation of this program was anticipated in such a short period of operation, but informal assessments from a variety of sources seemed desirable and even necessary for charting its future course. Accordingly, the project team and the consulting psychiatrist, the school principal, the aides, and the teachers involved in the program were all solicited for impressions. In general, the project team and consulting psychiatrist were impressed by what the aides were able to accomplish with specific children. They felt that the teachers had not been as active in communicating their feelings about the program as they might have been, or even would have to be if optimal relations were to develop, but generally agreed that the program showed promise and merited continuation. The school principal, who had been enthusiastically supportive of the aims of the program and the form it was taking, felt that it should be continued. He saw positive changes in some needy children although it was not always easy to attribute these directly to the aides because other efforts were being made in conjunction with this program to promote better adjustment.[16]

It was during a final series of three evaluative meetings with the teachers that their own strong feelings about the program found voice. The teachers continued to applaud the goals of the program, but objected quite strenuously to the form in which it was cast. Specifically, they felt that the aide's presence in the room was too disruptive and, when asked to elaborate, spoke heatedly about the way in which the role assumed by many aides undermined the teachers' own relationships with their pupils. As one teacher put it, "I had the feeling that she was the 'good mother' and that I was the ogre." Teachers saw themselves as responsible for teaching a curriculum and setting the acceptable limits of the classroom situation, while the aides, unfettered by such responsibilities, were capturing the open affection of the children. Some children were seen to be especially drawn to aides for attention so that their focus on schoolwork was disrupted. In cases in which children had clearly demonstrated improved adjustment, teachers attributed this to favorable changes in external circumstances or to a concurrent after-school activity program[16] rather than to the efforts of aides. Their reactions were so negative on these counts that they insisted that the program could not work with the aide present in the room. Their strong suggestion was that aides be made available outside the room to deal with children who needed individual attention.

Taking advantage of the wisdom hindsight affords, we can distinguish several inadequacies in the program as originally conceived. Perhaps its most basic weakness was a format that brought aides as a group and teachers as another but separate group together with resource and supervisory people. This tended to enhance the formation of allegiances to one's own work group, to underline relationship difficulties between aide and teacher, and, most important, to lose sight of the important goal of the relationship—the troubled child.

In retrospect, it would seem that a far more sensible approach would be always to bring a single teacher together with a single aide over a child or children regarding whom both share certain objectives. Such an approach would minimize concern over frictions that are inevitable when role relationships are still to be worked out and would focus attention where it most properly belongs, on the troubled child, who, all agree, often needs more help than a busy teacher can provide him.

Another major failing, closely related to the problem just discussed, was that too little time was spent preparing teachers for the program. The aides were provided with a five-week training period, however brief and superficial, which apparently served the intended purpose of giving them a feeling of security about what was to come. The teachers, on the other hand, knew about the training the aides were receiving but received none themselves. This undoubtedly promoted a strong "outgroup" feeling among the teachers and a certain amount of antipathy toward project personnel, who were perhaps viewed as having somewhat neglected them even though they looked for their co-operation in taking on the extra challenges demanded by the program.

Parenthetically, it might be added that part of the preparation of teachers for the program should have been provided before the teachers were even invited to participate. The fact that all six of the elementary-grade teachers in this program volunteered to accept aides without much questioning probably reflected a response based more on various group pressures than on a well-reasoned decision made after a clear understanding of all relevant details. This feeling of being somehow unable to resist being drawn into a program that complicates their already difficult task bids fair to set a negative tone to the participation of teachers.

Training for teachers might have proceeded along lines similar to those that characterized the program for the aides. In addition, it might have been very useful to introduce case material in the form of records of children of advanced grades in the school who had needed an abundance of attention from mental health clinical services. (These often display graphically how the child's difficulties were manifest while he was still in the early grades.) Discussions could profitably be oriented around the question of what early interventions might have been beneficial to such children.

Finally, participating teachers should probably have also been rewarded in some material way for having taken part in the program. This might most realistically have taken the form of some sort of credit for in-service training. Their participation in the program might thus have been granted an element of status which it seemed to lack and to which the teachers were probably also reacting.

Despite these specific reservations about the program in operation, the teachers nevertheless felt that its aims were highly desirable, and that some variant accommodating specific criticisms merited further trial.

Future plans for the teacher-aide program call for the institution of all of the modifications described as being necessary to the success of such a program. In addition, the practice of basing the aide directly in the classroom has been eliminated, in keeping with the strong wishes of participating teachers. In the future operation of the program, the aides will be based in some central location within the school and will be available to work with children who are referred to them by teachers. Perhaps a single aide will work with two teachers, permitting her to become familiar with the children in two specific classes. It is anticipated that at times a child will be referred who has already developed a relationship with an aide who happens to be off duty at that particular time. In such cases, the child will be seen by an aide who is on duty and, if necessary, can return the next day to see the aide with whom he is familiar. Care has been taken to attempt to plan the details of the program with the teachers themselves, who have been encouraged to spell out the ways they would be able to use such a resource.

It should be added that, despite the sobering experience of the first few months of this program and the recognized need to make adjustments in our particular setting, those connected with the project continue to feel that the underlying concept and assumptions of the teacher-aide program have merit. The experience of this pilot program has been valuable in highlighting the pitfalls that inevitably arise in the institution of such a new program. Hopefully, future reports will reflect how this experience has led to workable revisions of a program that is making an impact on children who are embarking shakily on their school experience.

REFERENCES

1. Joint Commission on Mental Illness and Health: Action for Mental Health. New York, Basic Books, 1961.
2. Albee, G. W.: Mental Health Manpower Trends. New York, Basic Books, 1959.

3. Albee, G. W.: American Psychologist, 18:90 (February), 1963.
4. Rioch, M. J., Elkes, C., and Flint, A. A.: Pilot Project in Training Mental Health Counselors. Public Health Service Publication No. 1254. Washington, D. C., U. S. Government Printing Office, 1965.
5. Sanders, R.: New Manpower for Mental Hospital Service. Paper read at conference on Emergent Approaches to Mental Health Problems, University of Rochester, N. Y., June 1965.
6. Community Apprentice Program: Disadvantaged Youth in Human Services. Washington, D. C. Center for Youth and Community Studies, Howard University, 1965.
7. Holzberg, J. D.: American Psychologist, 18:224 (April), 1963.
8. Reissman, F.: The Neighborhood Service Center: An Innovation in Preventive Psychiatry. Paper read at conference on Emergent Approaches to Mental Health Problems, University of Rochester, Rochester, N. Y., June 1965.
9. Umbarger, C. C., et al.: College Students in a Mental Hospital. New York, Grune and Stratton, 1962.
10. Cooperstock, H.: A Mental Health Consultative Service to Public Schools in Rockland County; A Report on Its First Two Years. Rockland County, N. Y., Rockland County Mental Health Association, Inc., 1960.
11. Cutler, R. L.: American Journal of Orthopsychiatry, 31:339 (April), 1961.
12. Gildea, M. C. L., et al.: American Journal of Psychiatry, 114:970 (May), 1958.
13. Donahue, G. T., and Nichtern, S.: Teaching the Troubled Child. New York, Glencoe Free Press, 1965.
14. Cowen, E. L., et al.: Journal of Psychology, 56:307 (July), 1963.
15. Cowen, E. L., et al.: Journal of Consulting Psychology (in press).
16. Cowen, E. L., Zax, M., and Laird, J. D.: Community Mental Health Journal (in press).

43.   Preschool Programs: Preliminary Findings[1]

David P. Weikart

Which type of preschool program for the disadvantaged child is more effective—the traditional nursery school program with its emphasis on social, emotional and motor development, or the more specific task-oriented program with its emphasis on cognitive devel-

The Journal of Special Education, 1967, 1, 163–181. Reprinted with the permission of the publisher and author.
[1] This article was adapted from a paper presented at the University of Kansas Symposium on the Education of Culturally Disadvantaged Children, May 5–6, 1966.

*opment? What are the three crucial stages in teaching
the disadvantaged? These are the issues which Dr.
Weikart examines in his critical review of preschool
programs for impoverished youth.*

On the final day of the 1961 annual convention of the American Association on Mental Deficiency, a panel of child development experts presented a series of papers on the educational problems of the disadvantaged child. The consensus of the panel was that a preschool intervention program might be what was needed to correct the intellectual deficits with which disadvantaged children start out in school.

When this group met, such thinking was largely speculative. The panel little anticipated what was to come: the massive adoption of preschool intervention as a nation-wide answer to the educational problems of the disadvantaged child. Yet in 1965 more than 500,000 four- and five-year-olds attended six to eight weeks of preschool financed by more than $90,000,000 of Federal funds, and Operation Head Start had moved into the national conscience as a national "good."

It is generally agreed that intervention before the disadvantaged child attends regular school is the most promising area for action. Bloom (1964) pointed out in his summary of the research on child development that the period before four years of age is the time of greatest intellectual growth and is therefore the optimal time for training. Scott (1962), working with animals. developed the concept of "critical period." Observing the effect of various kinds of deprivation, such as isolation, on lambs and puppies, he concluded that timing was a crucial factor in early environmental conditions and hypothesized that various kinds of experiences have a major effect when they occur at one period in time but not when they occur at another period. "Organization can be strongly modified only when active processes of organization are going on." Krech (1960), Rosenzweig (1964), Bennett (1964), and others have successfully identified and measured physiological changes in the brain that relate directly to early experiences in carefully controlled studies with laboratory rats.

Pasamanick & Knoblock (1961) have documented the impact of deprivation most vividly in their study of infant development. Employing samples of Negro and White infants selected for equal birth weights and absence of defects of premature birth, and using the Gesell Development Scale, they found no significant difference between the two groups at 40 weeks of age; the White babies obtained a developmental quotient of 105.4 and the Negro babies as DQ of 104.5. At age 3, the first 300 of the original 1,000 children studied were retested and a highly significant difference was found. The developmental quotient of the White children rose to 110.9, while the DQ of the Negro children fell to 97.4. Bayley (1965) found no differences between 1 to 15-month-old Negro and White babies nor between boys and girls, first-born and later born, or babies from different cultural backgrounds and geographical locations.

In view of research evidence such as the above, then, preschool intervention between 10 months and age 5 ought to prevent or correct the cognitive deficits found in disadvantaged children. What results support this conclusion?

Preschools are not virgin territory. They are inhabited, traditionally, by successful and intelligent middle-class children and taught by university-trained teachers. The teaching methods traditionally employed are child-centered and permissive. Sears & Dowley (1933, p. 814) characterize these methods as ". . . watching and waiting for the child's needs to emerge and determine the timing of different activities . . ." The specific aims of the traditional nursery program are seen as (p. 822): (a) meeting organic needs and establishing routine habits; (b) developing motor skills and confidence; (c) developing manipulatory skills; (d) developing control and restraint; (e) developing appropriate behavior; (f) psycho-sexual development; (g) language development; (h) intellectual development.

Research on programs with these traditional curriculum goals has produced varied results. Reviews of the literature by Fuller (1960), Sears & Dowley (1963), and Swift (1964) indicate that for middle-class children, on the whole, there is no difference on any characteristic or dimension between control and experimental groups by the time the groups reach the third grade. There are indications, however, from the early and extensive work of Skeels (1966), Skodak (1949), and others at the Iowa Child Welfare station and from Kirk's (1958) more recent study with mentally handicapped children that children who are labelled as culturally deprived may be directly and permanently aided by preschool experiences. Recent reviews by Robinson (1966) and Fowler (1966) also support cautious optimism in respect to such improvements.

With this background we come to the present and a major wave of studies focused entirely on disadvantaged preschool children.

THE RESEARCH

The current research can be categorized by the specific disadvantaged population studied, by the range of services provided, and by the program or curriculum methods used in the treatment phase of the project. Unfortunately, many current projects are either short-term programs without planned follow-up or are still in progress, so that long-term data on effectiveness of intervention are not available. For critical evaluation, most studies include social, emotional, and cognitive factors. A few have planned for the use of standardized achievement tests as long-term criteria.

The various populations under study are Northern Negro in great city slum areas and metropolitan fringe cities, Southern Negro, Northern White, and institutionalized mentally retarded.

The project services range from simple short-term programs with limited objectives to ambitious programs aiming at a total impact. A typical short-term project would be one of these: a several-days-a-week nursery, a six-to-eight-week summer preschool, or a concentrated reading-readiness program. A total impact project would include all of these: at least two

years of preschool experience, carefully planned parent education programs, regular home visits by teachers and social workers, and medical
services.

For the purposes of this review, various projects will be summarized
and grouped on the basis of their specific curriculum orientation. It is this
orientation, rather than the over-all project services rendered, that seems
to determine the results.

Three different basic preschool teaching methods are used, which can
be summarized as follows:

1. *Traditional nursery school methods.* "Watching and waiting for
the child's needs to emerge and determine the timing of different activities." The primary goals are for social, emotional, and motor development.

2. *Structured nursery school methods.* Carefully sequenced presenta-
tions of teacher-planned activities according to a specific developmental
theory. The primary goals are cognitive and language development. Traditional nursery school materials and activities are frequently employed,
but used to achieve pre-determined goals.

3. *Task-oriented nursery school methods.* Carefully sequenced pre-
sentations of teacher-planned program activities to accomplish specific predetermined goals such as reading, arithmetic, or logical thinking. New,
specifically designed, task-related activities and materials are employed;
those of the traditional nursery school are *not.*

The primary instrument for assessing the effectiveness of intervention
programs has been the Stanford-Binet Intelligence Scale. While the instrument has been criticized as being too culture-bound to be an effective test
of intelligence for disadvantaged children, no major scale has been available to effectively replace it with younger children. In addition, its predictive validity correlations with academic success in school and later job
attainment remain unimpeachable.

The critical results from intervention programs are not those associated with IQ change, of course, but with improvement in achievement.
Unfortunately, there is very little research information relevant to this
problem, as most studies have not investigated long-term effects of early
stimulation programs.

The following section of this paper presents examples of each of the
three intervention methods along with the available statistical data. Where
possible, the Stanford-Binet Intelligence Scale is used as the immediate
dependent variable or criterion of effectiveness, and achievement tests are
used as the intermediate dependent variable.

PROGRAMS EMPLOYING TRADITIONAL
NURSERY SCHOOL METHODS

Four programs will be discussed: (a) Alpern's Community Center Project;
(b) Henderson's Preschool and Primary Education Project; (c) Strodtbeck's Reading Readiness Project; (d) Operation Head Start.

It is inaccurate to classify all of these programs as traditional nursery
schools. Many new and varied techniques have been employed. The proj-

ects are presented in a rough continuum from those using the most to those using the least traditional methods.

ALPERN'S COMMUNITY CENTER PROJECT

Overview of Project and Program. Alpern (1966) evaluated an enrichment program for socially disadvantaged children sponsored by a community house which for many years has operated nursery school programs. Two groups of four-year-olds with 22 children in each group were formed before the start of school in the Fall of 1964. The groups were matched for sex, intelligence and "readiness" as measured by the Metropolitan Readiness Test, Form R. The curriculum goals of the school were to: (a) increase the children's language skills, (b) develop positive attitudes toward the concepts of *teacher, learning* and *school,* and (c) increase knowledge of middle-class values and experiences. The experimental group attended nursery school three times a week with an average attendance of 72 sessions. The control group did not have this experience.

Results. The first year results were (a) There were no differences in intelligence between the groups at the time of initial or second testing, (b) Both groups made significant gains in all three readiness measures for initial to second testing, and (c) There were no significant differences between the groups in any of the readiness tests. A follow-up is to be undertaken.

HENDERSON'S PRESCHOOL AND
PRIMARY EDUCATION PROJECT

Overview of Project. The Ford Foundation has sponsored several major preschool experimental programs. The Preschool and Primary Education Project of the Council for Human Services in Pennsylvania (Henderson, 1965) is an illustration of these. The project has two components: short-term summer schools and year-round programs that serve over 1,000 children. Included, too, are parent education pograms with educational visits to the home by teachers as often as twice a month and/or direct case service by trained social workers. The administrative control is widely diffused to each participating school district, and only the data collection is centralized at the project's headquarters in Harrisburg, Pa. The project is still underway.

The year-round program differed from the summer program in its greater stress on language development and in its more ordered and sequential introduction of new materials and experiences to the children. The actual curriculum and methods, however, were the responsibility of each individual teacher. To ascertain the focus the teachers gave to their individual programs, they were each asked to list the main accomplishments of the summer:

1. About two thirds of the teachers listed the main accomplishments of the program as either social, emotional, or motoric.

2. Fewer than one quarter listed the main accomplishments as intellectual (for example, cognition and language).

3. Half of the teachers did not list any cognitive or language accomplishments for the summer program.

4. Almost all of the teachers perceived the key learning problems to be of a social nature.

Results. The results of the summer project on standardized tests include data on the Illinois Test of Psycholinguistic Abilities (ITPA) and the Peabody Picture Vocabulary Test (PPVT). The Stanford-Binet Intelligence Scale was not employed. For those children who attended the summer preschool project augmented by a year of parent education and assistance from teachers and social workers, no significant differences between the experimental and control groups on the PPVT IQ and the ITPA Language Quotient were found.

The results of the year-round program are not much different. Measured after a year of preschool and three months of kindergarten, the experimental group *was* found to have a significantly higher PPVT score than its control group. The groups were not significantly different on the ITPA Language Quotient. A second group to have preschool experience was also compared with a control group. This time no significant differences were found between experimental and control groups on either PPVT or ITPA IQ.

At the entrance into first grade, experimental and control children were compared on the Metropolitan Readiness Test. The results indicate the experimental and control children are about equally "ready" for first grade instruction since no significant differences were found.

STRODTBECK'S READING READINESS PROJECT

Overview of Project. Strodtbeck (1963) initiated a reading-readiness nursery program for four-year-old Negro children. It was felt that the pre-school relationship with the family could be used to improve the child's later school adjustment and the mother's understanding of the educative process. The research design called for a continuing series of groups (about N-10 in each) to participate in a 13-week reading-readiness program. Testing was done three months before the child's entrance into the nursery, at entrance, and at end of nursery. This method used each child as his own control by testing three months before treatment.

Program. The program had various goals depending upon the methods and orientation of the different teachers in charge. This project is one of a few where two basic styles of curriculum were employed. Groups I and II (N-15) experienced a program described as "mothering while teaching." The teachers observed the children and noted the natural leadership in the group—teaching intervention centered about the spontaneously generated activity of the children. The teachers prided themselves on the development of maturity in the children's peer relations. These methods are those traditional to nursery schools.

Groups III, IV, and V experienced a different, more controlled teaching style. The teachers closely supervised free play activities and demonstrated to the children how to carry out the activities and projects. Verbal participation was greatly encouraged and emphasis was placed upon the noonday meal. The method closely parallels those of projects reported in the next section.

Results. The study is one of the few research projects which permit a tentative comparison for teaching methods on several replicated samples. There is a clear difference of 4.3 IQ points (significance level not available) between the attainment of the children in the readiness program taught by traditional methods and the readiness program taught by a somewhat structured method, in favor of those taught by the structured method.

OPERATION HEAD START

Overview of Project. Operation Head Start was a massive Federal program involving more than 500,000 children. While research was built into the program, much of the project study did not employ control groups. The project included six to eight weeks of preschool, parent involvement, medical services to children, and nutrition programs. The teachers for the project were not required to be certified preschool teachers, but all attended at least a week of paid orientation at universities and colleges throughout the country.

Program. While traditional-style nursery school methods seem to have been used in most programs, the general fervor with which the project was implemented produced many innovations.

Results. Allegato (1966), in reviewing the data released by the Head Start Headquarters, quotes Richmond, director of the project for the Office of Economic Opportunity, as saying that Head Starters gained an average of nine points in IQ (probably the PPVT). He also said that they were more proficient in learning, had more intellectual curiosity, and were better adjusted to the classroom. "Standard tests showed significant gains in the educational achievements and mental ability of Head Start children all across the country."

Sigel, however, in a personal communication, commented on the Merrill-Palmer findings in the Detroit Head Start groups. After one month of kindergarten in regular Detroit programs, there were no differences on the PPVT between those children who had attended Head Start and those from the same environment who had not. While these findings cannot be generalized to all 561,000 Head Starters, the implications are strong that eight weeks of summer school and four weeks of regular school *both* produce change in participating children.

DISCUSSION

Qualitative evaluation was included in most of the project reports. Nearly all reports contained an enthusiastic section discussing the general response of the children to the program. "He didn't talk for six weeks and now listen to him!" is a typical comment. Asking questions, use of new language, and, of course, social, emotional, and motor development, were also remarked upon by the teachers.

On the standardized tests, where carefully controlled research has been employed, the results are consistent. The total outcome of all projects using the so-called traditional methods of nursery school education with a disadvantaged population is that there are no statistically significant differences on standardized intelligence tests or achievement measures. Long-term follow-up data are not available. The absence of differences between groups may be altered by later growth by experimental groups or increased deficits in control groups. At this time no specific theoretical position can be substantiated.

PROGRAMS EMPLOYING STRUCTURED NURSERY SCHOOL METHODS

Five such programs will be described briefly: (a) Dawe's Institutional Training Program; (b) Kirk's Early Education of the Mentally Retarded Project; (c) Gray and Klaus's Early Training Project; (d) Deutsch's Preschool and Early Elementary Education Project; (e) Weikart's Perry Preschool Project.

While these five projects depart radically in some ways from the concerns of the traditional nursery school, the basic teacher-child relationship is preserved, with its focus on social adjustment, peer relations, good work habits, etc. The structure is derived from the programs' clearly-stated goals for specific cognitive and language development.

DAWE'S INSTITUTIONAL TRAINING PROGRAM

Overview of Project. Dawe (1942) conducted a short-term training program for orphanage children. She carefully matched 22 children and assigned one of each pair to an experimental group and the other to a control group. An extra child was placed in the experimental group. A special training program was offered to the experimental children over a 92-day period with an average of 50 hours for each child in sessions usually held on weekends.

Program. Dawe designed a program that emphasized factors related to superior language development. She had individual tutoring sessions in which classification of words by pattern and situation setting was stressed. There was informal conversation about words and their meanings, with attempts to give a referent for each word through its use in a variety of settings. There were small group sessions for story-telling, discussions about pictures, and excursions. She attempted to stimulate curiosity, to help the child think critically, notice relationships and cause and effect, and to eliminate careless thinking and careless use of language.

Results. The data from pre- and post-testing on the Stanford-Binet are presented in Table 1. Even though the contact with each child averaged only 50 hours, the experimental group gained 14.2 points in IQ (80.6 to 94.8). The control children, who experienced no substantial change in their environmnet, lost 2.0 points in IQ (81.5 to 79.5). The difference in final IQ scores is statistically significant. No further follow-up data are available, but Dawe also observed, from the daily lesson commentaries, that the children had improved in language ability, asked intellectual questions, and made more critical comments and analytical remarks.

KIRK'S EDUCATION OF THE MENTALLY RETARDED

Overview of Project. In 1958, Kirk reported on an extensive project, conducted over a five-year period, for mentally retarded children. The study included experimental and control groups drawn both from the community at large and from institutions. The project involved 81 children, whose retardation was related to organic development, cultural deprivation, or both.

The children, drawn from several cities in central Illinois, spent one to three years in a special preschool program and then entered either the first grade or special classes in the public schools.

It is from this study by Kirk that much of the current impetus for preschool education is derived.

Program. The specially designed program was constructed around (a) specific adaptation of materials and activities for each child, with careful attention to special individual needs as revealed by diagnositc study, and (b) individual tutoring in the areas of specific mental disabilities.

Results. The project used a number of tests to assess the progress of the children and included attempts to measure social development as well as intellectual change. Tests of statistical significance were run on change scores from initial to final tests. Experimental and control groups were not directly compared. Table 2 presents the results of the Stanford-Binet testing at the beginning and completion of the program and at the end of the first year of regular school attendance. All change scores are statistically significant for the experimental groups when compared to change scores obtained by control groups.

The over-all increase by the community experimental group was 11.7 IQ points derived primarily from the preschool experience. The increase by the community control group was 6.9 IQ points obtained after the year of school experience.

At the conclusion of the first grade, the Gates Primary Reading Tests were administered to all groups. The experimental and control groups did

TABLE 1. DAWE: EFFECTS OF INSTITUTIONAL TRAINING PROGRAM
STANFORD-BINET INTELLIGENCE SCALE

Time of Comparison	Experimental (*N*-12)	Control (*N*-11)	Difference	Significance
Pre-test	80.6	81.5	−0.9	n.s.
Post-test[a]	94.8	79.5	15.3	.01

[a] The post-test was given at the end of 92 days with the children in the experimental group averaging 50 hours of training.

TABLE 2. KIRK: EARLY EDUCATION OF MENTALLY RETARDED
STANFORD-BINET INTELLIGENCE SCALE

Community Groups Time of Comparison	Experimental (N-25)	Contrast (N-24)	Difference	Significance
Pre-test	72.5	75.8	−3.3	n/a*
Post-test[a], at end of Preschool	83.7	75.2	8.5	n/a
Post-test[b], at end of First Grade	84.2	82.7	1.5	n/a
Institution Groups Time of Comparison	Experimental (N-15)	Comparison (N-12)	Difference	Significance
Pre-test	61.0	57.1	3.9	n/a
Post-test[a], at end of Preschool	73.0	49.9	23.1	n/a
Post-test[c], at end of First Grade	71.2	50.6	20.6	n/a

[a]The preschool experience for each child ranged from one to three years.

[b]The first grade experience was provided in regular or special public school classrooms.

[c]The first grade experience was provided for six of the experimental children in regular or special public school classrooms. The remaining institutional children attended classes within the institution.

*Not available

not differ significantly in reading achievement at that time. The inability of the experimental group to "do better" than the control group was confirmed by teacher ratings of reading ability.

GRAY AND KLAUS'S EARLY TRAINING PROJECT

Overview of Project. One of the early studies in the current series was initiated by Gray and Klaus (1965) in Murfreesboro, Tenn. The Early Training Project involved carefully selected experimental and control groups of Negro children. One experimental group (N–20) had three summers of preschool experience and a second group (N–20) two summers of preschool experience of ten weeks each summer before entering regular first grade. Both groups were visited in their homes by a project visitor each week throughout the year between preschool experiences. A local community control group (N–20) was established as well as a distal control group (N–27) in a nearby community. Follow-up is still in progress.

Program. The curriculum was specifically designed to prevent the accumulation of deficits generally thought to occur in the development of disadvantaged children. The curriculum procedures were based upon a review of the literature on differences in social class, in child-rearing practices, in motivational patterns, in language, and in perceptual and cognitive development. Two classes of variables were employed in the day-to-day programing. The first class comprised attitudes toward achievement, especially as related to the kinds of activities expected in school, persistence, ability to delay gratification, and interest in typical school materials. The second class comprised aptitudes necessary for achievement, especially as related to perceptual and cognitive development and to language.

Results. The project was evaluated by several intelligence and achievement tests. Over the two-year period, the experimental groups gained an average of 7 IQ points while the control group lost an average of 5 IQ points. The difference in final scores is statistically significant. While the results of only two testing periods are given, a total of five Stanford-Binet or Wechsler Intelligence Scale tests were administered between 1962 and 1964.

The project reports that on first grade screening tests, the experimental children did "conspicuously" better than the controls. No statistical data are given.

DEUTSCH'S PRESCHOOL AND EARLY ELEMENTARY EDUCATION PROJECT

Overview of Project. The Institute for Developmental Studies of New York City under the direction of Deutsch (1965) has instituted a series of intensive and far-reaching studies on the preschool and early elementary education of disadvantaged children. The experiments on the preschool level involve a complex design of special treatments of varying lengths. The effect of both one- and two-year preschool programs are being tested, as well as the impact of specially designed kindergarten through third grade classes. The information available at this time involves youngsters in experimental groups who have participated in special classes at age 4 and then have moved into specially enriched kindergarten programs. The control children did not participate in preschool and entered kindergarten directly. Most of the children are Negro. The project is still in progress.

Program. The program has been described as having no single philosophic system or theory behind it (Deutsch, 1965). The approach is seen as flexible and exploratory. "Eclectic combinations of the developmental and educational theories advanced by such workers as Piaget, Hunt, Bruner, Montessori, Jensen among others" (p. 58) is the Annual Report's description of the classroom curriculum development efforts. The physical space of the classroom is ordered to help build the child's concepts of order and space. Efforts are made to enhance the child's self concept through the use of Negro dolls, stories involving Negro children, and photographs of the child himself. Language development is encouraged through classroom activities designed to elicit verbal responses. Auto-instructional devices have been developed and are employed at all program levels. These include the Listening Center with tape-recorded lessons and stories and the use of the Bell and Howell Language Master.

Attention is given to training in auditory and visual discrimination. The activities involved in the training also serve as a means of teaching concepts and imparting knowledge. Extensive supervision is provided for teachers of the experimental groups.

Results. Goldstein (1965) presented the results on two groups of children who had participated in the pre-kindergarten program (see

Table 3). For Group I, the net gain in the two years is 5.0 IQ points for the experimental group as contrasted with a loss of 7.0 IQ points for the control group. The second experimental group demonstrates a similar pattern, though the control group did not lose as much over the one-year period for which the data are available. The post-test score differences between the groups are statistically significant in all cases.

Large amounts of other data have been collected by the Institute, including that from the PPVT, the ITPA, and the Columbia Mental Maturity Scale. No information on achievement data are available at this time.

WEIKART'S PERRY PRESCHOOL PROJECT

Overview of Project. The Perry Preschool Project[2] is an experiment to assess the longitudinal effects of a two-year program designed to compensate for the mental retardation that is associated with cultural deprivation. The program consists of a cognitively oriented preschool, and home visits to involve mothers in the educative process. The project has been in operation since September, 1962 and is to be completed in December, 1967 (Weikart, 1964; Radin & Weikart, 1967).

The population from which each year's sample is selected consists of culturally deprived Negroes, diagnosed as mentally retarded. Control and experimental groups are equated for mean cultural-deprivation rating and mean Stanford-Binet IQ. Other measures include the Leiter International Performance Scale, the PPVT, the ITPA, the Parental Attitude Research Instrument (Radin Adaptation), and various achievement tests, teacher

TABLE 3. GOLDSTEIN: INSTITUTE OF DEVELOPMENTAL STUDIES STANFORD-BINET INTELLIGENCE SCALE

Group I Data Time of Comparison	Experimental (N-41)	Control (N-29)	Difference	Significance
Pre-test, entrance into Prekindergarten, 1962	98.9	99.0	−0.1	n.s.
Post-test, at end of Prekindergarten, 1963	102.2	93.3	8.9	.01
Post-test, at end of Kindergarten, 1964	103.9	92.0	11.9	.01
Group II Data Time of Comparison	Experimental (N-59)	Control (N-41)	Difference	Significance
Pre-test, entrance into Prekindergarten, 1963	93.2	95.1	−1.9	n.s.
Post-test, at end of Prekindergarten, 1964	98.8	94.0	4.8	.05

[2] The research reported herein has been supported since January 1, 1964, through the Cooperative Research Program of the Office of Education, U. S. Department of Health, Education, and Welfare, and since September 1, 1961 by the Ypsilanti Board of Education, the Washtenaw County Board of Education, State Board of Education of the State of Michigan.

ratings, and attendance records. The data to be discussed will include only the Stanford-Binet Intelligence Scale and achievement tests.

The program is a permissive but teacher-structured one, intended to guide the children toward increased cognitive development. Heavier emphasis is placed on verbal stimulation and interaction, dramatic play, and field trips than on social behavior and other traditional concerns of nursery schools.

The Instructional Program. The only requirements initially outlined for the instructional program were that it be designed to compensate for and prevent further cognitive deficits and that it operate five days a week for three hours a day. The project does not attempt to assess different methods of educational intervention. Waves 0, 1, and 2 (the pilot sample and the first two replication studies) experienced a gradually evolving program with an instructional method that can best be described as "verbal bombardment." In this method the teacher maintains a steady stream of questions and comments to draw the child's attention to critical aspects of his environment. This "bombardment" does not necessarily demand answers from the child. It is continued when rewarding a child for a good performance, when disciplining him, and when presenting academic material. The complexity of the language is increased as the child's verbal ability develops. An observer in the preschool receives the impression that the teacher is acting like a middle-class mother warmly interacting with her young children.

Wave 3 and succeeding waves of the project are experiencing a somewhat different program oriented towards Piaget's cognitive development theories. This program can be best described as an effort to firmly establish the precursors essential for the development of an adequate intellectual foundation to permit the growth of language and logical thought.

Results. The results available at this time are from Waves 0, 1, 2, and 3. Those presented here are from the Stanford-Binet Intelligence Scale and several follow-up achievement tests.

Tables 4, 5, 6, and 7 present the year-by-year testing data from the Stanford-Binet on each experimental and control group for a three-year period. Three patterns emerge. There is an over-all pattern of increased IQ

TABLE 4. WEIKART: PERRY PRESCHOOL PROJECT STANFORD-BINET INTELLIGENCE SCALE WAVE 0 DATA

Time of Comparison	Experimental (*N*-13)	Control (*N*-15)	Difference	Significance
Fall, 1962—Entrance into preschool	78.4	75.0	3.4	n.s.
Spring, 1963—Completion of one year in preschool	91.1	82.2	8.9	.01
Spring, 1964—Completion of kindergarten	88.9	84.6	4.3	n.s.
Spring, 1965—Completion of first grade	90.7	84.6	6.1	n.s.

TABLE 5. WEIKART: PERRY PRESCHOOL PROJECT STANFORD-BINET
INTELLIGENCE SCALE WAVE I DATA

Time of Comparison	Experimental (N-10)	Control (N-9)	Difference	Significance
Fall, 1962—Entrance into preschool	79.1	78.3	0.8	n.s.
Spring, 1963—Completion of first year in preschool	90.6 (N-8)	77.8	12.8	.05
Spring, 1964—Completion of second year in preschool	88.9	80.1	8.8	n.s.
Spring, 1965—Completion of kindergarten	90.5	83.3	7.2	n.s.

TABLE 6. WEIKART: PERRY PRESCHOOL PROJECT STANFORD-BINET
INTELLIGENCE SCALE WAVE II DATA

Time of Comparison	Experimental (N-13)	Control (N-14)	Difference	Significance
Fall, 1963—Entrance into preschool	80.5	79.4	1.1	n.s.
Spring, 1964—Completion of first year in preschool	100.9	82.9	18.0	.001
Spring, 1965—Completion of second year in preschool	94.5	79.1	15.4	.001

TABLE 7. WEIKART: PERRY PRESCHOOL PROJECT STANFORD-BINET
INTELLIGENCE SCALE WAVE 3 DATA

Time of Comparison	Experimental (N-13)	Control (N-15)	Difference	Significance
Fall, 1964—Entrance into preschool	79.6	81.0	−1.4	n.s.
Spring, 1965—Completion of first year in preschool	94.4	81.2	13.2	.01

scores for all groups. Part of this pattern can be attributed to the regression phenomenon—the tendency of sample means upon repeated testing to regress toward the population mean. (See Goodenough, 1940, for preschool data on this point.)

Inasmuch as one of the criteria for children in the program was an IQ score considerably below the supposed population mean, the regression phenomenon must be considered. As the groups are controlled for parent occupational levels—Goodenough's suggestion in her criticism of the Iowa studies—the regression phenomenon is most likely not operating in this study to produce the obtained IQ score change patterns.

A second pattern is a tendency towards stability in IQ scores for the control groups who do not have school experience, followed by an immediate gain after one year of school attendance. A third pattern is a dramatic spurt, as much as 20 points, in IQ scores after one year of preschool, followed by a slight decline during the next year whether in preschool or in regular kindergarten classes.

Statistically significant differences between experimental and control groups are always obtained at the end of the first year of participation in the project. The mean increase in IQ scores for the experimental groups is 15.1 points (range 11.5 to 20.4), while the mean increase for the control groups is 3.1 points (range −0.5 to 7.2). Waves 1 and 2 are the only waves in which the experimental groups have attended two years of preschool while the control groups have remained in their disadvantaged home environments. The difference in combined experimental and control groups obtained IQ scores at the end of the second year is 12.9 points, a statistically significant difference (.001). Thus, for combined waves, the experimental groups maintain a statistically significant lead over the control groups after two years of preschool. But at the end of the kindergarten year, uncombined waves produce no significant differences between control and experimental groups.

The important findings of the project are from the first grade California Achievement Tests for Wave 0 (see Table 8). All subtests and total battery scores reach a level of statistical significance for the experimental group. The control group performs at the level traditional for the school in which they are enrolled where the class mean on national norms is the 5th percentile level. The experimental group, on the other hand, has achieved the 22nd percentile on national norms, a very important accomplishment for the experimental group and preschool!

PROGRAMS EMPLOYING TASK-ORIENTED PRESCHOOL METHODS

Unlike the programs outlined above, projects employing task-oriented methods have not been widely instituted. While other programs seek to remedy the developmental deficiencies of disadvantaged children through adjusted or enriched natural environments, the task-oriented preschool method attempts to achieve the same goals through artificially contrived procedures. Cazden (1966) calls these "non-natural" treatments.

Most of these programs have very direct goals. There is no climbing apparatus, no doll corner with social-dramatic play, and no juice time with one cookie on normal days and two when visitors are present. There are things to be mastered and the program is directly focused on the task at hand.

Perhaps the most highly developed task-oriented curriculum is that of Bereiter (1965, 1966) at the University of Illinois.

Overview of the Project. The project involves 15 disadvantaged four-year-old children in attendance at a University of Illinois preschool. The ITPA is employed as well as specially developed academic measures of

TABLE 8. WEIKART: PERRY PRESCHOOL PROJECT CALIFORNIA
ACHIEVEMENT TESTS WAVE O DATA

California Achievement Tests	Mean Percentile Rank			
	Experimental	Control	Difference	Significance
Reading	30	8	22	.05
Arithmetic	10	3	7	.05
Language Skills	39	16	23	.05
TOTAL	22	5	17	.05

the children's progress. There are three 20-minute sessions a morning, each devoted to the direct teaching of language, reading, and arithmetic. Each of these periods is separated by 30 minutes of refreshments, singing, and a shorter period of relatively unstructured play activity. "Each subject has its own teacher, who works with each of three groups of children in turn, as in a high school" (Bereiter, 1965, p. 3). All three subjects are taught at one time, with the groups of children rotating from teacher to teacher.

Program. The curriculum is academically oriented, based on two premises: (a) Mere enrichment of experience is not enough to enable the culturally deprived child to overcome his backwardness in the skills necessary for later academic success. (b) Training in the formal, structural aspects of language will have more value in the improvement of academic aptitude than will training directed toward facilitating social communication.

The curriculum uses direct instruction to achieve the specific goal of developing the information processes necessary for thinking.

The language program is organized to help the child acquire grammatical statement patterns and an understanding of the logical organization of these patterns. Precise pronunciation, a critical requirement, receives considerable emphasis. The child's language is regarded as being basically nonlogical and lacking in the formal properties necessary for organized thought. The teaching method for the language program derives from the techniques of modern oral methods of teaching foreign languages. "Pattern drill" is the basic technique employed.

The arithmetic and reading programs also use these methods with rules taught through the patterning of language. In arithmetic the emphasis is upon learning statement forms, such as $2 + 0 = 2$ (identity). The teaching of arithmetic operations places emphasis on the formal meaning and not on concrete objects generally used as a basis for arithmetic education. Reading instruction follows the same pattern, with emphasis upon a maximum amount of experience in the explicit handling of rules and statements. In teaching, "We demanded the children's attention by continual questioning; we demanded that they look and respond, with or without understanding" (Bereiter, 1965, p. 26). After the basic rules about words are learned, the children progress to phonic blending, etc., and then on to formal reading.

The task-oriented approach is best summarized by Bereiter in his comment, "Full participation of all children in the learning tasks is treated as a requirement to which the children must conform (much like the hand-washing requirement in the conventional nursery school)" (1965, p. 4).

Results. Results are not fully available at this time. Basically the project reports excellent success in obtaining the cooperation of the children, growth in general intellectual ability, and academic development.

DISCUSSION

Data from the projects discussed in this paper lead to a number of tentative conclusions about effective educational programming for disadvantaged children.

Traditional Versus Structured Methods

The selection of adequate criteria by which to judge effective programing has always been difficult in education (Ryans, 1960). The general debate in the nursery education field has tended to be that one must choose between a cognitive and language development program structured by teacher planning and a program that promotes the socio-emotional growth of the child and is structured by the child's expressed needs. Two sets of criteria have been proposed to assess curriculum effectiveness. For the first type of program, standardized achievement and intelligence tests have assumed prime importance. For the second type, the teacher's qualitative assessments of the child's social and emotional growth are used. Each position, and with some justification, sees little value in the other's criteria of success.

It appears from the data presented in this paper that those programs which aspire to the development of improved socio-emotional adjustment by the child do obtain that goal. It appears that programs which intend to produce cognitive and language development obtain the same goal of socio-emotional growth and produce the desired intellectual development as well. The extensive Henderson study in Pennsylvania points up very clearly that preschool teachers, left unsupervised, will focus on the child's social and emotional growth. This focus will produce no significant change in intellectual development. The Perry Project, the Deutsch projects, the Strodtbeck II groups, Dawe's program, and others all report the same kinds of social and emotional growth *and* record impressive success with intervention in intellectual development. The Perry Project also finds significant differences in later academic achievement.

The conclusion is that preschool projects with the disadvantaged child must provide planned teacher action according to a specific developmental theory in which the primary goals are cognitive and language development. It seems that good social and emotional adjustment are an essential condition for such development, but focus on adjustment alone does not automatically produce the desired intellectual growth.

WHEN SHOULD PRESCHOOL INTERVENTION OCCUR?

The timing of preschool experience has been viewed as critical. Bloom (1964) has predicted that 50% of the intelligence measured at age 17 is developed by age 4. He also suggests that a conservative estimate of the effect of extreme environments on intelligence is about 20 IQ points (1964, p. 89). Pasamanick & Knoblock (1961), however, document the occurrence of deprivation by age 3. It is reasonable to assume that:

1. The experiences provided by the environment to the disadvantaged child are inadequate for continued normal development after age 1.

2. The process of deprivation is probably insidious in that it deprives the child of key experiences necessary to establish the foundation for future development before the effects of the deprivation process are noticeable through performance tests.

From this viewpoint, all projects reported in this paper are remedial rather than preventive in that the services are offered after the deprivation has occurred. Several new projects are underway exploring the gap between age 1 and age 3. Projects by Caldwell at the University of Syracuse and Schaefer at the National Institute of Mental Health represent two of these. Data are not available from these at this time.

HOW STABLE ARE OBTAINED RESULTS?

A major point to be noted in considering projects is that after the first year's initial spurt in obtained IQ, there is a tendency for a drop the second year. This drop occurs whether the child is enrolled in a second year of a structured preschool or in a regular school. If a drop does not occur, no further rise is especially evident. Fowler (1966) attributed this second year drop to diffuse programing on the part of projects that find the phenomenon.

The basic problem may be that the education of the disadvantaged child passes through a number of stages that force different programing goals upon the teacher. The readiness to accept these stages varies greatly from teacher to teacher and project to project. For example, Riessman (1964) identified two crucial stages in teaching the disadvantaged. The first stage is simply to achieve some form of contact and communication with the child to win his attention and confidence. The second is to develop an educational program. Riessman points out that many teachers and programs feel they have succeeded when the goals of the first stage are attained and fail to move on to the second.

Looking at this point of view and the data beginning to be available from preschools, it is possible to suggest a natural evolution of preschool programs.

Stage One: Silence. During this stage the child is brought into contact with the environment of the preschool and the adults who operate the program. Just talk! Say anything! In Riessman's terms, the goal is the establishment of rapport with the child. This goal is suspiciously like that of the traditional nursery school curriculum. No real cognitive growth occurs, since the program is not oriented toward cognition and language development. The emphasis is upon expression of self and adjustment. This stage seems to be the focus of the teachers in the Henderson project, a good many Head Start programs and other general intervention programs. These are the projects that basically registered no long-term and few short-term gains in intellectual or achievement growth. This stage is necessary and absolutely essential if the second stage is to be undertaken. Once contact has occurred, education may begin.

Stage Two: "Des god damn peaches am burnin!" This now-famous quote from *Life* magazine's article on the Deutsch project illustrates the goal of the second stage. A "set" for learning, problem solving, and language growth is produced. Excitement with new things in new situations alerts the child mentally and prepares him for learning. Rapid short-term intellectual growth or an increased mental alertness results. Dawe obtained 14.2 points of IQ change in only 50 hours of instruction. Perry Project has obtained up to 20 points in eight months. The stimulation through exposure to new language and demands for critical thinking combine to produce in the child a new capacity for problem solving and alertness to the outside world. An obvious outcome is an increased ability to respond to problems presented by adults in their demand for language and attention and to handle situations such as intelligence tests more efficiently.

Stage Three: "These god damn peaches are burning!" Now alert, the child is ready to learn to participate in the full educational process that Riessman identifies. The rapport stage is fairly easy for good teachers to achieve. The development of a "set" or "alertness" for learning can be created with a well-defined and teacher-planned curriculum. The completion of the third stage, however—long-term and systematic educational programming—is what is essential but generally missing. Perry Project, Kirk's study, Deutsch's programs have all grappled with this problem. The girl must learn to transform her ghetto speech into educationally functional language. The "god damn" can stay because we're broadminded, but without the correct verb form the girl may be permanently handicapped in logical thinking.

It is the difficulty in implementing this third stage that seems to set the limits to the child's growth potential. We simply do not know what to do in order to speed up the development process and continue the growth rate. The problem sets a practical limit of eight months on preschool intervention programs. That is as long as is necessary to complete Stage Two and place the child at a new level of functioning. It may be that Bloom (1964) is right when he suggests that a 10-point change is all that is possible during early childhood, since that is the magnitude of the change that is being obtained in most programs.

Perhaps it may be concluded that the question isn't, "How stable are the obtained results?" but, "Why are they so stable?"

CURRENT DIRECTIONS IN PROGRAM DEVELOPMENT

There is increasing interest in the task-oriented approach to preschool education. Bereiter (1961 goes directly to the teaching of language, arithmetic, and reading. Gotkin (1966) has produced a series of activities designed to teach reading. Blatt (1966) has employed O. K. Moore's responsive environment to introduce reading at the preschool age. It may be, however, that these approaches are too specific to permit broad development of intellectual skills.

Many preschool teachers have turned to the early work of Montessori, McMillan, and others (see Braun, 1964). The outcome of these attempts is not known as yet, but the general observation seems to be that they are too narrow for current needs.

Basic cognitive and language skills have received increasing attention. A good example is Cazden's (1966) summary of the key areas and problems of language development of the disadvantaged child. Deutsch and his co-workers have been involved in the development of many specific methods that have wide application. The tape recorder listening center is a good example. Smilansky (1964) has suggested many practical ideas, especially the use of social-dramatic play.

Perhaps the most promising efforts, however, are the efforts to apply broad theories of intellectual growth and development to preschool curriculum (Garrison, 1966). Sigel (1964) and Almy (1966) have suggested methods of utilizing Piget's concepts. Bruner (1966) has suggested specific methods and outlined immediate goals. Guilford (1966) has designed a model to facilitate the teaching of cognitive processes. These efforts, collectively and individually, may hold the solutions to the development of adequate programs to accomplish the basic tasks of preschool education.

CONCLUSION

It may be premature, but the debate between the so-called traditional and structured curriculum methods seems to be over. The traditional nursery school methods, so effective in fulfilling Stage 1 of the educational process, are ineffective in accomplishing the basic goals of preschool intervention with the disadvantaged child. Programs should now pass rapidly through the first two stages outlined above and arrive at Stage 3, which is where the basic problems are. Additional research in the field is needed to explore the effectiveness of various curriculum methods and devices rather than the problem of preschool versus no preschool experience. Based upon the population sample, the control groups growth pattern and even the pattern of the experimental group growth with known curricula are predictable. Certainly the Skeels (1966) follow-up study places the long-term results on the side of any style of intervention, especially when the control groups remain in deprived environments.

While the timing of intervention apparently can be very flexible, much work needs to be done in exploring the use of the period between age 1 and age 3 for a preventive program. The use of teachers as tutors and educational consultants to disadvantaged families with preschool children on a long-term basis might prove to be effective.

The doors to preschool education for disadvantaged children are open, and funds are available for financing such education. Teachers and researchers concerned with early child development must turn to the serious study and implementation of sound cognitive development theories if the expected results in accelerated child growth are to be obtained.

REFERENCES

Allegato, R. *Preschool training program is partial success.* Detroit: Detroit Free Press, 1966. 10-B.

Almy, M. *Young children's thinking: some aspects of Piaget's theory*. New York: Teachers College, Columbia, 1966.

Alpern, G. D. The failure of a nursery school enrichment program for culturally disadvantaged children. *American Journal of Orthopsychiatry*, 1966, 36, 244–245.

Bayley, N. Comparison of mental and motor test scores for ages 1–15 months by sex, birth order, race, geographical location and education of parents. *Child Development*, 1965, 36, 379–411.

Bennett, E. L., Diamond, M. C., Krech, D., & Rosenzweig, M. R. Chemical and anatomical plasticity of brain. *Science*, 1964, 146, 610–619.

Bereiter, C., Osborn, J., Engelmann, S., Reidford, P. A. An academically-oriented preschool for culturally deprived children. Paper delivered at annual meeting of the American Educational Research Association, Chicago, January, 1965.

Bereiter, C., & Engelmann, S. *Teaching disadvantaged children in the preschool*. Englewood Cliffs, N. J.: Prentice-Hall, 1966.

Blatt, B. (Textbook on cultural deprivation.) Chicago: Science Research Associates (forthcoming.)

Bloom, B. S. *Stability and change in human characteristics*. New York: Wiley, 1964.

Braun, S. J. Nursery education for disadvantaged children: an historical review. Community Research and Services Branch, National Institute of Mental Health, 1964. (Duplicated.)

Bruner, J. S. *Toward a theory of instruction*. Cambridge, Mass.: Harvard University Press, 1966.

Cazden, C. B. Some implications of research on language development for preschool education. Paper delivered at Social Science Research Council Conference on Preschool Education. University of Chicago, February, 1966.

Dawe, H. C. A study of the effect of an educational program upon language development and related mental functions in young children. *Journal of Experimental Education*, 1942, 11, 200–209.

Deutsch, M. *Institute for Developmental Studies: Annual Report*. New York: New York Medical College, 1965.

Fowler, W. Longitudinal study of early stimulation in the emergence of cognitive processes. Paper delivered at Social Science Research Council Conference on Preschool Education, University of Chicago, February, 1966.

Fuller, E. *Values in early childhood education*. Washington, D. C.: National Education Association, 1960.

Garrison, M. Cognitive models and development in mental retardation. *Monograph Supplement to American Journal of Mental Deficiency*, 1966, 70, 4.

Goldstein, L. S. *Evaluation of an enrichment program for socially disadvantaged children*. New York: Institute for Developmental Studies, New York Medical College, 1965. (Duplicated.)

Goodenough, F. L., & Maurer, K. M. The relative potency of the nursery school and the statistical laboratory in boosting the IQ. *Journal of Educational Psychology*, 1940, 41, 541–549.

Gotkin, L. G. *Language lotto*. New York: Appleton-Century-Crofts, 1966.

Gray, S., & Klaus, R. A. An experimental preschool program for culturally deprived children. *Child Development*, 1965, 36, 887–898.

Guilford, J. P. Intelligence: 1965 model. *American Psychologist*, 1966, 21, 20–26.

Henderson, A. S. *1964–65 annual progress report to the Ford Foundation on the preschool and primary education project*. Harrisburg, Pa.: Council for Human Services, 1965.

Kirk, S. A. *Early education of the mentally retarded*. Urbana, Ill.: University of Illinois Press, 1958.

Krech, D., Rosenzweig, M. R., & Bennett, E. L. Effects of environmental complexity and training on brain chemistry. *Journal of Comparative Physiological Psychology*, 1960, 53, 509–519.

Pasamanick, B., & Knoblock, H. Epidemiologic studies on the complications of pregnancy and the birth process. In C. Caplan (Ed.), *Prevention of mental disorders in children*. New York: Basic Books, 1961. Pp. 74–94.

Radin, N., & Weikart, D. P. A home teaching program for disadvantaged preschool children. *The Journal of Special Education*, 1967, 2, 183–190.

Riessman, F. Teachers of the poor: a five point plan. In C. W. Hunnicutt (Ed.), *Urban education and cultural deprivation.* Syracuse, N.Y.: Syracuse University Press, 1964.

Robinson, H. B. The problems of timing in preschool education. Paper delivered at Social Science Research Council Conference on Preschool Education. University of Chicago, February, 1966.

Rosenzweig, M. R., Bennett, E. L., & Krech, D. Cerebral effects of environmental complexity and training among adult rats. *Journal of Comparative and Physiological Psychology,* 1964, 57, 438–439.

Ryans, D. G. *Characteristics of teachers.* Washington, D. C.: American Council on Education, 1960.

Scott, J. P. Critical periods in behavioral development. *Science,* 1962, 138, #3544.

Sears, P. S., & Dowley, E. M. Research on teaching in the nursery school. In N. L. Gage (Ed.), *Handbook of research on teaching.* Chicago: Rand McNally, 1963. Pp. . . .–864.

Sigel, I. S. The attainment of concepts. In M. L. Hoffman & L. W. Hoffman (Eds.), *Child development research.* New York: Russell Sage Foundation, 1964.

Skeels, H. M. *Adult status of two groups experiencing early intervention.* Washington, D. C.: National Institute of Mental Health, 1966.

Skodak, M., & Skeels, H. M. A final follow-up study of one hundred adopted children. *Journal of Genetic Psychology,* 1949, 75, 85–125.

Smilansky, S. *Progress report on a program to demonstrate ways of using a year of kindergarten to promote cognitive abilities.* Israel: Henrietta Szold Institute, 1964. (Duplicated.)

Strodtbeck, F. L. *Progress report: the reading readiness nursery.* The Social Psychology Laboratory, University of Chicago, 1963. (Duplicated.)

Swift, J. W. Effects of early group experience: the nursery school and day nursery. In M. L. Hoffman & L. W. Hoffman (Eds.), *Review of child development research.* New York: Russell Sage Foundation, 1964. Pp. 249–288.

Weikart, D. P., Kamii, C. K., & Radin, N. *Perry preschool progress report.* Ypsilanti, Mich.: Ypsilanti Public Schools. 1964. (Duplicated.)

44.   The Modification, Mediation and Utilization of Stress During the School Years*

Eli M. Bower

Deeply imbedded in our educational system is the philosophy that students should not have to face stressful situations. A contrasting viewpoint, cogently pre-

American Journal of Orthopsychiatry, 1964, 34, 667–674. Copyright, the American Orthopsychiatric Association, Inc. Reproduced by permission of copyright owner and author.

* Presented at the 1963 Annual Meeting.

sented by Eli M. Bower, Consultant, National Institute of Mental Health, contends that anxiety-producing experiences should be used to develop stress immunity rather than avoided. By anticipating normal crises, teachers can help their students to cope more adequately with stressful experiences.

Philosophers and scientists have always had difficulty communicating meaning at the more abstract levels of experience and thought. As a consequence of this difficulty, Aristotle advised his Grecian colleagues to give special attention to the use of metaphors in prose "for the resources of prose are less abundant than those of poetry." In support of Aristotle, Embler[4] points out that metaphors do indeed appear to be a highly effective way of making meaning and "giving to airy nothing a local habitation and a name." Once an idea has been given a home and a name, however, its identity and utility are to some degree fixed and circumscribed. For example, while man may indeed be conceptualized as a machine or a computer and society as a prison, a wasteland or a hospital, each of the metaphors serves to reduce the possibilities of meaning; so that while metaphors may be helpful in defining an abstruse idea, the idea itself is pinched off and limited by its conceptual framework.

This process has to some extent sandbagged and straitjacketed the metaphorical utility of "stress." Of all the metaphors the human behavioral sciences have borrowed from their sister sciences and from literature, none has been more in need of habitation and name than the concept of stress. Yet in the past its metaphorical habitation has mostly been in the house of hardship, retardation, insult and affliction, and its name has been synonomous with noxiousness. Yet, while physicians, biologists, physicists and engineers have equated stress with the storm-tossed, battle conditions of living, no less an authority than Hamlet, in his philosophical musings on life, spoke of his stress as that of the "thousand *natural* shocks that flesh is heir to."

THE NATURE OF STRESS

The gist of the problem lies in the fact that stress as the grand metaphor of life and living has found little if any place in a philosophy or psychology of normal development and health. If stress is a condition existing within elastic material (organic or inorganic) as a result of external forces, such a condition can be conceptualized as having two pathways, one leading to increased elasticity, the other to increased rigidity. Without pursuing the historical and metaphorical origins of stress beyond this confusing introduction, stress is herein defined as any stimulus or force that changes an organism in some significant way for better or worse however these value terms are defined. It is also apparent that, whatever stress is, its impact is on some molecular or cellular arrangement having sufficient flexibility inherent in its make-up to respond. Therefore, the process of living can be regarded as stressful, that is, responding to stimuli. Death (note the absence of a comparable word such as "deathing") is an absence of stress. In relating the concept of stress to health or illness, one then needs to differentiate degrees of stress, quality of stress, and its idiosyncratic nature in human experience (one man's meat being another man's poison). As an illustration of this principle, Fenichel[5] found that compulsive personalities tend to develop acute anxiety symptoms as a result of severe environmental stress, whereas persons burdened by chronic latent guilt tend to react to misery by becoming less anxious than before. Although it is common to perceive stress as a noxious or adverse force, the natural shocks Hamlet pondered can be conceived as normal peaks in growth and development—defined as crisis or disequilibrium by Caplan, developmental tasks by Havighurst, stages of psychosexual development by Freud, and nuclear modes of development by Erikson.

The relationship of stress to noxious stimuli may be helpful to the epidemiologist who is looking for significant clues in the host factors of a population or in biological, physical or psychological agents tending to lead to disease. However, what is needed is a turned-over epidemiologist— a salubriologist, who can focus the tools and techniques of his disease-oriented colleagues on how organisms utilize stress to expand, differentiate and integrate personality growth and mental health. As a result of epidemiological studies, it is known that exposure in small measure to certain noxious agents can prevent illnesses. Certainly, one does not need to demonstrate that unstressful, aseptic or antiseptic conditions in the physical or mental dimensions of living can be catastrophic to the organism. If one could conceive a science of salubriology as the other side of the epidemiological coin, one would be concerned with the mass aspect of health enhancement and its measurement. Some of the problems this somewhat nebulous but emerging field faces are (1) the lack of operational definitions of health, (2) conceptualizations of specific exposures or experiences that build health rather than prevent specific diseases, and (3) a map or description of what Meredith Willson calls "the territory."

THE NATURE OF MEDIATION

It seems likely that future inhabitants of this planet will face increased amounts of stimuli, tension, natural and unnatural stress. Are socialization and enculturation processes up to producing individuals who can mediate these stresses healthfully? Are there whetstones or fulcra for sharpening and enhancing personality strength through healthy mediation of stress and can these be programmed into schools? Dark as the tunnel between stimulus and response may be, are there nevertheless some pretty good hunches about what can be done to make the entering symbols and signals emerge in appropriate and effective responses?

One such hunch lies in further implementation of the mediating personality construct called ego processes. Such processes of the personality mediate or interpret the events, symbols and significant signals in the external and internal worlds and indicate to the organism its most effective and economical response. Ego processes move the individual away from pain, danger or noxious stimuli. To do this the perception of stimuli may be altered, inhibited, shut off or distorted; adequate responses may be repeated or restricted, or they may completely vanish. As a result individuals develop a "hardening of the perceptual categories" or a closing and narrowing of response veins and response alternatives. Although such ego processes may be acting for the best interests of the individual, the result of any or all of these processes is a diminution or restriction of the degrees of freedom in perception, conception, response and behavior. Therefore, to some extent, one suffers a loss in degrees of freedom in any process of socialization and enculturation in much the same manner as a participant in a game gives up certain freedoms in accepting the rules by which he is to function with others. Ego or mediating processes that can help the individual mediate stress constructively might be learned in a play setting where stress is placed on game processes in addition to outcomes. For example, in the playing of games children learn to take defeat without being defeated, to evaluate the consequences of breaking the rules, to resolve conflict in ways acceptable to both sides, to consider the consequences of past actions in planning next moves and to utilize the tension of play in learning to play better.

The channeling of activity in games is based on an agreement often implicit in the rules of play. Children who cannot play games, that is, who cannot abide by the rules, who play unfairly, cheat, or are fearful of the consequences of their action, find less and less opportunities for this kind of social experience. Some specific possibilities for ego development in this field of action can be given.

THREE POTENTIAL STRESS-IMMUNITY BUILDING PROGRAMS

What follows are brief descriptions of potential foci or programs in the utilization of the "natural shocks" that children face to increase their chances of school success. It is not intended that these specific programs take on the full burden of these tasks. As a start, one needs to assume that the school is providing pleasant and enticing encounters between children and curriculum, that the teachers are trained, competent professionals with reasonably sized classes and that the school functions in an atmosphere of concern for money and children, with the latter slightly in the lead. However, in implementation of the theories discussed earlier, three focuses of action will be outlined which seem to have developmental potential for programs that can be operationally defined and replicated in a number of localities.

The crisis of school entrance. Among the stresses all children face are the slow or sometimes rapid separation from family dependency to a dependency on self and peers. A major stress point in this experience is the child's first few days, weeks and months in school.

School entry as a place to hang one's action hat in helping children mediate stress has been accorded theoretical body and life by a number of investigators. The conceptual model of the Boston group[7,8,10] is that school entry is a period of rapid change and role transition for children and parents that causes a rise in tension, a degree of functional disorganization in both children and parents (to say nothing of the teacher) and a searching by children for resources with which to cope or defend. One game has ended and another has begun; the child searches anxiously to discover the rules by which this new game is played and to assess his personal competencies as a player. He is like the rookie ready to play any position and run like a deer to get on the team. As a result, a little supportive coaching can go a long way *at this time*. In addition, the parents of such children view the situation anxiously to find out how successful or unsuccessful their child will be in this new and important game of life. Responsibility, the *bete noire* of parenthood, is happily accepted when the child is successful at his school tasks; failure, or not doing as well as expected, may produce the kind of guilt and discomfort in parental egos that increases stress and distress on an already vulnerable child.

A child's entering school is often the first family experience with an agency initiated on a jointly positive basis to last for at least ten years. Yet, in all but a few school systems in the U.S., children usually come to school having had a physical and the necessary immunizations to contagious diseases, but there has been little or no planned preparation for the teacher, the child or the parent.

To utilize the stress of school entrance positively for the child and his family, a specific program must be planned and carried out by the school. The objectives of the program should be communicated to all parents prior to the meeting of child and school. One aspect of the program might be an assessment of each child prior to kindergarten entry or during his kindergarten experience, so that the school can plan more effective challenges for the child. In the preschool checkup the child may take the Stanford-Binet test, work with clay and fingerpaints, play in a play house and participate in some simple games with other children. The child's developmental and social history will be obtained from the parents by a school social worker. In the testing and play, the child's behavior and personality will be evaluated by observing the nature of separation from his parents, his affective control and spontaneity, any unusual behavior and the degree of dependency on the adult present. During games the child's ability to function with others will be observed: Can he abide by social rules such as taking turns; how does he deal with impulses and fantasies; is his curiosity acted upon or inhibited; to what extent can he tolerate frustration and tension; can he show joy or anger without losing control; and to what extent can he adapt to new games and new persons?

Both parents would probably be asked to attend one weekly two-hour meeting with seven other parents to keep in touch with their child's progress, his growing edges and his problems, if any. Children who might have some difficulty in school would be assessed individually for sensory, motor or emotional handicaps and appropriate adjustments made for them at school entrance. A school social worker would be assigned to those children or families who require additional help at this time, to work with them during the planning period.

Other resources employed by the school would be a carefully selected group of kindergarten and first-grade teachers, including men teachers, sufficient time for them to prepare and meet with parents in the late afternoon or early morning, and sufficient consultation assistance by curriculum and pupil personnel workers when required. By mid-semester the school and parents should have become a friendly, communicative group in which ideas, reactions and problems are wrestled with freely and openly. At the same time, teachers will have had a chance to identify the strengths and weaknesses of their classes, feed back information on some of the preschool checkup assessments, plan and carry out appropriate experiences to increase the adaptive skills of some of the children, enrich the skills of others, and increase the range of experiences for all.

What has happened as a result of this program? Families and their children who are entering a normal period of rapid change and stress have been attended to and presumably helped to mediate this transition in a strengthening and integrating manner. In this first encounter with the school, each child has found the school ready with an appropriate "match" for those experiences and skills he has already assimilated into his repertoire. Where necessary, mental health workers have established liaison with righ-risk families and children. All children have gotten off to a good start in school.

Junior high child study classes. Puberty and junior high school (seventh and eighth grades) go together like ham and eggs. Often, earlier psychological conflicts and problems are rekindled, and ominous developmental tasks loom large on the horizon. Boys play more realistically at being men; girls aren't fooling about becoming women. Growth and change are flowing swiftly into bodies and psyches, which need to muster all their resources and wits to manage and mediate the current. A social studies program at this level might include two half-days of work each week in a child care center run by the school district for young children. The goals of the program for the students would be: (1) to enjoy children; (2) to learn how to communicate and relate to young children; (3) to discover how to teach children new skills; (4) to enjoy helping children to eat, read, rest, work and play; (5) to discover ways of understanding the behavior of children; (6) to develop ideas about human behavior that apply to the students themselves.

Each student in the class might be assigned to a child and given an initial observation guide for study. The students would meet with the child-care staff to learn the rules and procedures in working with the children. During this period the staff would discuss with the students how adults supervise children, how to tell a story to a child, how children are prepared for naps, what to do when a child wets, how to handle fights and what to do with a child who is unhappy. Back in the social studies class, the teacher and her asssistant (psychologist, psychiatrist or social worker) would present and discuss in general terms what is known about human behavior, how it develops, what makes children act like children, how children relate to adults, and how adults relate to children. As the students began to have experiences with individual children, the discussion would be focused on student-centered contributions. One student may find his child to be somewhat lonely; another may find he has a baby-faced assassin on his hands; a third student may be puzzled by his inability to establish any control over his charge. These and other examples would be presented and discussed by the class. Students would be asked to suggest ways of helping a lonely child feel more comfortable with the others, what they might do to channel the energies of the potential fighter and some ideas on how to help children "mind."

In the last quarter of the class such new problems would be posed to the students as: What did you feel you did best with children? Why? What did the children like about you? What didn't they like about you? Which child did you find most interesting? Why? Which children showed creative abilities? What specific examples can you cite? Have you found any children you didn't like? Why? Which children were leaders? How did these children differ from the others? How does one help a child grow up? What kinds of things frighten children? What pleases them? What did they do that pleased you?

In effect, this program utilizes a natural human behavior laboratory for experiential learning by students. Behavior of self and others (including parents) previously viewed as "surface" and monolithic in origin may, as a result, become a kaleidoscope of possibilities. For example, early in the program one group of students might propose and discuss two or three possible reasons for the behavior of a withdrawn, nonparticipating child. Later the same group can often suggest ten possible reasons for such behavior, such as: (1) maybe he just didn't know how to play some of the games, (2) maybe he was frightened of failure, (3) he could have been tired, (4) he may have a language difficulty, (5) maybe he doesn't get a chance to play with others, (6) perhaps he is just shy, (7) since he always carried a bear around with him perhaps he is more comfortable with that than with the kids, (8) perhaps some of the kids have bullied him, (9) his parents may encourage him not to play with others, (10) maybe he just doesn't understand about games.

Another possible outcome for the student can be learning how to communicate affective responses to others and the development of confidence and safety in allowing trusted peers and adults to share one's feelings. That this may be an important kind of learning is illustrated by a study of family relationships of creative children. The investigators found that such families were frank about their conflicts and feelings and were able to express their emotions openly to each other, sometimes with explosive intensity.[11] Such acceptance and learning of techniques of affective communication in families were found helpful to children in building stress-mediating experiences. As a rule, children and adolescents are shielded from learning about feelings or how they can be communicated or understood. Frank[6] suggests that a family or a school offers the best setting for children to attempt to learn how to resolve emotional stress and conflict. If building stress immunity in children is a worthy objective, then sibling rivalry might be a desirable rather than an undesirable experience, depending on how the conflict is mediated by the child and perceived by the adult. The successful mediating of such conflict may, as Frank believes, strengthen character in a number of ways. The child learns to handle defeat and victory, discovers hidden resources (I didn't know I had it in me), learns the relationship between conviction and action, develops self-discipline and learns to play the game of life against challenging problems or worthy opponents with satisfaction and zest.

Use of games in building stress immunity. Whatever the source of man's gregarious nature, one finds him clustered in groups in houses, at work and at play, and on roads to and from these places. To manage and enhance these myriad activities and the resulting astronomical social transactions of living, man has established rules or laws and a corps of blue-clad referees to blow the whistle when necessary. The values (goals) and ethics (sportsmanlike conduct of play) inherent in laws are no less present in the rules of children's games. One learns in time that the signal quality of a law is that it cannot be broken with impunity; similarly a rule of a game cannot be transgressed without penalty. Albee[1] illustrates this notion in *Who's Afraid of Virginia Woolf?*, as it exists in the idiosyncratic game of marriage played by George and Martha. In this relationship between husband and wife, the game has required, in part, the "conception" of a fantasied son and his fantasied growth and development. The rule, however, was that this was to be a two-person game and not shared with others. Martha, in a moment of despair or triumph breaks the rule, whereupon George "kills" their son:

Martha: No! No! You cannot do that. You cannot decide that for yourself, I will not let you do that!

George: You know the rules, Martha. For Christ Sake, you know the rules. . . . You broke our rule, baby.

One cannot, as Martha says, let others decide for you; on the other hand, as George points out, one cannot play any game without adhering to the rules.

Albee's play illustrates the bean-bag, hop-scotch nature of adult transactions and the emphasis that both child and adult societies place on the unshakable nature of rules. Play is ended when a rule is transgressed. "Thus," as Berne[2] deftly points out, "play may be deadly serious or even fatally serious but the social consequences are only serious if the rules are abrogated."

Often rules are broken because they are not known or one lacks sufficient skill to play the game. For example, small children can play together for only short periods of time since they lack sufficient rule-abiding mechanisms. Lower-class children find the game of "middle-class school" difficult to manage since no such games are played at home or in their neighborhood. In nursery school settings it is not at all surprising to find the disturbed or inadequate child unable to function in a game setting; he is probably easily recognizable as a child in trouble by this fact.

The application of game theory procedures in the high school has been suggested by Coleman[3] and has been developed by Suchman[9] for the elementary science curriculum. Suchman's Inquiry Training Project is a game similar to "Twenty Questions," in which young children attempt to explain the meaning of an observed scientific phenomenon in a "yes" or "no" inquiry structure. At the adolescent level some kind of "game" experience may be helpful in managing the changing of the rules from the high school to the college game.

Games may also provide a helpful and effective match in the initial introduction and motivation of children from lower-class families into the school institution. For these children, games can provide rapid pay-offs for choices, an ongoing system of reinforcement and continuously evolving, rather than future-oriented, rewards. For some children who can't function in an open competitive relationship, one can circumvent such group deterrents by an individual game approach to learning.

SUMMARY

Metaphorically and behaviorally stress must be regarded as a neutral force that can be utilized for growth and health. The school can plan stress-managing experiences in the curriculum by utilizing the normal stress of transition from home to school, from latency to adolescence and from one "game" setting to another.

REFERENCES

1. Albee, E. 1962. Who's Afraid of Virginia Woolf? Atheneum, New York, N. Y., 235–236.
2. Berne, E. 1961. Transactional Analysis in Psychotherapy. Grove Press, New York, N. Y., 88.
3. Coleman, J. S. 1961. The Adolescent Society. The Free Press. Glencoe, Ill.
4. Embler, W. 1963. Five metaphors from the modern repertory. A Review of General Semantics 19(4), 403–426.
5. Fenichel, O. 1945. The Psychoanalytic Theory of Neurosis. W. W. Norton & Co. New York, N. Y.
6. Frank, J. 1957. Are you a guilty parent? Harpers Magazine (April), 56–59.
7. Klein, D. and E. Lindemann. 1961. Preventive intervention in individual and family crisis situations. In Prevention of Mental Disorders in Children, G. Caplan, Ed. Basic Books, Inc. New York, N. Y., 283–306.
8. Klein, D. and A. Ross. 1958. Kindergarten entry, a study of role transition. In Orthopsychiatry and the School, M. Krugman, Ed. American Orthopsychiatric Association, Inc. New York, N. Y.
9. Suchman, J. R. 1960. Inquiry training in the elementary school. Science Teacher 27: 42–47.
10. Waldfogel, S. and G. Gardner. 1961. Intervention in crises as a method of primary prevention. In Prevention of Mental Disorders in Children, G. Caplan, Ed. Basic Books, Inc. New York, N. Y., 307–322.
11. Weisberg, P. S. and K. J. Springer. 1961. Environmental factors in creative function. Arch. Gen. Psychiat. 5: 544–64.

45.   Mental Health Consultation in Schools as a Means of Communicating Mental Health Principles

I. N. Berlin

Mental health consultation in the schools is designed to serve a dual purpose—to assist in the solution of the professional manpower shortage and to offer a prevention-oriented mental health program. Rather than working directly with the problem child, the consultant works instead with the teacher who, as a consequence, is not only better prepared to cope with the particular difficulty at hand but to forestall future problems. In the following selection, Dr. Berlin gives us some insights into how this task-oriented consultation process works.

The Mental Health Consultant in a school system often has a unique opportunity to communicate and sometimes to demonstrate mental health principles to teachers.

Perhaps the most important principle he can communicate to school people is the fact that all human feelings can be talked about without shame, blame, or passing judgment on the teacher as a "bad" person. The consultant, by his attitude of concern, attentiveness, and respect for his professional colleague, demonstrates his relationship to the teacher as a colleague whose problems with their attendant mixed feelings are of mutual concern. The consultant's encouragement of verbal expression of all feelings of the teacher about his work is greatly enhanced in my experience as the consultant progressively clarifies that he is not there to analyze the teacher, to pry into hidden motivations, or to uncover skeletons about the teacher's personal problems. He demonstrates in many ways that his job as an expert in interpersonal relations is to help the teacher understand

Journal of the American Academy of Child Psychiatry, 1962, 1, 671–679. Reprinted with the permission of the publisher and author.

himself in terms of the job he is doing, and, in particular, to help him be consciously aware of his feelings about the particular child who is a problem for him. The purpose is always to enable the teacher to do his work more effectively.

Another mental health principle the consultant can demonstrate effectively is that every person has limitations both professionally and personally. Unreal self-expectations and their aftermaths of tension and exhaustion from increasing conflict may seriously interfere with teaching. Thus the understanding, acceptance, and assessment of one's own limitations are important for good mental health.

A third vital principle that can be demonstrated by the consultant centers around authority. Workers in a hierarchical setting need to be able to accept constituted authority and to work under regulations without undue conflict. This may be especially important for mental health when as sometimes occurs the authority is unjust and the regulations are restrictive. Rebellion and its attendant repercussions in the teacher's teaching frequently only increase the tensions between teachers and administrators.

COMMUNICATION OF MENTAL HEALTH PRINCIPLES TO SCHOOL PEOPLE

Two experiences illustrate the consultant's role in demonstrating the mental health principle that all feelings aroused by a pupil can be talked about. A third-grade teacher and her principal asked to talk with me about a nonlearning Negro youngster whose size and aggression made him a terror in the classroom and out of it. The principal described the boy's behavior in the classroom and schoolyard and the difficulties of the teacher and the administrator in handling the boy. While the principal talked the teacher sat very quietly by and appeared frozen. When asked to add her comments to the principal's, she remarked in a barely audible voice that it had all been said and sat stiffly in her chair. As I began to comment about what a handful this must be for the teacher to contend with all day and that we psychiatrists were pretty lucky because at the worst we had to deal with such a child for only an hour once or twice a week, the teacher grinned tightly. I then talked about a learning experience of my own of which this child had reminded me. This was a severely hostile, aggressive ten-year-old boy who presented a constant dilemma in the early weeks of treatment. If I tried to stop him from attacking me and breaking up the playroom *before* he got started, he accused me of jumping him before he had done anything, and I felt guilty and uncomfortable about being unfair to such a disturbed child. If I waited until things did get started, it required all my efforts to contain him, and I found myself full of mounting rage and revengeful feelings as I struggled to prevent him from hurting me or destroying equipment. After seven or eight sessions, in one hour I found myself full of murderous fury having been hurt by him and finally finding myself on the floor with a scissor lock around his legs and arm locks holding this ten-year-old down. I was working very hard only to restrain him and not to hurt him.

Beside myself with impotent rage, I told this boy how terribly angry I felt and of my own fear that the anger he provoked in me might cause me to hurt him. If that happened I would feel very guilty and sorry. I told him further that to avoid this possibility I had just decided to restrain him the moment he even looked as if he were about to be violent and that I was quite prepared to be unfair to him at times. I was determined to continue this until he had shown me that he could begin to control himself. After three more hours of testing and protesting as I restrained him at every sign of incipient trouble, he began to settle down and express his feelings through the materials in the playroom.

As I was talking I could see this teacher's face relax; there were little nods as I described my own feelings in the playroom with respect to the child and when I finished she sighed mightily and began to talk rapidly of her own fears, the anger, hatred, and helpless feelings occasioned by this boy's behavior. She accepted my suggestion that she try to anticipate this boy's beginning unrest and stay with him, helping him do schoolwork. Her personal attention at such moments rather than a half hope from a distance that the ominous signs might not bring their inevitable result might slowly begin to help this child. Also she might in time aid this boy to begin to communicate in words his feelings and to find a way out of his tension through beginning successes in schoolwork. On my next trip to this school about six weeks later, the administrator commented that a great change had taken place in the teacher. Since the consultation in which the administrator had participated the teacher seemed more able to talk with the administrator about her problems. The boy, although still a school and classroom problem, was gradually settling down.

On another level, a male high school teacher, after several conversations around other problems, recounted his difficulties with several huge, explosive boys who seemed to dare him to stop them. Although no weakling himself, he found himself indecisive. He feared a fight and riot if he interfered and tried to stop the hostile, provocative behavior and he felt ineffectual and at the boys' mercy if he did not take some action. Involved in this also was his feeling that he could not ask the administrator's help with this recurring problem lest he be thought a poor teacher. As the teacher recounted his experiences the Dean of Boys who sat by became more and more uncomfortable.

My comment that this was a hell of a fix to find oneself in brought a "You ain't kidding" from the teacher and a nod from the Dean. I then recalled a particularly difficult situation in the army with a psychotic soldier who had been a wrestler as well as a much-decorated paratrooper. He terrorized the psychotic ward and was reigning as king when I took over the service. During the first ward rounds he made his stand clear as he towered over me flexing his muscles, saying, "I am running things, see." Since my fear was evident to all in my trembling hands and legs, there seemed no point in denying it. I told this psychotic patient that I was scared of him and what he might be able to do physically to me, but that I could not let him run the ward; I was prepared personally and with all the M.P.s in the hospital if necessary to run it as it must be run. The man glared at me for an interminably long minute. I did my best to meet his gaze. Finally, he shrugged his shoulders and disdainfully said, "Okay, have it your way," and returned to his bedside. I had felt that being painfully honest about my fears as well as clearly demonstrating my determination to carry out my job by whatever means were necessary had been the effective elements of this interchange.

Both teacher and Dean then began to discuss how they could work together to help these youngsters settle down in the classroom. It was clear to me from the Dean's avid following of my account and from his relieved look when our discussion began that he had felt as stymied as the teacher by these boys and therefore unable to be of much help. The humorous aftermath of this consultation came when the Dean, weeks later, commented that this teacher now had a reputation among the tough youngsters for great fearlessness because he could admit being scared.

The following illustrates how the consultant's attitudes toward others and himself may help reduce unreal self-expectations and lead to greater acceptance of realistic limitations.

A typical interchange among teachers, overheard after a group consultation is: "Well, Berlin wasn't really much help today, but it's kind of nice to hear a psychiatrist say he doesn't know something." The honest, "I don't know," or "This is out of my line," in answer to insoluble problems on matters of curriculum and other subjects in which the consultant has no special competence seem to help others not to have to know and be able to cope with everything.

In many instances this begins to help the educator to delineate his job to the kind of work, that is, educating, that he can do. It may also make it possible for the teacher to ask for help from administrators, to call in parents, etc., when necessary, without feeling that such a call for help is an admission of failure. Thus some problems may get worked with earlier rather than at the point of impasse, when both teacher and students are emotionally so disturbed that it becomes difficult to find ways of continued work.

Despite their best efforts, teachers will sometimes fail to help a disturbed child, and they need to be able to accept such failure. The consultant's readiness to illustrate from his own experience that he too has on occasions failed to be helpful demonstrates his understanding of their problem. It seems to me to be helpful to the teacher when the consultant in his comments shows that one can fail with a clear conscience after one has literally done everything one could do within one's own present scope of knowledge and professional development. As many of us have experienced, the readiness to give up and to admit failure often frees both people in a working relationship to try again. I have often witnessed that the consultant's understanding and acceptance of the administrator's and teacher's desire to exclude a child from school because they are at the end of their rope with the child resulted in the teacher's relief. Thus the contemplated action about which the teacher or administrator feel some guilt is accepted as reasonable in the light of the situation which has been discussed. Often later in the same discussion, after close examination of the problems and their possible causes, the teacher has reconsidered the exclusion and has been willing to try to work with the child again.

In my experience, the consultant can often demonstrate that one can accept constituted authority and its regulations even when they are unfair and that one can find ways of working within such a framework. In my own work I have insisted that administrators be present in consultation to decide about the action to be taken after our discussion of the problems involved.

Sometimes teachers are temporarily angered when the consultant does not side with their rebellion against short-sighted regulations or strongly biased administrators. In such instances, it has been possible to help some of these teachers to focus on using their energies more effectively in doing a good job of teaching and working with their pupils. As such energies are withdrawn from their usually fruitless rebellion and transferred to more effective teaching, one begins to recognize how often the problems with authority served other purposes. Most frequently, in my experience, such rebelliousness served as a rationalization for the actual poor job of teaching that was being done. An interesting paradox is often seen. The hostile, angry rebelliousness of many teachers does not become channeled into rational action as citizens or teachers through the organization appropriate for such action until they begin to teach more effectively, with consequent reduction of the irrational aspects of their rebellion.

A number of teachers and administrators have commented that my own acceptance of severe limitations in consultation imposed by frightened, unfriendly administrators has been of help to them. They have watched to see whether I would adhere strictly to the rules that were laid down. It became clear to them that I could and did function under these restrictions until as a result of my behavior the administrator felt less threatened and relaxed the restrictions. One vice-principal who later went on to an important job in another school system said that such a demonstration helped him resolve a problem he had been struggling with for years and made his advancement possible.

DISCUSSION

Mental health consultation is a term made meaningful by Gerald Caplan of the Harvard School of Public Health and used by him to describe particular consultative processes previously written about under many headings. In this process a consultant using specific consultative methods attempts to help a consultee whose internalized conflicts interfere with effective performance of some aspect of his job.

The dynamics of the mental health consultation process are being studied by a number of workers. This paper is concerned with the particular way in which the consultation process lends itself to the communication of certain mental health principles to the teacher and administrator and often through them to other members of the school faculty. In addition, these experiences highlight several aspects of the dynamics of mental health consultation.

The consultant demonstrates in many ways his understanding of the consultees' problems and his assessment of these as work problems. When he relates similar experiences of his own and indicates the mental health principles involved which he, an authority in interpersonal matters, also had to learn, then feelings of turmoil, hate, anger, rebellion, and self-righteousness which were largely covert can become more overt. As some of the defenses against the eruption of such feelings are reduced, the teacher begins to feel that his problems can be resolved and is ready to listen to the methods others have used to deal with similar problems. Frequently a teacher who has been helped will talk frankly and eagerly with colleagues and will emphasize the mental health principles he has learned.

In my own work I have insisted on the presence of administrators at most of the consultations. It reduces opportunities for divisive comments by teachers against administrators when they misquote the consultant to other faculty members. An even more important reason is that in my experience, the consultant is often called in because the administrator has not been able to help his teacher with some particular problems, which may indicate some difficulties on the administrator's part in doing his job effectively. As the administrator listens to the consultative sessions he becomes aware of the consultant's attitudes which seem to help the teacher. He also vicariously identifies with the teacher's work problems. Usually the principal has failed to help his teacher with problems in areas where he is also in conflict. Once he is once removed from the direct consultation, he gains relief and help with his problems without their ever being made explicit. Subsequently he often communicates what he has learned to other teachers and even to fellow administrators. This is especially true of problems concerned with authority and the acceptance of one's own limitations, areas of special concern to administrators.

Experienced consultants have come to recognize how often teacher consultees present the problems they are unable to deal with by behaving toward the consultant as their difficult students have behaved toward them. In my experience, this is especially true in instances of hostile, provocative behavior or when the incessant demands of one or more students for exclusive attention has exhausted the teacher. The teacher finds himself in conflict about what is fair to the demanding student, to the class, and lastly, if at all, to himself. These teachers may come to consultation with a hostile, demanding, provocative, and sometimes belligerent pounding at the consultant for answers to their problems. One senses the teacher consultee's wary, anxious observation of the consultant and the close scrutiny of his methods as he handles this situation. In these instances there is the clearest identification with the consultant and incorporation of his attitudes and methods of handling problems.

In almost all mental health consultation, identification with the consultant and incorporation of his attitudes and methods of working with problems are part of the process of ego integration. From my point of view, mental health consultation is essentially conducted at the ego level. In my own work in mental health consultation during the past twelve years, I have tried to apply the growing insights from ego psychology to refine the consultation process. These insights concern an awareness of the integrative capacities in all human beings, even those who are very sick; efforts to understand the individual's malintegrative behavior in the current situation and to assess that behavior in terms of the current realities; a detailed examination of the problems so that through the atttention to the minute details of the current difficulties in functioning one may begin to elucidate methods of resolution usually inherent in the troubles; help in the resolution of conflicts by honest assessment of the reality facing the person and a step-by-step analysis of the ways in which certain obstacles to resolution were noted, understood, and handled by the person. Thus the consultant is task oriented; this helps reduce the regressive helplessness of the consultee and enlists him as a collaborator, not a patient, to work together with the consultant to resolve the particular work problems. The consultant's understanding of the consultee's neurotic conflicts, which make for his work problems, is used to find the dynamically appropriate comments which will help reduce the central anxieties and permit the collaboration to occur.

Inherent in all of this is an underlying thesis in ego psychology: that the conflict between unconscious forces results from malintegrative experiences during infancy and childhood. These conflicts usually become manifest as a struggle between regression and helplessness versus mastery and integrative productive behavior. In the consultative situations involving rebellious feelings and behavior toward authority these aspects are perhaps most clearly seen. The consultee may begin by presenting his own problems of helplessness in handling hostile or rebellious behavior in his students and then go on to talk of his anger and hatred toward the unfair, punitive administrator, etc. In such comments the genesis of the conflicts in early experience often becomes clear. After listening carefully, if one returns to a close examination of the classroom events and especially inquiries about how the teacher handles other classroom problems, one gets a sense of the capacity for effective teaching that is present. A detailed assessment of the actual problems with the rebellious student often gives one clues to the teacher's momentary awareness of choices at critical points of dealing with the youngster—choices that were not heeded, so that the helpless, regressive feeling overwhelmed the teacher with resulting havoc. At this point some effort to externalize the situation by using experiences of others or one's own may illustrate why such moments of choice are difficult to detect and to use, how one's anger with authority may make such work more difficult. Finally, one can illustrate that other solutions might be possible if these critical moments were recognized and then handled differently.

The above elucidates some dynamics of the mental health consultation process. The development of methods of effective mental health consultation and of understanding its dynamics is one of the most interesting and challenging areas of the application of dynamic psychiatric and psychoanalytic thinking.

46. Incorporating Psychological Concepts in the School Curriculum

Ralph H. Ojemann

Some workers believe that one of the most effective ways to promote better mental health entails the incorporation of psychological concepts into the curriculum. Since 1941, Ojemann and his associates have developed and evaluated a curriculum approach to mental health which emphasizes a causal approach to the social environment. The basic rationale is that a person who becomes more fully aware of the motivations of human behavior is better able to cope with personal and social crises. The following selection reviews the results of this approach.

It seems helpful to begin by citing some data which suggest both the need for teaching psychological or behavioral science concepts at the elementary and secondary levels and some of the difficult aspects of the problem. As a back-ground for this discussion I should like to make use of two phrases to designate two contrasting approaches to behavior. On the one hand we may emphasize the outward or overt aspects of a given action and make an approach to it in those terms. For example, if a child takes some article belonging to another we may think of this as a violation of property rights and as something that is detrimental to society and we may classify it as a case of stealing. But when we do so we have considered the behavior only as it appears from the outside. If we make some judgment of it using only its overt form we are making essentially an arbitrary judgmental approach.

In contrast to this approach we may think of the behavior in more dynamic terms. We may ask why the child acted as he did. We may ask

Journal of School Psychology, 1967, 5, 195–204. Reprinted with the permission of the publisher and author.

what motive lay behind the behavior and how it happened that the child used the particular method he did for satisfying his motive and use these data in determining what to do.

The first approach which considers behavior as it appears in its outward form and neglects consideration of its courses we may call a surface or arbitrary judgmental approach to behavior. The second which considers behavior in terms of its underlying dynamics we may call a causal approach.

IMPORTANCE OF INCORPORATING PSYCHOLOGICAL CONCEPTS IN THE SCHOOL CURRICULUM

In some of our experimental work in studying the effects of teaching psychological concepts we tested children at the beginning of an experiment—usually in the fall of the year—and again in the spring. In a study reported in 1955 (Ojemann, *et al.*) involving children at the fourth-, fifth-, and sixth-grade levels, we used among others a test to measure tendencies toward arbitrary punitiveness. We found that our experimental groups showed a reduction in the tendency to resort to surface or arbitrary punitive procedures, but that the control group showed a tendency to increase in this dimension. In other words, there was a tendency for the control group to be, if anything, *more* arbitrarily punitive at the end of the year than at the beginning.

In a study published in 1964 (Ojemann and Snider) we obtained similar evidence. In this study we used scores obtained by trained observers who noted the children's actual behavior in daily situations. The actual behavior scores showed that the children growing up in the *ordinary* classroom—not in an experimental classroom where we introduced psychological concepts, but in the ordinary classroom—tended to be more arbitrary and *non-causal* in their approaches to behavior at the end of the year than they were at the beginning.

What is the meaning of these findings? It is well known that workers with various groups of adults have observed strong tendencies toward arbitrary judgments of human behavior at that age level. Investigators of teacher education programs have observed such tendencies in teachers in training (Prescott, 1957). Those who have been concerned with the training of school counselors have had to devote considerable energy to training prospective candidates to proper non-judgmental anecdotal records (Traxler, 1957). Those who have attempted to educate parents have often found that the first thing they have to do is to help the parent unlearn the arbitrary judgmental way of thinking. This may take considerable time and may give rise to guilt feelings (Spock, 1955). Workers in the field of mental health have had to contend with an arbitrary judgmental approach toward the mentally ill. In recent attempts to teach mental health principles to industrial executives, it has been found necessary to devote the first sessions to developing an understanding approach to behavior.

Enough is known about child and adult development to assure us that adults were not born with such arbitrary judgmental-noncausal tendencies. The evidence from our studies strongly suggests that they learned it as they were growing up in our present schools and homes. It appears, in other words, that we have a culture which is "infected" with an arbitrary judgmental approach to behavior and this infection is being transmitted from one generation to the next. We are teaching each on-coming generation an approach to behavior that is essentially non-causal in nature and not grounded in an understanding and appreciation of the dynamics of behavior.

If we are interested in increasing the understanding and appreciation of behavioral science it is most important that those parts of the school curriculum which deal with human behavior be changed so that instead of continuing the arbitrary judgmental approach they develop a more causal orientation.

We have found we can incorporate behavioral science concepts into the school curriculum and educate teachers to teach them. We have some evidence that such teaching develops in the student a greater sensitivity to the dynamics of behavior. Our further hypothesis is that helping a child to gain an understanding and appreciation of the dynamics of human behavior—in other words, of the forces operating in the social environment —will facilitate his interaction with that environment. We have some evidence for this hypothesis also.

EXAMPLES OF INCORPORATING PSYCHOLOGICAL CONCEPTS

A few examples showing how psychological concepts have been incorporated into the curriculum may be helpful at this point. This will be followed by a brief description of some of the effects on the child's development, especially as they relate to his interactions with his social environment.

To help the primary child develop an appreciation of the differences between the non-causal approaches we have used a variety of materials. One type of material consists of narratives in which the surface and causal procedures are contrasted. The narratives are read by the teacher at the kindergarten and first grade levels. In the later grades the child can read them for himself.

Each narrative describes some behavior situation. After the situation has been set forth, some character in the story begins to make a surface approach to it, then rethinks his proposed reactions and makes a more causal approach. Some of the ways in which the behavior may have developed come out and one of the characters in the narrative acts in the light of these data.

The situation has a reality about it in that someone begins to make a surface approach which children in our culture experience quite frequently. But the story also introduces a more effective way of living—a way that takes account of the meaning or the causes of behavior instead of its overt form.

To encourage the child to develop a more generalized conception and to prevent him from thinking only of incidents involving himself, situations are described involving children older and younger than himself and children from quite different environments. There is some observational evidence that situations involving people different from the child tend to be less emotionally charged and, therefore, less difficult for the child to consider causally in the early discussions.

Each narrative is preceded by a short introduction for use by the teacher. After the reading of the story, there is a discussion. The purpose of this discussion is not only to recall the incidents of the story but also to bring out the differences in procedure when one thinks of causes as contrasted with principal attention to the overt form of behavior. The discussion is also designed to consider alternative ways of meeting situations and some of the probable effects of these alternatives.

It is suggested to the teacher that this material furnish part of the offerings in the regular "story period." Under usual school conditions the material read in the story period deals with various objects and events in the child's environment. Some of it deals with physical objects; some of it deals with people. Our suggestion is that material dealing with people give more consideration to the dynamics of behavior. Much of current material deals with what people do, not why they do it. The causally oriented stories thus expand and enrich the content of the primary child's story period.

Another type of material we have used consists of expositions to help the child understand and appreciate the behavior of persons with whom he interacts directly. One person with whom he interacts extensively is the teacher. We prepared a leaflet entitled "The Work of the Teacher." This was a simplified discussion contrasting the conception of the teacher as "someone whose main job is to check up on you" with the conception of "a guide to help you learn." This material was designed to be read by the teacher to the class and discussed with them. The logical implications of the "guide to help you" concept are described, including what alternatives are available to the child and their respective probable consequences when he finds his learning experiences not challenging. Included also is a discussion of how it may help the teacher to "tell her when something is worrying you."

In this connection it is important to note that how the teacher handles the day-to-day social situations that arise in the classroom and on the playground, the extent to which the teacher seeks to know the child's ambitions, concerns, and abilities and makes use of this information in planning his program of work and understanding his behavior before dealing with it are examples of additional experiences that affect the growth of a causal orientation. If the teacher deals with the daily situations in an arbitrary way without attempting to understand the forces involved, the child will witness a demonstration of a non-causal approach. This demonstration is comparable to demonstrations in any subject matter area in the sense that the child learns from it. If the demonstration is that of a non-causal approach it will tend to teach the child to do likewise. On the other hand, if the teacher tries to understand before deciding, his behavior will demonstrate a more causal approach.

We have put considerable emphasis on educating the teacher to live the causal approach in the classroom. Developing a causal orientation in the pupil requires attention to both cognitive and emotional aspects. Observing and interacting with a teacher who deals with daily classroom situations in an understanding way provides both an intellectual and emotional experience. It "feels good" to experience an interaction with a teacher whom the pupil feels confident will try to understand.

At the secondary level, as well as at the elementary level, the social science area—including such divisions as civics, history, geography, government, and economics—can be based on a study of the forces operating in the behavior of the people involved. The basic problem of building communities and governments that help people meet the motivating forces stirring in the human personality can be a continuing theme.

The study of English literature can be made an adventure in gaining more insight into the feelings and other factors that operate in human strivings. Carefully selected material can also help to stimulate the process of thinking of a variety of alternatives in working out social situations, considering the probable effects of each and using these data to plan a course of action.

As the student acquires an understanding and appreciation of factors affecting behavior he can learn to apply this knowledge to the guidance of his *own* growth. By the time he reaches the end of the secondary period, he can have had considerable practice in becoming a self-guiding individual. We have developed various kinds of material and learning exercises to facilitate his growth in this dimension.

The student can learn to make extended applications of the casual approach in developing his plans for dating, marriage, and family life. A background in causal thinking can be laid in the early years. This foundation can then be used in preparation for marriage, parenthood and the responsibilities of maturity.

At the secondary level also, each instructor, whether he teaches social studies, English, mathematics, science, or any other subject, can practice the causal orientation in the daily interaction in the classroom and thus provide a demonstration from which the student learns.

It is not only social science and English that play a part. An important aspect of a causal orientation toward human behavior is the ability to apply the elements of probability thinking in behavior situations. We are all aware that the dynamics underlying a given incident of behavior may be quite complex and that one's knowledge of the underlying factors in a given situation is often quite incomplete. When one has to make a decision in a situation in which one's knowledge of the forces operating is incomplete the logical procedure is to gather as much data as one can, put the estimate in probability terms and proceed with the decision. There is a recognition that there is a margin of error in one's estimate as to the best course of action. Furthermore, one is alert to any additional data that may become available as one proceeds and one tries to incorporate into a revised estimate any additional data as it becomes available.

Thus, facility in using probability thinking in everyday situations is an important item in applying knowledge of behavior dynamics in daily social interactions.

We have evidence (Ojemann, Maxey, & Snider, 1965a, 1965b) that we can devise experiences which can help the child in the elementary school develop a beginning ability to think in probability terms and that this increases his ability to deal with such problems as ambiguous situations and "trial and error" situations. The ability to think in probability terms is an important ingredient in a causal orientation toward the social environment. We can see a role for such subjects as mathematics, social science and natural science in developing this way of thinking.

EFFECTS OF TEACHING PSYCHOLOGICAL CONCEPTS

There are two aspects to the question, what are the effects of teaching psychological concepts as an integral part of the curriculum? Is such teaching effective in increasing the understanding and appreciation of the dynamics of behavior? If so, what is the effect on the child's development of such an increase in causal orientation?

A study by Ojemann *et al.* (1955) provides data on the first point. This investigation was conducted at the fourth-, fifth-, and sixth-grade levels in a public school in a community of 80,000. There were 19 subjects in each of the four experimental classes (one fourth-grade, one fifth-grade, and two sixth-grade groups) and 25 in each of the corresponding control classes. A variance analysis of IQ scores at the beginning of the investigation indicated no significant differences among the experimental and control classes in this dimension.

A causal test (CT) was developed which consisted of eight descriptions of behavior, each followed by a series of true-false items. The test attempted to tap the child's awareness of the complex and dynamic nature of human behavior. It has a Kuder-Richardson reliability of .63 and correlates $-.36$ with intelligence. The test is scored inversely; that is, the lower the score, the more causally oriented the subject.

An analysis of the pre- and post-test scores of both experimental and control groups indicated that the experimental groups made significant changes in their understanding of the dynamics of behavior as measured by this test.

A study by Snider (1957) indicated that children who at the beginning of the program scored in the lower third of the range of scores on a security-insecurity test devised by Kooker (1951) gained as much in causal orientation as those in upper third of initial security-insecurity scores. In other words, the children giving many behavioral evidences of insecurity gained as much as those who gave few such indications. Snider used six classes, two at the fourth-grade level, one at the fifth, and three at the sixth.

What is the effect when the understanding of behavior dynamics is extended in this way? The study by Ojemann and others cited previously included, in addition to the causal test, a test of readiness to use immediate punitiveness in dealing with daily situations (PST or Problem Situation Test). This is a 22-item multiple-choice test in which the subject is faced with a number of behavior situations and six possible ways of dealing with each situation, three punitive and three nonpunitive. The score is the number of punitive responses. It has a test-retest correlation of .71 and correlates with intelligence $-.29$ at the fifth-grade level. The results showed a significant difference between the experimental and control groups on this test. The more causal subjects were less ready to use immediately punitive methods than the control subjects.

Stiles (1950) had shown in an earlier study, which investigated changes in methods used by fourth-, fifth-, and sixth-grade children in handling daily behavior situations brought up for consideration in the "room council," that the causal learning program produced a significant change in the direction of decreased punitiveness and increased concern for understanding before deciding.

Levitt (1955b) has shown in an analysis of data from 278 subjects that there is a significant relationship between causality and the tendency to be judgmentally punitive. The correlations between the two sets of scores with IQ held constant varied from .37 to .51, all significant at the 1 per cent level of confidence.

A further study by Levitt (1955a), provided data comparing causally trained and control groups at the fourth-, fifth-, and sixth-grade levels on the Children's Anti-Democratic Attitude Scale (CADS). This scale had been shown by Gough and others (1950) to be related to children's ethnic attitudes. The causally trained groups studied by Levitt showed significantly lower authoritarian scores at all three grade levels when compared with the control groups.

A study by Muuss (1960b) of fifth- and sixth-grade children reported significant differences on the Kooker Security-Insecurity Scale between high causally oriented and low causally oriented subjects. The Kooker scores in Muuss' study were obtained by trained observers who were not the subjects' teachers and who had nothing to do with the preparation of teaching material or other aspects of the experimental program.

Muuss also found significant differences in scores on the Children's Manifest Anxiety Scale at both the fifth- and sixth-grade levels. The Childen's Manifest Anxiety Scale has a built-in "lie scale" consisting of 11 items. The high and low causality subjects also differed significantly on this test.

In the previously mentioned study by Muuss (1960b), using a sequence of unfinished pictures, it was demonstrated that high causally oriented subjects evidenced more tolerance toward ambiguous stimuli. The high causality child might make a guess on the basis of partial information, but he was more inclined to do so in terms of probability and was more aware of the tentative nature of the response than the low causality subject. Muuss also found that high causality subjects were more likely to reject verbal suggestions indicative of intolerance of ambiguity.

In a further study by Muuss (1960a) 25 subjects who had participated in the causal learning program for two years were matched individually with 25 subjects who had been in the program for one year and with 25 subjects from control group on IQ, sex, and grade. The subjects who had been in the program for two years showed a significant gain over the one-year subjects on the PST, which, it will be recalled, is a measure of tendency to use immediate punitiveness; on the Children's Anti-Democratic Scale and on the certainty scores of the test for intolerance of ambiguity.

Bruce (1958) reported that sixth grade pupils with high self-ideal discrepancy scores who had been in the causally oriented program for two years evidenced significantly less manifest anxiety on the Children's Manifest Anxiety Scale than control subjects with equally high self-ideal discrepancy scores. In other words, it appeared that the usual finding that high self-ideal discrepancy scores are associated with high manifest anxiety scores has to be modified. It appears to hold only for subjects low in causal orientation. A growth in causal orientation may change this relationship.

A study of the child's conception of the teacher (Ojemann and Snider, 1963) compared the growth of fourth- and fifth-grade pupils in matched experimental and control groups using a test designed to measure four aspects of the child's conception of the teacher. The four aspects included:

1. The child's conception of the role a teacher is expected to play.
2. The child's conception as to the nature of the teacher's behavior, i.e., does he think of the teacher's behavior in arbitrary judgments, or non-causal terms, or does he recognize the possibility of many factors underlying the teacher's behavior?
3. The child's idea as to the degree of causality a teacher is expected to show toward pupils (and other school personnel).
4. The child's confidence that the teacher will proceed causally in interactions with others, including the child himself.

A significant difference between the E and C groups in scores on the total test was obtained at both the fourth- and fifth-grade levels.

Thus, there is experimental evidence which suggests that pupils who have increased their understanding and appreciation of the dynamics of behavior tend to be less ready to use immediately arbitrary punitive measures, show less anti-democratic attitudes, show less manifest anxiety and observational evidences of insecurity and more tolerance of ambiguity.

SIGNIFICANCE OF THE FINDINGS

It appears from the data reported above that it is possible to incorporate in a genuinely functional way important psychological concepts throughout the school curriculum and that the teaching of these concepts can be effective. It also appears that the extension of the child's understanding and appreciation of the dynamics of behavior is accompanied by significant changes in such dimensions as manifest anxiety, tendency to immediate arbitrary punitiveness, anti-democratic tendencies, conception of the teacher and tolerance of ambiguity.

These data suggest that it is not necessary to allow the future parent or teacher or employer to develop the arbitrary non-causal way of thinking in childhood and then attempt to change this way of thinking after the individual has arrived at the adult years. A more logical arrangement is to develop a foundation in the causal approach to behavior in all children beginning in the early years. Then, as the child approaches adulthood, he can build on this foundation and make the specialized applications to the study of marriage and family relationships, teacher-child relationships, employer-employee relationships, doctor-patient relationships, and many others.

In addition to laying this foundation for future development of the child, there is, as we have seen, evidence that this orientation helps a child during his childhood years to deal with daily situations in less authoritarian and less anxiety-producing ways. He seems to be more at home in his social environment and able to deal with it more logically and with more confidence.

Thus, there are two significant contributions of an increased understanding and appreciation of the dynamics of behavior: it helps the child now and it provides a needed foundation for later development.

REFERENCES

Bruce, P. Relationship of self-acceptance of other variables with sixth grade children oriented in self-understanding. *J. educ. Psychol.*, 1958, 49, 229.

Gough, H. G. *et al.* Children's ethnic attitudes: I. Relationship to certain personality factors. *Child Develpm.*, 1950, 21, 83.

Kooker, E. W. An investigation of security, insecurity, achievement and boredom in elementary school children. Unpublished doctoral dissertation, State University of Iowa, 1951.

Levitt, E. E. Effect of a causal teacher-training program on authoritarianism and responsibility in grade school children. *Psychol. Rep.*, 1955a, 1, 449.

Levitt, E. E. Punitiveness and causality in grade school children. *J. educ. Psychol.*, 1955b, 46, 494.

Muuss, R. E. The effects of a one- and two-year causal-learning program. *J. Pers.* 1960a, 28, 479–491.

Muuss, R. E. The relationship between causal orientation, anxiety, and insecurity in elementary school children. *J. educ. Psychol.* 1960b. 51, 122–129.

Ojemann, R. H., Maxey, E. J., & Snider, B. C. F. Effects of guided learning experiences in developing probability concepts at the fifth grade level. *Percept. Mot. Skills*, 1965a, 21, 415–427.

Ojemann, R. H., Maxey, E. J., & Snider, B. C. F. The effect of a program of guided learning experiences in developing probability concepts at the third grade level. *J. exp. Educ.* 1965b, 33, 321–330.

Ojemann, R. H., *et al.* The effects of a causal teacher-training program and certain curricular changes on grade school children. *J. exp. Educ.* 1955, 24, 95–114.

Ojemann, R. H., & Snider, B. C. F. The development of the child's conception of the teacher. *J. exp. Educ.*, 1963, 32, 73–80.

Ojemann, R. H. & Snider, B. C. F. The effect of a teaching program in behavioral science on changes in causal behavior scores. *J. educ. Res.*, 1964, 57, 255–260.

Prescott, D. A. *The child in the educative process.* New York: McGraw-Hill, 1957.

Snider, B. C. F. Relation of growth in causal orientation to insecurity in elementary school children. *Psychol. Rep.*, 1957, 3, 631.

Spock, B. Values and limits of parent education, in *Communication in parent education: proceedings of the ninth annual institute of workers in parent education.* New York: Child Study Association of America, 1955.

Stiles, F. S. Developing an understanding of human behavior at the elementary school level. *J. educ. Res.*, 1950, 43, 516–524.

Traxler, A. E. *Techniques of guidance.* New York: Harper, 1957.

47.   Children's Literature Can Affect Coping Behavior

Patricia Jean Cianciolo

Bibliotherapy is one means by which the teachers can give children an assist toward better mental health. Books, if carefully selected to suit the child's developmental level and cultural background, can provide not only an outlet for psychological tensions but also offer the student insight into his behavior. This selection by Patricia Jean Cianciolo includes reports of research as well as a bibliography on children's literature that could be used for therapeutic or preventive purposes.

Regardless of when children grow up they have numerous problems to cope with in the process; they must learn to identify, and then take directly into account and do something about the presence of such barriers as alienation, cultural pluralism and pressures. The gratification children get from their areas of security helps them handle anxieties that face them, helps them through the ups and downs of development (Murphy, 1956). For each child there exists different states of temporary tensions, different degrees of attraction or repulsion between specific subjects, people or situations (Murphy, 1956).

Some of the normal, expectable sources of stress for children growing up stem from the things that are done to them or happen to them, others arise within them. Such things as operations, childhood diseases, the uprooting from friends and a familiar neighborhood, war anxieties, separations from parents and tensions between parents constitute things that happen or are done to the child. Some of the problems that may arise chiefly within the child constitute the following—discrepancies between the child's abilities and his goals, instabilities related to defects in the physical or psychological equipment of the child or feelings of being different

Personnel and Guidance Journal, May 1965, 897–903. Reprinted with the permission of the publisher and author.

from brothers and sisters or other children who may seem to receive more attention, love, or approval (Murphy, 1957).

INTERACTION BETWEEN THE READER AND LITERATURE

The story and pictures of a book might be the source of psychological relief from the various pressures and concerns cited above. In general, a teacher or counselor may use bibliotherapy, a process of dynamic interaction between the personality of the reader and literature (Russell & Schrodes, 1950), in one of two ways. First, he may attempt to solve a child's actual and existing emotional problems and pressures by bringing him a similar experience vicariously through books. Through recognition of a problem and its solution in literature the individual gains new insights into his own problem and presumably is then able to take a step toward solving it. Second, the teacher or counselor may use literature for preventive bibliotherapy. This technique involves the theory that a child is able to make a satisfactory adjustment when a problem eventually arises in his own life because he met one similar to that which was depicted in the literature that he read in the past. This latter defined technique is analogous to that of an inoculation to prevent the contagious disease. "A little vicarious injection of experience with a problem in a book is to prevent a hard case of this same kind of experience in the young reader's development" (Darling, 1962, p. 293).

More specifically, bibliotherapy can help the individual in a variety of ways. The process may be used to help the reader (1) to acquire information and knowledge about the psychology and physiology of human behavior, (2) to live up to the injunction "know thyself," (3) to become extroverted and find interest in something outside himself, (4) to effect a controlled relief of unconscious difficulties, (5) to use the opportunity for identification and compensation, and (6) to clarify difficulties and to acquire insight into his own behavior.

The process by which the reading of a book affects a child should not be oversimplified, for the child is not quite so plastic a creature that he is easily changed by what he reads. Furthermore, the numerous variations and the factor of unexpectedness which is characteristic of human relationships prevents the categorizing of children as specific psychological types. The therapeutic effect that results from the process of dynamic interaction between the personality of the reader and literature is usually theorized in terms of *identification, catharsis* and *insight. Identification,* or the act of affiliating some real or fictional character in literature with oneself or associates, is an almost universal experience of young readers. The *cathartic effect* occurs as the reader achieves identification with the character who works through his problem and releases his emotional tension. The book's solving of the emotional situation provides a purge for the emotions of the reader. When the reader realizes his identification with the book character he is able to see the motivation of his own behavior more clearly. Purged of some of his own emotional tension the way is cleared to make a more intellectual approach to his problem. Thus, there is an integration of intellectual perception and emotional drive and the final component of the process of bibliotherapy, namely, *insight,* is achieved.

To a limited degree bibliotherapy is an activity that lies within the province of every teacher working with children who are not seriously maladjusted and in need of clinical treatment. Since one recognized objective of the elementary school program is to contribute to the provision of the basic needs of the learner it appears logical that teachers would make use of this technique. Studies have shown that through experiences in which literature is involved children can be helped to solve the developmental problems which they face.

SELECTING AND USING BOOKS TO AFFECT COPING BEHAVIOR

In advocating the use of biblotherapy the writer does not mean to imply that there should be a return to the didactic literature that characterized the fiction of a century ago. Books that are to be used to change an attitude or aid in understanding other people should exemplify good literature. The characters of the books should be lifelike and complete—yet individual entities. Regional, racial, religious or nationality groups should be pictured in an atmosphere which is accurate, showing the traditions and customs and the origination of each. Fiction, biography, drama, and poetry can effectively contribute to the social education of the readers.

Learning activities in which trade books are used to foster cosmopolitan sensitivity and growth in human understanding may be used in integrated activities of social studies units and they may be used with individuals in personal reading activities. The teacher or librarian desiring to offer learning experiences for the purpose of socializing the child should be diplomatic in offering him these books. Too, using books in this manner often calls for a discussion or other interpretative activity to follow-up the reading itself. If there is not an opportunity for cooperative sharing of a book, at least the readers should be encouraged to mull over, interpret, compare, and contrast the situations depicted.

It was reported that teachers have discovered during action research in their classrooms that discussion has a cumulative effect on the building of concepts and the extending of sensitivity; these discussions should have a sequence of questions or considerations. Heaton and Lewis provided steps for the sequence and stated that these steps had important psychological implications. There should be a retelling of what occurred in the story itself and the incidents, feelings, and relationships that are relevant to human relationships should be highlighted. There should occur a probing into what happened in feeling, in shift of relationship and change of behavior in order to make more vivid the identification with the feelings of the book characters. There should occur a stimulation to identify similar incidents relative to the experience of the students or from other stories in order to lend validity to the concept that literature can extend experience. The reader should be provided an opportunity to explore the consequences of certain behaviors or feelings, thus he can recapitulate what happened in a specific situation as a result of some specific behavior or consequences. There should be an opportunity to arrive at a conclusion or generalization about the consequences of certain behaviors or feelings in order to determine whether or not certain situations, behaviors, or feelings encourage improved human relationships and happiness. The reader is also encouraged to determine the desirability or helpfulness of several alternatives (Heaton & Lewis, 1955).

The very nature of some of the problems and pressures of the children and about which the books pertain makes a direct approach to the children difficult; older children are less likely to confide their problems as freely as younger children. This approach calls for a teacher who is patient and friendly and does not pry. She must be informed about the numerous activities and devices that help the readers to identify themselves with the characters in the books.

Kircher was one of the first to study carefully the effectiveness of trade books as an intrinsic aid in treating the child with a social or an emotional problem. The author reported that the children with whom she worked insisted on making their own selection of books; they often refused any book the therapist offered. She described some of the techniques a teacher might use to guide a child into selecting a book that had potential in helping the reader understand himself or others better (Kircher, 1945).

Except for the Kircher study there have been literally few solid studies about activities in which books are used in this manner. There have been a few master's studies done in connection with graduate work in library science; a few action research projects that have been conducted by classroom teachers were reported in the professional periodicals.

The Fischer study resulted in a bibliography of available literature that was deemed useful in the solution of emotional problems. Suggestions as to how teachers and librarians might use each of the books were also presented. The titles were classified in relation to the major emotional problems faced by children today and an approximate reading level was assigned to each book. The bibliography was sufficiently extensive in terms of number and classification to permit self-selection by children interested in reading about these problems (Fischer, 1956). Fischer's bibliography would make an excellent supplement to the one developed by Kircher some 11 years earlier.

Biair analyzed recommended books for children in terms of one criterion; namely, the teacher or librarian, sensitive to the distributed behavior characteristics of the preadolescent developmental stage, should use realistic literature in fiction form so that the child can vicariously meet others who share his unexpressed problems and gain an insight into how these problems might be solved. The factors that determined suitability of the books that were included as appropriate reading material for nine-, ten-, and eleven-year-old children were similar to those presented by Kircher and the other authors who have written about this kind of activity with books. They include the following: The books should be written on the child's independent reading level. The author should recognize characteristics of the children that are in keeping with research and he should deal with problems in a manner that can be supported by research. The problem faced by the book character should be brought out as a main issue and it should be presented without moralizing. The book should be about the modern child or it should be so universal in appeal that the difference in time or locale is of little importance (Biair, 1951).

There are several other studies, the findings of which serve to throw some light on the effects of learning activities in which trade books were involved for the purpose of influencing behavioral change. Comer read stories from carefully selected books to determine whether or not literature would help children to get to problems that needed discussing. This study involved group procedures and involved reading about problems common to many of the children in the class. The chief selection aid for appropriate titles was *Reading Ladders for Human Relations,* an extensive bibliography of trade books that can be used in learning activities designed to influence changed behavior (Comer, 1959).

Boone carried out a program on extending children's experience through literature under the theme of "Family Living—the Responsibilities of the Members to Each Other and the Individual Member to Himself." *Reading Ladders* was used to select books for this study, also. Some elaboration, discussions, and summaries of the book content were made in order to stimulate interest in the various titles. Discussions followed the reading of the books and the children were encouraged to relate these situations to their personal experiences. Role-playing techniques were used as were essays on open-ended questions. Children were also asked to write stories about pictures which depicted various human relations situations. Some change in behavior was noticed. This change was slow but continuous; the children developed a sensitive reading interest (Boone, 1959).

Timm reported that in her bibliotherapy program she made use of story hours, dramatizations with puppets, book displays; discussions about books, authors and illustrators; and guided "free" reading. The realistic and psychological novels that were involved in these learning activities were about economic problems, social relationships of individuals, family conflicts, and development of personality and character. Timm stated that the chief value of using books of this kind with the types of activities she chose was that the child could find a frankness in them that he was not likely to get from his family and acquaintances (Timm, 1959).

In an important study, the staff of the Materials Center of the University of Chicago sought to determine whether or not the reading of certain books and identification with characters can have a deep-seated effect on the child. Fifty of the most popular books of fiction were selected for use in this study; 25 of the books were written for the later childhood age group and 25 were for the early adolescent age group. The books were selected because they seemed to reflect the current patterns of social experiences, inter-personal relations, and problems of childhood and youth. In studying the effects of books on youth, three techniques were employed, namely, the focused interview, a story projective technique, and a sociometric technique. With each technique the reader was expected to reveal his identification with or rejection of the characters in the book together with the negative or positive qualities that he attributed to these characters. The directions of the findings were reported in *Youth, Communications and Libraries* (Brooks, 1959) and are as follows. The effects of the developmental values in a book are of a contributory sort; they will not produce dynamic changes but they do contribute to these changes. The vicarious experiences gleaned from reading are part of an overall pattern of forces, but to be effective the experiences or the values in the books must be appropriate to the developmental level of the reader. Children from different socio-economic levels and cultural groups responded to different values. Responses varied from individual to individual also, and depended on the needs and receptivity of each child.

The implications of these findings are numerous, but there are two that are most significant and should be kept in mind by teachers who are using books in learning activities designed to change social and emotional behavior. One, children's literature has a place in changing behavior but the books should be carefully chosen for content and style. Two, reading of the books should be accompanied by follow-up activities if a significant amount of change is to occur. The statement below defines more clearly aspects of this implication.

> The identification of developmental values in children's literature is an adult process in which children rarely play a conscious part either in their selection of what they read or in their post-reading discussions. Children are reading because of interest factors and not "to be developed." The elements that contribute to a good story and to the book as a creative literary piece still remain among the major factors in our appraisal of books for children. Without them the developmental values of books would exist in a vacuum completely removed from the "child world" in which we wish to have them play their part (Brooks, 1949, pp. 60–61).

This statement would lend support to the emphasis on follow-up activities for this kind of reading. This same emphasis was apparent in the reports by Heaton and Lewis and Fischer. Because the primary objective of these activities is to develop a sensitivity to human relations, the trade books that were used with these activities were chosen primarily for their pertinent content. By and large, however, the selection of books that the writers listed in their reports did not appear to be inferior didactic literature. Indeed some had titles of very excellent books. Nonetheless, if the teacher or librarian becomes too preoccupied with selecting books in relation to the topic and ignores the literary quality her ultimate goal of changing behavior through the use of trade books is unlikely to materialize. It was the investigator's experience when reviewing books for the latest edition of *Reading Ladders for Human Relations* (Crosby, 1963) that many of the books that were read for possible listing in this annotated selection aid could not be used. Although the topics of the books were appropriate for one or the other "Ladder Themes" it was decided that little or nothing would be accomplished by reading them because of the inferior literary quality.

BOOKS THAT AFFECT COPING BEHAVIOR

The investigator has identified a sampling of recent publications in the field of children's literature that might be used to affect coping behavior. These books could be used to enable the reader to recognize his own problems and pressures, find possible solutions for them; if not a solution then a realistic, wholesome view of these problems. These books might also be the source of understanding the behavior of others.

BIBLIOGRAPHY

Abaunza, Virginia. *Sundays from two to six.* Indianapolis: Bobbs-Merrill Co., 1956 (divorce), 13–16 years.

Apsler, Alfred. *Northwest pioneer.* New York: Farrar, Straus & Cudahy, Inc., 1960 (minority religious group—Jewish), 9–13 years.

Armer, Alberta. *Screwball.* Cleveland, Ohio: World Publishing Co., 1963 (family relationships, mobility), 9–14 years.

Arora, Shirley. *What then, Raman?* Chicago: Follett Publishing Co., 1960 (value of ed., family relationships, responsibility, conflict between cultures), 10–14 years.

Benedict, Steve. *The little house on wheels.* Tell-Well Press, 1953 (mobility), 6–8 years.

Biesterveld, Betty. *Run, Reddy, run.* New York: Thomas Nelson & Sons, 1962 (mobility), 9–13 years.

Brenner, Barbara. *Barto takes the subway.* New York: Alfred A. Knopf, Inc., 1961 (language barrier, mobility), 6–8 years.

Brooks, Gwendolyn. *Bronzville boys and girls.* New York: Harper and Bros., 1956 (poetry—all aspects of growing up), 7–12 years.

Buck, Pearl S. *The beech tree.* New York: John Day Co., Inc., 1955 (family relationships, death, conflict between generations), 9–13 years.

Buckley, Helen. *Grandfather and I.* New York: Lothrop, Lee & Shepard Co., Inc. 1959 (differences between generations), 5–8 years.

Buckley, Helen. *Grandmother and I.* New York: Lothrop, Lee & Shepard Co., Inc., 1961 (differences between generations), 5–8 years.

Buckley, Helen. *My sister and I.* New York: Lothrop, Lee & Shepard Co., Inc., 1964 (family relationships), 5–8 years.

Bulla, Clyde Robert. *Indian hill.* New York: Thomas Y. Crowell Co., 1963 (conflict between cultures and generations, modern American Indian), 10–14 years.

Butterworth, Oliver. *The trouble with Jenny's ear.* Boston: Atlantic, Little, Brown & Co., 1960 (family relationships), 8–12 years.

Calhoun, Mary. *Honestly, Katie John!* New York: Harper and Row, 1963 (sex role), 8–14 years.

Carroll, Ruth & Latrobe. *Tough enough and sassy.* New York: Henry Z. Walck, Inc., 1958 (family relationships, economic security), 7–9 years.

Clark, Billy. *River boy.* New York: G. P. Putnam's Sons, 1958 (commitment to change), 9–13 years.

Clayton, Barbara. *Tomboy.* New York: Funk and Wagnalls Co., Inc., 1961 (sex role), 13–16 years.

Cleary, Beverly. *Beezus and Ramona.* New York: William Morrow & Co., Inc., 1955 (family relationships), 8–12 years.

Cloutier, Helen. *The many names of Lee Lu.* Chicago: Albert Whitman & Co., 1960 (minority race—Chinese, need to belong), 6–8 years.

Davis, Clyde B. *The newcomer.* Philadelphia: J. B. Lippincott Co., 1954 (mobility, minority race—Negro), 15–18 years.

DeJong Meindert. *The house of sixty fathers.* New York: Harper & Bros., 1956 (wartime pressures and separation from family), 10–13 years.

DeLeeuw, Adele. *The barred road.* New York: The Macmillan Co., 1954 (minority race—Negro), 10–16 years.

Duncan, Lois. *The littlest one in the family.* New York: Dodd, Mead & Co., Inc., 1960 (family relationships), 4–8 years.

Enright, Elizabeth. *The Saturday's.* New York: Harcourt, Brace & Co., Inc., 1941 (family relationships, one parent), 9–12 years.

Estes, Eleanor. *The hundred dresses.* New York: Harcourt, Brace & Co., Inc., 1944 (minority nationality—Polish, need to belong, economic security), 9–11 years.

Estes, Eleanor. *A little oven.* New York: Harcourt, Brace & Co., Inc., 1955 (family relationships), 5–8 years.

Felt, Sue. *Hello-goodbye*. New York: Doubleday & Co., Inc., 1960 (mobility-need to belong), 6–8 years.

Fletcher, David. *The king's goblet*. New York: Pantheon Books, Inc., 1962 (peer pressure, set of values), 13–16 years.

Foster, Genevieve. *Teddy Roosevelt*. New York: Charles Scribner's Sons, 1954 (peer relationships, fears, physical problems), 9–11 years.

Friedman, Frieda. *The janitor's girl*. New York: William Morrow & Co., Inc., 1956 (family relationships, social status), 9–12 years.

Garthwaite, Marion. *Shaken days*. New York: Julian Messner, Inc., 1952 (orphaned), 9–13 years.

Gates, Doris. *Blue willow*. New York: Viking Press, Inc., 1941 (mobility), 10–16 years.

Gebhardt, Hertha von. *The girl from no where*. New York: Criterion Books, Inc., 1959 (separation from parent, need to belong), 9–12 years.

Godden, Rumer G. *The fairy doll*. New York: Viking Press, Inc., 1956 (family relationships), 7–10 years.

Govan, Christine. *Willow Landing*. Cleveland: World Publishing Co., 1961 (sex role), 13–16 years.

Graham, Lorenz. *South Town*. Chicago: Follett Publishing Co., 1958 (desegregation, family relationships), 12–16 years.

Gruenberg, Sidonie M. *The wonderful story of how you were born*. New York: Doubleday & Co., Inc. (sex education), 6–12 years.

Haywood, Carolyn. *Here's a penny*. New York: Harcourt, Brace & Co., Inc., 1944 (adoption), 7–9 years.

Hoban, Russell. *Bedtime for Francis*. New York: Harper & Row, 1960 (family relationships), 6–8 years.

Hoban, Russell. *A baby sister for Francis*. New York: Harper & Row, 1964 (family relationships), 6–8 years.

Juline, Ruth Bishop. *A place for Johnny Bill*. Philadelphia: Westminster Press, 1961 (mobility), 9–13 years.

Justus, May. *New boy in school*. New York: Hastings House, 1963 (integration of minority racial group—Negro), 8–14 years.

Knight, Ruth Adams. *First the lightning*. New York: Doubleday & Co., Inc., 1955 (peer pressure, set of values), 13–16 years.

Krumgold, Joseph. *Onion John*. New York: Thomas Y. Crowell Co., 1959 (commitment to change), 12–16 years.

Latham, Jean Lee. *Carry on Mr. Bowditch*. Boston: Houghton Mifflin Co., 1955 (value of education, sense of responsibility), 11–14 years.

Lattimore, Eleanor F. *Molly in the middle*. New York: William Morrow & Co., Inc. 1956 (family relationships), 7–9 years.

L'Engle, Madeline. *Meet the Austins*. New York: Vanguard Press, 1959 (family relationships), 11–14 years.

Lenski, Lois. *Judy's journey*. Philadelphia: J. B. Lippincott Co., 1947 (economic security—mobility), 9–11 years.

Lenski, Lois. *Shoo fly girl*. Philadelphia: J. B. Lippincott Co., 1963 (minority religious group: Amish), 8–12 years.

Lenski, Lois. *Strawberry girl*. Philadelphia: J. B. Lippincott Co., 1945 (family relationships and responsibility, economic security), 9–11 years.

Lewiton, Mina. *Candita's choice*. New York: Harper & Bros., 1959 (language barriers), 9–13 years.

Lindgren, Astrid. *The children on Troublemaker Street*. New York: The Macmillan Co., 1964 (sibling relationships; swearing), 7–11 years.

Lionni, Leo. *Little Blue and Little Yellow*. Oblensky, 1959 (feeling of rejection), 4–6 years.

Martin, Patricia Miles. *The pointed brush*. New York: Lothrop, Lee & Shephard Co., Inc., 1959 (minority racial group—Chinese; value of education), 5–8 years.

McCloskey, Robert. *One morning in Maine*. New York: Viking Press, Inc., 1952 (family relationships), 5–7 years.

Means, Florence Co. *The moved outers.* Boston: Houghton Mifflin Co., 1945 (minority race—Japanese), 13–16 years.

Neville, Emily. *It's like this, Cat!* New York: Harper & Row, 1963 (family and peer relationships), 9–14 years.

Olson, Gene. *Tin goose.* Philadelphia: Westminster Press, 1962 (conflict between generations), 13–16 years.

Raftery, Gerald. *Twenty-dollar horse.* New York: Julian Messner, Inc., 1955 (minority race—Negro), 9–13 years.

Randall, Blossom. *Fun for Chris.* Chicago: Albert Whitman & Co., 1956 (racial differences), 4–7 years.

Rutgers, vander Loeff, Anna. *Oregon at last.* New York: William Morrow & Co. (sibling relationships, responsibility), 10–16 years, 1962.

Schlein, Miriam. *Laurie's new brother.* New York: Abelard-Schumann, Ltd., 1961 (family relationships), 6–8 years.

Selz, Irma. *Katy be good.* New York: Lothrop & Lee & Shepard Co., Inc., 1962 (minority, religious group—Amish), 5–8 years.

Selz, Irma. *Wonderful nice.* New York: Lothrop, Lee & Shepard Co., Inc., 1960 (minority religious group—Amish), 5–8 years.

Seredy, Kate. *A tree for Peter.* New York: Viking Press, Inc., 1941 (economic security), 9–12 years.

Sheburne, Zoa. *Jennifer.* New York: William Morrow & Co., Inc., 1959 (alcoholism), 13–17 years.

Sheburne, Zoa. *Stranger in the house.* New York: William Morrow & Co., Inc., 1963 (mental illness), 13–17 years.

Shotwell, Louisa R. *Roosevelt Grady.* Cleveland: World Publishing Co., 1963 (mobility), 9–12 years.

Sorensen, Virginia. *Plain girl.* New York: Harcourt, Brace & Co., 1955 (minority religious group—Mennonite), 9–11 years.

Sorensen, Virginia. *Miracles on Maple Hill.* New York: Harcourt, Brace & Co., Inc., 1956 (family relationships, emotional disturbance), 10–12 years.

Steele, William O. *The perilous road.* New York: Harcourt, Brace & Co., Inc., 1959 (conflict in political values, family relationships), 10–13 years.

Sterling, Dorothy. *Mary Jane.* New York: Doubleday & Co., Inc., 1959 (desegregation), 10–14 years.

Stinetorf, Louise A. *Musa, the Shoemaker.* Philadelphia: J. B. Lippincott Co., 1959 (physical handicap), 9–12 years.

Stolz, Mary. *Belling the tiger.* New York: Harper & Bros., 1961 (leadership of group activities), 8–10 years.

Stuart, Jesse. *The beatinest boy.* New York: McGraw-Hill Book Co., 1953 (relationships between generations, orphaned), 9–11 years.

Summers, James L. *Off the beam.* Philadelphia: Westminster Press, 1955 (gang pressures, development of sense of values), 13–16 years.

Udry, Janice May. *Let's be enemies.* New York: Harper & Bros., 1961 (peer relationships), 4–6 years.

Vance, Marguerite. *Windows for Rosemary.* New York: E. P. Dutton & Co., 1956 (physical handicap), 9–11 years.

Waltrip, Lela & Rufus. *The quiet boy.* New York: Longmans, Green & Co., Inc., 1961 (conflict of generations and culture patterns, value of education, modern American Indian), 9–14 years.

Waltrip, Lela & Rufus. *White harvest.* New York: Longmans, Green & Co., Inc., 1960 (mobility), 9–13 years.

Wier, Ester. *The loner.* New York: David McKay Co., Inc., 1963 (mobility, need for love and acceptance), 12–16 years.

Wojciechowska, Maria. *Shadow of a bull.* New York: Atheneum Publishers, 1964 (overcoming fears, selecting a vocation), 11–14 years.

Wooley, Catherine. *A room for Cathy.* New York: William R. Morrow & Co., Inc., 1956 (family life, economic security), 9–12 years.

Yashima, Taro. *Crow boy.* New York: Viking Press, Inc., 1955 (introverted, talented boy), 6–8 years.

Yashima, Taro. *The golden footprints*. Cleveland: World Publishing Co., 1960 (family relationships, meaning of freedom), 8–11 years.
Zolotow, Charlotte. *Big brother*. New York: Harper & Bros., 1960 (family relationships), 4–6 years.

REFERENCES

Blair, Virginia B. Directed reading through the library for improving the social adjustment of older children. Unpublished master's thesis, School of Library Science, Texas State College for Women, 1951.
Boone, Robert. Using literature to extend children's experiences. *Element. English*, May, 1959, 36, 314–318.
Brooks, Alice. Developmental values in books. In *Youth, communications and libraries*, papers presented before the Library Institute at the University of Chicago, August 11–16, 1947. Chicago: American Library Association, 1949.
Comer, Dorothea. Using literature to extend children's experiences. *Element. English*, January, 1959, 36, 28–34.
Crosby, Muriel (Ed.). *Reading ladders for human relations*. Fourth edition. Washington, D. C.: American Council on Education, 1963.
Darling, Robert L. Mental hygiene and books: bibliotherapy as used with children and adolescents. In Trinkner, Charles L. (Ed.), *Better libraries make better schools*. Hamden, Conn.: Shoe String Press, 1962.
Fischer, Laurel J. Emotional needs of children as a basis for reading guidance. Unpublished master's thesis, Graduate Library School, Kent State Univ., 1956.
Heaton, Margaret M., & Lewis, Helen B. *Reading ladders for human relations*. Third edition, revised. Washington, D. C.: American Council on Education, 1955.
Kircher, Clara J. *Character formation through books: a bibliography*. Second edition, revised. Washington, D. C.: The Catholic Univ. of America Press, 1945.
Murphy, Lois B. *Personality in young children*. Vol. 1. New York: Basic Books, 1956.
Murphy, Lois B. Learning how children cope with problems. *Children*, July–August, 1957, 4, 132–133.
Russell, David H., & Schrodes, Carolina. Contributions of research in bibliotherapy of the language arts program. *School Rev.*, September, 1950, 58, 338–342.
Timm, Charlotte P. Reading guidance. *Wilson Library Bull.*, October, 1959, 34, 146–148.

48.   The Academic-Activity Program at Hawthorne: A Specially Designed Educational Program for the Troubled Adolescent

Herbert Cohen

Is it feasible to have educational programs for maladjusted youth once they have reached adolescence? If so, what kinds of educational program are most mean-

Exceptional Children, October, 1963, 74–79. Reprinted with the permission of the publisher and author.

ingful and viable? In the following selection, Herbert Cohen describes curricular modifications designed to challenge troubled adolescents in an institutional setting. Do you think that similar results could be obtained in a public school setting?

For many years, the antisocial, nonacademic child has been a problem to himself, his peers, and adults. He has presented a picture to the world about him of a sneering, hostile, defiant youngster who swaggers around wearing the proverbial chip on his shoulder. School has always been a succession of failures for him and he has resisted violently the traditional type of classroom education.

Every institution for disturbed or delinquent children has its share of such children. Lonely, feeling worthless, retarded in basic school subjects, these students have posed severe program problems to educators in institutional settings. For many years, this was also true at Hawthorne Cedar Knolls School.

We struggled with a group of such boys who had little or no interest in academic subjects and who wandered from one program to another. They ranged in age from 13 through 16 and functioned three to six years below their normal achievement level. These boys usually would be assigned to the dining hall, the truck, the farm, the kitchen, and other service jobs at Hawthorne. Even in this limited type of program they soon became bored and frustrated and after a short period would ask for another program change.

Some of the pupils had as many as fifteen program changes in a six-month period. They resisted any type of remedial help and insisted that they wanted no more of school. Even our shop program did not hold any challenge and motivation for these boys. They were the problem children of Hawthorne.

After much soul searching and discussion, we decided to set up a modified form of an academic program within an industrial arts setting. We felt that a shop teacher—a man who worked with his hands and mind and who dignified work—would represent to these boys a different picture from that of school teachers whom they had known in the past.

The class setting was to be an industrial arts general shop. We outfitted this shop with a classroom section which contained tables and chairs, maps, globes, and other facilities of an academic classroom. The first class we chose consisted of ten boys ranging in age from 13 to 15, who functioned from the second to the fifth grade level in reading and from the second to the sixth grade level in mathematics. These ten pupils had had a total of 64 different program changes in the past four months.

This class was to be assigned on an all-morning basis to an industrial arts teacher. The first period in the morning, from 9:20 to 10:25, was scheduled for academic subjects, and the second period, following a short recess, ran from 10:35 to 11:45 and was to be a shop period.

The academic work was to be as follows:
Monday—Current Events and Social Studies
Tuesday—Mathematics
Wednesday—Science
Thursday—English
Friday—Job Information.

The class would have approximately 35 hours per subject during the year and as a result, all minor details would have to be left out and most attention given to the major areas in that particular subject field. As far as possible, all of the academic subjects were to be integrated with industrial arts. Within the shop environment, it is possible to use actual shop problems to teach all of the subject areas. Although it is much easier to relate mathematics and science to industrial arts, we found many ingenious ways to use English and social studies in these classes.

One of the most important elements in this program was the immense task of preparing the special material that was needed in the classroom. Over 150 work sheets were produced during the first year, and many of them were revised after testing them in a class situation. We found it necessary to prepare much of our own materials after thoroughly searching the field and finding very little material that could be purchased which would meet the needs of these pupils. All commercial material that was used had to be carefully screened to make sure that it did not contain pictures of very small boys and girls, which would prove to our adolescents that they were functioning on a childlike level. We are now engaged in the third year of this type of program, and we have several academic-activity classes on various levels. In addition, a whole new approach toward teaching the various academic subjects with an industrial arts emphasis needed to be developed, and the problem of retraining an industrial arts teacher to teach academic subjects was a formidable one.

We found that all of the boys had huge voids in their backgrounds. Most of them did not know how to read a map and had no idea, in most cases, of the location of the Atlantic Ocean, Pacific Ocean, Europe, Asia, etc. Since most of them never took the opportunity to read a newspaper, they really did not know what was going on in our world. This, too, was a major area that had to be explored. Although many of the boys realized that some day they would have to work for a living, they had no idea of job opportunities, salary, unions, social security, income tax, and what would be expected of them in a job. Their interest and motivation were extremely low and most of them were wandering in an effortless way.

SOCIAL STUDIES

In working out the social studies curriculum, it was decided that the first 12 weeks, or 12 actual periods, would be devoted to basic geography. Geography was emphasized primarily in terms of location of minerals and other materials used in the shop situation. They studied the broad areas of the world, the continents and hemispheres, as related to sources of our raw materials. This included the study of transportation across oceans and the work necessary to obtain these materials. We found that we had materials from 17 nations in the shop. The boys learned how to read a map and to locate the important features of the earth. Visual displays of many of the materials used in the shop were labeled by country of origin as an important part of this unit.

The next 14 weeks of the social studies curriculum concerned itself with the study of New York City and New York State. Again, the stress was primarily on the materials of industry, where they were to be found, and how they were transported to the various manufacturing centers of the state. After studying New York City for several sessions, the class was taken on a bus tour of the city, which culminated in a visit to a clothing manufacturing plant. This was the forerunner of many such trips. A discussion preceded each trip and a follow-up was completed by the group at the end of it. This was written or was tape recorded by members of the group who did not yet possess enough ability to put their thoughts in writing.

The last 15 weeks of social studies were devoted to the United States as a whole. The broad areas were discussed with the emphasis again on the differences in the various areas and what each provided to the manufacturing economy of our country. Films and filmstrips helped to give the boys a "trip" to the various parts of our country. Map and globe work was an important aspect of this part of the curriculum. In addition, many of our staff members who had visited various facilities in different parts of our country spoke to the group. Some boys made scrapbooks of various materials that came from different states.

Some of the pupils were interested enough to send letters to the various states requesting information. This was incorporated as part of the English curriculum. Throughout the social studies curriculum, the theme of crafts and materials was stressed. We found that the boys were able to relate to this area because the things they used and talked about were meaningful to them.

Each social studies session opened with a ten minute discussion on current events of the week. We found that the *New York Times* news supplement was our best source of information for this. The teacher would read a digest of the most interesting articles of the week to the class. After a slow start, many of the boys became interested enough to listen to news on the radio and read newspapers so that they would have something to contribute to this part of the session. In this way, we were able to acquaint the boys with some of the important world happenings.

The social studies outline, broken down into its various units and time sequences, follows:
1. Geographical orientation—twelve weeks
2. New York City and state—ten weeks
3. United Nations—three weeks
4. United States economic and manufacturing regions—ten weeks
5. Current events (weekly)—ten minutes

MATHEMATICS

We found the area of mathematics an extremely easy area to integrate with the activity program. This subject is meaningful to the boys in many respects. The basic facts of addition, subtraction, multiplication, and division were all taught in relation to shop processes and projects. The entire problem of mensuration was given a high priority, and many basic skills were taught through the use of the ruler and calipers. We found it necessary to divide the class into two groups for this subject and used a work text for the basic course of study. As the class progressed, we used simple geometry represented by flat, round and square shapes in both wood and metal working. Fractions were discussed in terms of cutting correct pieces of material according to plan and figuring out how many pieces were needed for a project. Each boy was expected to figure out the cost of each project that he was working on during the shop period, and this, too, became a meaningful thing to the class. It soon became apparent to many of the boys that if they were to gain skill in any particular medium, mathematics was a vital subject. It was in this area that the pupils first started asking for extra assignments. This was the beginning of homework for this particular class. Although each boy had only 35 hours of actual class time in mathematics, most of them did at least the same amount in homework and extra assignments. Many of the extra assignments in class were manipulative in nature. As part of the curriculum, pupils used the ruler and calipers to measure various materials and then were able to use these instruments to create a project of their own choosing. It was necessary to develop many separate information sheets for this subject area. We found that most of our pupils were retarded in basic skills in mathematics and as a result, could not measure accurately any of the work done in the shop. Therefore, the curriculum outline for mathematics consisited primarily of basic skills as applied to practical mensuration and daily use.

SCIENCE

The area of science was also found to be easily integrated with industrial arts. This course of study included the study of simple and complex machines, magnetism and electricity, our solar system, and air pressure. All of these areas were given meaning and usefulness when it was shown that everyday living contains working examples of them. Most of the time the equipment of the shop was used to demonstrate the theories and principles used in these areas. The machines and tools were used to show practical uses of scientific knowledge. The race for space proved to be very interesting when the group studied the solar system and its implications for daily life. In many of the sessions, the class was divided into three groups of four boys each, which carried out various experiments to illustrate scientific principles. When the class studied electricity and magnetism, electrical answer games were made using the principles that were being studied at the present time. Telegraph sets were built as part of the shop curriculum and four of the boys became interested enough to learn Morse Code and later demonstrated this to the class by hooking up sending and receiving sets across the classroom area. Here, too, visual aids were extremely important in illustrating many scientific principles. This was the second area in which members of the class asked for extra assignments.

In addition, we brought in many simple texts, films and filmstrips which had been carefully screened so that they did not contain pictures or illustrations of small children doing science experiments. This was extremely important because it was necessary for these boys to feel that they were doing work commensurate with their age and not, as in many cases, with their reading ability.

The following books were included in the science bibliography: *The World About You,* by Ware and Hoffsten, Austin, Texas: Steck Publishing Co.; *This Earth of Ours,* by Ware and Hoffsten, Steck Publishing Co.; *Elementary Science Charts,* by Milton O. Pella, Chicago, Illinois: J. Nystrom and Company; *Fun with Science,* by Mae and Ira Freeman, New York: Random House; *First Book of Science Experiments,* by Wyler, New York: Franklin Watts. It wasn't long before the boys asked to borrow these books so that they could read them in the cottage. In the 35 sessions given to this subject area, many worthwhile principles were learned and many pupils attempted to go beyond the scope of the curriculum on their own.

The science area, which was divided into six basic units, is outlined below:
1. Sound—six weeks
2. Magnetism and electricity—six weeks
3. Weather—six weeks
4. The changing earth—six weeks
5. Simple and complex machines—six weeks
6. Living things—five weeks.

ENGLISH

The subject of English, which we felt would be least related to industrial arts, proved to be a pleasant surprise to us. We found, for instance, that letter writing became a rewarding project when a reply was received. Each boy, in the process of learning how to write a letter, wrote to various trade and industrial concerns, all of which replied. Many of them, in addition, sent samples of their materials and other literature relating to phases of industry. In this way, many of the students read articles on industry and products, and for many boys this was the only literature they had read for a long time. It was again necessary to develop our own work sheets in order to teach the simple rules of grammar, which very few of the pupils knew. All of the language was slanted in the direction of industrial arts. An example of this approach would be one of the questions that was on a simple work sheet, "We placed the work (into, in) the lathe." We found that there was very little resistance to this type of methodology, and that boys who would ordinarily resist doing English exercises actually clamored for more when the work was placed in this type of setting. The boys were taught how to make a simple report on such topics as the story of inventions, discoveries, or basic industrial processes. After visits to industrial plants, the boys learned how to make simple oral and written reports.

When dictionary work was introduced, it was surprising to discover how many boys had never used a dictionary before. We went on from this to a telephone directory and finally an encyclopedia. Simple articles in *Popular Science, Popular Mechanics,* and similar publications were read, and many of the boys made reports on articles which interested them. The teacher carefully screened the material that each boy would read to make sure that each would have a successful experience with the article he had chosen. In some cases it was necessary to let a boy fail to reinforce the teacher's contention that he was not quite ready for this level of work. Although only 35 hours of class time were involved in the English curriculum, many of the boys went far beyond this in their homework. Having a series of work sheets prepared in advance proved to be the key to teaching this subject. Each boy was able to move at his own pace. The initial fear that English would present a difficult situation for this class was dissipated.

The course outline for the English curriculum follows:
1. Basic language skills—fifteen weeks
2. Study and reference skills—five weeks
3. Reports, letter writing, composition work and literature—fifteen weeks.

Spelling was given every week for the first 15 minutes of each English lesson. The spelling word list consisted of the technical terms used in everyday shop practice plus the words most commonly misspelled in daily use. The New York State spelling word lists for the fourth, fifth and sixth grades were used for the latter.

JOB INFORMATION

The area of job information intrigued our boys from the very start. This represented to them an approach to the adult world and the realization that they were being prepared to do a man's job. Various films were used to illustrate the different processes of industry and the skills required to obtain jobs in the various fields. Guest lecturers representing the areas in which our boys could work were invited to speak to the class. During the first year, the personnel manager of a supermarket, the owner of a gas station, a representative of the United States Employment Service, a representative of the carpenter's union, and a representative of the U.S. Armed Forces spoke to the group. In addition, the boys learned to fill out a job application form and write a short resume, and we play-acted several employment interviews. The boys were attuned to the realistic requirements for jobs that they could hope to get when they first started out to work. Our trips to various plants helped in this respect as many of the boys saw jobs that they could fill when they were ready to work. At the same time, it soon became apparent that there are many processes that require a greater degree of education and skill than our pupils possessed. This had the dual function of urging some of the boys to work harder and causing others to revise some of their goals. Taxes, social security, unions and other topics were explained simply and many interesting questions were raised and discussed. In many cases, we used simple literature that was obtained from many sources including those of the U.S. Armed Forces. Each member of the group was given a battery of aptitude and inventory tests. This, too, helped to sharpen the boys' focus of where they would fit in the working world.

The job information area was broken down into the various aspects listed below:

1. Job opportunities—ten weeks
2. Field trips—seven weeks
3. Taxes, social security, unionization—five weeks
4. Industrial processes—eight weeks
5. Job interviews, guest lecturers, films—five weeks.

ACADEMIC ACHIEVEMENT

Each pupil in this group had been tested prior to admission, at midyear, and finally at the end of the school year. They averaged a 2.7 increase in reading and a 2.3 increase in mathematics for the year. Of the original group of twelve boys, only one had dropped out because of lack of interest and two others had been added during the year. Seven of the group had requested remedial reading or remedial mathematics some time during the school year. Emphasis in the remedial reading program was in the field of industrial arts. The rest of the daily program consisted of industrial arts shops, where it soon became apparent that the boys' interest remained high, as opposed to previous years in which they had become easily frustrated and bored. It was interesting to note that as the year progressed, many of these pupils were able to relate in a more positive fashion to their peers and to adults. They did not possess the same sense of worthlessness that had characterized their previous apathetic and belligerent behavior. No longer did these boys feel that they were at the bottom of the school ladder when it came to achievement. For the first time in their lives, these boys proudly carried books to school and actually looked forward to doing homework in the evening. Until this type of education became available to them, they were the ones who used the evenings in the cottage to watch television or wander aimlessly around bothering those other boys who were engaged in doing homework. Now they, too, took their place at the study table and had something worthwhile to contribute to the cottage life.

49.   Educational Engineering with Emotionally Disturbed Children

Frank M. Hewett

Based upon a behavior modification model, Frank Hewett's engineered classroom is designed to implement a hierarchy of educational tasks, a hierarchy that takes into account normal stages of psychoeducational development in which disturbed children are often deficient. This theoretical framework of teacher-pupil interaction allows the teacher to adopt a developmental viewpoint and to set realistic educational goals for emotionally disturbed children with learning disabilities. Implications for such germane issues as educational sequencing, pupil motivation and classroom management are presented.

As educational programs for emotionally disturbed children receive increased federal, state, and local public school support and become more widespread, several models for establishing these programs are available to teachers. There is the psychotherapeutic model with a psychodynamic, interpersonal emphasis; the pathological or medical model, which focuses on brain pathology and treatment of measured or inferred organic causal factors; and the pedagogical model, concerned with intellectual development, remedial techniques, and academic goals. Each model has influenced school programs for emotionally disturbed children, and, depending on the intuitive, diagnostic and curriculum skill of the teacher, has been useful to some degree. The need still exists, however, for a more generally applicable model to handle the ever increasing number of inattentive, failure prone, and resistant children who are being separated from their more readily educable peers for special education. Such a model must be

Exceptional Children, March 1967, 459–467. Reprinted with the permission of the publisher and author.

understandable to the teacher, translatable to the classroom, and hold promise for more effectively educating the emotionally disturbed child.

Recently, a model called behavior modification has demonstrated usefulness with exceptional children. Rather than view the emotionally disturbed child as a victim of psychic conflicts, cerebral dysfunction, or merely academic deficits, this approach concentrates on bringing the overt behavior of the child into line with standards required for learning. Such standards may include development of an adequate attention span; orderly response in the classroom; the ability to follow directions; tolerance for limits of time, space, and activity; accurate exploration of the environment; and appreciation for social approval and avoidance of disapproval. Promoting successful development of these standards as well as self care and intellectual skills through assignment of carefully graded tasks in a learning environment which provides both rewards and structure for the child in accord with principles of empirical learning theory (Skinner, 1963) are the basic goals of the behavior modification model.

According to Ullmann and Krasner (1965), the behavior modifier has three main concerns: (a) defining maladaptive behavior, (b) determining the environmental events which support this behavior, and (c) manipulating the environment in order to alter maladaptive behavior. In the case of the emotionally disturbed child, his maladaptive behavior is readily distinguished in the classroom by poor concentration, hyperactivity, acting out, defiance, avoidance, withdrawal, and other manifestations that make him a poor candidate for learning. Environmental events which maintain these behaviors might include positive reinforcement and recognition for misbehavior; association of school, teacher, and learning with failure and negative reinforcement; and assignment of learning tasks inappropriate to the child. The third concern, what can be done to change school to remedy both the emotionally disturbed child's maladaptive behavior and its environmental supports, is the subject of this paper.

THE ENGINEERED CLASSROOM

In the engineered classroom, the teacher is assigned the role of behavioral engineer; she attempts to define appropriate task assignments for students, provide meaningful rewards for learning, and maintain well defined limits in order to reduce and hopefully eliminate the occurrence of maladaptive behavior. The teacher, then, engineers an environment in which the probability of student success is maximized and maladaptive behavior is replaced by adaptive behavior. The role of behavior engineer has been previously described by Ayllon and Michael (1959), with reference to application of behavior modification theory by nursing personnel working with psychotic patients. The engineered classroom concept has been explored by Haring and Phillips (1962), Whelan and Haring (1966), and Quay (1966) with emotionally disturbed children, and by Birnbrauer, Bijou, Wolf, and Kidder (1965) at the Rainier School in Washington. The latter research project was visited by the author and aspects of the engineered design described here stem from these observations. Other authors, such as Staats, Minke, Finley, Wolf, and Brooks (1964), Zimmerman and Zimmerman (1962), and Valett (1966), have applied modification principles to academic teaching.

One of the problems inherent in introducing theoretical concepts and research findings into the classroom is the inevitable involvement of a specialized and often alien vocabulary, as well as a frame of reference for implementation not usual to the educational background of the teacher. This dilemma arises in the psychotherapeutic and pathological models mentioned earlier, where libido, ego strength, and psychosexual development, or dyslexia, perceptual motor dysfunction, and strephosymbolia may be impressive but not always useful terms in the classroom. Successful application of behavior modification principles also requires understanding of such concepts as reinforcement, contingencies, and scheduling; while simple and clear cut in intent, they are not always easily grasped or accepted by teachers.

The engineered classroom design currently under investigation was introduced in the public school (Hewett, 1966), by a teacher who had no previous exposure to behavior modification theory. It attempts a translation of this theory—not rigidly, but pragmatically—to the school setting. Behavior modification principles are organized in terms of a learning triangle, the sides of which represent the three essential ingredients for all effective teaching: selection of a suitable educational task for the child, provision of a meaningful reward following accomplishment of that task, and maintenance of a degree of structure under the control of the teacher. Figure 1 illustrates the relationship of certain behavior modification principles to these three factors.

The engineered classroom design creates an environment for implementation of the learning triangle. Suitable educational tasks are selected from a hierarchy, presented in Figure 2, which describes seven task levels. The first five are readiness levels, largely mastered by normal children before they enter school. The final two are concerned with intellectual skill development which constitutes a primary educational goal with all children.

Emotionally disturbed children are usually not ready to be in school because they are unable to pay attention, follow directions, explore the environment, or get along with others. For this reason, suitable educational tasks for these children must often be selected from the five readiness levels. The hierarchy encompasses many fundamental concepts of the psychotherapeutic, pathological, and pedagogical models discussed earlier. However, it attempts to define these concepts in terms of educational operations rather than by psychoanalytic, neurological, or narrow academic nomenclature. In this regard the present hierarchy is a revision of one earlier described (Hewett, 1964). Table 1 summarizes the seven task levels of the hierarchy, children's problems relating to each, the type of learner rewards available, and the degree of structure inherent at each level.

An assessment procedure enables the teacher to rate the child in terms of specific deficits on the hierarchy shortly after he enters the engineered classroom. This assessment becomes the basis for establishing an educational program for him and provides the teacher with an understanding

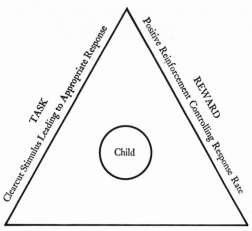

Withholding of Positive Reinforcement or Administration of
Negative Reinforcement Following Inappropriate Responses

Scheduling of Positive Reinforcement

Setting of Contingency for Receipt of Reinforcement

STRUCTURE

FIGURE 1.   The Learning Triangle

of his basic learning deficits. This procedure is ongoing and is repeated three times each semester.

In helping an emotionally disturbed child get ready for intellectual training the teacher can profitably use the behavior modification principle of shaping; rather than holding out for the ultimate goal (e.g., student functioning appropriately on the mastery and achievement levels), successive approximations of that goal (e.g., functioning at attention, response, order, exploratory, and social levels) are recognized achievements. The engineered classroom design attempts to provide an environment and program for shaping appropriate learning behavior.

CLASSROOM DESCRIPTION

The engineered classroom should be a large, well lighted room (ideally 1200 to 1500 square feet) with a double desk (2' x 4') for each of nine pupils. The class is under the supervision of a regular teacher and a teacher aide. The aide need not be certified or specifically trained. High school graduates and PTA volunteers have been effective.

The physical environment can be described as having three major centers paralleling levels on the hierarchy of educational tasks. The mastery-achievement center consists of the student desk area where academic assignments are undertaken. Adjacent to and part of this center are two study booths or offices where academic work may be done without visual distraction. These are carpeted and outfitted with desks and upholstered chairs. An exploratory-social center with three distinct areas is set up near

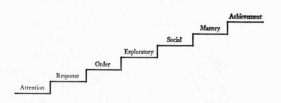

FIGURE 2.   A Hierarchy of Educational Tasks

the windows and sink facilities. Equipment for simple science experiments is available in one area, arts and crafts activities in another. Social skills are fostered in the communication area of the exploratory center where group listening activities and games are provided. The attention-response-order center is in an opposite corner of the classroom and consists of two double desks and a storage cabinet where puzzles, exercises, and materials for use in emphasizing paying attention, responding, and routine are kept. Thus each level on the hierarchy has a designated area in the room where specific types of tasks may be undertaken by the child.

Mounted by the door is a work record card holder displaying individual work record cards for each student. The room has limited bulletin board displays and looks much like any elementary classroom. The hypothesis that all emotionally disturbed children need a drab, sterile, nonstimulating school environment is rejected in this design.

The class operates five main periods in the minimum 240 minute day required by California for programs for the educationally handicapped. Period I is a 10 minute order period (attention, response, and order levels); Period II consists of reading and written language (mastery level) and lasts 60 minutes; Period III is devoted to arithmetic (mastery level) and is 60 minutes in length; Period IV is a 20 minute physical education session; and Period V is for science, art, and communication (exploratory and social levels) and lasts 60 minutes. In addition, a recess, nutrition break, and evaluation period round out the class day.

A floorplan of the engineered classroom is illustrated in Figure 3.

STUDENTS

Two types of students have been enrolled in experimental engineered classrooms to date: public school children with essentially normal intelligence from Santa Monica and Tulare in California and the Palolo School district in Oahu, Hawaii, identified as educationally handicapped (underachieving due to emotional, neurological, or learning disability factors) and emotionally disturbed children hospitalized on the Children's Service of the UCLA Neuropsychiatric Institute and enrolled in the Neuropsychiatric Institute School. The public school population consisted mostly

TABLE 1. DESCRIPTION OF THE HIERARCHY OF EDUCATIONAL TASKS

Hierarchy Level	Attention	Response	Order	Exploratory	Social	Mastery	Achievement
Child's Problem	Inattention due to withdrawal or resistance	Lack of involvement and unwillingness to respond in learning	Inability to follow directions	Incomplete or inaccurate knowledge of environment	Failure to value social approval or disapproval	Deficits in basic adaptive and school skills not in keeping with IQ	Lack of self motivation for learning
Educational Task	Get child to pay attention to teacher and task	Get child to respond to tasks he likes and which offer promise of success	Get child to complete tasks with specific starting points and steps leading to a conclusion	Increase child's efficiency as an explorer and get him involved in multisensory exploration of his environment	Get child to work for teacher and peer group approval and to avoid their disapproval	Remediation of basic skill deficiencies	Development of interest in acquiring knowledge
Learner Reward	Provided by tangible rewards (e.g., food, money, tokens)	Provided by gaining social attention	Provided through task completion	Provided by sensory stimulation	Provided by social approval	Provided through task accuracy	Provided through intellectual task success
Teacher Structure	Minimal	Still limited	Emphasized	Emphasized	Based on standards of social appropriateness	Based on curriculum assignments	Minimal

of boys with conduct disturbances, neurotic traits including long standing school phobias, psychosomatic and borderline psychotic problems, as well as minimal neurological impairment. The hospitalized group represented more serious emotional problems and included grossly psychotic and more markedly neurologically impaired individuals. All students were in the age group from 8 to 12.

ENGINEERED CLASSROOM OPERATIONS

As can be seen from Table 1, the range of rewards possible to offer the child in school includes tangible rewards, social attention, task completion, sensory stimulation, social approval, and task accuracy and success. Normal children arrive in the classroom ready to learn in anticipation of such rewards as approval and accuracy, but emotionally disturbed children often are not motivated in the same manner. Levin and Simmons (1962) found that emotionally disturbed boys were more effectively motivated by tangible rewards of food than by social praise.

Since a meaningful reward for learning is essential in a successful teaching situation and emotionally disturbed children differ so greatly with respect to what is rewarding for them, the engineered classroom operates on the most basic reward level in an effort to insure gratification in school for even the most resistant learner.

As each student enters in the morning he picks up his individual work record card which is ruled into 200 squares. As he moves through the day the teacher and aide recognize his work accomplishments and efficiency to function as a student by checking off squares on the work record card. The student carries his card with him wherever he goes in the room. Checkmarks are given on a fixed interval, fixed ratio basis every 15 minutes. A time rather than a task contingency is used because it standardizes the total number of possible checkmarks in a single day, reduces competition, and is useful in alerting the student to the work efficiency orientation of the classroom. Intermittent schedules for rewarding children may be more powerful but, in the author's experience, they have not proven as manageable and practical for the teacher.

Checkmarks are given in very specific ways. Normally, a maximum of 10 is given for any 15 minute period. Two checkmarks are given for starting the assignment (attention level), 3 for following through (response level), and a possible 5 bonus given for being a student (order, exploratory, social, or mastery levels, depending on child's learning deficits). In addition, extra checkmarks might be given a particular child when necessary for motivation. In the main, however, the checkmarks are awarded conservatively by the teacher and attention is called to the specific reasons

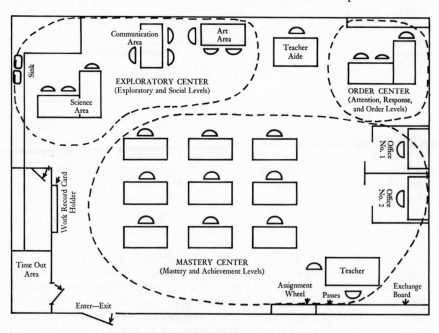

FIGURE 3.   Floorplan of an Engineered Classroom

for the checkmarks being given or withheld. Since social reinforcement may actually be aversive for some emotionally disturbed children, the checkmark system functions as a neutral, nonconflictual meeting ground for teacher and student. The teacher attempts to convey the notion that checkmarks are objective measures of accomplishment and literally part of a reality system in the classroom over which she has little control. In this regard the teacher functions as a shop foreman who pays workers what they actually earn according to standards set by the plant system. The teacher's message to the child is in essence: "That's just the way it is. I work here too." Students save completed work record cards and exchange them on a weekly basis for candy, small toys, and trinkets. An exchange board in the room displays the tangible rewards available for 1, 2, or 3 cards filled with checkmarks.

While the checkmark system remains constant as the primary source of reward in the classroom, every effort is made to provide rewards at the higher levels of the hierarchy. The attention-response-order center offers activities such as tachistoscopic training, decoding exercises with symbol and flag code messages, puzzle making, simple construction kits, design copying with beads, blocks, and many other tasks useful in getting the child to pay attention, respond, and follow directions.

The concept of order is also emphasized through the use of a system of passes to facilitate assignments to the offices and other centers in the room. When the child is assigned to a center he picks up at the teacher's desk a pass which designates the area to which he will move. This pass is hung on the wall by the center during the period of time the child is away from his desk.

The exploratory-social center provides opportunities for multisensory exploration of the environment and communication. Materials for science experiments and demonstrations in electricity, magnetism, animal care, and basic chemistry are available in one section. A listening post, Morse code activities, simple games for 2 or 3 children, and a tape recorder are in another section for communication and social tasks. Arts and crafts materials are available in another section. One of the main periods of the class day takes place at this center. Usually the teacher demonstrates several different science experiments each week. These experiments are pictorially illustrated on large cards with simple directions and filed at the center where they may be replicated by students assigned to the center at other times during the class day. Each day, students participate in art and communication tasks as part of the exploratory period.

The mastery and achievement center seeks to engage each child in a certain amount of academic work each day because in a majority of cases emotionally disturbed children have failed to keep pace in acquiring reading, written language, and arithmetic skills. A reading period is held three times weekly and consists of three different activities—individual oral reading with the teacher, independent activity reading for comprehension and development, and word study for review of reading and spelling words. Story writing takes the place of the reading period twice a week. Arithmetic assignments are individually prepared and based on diagnostic achievement test results. Assignment of mastery tasks coincides with the time contingency used as a basis for the checkmark system. Different tasks are assigned individual students every 15 minutes.

INTERVENTION

In accordance with principles of behavior modification the teacher in the engineered classroom attempts to alter the environment to change maladaptive behavior patterns of students and to foster the development of more adaptive patterns through manipulation of assigned tasks and provision of success and rewards. The basic goal is to keep every child functioning as a student. So long as the child respects the working rights of others and displays a reasonable tolerance for limits of time, space, and activity, he earns a full quota of checkmarks regardless of what type of task he is assigned in the room. In order to help individual children earn as many checkmarks as possible, a series of interventions must often be used to alter the learning environment including the nature of the assigned task, type of reward, and degree of structure. These interventions are divided into two categories, student and nonstudent, and involve descending the hierarchy of educational tasks until a level is found that enables the child to function successfully or provides for his exclusion from class.

If at any time during the class day the student begins to display signs of maladaptive learning behavior (e.g., inattention, day dreaming, boredom, disruption) his assignments are quickly changed. Table 2 summarizes the interventions which may be used in an attempt to foster adaptive student functioning. The teacher may select any intervention seen as appropriate or may try the student at each intervention level until his behavior improves. As long as the child is able to stabilize himself during any of the student interventions, he continues to earn checkmarks on a par with those students successfully pursuing mastery level assignments. He is in no way penalized for the shift in assignment. There appears little need to worry about other children reacting to what might be seen as inequality. They have seemed content to accept the teacher's explanation that "Johnny needs a different kind of assignment to help him learn right now."

When one to one tutoring on the attention level cannot be provided or is ineffective, the child loses his opportunity to earn checkmarks, is considered a nonstudent, and sent out of the room for a short period of isolation. Use of such isolation as an intervention has been described by Whelan and Haring (1966). If the child can successfully tolerate this period (usually 5, 10, or 15 minutes) his card is immediately returned and he may be reassigned at any level depending on the teacher's assessment of his capacities for adaptive behavior at the moment. No lecturing or demand he "promise to be a good boy" is given.

With respect to interventions, a question may arise regarding whether or not removing a child from a more demanding task and assigning him a less demanding task in the classroom actually constitutes rewarding inappropriate behavior. Will not some children misbehave in order to be reassigned to a more inviting exploratory or order activity? In the author's experience with the engineered classroom this has occurred only rarely.

When it does, the child is not permitted the choice of an alternative activity, but is directly placed in an isolation intervention. In most cases, teachers anticipate such problems by limiting the amount of mastery work given the child, assigning him to an alternate center before his behavior becomes maladaptive.

With most children who become restless and resistant the teacher approaches the child and says, "You seem to be having trouble with this assignment. I want you to earn all of your checkmarks this period so go get a pass for the exploratory (or order) center and I'll give you a different assignment there." This is an expression of the basic philosophy of the engineered classroom which in essence tells the child: "We want you to succeed at all costs. If you will meet us half way and function reasonably well as a student we will give you tasks you can do, need to do, and will enjoy doing, and we will reward you generously for your efforts."

DISCUSSION AND IMPLICATIONS

The engineered classroom design has been developed and observed in four public school systems and a hospital setting for the past two years. It has

TABLE 2. HIERARCHY OF INTERVENTIONS TO MAINTAIN STUDENT ROLE

Level	Student Interventions
1. Achievement	Assign student to study booth to pursue mastery work.
2. Mastery	Modify mastery assignment and have student continue at desk or in study booth.
3. Social	Verbally restructure expectation of student role (e.g., respect working rights of others, accept limits of time, space, activity).
4. Exploratory	Remove mastery assignment and reassign to exploratory center for specific science, art, or communication activity.
5. Order	Reassign to order center for specific direction following tasks (e.g., puzzle, exercise, game, work sheet).
6. Response	Remove child from classroom and assign him to a task he likes to do and can do successfully outside (e.g., running around playground, punching punching bag, turning specific number of somersaults on lawn).
7. Attention	Remove child from classroom, put on a one to one tutoring relationship with teacher aide, and increase number of check marks given to obtain cooperation, attention, and student behavior.
	Nonstudent Interventions
8. Time Out	Take away work record card and explain to child he cannot earn check marks for a specific number of minutes which he must spend in isolation (never use more than three times in one day).
9. Exclusion	If child requires more than three time-outs in one day or fails to control himself during time out, or if he is verbally or physically abusive to teacher, immediately suspend him from class for rest of day and, if possible, send home.

constantly been reassessed and changed and still is undergoing alteration in an effort to arrive at a practical and useful model for educating emotionally disturbed children. Preliminary observations suggest that changes in work efficiency and adaptive behavior occur quickly. One of the aspects that most impresses observers is the purposeful, controlled, and productive atmosphere in the classrooms. Despite the requirements for a teacher aide, a well organized classroom, and use of tangible rewards, it appears to be a feasible design for use in a public school.

Some educators are reluctant to use the behavior modification model because it has emerged from the experimental animal laboratory and some feel that tangible rewards for learning represent an unwholesome compromise with basic educational values. However, if one objectively and realistically views the emotionally disturbed child as a unique learner, not initially responsive to a conventional learning environment, and often not rewarded by traditional social and intellectual rewards, then reducing one's goals so that he may be included, not excluded, from school, is just good common sense. To fail to teach a child because he lacks capacity to learn is one thing, but to fail because of a lack of flexibility and a realistic assessment of a child's needs, is quite another.

The engineered class design is not viewed as an end in itself. Observations suggest that the value of checkmarks and tangible exchange items soon gives way to the satisfaction of succeeding in school and receiving recognition as a student from peers, teachers, and parents. Transition programs have been worked out where children started in the engineered classroom have gradually been reintroduced into regular classes. While this stage is not wholly developed, it appears to be a natural evolutionary development in the program.

Some criticism of this approach has discounted improvements seen in the adaptive functioning of the children as merely the result of the Hawthorne effect (Roethlisberger and Dixon, 1939); that is, anything novel or different in the environment produces an initial change in behavior. Even though some children have continued to improve for a full year in the engineered classroom, this possibility still exists. The answer to such a criticism is simply, "So what?" If one can create a unique learning environment that produces more adaptive learning behavior in emotionally disturbed children, perhaps we should capitalize on the Hawthorne phenomenon in special education and continuously introduce more stimulating and novel approaches with all exceptional children.

One major problem which has arisen from presenting the engineered classroom design to teachers in the field bears mention. Some of them are so desperate for ideas and directions to increase their effectiveness with emotionally disturbed children that they react to superficial aspects of the design and somewhat randomly apply them in the classroom. It is not uncommon to hear of a teacher rushing out, buying a large stock of M and M candies which are often used as exchange items, beginning to pass them out rather haphazardly in the classroom, and then waiting for a miracle to occur. Needless to say, such a teacher will have a long wait. Checkmarks and candy are only a small part of the entire design. There is nothing new in the use of gold stars and extrinsic rewards in education, but there is a great deal that is unique in the systematic use of these to foster development of more adaptive learning behavior on the part of resistant and often inaccessible learners.

Behavior modification theory is a systematic theory, not a faddist theory based on gimmicks. To be useful, it must be understood and adhered to systematically, not sporadically. We are still trying to increase our understanding of its effectiveness in the engineered classroom, anticipating considerably more evaluation, exploration, and experimentation before we can be certain of its applicability.

REFERENCES

Ayllon, T., and Michael, J. The psychiatric nurse as a behavioral engineer. *Journal of Experimental Analysis of Behavior*, 1959, 2, 323–334.

Birnbrauer, J., Bijou, S., Wolf, M., and Kidder, J. Programmed instruction in the classroom. In L. Ullman and L. Krasner (Eds.), *Case studies in behavior modification*. New York: Holt, Rinehart and Winston, 1965.

Haring, N., and Phillips, E. *Educating emotionally disturbed children*. New York: McGraw-Hill, 1962.

Hewett, F. A hierarchy of educational tasks for children with learning disorders. *Exceptional Children*, 1964, 31, 207–214.

Hewett, F. The Tulare experimental class for educationally handicapped children. *California Education*, 1966, 3, 6–8.

Levin, G., and Simmons, J. Response to food and praise by emotionally disturbed boys. *Psychological Reports*, 1962, 11, 539–546.

Quay, H. Remediation of the conduct problem in the special class setting. *Exceptional Children*, 1966, 32, 509–515.

Roethlisberger, F., and Dixon, W. *Management of the worker*. Cambridge: Harvard University Press, 1939.

Skinner, B. Operant behavior. *American Psychologist*, 1963, 18, 503–515.

Staats, A., Minke, K., Finley, J., Wolf, M., and Brooks, L. A reinforcer system and experimental procedures for the laboratory study of reading acquisition. *Child Development*, 1964, 35, 209–231.

Ullman, L., and Krasner, L. *Case studies in behavior modification*. New York: Holt, Rinehart, and Winston, 1965.

Valett, R. A social reinforcement technique for the classroom management of behavior disorders. *Exceptional Children*, 1966, 33, 185–189.

Whelan, R., and Haring, N. Modification and maintenance of behavior through systematic application of consequences. *Exceptional Children*, 1966, 32, 281–289.

Zimmerman, E., and Zimmerman, J. The alteration of behavior in a special classroom situation. *Journal of Experimental Analysis of Behavior*, 1962, 5, 59–60.

CHAPTER 11.

Intervention Procedures in the Community

50. Community Psychiatry—The Newest Therapeutic Bandwagon

H. Warren Dunham

What is community psychiatry? How has the widening definition of emotional disturbance influenced its development? What historical forces have led to its development? Will it prove to be a viable model upon which to base intervention efforts? H. Warren Dunham explores these issues in his critical evaluation of "the newest therapeutic bandwagon."

The proposal to add community psychiatry to the ever-widening list of psychiatric specialties deserves a critical examination. Thus, my purpose in this paper is fourfold. First, I intend to examine the nature of community psychiatry as it is taking shape. Second, I want to consider our continuing uncertainty about mental illness which is manifested in a widening of its definition. Third, I discuss some of the historical landmarks and cultural forces that have brought about the proposal for this new subspecialty of psychiatry. Finally, I examine some of its hidden aspects with respect to the future role of psychiatry.

COMMUNITY PSYCHIATRY: THE NEWEST SUBSPECIALTY

Let us begin by examining the nature of community psychiatry that is apparently emerging as judged by a mounting chorus of voices from those

Archives of General Psychiatry, 1965, 12, 303–313. Reprinted with the permission of the publisher and author.

Read before the staff of the Institute for Juvenile Research, Chicago, May 19, 1964.

who jump on any bandwagon as long as it is moving. In doing this I will focus first on community psychiatry in relation to community mental health and the various programs, plans, and social actions that are currently getting under way, with emphases that are as varied as the cultural-regional contrasts of American society.

A pattern concerned with maximizing treatment potential for the mentally ill is gradually taking shape. This newest emphasis points to a declining role of the traditional state hospital and the rise of the community mental health center with all of the attendant auxiliary services essential for the treatment of the mentally ill. In its ideal form the community mental health center would provide psychiatric services, both diagnostic and treatment, for all age groups and for inpatients and outpatients in a particular community. In addition, the center would have attached closely to it day and night hospitals, convalescent homes, rehabilitative programs or, for that matter, any service that helps toward the maximizing of treatment potential with respect to the characteristics of the population that it is designed to serve. Also attached to this center would be several kinds of research activities aimed at evaluating and experimenting with old and new therapeutic procedures. In the background would still be the state hospital which would, in all likelihood, become the recipient for those patients who seemingly defy all efforts with available therapeutic techniques to fit them back into family and community with an assurance of safety to themselves and others. This reorganization of psychiatric facilities as a community mental health program also implies an increased and workable coordination of the diverse social agencies in the community toward the end of detecting and referring those persons who need psychiatric help.

This ideal structure does appear to be oriented toward the urban community. Therefore, the need arises to clarify the size and type of the population that would be served. Further, a breakdown of the population into the several age and sex categories along with several projected estimates of the number of mentally ill persons that will occur in these population categories would be required. Estimates should be made for the psychoneuroses, the psychoses, the psychopathies, the mentally retarded, and the geriatrics cases that will be found in a community.

Indeed, we should attempt to mobilize and to organize our psychiatric resources in such a manner that they will maximize our existing therapeutic potential for any community. At all events, such a structure seems to suggest to certain professionals at the National Institute of Mental Health that if there comes into existence a realistic community mental health program, there must be a community psychiatry that knows how to use it. While the logic here escapes me, it seems to be quite clear to Viola Bernard who states that, "Recognition of the need to augment the conventional training for mental health personnel to equip them for the newer function of community mental health practice parallels wide-scale trends toward more effective treatment methods at the collective level to augment one-to-one clinical approaches."[1] Dr. Bernard goes on to say that community psychiatry can be regarded as a subspecialty of psychiatry and that it embraces three major subdivisions—social psychiatry, administrative psychiatry, and public health psychiatry.

While Dr. Bernard may see clearly the nature of a community psychiatry that transcends the traditional one-to-one clinical approach, this is not the case with departments of psychiatry in some medical schools as the recent National Institute of Mental Health survey attests.[2] In reviewing the limited literature it is all too clear that different conceptions abound as to what community psychiatry is and while these conceptions are not always inconsistent they nevertheless attest to the fact that the dimensions of the proposed new subspecialty are by no means clear-cut. These conceptions range all the way from the idea that community psychiatry means bringing psychiatric techniques and treatments to the indigent persons in the community to the notion that community psychiatry should involve the education of policemen, teachers, public health nurses, politicians, and junior executives in mental hygiene principles. A mere listing of some of the conceptions of what has been placed under the community psychiatry umbrella will give a further notion of this uncertainty. Community psychiatry has been regarded as encompassing (1) the community base mental hospital, (2) short-term mental hospitalization, (3) attempts to move the chronically hospitalized patient and return him to the community, (4) the integration of various community health services, (5) psychiatric counseling and services to nonpsychiatric institutions such as schools, police departments, industries, and the like, (6) the development of devices for maintaining mental patients in the community, (7) reorganization and administration of community mental health programs, and finally (8) the establishment of auxiliary services to community mental hospitals, such as outpatient clinics, day hospitals, night hospitals, home psychiatric visits, and the utilization of auxiliary psychiatric personnel in treatment programs.[2]

Perhaps we can come close to what someone visualizes as the content of community psychiatry by quoting an announcement of an opening for a fellowship in community psychiatry in Minnesota. In the announcement the program is described as follows: "One year of diversified training and experience, including all aspects of community organization, consultation, and training techniques, administration, research and mass communication media." Such a psychiatric residency program certainly represents a great difference from the more traditional training program and points to a type of training that might be more fitting for a person who wants to specialize in community organization.

There is no clearer support for this conception than Leonard Duhl's paper[3] where he discusses the training problems for community psychiatry. In this paper he speaks of three contracts that the psychiatrist has, the traditional one with the patient, the more infrequent one with the family, and still more infrequent one with the community. In connection with his community contract, the psychiatrist states, according to Duhl, "I will try to lower the rate of illness and maximize the health of this population." Duhl continues, and I quote, because the direction is most significant.

In preparing psychiatrists for these broadened contracts, a new set of skills must be communicated. For example, he must learn how to be consultant to a community, an institution, or a group without being patient-oriented. Rather, he must have the community's needs in central focus. He must be prepared for situations where he is expected to contribute to planning for services and programs, both in his field and in others, that are related: what information is needed; how it is gathered; what resources are available and so forth. Epidemiology, survey research and planning skills must be passed on to him. He must be prepared to find that people in other fields, such as the legislature, often affect a program more than his profession does. He must find himself at home in the world of economics, political science, politics, planning, and all forms of social action.[3]

While these remarks of Bernard and Duhl may not represent any final statement as to what community psychiatry will become, they point to a probable direction that this newest addition to psychiatric subspecialties may take. However, in this conception of the community psychiatrist as a person skilled in the techniques of social action there lie so many uncertainties, unresolved issues, and hidden assumptions that it is difficult to determine where it will be most effective to start the analysis, with the role of the psychiatrist or with the nature of the community.

Perhaps sociologists can garner some small satisfaction in the fact that the psychiatrist finally has discovered the community—something that the sociologist has been studying and reporting on for over half a century in the United States. However, once the psychiatrist makes this discovery he must ask himself what he can do with it in the light of his professional task, how the discovery will affect his traditional professional role, and how working on or in the community structure can improve the mental health level of its people. Now, it seems that those leaders of psychiatry who are proposing this new subspecialty imply several things at the same time and are vague about all of them. They seem to be saying, in one form or another, the following:

1. We, psychiatrists, must know the community and learn how to work with the various groups and social strata composing it so that we can help to secure and organize the necessary psychiatric facilities that will serve to maximize the treatment potential for the mentally ill.

2. We must know the community because the community is composed of families which, through the interaction of their members, evolve those events and processes that in a given context have a pathic effect upon some of the persons who compose them.

3. We must know the community in order to develop more effective methods of treatment at the "collective level," to eliminate mentally disorganizing social relationships, and to achieve a type of community organization that is most conducive to the preservation of mental health.

4. We must know the community if we are ever to make any headway in the prevention of mental illness. For we hold that in the multiple groups, families, and social institutions which compose the community, there are numerous unhealthy interpersonal relationships, pathological attitudes and beliefs, cultural conflicts and tensions, and unhealthy child training practices that make for the development of mental and emotional disturbances in the person.

An analysis of our first implication shows that no new burden is placed upon the psychiatrist but it merely emphasizes his role as a citizen —a role that, like any person in the society, he always has had. It merely emphasizes that the psychiatrist will take a more active part in working with other professionals in the community such as lawyers, teachers, social workers, ministers, labor leaders, and business men in achieving an organization of psychiatric facilities that will maximize the therapeutic potential in a given community. To be sure, it means that in working with such persons and groups, he will contribute his own professional knowledge and insights in the attempt to obtain and to organize the psychiatric facilities in such a manner as to achieve a maximum therapeutic potential. Thus, this is hardly a new role for the psychiatrist. It only becomes sharper at this moment in history when a social change in the care and treatment of the mentally ill is impending, namely, a shift from a situation that emphasized the removal of the mental patient from the community to one that attempts to deal with him in the community and family setting and to keep active and intact his ties with these social structures.

The second implication is routine in the light of the orientation of much of contemporary psychiatry. Here, attention is merely called to the theory that stresses the atypical qualities of the family drama for providing an etiological push for the development of the several psychoneuroses, character disorders, adult behavior disturbances and in certain instances, psychotic reactions. Thus, it follows that to change or correct the condition found in the person, some attention must be paid to the family as a collectivity, in order to grasp and then modify those attitudes, behavior patterns, identifications, and emotional attachments that supposedly have a pathogenic effect on the family members. From the focus on the family the concern then extends to the larger community in an attempt to discover the degree to which the family is integrated in or alienated from it.

However, it is in the third implication that many probing questions arise. For here the conception is implicit that the community is the patient and consequently, the necessity arises to develop techniques that can be used in treating the community toward the end of supplementing the traditional one-to-one psychiatric relationship. This position also implies a certain etiological view, namely, that within the texture of those institutional arrangements that make up the community there exist dysfunctional processes, subcultures with unhealthy value complexes, specific institutional tensions, various ideological conflicts along age, sex, ethnic, racial and political axes, occasional cultural crises, and an increasing tempo of social change that in their functional interrelationships provide a pathogenic social environment. Thus, when these elements are incorporated into the experience of the persons, especially during their early and adolescent years, they emerge as abnormal forms of traits, attitudes, thought processes, and behavior patterns. In a theoretical vein, this is the Merton[4] paradigm wherein he attempts to show the diverse modes of adaptation that arise as a result of the various patterns of discrepancy between institutional means and cultural goals.

The influence of the social milieu in shaping, organizing, and integrating the personality structure, of course, has been recognized for a long time. What is not so clear, however, is the manner in which such knowledge can be utilized in working at the community level to treat the mental and emotional maladjustments that are continually appearing. In addition, the nature and function of those factors in the social milieu contributing to the production of the bona fide psychotics are by no means established.

These issues point to some very pressing queries. What are the possible techniques that can be developed to treat the "collectivity"? Why do psychiatrists think that it is possible to treat the "collectivity" when there still exists a marked uncertainty with respect to the treatment and cure of the individual case? What causes the psychiatrist to think that if he advances certain techniques for treating the "collectivity," they will have community acceptance? If he begins to "treat" a group through discussions in order to develop personal insights, what assurances does he have that the results will be psychologically beneficial to the persons? Does the psychiatrist know how to organize a community along mentally hygienic lines and if he does, what evidence does he have that such an organization will be an improvement over the existing organization? In what institutional setting or in what cultural milieu would the psychiatrist expect to begin in order to move toward more healthy social relationships in the community? These are serious questions and I raise them with reference to the notion that the community is the patient.

If a psychiatrist thinks that he can organize the community to move it toward a more healthy state I suggest that he run for some public office. This would certainly add to his experience and give him some conception as to whether or not the community is ready to be moved in the direction that he regards as mentally hygienic. If he should decide on such a step he will be successful to the extent that he jokingly refers to himself as a "head shrinker" and that he becomes acceptable as "one of the boys." But if he does, he functions as an independent citizen, in harmony with our democratic ethos, bringing his professional knowledge to bear on the goal he has set for himself and his constituents. However, successful or not, he will certainly achieve a new insight concerning the complexity involved in treating the community as the patient.

While I have poked at this proposition from the standpoint of politics, let me consider it with respect to education. If this becomes the medium by which the pathology of the community is to be arrested, one can assume that it means adding to and raising the quality of the educational system in the community. The dissemination of psychiatric information with respect to signs and symptoms, the desirability of early treatment, the natural character of mental illness, the therapeutic benefits of the new drugs, and the correct mental hygiene principles of child training have been going on not only through the usual community lectures and formal educational channels but also by means of the mass media—radio, television, the newspapers, and the slick magazines. I hasten to add, however, that this may not be to the advantage of the community, for it may do nothing else but raise the level of anxiety among certain middle-class persons, who, when they read an article on the correct procedure for bringing up children, realize that they have done all the wrong things. Also, the media are frequently sources of misinformation and sometimes imply a promise that psychiatry cannot fulfill.

Further, I observe that in this proposal for a community psychiatry, the psychiatrist seems to be enmeshed in the same cultural vortex as is the professor. For it is becoming fashionable for a professor to measure his success in having hardly any contact with students—he is too busy on larger undertakings, research, consultations, conferences, and the like. Likewise, some psychiatrists think that they have arrived if they have no contact with patients. For example, I have heard of one psychiatrist who has not seen a patient for several years—he spends his time educating teachers, nurses, policemen, business men, and the laity in psychiatric principles.

The third and fourth implications of the new focus provided by community psychiatry are closely related because each position partially views the structures and processes of the community as containing certain etiological elements that make for the development of certain types of mental and emotional illness. However, the third implication, as we have shown, points to the development of treatment techniques on the collective level, while the fourth emphasizes that knowledge of the community is essential if mental illness is ever to be prevented.

There is no doubt that the word prevention falling on the ears of well-intentioned Americans, is just what the doctor ordered. It is so hopeful that no one, I am sure, will deny that if we can prevent our pathologies this is far better than sitting back and waiting for them to develop. But, of course, there is a catch. How are we going to take the first preventive actions if we are still uncertain about the causes of mental disorders? How do we know where to even cut into a community's round of life? And if we did cut in, what assurance do we have that the results might not be completely the opposite to those anticipated? Of course, there is always secondary prevention—that is, directing our efforts to preventing a recurrence of illness in persons who have once been sick. This is a laudable goal but in connection with mental and emotional disturbances we are still uncertain as to the success of our original treatment efforts.

PREVENTION OF BEHAVIORAL PATHOLOGY—SOME PREVIOUS EFFORTS

There is no doubt that the possibility of prevention is something that will continue to intrigue us for years to come. Therefore, it is not without point to take a look at several other programs that, while they have not all been exclusively oriented toward the treatment of the community, have been launched with the hope of preventing the occurrence of certain unacceptable behavior on the part of the members of a community. I cite two experiments which are widely known with respect to the prevention of delinquency.

The first is Kobrin's statement concerning the 25 year assessment of the Chicago Area Project.[5] Kobrin has presented us with a straight forward, modest, and sophisticated account of the accumulated experience provided by this project in the efforts to bring about a greater control of delinquency in certain areas of Chicago. This project has been significant on several counts, but in my judgment its greatest significance was that it helped to initiate various types of community organizational programs that logically proceeded from an empirically developed theory of delinquency. This theory, in general, viewed delinquency as primarily a "breakdown of the machinery of spontaneous social control." The theory stressed that delinquency was adaptive behavior on the part of adolescents in their peer groups in their efforts to achieve meaningful and respected adult roles, "unaided by the older generation and under the influence of criminal models for whom the intercity areas furnish a haven." This theory, in turn, rests upon certain postulates of sociological theory which emphasize that the development and control of conduct are determined by the network of primary relationships in which one's daily existence is embedded.

The significance of this experiment was that this theory of delinquency provided a rationalization for cutting into the community at certain points and seeking persons there who were ready to organize themselves to secure a higher level of welfare for themselves and their children. The results of this experiment are relevant to those advocators of the preventive function of a community psychiatry because there was not only the difficulty of determining what actually had been accomplished in the way of the prevention of delinquency but also a difficulty in assessing the experience in relation to community welfare.

Kobrin, in his opening sentence, has stated this problem most cogently:

> The Chicago Area Project shares with other delinquency prevention programs the difficulty of measuring its success in a simple and direct manner. At bottom this difficulty rests on the fact that such programs, as efforts to intervene in the life of a person, a group, or a community, cannot by their very nature, constitute more than a subsidiary element in changing the fundamental and sweeping forces which create the problems of groups and of persons or which shape human personality. Decline in rates of delinquents—the only conclusive way to evaluate delinquency prevention—may reflect influences unconnected with those of organized programs and are difficult to define and measure.[6]

The point here is that in a carefully worked out plan based upon an empirically constructed theory it is difficult to determine what has been achieved. One can hazard the observation that if this is true with respect to delinquent behavior where mounting evidence has always supported the idea that its roots are deeply enmeshed in the network of social relationships, how much more difficult it will be in the field of psychiatry to make an assessment in preventive efforts when we are much more uncertain concerning the etological foundations of those cases which appear in psychiatric offices, clinics, and hospitals.

The well-known Cambridge-Summerville Youth Study[7] provides the second example of a delinquency prevention program. While this study did not focus upon the community as such but rather on certain persons therein, it did proceed from a conception of a relationship between a person's needs and a treatment framework for administering to those needs. In this study an attempt was made to provide a warm, human, and continuing relationship between an assigned counsellor and a sample of delinquents and to withhold this relationship from another comparable matched sample. These relationships with most of the boys in the treatment group lasted for approximately eight years. At the conclusion of the experiment there was an attempt to assess the results. These were mainly negative. The number of boys in the treatment group appearing before the crime prevention bureau of the police department were slightly in excess of the number of boys making such appearances in the control group. The only positive note was that the boys in the control group were somewhat more active as recidivists than were the boys in the treatment group.

Although the results of this study were inconclusive and told us nothing particularly about the communities to which these boys were reacting, they did document the failure of one type of relationship therapy to reduce delinquency. While these results provide no final word they do point up the necessity for the various techniques in psychiatry to first acquire a far greater effectiveness than they now possess before starting to operate on a community level where there will be a great deal of fumbling in the dark before knowing exactly what to do.

It seems most appropriate in the light of the task envisioned for community psychiatry to call attention to the professional excitement that was engendered when the Commonwealth Fund inaugurated a child-guidance program in 1922. The Child Guidance Clinic was hailed as a step that eventually should have far-reaching consequences. For who saw fit to deny at that time in the light of certain prevailing theories and the optimism provided by the cultural ethos of the United States that if emotional, mental, and behavioral disturbances were ever to be arrested and prevented at the adult level it would be necessary to arrest these tendencies at their incipient stage, namely, in childhood. This all appears most logical and reasonable. However, 40 years after the opening of the first child guidance clinic we have such clinics in almost every state and they are very much utilized as evidenced by the long waiting lists. Nevertheless, not only does juvenile delinquency remain a continuing community problem but also the adult incidence rates of at least the major psychoses appear to remain approximately constant during this period, especially if the study by Goldhamer and Marshall[8] is accepted as valid.

I cite these three different kinds of experience primarily for the purpose of emphasizing the necessity to review our past efforts in attacking certain behavioral problems at a community level and also to point to some of the difficulties that are inherent in any proposal that emphasizes the development of psychiatric treatment techniques for the "collective level."

THE WIDENING DEFINITION OF MENTAL ILLNESS

Efforts in the direction of carving out a subspecialty of psychiatry known as community psychiatry take place in a cultural atmosphere which has seen a definite attempt to widen the definition of what constitutes mental illness. This is shown by the tendency in our society to place any recognized behavior deviant into the sick role. By doing this we not only supposedly understand them, but we can also point to therapies which will be appropriate for their treatment. Thus, the past two decades have witnessed attempts to place in the sick role delinquents, sex offenders, alcoholics, drug addicts, beatniks, communists, the racially prejudiced, and in fact, practically all persons who do not fit into the prevailing togetherness that we like to think characterizes middle-class American life. The danger here is that we only add to our state of confusion because the line between who is sick and who is well becomes increasingly a waving, uncertain one. Thus, we appear to be constantly moving the cutting point toward the end of the continuum that would include those persons who in some subcultural milieus are accepted as normal.

There is much current statistical evidence that supports this notion of a widening definition for mental illness. For example, if one examines the community epidemiological surveys of mental illness in the 1930's and compares them with the community epidemiological surveys in the 1950's one is struck with the fact that four to five times more cases are reported in the latter years.[10] In my own epidemiological study of schizophrenia, where I have examined many epidemiological studies from all over the world I have noted the great differences that are reported with respect to total mental disorders in the surveys, a marked decrease in the differences between the surveys when only psychoses are reported and a still further decrease in the rate variations when the reports are based upon only one mental disorder, namely, schizophrenia. In this latter case, the variations are slight and all of the rates are quite close together. One might point to the Mid-Town Manhattan Survey[11] where two psychiatrists reviewing symptom schedules on a sample population as collected by field workers found that approximately 80% of the sample were suffering from some type of psychiatric symptom. This extreme figure can be contrasted with the 20% reported as incapacitated. The providing of adequate psychiatric services for even the latter figure would place an impossible burden on any community.

Several factors help to explain this widening definition of mental illness which has been so apparent during the past two decades. One factor, of course, has been the adaptation of psychiatry to office practice following World War II.[12] Another factor is that the mounting frustration resulting from the failures to achieve therapeutic results with the bona fide psychotics has led to a widening of the psychiatric net in order to include those persons with minor emotional disturbances who are more responsive to existing treatment techniques. These people are suffering from what has been termed "problems of living," and they do not represent the bona fide mentally ill cases.[13] In this connection it is interesting to note that George W. Albee, at an American Medical Association meeting in Chicago, stated:

> What we clearly do not need more of in the mental health profession are people who go into private practice of psychotherapy with middle-aged neurotics in high income suburbs. While there are

humanitarian and ethical reasons for offering all the help we possibly can to individuals afflicted with mental disorders, it seems unlikely that we will ever have the manpower to offer individual care on any kind of manageable ratio of therapists to sufferers.*

In the light of Albee's observation it is instructive to note Paul Hoch's evaluation[14] of the therapeutic accomplishments of mental health clinics in New York State. With respect to psychotherapeutic techniques he states:

> I do not mean to deny that psychotherapy brings relief to those suffering from emotional disorders or that it may not be the treatment of choice in certain cases. What I am questioning is the preoccupation with intensive psychotherapy in clinics which are part of the community health program. After more than fifty years of its utilization we still have no foolproof of its effectiveness, of its superiority over other forms of treatment or even a long term is better than brief psychotherapy.[14]

He goes on to point out that while in the previous year 30,000 patients were released from the state hospital, nevertheless, only 8% of the cases that were terminated by psychiatric clinics came from inpatient facilities. He notes also that the volume of patients being treated in the state hospitals is greater than ever before, in spite of an almost unanimous need to develop alternatives to state hospital care. His evidence supports this contention of a widening definition of mental illness, implying that the outpatient clinics are not treating cases that are likely to need hospital care but are treating numerous cases that are experiencing emotional problems. These are, for the most part, tied up with the daily round of human existence and can never be completely eliminated except in a societal utopia. One conclusion appears inescapable—the more clinics, the more patients. In addition, this widening definition of mental illness has served as a type of fuel for the development of the idea of a community psychiatry.

HISTORICAL AND CULTURAL INFLUENCES

There is the problem as every historian recognizes of how far back one should go in enumerating those events which helped to shape a present situation, because every historical event is both a consequence of some previous happening and a cause of something that is to take place in the future. However, I begin my history of the proposal for a community psychiatry with the accumulated psychiatric experience which came out of World War II. Psychiatric experience during the war showed that a large number of inductees were afflicted with various types of neuropsychiatric disorders. This finding was reported by Dr. William Meninger, head of psychiatric services of the United States Armed Forces, in a book dealing with his war experience and anticipating the uses to which psychiatry might be put in meeting the new problems and tensions that were arising in American society and in the societies throughout the world. In this volume Meninger[15] asks if psychiatry after the war is to continue its

---

* See Hoch, P.[14]

preoccupation with the end results of mental disease or is "to discover how it can contribute to the problems of the average man and to the larger social issues in which he is involved." Thus, Meninger anticipated that the new role for psychiatry would be expanded to deal with family problems, industrial conflict, community conflict, and in fact, any situation where conflict, difficulties, and tensions arise between people. Thus, the publication of this work seemed to play a role in turning psychiatry away from its traditional concerns and in directing its attention to problems of the community.

The work of Meninger, Thompson[16] and others tended to anticipate a more positive and frontal attack upon mental health problems in American society. The writings of these men set the stage for the passage of the National Mental Health Act in 1948 which has played a significant role in stimulating professional training, research, and treatment programs in psychiatry and its allied fields. After the passage of this act which raised mental health to the status of a public health problem numerous events followed swiftly. Certainly the new monies available through the Federal Government and foundations made it possible for scholars from all over the United States and Europe to meet more often to deal with specific problems in the mental health field. This exchange of scholars acquainted psychiatric workers in the United States with the various programs and plans that were being carried on in Eurpoe for handling mental health problems, such as Querido's program for community psychiatry in Amsterdam, the development of the open door hospital in England, auxiliary psychiatric units such as night- and day-hospitals, rehabilitation houses, and various kinds of industrial units to train the mental convalescent for jobs. All of these developments proved most exciting and interesting, stimulated thinking, broke through conventional and traditional notions of the past, and paved the way for taking many new looks as to how we could more adequately treat the mentally ill in order to more quickly return them to their families and communities.

In fact, these developments began to undercut various conceptions of chronicity and we recognized that hospitalization for mental illness need not be a lifetime affair. We should call attention also to the research on the mental hospital conducted by social scientists which provided a rationale for the hospital as a therapeutic community, a development that Maxwell Jones[17] in his work in England has already anticipated. However, these studies that came during the 1950's in the work of Stanton and Schwartz,[18] Dunham and Weinberg,[19] Belknap,[20] John and Elaine Cumming,[21] and W. Caudill[22] increasingly began to pose the issue as to whether the therapeutic community could be considered as a real factor in the treatment process. These studies further called attention to the rigid traditional structure of the state hospital and how it actually contained within itself those cultural forms that tended to discourage patients towards moving to a level of acceptable behavior. Finally, there came the report of a Joint Commission on Mental Illness and Health[23] in 1961, along with the Surgeon General's recommendation in January, 1962, that the states explore a more complete utilization of all community resources dealing with the mentally ill towards achieving a maximum in the prevention and treatment of such illnesses. And as a final stimulus came the speech of the late President Kennedy[24] to Congress in October of 1963 in which he outlined a broad program with respect to community centered hospitals, research and training, covering both mental illness and mental retardation.

In the above account I have attempted a cursory examination of the central historical events that have led to the development of community psychiatry. However, in a broader perspective these events can be regarded as the consequences of the cultural forces embodied in certain beliefs and traditions that are deeply embedded in the texture of American society. In a sense the emergence of community psychiatry as a subspecialty of psychiatry is a reflection of the cherished American belief that all problems are capable of solution if we can just discover the key by means of the scientific methodology at our disposal. The ever-multiplying programs of health insurance during the past 20 years have also laid an economic foundation making it possible to bring mental patients out in the open instead of hiding them away as we have done in the past. Under these conditions the essential qualities of American culture, individualism, optimism, humanism, and the equalitarianism have merely provided the additional push for the emergence of community psychiatry.

SOME HIDDEN ASPECTS FOR THE ROLE OF PSYCHIATRY

In this account I have pointed to the several conceptions which seem to be implied in the development of a community psychiatry. I have emphasized that the tieing of community psychiatry with the several evolving plans throughout the country to reorganize the mental health facilities toward the end of maximizing treatment potential is a significant move. While there is the question as to whether community psychiatry extends beyond current psychiatric practices there may be a gain in identifying the psychiatrist more closely with the different community services and breaking down the isolation in which both the psychoanalytic practitioner and the hospital practicing psychiatrist have been enmeshed. This would move the psychiatrist not only closer to the patient but what is more important, closer to the entire network of interpersonal relationships of the family and the community in which the patient is involved.

However, it is in the other visions that have been held up for community psychiatry wherein I think, as I have indicated, great difficulties are in the offing. Here I am most skeptical concerning the adequacy of our knowledge to develop significant techniques for treating social collectivities or for developing techniques on the community level that will really result in a reduction of mental disturbances in the community. It seems that such expectations are likely to remove the psychiatrist still further from the more bona fide cases of mental illnesses that develop within the community context. Much of his effort will be spent on dealing with the noncritical cases. This trend has already been going on for some time as I have indicated in discussing the widening definition of mental illness. Until we have a more sound knowledge which will indicate that the minor emotional disturbances are likely to develop into the more serious types of mental disturbances we will be dissipating much of our collective psychi-atric efforts.

Then, too, there is another hidden aspect of these projected con-ceptions of community psychiatry which deserves careful exploration. I refer to the implication that the psychiatrist will be able to move into the ongoing power structure of a community. The profession must confront the issue as to whether its effectiveness will be less or greater if some of its members should succeed in obtaining roles within the power structure of any community. Here, I would suggest that such a psychiatrist would find himself in a system where his professional effectiveness would be con-siderably reduced because he would be involved in a series of mutual ob-ligations and expectations in relation to the other person composing the power structure. He would thus lose the role that in general characterizes the professional in other areas, that of being an adviser and a consultant with respect to any psychiatric problems or issues that the groups, institu-tions, and associations of the community confront. What I am trying to indicate is that in becoming a part of the power structure he is likely to lose more than he gains. That is, his gains would be in respect to power, personal prestige, and recognition but his losses would be in the growing rustiness of his diagnostic and therapeutic skills with patients.

Another implication of these aspects of community psychiatry is the fact that psychiatrists are being pushed in a direction not entirely of their own making. The national efforts and monies that are being directed to the states and communities for the reorganization of the mental health facilities have engendered a high degree of excitement among professional social workers, mental health educators, psychiatric nurses, and numerous well-intentioned persons who see new professional opportunities for serv-ice and careers. Thus, the psychiatrist is led to think, because of these pressures, that he should prepare himself with new skills in order to pro-vide the required leadership to these various professionals who are plan-ning to work towards this new vision to maximize the treatment potential in the community for the mentally ill.

Finally, there is the implication that psychiatry is being utilized to move us closer in the direction of the welfare state. This may not be un-desirable in itself but it seems most essential that psychiatrists should be aware of the role that they are asked to play. We can anticipate that while the doctor-patient relationship will still be paramount in most medical practice the psychiatrist is likely to move into roles unforeseen but which will be required by the new structural organization of psychiatric facilities with the proposal for a community psychiatry. In such new roles the psychiatrists may become agents for social control, thus sacrificing the main task for which their education has fitted them.

In this paper I have attempted to show the link between community psychiatry and the new evolving community mental health programs. While one can see in this linkage a most significant development I am somewhat skeptical toward those emphases in community psychiatry which aim at the development of treatment techniques on the community level. In discussing the widening definition of mental illness I have tried to show that this is one of the crucial factors that has accounted for this movement towards a new type of psychiatric specialty. I have seen, in this widening definition, an opportunity to overcome a frustration that engulfs psychiatrists with respect to their inability to make much therapeutic headway with the traditional mental cases. Finally, I have attempted to consider some of the hidden implications for psychiatry in the proposal for this new psychiatric specialty.

Thanks for critical comments on the manuscript are extended to the following colleagues at Lafayette Clinic; Jacques Gottlieb, MD, Director of Lafayette Clinic; Elliott Luby, MD, Assistant Director in Charge of Clinical Services; Paul Lowinger, MD, Chief, Adult Out-Patient Services; Garfield Tourney, MD, Assistant Director in Charge of Education.

REFERENCES

1. Bernard, V. "Some Interrelationships of Training for Community Psychiatry, Community Mental Health Programs and Research in Social Psychiatry," in Proceedings of Third World Congress of Psychiatry, Montreal, Canada: McGill University and University of Toronto Press, 1961, vol. 3, pp. 67–71.
2. Goldston, S. E. Training in Community Psychiatry: Survey Report of Medical School Departments of Psychiatry, Amer. J. Psychiat. 120:789–792 (Feb.) 1964.
3. Duhl, L. J. Problems in Training Psychiatric Residents in Community Psychiatry, paper read before the Institute on Training in Community Psychiatry at University of California, Texas, Columbia, and Chicago, mimeographed, Fall-Winter, 1963–1964, p. 6.
4. Merton, R. K. "Social Structures and Anomie," in Social Theory and Social Structure, Glencoe, Ill.: The Free Press, 1949, pp. 125–150.
5. Kobrin, S. Chicago Area Project—25-Year Assessment, Ann. Amer. Acad. Political Soc. Sci., 322:20–29 (March) 1959.
6. Kobrin, S.[5]
7. Powers, E., and Witmer, H. Experiment in Prevention of Delinquency, New York: Columbia University Press, 1951.
8. Goldhamer, H., and Marshall, A. Psychoses and Civilization, Glencoe, Ill.: The Free Press, 1953.
9. Dunham, H. W. Sociological Theory and Mental Disorder, Detroit: Wayne State University Press, 1959, chap. 6.
10. Plunkett, R. J., and Gordon, J. E. Epidemiology and Mental Illness, New York: Basic Books, Inc., Publishers, 1960, p. 90.
11. Srole, L., et al. Mental Health in Metropolis: Midtown Manhattan Study, New York: McGraw-Hill Book Co., Inc., 1962, vol. 1.
12. Barton, W. E. Presidential Address—Psychiatry in Transition, Amer. J. Psychiat. 119:1–15 (July) 1962.
13. Szasz, T. S. Myth of Mental Illness: Foundations of Theory of Personal Conduct, New York: Paul B. Hoeber, Inc., Medical Division Harper & Brothers, 1961.
14. Paul H. Hoch: in Therapeutic Accomplishments of Mental Health Clinics, Ment Hygiene News, June, 1963, pp. 1–3.
15. Meninger, W. Psychiatry in Troubled World, New York: The Macmillan Company, 1948, chap 13.
16. Thompson, C. B. Psychiatry and Social Crisis, J. Clin. Psychopath 7:697–711 (April) 1946.
17. Jones, M. Therapeutic Community: New Treatment Method in Psychiatry, New York: Basic Books, Inc., Publishers, 1953.
18. Stanton, A., and Schwartz, M. S. Mental Hospital: Study of Institutional Participation in Psychiatric Illness and Treatment, New York: Basic Books, Inc., Publishers, 1954.
19. Dunham, H. W., and Weinberg, S. K. Culture of State Mental Hospital, Detroit: The Wayne State University Press, 1960.
20. Belknap, I. Human Problems of State Mental Hospital, New York: Blakiston, Medical Division McGraw-Hill Book Co., 1956.

21. Cumming, J., and Cumming, E.: Closed Ranks: Experiment in Mental Health Education, Cambridge Mass: Harvard University Press, Commonwealth Fund, 1957.
22. Caudill, W.: Psychiatric Hospital as a Small Society, Cambridge, Mass.: Harvard University Press, 1958.
23. Joint Commission on Mental Illness and Health: Action for Mental Health, New York: Basic Books, Inc., Publishers, 1961, p 338.
24. Kennedy, J. F.: Message From President of United States Relative to Mental Illness and Mental Retardation: February 5, 1963, Amer. J. Psychiat. 120:729–737 (Feb.) 1964.

51. Three Approaches to Delinquency Prevention: A Critique

John M. Martin

Delinquency remains one of the critical social problems in our society. In the following selection, three basic approaches to delinquency prevention are treated: improvement of the general societal welfare, programs at the community level, and rehabilitation of individual delinquents. After weighing the relative merits of each approach, John M. Martin concludes that the community-centered approach provides the most efficient means for tackling the problem of delinquency. Why does he believe this to be true? What is your reaction to his conclusion?

Aside from punishment and strict repression, delinquency prevention is usually defined in these three different ways:

1. Delinquency prevention is the sum total of all activities that contribute to the adjustment of children and to healthy personalities in children.

Crime and Delinquency, January, 1961, 16–24. Reprinted with the permission of the publisher and author.

*Adapted from the author's book, *Juvenile Vandalism: A Study of Its Nature and Prevention,* Charles C Thomas, Springfield, Ill., 1961.

2. Delinquency prevention is the attempt to deal with particular environmental conditions that are believed to contribute to delinquency.

3. Delinquency prevention consists of specific preventive services provided to individual children or groups of children.[1]

GENERAL DESCRIPTION

The logic underlying preventive activities of the first type is disarmingly simple: anything that contributes to the adjustment of children and to their healthy personality development prevents delinquency. Basically this approach links delinquency prevention with general improvements in the institutional fabric of our society, particularly as these affect child welfare. In large part this approach rests on a continuation and extension of measures, now commonplace on the American scene, which are designed to reduce the economic inequities of our social system. Such activities include procedures for raising the income levels of poverty stricken families, better low-rent housing, improving job tenure and work arrangements, and other means for reducing the rigors of poverty and economic insecurity. The approach also embraces attempts to reduce prejudice and discrimination against minority group people, increase the educational achievements of oncoming generations, improve marital relations by premarital counseling and family social work, and increase the impact of religious doctrines on both adults and children.

Preventive activities of the second type, by and large, aim to overcome factors in the immediate environment of children that seem to contribute to their delinquency. Such activities include attempts at community organization, such as the Chicago Area Projects (to be discussed later in this article); work by "coordinating councils" for harmonizing the efforts of welfare and child care agencies in delinquency prevention; the work of recreational and character-building agencies of all types; and attempts to reduce the commercial activities of adults which are clearly illegal and detrimental to the welfare of children who may get caught up in such traffic as, for example, the sale of liquor to minors, dope peddling, and receiving stolen goods.

Preventive activities of the third type include probation and parole services to children and youths, the programs of residential institutions and special schools for delinquents, child guidance clinics insofar as they are concerned with the diagnosis and treatment of delinquents, direct work with antisocial street gangs, and a variety of other services whose principal purpose is the adjustment of individual children or groups of children.

RELATIVE MERITS

It would be enormously difficult, if not impossible, to measure the effectiveness of these three types of preventive activities in terms of their ability

---

[1]H. A. Bloch and F. T. Flynn, *Delinquency: The Juvenile Offender in America Today*, New York, Random House, 1956, p. 512.

actually to reduce delinquency, and no attempt will be made to do so here. However, general comment will be made about the relative merits of the three approaches.

In the main it is correct to conclude that improvement in the collective welfare, particularly in the welfare of depressed minority people, will reduce delinquency. In areas such as metropolitan New York the reduction of juvenile delinquency is most intimately liked with the successful assimilation of low-status groups, in particular the ever increasing number of migrant and uprooted Negroes and Puerto Ricans.[2] Whatever contributes to the welfare and assimilation of these people reduces the delinquency rate among their children and, correspondingly, in the communities in which they live; conversely, whatever impedes their progress inflates the delinquency rate in those areas.

But the relationship between delinquency and improvement in the general welfare is more complicated than it appears at first glance. For example, although it is tempting to claim that improved housing and the reduction of poverty will reduce both crime and delinquency, evidence that delinquency is highest during periods of extreme prosperity and *not* during depressions, as well as awareness of the variety and number of offenses committed by middle- and upper-class persons, should warn us against the facile assumption that the elimination of poverty is the Rosetta stone of crime prevention.

The relationship between delinquency, at least in terms of official statistics, and poverty and poor housing has, of course, long been noted by students of social problems. However, it is erroneous to conclude that the abolishment of these living conditions will also abolish delinquency among low-status children. As Bernard Lander pointed out in his study of differential juvenile delinquency rates by census tracts in Baltimore,[3] delinquency appears to be fundamentally related to social instability or *anomie* and not basically to poverty and poor housing.

It is within this context that we can best understand the disillusionment of those who expected too much by way of delinquency prevention from public housing. Their disappointment is well reflected in the pungent remark reportedly made by one student of New York's slums: "Once upon a time we thought that if we could only get our problem families out of those dreadful slums, then papa would stop taking dope, mama would stop chasing around, and Junior would stop carrying a knife. Well, we've got them in a nice apartment with modern kitchens and a recreation center. And they're the same bunch of bastards they always were."[4]

Emphasis upon *anomie* or social disorganization as a basic contributing factor to the high delinquency rates characteristic of some urban areas, with a concomitant de-emphasis of the obvious poverty of these areas as the underlying factor in their high delinquency rates, would, then, appear

---

[2] For an excellent discussion of this point, see O. Handlin, *The Newcomers*, Cambridge, Mass., Harvard University Press, 1959, especially chap. 4

[3] See B. Lander, *Towards an Understanding of Juvenile Delinquency*, New York, Columbia University Press, 1954, especially p. 89.

[4] D. Seligman, "The Enduring Slums" in the Editors of Fortune, *The Exploding Metropolis*, Garden City, N.Y., Doubleday, 1958, pp. 111-132.

to be of cardinal importance for understanding and preventing delinquency in such places.

ANOMIE AND DELINQUENCY

Useful as Lander's statistical analysis of census tracts in Baltimore may be for destroying the myth that poverty and inadequate housing are the root causes of delinquency, the relationship between *anomie* and delinquency may also be more complicated than it seems. Lander emphasized the "internal" disorganization characteristic of high delinquency areas. Yet relatively *stable* neighborhoods may also be characterized by comparatively high rates of delinquency. A good example of just such a neighborhood is the tightly knit Italian slum of "Eastern City" examined by William Foote Whyte in his classic, *Street Corner Society*.[5]

The existence of stable but delinquent neighborhoods suggests that there are at least two kinds of areas that produce delinquency.

One is the rapidly changing and thoroughly chaotic local area of the kind isolated by Lander, perhaps best illustrated by New York City's recially mixed and tension-ridden Spanish Harlem so well described by Dan Wakefield in *Island in the City*.[6]

The other is the rather well-organized neighborhood such as the Italian ethnic community studied by Whyte, "disorganized" primarily in the sense that the way of life there is judged "out of step" when contrasted with the essentially middle-class culture of the greater society.[7]

It is in the second kind of area particularly that well-developed relationships are likely to exist between criminally precocious adolescents, corrupt politicians, and the seemingly inevitable racketeers. These relationships go far in explaining the easy transition many delinquents make from juvenile misbehavior to the more sophisticated forms of adult criminality. It is in this type of area, too, that personality and family structures are less likely to split and disintegrate under the stresses and strains characteristic of more chaotic and tension-ridden neighborhoods.

But distinctions of this sort, important as they may be for understanding differences in the social structure of delinquency areas, must not obscure a more basic fact: quite aside from the stability or instability of social relations in delinquency-prone areas, the traditions, standards, and moral sentiments of such areas are notoriously delinquent and criminal in "complexion" and "tone." This peculiar cultural climate has long been recognized by students of urban life, particularly by the ecologists and social psychologists of the "Chicago School" of American sociology.[8]

---

[5] W. F. Whyte, *Street Corner Society*, enlarged edition; Chicago, University of Chicago Press, 1955.

[6] D. Wakefield, *Island in the City*, Boston, Houghton Mifflin, 1959.

[7] For a further discussion of these two kinds of delinquency areas, see W. F. Whyte, "Social Organization in the Slums," *American Sociological Review*, February, 1943, pp. 34–39.

[8] For an excellent survey of studies in the "social ecology" of crime conducted during the past 150 years, see T. Morris, *The Criminal Area*, London, Routledge and Kegan Paul, 1958, chaps. 1–6.

Recently this recognition has linked up with a more general discussion of social-class subcultures and particularly with more detailed analyses of lower-class culture as a breeding ground for delinquency. A good example of this is found in an article by Walter B. Miller which called attention to the delinquency proneness of lower-class culture in a discussion of the "focal concerns" of the urban lower-class way of life.[9] Miller's emphasis is not upon the so-called "subculture of the delinquent gang" as discussed by Albert K. Cohen,[10] but upon the content of the whole mode of existence of urban lower-class people. Miller believes that in the lower class, in contrast with the middle class, people are likely to have commitments to focal concerns such as physical "toughness," "smartness" interpreted as the ability to "con" or dupe others, and "excitement" in terms of seeking thrills, taking risks, and courting danger. When these commitments are combined with the intense need for "in-group" membership and status or "rep" so characterisic of lower-lass adolescents, Miller feels that conditions are especially ripe for the development of juvenile misconduct, particularly gang delinquency.

Thus the concept of social disorganization can be used to describe both stable and unstable delinquency areas. If we accept such disorganization as basic to an understanding of law violation in both kinds of areas, then we must question the value of other delinquency prevention methods besides those aimed at the reduction of poverty. In particular we should examine the limitations inherent in current attempts to prevent delinquency by the use of "individual-centered" techniques such as social casework and related psychological-psychiatric services.

"INDIVIDUAL-CENTERED" TECHNIQUES

Practitioners of such techniques work toward individual adjustment, not social change. Seldom do they try to reduce the delinquency-producing features of the delinquent's environment, especially his extrafamilial environment; instead they emphasize adjustment to prevailing environmental conditions. For most delinquents, who are generally without emotional disturbance and who reflect the patterned deviancy so often found in their lower-class neighborhoods,[11] this means that they are expected to make a nondelinquent adjustment to a highly delinquent life situation. Our recidivism rates testify that at best this adjustment is precarious. Furthermore—and this is perhaps the more basic point—because such efforts fail to come to grips with the underlying social and cultural conditions giving rise to delinquency, they do little to prevent the outcropping of delinquency in the first instance. Most try to take hold only after maladjustment, even delinquency itself, has become manifest in the lives of the youngsters they seek to help.

---

[9] W. B. Miller, "Lower Class Culture as a Generating Milieu of Gang Delinquency," *The Journal of Social Issues*, Vol. 14, No. 3, 1958, pp. 5–19.

[10] See A. K. Cohen, *Delinquent Boys: The Culture of the Gang*, Glencoe, Ill., The Free Press, 1955.

[11] For a recent discussion of this crucial point, see W. C. Kvaraceus *et al.*, *Delinquent Behavior: Culture and the Individual*, Washington, D.C., National Education Association of the United States, 1959, chap. 7.

This, however, should not be taken as a rejection of probation and parole, of training schools and reformatories, of child guidance clinics, and of other kinds of institutions and agencies given over to the care and "correction" of delinquents. Far from abandoning this line of approach, we must work hard at improving existing facilities of this sort and act imaginatively regarding the "invention" of new ones. Furthermore, we must, as we have seldom paused to do in the past, rigorously test and verify the effectiveness of various approaches aimed at the rehabilitation of individual delinquents. In this regard the basic question still to be answered is: To what extent and under what conditions do our correctional agencies really correct?

But despite all of this, we must not be so carried away by our desire to rehabilitate delinquents that we fail to see individual treatment in a proper perspective, lose sight of its limitations, and ignore the fundamental proposition that *the prevention of delinquency should include both individual treatment and general or social prevention.* Unfortunately this is just what has happened. To a truly remarkable degree public and private delinquency prevention agencies have spent comparatively little money or energy on community-centered programs of social prevention. For decades most of these agencies have put their effort into establishing various kinds of facilities for rehabilitating delinquents on a case-by-case basis, with the "model" and most prestigeful approach in recent years being that of the psychiatrically-oriented child guidance clinic.

In sum, if we grant the primary role social disorganization plays in the development of delinquency, then the prevention of delinquency is not fundamentally a problem of bettering the general welfare of children or rehabilitating individuals, although the wisdom of continuing our attempts at both seems obvious. Nor for that matter is delinquency prevention essentially a problem of coordinating the activity of welfare agencies, although, like the application of "individual-centered" techniques, this too has an important role to play in prevention. (The coordination of agency activity is particularly valuable insofar as it enables accurate statistics on reported delinquency to be gathered in various jurisdictions, for it is only on the basis of such statistics that a community can determine the trend of its delinquency and measure the effectiveness of its preventive efforts. Agency coordination is even more valuable when it serves to bring various preventive programs and techniques to bear on potential delinquents before their deviancy becomes well established.)

Basically, the problem of delinquency prevention is a problem of social organization or reorganization, and other approaches have merit only to the degree that they contribute to such reorganization.

SOCIAL REORGANIZATION

How can social reorganization best be accomplished? Although we may be both unable and unwilling to reduce substantially the drift toward *anomie* that Robert K. Merton[12] and others have suggested is a pervasive

---

[12] See R. K. Merton, *Social Theory and Social Structure*, Glencoe, Ill., The Free Press, 1949, chap. 4.

characteristic of American society, we may be able to make partial inroads upon such disorganization, particularly insofar as it is related to the problem of juvenile delinquency, if we focus directly on the local areas in which delinquency is most pronounced. The logic underlying this proposal is that a local area "does not need to control the entire culture of a nation (which would be impossible) in order to control its delinquency rate. The things that need to be done are local and relate to personal interaction rather than to the larger institutions."[13] The essence of this approach to social reorganization, then, is to stimulate social change in delinquency-prone neighborhoods.

Unfortunately we have no rich arsenal of tried and proven techniques for accomplishing such change. Much needs to be learned and many innovations need to be developed toward this end. Despite these difficulties, however, we do know much about stimulating change in delinquency areas. The framework within which the reorganization of such neighborhoods can be accomplished has been well described by Frederic M. Thrasher in his outline of a proposal for coordinating neighborhood activity for delinquency prevention.[14]

This proposal envisions that any attempt to prevent delinquency in local areas must fix responsibility for social change at the neighborhood level where such changes can be implemented by local community leaders assisted by experts. Implicit in this approach is the assumption that in even the most delinquency-prone neighborhoods not all the residents are criminals or delinquents, and that in such areas there is actually a duality of conduct norms—one favoring law-abiding behavior, the other favoring delinquency.[15]

Although Thrasher's plan utilizes, as subsidiary techniques, the best services offered by the usual community agencies—especially those of school, court, training institutions, and child guidance clinic—his proposal "represents a radical departure from the methods of social work and community organization as formerly conceived."[16]

This comment made almost three decades ago is nearly as applicable now as it was then. When one surveys current social work efforts at community organization, it becomes abundantly clear that, far from being focused in local areas, this activity is largely country- or city-wide in scope. Furthermore, all too often "community organization" in social work means that professional social workers meet with one another and with upper- and middle-class laymen for the purposes of mapping fund-raising campaigns, educating the public, coordinating agency activity, and similar objectives. Even when particular neighborhoods are the target for

---

[13] E. H. Sutherland, "Prevention of Juvenile Delinquency" in A. Cohen et al. (eds.), The Sutherland Papers, Bloomington, Indiana University Press, 1956, pp. 131–140.

[14] F. M. Thrasher, "Some Principles Underlying Community Co-ordination," The Journal of Educational Sociology, March, 1945, pp. 387–400.

[15] For a discussion of the duality of conduct norms in delinquency areas, see S. Kobrin, "The Conflict of Values in Delinquency Areas," American Sociological Review, October, 1951, pp. 653–661.

[16] F. M. Thrasher, The Gang, second revised edition; Chicago, University of Chicago Press, 1936, p. 538.

such organization, seldom is the basic responsiblity for such work placed in the hands of leaders who are truly representative of the people living in such areas.

Fundamentally the difference between the kind of plan outlined by Thrasher and traditional social work proposals for community organization is that in the former the real work is done by local residents who, banded together in a committee or council, act to (1) get the facts about delinquents and delinquency in their neighborhood; (2) organize existing preventive forces serving their neighborhood; (3) stimulate the development of new programs and services as required; and (4) in cooperation with professional agencies, look to the adjustment of their own delinquents, organize the leisure-time activities of their own children and young people, and improve the neighborhood environment, particularly by encouraging the enforcement of laws outlawing the activities of "slum landlords," petty racketeers, and other adults that are clearly detrimental to the welfare of their neighborhood and their children.

Other sociologists besides Thrasher have also foreseen the urgency of organizing the local community for delinquency prevention. Thus Edwin H. Sutherland, for example, endorsed local community organization as the most effective means for preventing delinquency, emphasized the need for placing responsibility for such organization in the hands of those whose children are the most likely to become delinquent, and cited the necessity of including juveniles themselves as participants in such organization.[17]

The inclusion of children and youths in neighborhood organizations for delinquency prevention is most vital. Too often they are simply left out of the planning and management phases of such activity. As a result, the isolation of their adolescence is compounded and a real opportunity for establishing closer ties between the generations is overlooked.

CHICAGO AREA PROJECT

Perhaps the best known of the relatively few delinquency prevention programs predicated on local community organization that are actually in operation are the Chicago Area Projects developed by Clifford R. Shaw and his associates.[18] Basically these projects aim at producing internal cohesiveness and conventional behavior in delinquency areas through the development of *indigenous leadership*. Outside professional leadership is minimal. Chiefly it is used to interest and develop local talent. Program activities are not ends in themselves but are used to achieve local unity. Some direct work is done with children and adolescents on a one-to-one counseling basis, and psychiatric and other types of referrals are made when needed. But the central aim is to draw local youngsters into various project activities

---

[17] Sutherland, "Prevention of Juvenile Delinquency," *op. cit.*

[18] For detailed descriptions of the Chicago Area Projects, see A. Sorrentino, "The Chicago Area Project after Twenty-five Years," *Federal Probation*, June, 1959, pp. 40–45; S. Kobrin, "The Chicago Area Project–A Twenty-five-Year Assessment," *The Annals of the American Academy of Political and Social Science*, March, 1959, pp. 20–29.

so that they will identify with conventional rather than with delinquent groups and cultural patterns.

Outside leaders have a definite but limited role. This approach to area reorganization places principal emphasis on the role of natural community leaders who are carriers of conventional conduct norms. Not only do such leaders serve as nondelinquent models for emulation by youngsters attracted to programs offered by projects of this type, but because these indigenous leaders have prestige in the local area, they easily attract adults, as well as children and youths, to project programs in the first instance. It is around natural community leaders, then, that legitimate social structures can be germinated and multiplied in delinquency-prone areas. And it is in relationship with such leaders and within such structures that youngsters can develop the close and intimate attachments with conventional models, achieve the satisfactions, and acquire the sense of personal worth and purpose necessary to counter the drift toward delinquency characteristic of their life situations.

SOME BASIC QUESTIONS

Two basic questions arise relative to preventive programs like the Chicago Area Projects: First, *can they be established, and once established will they last? Second, do they actually prevent delinquency?*

In regard to both parts of the first question, the answers seem to be definitely affirmative. Thus, in their recent evaluation of the Chicago Area Projects, Witmer and Tufts found that:

1. Residents of low-income areas can organize and have organized themselves into effective working units for promoting and conducting welfare programs.

2. These community organizations have been stable and enduring. They raise funds, administer them well, and adapt the programs to local needs.

3. Local talent, otherwise untapped, has been discovered and utilized. Local leadership has been mobilized in the interest of children's welfare.[19]

A definite answer to the second question is much more difficult to obtain. However, two types of evidence tentatively suggest that it too may be affirmative. First, statistics from 1930 to 1942 indicate that delinquency rates declined in three out of four of the communities in which projects were then being carried on; second, in some of the projects, work with men and boys on parole from institutions has been very successful, with one project noting that out of forty-one parolees worked with between 1935 and 1944, only one was recommitted to an institution.[20] However, evidence such as this, without comparable controls, must obviously remain inconclusive. As has been remarked elsewhere, "the role of any preventive agency is likely to be most difficult to assess."[21] The Chicago Area Projects are no exception.

---

[19] H. L. Witmer and E. Tufts, *The Effectiveness of Delinquency Prevention Programs*, Children's Bureau, United States Department of Health, Education and Welfare, Publication 305, Washington, D.C., Government Printing Office, 1954, p. 15.

[20] *Ibid.*, p. 16.

[21] Bloch and Flynn, *op cit.*, p. 514.

Another question that arises with respect to delinquency prevention programs geared to local leadership is: *How can they best be originated?* In this regard Walter C. Reckless has warned against waiting for the "spontaneous generation of experimental action"; outside help must get such programs started by stimulating local leaders to action.[22] Likewise it seems necessary that outside assistance should also include sufficient money, at least in the beginning, to help defray costs. Again and again programs of this type have foundered because the few hundred dollars raised by raffles, cake sales, thrift shops, and local donations were simply not enough to meet day-to-day expenses.

Who should provide such assistance? To this there are a number of answers. The potential role of private foundations, boards of education, fraternal organizations, and private industry and labor unions in supporting or initiating such activity is enormous. Of special significance is the potential but presently underdeveloped role urban churches can play in this field. The force of organized religion in the prevention of delinquency will be more fully realized if, and only if, more churches make realistic financial appropriations for such purpose and if, on the personal level, more churchmen base their approach to delinquency on love, direct service, intimate communication, and example, instead of on benign indifference, social distance, and exhortation.[23]

Assistance should also be available from other sources. For example, communities in states with Youth Authority plans might well call upon such authorities for help insofar as these state agencies actually make provision for realistic assistance to local communities; and in New York the new State Youth Division, one purpose of which is to stimulate communities to take action with regard to delinquency, should be a prime source of both money and advice, as should the Youth Board in New York City. Although the Federal Youth Corrections Act makes no provision for rendering assistance to local communities, the capacity of the federal government in this and other facets of community programs for delinquency prevention is tremendous. Finally, professional social workers themselves, as citizens, as agency representatives and educators, and as spokesmen for their highly influential professional associations, might becomes less remiss about endorsing, inaugurating, and experimenting with community-centered crime prevention programs.

In any event, if neighborhood programs run by residents are to develop to their full potential, it seems almost axiomatic that outside assistance must be provided.

---

[22] W. C. Reckless, *The Crime Problem*, New York, Appleton-Century-Crofts, 1950, pp. 524–525.

[23] For excellent descriptions of religious programs in which churchmen have established intimate relationships with gang members and other residents of delinquency-prone neighborhoods, see C. K. Myers, *Light the Dark Streets*, Greenwich, Conn., Seabury Press, 1957, and H. J. Rahm and J. R. Weber, *Office in the Alley: Report on a Project with Gang Youngsters*, Austin, University of Texas, Hogg Foundation for Mental Health, 1958.

IN SUMMARY

Students of delinquency are becoming increasingly aware of the necessity of reaching out beyond the child and his family in their efforts at prevention. It is submitted that the most efficacious approach for modifying the operating milieu of the bulk of our delinquents is through the widespread establishment of community-centered programs of prevention. Supported by continued improvement in the collective welfare—particularly in terms of the succesful assimilation of low-status groups—and incorporating the best of "corrections" and individual treatment, the community-centered approach offers the most hope for reducing law-violation by our children and adolescents.

52.   Preschool Intervention Through a Home Teaching Project[a]

David P. Weikart and Dolores Z. Lambie

Educators today are keenly aware that the role played by the family is a crucial one in the pupil's attitudes, motivations and readiness to learn. The influence of child-rearing practices on school adjustment is particularly critical in the case of culturally disadvantaged pupils, since their parents as a group fail to reinforce

[a] Paper presented at the 1968 convention of the American Educational Research Association. The research reported herein was supported by Section 4 funds of the 1966 State Aid Act of the State Board of Education, State of Michigan and the Ypsilanti Board of Education. An extensive replication of the project is planned for the spring of 1967 funded by the State of Michigan Board of Education and the Ypsilanti Board of Education. Special appreciation is extended to Mr. Benjamin Hamilton of the State Department of Education for his extensive support and assistance. For their professional pioneering, the teachers who worked in the study, Mrs. Judy Borenzweig, Mrs. Patricia Moss, Mrs. Linda Rogers, and Mrs. Gail Wilkins deserve recognition for their excellent service.

A full account of the project is to be published in Hellmuth, J. (Ed.) The Disadvantaged Child, Vol. 2. Special Child Publications, Seattle, Washington. Reprinted with the permission of the author.

the efforts of the school. Although educators recognize that efforts must be made to strengthen the relationship between home and school, research and practice have been overwhelmingly concentrated on attempts to change the disadvantaged child directly, to the neglect of changes needed in the disadvantaged parent. Contrary to this trend, David Weikart and Dolores Lambie developed a home teaching program designed to alter parent-child interaction in an effort to promote the intellectual development of four-year-old deprived children. What is your reaction to their imaginative approach?

INTRODUCTION

Preschool intervention programming has been widely hailed as an effective technique for preventing the academic and intellectual deficits agreed to be common among culturally disadvantaged children. The basis for the interest in the preschool period is that early childhood seems to be the most promising time for effecting desired improvement in intellectual development patterns. While this basis would seem to suggest an unusual potential for success through preschool education, the research in the field is equivocal. Reviews of the research report few if any differences between groups attending or not attending preschool by the time the groups reach third grade. Results from the current efforts with disadvantaged children are still preliminary. The most recent data from the five year Ypsilanti (Perry) Preschool Project in Ypsilanti, Michigan, as representative of the current studies, indicate that preschool experiences for groups of children from disadvantaged homes will not greatly change measured intellectual level but may provide the foundation necessary to produce improved academic achievement (Weikart, 1967).

The difficulty in maintaining a long term pattern of intellectual growth may come from several sources. 1) It may be that the general inability of present preschool programs to "cure" the deficits present in deprived children stems from the failure to start early enough to alter the child's environment. 2) It may be that preschool programs tend not to succeed because they have not evolved adequate curricula to meet the needs of the deprived child. 3) It may be that the preschool follow up data are discouraging because elementary schools are not willing to alter curricula so that children given a start in preschool can continue to progress with the assistance of programs designed especially for them. 4) Or it may be that preschools are attacking the wrong problem with the wrong person. Rather than provide enrichment and training to a disadvantaged child, it might be better to regard his learning deficits as a symptom of basic child rearing problems and take ameliorative action by retraining his mother in areas essential for cognitive development. The problem does not seem to be one of providing enrichment opportunities for the child or even child welfare information to the mother, but of restructuring the mother-child interaction pattern. It is to this restructuring that preschool education must give some attention.

This paper reports the results of a 12 week preschool intervention pilot project conducted in the homes of 35 culturally disadvantaged families to determine the feasibility and immediate effectiveness of a program designed to improve the cognitive growth of disadvantaged children. The specific goals of this initial project were 1) to demonstrate the impact of a home teaching program on the intellectual development of four year old children, and 2) to determine the acceptability of a home teaching project to these mothers. This project is one of a series oriented toward altering the behavior of mothers in essential areas such as language patterns, teaching methods, and child control techniques. (The current work in this series is a two year infant education project for babies 3–12 months of age funded by the Carnegie Corporation.)

METHOD

A sample was drawn from available four year old disadvantaged children in Ypsilanti School District. Matched experimental and control groups were established after all children were tested on the Stanford-Binet Intelligence Scale and the Peabody Picture Vocabulary Test. See Table 1 for general characteristics of experimental and control groups. The gen-

TABLE 1. CHARACTERISTICS OF THE EXPERIMENTAL AND CONTROL GROUPS

Characteristic	Experimental (N-35)	Control (N-29)[a]
Stanford-Binet IQ (mean)[b]	95.3	98.6
Peabody Picture Vocabulary IQ (mean)	89.0	94.1
Cultural Deprivation Rating (mean)[b]	9.5	9.8
Boys (per cent)[b]	48.5%	72.4%
White (per cent)[b]	74.2%	58.6%
Father in home (percent)	77.1%	82.7%
Education of mother (mean grade attained)	10.3	10.3
Education of father (mean grade attained)	9.1	10.0
Occupation of father		
unskilled-unemployed	77.1%	68.9%
semiskilled	17.1%	31.0%
skilled	2.8%	0 %
professional	0 %	0 %
Number of children (mean)	3.5	3.8
Welfare assistance (per cent)	22.8%	20.6%
Number of rooms (mean per person)	1.06	1.04
Number of persons in home (mean)	5.6	6.2

[a] Six control children are not included in the analysis. One family moved, one child was found to be too young and four families had incomplete data.

[b] Characteristics considered in the original matching of the two groups.

eral attitude of the mother toward education was assessed by the Weikart Educational Attitude Test (1966). Various environmental and demographic variables were collected through interview and observation by the teachers during the initial contact and follow up home teaching sessions.

The basic educational procedure of the project was a one-and-a-half hour per week home visit to each participating family. The visits allowed a carefully individualized program to be initiated involving the mother and her four year old child. The contact was to permit the systematic development of the foundations necessary for intellectual functioning by the child through direct tutoring and to give occasion for the development of the language, teaching and child management skills by the mother. The project operated with four state-certified elementary school teachers without any previous training in home teaching and a curriculum development supervisor who worked directly with each teacher in her program planning.

The curriculum employed in the project was organized around five basic areas: 1) Manipulative activities, 2) Dramatic play, 3) Perceptual discrimination, 4) Classification, and 5) Language. While no single source can be identified as influencing the specific curriculum content, liberal use was made of the ideas from Piaget (Inhelder, 1958), Deutsch (1965), Smilansky (1964), Peel (1960); and others. The project also drew heavily upon the ideas the staff had developed in prior work with children. The specific curriculum was not fully developed before the project began, but was evolved as the teachers worked with the curriculum supervisor to resolve the very real poblems faced in the teaching sessions.

While the poject curriculum was specifically designed by the staff, the program did meet the criteria necessary in successful preschool programming for disadvantaged children. The curriculum provided step-by-step opportunities for each individual child to proceed at his own rate toward predetermined cognitive goals, i.e., a structured curriculum. And the curriculum was closely supervised so that an individual teacher could maintain a perspective of the objectives to be obtained. The unique teacher-mother-child interaction situation permitted wide latitude for individualized programming, of course.

RESULTS

Table 2 presents the data from the Stanford-Binet Intelligence Scale and the Peabody Picture Vocabulary Test on the pre and post test assessments of the experimental and control groups. The experimental group obtained a statistically significant greater change score (8.2) than did the control group (0.9) on the Stanford-Binet. Because of the difference in initial group means, an analysis of co-variance was run and the adjusted group means indicate a significantly higher mean for the experimental group ($p < .01$). There were no significant differences on the Peabody.

It is generally accepted that environmental factors greatly influence the expression of intellectual ability. In a correlational analysis of environmental variables and IQ scores, presented in Tables 3 and 4, several points

TABLE 2. COMPARISON OF GROUPS ON INTELLIGENCE SCALES

Scale	Experimental (N-35)	Control (N-29)	Difference	t-Test
Stanford-Binet				
Pre test, March '66	95.3	98.6	−3.3	−.839
Post test, June '66	103.3	99.4	3.9	.902
Change score	8.0	0.9	7.1	2.925**
Peabody				
Pre test, March '66	89.0	94.1	−5.1	−.762
Post test, June '66	98.9	98.0	0.9	.141
Change score	9.9	4.0	5.9	1.242

**p< .01

emerge. First is that general environmental determiners of intellectual growth such as parent education, developmental "mile-stones," birth conditions, etc. hold true for these two samples of culturally deprived children. Second is that a far stronger relationship between environmental variables and IQ is obtained for the control group from the post test than from the pretest scores even though there was only a 0.9 IQ point gain in group mean. This finding would tend to indicate that a test experience or "rehearsal" allows more accurate individual scores than are obtainable at an initial testing. Third, for those children participating in the home teaching program, the pattern is one of decreased correlation with environmental variables after the 12 week intervention. It would seem from these data that the home teaching program has the effect of "freeing" the culturally disadvantaged child from the environmental determiners of intellectual growth.

Weekly, systematic home teaching ratings were made by teachers. These ratings included an adjective rating scale similar to a semantic differential scale, assessing extent of mother participation, general cooperation, etc. Correlations of the adjective ratings and initial Stanford-Binet IQ indicated that mothers seen as "good" by the teachers had children with high IQ scores (see Table 5). Ratings of *deep, going somewhere, sensitive, fresh,* and *together* were positively and significantly correlated with IQ. Upon completion of the program, there were no significant relationships between teacher ratings of mothers and IQ of children. However, mothers rated as *bad, erratic, shallow, hard, insensitive, stale,* and *cloudy* had children who obtained significantly higher IQ gains as a result of the program. On all adjective pairs, high IQ gain was associated with qualities in mothers that teachers regard as "bad." In addition, mothers who tended to be the least cooperative had children who had high IQ gain scores. Also, high IQ gain children tended to come from families who were worse off in terms of general environmental variables.

The attitude toward education was measured by the Weikart Educational Attitude Test. Of the eight areas assessed by the test only one attitude area was changed significantly as a result of the intervention program. Mothers in the home teaching experimental group attributed to teachers

TABLE 3. CORRELATION OF FAMILY HISTORY DATA AND
INTELLECTUAL DEVELOPMENT
CONTROL SAMPLE

Variable	N	Pre test S-B	Post test S-B	Pre test PPVT	Post test PPVT
Education of mother, years	29	.30	.16	.23	.39*
Education of father, years	28	.21	.36*	.08	.22
Cultural deprivation rating, low to high	29	.28	.43*	.18	.36*
Number of children home	29	−.39*	−.37*	−.38*	−.42*
Number of younger children	17	−.48*	−.35	.01	−.11
Number of older children	23	−.47*	−.63**	−.41*	−.42*
Labor severity, easy to hard	26	−.12	−.21	−.03	.01
Labor length, short to long	26	−.26	−.29	−.21	−.07
Birth weight, ounces	28	−.34	−.48**	−.31	−.43*
Age walking, months	27	.13	.40*	.27	.38*
Age talking, months	25	.08	.30	.46*	.49**
Age first tooth, months	22	.53**	.21	.27	.38
Age of toilet training, slow to fast	26	.22	.03	.02	−.15

*p < .05
**p < .01

TABLE 4. CORRELATION OF FAMILY HISTORY DATA AND
INTELLECTUAL DEVELOPMENT
EXPERIMENTAL SAMPLE

Variable	N	Pre test S-B	Post test S-B	Pre test PPVT	Post test PPVT
Education of mother, years	35	.27	.09	.25	.22
Education of father, years	31	.33	.29	.37*	.43*
Cultural deprivation rating, low to high	35	.25	.18	.23	.21
Number of children home	35	−.23	−.19	−.37*	−.32*
Number of younger children	23	.22	.19	.32	.03
Number of older children	25	−.16	−.13	−.32	−.21
Labor severity, easy to hard	35	−.17	−.26	−.30	−.23
Labor length, short to long	35	−.18	−.24	−.21	−.09
Birth weight, ounces	35	.04	.00	−.07	.03
Age walking, month	32	−.13	−.00	.03	−.11
Age talking, month	31	−.19	−.19	−.14	−.14
Age first tooth, month	28	−.26	−.15	−.09	−.11
Age of toilet training, slow to fast	34	.21	.16	.10	.09

*p .05

more favorable attitudes toward mothers than did mothers of control
children (F ratio = 10.23, p <.01).

CONCLUSIONS

This project demonstrated that home teaching is a feasible method of
preschool intervention with disadvantaged families. The 12 week program
with about 15 hours of contact produced significant IQ gains, as mea-

TABLE 5. CORRELATION OF ADJECTIVE SCALE RATING OF MOTHER AND INTELLECTUAL GROWTH

Variable[a]	Pre test S-B	Post test S-B	Change S-B	Pre test PPVT	Post test PPVT	Change PPVT
bad-good	.32	.10	−.38*	.00	.12	.15
erratic-steady	.25	.07	−.34*	.02	.04	.03
shallow-deep	.45**	.22	−.37*	.18	.18	−.03
hard-soft	.20	.01	−.34*	.00	.11	.14
dead-alive	.26	.16	−.16	.07	.12	.04
aimless-going somewhere	.34*	.26	−.11	.20	.09	−.17
tight-loose	.02	.00	−.10	−.01	.21	.27
uncooperative-cooperative	.21	.05	−.31	−.01	.06	.09
insensitive-sensitive	.36*	.13	−.38*	.13	.12	−.04
stale-fresh	.35*	.16	−.33*	.09	.13	.03
cool-warm	.19	.09	−.17	.03	.05	.02
closed-open	.26	.18	−.12	.13	.12	−.04
dry-wet	−.13	−.15	−.03	−.18	−.22	−.02
cloudy-sunny	.30	.10	−.37*	.01	.15	.17
apart-together	.37*	.23	−.22	.13	.22	.08
passive-active	.18	.14	−.03	.12	−.04	−.21

[a] Scale was from 1 to 7, e.g., bad, erratic—1; good, steady—7. Eleven dimensions have been reversed to facilitate reading of table.
* p .05

sured by the Stanford-Binet Intelligence Scale, in experimental children. The children who came from the more environmentally deprived homes and who had mothers rated as "bad" had the highest IQ gain. This finding supports the contention that deprivation is a function of the environment created in the home by the mother rather than a general socio-economic condition. Teachers without special training can effectively work in the homes of disadvantaged families even when the family is seen as inadequate.

It is recommended that serious consideration be given to exploring the potential of home teaching programs for improving the cognitive development of disadvantaged children and for altering the child rearing styles of their mothers.

REFERENCES

1. Deutsch, M. *Institute for developmental studies: Annual Report 1965.* New York: New York Medical College, 1965.
2. Inhelder, B., & Piaget, J. *The growth of logical thinking from childhood to adolescence.* New York: Basic Books, 1958.
3. Peel, E. A. *The pupil's thinking.* London: Oldbourne Book Co., 1960.
4. Smilansky, S. Progress report on a program to demonstrate ways of using a year of kindergarten to promote cognitive abilities. Henrietta Szold Institute, Israel. Unpublished manuscript, 1964.
5. Weikart, D. P. A semi-structural projective test for measuring educational attitudes. Unpublished doctoral dissertation, University of Michigan, 1966.
6. Weikart, D. P. (Ed.) *Preschool intervention: Preliminary report of the Perry Preschool Project.* Ann Arbor, Michigan: Campus Publishers, 1967.

53.   National Institute of Mental Health Pilot Study
in Training Mental Health Counselors*

Margaret J. Rioch, Charmian Elkes, Arden A. Flint,
Blanche Sweet Usdansky, Ruth G. Newman, and Earle Silber

*In this article, a fundamental question is explored: Can
carefully selected, mature housewives, if given practical training over a two year period, do psychotherapy
under limited conditions? The results were encouraging, as you will see in the following selection by
Margaret J. Rioch and her colleagues.*

In the spring of 1960 a pilot study was begun in the Adult Psychiatry
Branch of the National Institute of Mental Health to explore one means of
alleviating the shortage of trained workers in the mental health field and
of filling some of the community's needs for low-cost psychotherapy. The
idea behind the experiment is that, even as the Public Health nurse can
perform many duties with and for patients, thereby freeing the medical
officer for tasks requiring greater training, so also a corps of workers
could be trained in the mental health field, thereby freeing a significant
amount of the psychiatrist's time.

One of the best reservoirs of people gifted for this kind of work consists of married women of about 40 who are looking for a constructive
activity outside the home to take the place of the job of child rearing. To
exploit this gold mine of psychological talent would be to kill two birds
with one stone. The need for low-cost therapy could be alleviated and
the mature woman's need to be useful could in some cases be filled. This
latter would not be a salvage operation for neurotic middle-aged ladies,
but rather the appropriate deployment of people who have performed suc-

* Presented at the 1962 Annual Meeting.
American Journal of Orthopsychiatry, 1963, 33, 678–689. Copyright, the American
Orthopsychiatric Association, Inc. Reproduced by permission of copyright owner
and senior author.

cessfully in one phase of life and who are now passing to another. These women have an inestimable advantage over the usual beginning psycho-therapist; they have resided for a considerably longer time on this planet and have been engaged in the highly complex interpersonal training ground of child rearing and family living. By virtue of this they are less self-absorbed than their more youthful counterparts and have a larger pool of experience from which to draw.

The objective of this study is in line with the recommendation of the Report of the Joint Commission on Mental Health and Illness "that non-medical mental health workers with aptitude, sound training, practical experience and demonstrable competence should be permitted to do general, short-term psychotherapy—namely, the treating of persons by objective, permissive, nondirective techniques of listening to their troubles and helping them resolve these troubles in an individually insightful and socially useful way."

The experiment can be divided into four phases. The first two, Recruitment and Selection, have been completed. The third, Training, is in process. The fourth, Evaluation, has been accomplished for the first year's work, and will be repeated with variations for the second year, in June 1962. A follow-up study is being planned for the years following the experiment itself.

The hypothesis, which was tested in the recruitment stage, was that there is a large unexploited reservoir of talent among middle-aged women, waiting and eager to be used. This was amply demonstrated, at least for the Washington area.

The recruitment lasted approximately six weeks. During this short period by means of 60 telephone calls and six short public speeches, 80 women became sufficiently interested to request application blanks. Forty-nine applications were returned filled out. No blank was sent out before a 10-minute telephone conversation had taken place with the applicant, explaining the program and emphasizing its experimental character. Applicants were told that there would be no financial recompense during the two-year training period, and that there was no guarantee of success, or of future employment. The insecurity that we were obliged to emphasize with regard to our experimental program limited its appeal to people who could and would take a risk. They were all from the middle class and most of them had been to college. We thought the program might well appeal to many from the lunatic fringe, but, of the 42 women who came to the NIH for the selection procedures, at most three might be thought to fall into this category; even including these, all were capable people whose services could and should be used in some form in the community.

We began the selection phase by asking for an autobiography of about 1,500 words from each applicant. The 42 women who complied with this request were invited to come to the National Institutes of Health in groups of approximately eight for a day of group procedures, including tests and discussions. On the basis of these, the Committee on Selection*

---

* The Committee consisted of Drs. Margaret Rioch, Chairman, Charmian Elkes, Arden Flint, Nathene Loveland, David Hamburg, Beatrix Hamburg.

chose 20 who were given individual interviews and tests and from whom eight were finally chosen as the successful candidates. Their median age was 40–44. One was widowed; all the others were living with their husbands. All had children, the average number being 2.4 Their husbands were all either professionals or executives. They were all college graduates; three had advanced degrees. Of their undergraduate majors, four were in the behavioral sciences, three in the humanities, one in biology. Six had held paying jobs at a professional level. Four had been psychoanalyzed.

The hypothesis to be tested by this phase was that, by the various group and individual procedures used, a number of candidates could be selected who would have good general intelligence, perceptiveness, integrity and sufficient emotional maturity to be able to operate effectively together and to cope with the stresses of psychotherapeutic work. To be complete, this hypothesis should include the statement that the selectors were for the most part the teachers in the Training Program.

This hypothesis has proved correct at least to the extent that all eight of the selected candidates have remained in the program and intend to continue in this field.* Further, the staff has not wished to recommend dismissal of any one of them. It cannot, of course, be claimed that the procedures used selected the best of the applicants. We have no way of knowing how much better some of the rejectees may have been than the selected candidates.

The training began in September, 1960, and is to run officially for four semesters. Actually, from what we know of the eight women in this experiment, they will continue their training indefinitely in one form or another. The two years we are offering them constitute only a beginning of their awareness of themselves as therapeutic instruments. This report will deal with the two semesters completed in June, 1961.

In planning our program, we had to decide at the start whether we were training professionals or technicians. In other words, should we expose our students to a variety of theories and practices with the intention of helping them gradually to find their own way, or should we teach them to follow directions according to a set method? We agreed on the former course. The statement was made explicitly to the students that there is no one "right way" to do therapy but that each person develops his own style, which is right for him because it is an integral function of his own personality. The instructors, including the consultants, are people with a variety of backgrounds: Some are psychoanalysts, some psychiatrists, some psychologists. All of them hold a broad, more or less eclectic point of view with regard to theory and practice. We are unable to make a sharp distinction between counseling and therapy. Our students are called Mental Health Counselors for lack of a better term. What they do in their interviews varies a great deal from one to another, from one phase of their development to another, and from one patient to another. Sometimes they listen sympathetically and supportively; sometimes they "represent reality" or give common-sense advice; sometimes they engage in a

---

* One was absent from the city during the second semester, which she had told us might occur. She has returned for the second year.

process of exploration of the patient's feeling and attitudes with a view to a better understanding of them; and occasionally they are able to draw out into the open some aspect of a patient to which he had previously been blind, and to help him become more aware and accepting of this aspect. In our teaching we have emphasized that the patient's problem has something to do with distorted perceptions of himself and others and that he would be able to see more clearly if the anxiety in these areas were reduced. We have also emphasized the need to listen to the patient on more than one level, to hear the unspoken messages and to respond to them as well as to the spoken ones. And we have stressed above all the importance of self-awareness.

Our training is narrow but intensive; it is sharply focused on psychotherapy, and only on psychotherapy. This differentiates it from training for social work, psychology and psychiatry. Members of all three of these professions engage in psychotherapy, but their education includes many other things. Our hypothesis is that the intensive training offered to carefully selected applicants can produce in a relatively short time people qualified to do this particular task for which the need is so great.

In setting up our program we tried to allow ourselves maximum flexibility, but we did have certain notions about how it would be structured. One was that the students should be thoroughly and frequently supervised and supported in their work; a second was that they should be given a broad, undogmatic point of view with as little jargon as possible. A third was that the work would be primarily practical, on-the-job training, and only secondarily theoretical. These have all been carried out.

We had some other intentions, however, which have been modified. First, we planned that the training would be 20 hours a week, or half time for two years. But the students have worked so hard that they have turned it into what is now practically a full-time program. Second, we thought that we would limit the type of patient to be seen, so that the training would be more intensive in one area. We chose college students partly because of the already existing interest in the Adult Psychiatry Branch; partly because we thought they would be easy to treat and by and large not so very sick, and thus appropriate for a first experiment; and partly because, from the general mental health point of view, this seemed like a good age for preventive psychiatry. For practical reasons having to do chiefly with geography and transportation, we were unable to carry out this intention. Not enough college students were available to the outpatient service at the NIH, so we included high school students and their parents. Then other adults came seeking help, bringing the age range of our patients to between 15 and 55. There has been a preponderance of adolescents and their parents, however, and we have emphasized in our course work the problems of this developmental phase.

Third, we intended to have our students see patients with relatively minor disturbances. This intention has gone the way of unrealistic expectations, since practically none of the patients who have sought out our services has been really easy to treat. We think that in general it is best to screen out those patients who are schizophrenic, those who act out a great deal and those who would probably develop a very demanding and possessive sort of transference relationship. In some cases we have taken a calculated risk because there was no other possibility for treatment. In some cases in which our screening was faulty, the trainee performed the useful service of helping the patient and his family, through a series of introductory interviews, to accept more intensive and experienced therapy than we could offer.

Fourth, we intended to screen all patients for the trainees. While this still occurs consistently at NIH, initial interviewing is now being done by some of the trainees in their community placements.

The training covered the following five areas:

1. The first was practical work at NIH. This consisted of interviewing normal subjects and patients, group therapy for adolescents and their parents, individual and group supervision including listening to the playback of the trainees' own tape-recorded interviews. This was the most important part of the work.

The trainees began by interviewing the normal control subjects who live at the Clinical Center of the NIH and are studied by the various institutes. Most of them were college students. It was a great advantage to have this resource in the initial period, especially in an untried pilot program. Since a number of these "normal" people had very serious problems, we became aware that our trainees were able to cope with a greater degree of emotional disturbance than we had originally intended to have them handle. Before the end of the first semester each trainee had been assigned at least one real patient.

From the very beginning all the interviews were tape-recorded. Each trainee listened to her own interviews, not only by herself and with a supervisor, but with the whole group. One of the remarkable aspects of the first year's work was the way in which an atmosphere of mutual support developed among the students, making it possible for them to expose their floundering and blundering to each other without essential loss of self-esteem.

The supervision took place at scheduled times both individually and in groups of four or eight. In addition, it was made clear that the supervisors were always available to their students in case of need. The need might be a matter of supporting the trainee in dealing with a demanding patient, answering a practical question of how to refer a patient's relative to a psychiatrist, or sitting down for an extra session with the tape recording and working through the anxiety about a given situation. It is fair to say that the trainees felt confident that they could rely upon their supervisors for prompt assistance in a crisis and for a generally benign attitude in dealing with their difficulties. This does not imply that the supervisors were uncritical or that the process of supervision was anxiety-free. It does imply that we had a fair measure of success in establishing what might reasonably be called a therapeutic environment, although no formal therapy (group or individual) of the trainees was ever undertaken in the program. It should be mentioned here, however, that during this first year one trainee continued until late winter her previously begun analysis. Two returned to therapists with whom they had earlier terminated. One began therapy for the first time. This indicates that the program stirred up considerable anxiety. It is our opinion that this was by and large constructive in that it led the trainees to work through problems that would otherwise have limited their effectiveness as therapists. Those who were or had been in therapy learned at first hand what it is like to be a patient. If the students had been unable, for financial or other reasons, to arrange treatment for themselves when needed, it would have been advisable to proceed differently. Group therapy could be made part of the regular schedule, or the program could be maintained at a lower level of anxiety. In the latter case there might be some loss in effectiveness.

2. The second area of training was observation of group, family and individual therapy.

3. The third consisted of lectures and seminar discussions.

4. The fourth was outside reading and report writing.

5. And the fifth was community placements. These were arranged partly to broaden the experience of the trainees and partly to open doors that might lead to future employment. This was the beginning of a feeling-out process to see how the community would react to the trainees and how the trainees would fit and function in the community. We met with a remarkably open-hearted and open-minded welcome on the part of most, though not all, of the agencies with which we had contact. Only two of the ten agencies we approached declined to accept any trainees. The placements for the first year were in one federal probation office, two juvenile courts, three clinics, one university counseling center and one social service agency. The trainees were especially warmly welcomed and well thought of in the probation office, the juvenile courts, and two of the clinics. In one clinic the attitudes of the staff were mixed and shifting. The university was very warmly hospitable but not enthusiastic about future employment. The social service agency turned out to be an unsuitable placement. For the second year we have trainees placed in seven clinics, two public high schools, one public junior college, two universities and one college.

The evaluation phase of the work will not, of course, be complete until the second year of training is over. The follow-up study will, we hope, present additional material. The results of the first year's evaluation are being presented now as part of a progress report.

We are aware that there is no recognized standard method of measuring the amount learned in this field or the degree of competence of a psychotherapist or the success of anyone's therapeutic endeavors. We have tried to approach the problem in five different ways.

1. In an effort to obtain an objective judgment of the trainees' work, uncolored by the personal investment of the teachers in the project, we obtained the services of four raters from outside the Washington area who, without knowing anything about the program or the background of the trainees, agreed to do blind ratings of tape-recorded therapeutic interviews.* After listening to and rating each tape, the rater was to open a sealed envelope containing an autocriticism of the interview by the

---

* We are indebted to Drs. Roy R. Grinker, Jr., LeRoy P. Levitt, Melvin N. Seglin from the Michael Reese Hospital, Chicago, and to Miss Nea Norton, Assistant Professor of Psychiatry, Yale University, for their help in this part of the evaluation.

Since one trainee was absent for the second semester, the evaluation of the first year's work is based on the accomplishment of the other seven.

trainee. This also was to be rated on several criteria, as well as on global impression. The results of this procedure are summarized in Tables 1, 2 and 3. Two ratings on each of two interviews are not enough to represent a valid judgment of any one interviewer, but the average of 28 judgments is a reasonable assessment of the group of trainees as a whole.†

TABLE 1.* RATING OF INTERVIEW

Name of rater: _____

Code no. of interview: _____

	Excellent 5	Good 4	Satis-factory 3	Passable 2	Poor 1
1. Global impression of interview	3	5	12	4	4
2. Respect for the patient	2	15	8	1	2
3. Interest in the patient	4	14	7	3	0
4. Understanding of the patient	4	4	9	8	3
5. Success in drawing out affect	2	5	6	11	3
6. Beginning of interview	1	3	7	10	4
7. End of interview	1	7	2	10	4
8. Professional attitude	3	18	4	3	0
9. Skill in using patient's cues	1	7	4	10	6

	Very Easy	Easy	Medium	Difficult	Very Difficult
Patient's accessibility to therapy (i.e., an easy or difficult patient)	2	3	7	14	1

Remarks:

*Tables 1 and 2 are reproductions of the rating blanks sent to the raters. The numbers in each box represent the number of times a rating was assigned to that box. Totals are not always the same because occasionally a rater did not rate, if the recording was not clear enough to allow him to form a judgment.

TABLE 2. RATING OF AUTOCRITICISM

Name of rater: _____

Code no. of interview: _____

	Excellent 5	Good 4	Satis-factory 3	Passable 2	Poor 1
1. Global impression	5	10	10	2	1
2. Shows awareness of major weakness or weaknesses	5	6	9	5	2
3. Shows awareness of the main points at which communication broke down	7	4	8	6	2
4. Shows awareness of how and where communication was facilitated	3	10	6	5	3
5. Shows awareness of her own "inner workings"	4	12	5	5	2

Remarks:

†We owe the clear formulation of this idea to a personal communication from Dr. Roy Grinker.

TABLE 3*

Rating of Interviews	Average Score
1. Global impression of interview	3.4
2. Respect for the patient	4.0
3. Interest in the patient	4.0
4. Understanding of the patient	3.4
5. Success in drawing out affect	3.2
6. Beginning of interview	2.7
7. End of interview	2.9
8. Professional attitude	4.2
9. Skill in using patient's cues	3.0
Rating of Patient's Accessibility to Therapy (i.e., an easy or difficult patient)	3.2

    5—very easy
    4—easy
    3—medium
    2—difficult
    1—very difficult

Rating of Autocriticism	
1. Global impression	4.0
2. Shows awareness of major weakness or weaknesses	3.7
3. Shows awareness of main points at which communication broke down	3.7
4. Shows awareness of how and where communication was facilitated	3.6
5. Shows awareness of her own "inner workings"	3.8

*Table 3 shows the average scores on the blind ratings, first year: 5—excellent; 4—good; 3—satisfactory; 2—passable; and 1—poor.

It is important to remember that the "reference interview" done by a professional therapist was given an average rating of 3 by six judges.

The average rating on the global impression of all the interviews was 3.0, that is, in the middle range of the scale. The average rating on the global impression of the autocriticisms was 3.6. Since no one's average rating was below 2, or passable, and since 3, or the middle range of the scale, represents satisfactory performance, this part of our evaluation procedure has shown positive results.

2. We have tried to assess the changes that took place in the patients seen by the trainees at NIH, considering at the same time the kind of patient and the degree of difficulty of the treatment. Table 4 summarizes the work. As in all such assessments of change under therapy, there is no way of knowing how much of this might have occurred without any intervention whatsoever.

There were in all 49 patients—18 males, 31 females, 21 adolescents, 28 adults. Each trainee saw an average of seven patients once a week. The diagnoses were distributed as follows: 20 personality trait disorder, 12 neurotic reaction, 6 schizoid or borderline schizophrenic, 5 immature or unstable personality, 4 adjustment reaction of adolescence, 2 diagnosis doubtful. None of these patients changed for the worse. In 19 there was no change. Thirty, or 61 per cent, showed some change. Seventeen showed a

TABLE 4. OVER-ALL SUMMARY OF WORK WITH NIH PATIENTS
BY ALL SEVEN TRAINEES

	N	
Number of Patients		
Males	18	
Females	31	
Young adolescents (ages 15–16)	7	
Older adolescents (ages 17–19)	14	
Young adults (ages 20–25)	5	
Mature adults (ages 30–55)	23	
Average no. of patients per trainee	7	
Total number of patients	49	
Number of interviews		
Average no. of interviews by each trainee	77	
Range of no. of interviews with a single patient	1 to 26	
Average no. of interviews with a single patient	10	
Total no. of interviews	539	
Diagnoses of patients		
Personality trait disorders	20	
(14 of these were patients who came for help ostensibly because of their children)		
Neurotic reaction	12	
Schizoid or borderline schizophrenic	6	
Immature or unstable personalities	5	
Adjustment reaction of adolescence	4	
Diagnosis doubtful	2	
Rating of patients' improvement or nonimprovement in the course of therapy		%
Marked improvement	3	6
Moderate improvement	10	20
Slight improvement	17	35
No change	19	39
Rating of patients according to difficulty of treatment		
Very difficult	13	
Difficult	21	
Medium	10	
Easy	5	
Very easy	0	

slight improvement; ten showed a moderate improvement; three, marked improvement. In evaluating the results it is important to remember that 69 per cent of the patients were "difficult or very difficult to treat," and that the length of treatment at the time of our evaluation was in no case more than six months, and, on the average, ten weeks. That the patients themselves were favorably impressed is demonstrated by the fact that of those who came asking for help, only one dropped out of therapy.

3. We asked the supervisors in ten community placements to rate the trainees who worked with them. The ratings are shown in Table 5. The general results here are highly favorable. The average rating is "good," and none is lower than "satisfactory."

4. We asked the trainees themselves to evaluate the program. There was general agreement on their part that it had been important to have one systematic, very well-given background course in personality develop-

TABLE 5*

Name of agency: _____

Name of trainee: _____

	Excellent 5	Good 4	Satisfactory 3	Passable 2	Poor 1	Insufficient Information	Average Score
The trainee did the work assigned to her in a way which was: (Please use other students in training as a yardstick)	4	4	1				4.3
The trainee fitted into this agency in a way which was:	4	4	1				4.3
The trainee made progress during the time she was with this agency in a way which was:	4	1	4				3.9

Comments:

Signature: . . . .

*This table reproduces the blank sent to the supervisors in the various agencies, except that the last column on the right has been added to represent an average rating. The numbers in each box represent the number of times it was checked by a supervisor with regard to one trainee. One supervisor placed no check marks giving as the reason: "Assignments for direct service were so limited (due to limitations in time she was available and suitable assignments for a beginning trainee) that I feel it impossible to make an appraisal of patterns of her relating to families, staff and supervisor."

The table is incomplete since one supervisor has not yet returned his rating. Some trainees had more than one placement during the year.

ment. There was general appreciation of a "human" attitude on the part of instructors who were willing to expose their own fears and failings, especially in their therapeutic work. They liked it particularly when theory and practice were brought close together, as in a course on family interaction patterns that was integrated with the group therapy for adolescents and their parents. The practical work was considered the "guts" of the program and wishes were expressed for more opportunities to listen with the supervisors to selected tapes of their own interviews and to observe more interviews by experienced therapists. Some of the placements were considered useful; some, more or less time wasting.

For all of the trainees the program has been an important step in their lives. Although they were warned *ad nauseum* that it is an experiment with no guarantee of success or future employment, they are, without exception, looking forward to using this training in serious work. They have raised the question whether a degree or certificate of some kind might be obtained that would enable them to identify themselves in any community in which they might live as being equipped to do the kind of work for which they have been trained. For all of them, the program supplied something they needed in that it filled satisfyingly a vacuum left by their children's growing up.

5. The teachers in the program have reported their impressions. Not all of the instructors are in a position to pass judgment on the clinical competence of all the trainees, but there has been a consensus on the part of those who have worked with them that they are a responsive, intelligent, conscientious group of people. During the first semester, comments were made several times to the effect that their "receptors" were good although the "broadcasting" was often awkward. From the beginning they impressed observers with their perceptiveness. One of the consultants observed with pleased surprise that when he asked for a description of a patient he really got it, in full detail.

As therapists they have all performed some useful services to patients during this past year, and none of them has done anyone any harm. They have improved considerably since the beginning of the course in their ability to draw out troublesome material and to respond appropriately to patients' cues.

Their greatest fault has been a tendency to follow the dictates of polite society. In other words, they pleasantly reassure, protect and sympathize when it would be better to question more deeply and seriously. A second fault is a tendency to try to deal on a surface, common-sense level with problems that are soluble only by eliciting unconscious conflicts.

We do not contend that the work of the trainees with their patients was highly skillful. Some of it was skillful; some was adequate; some was awkward. The fact of the matter is that favorable change sometimes occurred in spite of awkward, blundering work.

It is, of course, not yet possible to form a judgment about the degree of usefulness these women will demonstrate when they have finished the two-year course and are away from the protection of the group and their familiar teachers. Their future employment is uncertain and the quality of their performance will no doubt depend upon the kind of settings in which they find themselves, as well as upon what they will take with them at the end of the course. We hope to arrange a weekly seminar for them for the years following the training, not only for the purpose of continuing education, but also because it will be important from the point of view of morale so long as their identity in the field is an uncertain one.

What, now, are the implications of this pilot study for the general field of mental health?

First, there is a potential reservoir of workers in the age group we have tapped that is not presently being exploited. There may well be others, such as retired persons, who could also be used in various ways.

Second, we have anecdotal evidence to the effect that the 40-year-old married woman with children is reluctant to embark upon the regular training programs set up for young graduate students, and in some cases she is not welcomed in them. She does respond eagerly to a program tailored flexibly to her situation.

Third, there is the large and complex question of whether there is need and space for a new profession in the field of mental health. Many people have been concerned that the training for psychotherapy as a major professional activity is not optimally served in psychiatry, psychology or social work.* The present study is not by any means an attempt to prepare doctors of psychotherapy who would be licensed to practice independently. Our goal is a far more modest one. If such people as our trainees can perform useful services to patients—and in their first year of training they have done just that—then it should be possible for departments of psychiatry, psychology or social work to offer a subcurriculum something like this one, with emphasis upon practical work, which would train people in psychotherapy. The students in such curricula would no doubt arrive at varying levels of competence, ranging from listening sympathetically and giving common sense advice, to skillful therapeutic interviewing with optimal use of unverbalized messages, and so on. They could be employed in settings in which they need not work above or beyond the limits of their competence. There will, of course, be no rigorous proof that this NIH pilot project can be replicated unless and until it is tried elsewhere. But there is no essential element in our program that could not be reproduced in other centers with good universities and clinics. A double purpose would be served if this could occur: More patients could be seen and more people could find a constructive use for their talents.

54. Helping Disturbed Children: Psychological and Ecological Strategies[1]

Nicholas Hobbs

(1) Intensive short-term intervention. (2) The use of teacher-counselors. (3) A focus on behavior and personal competence. (4) Mobilization of community resources. (5) Reduced treatment costs. These are just

---

* See L. S. Kubie, "The Pros and Cons of a New Profession: A Doctorate in Medical Psychology," *Texas Reports on Biology and Medicine*, 12(3): 125–170.

American Psychologist, 1966, 21, 1105–1115. Copyright 1966 by the American Psychological Association. Reprinted with the permission of the copyright owner and author.

[1] Address of the President to the Seventy-Fourth Annual Convention of the American Psychological Association, New York, September 3, 1966.

some of the innovations characteristic of the bold new
approach to institutional treatment depicted in Nicho-
las Hobbs' report on "Project Re-ED."

Honoring a long tradition, I have the privilege tonight to present to you, my colleagues in psychology, an account of my own work in recent years.[2]

I wish to present a case study in institution building, an account of a planful effort at social invention to meet an acute national problem, the problem of emotional disturbance in children.

I should like to cast this account in large context as an example of the kind of responsibility psychologists must assume in order to respond to a major challenge of our time: to help increase the goodness of fit between social institutions and the people they serve. This commitment demands that we invent new social arrangements designed to improve the quality of human life, and, in doing so, to adhere to the exacting traditions of psychological science: that is, to be explicit about what we are doing, to assess outcomes as meticulously as possible, to relate practice and theory to the benefit of both, and to lay our work open to public and professional scrutiny.

Let me acknowledge here that the work I report is the product of a cooperative effort to which a number of psychologists have contributed, notably Lloyd M. Dunn, Wilbert W. Lewis, William C. Rhodes, Matthew J. Trippe, and Laura Weinstein. National Institute of Mental Health officials, mental health commissioners, consultants, and especially the teacher-counselors, have invented the social institution I shall describe. If on occasion I seem unduly enthusiastic, it springs from an admiration of the work of others.

THE PROBLEM

"Project Re-ED" stands for "a project for the reeducation of emotionally disturbed children." Re-ED was developed explicitly as a new way to meet a social need for which current institutional arrangements are conspicuously inadequate. It is estimated that there are some 1½ million emotionally disturbed children in the United States today, children of average or superior intelligence whose behavior is such that they cannot be sustained with normal family, school, and community arrangements. There is one generally endorsed institutional plan for the care of such children: the

[2] The work here reported was made possible by Grant No. MH 929 of the United States Public Health Service, and by funds provided by Peabody College, the State of Tennessee, and the State of North Carolina. We are grateful for the support and wise counsel of Commissioner Joseph J. Baker and Commissioner Nat T. Winston, Jr., of Tennessee, Commissioner Eugene A. Hargrove and Sam O. Cornwell of North Carolina, Leonard J. Duhl and Raymond J. Balester of NIMH, and Paul W. Penningroth and Harold L. McPheeters of the Southern Regional Education Board.

psychiatric treatment unit of a hospital. But this is not a feasible solution to the problem; the costs are too great, averaging $60 a day, and there are not enough psychiatrists, psychologists, social workers, and psychiatric nurses to staff needed facilities, even if the solution were a good one, an assumption open to question. There is a real possibility that hospitals make children sick. The antiseptic atmosphere, the crepe sole and white coat, the tension, the expectancy of illness may confirm a child's worst fears about himself, firmly setting his aberrant behavior.

But worse things can happen to children, and do. They may be sent to a state hospital to be confined on wards with psychotic adults. They may be put in a jail, euphemistically called a detention home, or committed to an institution for delinquents or for the mentally retarded; or they may be kept at home, hidden away, receiving no help at all, aggravating and being aggravated by what can become an impossible situation.

The problem is further complicated by the professional advocacy of psychotherapy as the only means of effecting changes in behavior and by the pervasive and seldom questioned assumption that it takes at least 2 years to give any substantial help to a disturbed child. Finally, the availability of locks and drugs makes children containable, and the lack of evaluative research effectively denies feedback on the adequacy of approved methods. We became convinced 8 years ago that the problem of the emotionally disturbed child cannot be solved by existing institutional arrangements. The Re-ED program was developed as one alternative, surely not the only one or even the most satisfactory one, but as a feasible alternative that deserved a test.

THE RE-ED SCHOOLS

The National Institute of Mental Health made a test possible by a demonstration grant in 1961 to Peabody College to develop residential schools for disturbed children in which concepts of reeducation could be formulated and tried out. The States of Tennessee and North Carolina, represented by their departments of mental health, joined with Peabody College to translate a general idea into an operational reality. The grant further provided for a training program to prepare a new kind of mental health worker, called a teacher-counselor, and for a research program to evaluate the effectiveness of the schools to be established.

Cumberland House Elementary School in Nashville received its first students in November of 1962, and Wright School of Durham in January of 1963. The schools are located in residential areas not far from the universities (Vanderbilt and Peabody, Duke and North Carolina) that provide personnel and consultation. They are pleasant places, open, friendly, homelike, where children can climb trees and play dodge ball, go to school, and, at night, have a good meal, and a relaxed, amiable evening.

Both schools have nearby camps that are used in the summer and on occasion throughout the year. The camps are simple, even primitive, with children erecting their own shelters, preparing their own meals, making their own schedules. For staff and children alike there is a contagious serenity about the experience. Cooking is a marvelously instructive enterprise; motivation is high, cooperation is necessary, and rewards are imme-diate. Children for whom failure has become an established expectation, at school and at home, can learn to do things successfully. Nature study is a source of unthreatening instruction. And there is nothing quite like a campfire, or a dark trail and a single flashlight, to promote a sense of com-munity. In this simpler setting, where avoidant responses are few or weakly established, the child can take the first risky steps toward being a more adequate person.

At capacity each school will have 40 children, ages 6 to 12, grouped in five groups of 8 children each. Each group is the responsibility of a team of two teacher-counselors, carefully selected young people, most of whom are graduates of a 9-month training program at Peabody. The two teacher-counselors, assisted by college students and by instructors in arts and crafts and physical education, are responsible for the children around the clock. Each school has a principal and an assistant principal, both edu-cators, a liaison department staffed by social workers and liaison teachers, and a secretarial and house-keeping staff, who are full partners in the reeducation effort. The principal of a Re-ED school has an exacting job of management, training, interpretation, and public relations. The two schools have developed under the leaderships of four able men: John R. Ball and Neal C. Buchanan at Wright School and James W. Cleary and Charles W. McDonald at Cumberland House.[3]

Of course, the teacher-counselors are the heart of Re-ED. They are young people, representing a large manpower pool, who have had experi-ence in elementary school teaching, camping, or other work that demon-strates a long-standing commitment to children. After careful screening, in which self-selection plays an important part, they are given 9 months of training in a graduate program leading to the Master of Arts degree. The program includes instruction in the characteristics of disturbed children, in specialized methods of teaching, including evaluation and remediation of deficits in reading, arithmetic, and other school subjects, in the use of consultants from mental health and educational fields, and in arts and crafts and games and other skills useful on the playing field, on a canoe trip, in the living units after dinner at night. They get a thorough intro-duction to child-serving agencies in the community and to the operation of a Re-ED school through an extensive practicum. Finally they are challenged with the task of helping invent what Re-ED will become.

But most of all a teacher-counselor is a decent adult; educated, well trained; able to give and receive affection, to live relaxed, and to be firm; a person with private resources for the nourishment and refeshment of his own life; not an itinerant worker but a professional through and through; a peson with a sense of the significance of time, or the usefulness of today and the promise of tomorrow; a person of hope, quiet confidence, and joy; one who has committed himself to children and to the proposition that

---

[3] So many people have worked to make Re-ED a reality it is impossible even to record their names. They will have received recompense from seeing children flour-ish in their care. Yet Alma B. McLain and Letha B. Rowley deserve special recogni-tion for long service and uncommon skill and grace in managing many problems.

children who are emotionally disturbed can be helped by the process of reeducation.

The total school staff, and especially the teacher-counselors who work directly with the children, are backed by a group of consultants from psychiatry, pediatrics, social work, psychology, and education, an arrangement that makes available to the schools the best professional talent in the community and that has the further attractive feature of multiplying the effectiveness of scarce and expensive mental health and educational personnel.[4]

THE CHILDREN

What kind of children do the teacher-counselors work with? It can be said, in general, that diagnostic classification has not been differentially related to a successful outcome; that the children are normal or superior in intelligence but are in serious trouble in school, often retarded 2 or 3 years in academic development; that they do not need continuing medical or nursing care, and that they can be managed in small groups in an open setting. Re-ED is not a substitute for a hospital. There are children too disturbed, too out of touch, too aggressive, too self-destructive to be worked with successfully in small groups in an open setting. However, Re-ED schools do take many children who would otherwise have to be hospitalized.

Susan was 11, with a diagnosis of childhood schizophrenia. She had attended school 1 day, the first day of the first grade, and had been in play therapy for 4 years. She was a pupil at Cumberland House for a year, staying longer than most children. She has been in a regular classroom for 3 years now, an odd child still but no longer a prospect for life-long institutionalization. Ron was a cruelly aggressive child, partly an expression of inner turmoil and partly an expression of class values and habits; he is much less destructive now, and is back in school. Danny was simply very immature, so that school was too much for him; his problem could be called school phobia if that would help. Dick was extremely effeminate, wearing mascara and painting his nails. Both boys responded to masculine activities guided by a trusted male counselor. Billy was a gasoline sniffer and an ingenious hypochondriac; he returned to a reunion recently much more mature though still having trouble with school work. Larry, age 12, was quite bright yet unable to read; nor were we able to teach him to read. So we failed with him. It is such children as these that we aspire to help. To call them all "emotionally disturbed" is clearly to use language to obscure rather than to clarify. Nonetheless, they are all children who are in serious trouble, for whom the Re-ED idea was developed.

[4] The consultants have meant much more to Project Re-ED than can be recorded in this brief account. We here inadequately recognize the invaluable contribution of our colleagues: Jenny L. Adams, MSW, Gus K. Beil, PhD, Lloyd J. Borstelmann, PhD, Eric M. Chazen, MD, Julius H. Corpening, BD, Jane Ann Eppinger, MSW, John A. Fowler, MD, Ihla H. Gehman, EdD, W. Scott Gehman, PhD, Maurice Hyman, MD, J. David Jones, MD, and Bailey Webb, MD.

During the past summer, under the direction of William and Dianne Bricker and Charles McDonald, we have been working at Cumberland House with six of the most severely disturbed children we could find, mostly custodial cases from state institutions. Regular Re-ED activities are supplemented by a 24-hour schedule of planned behaviors and contingent rewards, the staff being augmented to make such individualized programming possible, but still using inexpensive and available personnel, such as college students. While it is too early to assess the effectiveness of this effort, we are pleased with the progress that most of the children are making, and we are certain we are giving them more of a chance than they had when their principal challenge was to learn how to live in an institution.

ECOLOGICAL CONCEPTS

Let us turn now to an examination of the theoretical assumptions and operational procedures involved in the process of reeducation. We do not, of course, make use of the principles involved in traditional psychotherapy; transference, regression, the promotion of insight through an exploration of inner dynamics and their origins are not a part of the picture. The teacher-counselor is not a psychotherapist, nor does he aspire to be one.

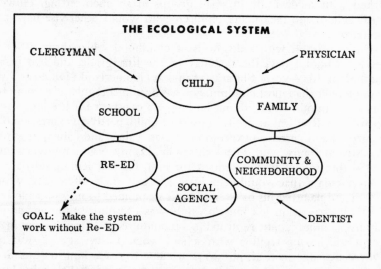

FIGURE 1.   Chart of ecological system, the smallest unit in a systems approach to working with a disturbed child.

We have become increasingly convinced that a major barrier to effective national planning for emotionally disturbed children is the professional's enchantment with psychotherapy. Everything in most model institutions revolves around getting the child to his therapist 1, 2, or maybe 3 hours a week. A few superb treatment centers combine psychotherapy with a program of daily activities conducive to personal growth and integration. But these are rare indeed. It is not uncommon to find children locked 15 stories high in steel and glass, with a caged roof to play on, drugged to keep them from doing too much damage to the light fixtures and air conditioning, while they await their precious hour, guarded by attendants who think disturbed children must scream, fight, climb walls, cower in a corner. Most frequently, of course, therapy is not available; most hospitals hold children hoping somehow they will get better.

An overcommitment to individual psychotherapy seems to us to stem from an uncritical acceptance of "cure" as the goal in working with a child, a consequence of defining the problem initially as one of "illness." That some disturbed children are "ill" in the usual sense may be accepted, but to define them all as such leads, we think, to a host of unvalidated and unquestioned assumptions; to a preoccupation with the intrapsychic life of the child, with what goes on inside his skull; to an easy use of drugs without knowledge of their long-term effects on character development; to the extended isolation of children from their families, the presumed source of contagion; to a limitation of professional roles; to the neglect of schools and of schooling, and so on. The preemptive character of a definition and the semantic sets that ensue are major barriers to innovation in working with disturbed children.

Of course we have our own ways of talking about the problem, and our metaphors are no less preemptive, making it all the more important for us to be explicit about definitions. We prefer to say that the children we work with have learned bad habits. They have acquired nonadaptive ways of relating to adults and to other children. They have learned to perceive themselves in limiting or destructive terms and to construe the world as an uncertain, rejecting, and hurtful place. We also recognize that the child lives in a real world that often falls short in giving him the affection, support, and guidance he needs. So we deal directly with social realities as well as with private perceptions.

This kind of thinking has led us gradually to a different way of defining our task, a definition of considerable heuristic merit (see Figure 1). For want of a more felicitous phrase, we have been calling it a systems approach to the problem of working with a disturbed child. We assume that the child is an inseparable part of a small social system, of an ecological unit made up of the child, his family, his school, his neighborhood and community. A social agency is often a part of the picture when a child has been designated emotionally disturbed, and other people—a physician, a clergyman—may be brought in as needed. The system may become "go" as a result of marked improvement in any component (the father stops drinking and goes back to work, a superb teacher becomes available, the child improves dramatically), or it may work as a result of modest improvement in all components. The effort is to get each component of the system above threshold with respect to the requirements of the other components. The Re-ED school becomes a part of the ecological unit for as brief a period of time as possible, withdrawing when the probability that the system will function appears to exceed the probability that it will not. We used to speak of putting the child back into the system but we have come to recognize the erroneous assumptions involved; the child defines the system and all we can do is withdraw from it at a propitious moment.

Once we abandoned cure as a goal and defined our problem as doing what we can to make a small social system work in a reasonably satisfactory manner, there ensued a number of operational patterns that contrast sharply with the practices of existing residential treatment centers for childen.

For one thing, parents are no longer viewed as sources of contagion but as responsible collaborators in making the system work. Parents are involved in discussion groups and are helped to get assistance from mental health centers. They actively participate in the ongoing program of the school. They organize an annual reunion, publish a parent's manual, sew for the children, and in many ways assume responsibility for reestablishing the child as quickly as possible in his own home, school, and community.

The children go home on weekends to keep families and children belonging to each other, to avoid the estrangement that can come from prolonged separation, and to give the child and his parents and brothers and sisters an opportunity to learn new and more effective ways of living together. Visitors ask "Aren't your Mondays awful?" They are, indeed, but we cherish their chaos as a source of new instruction; we try to keep in mind that our goal is not to run a tranquil school but to return the child as quickly as possible to his own home and regular school.

The ecological model requires new strategies to involve home, neighborhood, school, agency, and community in a contract with us to help a child. It requires new patterns for the deployment of personnel, and it has led to the development of a new kind of mental health worker: the liaison teacher. The liaison teacher is responsible for maintaining communication with the child's regular school, again to prevent alienation and to arrange optimum conditions for the child's early return to a regular classroom. For example a liaison teacher may personally accompany a child to a new school to which he has been transferred in order to increase the probability that that component of the ecological system will function effectively.

The social worker in Re-ED honors an early heritage of his profession, before the lamentable sit-behind-the-desk-and-do-psychotherapy era got established. He reaches out to the family, to community agencies, and to individuals—to any reasonable source of help for a child in trouble. Again, the goal is to make the system work, not simply to adjust something inside the head of the child.

THE PROCESS OF REEDUCATION

Now, let us turn to the child himself, to our relationships with him, and to what is meant operationally by the process of reeducation. Here are an even dozen underlying concepts that have come to seem important to us as we try to talk about what goes on in a Re-ED school.

Item 1: Life is to be lived, now. We start with the assumption that each day, that every hour in every day, is of great importance to a child, and that when an hour is neglected, allowed to pass without reason and intent, teaching and learning go on nonetheless and the child may be the loser. In Re-ED, no one waits for a special hour. We try, as best we can, to make all hours special. We strive for immediate and sustained involvement in purposive and consequential living. We constantly test the optimistic hypothesis that if children are challenged to live constructively, that if they are given an opportunity for a constructive encounter with other children and with decent adults, they will come off well—and they do, most of the time. They learn, here and now, that life can be lived on terms satisfactory to society and satisfying to themselves. Our task is to contrive each day so that the probability of success in this encounter clearly outweighs the probability of failure. I paraphrase Jessie Taft when I say, in the mastery of this day the child learns, in principle, the mastery of all days.

Item 2: Time is an ally. We became convinced, in the early stages of planning the project, that children are kept too long in most traditional treatment programs. The reasons for this are many. The abstract goal of cure through psychotherapy leads to expectations of extensive personality reorganization, of the achievement of adequacy in a wide array of possible life roles. It thus takes a long time either to succeed in this ambitious endeavor or to become aware that one has failed. Staff and children become fond of each other, making separation difficult. The widespread practice of removing the child from his home for extended periods of time causes a sometimes irreparable estrangement; the family closes ranks against the absent member. While everyone recognizes the importance of school in the life of the child, mental health programs have neither operational concepts nor specialized personnel necessary to effect an easy transition for the child from the institution back to his own school. Furthermore, the expectation of a prolonged stay in a treatment center becomes a self-validating hypothesis. A newly admitted child asks "How long do kids stay here?" He is told "about 2 years," and he settles down to do what is expected of him, with full support of staff and parents who also "know" that it takes 2 years to help a disturbed child. Myriad other constraints get established; for example, the treatment center hires just enough secretaries to move children in and out of a 2-year cycle, and it is not possible, to speed the process without hiring more secretaries, a restraint on therapeutic progress that is seldom identified. So before we admitted the first child, we set 6 months as the expected, average period of stay, a goal we have now achieved.

Time is an issue of importance in the process of reeducation in yet another way. We work with children during years when life has a tremendous forward thrust. Several studies suggest that therapeutic intervention is not demonstrably superior to the passage of time without treatment in the subsequent adjustment of children diagnosed as emotionally disturbed (Lewis, 1965). Treatment may simply speed up a process that would occur in an unknown percentage of children anyway. There is a real possibility that a long stay in a treatment center may actually slow down this process. Furthermore, in ecological perspective, it is clear that children tend to get ejected from families at low points in family organization and integrity. Most families get better after such periods; there is only one direction for them to go and that is up. The systems concept may entail simply observing when the family has regained sufficient stability to sustain a previously ejected child. The great tragedy is that children can get caught up in institutional arrangements that must inexorably run their course. In Re-ED we claim time is an ally and try to avoid getting in the way of the normal restorative processes of life.

Item 3: Trust is essential. The development of trust is the first step in reeducation of the emotionally disturbed child. The disturbed child is conspicuously impaired in his ability to learn from adults. The mediation process is blocked or distorted by the child's experience-based hypothesis that adults are deceptive, that they are an unpredictable source of hurt and help. He faces each adult with a predominant anticipation of punishment, rejection, derision, or withdrawal of love. He is acutely impaired in the very process by which more mature ways of living may be acquired. A first step, then, in the reeducation process, is the development of trust. Trust, coupled with understanding, is the beginning point of a new learning experience, an experience that helps a child know that he can use an adult to learn many things: how to read, how to be affectionate, how to be oneself without fear or guilt.

We are intrigued by the possibility, indeed are almost sure the thesis is true, that no amount of professional training can make an adult worthy of the trust of a child or capable of generating it. This ability is prior to technique, to theory, to technical knowledge. After seeing the difference that teacher-counselors in our two schools have made in the lives of children I am confident of the soundness of the idea that some adults know, without knowing how they know, the way to inspire trust in children and to teach them to begin to use adults as mediators of new learning.

Item 4: Competence makes a difference. The ability to do something well gives a child confidence and self-respect and gains for him acceptance by other children, by teachers, and, unnecessary as it might seem, even by his parents. In a society as achievement oriented as ours, a person's worth is established in substantial measure by his ability to produce or perform. Acceptance without productivity is a beginning point in the process of reeducation, but an early goal and a continuing challenge is to help the child get good at something.

What, then, in the process of reeducation, does the acquisition of competence mean? It means first and foremost the gaining of competence in school skills, in reading and arithmetic most frequently, and occasionally in other subjects as well. If a child feels that he is inadequate in school, inadequacy can become a pervasive theme in his life, leading to a consistent pattern of failure to work up to his level of ability. Underachievement in school is the single most common characteristic of emotionally disturbed children. We regard it as sound strategy to attack directly the problem of adequacy in school, for its intrinsic value as well as for its indirect effect on the child's perception of his worth and his acceptance by people who are important in his world. A direct attack on the problem of school skills does not mean a gross assault in some area of deficiency. On the contrary, it requires utmost skill and finesse on the part of the teacher-counselor to help a disturbed child move into an area where he has so often known defeat, where failure is a well-rooted expectancy, where a printed page can evoke flight or protest or crippling anxiety. The teacher-counselor need make no apologies to the psychotherapist with reference to the level of skill required to help a disturbed child learn.

So, in Re-ED, school keeps. It is not regarded, as it is in many mental health programs, as something that can wait until the child gets better, as though he were recovering from measles or a broken leg. School is the very stuff of a child's problems, and consequently, a primary source of instruction in living. Special therapy rooms are not needed; the classroom is a natural setting for a constructive relationship between a disturbed child and a competent, concerned adult.

Much of the teaching, incidentally, is through the unit or enterprise method. For example, a group of boys at Cumberland House was invited to go camping with some Cherokee Indian children on their reservation. The trip provided a unifying theme for 3 months' instruction in American history, geography, arithmetic, writing, and arts and crafts. At Wright School, rocketry has provided high motivation and an entrée to mathematics, aerodynamics, and politics. The groups are small enough to make individualized instruction possible, even to the point of preparing special programmed materials for an individual child, a method that has been remarkably effective with children with seemingly intractable learning disorders. The residential character of the Re-ED school means that the acquisition of competence does not have to be limited to increased skill in school subjects. It may mean learning to swim, to draw, to sing; it may mean learning to cook on a Dakota Hole, to lash together a table, to handle a canoe, to build a shelter in the woods; it may mean learning to talk at council ring, to assert one's rights, to give of one's possessions, to risk friendship, to see parents as people and teachers as friends.

Item 5: Symptoms can and should be controlled. It is standard doctrine in psychotherapeutic practice that symptoms should not be treated, that the one symptom removed will simply be replaced by another, and that the task of the therapist is to uncover underlying conflicts against which the symptom is a defense, thus eliminating the need for any symptom at all. In Re-ED we contend, on the other hand, that symptoms are important in their own right and deserve direct attention. We are impressed that some symptoms are better to have than other symptoms. The bad symptoms are those that alienate the child from other children or from the adults he needs as a source of security or a source of learning. There is much to be gained then from identifying symptoms that are standing in the way of normal development and working out specific plans for removing or altering the symptoms if possible. The problem is to help the child make effective contact with normal sources of affection, support, instruction, and discipline. We also work on a principle of parsimony that instructs us to give first preference to explanations involving the assumption of minimum pathology, as contrasted to professional preference for deep explanations and the derogation of all else as superficial.

Item 6: Cognitive control can be taught. Though little emphasis is placed on the acquisition of insight as a source of therapeutic gain, there is a lot of talking in Re-ED about personal problems and how they can be managed better. The teacher-counselor relies primarily on immediate ex-

perience, on the day-by-day, hour-by-hour, moment-by-moment relationship between himself and the child; he relies on specific events that
can be discussed to increase the child's ability to manage his own life. The
emotionally disturbed child has fewer degrees of freedom in behavior
than the normal child, yet he is not without the ability to shape his own
behavior by self-administered verbal instruction. He can signal to himself if he can learn what the useful signals are. The teacher-counselor
works constantly to help a child learn the right signals. The focus of this
effort is on today and tomorrow, not on the past or the future, and on
ways for the child to signal to himself to make each day a source of instruction for the living of the next. At the council ring at night, at a
place set apart from the business of living, children in a group are helped
to consider what was good about the day just past, what went wrong that
might be handled better tomorrow, and what was learned, especially in
successes and failures in relationships among themselves. Possibly more
important than the solving of particular problems is the acquisition of the
habit of talking things over for the purpose of getting better control over
events, a habit that can frequently be carried over into the child's home
and become a new source of strength for his family.

Item 7: Feelings should be nurtured. We are very interested in the
nurturance and expression of feeling, to help a child own all of himself
without guilt. Children have a way of showing up with animals and we are
glad for this. A child who has known the rejection of adults may find it
safest, at first, to express affection to a dog. And a pet can be a source of
pride and of sense of responsibility. Anger, resentment, hostility are commonplace, of course, and their expression is used in various ways: to help
some children learn to control their violent impulses and to help others
give vent to feelings too long repressed. In Re-ED schools one finds the
familiar ratio of four or five boys to one girl, a consequence in part, we
believe, of a lack of masculine challenge in school and community today.
Thus we contrive situations of controlled danger in which children can
test themselves, can know fear and become the master of it. The simple
joy of companionship is encouraged. We are impressed by the meaning-
fulness of friendships and how long they endure. The annual homecoming
is anticipated by many youngsters as an opportunity to walk arm-in-arm
with an old friend associated with a period of special significance in their
lives. And we respect the need to be alone, to work things through without intrusion, and to have a private purpose. Feelings also get expressed
through many kinds of creative activities that are woven into the fabric of
life in a Re-ED school. Throwing clay on a potter's wheel gives a child a
first sense of his potential for shaping his world. A puppet show written
by the children may permit freer expression than is ordinarily tolerable.
Drawing and painting can be fun for a whole group. And an object to
mold gives something to do to make it safe for an adult and child to be
close together.

Item 8: The group is important to children. Children are organized in
groups of eight, with two teacher-counselors in charge. The group is kept
intact for nearly all activities and becomes an important source of motiva-

tion, instruction, and control. When a group is functioning well, it is extremely difficult for an individual child to behave in a disturbed way. Even when the group is functioning poorly, the frictions and the failures can be used constructively. The council ring, or powwow, involving discussion of difficulties or planning of activities, can be a most maturing experience. And the sharing of adventure, of vicissitudes, and of victories, provides an experience in human relatedness to which most of our children have been alien.

Item 9: Ceremony and ritual give order, stability, and confidence. Many Re-ED children have lived chaotic lives, even in their brief compass. They may come from homes where interpersonal disarray is endemic. We have stumbled upon and been impressed by the beneficence of ceremony, ritual, and metaphor for children and have come to plan for their inclusion in the program. The nightly backrub is an established institution with the Whippoorwills, a time of important confidences. Being a Bobcat brings a special sense of camaraderie and has its own metaphorical obligations. And a Christmas pageant can effect angelic transformation of boys whose ordinary conduct is far from seraphic.

Item 10: The body is the armature of the self. We are intrigued by the idea that the physical self is the armature around which the psychological self is constructed and that a clearer experiencing of the potential and the boundaries of the body should lead to a clearer definition of the self, and thus to greater psychological fitness and more effective functioning. The Outward Bound schools in England, developed as an experience for young men to overcome the anomie that is the product of an industrial civilization, are built around the concept. Austin Des Lauriers' ideas about treatment of schizophrenia in children emphasize differentiating the body from the rest of the world. Programmatically, in Re-ED, the idea has been realized in such activities as swimming, climbing, dancing, tumbling, clay modelling, canoeing, building a tree house, and walking a monkey bridge.

Item 11: Communities are important. The systems concept in Re-ED leads to an examination of the relationship of the child to his home community. Many children who are referred to our schools come from families that are alienated or detached from community life or that are not sufficiently well organized or purposeful to help the child develop a sense of identity with his neighborhood, his town or city. He has little opportunity to discover that communities exist for people and, while the goodness of fit between the two may often leave much to be desired, an important part of a child's education is to learn that community agencies and institutions exist for his welfare and that he has an obligation as a citizen to contribute to their effective functioning. This is especially true for many of the boys referred to Re-ED, whose energy, aggressiveness, lack of control, and resentment of authority will predispose them to delinquent behavior when they are a few years older and gain in independence and mobility. This idea has a number of implications for program planning. Field trips to the fire, police, and health departments are useful. Memberships in the YMCA, a children's museum, a playground group, or a community center may be worked out for a child. Church attendance may be encouraged and a clergyman persuaded to take special interest in a family, and a library card can be a proud possession and a tangible community tie.

Item 12: Finally, a child should know joy. We have often speculated about our lack of a psychology of well-being. There is an extensive literature on anxiety, guilt, and dread, but little that is well developed on joy. Most psychological experiments rely for motivation on avoidance of pain or hunger or some other aversive stimuli; positive motivations are limited to the pleasure that comes from minute, discrete rewards. This poverty with respect to the most richly human of motivations leads to anaemic programming for children. We thus go beyond contemporary psychology to touch one of the most vital areas of human experiencing. We try to develop skill in developing joy in children. We believe that it is immensely important, that it is immediately therapeutic, if further justification is required, for a child to know some joy in each day and to look forward with eagerness to at least some joy-giving event that is planned for tomorrow.

COSTS AND EFFECTIVENESS

Now, let us turn to the practical questions of cost and of effectiveness.

A re-ED school costs about $20 to $25 per child per day to operate. Thus the per-day cost is about one-third the cost of the most widely accepted model and perhaps four times the cost of custodial care. Cost per day, however, is not the best index to use, for the purpose of a mental health program is not to keep children cheaply but to restore them to home, school, and community as economically as possible. In terms of

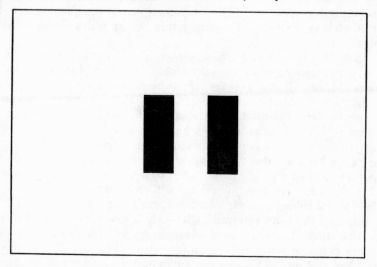

FIGURE 2.   Geometric felt figures used in replacement technique (after Weinstein, 1965).

FIGURE 3.   Human felt figures used in replacement technique (after Weinstein, 1965).

cost per child served, the cost of a Re-ED program is equivalent to or less than the cost of custodial care. The cost per child served is approximately $4,000. If Re-ED can prevent longer periods of institutionalization, this is a modest investment indeed.

Appropriate to the systems analysis of the problem, most of our studies of effectiveness of Re-ED schools have employed ratings by concerned observers: mother, father, teacher, our own staff, and agency staffs, all important persons in the ecological space of the child. However, Laura Weinstein (1965) has been interested in the way normal and disturbed children construct interpersonal space, as illustrated by the accompanying representations of felt board figures. She used two techniques. In the first (the replacement technique), each of two figure pairs—a pair of human figures and a pair of rectangles—is present on a different board and equally far apart (Figures 2 and 3). The child is asked to replace the felt figures "exactly as far apart as they are now." Normal and disturbed children make systematic errors, but in opposite directions: normal children replace human figures closer together while Re-ED children replace human figures farther apart (Figure 4). In the second technique (the free placement technique), human figures are used, representing mothers, fathers, and children. The children are asked to place the figures on the board "any way you like." Again systematic differences occur. Normal children place the child very close to the mother. Re-ED children place greater distance between the mother and the child than between any other human pair (Figure 5). The mother-child relationship is clearly crucial in the life space of the 6- to 12-year-old children with whom we work. It is gratifying to report that children after the Re-ED experience put the child figure closer to the mother than they did before; that is, they structure interpersonal space as normal children do.

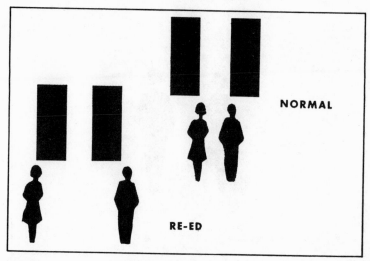

FIGURE 4.   Placement of geometric and human felt figures by normal and disturbed children (after Weinstein, 1965).

The basic design for evaluating the effectiveness of the Re-ED schools involves observations taken at time of enrollment and repeated 6 months after discharge. Preliminary results present an encouraging picture. A composite rating of improvement, based on follow-up information on 93 graduates provided by all evaluators, gives a success rate of approximately 80%. We are in process of obtaining comparison data from control groups to determine the extent to which the reeducation effort is superior to changes that occur with the passage of time.

Detailed analyses show that mothers and fathers independently report a decrease in symptoms such as bedwetting, tantrums, nightmares, and school fears, and an increase in social maturity on a Vineland type check list. School adjustment as rated by teachers shows the same favorable trends. On a semantic differential measure of discrepancy between how the child is seen and parental standards for him, there is an interesting and dynamically significant difference between fathers and mothers. Both see the child as having improved. For fathers the perceived improvement results in lower discrepancy scores between the child as seen and a standard held for him. For some mothers, however, improvement results in a raising of standards so that discrepancy scores frequently remain high. This is not true of all mothers but it is more frequently true of mothers than of fathers.

But T tests seldom determine the fate of institutions; public and professional acceptance is crucial.

To obtain an informed and mature professional appraisal of Re-ED, we have established a panel of visitors composed of men whose judgment is held in high esteem: Eli M. Bower, psychologist; Reginald S. Lourie, psychiatrist; Charles R. Strother, psychologist; and Robert L. Sutherland, sociologist. Members of the panel have been visiting the schools regularly since their inception and will make public their final appraisal at the end of the project period. It is enough to say now that they are all strong supporters of the Re-ED idea.

A test of public support of the Re-ED idea was adventitiously obtained when the Legislature of the State of North Carolina last June terminated state funds for the support of Wright School after July 1, 1966. Protest from all over the state was immediate and strong; in less than 3 years of operation the school had won impressive public support. Funds have been raised to continue Wright School in operation until the Legislature convenes again.[5] The Governor has assured the mental health officials of North Carolina that he will support legislative measures to restore state funds for the operation of Wright School. Fortunately the Tennessee school has not been put to such public test but professional and political endorsement is evident in the decision to build two new schools, one in Memphis and one in Chattanooga, that will be operated as reeducation centers. Finally, it is encouraging that several other states have committees working to establish Re-ED schools.

Our aspiration and our growing confidence are that the Re-ED model will be replicated in many states, that it will have its influence on the character of more traditional treatment programs, and that the beneficiaries will be the disturbed children of America.

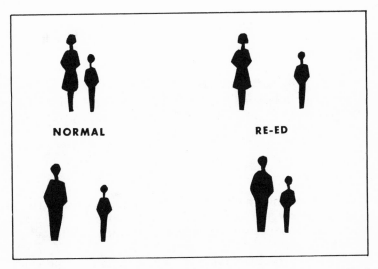

FIGURE 5.   Mother, father, and child felt figures as placed by normal and disturbed children (after Weinstein, 1965).

[5] Among the major contributors are the Wright Refuge Board, the Sarah Graham Kenan Fund, the Mary Duke Biddle Foundation, the Hillsdale Fund, and the Stanley County Mental Health Association. Many gifts have come from churches, mental health associations, civic organizations, and individuals. We gratefully acknowledge their help in keeping Wright School in operation.

We further think of Re-ED as an institution that exemplifies, in its development, the contemporary challenge to psychologists to concern themselves with the invention of social arrangements that put psychological knowledge to use to improve the quality of human life.

REFERENCES

Hobbs, N. Mental health's third revolution. *American Journal of Orthopsychiatry,* 1964, 34, 822–833.

Lewis, W. W. Continuity and intervention in emotional disturbance: A review. *Exceptional Children,* 1965, 31(9), 465–475.

Weinstein, L. Social schemata of emotionally disturbed boys. *Journal of Abnormal Psychology,* 1965, 70, 457–461.

55. Professional Deployment in the Mental Health Disaster: The Range Mental Health Center

D. F. Muhich, W. F. Hunter, R. I. Williams,
W. G. Swanson, E. J. DeBellis, and J. M. Moede

The provision of mental health services to areas lacking in professional facilities remains a critical problem. In the following article, Dr. Muhich and his colleagues describe one approach to this dilemma.

The Range Mental Health Center, Virginia, Minnesota, makes an effort to use mental health specialists in a unique way, realizing that there will never be enough mental health specialists to meet the needs of the acutely and chronically distressed.

Mental health specialists can offer more to an area by providing consultation to other caretaking persons than by devoting the same time to direct therapy. These community caretakers are usually the people naturally turned to for help in an emergency. The aim of consultation should be to help these caretakers handle the mental health problems presented to them in a way that will lead to the strengthening of the distressed person.

Community Mental Health Journal, 1965, 1, 205–207. Reprinted with the permission of the publisher and senior author.

Thus, most of the effort of the Center is spent consulting with existing community caretakers, stimulating and coordinating agency efforts, providing inservice training, working regularly through all media for public education, offering direct service in acute or preventive type situations only when nobody else is willing or able, and evaluating these inputs into the several communities and into the area as a unit. In the program here outlined, 65 per cent of staff time is expended in consultation and inservice training activities.

Through all this, the major effort is towards the local handling of a distressed person, if at all possible, toward strengthening rather than breaking family ties, and toward developing the entire community in its therapeutic and preventive mental health role.

LOCALE

The Range Mental Health Center serves a population of 100,000 in the northern two-thirds of St. Louis County, adjacent to the Canadian border in Minnesota. The area covers a series of fourteen small mining towns strung out along the Mesabi Range iron ore vein. Eighty per cent of the population is within 30 miles of the Center offices. The area is isolated from large urban centers, and few social services and psychiatric facilities, other than our program, are present. Two district welfare offices do provide family-oriented casework services and assume responsibility for aftercare of state hospital dischargees. The medical and legal professions, school personnel, police, courts, and clergymen, represent the traditional caretakers in times of emotional stress and crisis in the life of an individual.

1. *Consultation.* Each of the staff members of the Center assumed responsibility for one group of caretakers to develop a consultative relationship between that portion of the community and the mental health center. Out of this evolved an ongoing consultation program so that everyone in the area who is in a caretaking position to an individual in emotional distress is seen in ongoing consultation in his own office approximately once every four weeks.

The members of the staff travel individually or as a team (depending upon the manpower needs in each area) to the office of the consultee, where an effort is made to increase the therapeutic skills of the individual consultee and to stimulate his interest in using himself in a psychotherapeutic manner. In addition to consultation, occasionally a staff member will participate in a joint interview with the consultee and his client.

This consultative function also places the staff in a position to serve as a liaison between various community agencies. As others have noted, we also have discovered that a number of people are involved with the same family, but are unaware of each other and do not communicate with each other. We serve to coordinate these efforts.

2. *Training.* Another important aspect of the program is to provide training seminars and workshops for these "front line" key people. The training program emphasizes human growth and development, psychological theories, interviewing techniques, psychopharmaceutical medications, therapeutic interactions, family interviewing, etc. Again, the needs

of different caretakers vary and the program has been tailored to meet the needs as the individual groups see them, with a general attempt to make the family the basic unit of inquiry, understanding, and interaction.

3. *Public Information.* In order to encourage public support and assistance in the development of the Center and other programs, all news media are used in public information work, and the Center staff spends considerable time speaking to a variety of social clubs and service organizations. Also the Center has developed a mental health library which is catalogued in each of the eight local libraries in the area, although the books reside in the Center offices.

4. *Direct Service.* The matter of direct service is an important consideration to any mental health facility, but it is especially important to a center such as this. A closed intake system has been designed, in that a case will be accepted only through consultation, and will be accepted for only one of six reasons. The priorities are: consultative value, preventive value, psychiatric reasons, staff development value, community coordination or public relations. All individuals applying directly to the Center are referred to a community caretaker for initial evaluation and, hopefully, definitive therapeutic intervention.

Cases are essentially triaged as in responses to disaster. No prolonged psychotherapy is available at the Center. A family or individual will not be seen continuously for months or years. Rather, patients are on a highly active status for a brief period and wherever possible the family is considered as a unit for both diagnosis and therapy. In each case, an attempt is made to return the family to the consultee for continued treatment as soon as possible or perhaps to refer them to some other community agent who is in a better position to continue therapy.

5. *Development of Resources.* The Center staff in assessing the needs of this area has attempted to stimulate, and continues to try to develop, needed mental health resources such as school psychology programs, special classes, day-night facilities, an adequate school for the physically handicapped (such as cerebral palsied, deaf, and blind) on a regional basis, and a number of other programs.

6. *Preventive Programs.* Although we recognize the preventive value of working with community caretakers and their involving themselves in therapeutic interactions early with clients, a more direct kind of preventive program is also necessary. The primary vehicle for this program is the fourteen school systems and we have designed and are developing adequate data collection systems within the school systems to allow identification of deviant populations in the first three grades. Subsequent controlled preventive programs will be developed from that data. In conjunction with the University of Texas Personnel Services Research Center, we are also engaged in a long-term study of the effectiveness of school mental health consultation.

METHODS OF ASSESSMENT

It is the responsibility of any community agency to examine its own operation, particularly a program such as ours, which has some novel features.

It seems important to attempt to assess our work and our effect as best we can and to make modifications when needed. To meet this end, a four-phase inquiry system has been designed.

Phase I concerns itself with the detailed examination of where the mental health center puts time and energy into the community, at what locations, with what individuals, concerning what ends. Phase II is an attempt to describe the cases we deal with purely through consultation. It is an attempt to see where they work, where they live, and size and kinds of families that they exist in, etc. Phase III attempts to perform the same task for those cases which are seen in direct service by the Center personnel. Phase IV is an attempt to assess the changes in behavior of our consultee population. The development and modification of the program rests directly on this series of data collection systems built into a feedback circuit. A fifth phase attempting to assess changes in the Center staff is still in design stages.

PROGRAM DEVELOPMENT

The initial difficulty facing this community mental health program was that of obtaining sufficient time for organization, and during this period withstanding the pressures for direct service from the community faced with immediate problems. If this community program had not been the coordinated development of both professional staff and board (the representatives of the community) such time would not have been obtained. First, time was spent acquainting ourselves with the community and communicating basic ideas within this program to the community.

Overlapping with it was the procurement of what Caplan has called sanctions. This process of obtaining permission to work with a number of individuals within a variety of social systems and subsystems was occurring at the same time as the original organization. The procurement of sanctions is a constant, never-ending, and ever-changing operation of great interpersonal complexity.

The third phase seems to us to be the beginning of a cycle of development similar to that Erikson described for the individual. The initial problem at the beginning time is the establishment of trust. This, to be sure, began with the first day of the Center's existence, carried through with the establishment of sanctions, but has become the "phase specific task" of the Center when the consultative and training relationship with the various groups has begun.

This is also a never-ending task and it is an issue to which one must address oneself with each consultative contact. However, the first contacts are by far the most important. This is a period of consultee wariness and defensiveness, a period when many of the projections that others place upon mental health specialists can be identified and sometimes partially dealt with, and a period of consultant discomfort.

It is a period in which the usual diadic training of mental health specialists may seem woefully inadequate. The comfortable confines of the office are gone and the use of receptive silence is noticeably inappropriate. With the gradual establishment of trust, there follows the development and maturation of an ongoing consultative relationship.

The program is still somewhere in the "netherland" between the establishment of trust and the development of mature consultative relationships after two and one-half years of operation. In some selected areas within our community, trust is relatively established while in other areas the task remains before us.

As the program matures and the community develops, our consultation and training efforts will also need to adapt, and are likely to be on a more responsive than regular ongoing basis. Multiple and novel possibilities exist for reaching unserved segments of our population, such as through training bartenders, barbers, and beauticians. Programs that reach into the laundromat or pool hall are also within the realm of possibility. Whatever the direction the program goes, it is not likely to return to the traditional, uneconomic, and impractical method of trying to pose the private practice model as the best answer to professional deployment in the mental health disaster.

BIBLIOGRAPHY

REFERENCES FOR PART I

Bower, E. M. *The early identification of emotionally handicapped child in schools.* Springfield, Illinois: C. C. Thomas Press, 1960.

Bower, E. M. Mental health. In R. Ebel (Ed.), *Encyclopedia of educational research,* fourth ed. New York: Macmillan, 1969.

U. S. Children's Bureau. *Juvenile Court Statistics,* statistical series number 85. Washington, D. C.: U. S. Government Printing Office, 1966.

White, M., & Harris, M. *The school psychologist.* New York: Harper and Brothers, 1961.

REFERENCES FOR PART IV

Action for Mental Health: Final Report of the Joint Commission on Mental Illness and Health. New York: Basic Books, 1961.

Hobbs, N. Mental Health's Third Revolution. *American Journal of Orthopsychiatry,* 1964, 34, 822–833.

Redl, F., & Wattenberg, W. *Mental Hygiene in Teaching.* New York: Harcourt, Brace & World, Inc., 1959.

Smith, M. B. The Revolution in Mental Health Care—A "Bold New Approach"? *Transaction,* 1968, April, 19–23.

INDEX

INDEX

PRINTED IN U.S.A.